The Doctrine of the Work of Christ

ROBERT S. FRANKS
M.A.(Cantab.), D.Litt.(Oxon.), Hon. LL.D.(Brist.)
Formerly Principal of Western College
Bristol

Vexilla regis prodeunt
Fulget crucis mysterium

Wipf and Stock Publishers
150 West Broadway • Eugene OR 97401
2001

A History of the Doctrine of the Work of Christ

By Franks, Robert

ISBN: 1-57910-630-7

Reprinted by *Wipf and Stock Publishers*
150 West Broadway • Eugene OR 97401

Previously published by Thomas Nelson and Sons, 1962.

Previously titled The Work of Christ: *A Historical Study of Christian Doctrine*

THIS BOOK IS DEDICATED
TO MY FATHER

In order to enable the reader to get as near as possible to the original writers, I have included a good deal of quotation and translation. The translations, except where it is otherwise stated, are my own. In quotations I have not thought it necessary always to reproduce the exact orthography of the writers, which is very various, especially in eighteenth-century works.

As regards the theological principles which have guided me, I owe special gratitude to Weisse, 'Philosophische Dogmatik oder Philosophie des Christenthums' (1855–62), Harnack, 'Lehrbuch der Dogmengeschichte' (4th ed., 1909–10), Kaftan, 'Dogmatik' (3rd and 4th ed., 1901), and, last but not least, to Heim, 'Das Gewissheitsproblem in der systematischen Theologie bis zu Schleiermacher' (1911).

The reason why I have attempted no construction at the end of my work is the same as the reason given in the Introduction (p. 2) why I have omitted from it any account of the Biblical material of the subject: each would demand greater fullness of treatment than belongs to the scale of my history.

I take this opportunity of acknowledging the valuable help in the final preparation of my book for the press of the Rev. H. Morgan, M.A., and the late Rev. A. Gaunt, M.A., B.Litt.

ROBERT S. FRANKS

WESTERN COLLEGE, BRISTOL

PREFACE

It is stated in the Introduction to this work (pp. xv–xvi) that its purpose is to trace the antecedents of the modern doctrine of the work of Christ. The result of my investigation is to show that this doctrine in its most typical form, as developed by Schleiermacher and Ritschl, is no arbitrary opinion on the subject, but that the whole course of doctrinal development has led to it by an immanent necessity.

This course of development has its nodal points in the four great syntheses (pp. xviii–xx) in which the various factors that have contributed to the doctrine of the work of Christ have from time to time found a relative settlement. Into these syntheses the threads of doctrine are gathered up, and out of them again they diverge. The gist of my book is accordingly to be found in the sections which treat of these syntheses (pp. xiv–xx, 202–5, 233–5, 347–51, 355–7, 644–8); in order however to apprehend the full significance of these highly condensed summaries, the rest of the book must be read.

In my research for material I have naturally been greatly indebted to the two chief works dealing with the whole of my subject: Baur, 'Die christliche Lehre von der Versöhnung in ihrer geschichtlichen Entwicklung von der ältesten Zeit bis auf der neueste' (1838); and Ritschl, 'Die christliche Lehre von der Rechtfertigung und Versöhnung', Erster Band: Die Geschichte der Lehre (3rd ed., 1889). As regards the modern period I also owe guidance particularly to Kattenbusch, 'Von Schleiermacher zu Ritschl' (3rd ed., 1903), Tulloch, 'Movements of Religious Thought in Britain during the Nineteenth Century' (1885), and Scott Lidgett, 'The Spiritual Principle of the Atonement' (2nd ed., 1898). I have, however, everywhere, except in a very few less important instances, investigated the original sources for myself. This was the more necessary as my purpose to treat the special doctrine of the work of Christ from the point of view of the whole of theology (pp. xvff.) involved in many cases a fresh selection of material.

vii

CONTENTS

Part I   The Patristic Theology

xi

CONTENTS

Part II The Mediaeval Theology

Part III The Older Protestant Theology

Part IV   Modern Protestant Theology

CONTENTS

PART I
THE PATRISTIC THEOLOGY

CHAPTER 1

THE SUB-APOSTOLIC AGE

THE first period of our doctrine stretches as far as Irenæus. Its general characteristic is a freedom of development, due to two important facts, that separate it from all later ages of the Church. The first was the existence of a charismatic ministry, whose utterances were regarded as possessing the value of inspiration. Such utterances were naturally influenced and guided by apostolic tradition; but the tradition was not regarded as altogether limiting and determining the free utterances of the spirit. The second fact was that the written revelation, originally employed by Jesus and the Apostles for the proof of doctrine, was the Old Testament; while the Scriptures of the New Testament, though read in the churches for edification, were not yet generally recognised as canonic in the same sense with the Old. The Old Testament was a pillar of monotheism. But beyond this it was hardly calculated to restrict the development of Christian doctrine; which, however, on the other hand it might assist, inasmuch as there had been handed down along with it from the Apostles the allegorical exegesis and the method of proof from prophecy, which made it serviceable for Christian purposes.

It is not surprising therefore that we find a great variety of doctrinal positions in the primitive Church. We shall adequately cover the ground, so far as our particular subject is concerned, by distributing the material according to the following scheme:

(1) The original form of the Apostles' Creed (from A.D. 100–150).

(2) The Apostolic Fathers (A.D. 90–140), with a particular reference to Ignatius.

(3) The Apologists of the second century, especially Justin (d. *c.* A.D. 165).

(4) The Gnostics of the first and more particularly the second century, including Marcion (*fl. c.* A.D. 140).

3

THE APOSTLES' CREED

We take as our first testimony as to the doctrine of the work of Christ existing in the early Church the original form of the Apostles' Creed (A.D. 100–150), which is known to us in the third century as the creed of the Roman Church, but may have originated either in Rome (Kattenbusch, Harnack) or in Asia Minor (Zahn, Loofs). There is some uncertainty as to the exact wording of the oldest form of the creed, but that doubt does not touch the point with which we are here concerned, viz. that the Second Article appended to the name of Jesus Christ a recital of the facts of His Incarnate life from His birth to His ascension concluding with the assertion of His present exaltation and of His future coming to judgment. This passage ran as follows:

'Who was born of Holy Ghost and Mary the Virgin, who was crucified under Pontius Pilate and was buried, and on the third day rose again from the dead, who ascended into heaven, and sitteth at the right hand of the Father, whence He cometh to judge the quick and the dead.' [1]

Upon the theological significance of this passage I will let Kattenbusch speak.

'As regards its positive content, I feel compelled to understand the Roman Creed as a kind of positive precipitate of Paulinism. This is clearest in the Christological portion. For here Jesus is spoken of as though He was born, only to die and enter into His glory. All that which according to the evangelists filled the earthly life of Jesus till His death is wanting. There is not a word on His preaching ministry, His miracles, His inner character. Nevertheless the Roman Creed also reminds us of the Gospels, above all the Synoptic Gospels. It operates like these, through the mere narrative recital. No theory of the "work" of Jesus is given. No word of interpretation accompanies the reference to what befel Him. As in the Gospels a picture of Him is brought before our eyes. His history appears to be intended to operate immediately like a sermon upon Him.' [2]

[1] See Loofs, D.G., 4th ed., p. 88, n.

[2] 'Der geschichtliche Sinn des apostolischen Symbols', in 'Zeitschrift für Theologie und Kirche', 1901, Heft 5, p. 416.

The Apostolic Fathers

Our second witness as to the doctrine of the early Church upon the work of Christ comes from the writings of the so-called 'Apostolic Fathers' (A.D. 90–140). Under this head are included the Epistle of the Roman Church to the Corinthians (First Epistle of Clement), the seven genuine letters of Ignatius, the Epistle of Polycarp to the Philippians, the doctrinal work known as the Epistle of Barnabas, the Shepherd of Hermas (an apocalypse), the homily known as the Second Epistle of Clement, and since its publication in A.D. 1883, the Didache or Teaching of the Twelve Apostles. If we except the case of Ignatius, presently to receive special treatment, the theological elements to be found in the Apostolic Fathers are so germinal and sporadic that the following summary of their teaching may well produce the impression of a more developed doctrine than really exists in their writings. The Christianity which these represent is of a simple and untheological type. The fundamental conception of the Christian religion to be found in them is that it includes the knowledge of God ($\gamma\nu\hat{\omega}\sigma\iota\varsigma$), and of His law ($\nu\acute{o}\mu o\varsigma$), along with the promise of immortality ($\zeta\omega\acute{\eta}, \dot{\alpha}\phi\theta\alpha\rho\sigma\acute{\iota}a$), all these being revealed by Jesus Christ.[3]

As passages typical of this point of view may be cited the following:

1 Clem. xxxvi, 2: 'By Him we look steadfastly unto the heights of heaven. By Him we behold, as in a mirror, His immaculate and most excellent visage. By Him the eyes of our hearts were opened. By Him our foolish and darkened understanding blossoms up anew towards His marvellous light. By Him the Lord has willed that we should taste of immortal knowledge.'

Didache ix, 3: 'We give thanks unto Thee, our Father, for the life and knowledge, which Thou hast made known unto us through Jesus Christ, Thy servant.'

2 Clem. xx, 5: 'To the only invisible God, the Father of truth, who sent forth unto us the Saviour, the leader of our incorruption, through whom also He manifested unto us truth and heavenly life, to Him be the glory for ages of ages.'

[3] Cf. Harnack, D.G., 4th ed., vol. i, pp. 188–91, 220–1 ; Loofs, D.G., 4th ed., pp. 90–3.

Hermas, 'Sim.' V, VI, 3: 'He therefore having cleansed the sins of the people, showed them the paths of life, giving them the law, which He received from His Father.'

The above point of view of the Apostolic Fathers may be generally described as a Christian moralism. Their doctrine is, however, not a pure moralism, but has in it a mystical element. For one thing a certain vagueness attaches to the idea of revelation by Jesus Christ, in so far as the Christological idea of the Apostolic Fathers includes both the historical Jesus and the spiritual Christ, without the establishment of any very clear relation between the two.[4] Again, the complete knowledge of God is conceived as very closely associated with eternal life. Compare the above quotations from the Didache and 2 Clement, also the phrase 'immortal knowledge' in the quotation from 1 Clement.[5] On the whole then, out of the different New Testament types of doctrine, it is the Johannine with which the Christianity of the Apostolic Fathers has most affinity, only that it is altogether less theological and more elementary.

The above view does not, however, exhaust all that the Apostolic Fathers have to say of the work of Christ. We find also the thought, though very indistinctly expressed, that Christ did not merely promise eternal life, but procured it by His Incarnation and Passion.

Cf. Barnabas v, 6: 'But He Himself, that He might bring to nought death and manifest the resurrection from the dead, because it was necessary that He should be manifested in the flesh, endured.' Here we have a hint of the (ultimately Pauline) type of doctrine presently to be more fully studied in Ignatius.

Moreover, in addition, the idea of Christ's death as a sacrifice and ransom is well represented in the Apostolic Fathers, but it is not expressed with any great distinctness. We appear to be dealing here mainly with an imperfectly assimilated tradition. Even the Epistle of Barnabas, which deals with this subject at considerable length from the point of view of the correspondence of Christ's death with Old Testament types, shows no real insight into the matter. 'Barnabas' says, however (v, 1):

[4] Cf. Seeberg, D.G., 2nd ed., vol. i, pp. 112ff.
[5] See also Harnack, D.G., 4th ed., vol. i, p. 189, n. 1.

'For to this end the Lord endured to give up the vessel of His flesh to corruption, that we might be sanctified through the remission of sins, which is effected through His blood of sprinkling.'

Cf. also VII, 3 : 'He Himself purposed to offer the vessel of the Spirit as a sacrifice for our sins.'

VII, 5 : 'When I shall offer My flesh for the sins of My new people.'

Very similar to these passages in Barnabas is Hermas, 'Sim.' V, VI, 2 : 'He Himself made purification of their sins, having laboured much, and undergone many labours.'

The above passages have affinity in the New Testament with the Epistle to the Hebrews. The parallel doctrine of 1 Clement on the other hand closely resembles the ' Paulinism' of 1 Peter.

Cf. 1 Clem. XLIX, 6 : 'Through the love He had for us Christ our Lord gave His blood for us by the will of God, and His flesh for our flesh, and His soul for our souls.'

1 Clem. VII, 4 : 'Let us gaze upon the blood of Christ and recognise how precious it is to God His Father, because it was shed for our salvation and obtained for all the world the grace of repentance.'

Harnack [6] says on 1 Clem. VII, 4 : 'The transformation of "the forgiveness of sins" into "the grace of repentance" shows clearly that the special value put upon the death of Christ for the procuring of salvation is with Clement a mere matter of tradition; for it is hardly possible to deduce the grace of repentance from the blood of Christ.' But clearly what we have here is just as in 1 Peter [7] a practical and untheological echo of Paulinism, which, passing over the intervening links, directly connects the moral results of the death of Christ with His sacrifice.

IGNATIUS

In the Ignatian epistles we find a somewhat more developed view of the work of Christ, which I will give in the words of

[6] D.G., 4th ed., vol. i, p. 222, n. [7] Cf. 'Man, Sin, and Salvation', pp. 143–4.

Loofs, who has given so admirable and succinct a statement of it that it must be given intact.

'In the centre of this general view of Christianity, which has exercised very great influence on the later development (though only in small degree by the direct effect of the Ignatian letters), stands Christ as (the Revealer of God and as) the Beginner of a new humanity, stands the dispensation whose end is the new man.[8] Before Christ humanity (or indeed the world) was under the power of Satan, the ruler of this present age,[9] and under the dominion of death.[1] But in silence God was preparing the new dispensation [2]—Judaism believed in Christianity [3]—and without the prince of this world surmising the meaning of what was taking place, with the earthly life—lying between the virgin birth and the death on the cross—of Jesus, who became perfect man,[4] begins the destruction of death.[5] Its accomplishment takes place in the bodily resurrection of Christ. As the Risen One, as He, who even after His resurrection is in the flesh,[6] Christ is the Beginner of a new humanity, the Founder of a community, which possesses incorruption.' [7]

With this passage, however, is to be taken another in which Loofs develops more fully another aspect of the view of Ignatius, which in it is only just indicated. This is the aspect of his teaching which resembles the common view of the Apostolic Fathers.

'The work of Christ is the mediation of knowledge and incorruption. He is the Knowledge of God, the Counsel of the Father.[8] It is He in whom God reveals Himself, and breaks His silence; who is His Word proceeding from silence,[9] the Mouth without falsehood, in whom the Father hath truly spoken.[1] This knowledge of God brought by Christ is itself (as in Jn 17:3) thought of as a doctrine of incorruption.' [2]

Taking the doctrine of Ignatius altogether as represented in these passages from Loofs, we have in it a suggestive and interesting combination of the Pauline idea of Christ as the Founder of a new humanity with the Johannine conception of

[8] 'Eph.' xx, 1. [9] *Ibid.* xix, 1. [1] *Ibid.* xix, 3. [2] *Ibid.* xix, 1–3.
[3] 'Magn.' x, 3. [4] 'Smyrn.' iv, 2 ; cf. 'Eph.' x, 3 ; xx, 1. [5] 'Eph.' xix, 3.
[6] 'Smyrn.' iii, 1. [7] 'Eph.' xvii, 1 ; Loofs, D.G., 4th ed., p. 99.
[8] 'Eph.' xvii, 2 ; iii, 2. [9] 'Magn.' viii, 2. [1] 'Rom.' viii, 2.
[2] 'Magn.' vi, 2 ; cf. 'Eph.' xvii ; Loofs, D.G., 4th ed., p. 101.

the revelation of God and the bringing of life and light by the Incarnation. This is what gives it importance in the history of doctrine. It must be pointed out, however, that the above systematisation of the ideas of Ignatius is due to Loofs, not to Ignatius himself; and it is a question whether it would have been made without the knowledge of the fuller and clearer presentation of the same type of doctrine in the later Greek theology. If we look back from this more developed statement to Ignatius, the outlines of it are plain enough in his epistles; they would not be so clear otherwise. The observation explains the position taken up by Harnack relatively to Loofs's construction of the theology of Ignatius. He admits that we have in the Ignatian epistles the first attempt in the post-apostolic literature closely to combine the historical propositions of the creed with the blessings which Jesus has brought. But he doubts 'if one can at all assign to this pathetic confessor any clearly conceived doctrine', and says that 'only the will of the writer is here clear, all the rest is in confusion'.[3] The truth then would seem to be that Ignatius is important as manifesting a tendency in the sub-apostolic age to the development of a type of doctrine afterwards formulated by Irenæus and his successors. His letters explain the character of the tradition under the influence of which Irenæus worked; but it was Irenæus in whose mind the tradition crystallised into definite form.

Before parting with Ignatius, let me call attention to the fact that in what he says about the destruction of death beginning in the silence of God, without the prince of this world understanding what was taking place, we have at least a suggestion of the later idea that the devil was deceived by God in the economy of redemption. I may also point out the existence in the Ignatian letters of the doctrine of the descent into hell, which is connected in his mind with the idea that Christ is our life.

'How can we live without Him, whom also the Prophets, His disciples in the Spirit, expected as Teacher? And therefore He, for whom they righteously waited, is come, and has raised them from the dead.'[4]

---

[3] See D.G., 4th ed., vol. i, p. 221, n. 1.   [4] 'Magn.' IX, 2, 3.

THE APOLOGISTS

By the Apologists the conception of the work of Christ as a revelation is further defined and related to the idea of revelation in general. Already in the Apostolic Fathers we meet with the point of view that the revelation made in Christ does but confirm that already given in the Old Testament.[5] But by the Apologists this revelation is identified, not only with that made in the Old Testament, especially through the prophets, but also with the revelation in the general reason of man. The combining idea is that of the Logos. The Logos or Reason of God is immanent in every man. The prophets spoke by His inspiration. In Jesus Christ He became incarnate; but He brings no new revelation. He does but confirm the revelation already made from the beginning in man's reason, but beclouded by the demons who have led men astray into idolatry and superstition, and enslaved them under the dominion of the senses. The prophets renewed this revelation in its pristine clearness. Jesus Christ finally completes their work by guaranteeing its truth. This He not merely does, however, by repeating the prophetic revelation of God, the essence of which is the knowledge of God and His law along with the promise of immortality; but also, by the actual correspondence of the historical events of His life with the predictions of the prophets, He gives the final proof of the truth of their doctrine.

This is practically the whole view of the Apologists with regard to the work of Christ. Only Justin Martyr forms some exception to the general rule. His main view indeed is essentially the same as that of the rest.

'According to the Apology and Dialogue of Justin, Christ accomplishes the conversion and restoration of humanity to its destination by His teaching as to the worship of the true God and a virtuous life in faith in the eternal reward of immortality, which He will bestow at His second coming.'[6]

Nevertheless we find also in Justin ideas that resemble the doctrine of Ignatius as to a Divine economy in the Incarnation whose purpose is the overthrow of death and Satan.

[5] Cf. Loofs, D.G., 4th ed., p. 92.
[6] Thomasius, D.G., 2nd ed., vol. i, p. 394, note by Bonwetsch.

10

'(Christ) having been made flesh submitted to be born of the Virgin, in order that through this dispensation the Serpent, who at the first had done evil, and the angels assimilated to him might be put down and death might be despised.'[7] In fact we find in Justin clear indications of the presence to his mind of the recapitulation theory, afterwards more fully developed by Irenæus, according to which Christ becomes a new head of humanity, undoes the sin of Adam by reversing the acts and circumstances of his disobedience, and finally communicates to men immortal life. Compare the sentence quoted by Irenæus from Justin's treatise against Marcion, 'The only-begotten Son came to us, recapitulating His creation into Himself'.[8] Compare also the following passage:

'He became man through the Virgin, in order that in the way that the transgression took its beginning from the Serpent, through that same way it might also take its destruction.'[9]

Apart from these passages in Justin, where as in Ignatius a Pauline element enters, the theology of the Apologists has again more affinity with the Johannine than with any other type of New Testament doctrine. Their central conception of the Logos they have in common with Jn 1:1–18, as also the way in which they apply it to unite the pre-Christian revelation with that made in Christ. That their working out of the Logos doctrine in detail differs considerably from that of the Gospel of John is of importance in connexion with the doctrine of the Person of Christ, but has no special significance for us. On the other hand, however, we are concerned with another difference between John and the Apologists, viz. that they simply identify Christianity with the prior Divine revelation, whereas John points out the contrast between the two.[1] It is part of the same difference of view that the Apologists fail to supplement the Logos doctrine, as John supplements it, with the intuitive contemplation of Jesus Christ in His historical life. Moreover, whereas the Apologists regard the revelation of the Logos as containing the knowledge of God and His law and the promise of immortality, the Johannine mysticism views immortality as already com-

---

[7] 'Dial.' 45.   [8] Irenæus, 'Adv. Hær.' IV, 6, 2, Harvey's ed., vol. ii, p. 159.
[9] 'Dial.' 100.   [1] Jn 1:17

11

municated to the believer by faith in Christ,[2] and views the keeping of Christ's commandment as involved in abiding in Him.[3] The doctrine of the Apologists is then purely moralistic, without the mysticism which balances the ethical interest in John.[4] There is here a retrogression in content from, if an advance in science upon the doctrine of the Apostolic Fathers in general, to say nothing in particular of Ignatius. The Apologists have in fact brought Christianity in its practical aspect down to the level of the philosophical Hellenism of their time, for which, just as for Pharisaism among the Jews, the idea of God as the Creator and Rewarder seemed to sum up the whole of religion. Compare my article 'Merit' in Hastings's 'Dictionary of Christ and the Gospels,' Vol. II, p. 168, and for the antecedents of this view in Greek religion my essay 'The Idea of Salvation in the Theology of the Eastern Church'.[5]

GNOSTICISM

The Gnostics regarded Christianity as primarily the revelation to the spiritual portion of humanity of their true nature and destiny as akin to the supreme God of the universe, and their deliverance by this knowledge from the dominion of the lower powers who rule this present world. To these powers, the chief among them being the Creator-God of the Jews, belongs the world of sense in opposition to the world of spirit, which appertains to the supreme God and the higher powers who emanate directly from Him. In the most highly developed Gnostic systems the lower powers themselves also emanate from the supreme God, but by means of a disruption in the world of spirit or a fall from it. The same pre-temporal fall of spirit into the realm of matter is also the cause of the imprisonment of the spiritual humanity in the present world. Those who compose it are partly of an earthly and partly of a heavenly origin. Their redemption consists in the deliverance of the spirit within them, from matter as well as from the powers that rule

---

[2] *Ibid.* 3: 36;17:3.   [3] *Ibid.* 15:1–10   [4] 'Man, Sin, and Salvation', pp. 167, 168.
[5] 'Mansfield College Essays', 1909, pp. 254, 259ff.

the material sphere. The knowledge by which they are delivered includes an ethic, usually an asceticism intended to wean the spirit from matter; but also various magic formulas or charms by which the power of the world rulers is broken.

It is evident that Christianity has here been very much philosophised. The conception of it as a redemption from the powers that rule this present world indeed plays a great part in the theology of Paul; but the dualism of spirit and matter, and the notion that the lower powers are emanations from the supreme God carries us altogether outside the borders of New Testament Christianity, dominated as it is by the monotheism of Israel. In these respects Gnosticism has amalgamated fresh elements drawn from the Hellenistic-Oriental syncretism of the age with the original Christian stock, elements which could only be incorporated by the expulsion of much that was fundamental in primitive Christianity.

In accordance with the main tendency of Gnosticism the work of Christ is construed as the bringing of the redeeming knowledge. This view is, however, accompanied by a peculiar theory of the Incarnation, which involves a very limited valuation of the humanity of Christ as regards His work. The Gnostics in general regard the Incarnation as the manifestation of an Æon or Spirit, who belongs to the upper world, in the man Jesus, who belongs to the world of sense. Since, however, their fundamental dualism allows of no real union between spirit and matter, the Gnostics either regarded the humanity of Jesus as only temporarily indwelt by the Divine Saviour, who descended upon it at the Baptism, but departed before the Crucifixion; or else they viewed the human Jesus as simply an appearance assumed by the Saviour for the end of Revelation. In consequence of these views, they could of course assign little significance to the sufferings and death of Jesus. Such as they had was only typical or symbolical. Either, as with Basilides, who deliberately denied that one man could suffer for another, they were typical of the purifying sufferings which all spiritual men must undergo.[6] Or else, as with the Valentinians, they symbolised the condescension of the spiritual Christ to the sphere of matter, in that just

[6] See 'Real-Encyclopädie', 3rd ed., vol. ii, p. 434.

as Jesus was extended over the Cross, so the Spiritual Christ extended Himself over the Æon Horos, or Stauros, that divided the upper from the lower world.[7]

MARCION

The only Gnostic, who in spite of its inconsistency with his dualistic Christology still conserved a doctrine of redemption through the sufferings of Jesus, was the Paulinist Marcion, who was indeed a Gnostic so far as his metaphysical dualism was concerned, but not in so far as in dependence upon Paul he viewed the work of redemption as no mere communication of knowledge. Marcion made the supreme God a God of love. Below Him, however, was the Creator-God, the giver of the Jewish law, who as a God of righteousness had to be satisfied by the death of Jesus before men could be redeemed from His power. Marcion's exact conception of redemption cannot now be with certainty established in detail. As represented by the Marcionite in the 'Dialogus de recta in deum fide,' 2 (in the works of Origen) the theory passes over into the notion that the Demiurge was deceived in the transaction.

'The Demiurge, seeing the Good One undoing his law, took counsel against him, not knowing that the death of the Good One was the salvation of men.' [8]

According to Esnik, an Armenian bishop of the fifth century, the Marcionite view was as follows:

'The Demiurge, since he had attacked the innocent Christ, and so had transgressed his own law, must give Christ satisfaction. He says: "Inasmuch as I have erred and in ignorance put Thee to death, because I knew not that Thou wert God, I give Thee as satisfaction all those who will believe on Thee, to lead them whither Thou wilt." Christ therefore delivers Paul and sends him to preach that we are redeemed with a price, and that every one who believes upon Jesus is ransomed from the Righteous One to the Good God.' [9]

[7] Baur, 'Die christliche Gnosis', 1835, p. 140.
[8] Origen's 'Opera', ed. Lommatzsch, vol. xvi, p. 304.
[9] Seeberg, D.G., 2nd ed., vol. i, p. 252, n. 1.

14

There is no doubt that the above passages give at least the general drift of Marcion's doctrine, which is a natural development enough from Paulinism, when once by the acceptance of the Gnostic dualism the constraint of Paul's Jewish monotheism had been removed. Paul himself represents the death of Christ as a ransom price.[1] Moreover, in Col. 2:14–15, he views it as annulling the bond of ordinances, by which the angels of the law [2] had power over men. This last idea is explained by Gal. 4:1–5, 8–10, and Col. 2:16–20, where all ceremonials, whether Jewish or pagan, are regarded as being enforced by angelic powers, to which God gave authority over men till the coming of Christ, and which, as opposed to Christ, who shares the life of God,[3] belong to this temporal world. It is only the firm monotheism in the background of Paul's thought that divides these conceptions from the doctrine of Marcion.

Finally, it may be pointed out that in 1 C. 2:8 we have the idea that the rulers of the world [4] crucified Christ in ignorance of the mystery of redemption, a thought which explains not only the Marcionite doctrine in the 'Dialogus', but also the Ignatian idea of the devil's being surprised by the Conception, Incarnation and the Crucifixion of Christ. For the Pauline angels of the law easily pass over in thought from a middle position like that of the Demiurge, to that of malignant demons. They are in fact Divinely appointed till the coming of Christ as the guardian spirits of the present order of the world; but when Christ comes they stand in the way of His kingdom, and their power has to be destroyed.[5]

The Transition
to the Further Theological
Development: the Question of the Proof of Doctrine

If we now review the situation in the early Church as represented by the above delineated types of doctrine, we see that great doctrinal variety reigned in it; as indeed in view of the existence of a charismatic ministry was naturally to be expected.

[1] 1 C. 6:20 ; 7:23   [2] Gal. 3:19.   [3] Col. 3:1–3.
[4] Undoubtedly spiritual powers, cf. Eph., 6:12.   [5] 1 C. 15:24–25 ; Rom. 8:38–39.

Nevertheless, in the midst of this variety are clearly discernible already the shapes of the fundamental types of doctrine destined to rule in the Ancient Catholic Church during the following centuries. These are three in number: (1) There is the idea of the work of Christ as revelation. He brings the knowledge of God and of His law, and the promise of immortality. This is the common doctrine alike of the Apostolic Fathers including Ignatius, of the Apologists, and of the Gnostics. (2) There is next the conception of the destruction of death and the endowment of humanity with immortal life through the Incarnation, Death, and Resurrection of Christ (Barnabas, Ignatius, Justin). (3) Finally there is the idea of Christ's death, either as a sacrifice to God (the Apostolic Fathers), or as a ransom from the spiritual power opposed to Him (Marcion), with suggestions that the opposing power (the Devil, or the Demiurge) was in some way deceived in the economy of redemption (Ignatius, Marcion).

There is then undoubtedly a common drift in the post-apostolic development of doctrine in spite of its charismatic variety. On the other hand, however, in spite of this common drift, there was also a drift apart upon one of the most important points in connexion with the doctrine of the work of Christ. This was with regard to the ultimate value for doctrine of the historical events of the life of Jesus. While the Creed, though giving no interpretation of these events, plainly presupposed that they are the very foundation of the Christian gospel, and Ignatius endeavoured to incorporate them into a theology, the Apologists gave them no direct value for salvation, and the Gnostics regarded them as of no saving value at all.

At this point our subject touches the general question of the significance of Gnosticism in early Christianity. This question we must now discuss, even if the discussion carries us temporarily away from our main theme; since no otherwise is it possible properly to apprehend the general conditions of the further development of doctrine. The advent of Gnosticism among the other types of Christianity precipitated a crisis.

Gnosticism, like the cuckoo in the sparrow's nest, tended first to grow big at the expense of the other occupants, and then remorselessly to shoulder out the original possessors. In other

16

words, it was a doctrinal development of Christianity which threatened to destroy the foundations of Christianity. All other types of doctrine left standing these foundations, viz. on the one hand the Old Testament and monotheism, and on the other the historical statements summed up in the Creed. Even the doctrine of the Apologists, though it made nothing of the Gospel facts except a confirmation of the doctrine of the prophets, did not touch them. But the Gnostics both attacked the Old Testament and sublimated the articles of the Creed. The question of the proof of doctrine, therefore, became urgent. It was not enough to appeal to the inspiration of the Spirit. There were many spirits in the Church. How was the true Spirit to be known? The Gnostics themselves led the way in the matter. In the first place, they criticised the Old Testament, the original basis of proof of Christian doctrine. A good example of their method is given in the famous letter of the Valentinian Ptolemæus to Flora. Ptolemæus recognises three fundamental powers, the supreme God, who is perfect, the Devil, who is evil, and the Demiurge, who is of an imperfect righteousness, midway between them. From the last emanates the law of Moses, which contains three different strata :

(1) That which in itself is perfect, and which Christ did not destroy, but fulfilled, e.g. the decalogue or pure moral law.

(2) The law, that is mixed with evil, which Christ has abolished, e.g. the *lex talionis*.

(3) That which is typical, i.e. the ceremonial law, of which Christ has brought out the true meaning.[6]

In the second place, however, the Gnostics began to appeal definitely to other sources of proof than the Old Testament. One was tradition. The appeal to tradition was indeed as old as Paul;[7] but the Gnostics gave it a new meaning. They propounded the doctrine of a secret tradition from the Apostles in excess of the common faith of the Church. This secret tradition the Gnostic teachers claimed as their own peculiar inheritance through various disciples of the Apostles. Its content was the very Gnosis or higher wisdom which they taught was the means

[6] See 'Real-Encyclopädie', 3rd ed., vol. xx, pp. 405ff.   [7] 1 C. 15:3.

17

of redemption. For the initiated or 'spiritual' Christians it replaced the common faith.

Their third appeal was to the Christian Scriptures, which were already being read for edification in the churches, but had not previously been definitely utilised as a doctrinal standard. In the Gnostic schools began the work of commenting upon and interpreting some of these writings; while Marcion actually formed a canon of Pauline Scriptures. The Gnostics found their doctrines in our present New Testament Scriptures, especially in the parables of Jesus, by means of an allegorical exegesis.[8] They in fact Gnosticised the original Christian tradition in the same way as the Church had already Christianised the Old Testament. They also, however, made use of scriptures themselves of a Gnostic tendency.[9]

Such then altogether was the elaborate system of proof established by the Gnostics. It is clear that in opposition to it the old method of appealing on the one hand to the Old Testament and on the other to the Spirit in the Church was insufficient. For the Gnostics by their method put the Old Testament almost altogether out of court: moreover, they claimed the Spirit pre-eminently for themselves. They declared in fact that they had the final revelation beyond even that given by the Apostles or Christ Himself. 'For even the Apostles, they say, had mixed what belongs to the law with the words of the Saviour: and not only the Apostles, but even the Lord Himself, now spoke by inspiration of the Demiurge, now again by that of the middle powers, sometimes again by that of the Highest: they themselves, however, know infallibly and without contamination and purely the hidden mystery: which is nothing else but in the most impudent way to blaspheme their Creator.'[1] The battle of the Church with the Gnostics had therefore to be joined on other than the old grounds.

It was the work of the great 'Anti-Gnostic' Fathers at the end of the second century, above all of Irenæus, next to him of Tertullian, to meet the Gnostic attack, subversive as it was of the original foundations of Christianity, and at the same time

---

[8] Cf. Irenæus, 'Adv. Hær.' i, 1, 5 ; i, 3, 1 ; i, 8, 4.   [9] Ibid. i, 20, 1.
[1] Ibid. iii, 2, 2.

18

to establish upon new foundations more definite than those of the past the doctrine of the Catholic Church, as the Church of the great body of Christians, opposed to Gnosticism, now came to be called.

(1) The new appeal was in the first place to the creed, which now first became definitely a standard of doctrine.[2] The creed presupposed by both Irenæus and Tertullian is essentially the Roman (or Apostles') Creed.

(2) In the second place, while the Old Testament was retained as the foundation of monotheism (the Gnostic criticism, as we shall presently see, was met by a theory of the historical development of revelation), a definitely Christian standard of doctrine, fuller than the Creed, was established by the formation of the Canon of the New Testament. The fact that the Canon was not entirely fixed in all details as at present till long after the time of Irenæus and Tertullian does not here concern us. The Four Gospels and the Pauline Epistles, the most fundamental sources of Christian doctrine, composed the body of the Canon from the first. The only work of first-rate doctrinal importance afterwards added to the Canon was the Epistle to the Hebrews, which was accepted (as Pauline) in the East by Clement, with reservations by Origen, then by Athanasius and the later Greek Fathers, but in the West was not so accepted till the time of Augustine and Jerome.

(3) The third appeal was to the bishops of the Apostolic Churches, (a) as the holders of the true tradition from the Apostles in opposition to the Gnostic secret tradition,[3] (b) as themselves, in opposition to the Gnostic teachers, the supreme repository of the 'charisma certum veritatis'.[4] This last criterion, the appeal to the bishops, is of the greatest importance, as it put out of court the Gnostic allegorisation of the statements either of the Creed or of the New Testament. It meant that not a Gnostic but a 'Catholic' Anti-Gnostic interpretation was to be placed upon these statements.

Upon these principles then, or a development of them, the

---

[2] *Ibid.* I, 10, 1 ; I, 21, 5 ; III, 4, 1. Tertullian, 'De præscr. hæreticorum', cap. 13.

[3] Irenæus, 'Adv. Hær.' III, 2, 2 ; III, 3, 1 ; III, 3, 4 ; III, 4, 1 ; IV, 33, 8. Tertullian, 'De præscr.' cap. 21, 32.

[4] Irenæus, IV, 26, 2 ; cf. also IV, 26, 5.

dogmatic work of the Ancient Catholic Church proceeded. It was not indeed all at once even among orthodox Christians that these principles were fully accepted. With Clement of Alexandria, for example, the rule of faith is the Scriptures of the Old and New Testament only, not the Scriptures and the Creed, while the true leader of the Church is not the bishop but the (true) Gnostic. Origen follows Clement, approximating, however, somewhat nearer to the Catholic view. He has prefixed to his great systematic work an extended Rule of Faith ('De Principiis', Præf.). But by the end of the third century or the beginning of the fourth the Catholic Church became a firm reality in all parts of the Roman Empire through the acceptance of the three norms of the Creed, the Scriptures, and the consensus of the Church. Only in general, however, was this system of authority established. The exact relation of its elements to one another remained uncertain.

(1) The Scriptures of the Old and New Testaments possessed a unique authority. From them every doctrine must be proved. Nothing that could not be proved from Scripture was universally regarded as a necessary part of the faith. To stand upon the Scripture alone was not in itself an uncatholic position.[5]

(2) But the essential content of the Scriptures was held to be contained in the Creed. In the West the Creed always meant from Tertullian onwards the Apostles' Creed. In the East, before the Council of Nicæa, it meant the baptismal confession of the particular Church (Jerusalem, Antioch, Cæsarea, etc.). After the Council of Nicæa it meant above all the Nicene Creed, till later on its place as the chief symbol was taken by the Nicæno-Constantinopolitanum. In the West correspondingly, while the Apostles' Creed remained, as above stated, the fundamental creed, first the Creed of Nicæa and later the Nicæno-Constantino-politanum became its authoritative interpretation.[6]

(3) The doctrine of Irenæus that the bishops of the Apostolic Churches were the repositories of the true tradition, and at the same time the possessors of the 'charisma certum veritatis', developed on the one hand into the general appeal to tradition (the Fathers), and on the other hand into the belief in the

---

[5] Cf. Harnack, D.G., 4th ed., vol. ii, p. 70.   [6] *Ibid.* pp. 87ff.

infallible authority of the great œcumenical councils from Nicæa onwards.[7]

In this way then the Church solved the problem as to the proof of doctrine, which had been so sharply formulated by the Gnostics. It is evident that the conditions of doctrinal development in the Catholic Church from Irenæus and Tertullian onward were very different from those of the charismatic post-apostolic Christianity. In the earlier age the source of doctrinal development had been either the free play of the mind of the Spirit, as is illustrated in Ignatius, or else the free exercise of reason, as is exemplified in the Apologists: the check of authority (the incipient creed, the incipient canon, tradition in general) was only very slightly felt. From Irenæus onwards, however, we have instead the endeavour rationally to systematise and comprehend a solid body of authoritative tradition, and as a consequence in the ensuing Catholic doctrine a more or less marked opposition of authority and reason. As, however, the exact relation between authority and reason varies from one theologian to another, any detailed study of this subject is best left to the following sections which deal in turn with the different doctors of the Ancient Church.

[7] *Ibid.* pp. 91ff.

Chapter 2

THE BEGINNINGS OF THE GREEK THEOLOGY

Irenæus

Irenæus (d. c. a.d. 200) is in every way the founder of the Greek system of theology, alike in principles, method, and matter. We have already seen how in opposition to the Gnostics he appealed to the Creed, the New Testament Scriptures, and the bishops of the Apostolic Churches. His theological method follows from this establishment of principles, but introduces a further point of view, in that it determines the way in which these norms of doctrine are to be applied in theology.

Irenæus starts first of all from the creed, taken in the sense of Catholic tradition ('Adv. Hær.' iii, 4, 1). He then proceeds to prove it point by point from the New Testament Scriptures, at the same time both refuting Gnostic perversions of the truth, and expanding the brief statements of the creed into a fuller theology, partly indeed derived from the Scripture proofs adduced, but partly going beyond the text of Scripture and developed upon its basis in original theological views of his own. Of these views Irenæus himself has nowhere given a single comprehensive statement, showing how they are finally to be joined together. They have indeed a strong family resemblance, and are almost even as they stand parts of a system. But they just fall short of absolute systematic unity. For one thing, we find the same theological view repeated again and again, yet with slight differences. For another, some links needful to a complete system are wanting. The reason is that the argument of Irenæus is determined primarily not so much by the direct endeavour to expand the creed into a theology, as by the attempt upon the basis of it and of the Scriptures to refute the Gnostics. The presentation of his own theology therefore tends to follow the form of the doctrines refuted rather than to take its own natural

22

lines. Nevertheless Irenæus is so much a theologian by nature, and so naturally inclined to see the whole in the parts, and the parts through the whole, that in spite of all we almost have a system in the end. It is to be observed, however, that the following account of his doctrine of the work of Christ represents a considerable systematisation of the material, although that material falls naturally into the arrangement adopted.

We find, in fact, in Irenæus the threefold type of doctrine which we have already noted as characteristic of the Ancient Catholic Church. Moreover, its outlines are much more firmly drawn in his theology than in that of the previous age.

(1) In the first place then Christ appears, just as in the doctrine of the Apologists, as the Incarnate Logos, who brings to men the knowledge of God and of His law and the promise of immortality.

'By this means the immeasurable and inapprehensible and invisible God gave Himself to the faithful, being seen and apprehended and measured, that He might give life to those who received Him and saw Him through faith.' [1]

'The manifestation of the Father, which is through the Word, gives life to those who see God.' [2]

'The Son is the measure of the Father, since He also contains Him.' [3]

Irenæus, however, has developed the doctrine of the revelation of God by the Logos in such a form as to distinguish more effectively than the Apologists had been able between the different stages of the revelation in nature, in the Old Testament, and in the New Testament. This part of his doctrine is of the greatest importance. Not only did it overcome the Gnostic separation of the Creator from the Redeemer and the Gnostic criticism of the Old Testament, but it also laid the foundations for all further theological development.

Irenæus distinguishes three covenants:

(a) The first was that of the original law of nature, which included the love of God and of our neighbour, and was essentially one with the content of the decalogue.[4]

(b) This law was renewed and embodied in a positive form

[1] 'Adv. Hær.' IV, 20, 5.   [2] *Ibid.* 20, 7.   [3] *Ibid.* 4, 2.   [4] *Ibid.* 13, 4.

23

in the decalogue, to which, however, on account of the sensuous nature of the people of Israel, the ceremonial precepts of the Jewish law were added. 'They received a servitude suitable to their lust, not indeed separating them from God, but governing them by the yoke of slavery.'[5] Under this covenant, however, the prophets foretold the Advent of Christ and the final revelation of God in Him.[6]

(c) In the third covenant Christ has renewed the original moral law of love.[7] The symbols of the Old Testament are done away in Christ, but not the moral law. This covenant is related to that of the Old Testament as freedom to bondage, and as fulfilment to prophecy. It is, however, not merely a renewal of the moral law of love, but adds to the natural law a fresh law of faith. Christians in fact have a severer law to obey than Jews; for they have more to believe. They have not only to believe in God the Father, but also in the Son, who has now appeared.[8]

It is to be observed that Irenæus in all this not only opposes the Gnostics, but also corrects the Apologists. It is made clear that the Incarnation did not merely confirm an existing revelation, but brought a further revelation beyond that of nature.

(2) If Irenæus in the doctrine of revelation is constructive of foundations for the future, he is even more so in what is as much his own central doctrine, as it is that of the Greek theology in general, viz. the doctrine of the destruction of death and the communication to humanity of immortality by the Incarnation. We come here to the famous Irenæan doctrine of Recapitulation (ἀνακεφαλαίωσις). The conception is that of Christ as the Second Adam, or second head of humanity, who not only undoes the consequences of Adam's fall, but also takes up the development of humanity broken off in him, and carries it to completion, i.e. to union with God and consequent immortality.

The general outlines of the idea are defined in III, 13, 7: 'It was God recapitulating the ancient creation of man in Himself, that He might slay sin, and annul death, and give life to man.' Also III, 18, 1: 'The Son of God, when He was incarnate and was made man, recapitulated in Himself the long line of men, giving us salvation compendiously (in compendio), so that what we had

---

[5] *Ibid.* 15, 1.   [6] *Ibid.* 23, 1.   [7] *Ibid.* 12, 2 and 5.   [8] *Ibid.* 28, 2.

lost in Adam, viz. that we should be after the image and similitude of God, this we should receive in Jesus Christ.'

Absolutely fundamental to Irenæus is the notion of humanity as an organism into which Christ enters, and in which all that He is and all that He does are as a leaven permeating the mass. Hence He gives us by His presence in humanity salvation *in compendio*. He Himself is 'salus, et salvator, et salutare' (III, 10, 3).

We must now, however, examine more in detail the two aspects of the *recapitulatio*. There is on the one hand the undoing of the consequences of Adam's fall, and on the other hand the communication to humanity of immortal life.

(*a*) We shall consider first the latter aspect, which is the more fundamental of the two. Christ by His very Incarnation communicates immortal life to our corruptible humanity. Here we meet with the conception of 'deification', so characteristic of the Greek theology. Its strict meaning is not that man is made God, but rather that he is made Divine, or a participator of immortality. Compare the following passages: 'Unless man had been united to God, he could not have been made partaker of incorruptibility' (III, 18, 7).

'For in no other way could we receive incorruption and immortality, except first we had been united to incorruption and immortality' (III, 19, 1). This deification then was the purpose of the Incarnation.

'Jesus Christ because of His immeasurable love was made what we are, that He might make us completely what He is' (*V*. Præf.).

'How could we be joined to incorruption and immortality, unless first incorruption and immortality had become what we were, so that the corruptible might be swallowed up by incorruption, and the mortal by immortality, that we might receive the adoption of sons?' (III, 19, 1).

Irenæus, however, by no means thinks only of a 'physical' redemption; he thinks of the gift of immortality as included in the gift of life in a wider sense. 'Life' also involves the knowledge of God. For the close association of the knowledge of God with immortality, cf. IV, 36, 7: 'The knowledge of the Son of God, which is incorruption.' Cf. also IV, 20, 2: 'That in the flesh of our

Lord that light of the Father may meet us, and from His ruddy flesh may come to us, and thus man may attain to incorruption, surrounded with the light of the Father.'

So also Irenæus like Ignatius [9] thinks of Christ as bringing life to the Old Testament saints by His descent into Hades, when He preached to them the Gospel and manifested Himself to them (IV, 22, 1).

But again the gift of life through the Incarnation has an ethical aspect. The notion of the ethical renewal of humanity by the Incarnation is not so clearly developed by Irenæus. It appears, however, in the famous passage (II, 22, 4): 'He came to save all through Himself: all, I say, who through Him are renewed unto God, infants, and little children, and boys and young men and older men. Therefore He passed through every age, and was made an infant for infants, sanctifying infants: among the little ones He was made a little one, sanctifying those having this very age, and at the same time being made an example to them of piety and righteousness and obedience: among young men He was made a young man, becoming an example to young men, and sanctifying them to the Lord. So also He was made an older man among the older men, that He may be the perfect master in all things, not only according to the exposition of the truth, but also according to the condition of age, thus also sanctifying equally those who are older, becoming an example to them also: finally He came even to death, that He may be the first-born from the dead, Himself holding the primacy in all things, the prince of life, first of all, and before all.'

In connexion with the above passage there are two things to be noted. The first is that the notion of moral renewal which it contains is naturally connected not merely with the Incarnation itself, but with all the subsequent stages of the life of Christ. The second is that it very readily passes over simply into the idea of example. The fact that Irenæus, however, includes the case of infancy in the list of the sanctifying effects of the Incarnation shows that his idea is not merely that of example; as does also the mention of Christ's resurrection at the close of the list.

[9] 'Magn.' IX, 3 ; cf. also Justin, 'Dial.' 72.

Neither Christ's infancy nor His resurrection can sanctify by example, but only in some more occult and mysterious way.

(b) We pass on to the second aspect of the idea of Recapitulation, viz. that Christ makes good Adam's fall. This Irenæus connects first of all with the temptation. Christ's victory here over the devil involves the victory over him of the human race. His obedience undoes the effects of Adam's disobedience.

Cf. v. 21, 2: (In the temptation) 'the transgression of the commandment, which had taken place in Adam, was paid for (*soluta*) by the commandment of the law, which the Son of man kept, not transgressing the commandment of God.'

But the death of Christ also is an act of obedience, which counteracts the transgression of Adam, and reconciles men to God.

'In the first Adam we had offended God, not doing His commandment: but in the second Adam we were reconciled, being made obedient unto death. For we were debtors to no other, but to Him, whose precept we had transgressed from the beginning' (v, 16, 3).

'For this reason in the last times the Lord restored us to friendship with God by His Incarnation, being made a mediator between God and man: on the one hand propitiating on our behalf the Father against whom we had sinned, and having mitigated (*consolatus*) our disobedience by His obedience; on the other hand giving us intercourse with our Maker and obedience' (v, 17, 1).

In this connexion the recapitulation theory is worked out into curious parallels between the tree by which Adam fell, and the tree by which Christ has redeemed us (v, 16, 3; v, 17, 3, 4), and again between Eve and Mary.

'What the virgin Eve bound by means of incredulity, this the virgin Mary loosed by faith' (III, 22, 4).

Fantastic as these parallels appear upon the surface, they nevertheless reflect clearly an important thought of Irenæus, viz. that the work of Christ was the exact undoing of the sin of Adam.

(3) This leads us to the last point of view from which Irenæus treats the work of Christ, that is the legal. Irenæus recognises a claim which must be settled before man can be freed. This view

27

is on the one hand expressed as an aspect of the doctrine that Christ by His death undoes the sin of Adam, and has accordingly been met with already in the passages above quoted, where it is said that Christ reconciles us to the Father, by atoning in His death for Adam's transgression. The legal aspect of the work of Christ is, however, much more fully developed by Irenæus in the form of a doctrine of redemption from the devil. To this doctrine we now therefore in the next place turn.

Irenæus teaches that, though the devil had at the first unjustly acquired dominion over the human race, yet it befitted God to deal with him by persuasion rather than by force.

Cf. v, 1, 1: 'The Word of God, mighty in all things, and not lacking in His justice, acted justly even against the Apostasy itself, redeeming from it those things which are His own, not by force, as the Apostasy gained possession of us at the beginning, insatiably seizing what was not its own, but by persuasion, even as it was fit that God should by persuasion and without employing force receive what He wished; so that neither the law of justice should be broken, nor the ancient creation of God perish.'

Christ therefore 'reasonably redeeming us with His blood, gave Himself as a ransom for those who had been led into captivity' (v, 1, 1). In this method of redemption there is a display both of justice and mercy.

'As regards the Apostasy, justly redeeming us from it by His blood; as regards us, who were redeemed, kindly' (v, 2, 1).

Such then are those main lines of the doctrine of Irenæus, which, however, not infrequently pass over into one another. We may, before we conclude our account of his theology, refer to a great passage in which Irenæus reflects upon the necessity of both the divinity and the humanity of Christ for the work of redemption.

'He united therefore, as we said before, man to God. For unless man had vanquished the adversary of man, the enemy would not have been justly vanquished; and again, unless God had granted us salvation, we should not have had it securely, and unless man had been united to God, he could not have beeen partaker of incorruption' (III, 18, 7). Here we come upon the very

28

nerve of the doctrine of Irenæus. Christ must be God to deify man, man to overcome man's enemy.

The above passage brings closely together the doctrine of redemption from the devil and that of the communication of immortality, just as the phrase previously quoted, 'the knowledge of the Son of God, which is immortality,' brings together the communication of immortality and the bringing of knowledge. The ultimate unity of the different lines of Irenæan doctrine is, however, practical. In so far as Christianity is on the one hand the gift of immortality and on the other hand the forgiveness of sins (reconciliation with God) or redemption from the devil, it is a religion of grace. But the grace is only for those who keep the law. By faith and baptism all the blessings of salvation are secured to the Christian: there remains the task of a life under the new law of Christ, of which these blessings are the final reward. Thus the standpoint of grace in practice alternates with the standpoint of law. In spite of the attempts of Irenæus to conceive the recapitulation as the communication of an ethical life to mankind, it is not subjectively realised as an ethical regeneration in the life of the individual in virtue of which he spontaneously keeps the law. Moreover, the experience of forgiveness is restricted to the washing away of previous sin at baptism.

For the above account of the practical aspect of the teaching of Irenæus, I may refer to Werner, 'Der Paulinismus des Irenæus', 1889, pp. 202ff. It may be observed that in his practical attitude, just as in his conception of the work of Christ, Irenæus both sums up the post-apostolic age, and is typical of the Greek Christianity of the future. From the beginning in the primitive Gentile Church, where Christianity was regarded as the knowledge of God and the law and the promise of immortality, the practical understanding of it was essentially the same as that of Irenæus. Baptism was held to assure or communicate the gift of immortality with the forgiveness of pre-baptismal sin: for the rest of his life the Christian was under the law.

Further communication of the gift of immortality in the Eucharist [1] in no way alters the legal relation to God. Only the

---

[1] φάρμακον ἀθανασίας, ἀντίδοτος τοῦ μὴ ἀποθανεῖν (Ign. 'Eph.' xx, 2 ; cf. the similar ideas in Irenæus, 'Adv. Hær.' IV, 18, 5).

Gnostics and Marcion endeavoured to understand Christianity entirely as a religion of grace. But as to this end they undermined the authority of the Old Testament and so discredited themselves, their procedure did but serve to strengthen the general apprehension of Christianity as law.

The above statement of the practical Christianity of Irenæus then serves to supplement his theoretical doctrine of the work of Christ and enables us to understand its true import. At this point, however, some questions of the greatest importance emerge. Irenæus undertook to build his theology upon the threefold basis of the Creed, the Scriptures, and tradition. What now is the relation to these doctrinal standards of his teaching on the work of Christ?

It is clear that the Creed is not the source of this doctrine, any further than that it emphasises the historical facts which Irenæus evaluates. Tradition is a positive source of the doctrine in so far as it develops the ideas of the Apostolic Fathers, especially Ignatius, and of Justin. Loofs has called this particular tradition 'the tradition of Asia Minor'. But what is the relation of the doctrine of Irenæus to the Scriptures? The Old Testament is for him as for the Apostolic Fathers and the Apologists the foundation of monotheism. The New Testament, however, has supplied Irenæus with his doctrinal proofs and his means of expanding the Creed and tradition. We proceed then to examine the relation of the doctrine of Irenæus to the New Testament.

In the first place, his doctrine of the work of Christ as revelation is more Johannine than that of the Apologists. Irenæus gives prominence to the fresh revelation of God brought by the Incarnation. Moreover, in him the moralism of the Apologists is to some extent qualified by the Johannine mysticism.

As regards the Recapitulation doctrine this is undoubtedly Pauline in origin. In Eph. 1:10 we have already a pregnant use of the word ἀνακεφαλαιόω, which at least suggests the Irenæan conception of ἀνακεφαλαίωσις. From Paul comes the opposition of the first and second Adam, of the destroying disobedience of the one, and the saving obedience of the other. In Paul's conception of salvation as union with Christ in His death and resur-

30

rection we have the idea of salvation as a victory over death and an establishment of eternal life, both already given in principle in Christ and imparted by faith and baptism to the Christian.[2] It is, however, a development which carries us beyond the Pauline doctrine, when Irenæus goes back behind Christ's death and resurrection and views salvation as already given in the Incarnation itself. Harnack speaks of an amalgamation here of the Pauline gnosis of the Cross with a gnosis of the Incarnation.[3] The new idea so characteristic of Irenæus and after him of the Greek theology is given in the sentence already quoted: 'Jesus Christ . . . was made what we are that He might make us completely what He is.'[4] We have certainly an anticipation of this point of view in the isolated Pauline passage 2 C. 8:9. But the idea that salvation is already given in the Incarnation is fundamentally Johannine,[5] only that where John interprets the idea through an intellectualistic mysticism,[6] Irenæus, while not without this interpretation, in the main like Paul in Rom. 6:1ff., is realistic. The Incarnation is thought of as a ferment in humanity which leavens it with incorruption and immortality.

Finally, as regards the Irenæan doctrine of the death of Christ as ransom, the Pauline origin of this has already been fixed in our discussion on Marcion.

In view of the above statements, it may seem strange to find that Werner totally denies that the Christianity of Irenæus is a genuine development of Paulinism. According to him Irenæus, though perpetually quoting Paul, has nothing of his spirit. 'This Irenæan doctrine of salvation, however frequently it appears to be punctuated with Paulinisms . . . nevertheless is in its entire character pseudo-Pauline.'[7] Werner's view turns partly on the way in which the centre of gravity of the theology of Irenæus is displaced from the cross to the Incarnation, partly on the difference in practical attitude between Paul and Irenæus.

'The positive blessing of salvation consists (for Irenæus) not in the believing trust of the heart upon God, but in the hyperphysical transformation of human nature as a preparation for immortality. We become not God's, but God. Salvation is in

---

[2] Rom. 6:1 ff.   [3] D.G., 4th ed., vol. i, p. 561, n. 1.   [4] V. Præf.
[5] Jn 1:1–18 ; 1 Jn 1:1–4.   [6] Ibid. 17:3.   [7] Op. cit. p. 211.

31

consequence not full possession in the present, but an earnest of and preparation for the fulfilment in the future. The possession of salvation is not the source of morality, but good works are the pre-condition of receiving the gift of salvation: the morality (of Irenæus) is therefore not a religious but a self-active morality' (p. 212).

Werner's verdict that the doctrine of Irenæus is pseudo-Pauline thus involves two points:

(1) His doctrine is gnosis of the Incarnation, not of the cross, and his conception of salvation is not the blessedness of trust in God, but deification. The centre of the Irenæan theology is certainly not the doctrine of the revelation of God's love in the cross making its appeal to human trust,[8] that Pauline doctrine which was central for Luther. But the doctrine of Irenæus that salvation is the communication of immortal life and the destruction of death, both given in Christ's death and appropriated to the believer by faith and baptism, is a Pauline doctrine. Only the retrogression to the Incarnation as itself containing the whole salvation is not Pauline, but Johannine.

It is, however, true that as regards the doctrine of the communication of life to the Christian through Christ, whereas in Paul's doctrine of union with Christ 'life' means equally immortality, righteousness, and the spirit of sonship,[9] in Irenæus the stress falls most of all, though by no means exclusively, upon the hyperphysical element of immortality. Loofs speaks of an abbreviation of the tradition of Asia Minor as taking place in Irenæus, i.e. of a tendency to narrow down the Pauline-Johannine tradition received through Ignatius and Justin:[1] the process of abbreviation is, however, already begun in Ignatius and Justin. The tendency to lay the chief stress on the gift of incorruption rather than on the gifts of righteousness or of faith (trust in God) marks the change experienced by Christianity in passing over from a Jewish to a Greek soil. From the very beginning of the Greek religion death is the object of a supreme fear.[2]

[8] 2 C. 5:19.
[9] I.e. it is at once hyperphysical, ethical, and religious ; cf. 'Man, Sin, and Salvation', pp. 95–7, 123–8.   [1] D.G., 4th ed., p. 203, n. 2.
[2] Cf. Chantepie de la Saussaye, 'Lehrbuch der Religionsgeschichte', 3rd ed., vol. ii, pp. 258, 259.

'Without a doubt the thought of death commonly filled the ancestors of the Greeks also with the deepest dread. . . . Millenniums of enlightenment were not able to free the Greeks from this fear.'

Due to the influence of Greek religious thought also is the identification of the communication of immortality with 'deification'.[3] In the history of Greek religion the idea of deification as union with the God and the impartation of immortality goes back to the religion of Dionysus.[4] Through the medium of Orphism it afterwards influenced Greek philosophy.[5]

(2) The second point in Werner's indictment of Irenæus amounts to this, that he has not the Pauline conception of justification as an abiding state of communion with God in which the believer rejoices in the forgiveness of sins and faith works by love. Here no doubt Irenæus misses the evangelical nerve of Paulinism, hence Werner's view that he has nothing of Paul's spirit. But it is only fair to add that Paul himself at times tends to regard the Christian as after baptism still under the law and awaiting a final justification after death.[6] Still on the whole the practical Christianity of Irenæus, like that of the Apologists, is a moralism very different from the Pauline Christianity. Here again the influence of the Greek *milieu* makes itself felt. Compare what has been said before on the Apologists.

The Paulinism of Irenæus is then certainly not quite a pseudo-Paulinism, but still it is a Paulinism modified very considerably by Greek influences. It is only right, however, to recognise that the modification of Paul in the direction of Greek thought is already begun in the New Testament itself in the Johannine theology with its centre in the Incarnation as a manifestation of the Divine life and light, its tendency to interpret faith as knowledge, and its increased stress on the ethical over against the religious aspect of Christianity.[7]

So much then for the relation of Irenæus to Paul and to the

---

[3] Jn 10:35 and the late 2 Pet. 1:4 furnish points of contact in Scripture.

[4] Cf. my Essay, 'The Idea of Salvation in the Theology of the Eastern Church', in 'Mansfield College Essays', 1909, p. 261.

[5] *Ibid.* pp. 261–4 ; cf. Harnack, D.G., 4th ed., vol. i, p. 138, n.

[6] 'Man, Sin, and Salvation', pp. 128–9.

[7] *Ibid.* pp. 172–9.

New Testament. The ultimate question, however, which is raised by the foregoing discussion is that of the interpretation of the New Testament as a standard of doctrine. The New Testament itself neither is nor contains a system of doctrine. It rather includes within itself a number of varying and even in a measure conflicting points of view, which the theologian is called upon in some way to unify. The theology of Paul, the fullest and most developed theology which it contains, alone includes many conflicting elements, to say nothing of further conflict between Paul and other New Testament writers.

One of the chief problems of theology therefore ever since the formation of the New Testament Canon, is the question of its doctrinal interpretation. The systematic theologian has to face the questions, which points of view in the New Testament are to be taken as fundamental, how the different elements within it are to be combined, in what hierarchy of principles they are to be arranged. From first to last since the fixing of the New Testament as a norm of doctrine, the Church has wrestled with this problem and different doctrinal systems have resulted from the different solutions which have been given of it.

We see that in this way in the new age of the Church beginning with Irenæus the old principle of doctrinal development under the guidance of the Spirit reasserts itself. The difference is that the sphere of the Spirit's operation is more closely defined.

CLEMENT OF ALEXANDRIA

It is essentially the theology of Irenæus with its threefold view of the work of Christ, which finally through Athanasius became dominant in the Eastern Church. Another influence, however, which helped to form the Greek theology was that of the school of Alexandria. We have here two theologians to consider, Clement and Origen.

Upon Clement (d. *ante* A.D. 216) we may be brief, for his theological influence on posterity was only through his disciple Origen. It is Origen therefore who mainly concerns us.

As we have already seen, the theological position of Clement as regards the norms of doctrine was more archaic than that of Irenæus. The only fresh authority which Clement recognises beyond those of primitive Christianity is the New Testament: the creed is not for him a doctrinal authority. He has therefore greater theological liberty than Irenæus, in so far as the New Testament is a less definite standard of doctrine than the creed. Moreover, though he repudiates Gnosticism so far as it is dualistic and so far as it refuses the authority of the Old Testament, yet he himself in his own way is a Gnostic, and recognises an esoteric Christianity. He treats the common Christianity of the Church as a first stage (Pistis), to which the stage of Gnosis succeeds as a higher and completer Christianity.

(1) The former aspect is connected with the Incarnation. The Logos Incarnate brings the knowledge of God and of His law and of eternal life as the reward of obedience to the law. Such revelation is the ground of the common Christianity, which is a religion of fear. To this lower stage of Christianity belongs the forgiveness of sins. Christ, however, forgives sins as God: as man, He teaches us not to sin ('Pæd.' 1, 3, 7). Clement repeats the Christian tradition of the sacrifice of Christ without any inner appropriation.[8]

(2) The higher stage, however, is where the Logos reveals Himself inwardly to the heart not as man but as God. This higher revelation is mystical: it is not law, but grace, conferring the perfect freedom which obeys God spontaneously in love. At this higher stage the Incarnation ceases to have significance. 'Love is not of Jesus, but of the Logos, the Ideal. Clement could not bear to think that the rose of Sharon could blossom on common soil.' [9]

Clement clearly has close affinity with the Apologists. Like them he regards not only the Old Testament, but also the philosophy of Greece as emanating from the Divine Logos. But he adds to their moralism the intellectualistic mysticism of the Gnostics. Where, however, the latter saw opposition and conflict between the religion of law and the religion of grace, Clement sees only a lower and a higher stage. Thus he overcomes the heretical gnosis by a Catholic gnosis.

[8] Cf. Seeberg, D.G., 2nd ed., vol. i, p. 399.
[9] Bigg, 'The Christian Platonists of Alexandria', p. 93.

The theology of Clement stands in sharp contrast with the realism of Irenæus. Bigg says of him (p. 75): 'The idea of the Recapitulation of all men in Christ as the Second Adam, so fruitful in the brooding soul of Irenæus, is strange to him.' He says indeed of Christ that 'having taken on the character of man and having fashioned Himself in flesh He enacted the drama of salvation'.[1] But he says again that 'the Word of God became man, that thou mayest learn from man, how man may become God'.[2] The Incarnate Logos is for us a teacher and an example only.

ORIGEN

Origen (d. A.D. 245), Clement's disciple, is the first Christian theologian who (in his work 'De Principiis') deliberately sets out to form a system or body of Christian doctrine. This he proceeds to do by the development of the elements of Christian truth which compose the Rule of Faith. Origen's Rule of Faith, however, is not an actual creed, but rather an elementary statement (of his own) of the fundamentals of Apostolic Christianity, as believed by the Church. The author of the faith is Christ, the Logos, who speaks not only in the Incarnation, but in the Old Testament and the Apostles. From the elements of the Rule of Faith the body of truth is to be developed either by addition of fresh elements from Scripture, or of deduction from what is given.[3]

Origen has devoted in 'De Principiis', Book VI, particular attention to the method of Scripture proof. It is necessary in order to refute Jews and heretics to recognise in Scripture not only a literal, but also a moral and a spiritual sense. Sometimes even there is no literal sense. By means of observing the spiritual sense of Scripture it is possible to attain to the wisdom of the perfect.

Origen thus in his theology is prepared to carry out the programme of Clement and understand Christianity as a Pistis advancing to Gnosis.

What then are Origen's results as far as concerns the doctrine of the work of Christ? His doctrine takes two forms. There is

---

[1] 'Strom.' 7, 2, 5. [2] 'Protrept.' ɪ, 8. [3] 'De Principiis', Præfatio.

first the treatment in the 'De Principiis', which we must regard as primary. It is, however, very limited in extent, occurring only in one or two short passages of his treatise. But besides this strictly scientific treatment, there is also a more extended form of doctrine to be drawn from his commentaries on the Scripture.

(1) *The doctrine of the 'De Principiis'.* This is virtually a repetition of Clement. In the first place Christ is for us in His Incarnation an example.

'On this account is Christ proposed for us as an example to all believers, because as He always, even before He knew evil at all, chose the good and loved righteousness, and hated iniquity and therefore God anointed Him with the oil of gladness; so also must each one, after a lapse or error, cleanse himself from stains, in view of His example, and taking Him as the guide of his journey, enter upon the steep way of virtue; that so perchance by this means, as far as possible, we may by imitating Him be made partakers of the Divine nature' (IV, 31).

Still even this is only living under the shadow of Christ. As our shadow repeats the movements of the body, so Christ's human soul repeats the movements of the Divine Word, and may be called His shadow. To imitate the human example of Christ is then to live under His shadow, and well befits this life of ours here in this world, which itself is a shadow. But beyond this life is one where there is no shadow, where we shall no longer live under the shadow of Christ, a state of things which the apostle anticipated through the Spirit when he said, 'Yea, though we have known Christ after the flesh, yet now henceforth know we Him so no more.' [4]

And now in this view of things what place for the cross? By the imitation of the Divine Word or Wisdom we become wise or rational. But Christ meets also the weak by condescending to their weakness, and by being through weakness crucified.[5] Thus the doctrine of the cross remains as comfort for those who are not yet strong enough to avail themselves of Christ's example.

The general background of this doctrine of the work of Christ in the 'De Principiis' is the view of the world as a place of discipline for fallen spirits: Origen held the fall to have taken

[4] Cf. II, 6, 7 and 2 C. 5:16.   [5] Cf. IV, 31.

place for each spirit in a state of pre-existence. In the present disciplinary state each spirit is subject to temptation from spirits worse than itself, especially the demons, but is helped by the example and influence of these better than itself. The Logos, who in His Incarnation has united Himself with a sinless human soul, appears as the Supreme Influence for good in a sinful world.

(2) From the doctrine of the 'De Principiis' we pass on to the extended doctrine of the commentaries on Scripture. It was the design of Origen to establish the Christian doctrine not only in systematic form, but also in the form of Scriptural exegesis. This form of treatment naturally brings his doctrine much nearer to the common ecclesiastical Christianity, since the letter of Scripture is not so constantly transmuted into its spiritual essence as in the 'De Principiis'. The work 'Against Celsus' also comes in here, in so far as its presentation of Christianity runs parallel with that in the commentaries, and stands nearer to the popular Christianity than that of the 'De Principiis'. But the 'De Principiis' helps us to see how the more extended doctrine is to be understood. For according to Origen the content of Scripture and the 'De Principiis' is the same; as IV, 14 practically indicates. Primary therefore is the doctrine of the work of Christ as revelation, secondary the doctrine of the cross.

(a) The former doctrine does not receive much expansion beyond what we have already found in the 'De Principiis'. There is first the thought of Christ as Teacher, Lawgiver, and example. The Gospel which He brings is a teaching, distinct from the ceremonial of Judaism. It is spiritual and universal ('Con. Cels.' VII, 26).

Origen distinguishes this 'spiritual law' ('Con. Cels.' v, 33) from the law of nature, as a law of faith ('In Rom.' IV, 4). Its essential content is the knowledge of God, faith in Jesus as the Son of God, the following of His commandments in a virtuous life, and the promise of reward and punishment.[6] Besides this Christ is an example of virtue.[7] But as in the 'De Principiis', it is taught that there is a point when the humanity of Jesus is transcended.

---

[6] 'Con. Cels.' v, 51–3 ; VII, 17, 48ff. ; VIII, 1, 51, 75.　　　[7] *Ibid.* VIII, 17, 56.

'Christ as flesh preaches the Gospel and calls to Himself those who are flesh, that He may first cause them to be transformed according to the Word made flesh, and after this may raise them to see Him as He was before He became flesh; so that they, receiving profit, and advancing beyond the preliminary teaching according to the flesh, may say, "even if we have known Christ after the flesh, we now know Him so no more".'[8]

(b) The doctrine of the cross in the commentaries and the work against Celsus. This takes a variety of forms.

(i) Christ overcomes the demons, who seduce and lead men astray, not only by His doctrine but by His death. According to the view of Origen the demons are in constant warfare with the Christian Church, and the Church is equally at war with the demons. Every triumph of the one constitutes a reverse of the other. Origen teaches, moreover, that in the deaths of the martyrs there is a mighty power which counteracts the dominion of the demons.[9]

A supreme instance of such victory over the forces of evil occurred when the demons crucified Christ. Origen supports his view of the demon-compelling power of our Lord's death by an appeal to the belief common in antiquity that innocent men by giving themselves up for the common weal have removed pestilences or other calamities from peoples or states.

Cf. 'Con. Cels.' I, 31: 'For it is probable that there is in the nature of things for certain mysterious reasons which are difficult to be understood by the multitude, such a virtue that one just man, dying a voluntary death for the common good, might be the means of removing wicked spirits, which are the cause of plagues, or distresses, or dangers to shipping, or similar calamities.'

Cf. again 'Con. Cels.' VII, 17: 'There is nothing absurd in a man having died, and in his death being not only an example of death endured for the sake of piety, but also making a beginning and advance of the destruction of that evil spirit, the devil, who had obtained dominion over the whole world.'

(ii) From this view it is not very far to that other which we find frequently in the commentaries of Origen and which continues

---

[8] *Ibid.* VI, 68. [9] *Ibid.* VIII, 44.

a development already begun by Irenæus, viz. that the death of Christ was a ransom-price paid by God to the devil, who had acquired a claim to men through their sin, which claim, however, he lost by accepting as a ransom the death of Christ.

Cf. 'In Rom.' II, 13 : 'If therefore we were bought with a price, as Paul also agrees, without doubt we were bought from some one, whose slaves we were, who also demanded what price he would, to let go from his power those whom he held. Now it was the devil who held us, to whom we had been sold by our sins. He demanded therefore as our price, the blood of Christ.' Cf. also 'In Exod.' VI, 9.

So far the doctrine agrees with Irenæus. But Origen has developed further the conception of which we have hints in 1 C. 2:8 (a text continually upon his lips), and again in Ignatius and Marcion (see above, p. 15), viz. that the devil was deceived in the transaction. Cf. 'In Matt.' XIII, 8, where 1 C. 2:8 is referred to. Above all cf. 'In Matt.' XVI, 8.

'But to whom did He give His soul as a ransom for many? Certainly not to God: why not then to the devil? For he had possession of us until there should be given to him the ransom for us, the soul of Jesus; though he was deceived by thinking that he could have dominion over it and did not see that he could not bear the torture caused by holding it.'

Again on Ps. 35 (34):8, Origen says of the words 'Let him fall into his own snare' as follows: 'I think that he speaks of the cross, into which the devil in ignorance fell. For if he had known, he would not have crucified the Lord of Glory.'

In another passage ('In Matt.' XIII, 9), the deceit is directly ascribed to God, that the demons 'might be laughed at by Him who dwells in the heavens, and might be ridiculed by the Lord, having received the Son from the Father unto the destruction of their own kingdom and rule contrary to their expectation'.

It is noteworthy in view of subsequent developments that Origen sometimes substitutes death for the devil. So in the continuation of the previous quotation ('In Matt.' XVI, 8), it is said that since the devil could not hold the soul of Christ 'death also that thought to have dominion over Him, has dominion no more, He being free among the dead and stronger than the power

40

of death'. So again in another passage ('In Matt.' xiii, 9) we have the words, 'his enemy death being brought to nought'.

(iii) Origen has also the idea of a sacrifice to God. Bigg [1] and Harnack [2] point out that he is the first theologian since Paul with a developed doctrine of sacrifice. In this he is epoch-making.[3]

Thus Origen writes: 'If there had not been sin, it had not been necessary for the Son of God to become a lamb, nor had need been that He, having become incarnate, should be slaughtered, but He would have remained what He was, God the Word; but since sin entered into this world, whilst the necessity of sin requires a propitiation, and a propitiation is not made but by a victim, it was necessary that a victim should be provided for sin.' [4]

Cf. also 'In Lev.' i, 2; iii, 1, and especially 'In Joh.' xxviii, 14: 'This man, purer than any living being, died on behalf of the people, who bore our sins and infirmities, since He was able to take upon Himself the sin of the whole world and to undo and to dissipate it and make it disappear, because he did no sin.'

Origen says that sin necessarily requires a propitiation, but he nowhere deduces the necessity of the propitiation from the righteousness of God. He comes nearest to doing so 'In Rom.' iii, 7, 8, but does not actually reach this idea.[5] Nor again does Origen's explanation of the nature of the propitiation lie in the idea of a satisfaction to God, but rather in the mysterious cleansing power of the shed blood of sacrifice. Cf. 'In Rom.' iii, 8 where he quotes Heb. 9:22. He says, however,[6] 'the death which is inflicted for sin by way of punishment is the cleansing of the very sin for which it is commanded to be inflicted. The sin therefore is remitted by the penalty of death.' This reminds one of Paul's doctrine in Rom. 6:7.

The idea of substitutionary suffering also is quite undeveloped in Origen. He often, however, speaks of Jesus as having suffered for man; and in one place ('In Lev.' i, 3) he says, 'He placed the sins of the human race upon His head. For Himself is the head

---

[1] 'Christian Platonists', p. 210.   [2] D.G., 4th ed., vol. i, p. 682, n. 3.
[3] Cf. Harnack, D.G., 4th ed., vol. ii, p. 177.   [4] 'In Num.' xxiv, 1.
[5] Cf. Baur, 'Die Christliche Lehre von der Versöhnung', p. 61, n. 1.
[6] 'In Lev.' xiv, 4.

of the body which is His Church.' This passage at least suggests that the explanation of the possibility of the substitution lies in the peculiar relation of Christ to His people.

Such then is Origen's extended and developed doctrine of the cross. There is no doubt that the cross meant much to Origen. On the other hand there is also no doubt that in the end it is a doctrine belonging only to the lower stage of Christianity. This is not merely to be proved by a reference to the essential doctrine of the 'De Principiis': the commentaries and the work 'Against Celsus,' in spite of their emphasis on the cross, leave us no doubt on the point.

Cf. 'Con. Cels.' III, 62: 'God the Word was sent as a physician to sinners, but as a teacher of the Divine mysteries to those already pure and no longer sinning.'

Also cf. 'In 1 Joh.' I, 22: 'Blessed are they, as many as needing the Son of God have become such as no longer need Him as a physician healing those who are ill, nor as a shepherd, nor as redemption, but as wisdom and word and righteousness, or anything else to those who through perfection can receive of Him what is best.'

The ultimate tendency of the doctrine of Origen both in its systematic and essential, and also in its extended and Scriptural form remains the same as with Clement. The practical difference between the two is that Origen is less confident than Clement of the ability of the individual to attain in this life to the higher or Gnostic stage.[7]

It is important to observe the exact relation of the different elements of the Origenistic to those of the Irenæan doctrine.

(1) Common to both is the idea of Christ as the Teacher and Lawgiver. But with Origen this belongs to the first stage of Christianity only, with Irenæus it is never in this life transcended.

(2) Common to both is the view of the first forgiveness of sins in baptism, based upon redemption from the devil or sacrifice to God.[8] This is for both systems the necessary preparation for a life under the law.

(3) The difference is in the doctrine of the communication of immortality or deification. With Irenæus this is, in spite of such

---

[7] Cf. Bigg, op. cit., p. 210. [8] *Ibid.* p. 211, n.

Johannine passages as 'the knowledge of the Son of God, which is incorruption' (above, p. 25), in the main realistically conceived as communicated to humanity by the Incarnation. Along with forgiveness this gift of immortality then forms the grace sacramentally conveyed to the individual at baptism, while at the same time it remains the ultimate goal of Christian obedience. Origen on the other hand, following Clement, spiritualises deification into the indwelling of the Logos in the individual Christian, which belongs to the higher or Gnostic stage of Christianity, which is a life beyond the law, but which is brought about through the teaching and example of Jesus. Origen, as Loofs says, could not ignore the doctrine of physical redemption, but he has spiritualised it away.[9] What the union of the Divine and human in the person of Jesus meant for him is made clear by the following passage:[1]

'Both Jesus Himself and His disciples desired that His adherents should not merely believe in His Godhead and miracles, as if He had not also been a partaker of human nature, and had not assumed the human flesh with lusteth against the spirit; but they saw also that the Power which had descended into human nature, and into the midst of human circumstances, and which had assumed a human soul and body, contributed by being believed in, along with things yet more Divine, to the salvation of believers, who see that from Him there began the union of the Divine with the human nature, in order that the human by communion with the Divine might become Divine, not in Jesus only, but in all those who not only believe, but also enter upon the life which Jesus taught, and which elevates to friendship with God and communion with Him everyone who lives according to the precepts of Jesus.'

Here deification is conceived, not as essentially the impartation of a hyperphysical gift of immortality, but rather as the union of the Logos with the humanity of Jesus which repeats itself in the religious and moral life of each of His true disciples. It is noteworthy in this connexion that Origen (following Clement), while retaining in his popular teaching realistic views of the Eucharist like those of Ignatius and Irenæus, in his doctrine

---

[9] D.G., 4th ed., p. 203.   [1] 'Con. Cels.' III, 28.

for the initiated altogether spiritualises this sacrament into a symbol of the inner gift of the Logos.[2]

Such then is the relation of the theology of Origen to that of Irenæus. Origen's influence on the following age was not through his aim, which was rejected, but through his actual development of doctrine. While in general the Irenæan and not the Origenistic scheme prevailed, yet the Greek theology enriched itself from the abundant stores of Origen, especially from his commentaries. Hence may be understood the words of Harnack: 'One must say in general that Origen has helped to trail into the Church an abundance of ancient (heathen) notions with reference to expiation and redemption, always finding some Biblical passages or other with which to connect them.' [3] The idea of the mysterious demon-compelling power of sacrifice is certainly a legacy from the ancient Greek (Chthonian) religion. Compare again my Essay, 'The Idea of Salvation in the Theology of the Eastern Church.' [4]

It is only right, however, to measure Origen not by his actual results, but by his aim. When we do this, there is no doubt that Origen, like Clement before him, has in his own way reproduced in his doctrine of the Christian Gnostic, the spirit of evangelical freedom from the law, which is altogether lost by Irenæus and is not found again so clearly expressed till we come to Luther.[5]

[2] Cf. Rauschen, 'Eucharistie und Busssakrament in den ersten sechs Jahrhunderten der Kirche', 1908, pp. 7–10.

[3] D.G., 4th ed., vol. i, p. 683, n.   [4] 'Mansfield College Essays', p. 262.

[5] The Christian Gnosticism of Clement and Origen has a contemporary pagan parallel in the Neoplatonism of Plotinus (A.D. 205–270), which, along with the also contemporary Manichæism of Mani (d. A.D. 276), deserves brief notice here, inasmuch as each of these systems later touches our subject at important points (v. infra, pp. 87, 207, 510). The Neoplatonic doctrine of salvation exhibits three stages of progressive deliverance from the world : (1) purification of the senses by virtue ; (2) participation in the νοῦς or Divine Reason : (3) union through ecstasy with the Transcendent Source of Being, of which the νοῦς is only the first emanation, intermediate between It and the world. As far as the second stage there is general agreement with the Alexandrian Gnosis : the third stage, however, goes beyond it. Clement and Origen were not mystics to this degree (cf. Bigg, op. cit., p. 99, n. 1). The resemblance of Manichæism is not to the new Catholic, but to the old heretical Gnosis (supra, pp. 12ff.). There are two ultimate principles, Light (good) and Darkness (evil), from whose mixture the world and man originate. The redemption of man is through knowledge and asceticism : hereby the elements of light in him are delivered from their dark prison.

CHAPTER 3

THE LATER GREEK THEOLOGY

ATHANASIUS

FROM Athanasius (d. A.D. 373) comes the first complete and systematic treatment of the doctrine of the work of Christ. In the case of Irenæus we had to gather our material from a series of different presentations in the work 'Against Heresies'. In that of Origen we had to supplement the very brief treatment of the subject in the 'De Principiis' by a survey of the doctrine of the commentaries and the 'Contra Celsum'. Athanasius, however, has devoted a special treatise to the subject of the work of Christ. in His 'De Incarnatione', written in his earlier years before the outbreak of the Arian controversy, he shows the necessity of the Incarnation of the Word, by means of a doctrinal statement which stands alone in the Early Church for completeness and clearness. It is based, certainly with modifications and developments, on the doctrine of Irenæus, but Athanasius has also appropriated further Pauline elements left unused by Irenæus. The idea of recapitulation, moreover, ceases to dominate the theological situation in the way that it does with Irenæus. What Athanasius retains from him is rather the conception of the deification of humanity through the Incarnation.

'It is a closely reasoned process of thought (*ein straffer Gedankengang*) which Athanasius develops.' [1]

Starting from the assumption of the existence of God, and of the activity of the Logos in creation and providence, Athanasius proposes to unfold the doctrine of the Incarnation (1, 1).

The doctrine of the Incarnation presupposes the doctrine of creation. Man's redemption by the Word fitly follows upon his creation by the Word (1, 4). God in His goodness made man by

---

[1] Kattenbusch, 'Lehrbuch der vergleichenden Confessionskunde', 1892, p. 297.

the Word, and has distinguished him above all other created
beings in further endowing him with the Logos, thus making him
rational and putting him who was naturally corruptible in the
way to incorruption (3, 3). But God made the retention of the
Logos and the promise of immortality involved in it consequent
upon man's obedience to a law, the command given in paradise
(3, 4). Man, however, transgressed this law and forfeited both
the Logos and the hope of incorruption. Death now reigned over
him as a king (4, 4), having in addition to its natural power over
men the additional hold given by the Divine commandment with
its threat of death to the transgressor (5, 2).

Here then was an unseemly state of things (6, 2). On the one
hand God's threat could not remain unexecuted without making
Him false (6, 3). Yet on the other it was unseemly that man whom
God had made rational and destined for incorruption should
perish (6, 4). Neither the deceit of the devil (6, 5), nor the folly
of man (6, 6), ought to avail to undo God's purpose.

What then was God to do? To demand repentance. Man's
repentance might undo his transgression (7, 2). But it would
fail, firstly, to guard what was reasonable with regard to God
(τὸ εὔλογον τὸ πρὸς τὸν θεόν) (7, 3); and, secondly, it would not
call man back from corruption (7, 4). These two things could
only be achieved by the Logos, who alone was able to recreate
everything, and was worthy to suffer on behalf of all, and to
be the ambassador of all with the Father (7, 5). In His love to
men, therefore, the Logos undertook both tasks, and for this
purpose assumed a body like our own (8, 1, 2).

This, moreover, in His loving kindness He gave over to death
in the stead of all, and offered it to the Father; (1) that all
being held to have died in Him, the law involving the ruin of
men might be undone, its power having been spent in the Lord's
body, and having no longer holding ground against men His
peers; (2) that by the appropriation of His body and by the
grace of the Resurrection He might quicken men to incorruption
(8, 4).

The Word did this, perceiving that the corruption of men
could no otherwise be undone except by death as a necessary
condition. In offering His own body He offered an equivalent

(ἠφάνιζε τὸν θάνατον τῇ προσφορᾷ τοῦ καταλλήλου) (9, 1); and He satisfied the debt by His death (ἐπλήρου τὸ ὀφειλόμενον ἐν τῷ θανάτῳ) (9, 2).

Moreover, the quickening of mankind begins with the Incarnation itself, though only in so far as this is the guarantee of the subsequent Death and Resurrection of the Lord.

'The Incorruptible Son of God, being conjoined with all by a like nature, naturally clothed all with incorruption by the promise of the Resurrection. . . . For now that He has come to our realm, and taken up His abode in one body among His peers, henceforth the whole conspiracy of the enemy against mankind is checked and the corruption of death, which before was prevailing against them, is done away. For the race of men had gone to ruin, had not the Lord and Saviour of all come among us to meet the end of death' (9, 2, 4).

Such a work was peculiarly suitable to the goodness of God, who had created man (10, 1). As Scriptural proofs are advanced 2 C. 5:14, Heb. 2:9f., 1 C. 15:21f. (10, 2–5).

There was, however, a second reason for the Incarnation. God, knowing that man in his weakness was not sufficient to know Him, made him in the image of the Word, that so, perceiving the Word, he might know the Father (11, 1–3). However, man despised this knowledge and fell into the superstition of idolatry and magic (11, 4–7). While the grace of the Divine image was itself enough to make known the Word and so the Father, God in His mercy to the weakness of man manifested Himself further in the creation, and then through the law and the prophets (12, 1, 2). Nor was the law for the Jews alone, nor yet the prophets: but these latter, sent to the Jews, and persecuted by them, were a school of the true knowledge of God for the whole world (12, 5). Nevertheless men were still seduced by sense and the demons (12, 6). Therefore God to renew in man the grace of His image sent His Image Himself, the Word, to recreate man afresh after the image (13, 7). Athanasius refers to Lk. 19:10. It was not sufficient that the Word should be manifested in the creation (14, 7). This manifestation had failed. Therefore the Word became incarnate, that those who would not know Him from His providence in the creation, 'may even from the works done by His actual body know the Word of God who is in the body, and through Him the Father' (14, 8). Athanasius quotes 1 C. 1:21 (15, 1).

Thus the Word met all man's errors: whether man was induced to worship nature, man, the demons, or the dead, He showed by His miracles His power over all these (15, 3–7). Moreover, seeing that man had fallen to things of sense, He met him here also, attracting their senses to Himself as man, showing by His miracles that He is God the Word (16, 1). Hence on coming into the world He did not immediately accomplish His sacrifice, but first did His miraculous works (16, 4). Christ's very birth from a virgin was the beginning of His miracles (18, 5). Moreover, even at His death on the Cross He showed His miraculous power in the eclipse of the sun and the earthquake (19, 3). By this transition Athanasius returns to the subject of Christ's death, which 'is the sum of our faith' (19, 4). He apologises for repetition; but in expounding the counsel of God it is better to incur the charge of repetition than to leave anything out (20, 3). He seeks now to show that the manner of Christ's death was the fittest possible. The most important point is that in accepting an ignominious death at the hands of His enemies, He all the more showed His triumph over death (24, 2, 3). Besides, in dying on the cross (1) He bore the curse for us,[2] since such a death is accursed;[3] (2) on it He held out His hand to unite Jews and Gentiles;[4] finally, by dying in the air He cleared the air of evil spirits,[5] and prepared the way for us to heaven.[6] That death is destroyed and that the cross is the victory over it, is shown by the faith and constancy of the martyrs, who now no longer fear death (27–29).

Moreover, the Risen Christ shows His power in the conversion of multitudes in all lands (30, 4), and in destroying the power of idols and of witchcraft (31, 2).

In chaps. 33–40 Athanasius now produces Old Testament proofs of the Incarnation against the Jews, and then in chaps. 41–55 rational proofs of it against the Greeks. The latter largely embrace the ground already covered.

---

[2] Gal. 3:13.   [3] Dt. 21:23.   [4] Eph. 2:14 ; Jn 12:32.
[5] Eph. 2:2.   [6] Heb. 10:20.

Finally, he describes his treatise as a rudimentary sketch and outline in brief compass of the faith concerning Christ and His Divine appearance in the world. It may be expanded from the inspired Scriptures. Athanasius has it himself by a sacred tradition from the past (56, 1, 2).

Scripture, however, tells us also of Christ's second coming to Judgment (56, 3). Both knowledge of the Scriptures and the eternal reward are for those who live a virtuous life and love God and the Father through our Lord Jesus Christ (57, 1, 2).

Such is in abstract the doctrine of the 'De Incarnatione'. The two following passages from the treatise are noteworthy as concentrating it in a few words:

'By His becoming man the Saviour was to accomplish both works of love; first in putting away death and renewing us again; secondly, being unseen and invisible, in manifesting Himself and making Himself known by His works to be the Word of the Father, and the Ruler and King of the Universe' (16, 5).

'He was made man that we might be made God (Αὐτὸς ἐνηνθρώπησεν, ἵνα ἡμεῖς θεοποιηθῶμεν); and He manifested Himself by a body, that we might receive the idea of the unseen Father' (54, 3).

The theory of Athanasius demands the most careful scrutiny, in view both of its intrinsic character and its historical results. If Origen is, as Harnack says, epoch-making in being the first after Paul to present a developed doctrine of the sacrifice of Christ, much more is Athanasius epoch-making, on the one hand in having reduced to the utmost clearness the Greek view of the work of Christ as the communication to humanity of incorruption and as the revelation of God, and on the other hand in having been the first after Paul to develop a doctrine of the death of Christ as a satisfaction of the Divine sentence. There is no doubt that as regards the last aspect of his doctrine Athanasius is Pauline through and through. We have to recognise in his theology a fresh influx of Paulinism into the history of our doctrine.

The following points now demand attention in detail.

(1) As regards the doctrine of the death of Christ as a satis-

faction of the Divine sentence, there is practically no difference
between Athanasius and Paul, except that the attribute which
demands the satisfaction is for Paul the Divine righteousness,[7]
for Athanasius the Divine veracity, and again that with Paul the
'law' which demands satisfaction is the law of Moses,[8] with
Athanasius the commandment given to Adam.[9] The idea of the
necessity of a satisfaction is, moreover, made explicit, whereas
with Paul it is only implied.[1] For the rest, Athanasius follows
Paul most closely, Christ's death is at once a sacrifice to God [2]
and a satisfaction of the Divine sentence:[3] it is a death for us,
and yet we die in Him.[4] In fact it cannot be said that just here
Athanasius has cleared up anything that Paul left undetermined.
He hardly does more than reproduce Pauline doctrine without
development. It will be remembered that he is sensible that he
repeats himself, but fears to lose any revealed truth.

(2) When we pass on to the doctrine of the Incarnation and
Resurrection as a destruction of death and a communication
to humanity of immortality, here once more Athanasius follows
Paul, but Paul as already interpreted by Irenæus. Even more
than in Irenæus is the 'abbreviation of the tradition of Asia
Minor' noticeable.[5] Attention is more than ever centred upon
incorruption ($\dot{a}\phi\theta a\rho\sigma i a$) as the great gift communicated to
humanity by the Incarnation.

'The thoughts of the doctrine of recapitulation, which
apprehend Christ as the Beginner of a new humanity, are as
good as entirely vanished; and in spite of Biblical reminiscences
in this physical doctrine of redemption the sinful state of
humanity almost entirely recedes behind the sentence of death:
"If there were only trangression and no consequence of
corruption, repentance were well enough" ' (7, 4).[6]

The moral and religious effects of the Resurrection in
awakening faith and hope are certainly not altogether overlooked
by Athanasius, but are very secondary in his argument.

(3) The view of Christ's work as the revelation of God is
very clearly expressed by Athanasius, but in reality contains

---

[7] Rom. 3:25.   [8] Gal. 3:13.   [9] Cf., however, Rom. 5:15–19.
[1] Cf., however, the deutero-Pauline passage Heb. 2:9, 10.   [2] Rom. 3:25.
[3] Gal. 3:13.   [4] 2 C. 5:14.   [5] Cf. Loofs, D.G., 4th ed., p. 231.
[6] Op. cit. p. 232.

nothing beyond what we have already found in the Apologists, Irenæus, and Origen.

(4) Athanasius develops his whole argument on the basis of reason (the Logos doctrine) and Scripture. He makes fully explicit the presupposition of Irenæus, viz. that the God of creation and redemption is one. Both creation and redemption are through the Logos. This fundamental character of the Logos doctrine serves to establish a general harmony between reason and authority. The problem as to where revelation transcends reason is not felt, as it is by later theologians.

(5) Finally, the practical view of Athanasius is that of Irenæus. He is at this point no more Pauline than his predecessor. Virtue and knowledge and the love of God and Christ prepare men for the eternal reward (57, 3).

To sum up, the significance of Athanasius lies, firstly, in the bringing in of fresh Pauline points of view; secondly, in the closely systematic character of his treatise; and, thirdly, in the harmonisation of authority and reason in his doctrine. He has gathered up and woven together the threads of doctrine which before him were floating loosely apart. In him the theology of the Eastern Church found its first clear expression.

One additional minor point may be noted for the sake of completeness. The doctrine of the price paid to the devil disappears in Athanasius in favour of the doctrine of the satisfaction of the Divine sentence. Yet Athanasius had not divested the death of Christ of all relation to the devil. According to him it took place in the air, not on the earth, our Lord being lifted up upon the cross, that He might clear the air of the malignity of the devil (the prince of the power of the air) and of demons of all kinds (25, 6). Here is the idea, already found in Origen, of the demon-compelling power of sacrifice.

THE NICENE CREED

The Nicene Creed (A.D. 325) falls after the 'De Incarnatione' of Athanasius, which was probably written in A.D. 318. We have now to estimate the significance of this fundamental creed for the doctrine of the work of Christ.

After the confession of God, the Father Almighty, Maker of all things visible and invisible, the Creed proceeds as follows:

'And (we believe) in One Lord Jesus Christ, the Son of God, only begotten of the Father, that is of the essence (οὐσίας) of the Father, God of God, Light of Light, very God of very God, begotten, not made, of one substance (ὁμοούσιον) with the Father, through whom all things were made, both the things in heaven and the things upon earth; who for us men and for our salvation came down and was made flesh, was made man, suffered and rose again on the third day, ascended into heaven, and cometh to judge the quick and the dead.'[7]

The importance of the Creed for our present study is that it further defines the Person of the Logos who became incarnate for human salvation, in the interest of asserting his true and essential Godhead. In opposition to the inflorioristic view of Arius, who for the sake of a philosophical explanation of the world made the Logos a creature, and conceded to Him a Godhead only of the second order, the Creed asserts that He is of one substance with the Father, and is true God. That the assertion was made in the direct interests of the Greek doctrine of redemption, is well shown by the apology of Athanasius for the term ὁμοούσιος in his 'Epistola de Synodis Arimini et Seleuciæ' written in A.D. 359.

'Again, if, as we have said before, the Son does not exist by participation (ἐκ μετουσίας), but, whilst all other things, being created, have by participation the grace of God, He, on the other hand, is the Wisdom and Word of the Father, in whom all things participate—it follows that He, being the deifying and illuminating (energy) of the Father, in Whom all things are deified and illuminated, is not of another substance (ἀλλοτριούσιος) from the Father, but of the same substance (ὁμοούσιος). For by participation of Him we are made participators of the Father, since He is the Father's own Logos. Wherefore, if He were by participation, and not of Himself, essential Godhead (οὐσιώδης θεότης) and the image of the Father, He could not deify, being Himself the subject of deification (οὐκ ἂν ἐθεοποίησε, θεοποιούμενος καὶ

---

[7] Hahn, 'Bibliothek der Symbole und Glaubensregeln der alten Kirche', 3rd ed., 1897, pp. 160ff.

αὐτός). For it is not possible that one who had Godhead by participation, could communicate to others what he himself had received, since it is not of himself that he has it, but of the Giver, and as to what he has received, he has hardly received sufficient grace for himself.' [8]

GREGORY OF NYSSA

The other great systematic treatment of the doctrine of the work of Christ which the Greek Church has produced beside the 'De Incarnatione' of Athanasius is contained in the 'Great Catechism' of Gregory of Nyssa (d. c. A.D. 394). It is a presentation of the subject less rounded and complete than the Athanasian, but shows further reflection on some important points. There is the same desire as in Athanasius to harmonise reason and authority. But Gregory is more conscious than Athanasius that the Incarnation cannot altogether be rationally explained. The sick man must not prescribe his cure. We cannot expect wholly to understand the Divine goodness till the next life. Still it is good to help faith by reason (17).

The Trinity having been established for the Greeks on the basis of common notions, and for the Jews on the basis of Scripture, Gregory proceeds (5) to the great stumbling-block of Greeks and Jews alike, viz. the Incarnation. Through the Logos God has created the world and in particular man, as it was not fit that there should be none to behold the Invisible Light and to enjoy the Divine goodness. Man is therefore made, by sharing to an extent the Divine nature, fit to participate in God. He is endowed with life, reason, wisdom, etc., above all with immortality: all these things are included in the Scriptural idea of the Divine image. Such and no other in view of the Divine goodness must have been the original state of man. His present passibility and mortality must have another cause. God in His goodness did not deprive man of that noblest grace, the exercise of free will, otherwise the Divine image would have been falsified.

The cause of trouble then was as follows (6): The Prince of this world envied the constitution of man, and persuaded him

[8] 'De Syn.' 51.

53

by fraud to become his own slayer. He led him to turn from God, his strength, and thus brought him to sin. The necessary result of sin, however, was misery and death. Just as virtue leads to life and impassibility, so vice necessarily leads to all evils.

Since man then was thus fallen, how was he to be restored to the first grace? Who but God, Who had first made him, could restore him? (8).

The difficulty, however, is that the way of salvation was the Incarnation with all that it involves. But why so much difficulty? Are birth, growth, etc., in themselves evil and unworthy of God? (9). Or again, if it be argued that the finite cannot contain the infinite, is not mind in a way infinite, and yet united to a finite body, and not thereby circumscribed? (10). We do not know how mind is united with body, nor Divinity with humanity; but the miracles of Christ show the fact of the union (11). If birth and death are marks of humanity, the virgin birth and the resurrection manifest Divinity (13).

What then was the cause of the Incarnation? (14). The answer is (15): our disease needed a physician, fallen man one to lift him up and restore him to life and to participation in the good, our darkness needed illumination, the captive needed a redeemer. But why did not God restore us to our pristine state directly by Divine omnipotence: why the circuit of the Incarnation? On the other hand, why not? There is nothing contrary to God in the creature, but only in darkness, death, and vice. But at least (16) the Incarnation implied the passion of the immutable. No: the Incarnation was a Divine action rather than passion. Christ's birth was an action; since it took place without lust. So also, therefore, was the life following upon it an action. Finally Christ's death as the separation of His soul and body was not a passion, unless the union of His body and soul was a passion. In His death His soul and body were separated, each being still united to His Divinity, that they might be reunited to each other. the dross of sin having been purged out of the vessel of humanity when it was broken (cf. 8). From the Incarnation this purging of sin by death proceeds to humanity in general, inasmuch as here also soul and body are united in a more general way by the Logos.

But why (17), if Christ had power to destroy death and confer life, the long circuit of the Incarnation? It is folly (18) to challenge the wisdom of the Incarnation. The works of Christ sufficiently show the fact of it, viz. the abolition of idolatry, the spread of the Church, its rites and its philosophy, also the Christian fearlessness of death.

From what point, however, must we start in a rational explanation of it? (19). All agree (20) that we must believe God not only to be powerful, but just, good, wise, and all that is excellent: moreover, none of these can be realised without the rest. They must then concur in the Incarnation. Its goodness is apparent in the salvation of fallen man: wisdom must be added, and also justice.

Man was created with free will (21), and fell deceived by the tempter. God, as good, pities him; as wise, He is not ignorant of the mode of redemption. Wisdom, however, is to know what is just. Justice demands (22) that as man of his free will had given himself to Satan, God must not use force to deliver us, but pay a price to him for us. What would Satan (23), who at first envied the happiness of man, and so fell, accept instead of him, but one better than he, i.e. Jesus, the virgin-born and the worker of miracles? Satan coveted to get this Divine power into his possession. If, however, he had perceived that it was Divine, he would rather have dreaded than coveted it. Therefore God needed to hide it beneath the veil of the flesh. Thus goodness is displayed in God's will to save, justice in the giving of a *quid pro quo*, wisdom in the devising that Satan might take what he could not retain. But where (24) are the Divine power and incorruption? The power of God is seen most of all in His achieving a thing so contrary to His nature as the humiliation of the Incarnation. On the other hand, however, as Satan could not bear the unshrouded Divinity, God veiled it in the flesh, and so Satan was taken as a greedy fish by the hook concealed in the bait. Thus life was introduced into the midst of death, light into the midst of darkness, and Divine life and light destroyed their opposites. Here then the Divine power directly works results according to its own nature. It is natural that if purity touches sin, life death, guidance those wandering from the way,

55

then the filth of sin should be purged, error remedied, and the dead restored to life. The purpose of the Incarnation (25) was then that human nature, mixed with the Divine nature, might, as being delivered from death and the devil, become Divine. Deliverance from death is the beginning of the reversion to immortal life.

But was not guile used in the Incarnation? (26). Yes; but this is a mark of wisdom, justice, and goodness—justice, in that the devil is rewarded after his desert; wisdom, in that by this retribution a better thing is brought about; goodness, in that the guile ends in human salvation.

It follows (27) that Christ in assuming human nature assumed all its properties; as the whole of human life from birth to death was stained by sin, Christ's healing nature came into contact with it all. We can see (29) that the Incarnation was suitably delayed till the disease of sin had reached its head. But why (30) after the remedy has been applied does not sin at once cease? Why does not God extend grace to all? The answer is that God respects human free will. Man without free will (31) were less than man.

But the death on the cross (32) remains a difficulty? Death belongs to human nature: if Christ was born, He must die, otherwise He could not have touched human nature in all its properties. Or rather, Christ was born in order to die. To raise our human nature from death, He must come to close quarters with death in His own body, and begin the resurrection of the race with His own resurrection. For Christ assumed flesh from our nature; which must be conceived as an organism, so that because of continuity the resurrection of one part passes over to the whole.

The application to the individual of the benefits of the Incarnation is, upon the presupposition of faith, through the sacraments of Baptism and the Eucharist. Gregory is the first firmly to interweave the doctrine of the sacraments into the systematic theology of the Incarnation, another epoch-making event in the history of doctrine. In Baptism we imitate the death and resurrection of Christ. Sin is washed away, and we anticipate the grace of the resurrection. Baptism is a small beginning of great goods (36). Again, as the soul is united to

Christ through faith, so the body is united to Him through the Eucharist. The antidote of redemption penetrates through our fleshly organism, and makes it immortal (37). Baptism, however, is ineffectual without conversion accompanying it (40). The Christian must strive for the eternal reward set in his view.

Such is in outline the argument of the 'Great Catechism'. The total view of Gregory is clear. He expresses the dominant tendency of the Greek theology with the utmost precision. The Incarnation is essentially a remedial process in humanity, whose beneficent results are communicated through the sacraments, yet so that the securing of these benefits depends upon a virtuous life lived in anticipation of the eternal reward. Negatively the remedial process destroys sin and death, positively it communicates life and light. When Gregory wishes to show explicitly the necessity of this process, he, however, substitutes for the physical conflict of life and light with sin and death a personal dealing of God with Satan. This twofold way of looking at the Incarnation as at once constituting the basis of a personal dealing with Satan and at the same time acting directly as an impersonal principle is of course not new. It has a Scriptural basis in the Pauline view of the death of Christ as at once a death to sin [9] and a satisfaction of the claims of the angels of the law.[1] A further Scriptural basis is found in the Fourth Gospel, where at once the Incarnation is conceived as light overcoming the darkness,[2] and the death of Christ is regarded as a victory over Satan.[3] Then again the interchange between the thoughts of the death of Christ as a victory over the devil and as a triumph over death is found in Irenæus and Origen. But in Gregory the transition between the two views is made particularly plain. Such oscillation between principle and person is common to the ancient world as a whole. We see how easy it is for Paul to conceive sin as quasi-personal.[4] But it is worthy of mention as explaining how natural the double point of view was to a Greek theologian, that the same oscillation is well marked in the ancient religion of Greece.[5]

'In the first place, suffering was regarded as occasioned by

[9] Rom. 6:6.   [1] Gal. 3:13 ; Col. 2:14, 15.   [2] Jn 1:5.
[3] *Ibid.* 14:30.   [4] Rom. 5:21 ; 7:9, 11.
[5] Cf. Gruppe, 'Griechische Mythologie und Religionsgeschichte', 1906, vol. ii, p. 886.

57

a deleterious substance, which was represented as animated and often raised to the rank of a demon. It was the next step, which was taken very early, to conceive these often death-dealing spirits as messengers of the underworld. . . . Gradually the custom grew of regarding suffering no longer as the mode of appearance of the demon, but only as his operation. . . . From this it was only a step to the world-view of the Epos, that suffering too is sent by the gods. Remains of each of these stages of development are, however, contained in those that follow, so that even the oldest is still clearly to be perceived in historical Greece.'

Here is the closest parallel to the oscillation between the different notions of corruption and death as a deleterious principle infesting humanity, of the personification of death as itself a demon, or once more, as we find in Athanasius though not in Gregory, of death as the result of a Divine sentence. The Greek theologians in fact moved at this point in just the same medium of thought as Paul and John, and hence had here no difficulty in working out their doctrine, whatever difficulty it may present to a later age.

The ancient Greek religion may also be brought in to explain the development of the idea of a deceit practised on the devil, which although it may have a Scriptural basis in 1 C. 2:8 is developed with such unscriptural exuberance in Origen and still more in Gregory.

Cf. Gruppe, op. cit. II, p. 903, on the deception of demons:

'The endeavour was to make oneself unrecognisable and distract the attention of the demon. This was done by there being put in the place of the threatened weak man, either another stranger, over whom the fiends could gain no advantage, or another animate or inanimate being, of which they might possess themselves instead of the man.'

To sum up, Gregory of Nyssa brings the Greek doctrine of the work of Christ to a highly systematic and very typical expression. If he is morally inferior to Athanasius in that he reverts from the doctrine of the death of Christ as a satisfaction of the Divine sentence to the view of it as a ransom to the devil, he nevertheless better expresses here the general Greek view. In one point, moreover, Gregory has amended the view of

Athanasius: he regards the effect of the Incarnation as a destruction not merely of death, but also of sin. Here he stands nearer to Paul.

GREGORY OF NAZIANZUS

Compared with Athanasius and Gregory of Nyssa, this father (d. A.D. 390) is of secondary importance. His main doctrine runs parallel with that of the two former theologians, but attains to no such systematic expression. A general statement of it occurs in a passage in the second oration 'De Pascha'.[6]

'We were created that we might be benefited. We were benefited after we were created. Paradise was committed to our charge, that we might live in bliss. We received a commandment that having kept it we might obtain a good repute, not that God did not know what would happen, but that He laid down the law of the free will. We were deceived because we were envied (by the devil). We fell, because we transgressed the commandment. . . . We had need of a God incarnate and put to death, that we might live. We were put to death with Him, that we might be cleansed. We rose again with Him, because we were put to death with Him. We were glorified with Him, because we rose again with Him.'

With this passage may be taken the following summary of Gregory Nazianzen's doctrine of salvation from Ullmann, 'Gregor von Nazianz', 1825, p. 451:

'This salvation he conceived as the sanctification, beatification, and deification of man, and he connected therewith the idea that God in Christ had therefore united Himself with all parts of human nature, in order that they all might by this union be consecrated and sanctified, and that the Divine nature united with the human nature might penetrate the latter as the leaven does the mass, strengthening and ameliorating it. . . . On this account Christ must pass through all earthly conditions and enter into all human relations, even to the point of the deepest shame and humiliation, in order that all that is human, even what is

[6] Oratio XLV, 28.

least, might be honoured and cleansed by this condescension of
the Godhead, and under all limitations the image of a Divine life
might be glorified and presented as an eternal pattern to
humanity.'

The above doctrine is summed up in the famous short
argument with which Gregory Nazianzen met the view of
Apollinaris that in the Incarnation the Logos assumed only
an imperfect human nature without νοῦς. This argument was
that what was not assumed was not cured: τὸ γὰρ ἀπρόσληπτον
ἀθεράπευτον.[7]

Another passage in which the same doctrine is focused is
Or. xxix, 19 :

'Man here below became God since he was united to God
and became one person, the stronger nature overcoming, so
that I might become God, just as much as He became man.'

Cf. further the passage, Or. xxxviii, 13 : 'I had a share in the
image. I did not keep it. He partakes of my flesh, that He may
both save the image and make the flesh immortal.'

In carrying out his idea of the cleansing and deification of
human nature, moreover, Gregory Nazianzen sometimes uses
very strong (Pauline) language to describe Christ's identification
with sinful humanity. Thus, for example, in Or. xxx, 5, he says:

'Just as He was called a curse for the sake of salvation, Who
dissolves my curse; and was called sin, Who takes away the
sin of the world, and instead of the old Adam is made a new
Adam, in the same degree He makes my rebellion His own as
Head of the whole body. As long, therefore, as I am rebellious
and seditious by the denial of God and by my passions, Christ
is called disobedient as far as I am concerned. But when all
things shall have been subjected to Him (now they will be
subjected both by knowledge and by transformation), then He
Himself will have fulfilled His subjection, bringing me, whom
He has saved, to God.'

A little farther on in the same section we read that when
Christ said, 'My God, my God, why hast Thou forsaken me',
He spoke in our person. 'For we were the forsaken and despised
before, but now we were taken up and saved by the sufferings

[7] Ep. 101 (ad Cledonium, 1).

of the Impassible. Similarly He takes to Himself our folly and sin; and says what follows in the Psalm.'

So also in the same oration, § 21, Gregory writes:

'He united to Himself what was condemned, in order to deliver the whole from condemnation, in that for all He became all that we are, sin except, body, soul, and mind, so far as death reaches.'

It would be easy to multiply further passages of this tendency. But they have not the same systematic character as the doctrinal statements of Athanasius, but are incidental and occasional, often merely suggested by the attempt to explain various Scripture passages. Therefore we will be content with those already given, which are sufficiently typical.

To the view of the Incarnation as a purifying process in human nature, Gregory Nazianzen, like the other great Greek theologians, naturally adds the further view of it as a revelation of God. Like Irenæus, Gregory regarded the Incarnation as necessary that the finite reason of man might comprehend the infinite God. Hence he frequently uses the expression, God became incarnate, ἵνα χωρηθῇ ὁ ἀχώρητος.[8]

The point at which Gregory Nazianzen shows originality is in his treatment of the doctrine of redemption from the devil. He does not object to the idea that the devil was deceived by the Incarnation.

Cf. Or. xxxix, 13: 'Since that Master of wickedness thought himself to be invincible, when he had enticed us with the hope of Divinity, he himself is enticed by the screen of the flesh, in order that he may attack God, thinking to be attacking Adam, and so the new Adam may rescue the old Adam and the curse upon the flesh be dissolved, since death is slain through the flesh (i.e. through the death of Christ in the flesh).'

But although Gregory can thus think of the Incarnation and death of Christ as a victory over Satan and death in which Satan was deceived, yet he cannot allow that in the transaction a ransom was paid to Satan. There is an important passage in which he expresses his view on this subject.

This is Or. xlv, 22, where he says: 'As an offering to whom

[8] Ullmann, p. 453.

and for what cause was the blood—I mean that precious and famous blood of God who was high priest and sacrifice at once—shed for our advantage? We were under the power of the evil one, in that we were sold under sin and we exchanged pleasure for misery. If now the ransom was given to no other than the possessor who had power over us, I ask to whom was it offered and for what cause? Was it to the evil one himself? Shame upon the blasphemy (φεῦ τῆς ὕβρεως)! Then doth the robber receive not only a ransom from God, but God Himself as a ransom, and thus an exceeding reward for his tyranny, for the sake of which ransom also it was right for us to be spared. But if to the Father, the question is here in the first place, how was this? For He did not hold us in His power. Again, what ground can one give why the Father should have taken delight in the blood of the only begotten Son, while He did not even accept Isaac, who was offered to him by his father, but changed the sacrifice, substituting a ram for the offering of a rational being? Or is it not manifest that the Father received the ransom, not because He either asked it, or needed it, but on account of the plan of salvation (διὰ τὴν οἰκονομίαν) and because man must be sanctified by the humanity of God; in order that He, overcoming the tyrant by force, might free us, and might bring us back to Himself by the mediation of the Son, who carried this out to the honour of the Father, to Whom He is seen in every way to submit?'

The above passage is important and interesting not only because of the rejection of the idea of a ransom paid to the devil, but also because Gregory equally rejects the notion that a price was paid to God. The need of the death of Christ is seen in the abstract necessity of the renewal of mankind by the Incarnation and of the overcoming at the same time of the devil.

CYRIL OF ALEXANDRIA

The later Greek theology practically adds nothing to the preceding development. For the sake of completeness, however, a brief account may be given of the ideas of Cyril of Alexandria and John of Damascus.

62

The view of Cyril (d. A.D. 444) is thus summarised by Schultz, 'Lehre der Gottheit Christi,' 1881, pp. 109f. :

'Humanity, apart from Christ, is dominated by the devil by means of sin and death—or without a figure: it is given over to sin and death, to the corruptibility and vanity of the world. Nor will God overcome the prince of the world by His superior power. . . . He goes into the battle as man, and overcomes the devil as the sinless and righteous One, therefore in a moral way. He delivers human nature from the corruptibility and weakness of the world, in that He assumes it and in His own person penetrates it with His Divine life and so in principle elevates it above the world and deifies it.

'This work of the Son of God is the decisive work. Humanity, in its head and representative, has now obtained a right against the devil; the law in the members is slain, and, therefore, the sinful worldliness of men overcome by a higher principle, as light overcomes darkness.'

This is just the same doctrine as we have had before from Athanasius, Gregory of Nyssa, and Gregory of Nazianzus, and requires, therefore, no comment. The only other point further to be noted in connexion with Cyril of Alexandria is the occurrence in his writings of passages speaking of the infinite worth of Christ's passion, an idea which indeed is sporadically found before his time.

Thus Cyril of Jerusalem (d. A.D. 386), 'Catech.' XIII, 33, says:

'Not so great was the lawlessness of sinners as the righteousness of Him that died for them: we had not sinned so much as He wrought righteousness, Who laid down His life for us.'

Chrysostom (d. A.D. 407) again writes in Ep. ad Rom. hom. 10:

'What Christ paid was far more than we owed, and so much more, as an infinite sea is greater than a small drop.'

Cyril of Alexandria has, however, developed the idea with greater fullness. He thus expounds Jn 1:29. The Lamb prefigured in the Old Testament is led to the slaughter for all, that it may take away the sin of the world, that it dying for it, may destroy death and dissolve the curse passed upon us. The Lamb has died, one for all, in order to bring back all to God. 'For when we were taken captive in many sins and, therefore, in debt to death and corruption, the Father gave His Son as a ransom for us (ἀντίλυτρον ὑπὲρ ἡμῶν), one for all; for all is in Him, and He outweighs all in value; One died for all, that we all might through Him attain to life.' [9]

So also in his 'De recta fide ad reginas,' II, 7, Cyril says with reference to Gal. 3:13 : [1]

'Christ has redeemed us from the curse of the law, having become a curse for us. . . . Inasmuch as the letter of the law declares him accursed who is taken in trangression and sin, He who knew no sin, that is Christ, has been brought under the judgment, having endured an unrighteous sentence and having suffered that which became those under the curse, in order that He who is of equal worth with the whole of humanity (ὁ τῶν ὅλων ἀντάξιος) might free all from the accusation of disobedience and therewith redeem the terrestrial world by His own blood. The One would not have equalled all, if He had simply been man; but if He be reckoned as Incarnate God suffering in His own flesh, the whole creation is small compared with Him, and what is required for the ransom of all that is under heaven is the death of this one flesh, for it belonged to the Logos begotten from God the Father.'

'Here', says Baur,[2] 'there is wanting to the full idea of satisfaction nothing but the express reference to God and the Divine righteousness. But this is just always the obscure point in the older ideas of satisfaction.' The fact is that these passages from Cyril of Alexandria, though fuller than those quoted from Cyril of Jerusalem and Chrysostom, are not really of great dogmatic importance. The anticipation in them of the idea of the infinite worth of Christ's passion is of course very interesting, but even in the most definite form in which it occurs, viz. in the last quoted passage, is still only suggestive rather than doctrinally complete. The most important point made is that the infinite value of Christ's death depends on His Divinity. But it is to be remembered that the above passages are after all rather homiletical than strictly dogmatic in character.[3]

[9] 'Opera', ed. Migne, VI, col. 192.   [1] *Ibid.* IX, col. 1344.
[2] 'Die Christliche Lehre von der Versöhnung', p. 103, n.
[3] Cf. Harnack, D.G., 4th ed., vol. ii, p. 174.

The Creed of Chalcedon

Upon our account of the theology of Cyril may fitly follow a note on the Creed of Chalcedon (A.D. 451), with which his name is so closely associated. The Council of Chalcedon set forth as standards of the true faith, first of all the original Nicene Creed with some additions; then the so-called Niceno-Constantinopolitan Creed (the Nicene Creed of the English Prayer Book), whose exact origin is unknown; finally, a new formula on the Person of Christ.

Neither the additions to the Nicene Creed, nor the Niceno-Constantinopolitan Creed, need detain us. There is nothing in them which adds materially to what was already given as a basis for the doctrine of the work of Christ in the Roman (Apostles') Creed, and in the original Nicene Creed. The new formula ran as follows:

'Wherefore, following the Holy Fathers, we all with one accord teach the confession of our Lord Jesus Christ as one and the same Son, the same perfect in Godhead, the same perfect in manhood, very God and very man, the same consisting of a reasonable soul and a body, of one essence with the Father as touching the Godhead and the same of one essence with us as touching the manhood, like us in all things, sin except; begotten of the Father before the worlds as touching the Godhead, the same in these last days, for us and for our salvation (begotten) of the Virgin Mary, the mother of God, as touching the manhood, one and the same Christ, Son, Lord, Only-begotten, being made known in two natures, without confusion, without change, without division, without separation; the distinction of the natures being in no wise done away by the union, but rather the characteristic property of each nature being preserved, and concurring into one Person and one hypostasis, Who is not parted or divided into two Persons, but one and the same Son and Only-begotten, God the Word, Lord, Jesus Christ.'[4]

What is important here for the doctrine of the work of Christ is that the exact metaphysical conception of His Person,

[4] Hahn, 'Bibliothek der Symbole und Glaubensregeln der alten Kirche', 3rd ed., 1897, p. 166.

which was to form its basis, was fixed for the subsequent orthodoxy both of the East and West, both Catholic and Protestant.

In opposition to the Nestorian view, that there were in the Incarnate Christ two persons, a Divine and a human, there was affirmed the absolute unity of His Person. Again, in opposition to the Eutychian view, that in the One Person after the Incarnation there was only one nature, a Divine-human, there was equally affirmed the continued distinction of a Divine and a human nature in one person. Finally, in opposition to the doctrine of Apollinaris, who taught in the interest of the speculative unity of Christ's Person that the Logos in the Incarnation assumed only an imperfect human nature, consisting of soul and body, but without the higher principle of reason ($\nu o \hat{v} s$), the Creed affirmed the perfection of the human as well as of the Divine nature after the Incarnation.

The definitions of the Chalcedonian Council were the result of two influences which crossed each other. One was that of the Greek doctrine of redemption. An interest in it lay behind Cyril's desire for the closest union between the Divine and human natures in the One Person (which desire at times led him very close to Eutychianism). The same interest also lay behind the opposition to Apollinarianism in the Greek Church, which was concentrated in the formula of Gregory of Nazianzus: 'What is not assumed is not cured.' [5]

The other influence was that of the theology of the West, which was exercised through the famous Tome of Leo of Rome, which lay before the Council. From the time of Tertullian onwards the West had always a great interest in the complete humanity of Christ, which was akin to Nestorianism. Western theology, as represented by Leo, therefore, even at the time of the Council of Chalcedon being less speculative than that of the East and less under the influence of the doctrine of the deification of human nature in Christ, was not afraid to assert strongly the distinctness of the Divine and human natures in the Incarnation, in spite of whatever speculative difficulties might be involved, and in spite of the fact that the doctrine of deification seemed

[5] Ep. 101 (ad Cledonium, 1).

to require as its natural correlate the closest fusion of the Divine and human natures in the Incarnate Logos.

The Creed of Chalcedon then leaves us with the problem how the unity of the Person can coexist along with the completeness and the distinction of the natures. The last word on the subject in the Greek Church was spoken in the formula of Leontius of Byantium (485–543), who taught 'that the human nature in Christ is not ἀνυπόστατος nor yet itself ὑπόστασις, but ἐνυπόστατος, i.e. it has its ὑποστῆναι in the Logos'.[6]

JOHN OF DAMASCUS

What is interesting and important about this writer (d. *ante* A.D. 754) is that in his 'Expositio Orthodoxæ Fidei' we have the first complete systematic treatise covering the whole of Christian doctrine since Origen's 'De Principiis'. John bases his doctrine on Revelation (1, 1), yet as far as possible supports it on rational grounds. The doctrine of God and even that of the Trinity have a rational basis. The doctrine of the Incarnation is seen to be a natural consequence of the doctrine of God in view of the fact of human sin.

As regards the details of the doctrine, John collects his material from previous theologians, especially the two Gregories and Cyril of Alexandria. As Schultz says,[7] 'John of Damascus gathers up in his doctrine of salvation the results of the theology since Athanasius.' We observe in his treatment, however, the influence of a new and important doctrinal factor, viz. the Gospel history. If we review the progress of the Greek doctrine of the work of Christ up to this point, we see that it really began in earnest with Irenæus, who depends on the Creed, but does not, as a matter of fact, very closely follow it from point to point, being rather concerned to refute the Gnostics than to expound the Creed. Still less does Origen adhere to the order of the extended Rule of Faith which he gives in 'De Principiis' (Preface). Athanasius and Gregory of Nyssa, on the other hand, have treated the Incarnation in a systematic order, determined not by history but by the exigencies of logical thought. With

---

[6] Loofs, D.G., 4th ed., p. 305.   [7] 'Die Lehre der Gottheit Christi', p. 130.

67

John, however, comes the great change that the facts, not merely of the Creed, but of the Gospel history, begin to be treated of in order. The implication is that the whole life of Christ has a saving significance. In fact, John begins to add reflections on the saving value of various historical elements, which before have found no place in the systematic treatment of our doctrine. He considers in turn the Incarnation, the actions and passions of Christ, His death, His descent into Hades, His resurrection, ascension, and sitting at the right hand of the Father; and everywhere has something to say on the saving significance of these facts.

He begins with the Incarnation itself (3, 1). When man had fallen, deceived by the devil, and death reigned in the world, the Creator and Lord Himself took up the battle for the creature. Since the enemy had deceived man with the hope of divinity, he himself is deceived by the flesh of Christ offered as a bait; and thus God shows at once His goodness, wisdom, justice, and power. His goodness appears in His not abandoning man, His justice in His taking him from the devil otherwise than by force, His wisdom in finding a suitable way in this difficult case. His power appears in the miracle of the Incarnation, the newest of all that is new, in fact the one thing new under the sun (Ec. 1:10). Thus the Word was made flesh of the Holy Ghost and the Virgin Mary, born without concupiscence of Adam's race; and was made obedient to the Father, that by that which He had assumed from us like ourselves, He might supply a cure for our disobedience, and give an example of obedience, without which salvation cannot be had.

The whole Divine nature was in the Person of Christ united to the whole human nature, that it might bring salvation to the whole. John reproduces Gregory Nazianzen: 'What has not been assumed cannot be cured' (3, 6). Christ assumed the whole man, and that up to the very part which was liable to death, that He might bestow salvation upon the whole (3, 18). In assuming human nature then Christ assumed its natural and guiltless passions. He assumed all to heal all. He was tempted, and overcame to give us the victory, and to enable us to overcome our enemy (3, 20). He grew in wisdom and grace, or rather He

68

gradually exhibited what was in Him, in order to share our nature (3, 22). He prayed as an example for us (3, 24). In Mt. 27:46, He prays as representing us. In the same way also is to be understood Gal. 3:13.

In all His passions, however, His Deity suffered through the flesh, not in itself (3, 26). Thus is to be understood the nature of Christ's death. As free from sin, He was not subject to death. But He died, undergoing death for the sake of our salvation, and offering Himself as a sacrifice to God, against whom we had sinned, and to whom the price of our redemption was to be paid, so that thereby we might be freed (3, 27).

John rejects like Gregory Nazianzen the idea of a price paid to the devil. 'God forbid that the blood of the Lord should have been offered to the tyrant.' But he is all the same unable to get very far away from the idea which he rejects.

'Death approaches, and eagerly swallowing the bait of the body is transfixed by the hook of the Divinity; and so having tasted that innocent and life-giving body, itself is destroyed, vomiting up all those whom it had previously swallowed. For just as darkness is dispelled when light is introduced, so corruption is driven back before the assault of life, and life comes to all, but to the destroyer destruction' (3, 27).

Putting this passage together with the above-mentioned reference in 3, 1 to the deceit practised on the devil through the Incarnation (cf. also 3, 18), we see that John, like Gregory Nazianzen before him, though he protests against the doctrine that a price was paid to the devil, cannot escape out of the circle of ideas therewith connected.

From the death of Christ John passes on to His descent into hell. After His death He deified soul [deified, because it remained, like His body, still in death united to the Word (3, 27)] descended into hell, that as before the Sun of righteousness had risen upon those on earth, now it might shine on those in darkness and in the shadow of death. As Christ had before preached deliverance on earth, so now He did the same in Hades; [8] and having delivered those who were bound, He returned from death to make a way for us to the resurrection (3, 29).

[8] 1 Pet. 3:19.

In 3, 28 John has already said that Christ gave resurrection and incorruption to our body through His body, becoming for us the firstfruits of resurrection and incorruption.

After His resurrection He ascended into heaven and sits at the right hand of the Father, caring for our salvation both in a Divine and a human manner; a Divine manner, in so far as He preserves and governs all things by His providence; a human manner, in so far as He remembers His life on earth, and sees and knows Himself the object of universal adoration (4, 1). Finally in 4, 4, John sums up in a general statement his whole doctrine of the Incarnation as the way of human salvation. As the Son of God created man in His image, i.e. endowed him with reason and free will, so also He gave him His likeness, i.e. endowed him with all virtues, as far as was possible to human nature. This He did by the communication of Himself, by which communication He also gave man the gift of immortality. By disobedience to the Divine command we, however, lost these gifts, and became subject to death. Therefore the Son of God took our nature to restore us to the glory of the image and the likeness. The purpose of the Incarnation was to teach us the way of a virtuous life, affording us an easy way to it through Himself (i.e. through His example). Its purpose was also by the communication of life to deliver us from death, Christ being made for us the firstfruits of resurrection, and renewing the vessel which had been marred. Finally it was to deliver us from the devil and to teach us to overcome him by humility and patience.

As regards the practical aspect of the doctrine of salvation, John teaches that salvation is mediated to us through faith and baptism. Through baptism we obtain the remission of sins, by faith the gift of the Spirit (4, 9). By the Eucharist the life thus communicated is further maintained (4, 13). The position attained by baptism must, however, be maintained by good works. To this end, however, we must strive with all our strength, lest, returning to the vomit like a dog,[9] we should again make ourselves the servants of sin (4, 9).

[9] 2 Pet. 2:22.

THE GREEK SYNTHESIS

With John of Damascus we reach the conclusion of our study of the Greek theology. Before we pass on to the next section, some remarks must be made on the Greek doctrine of salvation as a whole. We have already, in dealing with Irenæus, attempted to indicate its practical unity. It must be admitted, however, that an absolutely perfect theoretical synthesis corresponding to this practical unity is far from being attained by the Greek theologians. The different views which they propound are most intricately entangled with one another, as is particularly clear in the case of John of Damascus, who in his anxiety to include all good doctrine and reject none, ends with a statement which is most involved, far more involved indeed than can be gathered from the above summary of his doctrine.

In particular, however, we have to consider the relation in the Greek theology of two main aspects of doctrine. On the one hand salvation is regarded as the direct result of the Incarnation (a) as a Divine revelation, (b) as (along with the death and resurrection of Christ) a communication of life to mankind. Through the death and resurrection operates, according to this view, what is implicitly given already in the Incarnation itself.

On the other hand salvation is viewed as following from a certain negative pre-condition, either that of a sacrifice to God or of a price paid to the devil, a pre-condition the accomplishment of which removes the obstacles which stand in the way of God's desire to save men.

The problem now is of the relation of these two great points of view. It is generally admitted and has already been recognised that the former point of view, which regards salvation as implicitly given in the very constitution of the Person of Christ, is the central element in the Greek theology. The great proof of this is that only the doctrines of the Trinity and of the Person of Christ constituted properly the dogma of the Greek Church. In agreement with this fact, moreover, we find some startling things said by some Greek theologians as to the secondary importance of all else compared with the doctrine of the Person of Christ.

71

Irenæus [1] counts the question why the Word of God has become flesh and suffered among those things which, lying outside the *regula fidei*, belong simply to theological inquiry. And so Gregory Nazianzen says:

'You may philosophise about the world and worlds, about matter, about the soul, about reasonable natures better and worse, about resurrection, judgment, retribution, the sufferings of Christ, for in these matters success is not unprofitable and failure is harmless.' [2]

From passages like these we might at first be inclined to infer that the doctrine of the work of Christ mattered little or nothing to some at least of the Greek theologians. Obviously, however, the view which regards salvation as sufficiently guaranteed and established by the very constitution of the Person of Christ, implies a certain view also of His work. It involves in fact what in general may be called the Johannine view, the doctrine that Christ is the life and light of men. Thus the silent coefficient of the Greek emphasis on the dogma of the Person of Christ is the doctrine that in His Person the Logos has revealed God to men and has overcome in humanity sin and corruption and death. The latter point in particular is undoubtedly the central doctrine of the Greek Church on the work of Christ, but the view of the Incarnation as a revelation of God is always most closely connected therewith.

But now as to the doctrine of Christ's work as a sacrifice to God and as a redemption from the devil: Is it right to regard these views, as does for instance Harnack,[3] as merely circumferential? This can hardly be the case, since the idea of a sacrifice to God naturally corresponds to the practical belief of a forgiveness of sins bestowed in baptism, a very vital element in the religion of the Greek Church; though at the same time it must be admitted that the connexion between the two conceptions is not very clearly established by the Greek theologians, and that the forgiveness of sins is not infrequently, as by Gregory of Nyssa, derived from the purification of human nature which is the direct result of Christ's Incarnation, Death, and Resurrection.

---

[1] 'Adv. Hær'. I, 1, 30.   [2] Orat. XXVII, § 10, p. 495.   [3] D.G., 4th ed., vol. ii, pp. 174ff·

Moreover, the doctrine of redemption from the devil can hardly be regarded as unimportant. It is very tempting certainly to follow Schultz and others, who regard this doctrine as no more than a mythological variant upon the more abstract idea of the destruction of death and corruption by the Incarnate Divinity. It is indeed natural enough to a modern theologian thus to regard the doctrine, and there are many passages in the Greek Fathers themselves which might be quoted in support of the view of Schultz—passages in which the idea of redemption from the devil quickly passes over into the notion of a destruction of death and corruption by the Divine life. The truth is, however, that it is as much a case of death being personally regarded as of the devil being equated to an abstract principle. In general it cannot be doubted that to the Greek Fathers redemption from the devil was a great reality. This is borne out by the immense place which demons filled in the thought of the Hellenistic world, and the dread of their malign influence which was universally felt. Moreover, by the Christian Church the heathen gods were generally identified with the demons (cf. 1 C. 10:20). The right view therefore seems to be that of Kaftan, who emphasises the historical importance of the doctrine of redemption from the devil in addition to that of the dogma of the Incarnation as expressed in the creeds.

'It is not to be regarded as an accident that it originated in the ancient Greek theology. The general historical background of this doctrine is formed by the heathen environment of the Ancient Church, in which it saw the reign of Satan and his demons. It was therefore for the Ancient Church more than a mere doctrine: it was a living view.' [4]

It is to be observed also that the doctrine of redemption from the devil comes to have a direct practical significance through the exorcism and the renunciation of the devil which accompanied the rite of baptism in the Greek Church.

Cf. Cyril of Jerusalem: [5] 'Here (in baptism) the blood of the unblemished Lamb Jesus Christ is made the charm to scare evil spirits. . . . What then did each of you standing up say? "I renounce thee, Satan, thou wicked and most cruel tyrant!"

[4] 'Dogmatik', 3rd and 4th eds., 1901, p. 490.   [5] 'Catechetical Lectures', XIX, 3, 4.

meaning, "I fear thy might no longer; for Christ hath overthrown it, having partaken with me of flesh and blood, that through these he might by death destroy death, that I might not for ever be subject to bondage".'

Here the practical significance of the doctrine of redemption from the devil (and death) appears very clearly. No doctrine, however, which possesses practical significance can be regarded as unimportant.

CHAPTER 4

THE THEOLOGY OF THE LATIN FATHERS

THE development of doctrine during the first eight Christian centuries was in a certain sense a common Catholic development. Nevertheless the Greek and Latin Churches even before their final separation from one another were characterised by their own peculiar differences, at least from the time when, at the end of the second century, the Western Church ceased to be essentially Greek. With Tertullian begins at this time the distinctively Latin type of theology, which in the third century is continued by Cyprian and others. Even the theologians of the fourth century, Hilary, Ambrose, etc., who did so much to introduce Greek ideas into the West, nevertheless show themselves by no means mere imitators of the Greeks. Finally, with Augustine a fresh type, first of religion and then of theology, manifests itself in the West, not indeed altogether without previous preparation, but still of a marked originality; so that from Augustine onwards both the problems of theology and the outlook upon them differ very considerably from those of the East.

In regard to the doctrine of the work of Christ the most important Western development does not indeed begin till after the period above-named, viz. with the Schoolmen, especially Anselm and Abelard. Yet during the first eight centuries we find, firstly, a type of doctrine on this subject, already deviating more or less unconsciously from the Greek theology in directions afterwards taken by the Schoolmen, and, secondly, important theological developments taking place especially with regard to the practical view of Christianity—developments the reaction of which upon the doctrine of the work of Christ ultimately produced the Anselmic theory of the subject.

75

TERTULLIAN

In Tertullian (*c.* A.D. 150–*c.* 225) we find practically the same points of view with regard to the work of Christ as in Irenæus with the important difference that in Tertullian the mystic-realistic doctrine so central for Irenæus recedes into the background. 'He (Tertullian) has', says Harnack, 'taken over from Irenæus the mystical conception of redemption—the constitution (of the Person) of Christ is redemption—yet with a rationalistic interpretation.'[1]

Cf. 'Adv. Mar.' II, 27, where Tertullian says that the mystery of human salvation is in the Incarnate Son, who mingles in Himself man and God, that He may confer on man as much as He takes from God. But he adds: 'God lived among us, that man might be taught to do the things of God. God acted on a level with man that man might be able to act on a level with God.' The significance of the Incarnation according to this passage therefore reduces itself to that of Divine teaching and example.

Cf. also 'De Resurr.' 63, where Christ is called the most faithful mediator between God and man, who will restore (*reddet*) God to man and man to God. Harnack here bids us observe the future tense: in the view of Tertullian the union of man to God is not as with Irenæus a thing already accomplished in the very fact of the Incarnation, but a thing to be accomplished by the moral influence of the Incarnate Logos upon men.

On the other hand, however, Tertullian lays a greater stress than Irenæus on the death of Christ. 'In innumerable passages he has emphatically affirmed that the whole work of Christ is involved in His death on the cross, in fact that the death on the cross was the purpose of the mission of Christ.'[2]

Cf. especially 'Adv. Marc.' III, 8, where Tertullian says that if the flesh of Christ is taken to be a lie, His sufferings will not deserve faith. He goes on: 'Therefore is the whole work of God overthrown. The death of Christ, the whole import and blessing of the Christian name, is denied.'

Tertullian has indeed no definitely formulated doctrine of

[1] D.G., 4th ed., vol. i, p. 613, n. 3.
[2] Harnack, D.G., 4th ed., vol. i, p. 613, n. 3.

the death of Christ beyond that of Irenæus; nevertheless his peculiar insistence upon it is noteworthy. Here, as in many other cases, he strikes a note characteristic of the Latin theology throughout.

It is, however, by his treatment of the practical aspect of Christianity that Tertullian becomes indirectly of the greatest importance for the history of our doctrine. Not only does he agree with the Apostolic Fathers, the Greek Apologists, and Irenæus in regarding Christianity as a new law of Christ; but, as was natural to one who before his conversion had been a Roman *juris peritus,* he has made the idea of the new law more strictly legal and also more dominant than it was among the Greeks. With them the new law was essentially a new moral law and a new philosophy of life; but for the West, under the influence of the Roman tradition embodied in Tertullian, the new law was a law in the same sense as the law of the Empire. This applies not only to the Christian ethic, but also to the Christian faith. 'The dogma was always in the West more a law of faith than a philosophy of faith.' [3]

In this connexion it may be pointed out that the colligation of reason and authority, which we have also found in the Greek theology, begins already to assume in Tertullian the form of the dialectical opposition between them which characterises Western theology as a whole. In particular Tertullian, while he accepts the rational theology of the Greek Apologists, at the same time bases the doctrine of the death and resurrection of Christ purely on authority.

'To know nothing contrary to the Rule of Faith is to know all things.' [4]

'The Son of God died; it is certainly believable, because it is absurd: and having been buried, He rose again; it is certain, because it is impossible.' [5]

We return, however, to the practical attitude of the Christian in his relation toward God. Tertullian has systematised his legal view of the relation of the Christian to God by the use of the important terms merit (*meritum*) and satisfaction (*satisfactio*), both of which, together with their cognates, are common in

---

[3] Loofs, D.G., 4th ed., p. 335. [4] 'De præscr.' 14. [5] 'De carne Christi', 5.

Roman jurisprudence.[6] Here first we touch the beginnings of that great Western systematisation of the doctrine of grace and merit, the counterpart of which is not to be found in the theology of the East. The following account of Tertullian's doctrine on these points is largely dependent on the exhaustive and definitive articles of Schultz, 'Der sittliche Begriff des Verdienstes und seine Anwendung auf das Verständniss des Werkes Christi'.[7] I wish here once and for all to express my deep obligation to these articles, which I shall make use of not only in connexion with Tertullian, but with other Latin writers.

Tertullian regards God above all as the Lawgiver, and religion as a discipline ordained of God through Christ. God's will is rational: yet we must obey not because it is good, but because God has commanded it.[8] Thus we win merit (*promereri*).

God is the rewarder of all merit: 'If God is the acceptor of good works, He is also the rewarder . . . a good deed has God as its debtor, just as has also an evil deed, since the judge is the rewarder of every matter.'[9]

In general all service of God is meritorious: 'Artificium promerendi obsequium est.'[1] But in the stricter sense only non-obligatory performances are meritorious. God has ordained a sphere of liberty (*licentia*), in order to give an opportunity for such supererogatory works.[2] To this class belong patience, acts of voluntary penance, above all fasting, virginity, and martyrdom.[3] In all this region the rule is that of retribution according to law.

'Par factum par habet meritum.'[4]

'Majora certamina sequuntur majora præmia.'[5]

Such is Tertullian's doctrine of merit. He is indeed not the absolute originator of the view that supererogatory work constitutes merit. We find it already in Hermas, 'Sim.' V, III, 3:

'If thou doest aught good beyond the commandment of God, thou shalt gain to thyself a more exceeding glory.' Cf. also

---

[6] Cf. Dirksen, 'Manuale Latinitatis fontium juris civilis Romanorum', 1837.
[7] 'Theologische Studien und Kritiken', 1894, pp. 1–50, 245–314, 554–614.
[8] 'De pœn.' 4.   [9] *Ibid.* 2.   [1] 'De pat.' 4.
[2] 'De cultu femin.' 2, 10 ; 'De exhort. cast.' 8.
[3] 'De pat.' 15, 16 ; ' De jejun. adv. ps.' 7 ; 'De exhort cast.' 3 ; 'Ad Scap.' 4.
[4] 'De pat.' 10.   [5] 'Ad Scap.' 4.

'Mand.' 4, 4, 2 for similar ideas. In one point, moreover, Tertullian is unwilling to go as far in the development of the idea of merit as the general popular Christianity of North Africa. The prevailing view seems to have been that there was possible a transference of the merit not only of Christ, but also of the martyrs. But Tertullian says: 'Let it suffice the martyr to have cleansed his own sins. . . . Who has paid the death of others by his own, except the Son of God?' [6]

These things, however, must not blind us to the extreme importance of Tertullian at this point, in that he first codified the doctrine of merit, and gave it a firm substance, thereby stamping the doctrine of Western Catholicism with a permanently legal character.

The second legal term introduced by Tertullian is *satisfactio*, to the examination of which we now pass on. Where after baptism man by his sin has again become a debtor, he must 'per delictorum pœnitentiam . . . domino satisfacere'.[7]

'Every sin', says Tertullian, 'is discharged either by pardon (*venia*) or penalty (*pœna*), pardon as the result of chastisement (*castigatio*), penalty as the result of condemnation.' [8]

Here emerges a somewhat difficult problem. Does Tertullian regard *pœnitentia* (*satisfactio*) primarily as a meritorious work availing to pay the debt of sin, or rather as of the nature of punishment and as paying in this way for sin? The view of Schultz is that *satisfactio* is primarily to be regarded as a sub-species of merit. In the first place he appeals to the use of the term in Roman law. *Satisfactio* is here in the stricter sense that transaction by which one man meets otherwise than by *solvere* the legal claim of another, especially one that has arisen through damage done to him. Its sphere is that of obligations in private law. *Solvere* is the proper performance of the obligation, *satisfacere* the discharge of it by some other method agreeable to the claimant. In this usage *satisfacere* has no inner connexion with the idea of punishment, but has affinity rather with *solvere*. Where in Roman law the word stands in a wider sense, it means simply to meet the claim of one who possesses a right. Thus we find the phrases, *satisfacere sententiæ, judicato, stipulationi,*

---

[6] 'De pud.' 22.   [7] 'De pœn.' 5.   [8] 'De pud.' 2.

conditioni, edicto, etc. In this sense again, however, the word has no inner connexion with *pœna.*

In proof of these assertions Schultz brings forward an exhaustive list of passages from Roman legal authorities, for which he acknowledges indebtedness to his juristic colleague, Professor Merkel.[9]

In view of this usage he argues that to a Roman jurist like Tertullian *satisfactio* could not mean one form of punishment substituted for another, but could only mean a meritorious act applied to pay the debt of sin. The alternative is *aut solvere aut satisfacere;* again, it is not *aut pœna aut satisfactio,* but *aut pœna aut venia; pœnitentia* for sins after baptism is therefore *satisfactio* in the sense that by it man acquires merit, and so wins *venia* instead of *pœna.* If penance includes confession of sin, fasting, and above all martyrdom, these are to be regarded as meritorious acts.

Such then is Schultz's theory of Tertullian's doctrine of merit and satisfaction. Summed up in brief, it amounts to this. Merits are supererogatory works, which win reward from God. Where, however, a debt is occasioned by post-baptismal sin, they avail first to cancel the debt, and then if there is any excess, to win reward. This view has been widely accepted, and is no doubt on the whole correct; we actually find the phrase *merita pœnitentia.*[1] Nevertheless it is to be kept in mind that the penitential works, which avail as satisfaction, are in general of a penal character (*castigatio*), and Tertullian lays stress on this aspect of the matter. In a most fundamental passage [2] Tertullian describes penance as a self-humiliation or self-inflicted chastisement, by which we placate an angry God. It is to lie in sackcloth and ashes, to lay the spirit low in sorrow, to exchange the former life of sin for severe treatment: it is fasting, incessant prayer, and self-abasement. 'All this penance does, that it may enhance repentance, may honour God by fear of danger; may by itself pronouncing against the sinner take the place of God's indignation, and by temporal mortification, I will not say frustrate, but discharge eternal punishment. . . . So far as thou hast not spared thyself, so far, believe me, will God spare thee.'

---

[9] Op. cit. pp. 28–31.   [1] 'De pœn.' 2.   [2] *Ibid.* 9.

In spite, therefore, of the fact that satisfaction in Roman private law is opposed to punishment, and that Tertullian regards penitential satisfaction as a meritorious work paying the debt of sin, he also views it as an act of self-humiliation before God, and even as the endurance of temporal punishment instead of eternal. The unity of the two lines of thought lies in the fact that the satisfaction, so far as it is penal, is self-inflicted punishment: thus it combines in one the characters of active work or merit and passive endurance or chastisement.

The importance of the above theological development in Tertullian lies not only in the systematisation of the legal view of Christianity, as already described, but also in that here first we get a definite doctrine with respect to post-baptismal sin. Only when a clear doctrine of the implications of post-baptismal sin had been reached, could there be the possibility of an application to this sphere of the doctrine of the work of Christ, such as is wanting in the Greek theology.

Hilary and Ambrose

After Tertullian we get no new theology of the work of Christ, nor any important development of the general view of Christianity, till we come to the Graecising theologians, Hilary (d. A.D. 368) and Ambrose (d. A.D. 395).

Hilary, while recognising faith in God and the hope of immortality as belonging to the sphere of a rational religion, bases the doctrine of the Incarnation with all it involves upon the authority of the Gospel. Such things God intended that 'faith should not refuse to believe, because it could not understand, but should remember that it could understand if it believed'.[3]

Hilary, in his actual doctrine of the work of Christ, in the first place more closely reproduces that of the Greeks than does any other of the Western Fathers. We have from him the doctrine of the sanctification of humanity by the Incarnation.

'The Son of God was born of the Virgin and of the Holy Ghost for the sake of the human race . . . that being made man

[3] 'De Trinitate', i, 12.

of the Virgin, He might receive into Himself the nature of flesh, and that the body of the human race might through the fellowship of this admixture appear in Him as sanctified.' [4]

We have also the victory of Christ in His death and resurrection over death and the devil.

'He first Himself rising from the dead and discharging the sentence of death by which we before were held, in Himself who still among the dead remained eternal, thus fulfilled the dispensation of our salvation. But in that very thing that He is to us in Himself the author of life . . . He also made a show of all the hostile powers.' [5]

All this is good Greek doctrine. But we find all the same a new and distinctively Western note struck for the first time, when Hilary not merely like Tertullian lays stress on the death of Christ, but actually presents it under the view of a satisfaction to God. Christ's passion was 'voluntarily undertaken to satisfy a penal obligation' (officio satisfactura pœnali).[6]

Hilary further affirms the necessity of this procedure. 'It was necessary therefore that what took place should be done, because the adding of a curse did not permit the neglect of a sacrifice. From which curse Our Lord Jesus Christ redeemed us. . . . He offered Himself therefore to the death of the accursed, that He might undo the curse of the law, offering Himself voluntarily as a victim to God the Father.' [7]

We find a doctrine of the work of Christ parallel with that of Hilary also in Ambrose, in whom the Western type of theology is still more distinctly apparent.

Ambrose definitely rests the doctrine of the Incarnation upon revelation. He does not wonder that human knowledge should err in heavenly things, but wonders that it has not obeyed Scripture.[8] In such matters reason is of no avail.

'Non in dialecticâ complacuit Deo salvum facere populum suum.' [9]

Accordingly everywhere it is the death of Christ which is made central. In no Western theologian before or after is there greater emphasis on the cross.

---

[4] *Ibid.* II, 24. [5] 'Tract. in Ps.' LXVII, 23. [6] *Ibid.* LIII, 12.
[7] *Ibid.* 13. [8] 'De Fide', 4, 1, 1. [9] *Ibid.* 1, 5, 42.

This appears even where Ambrose continues the realistic mysticism of Irenæus.

'How except through the flesh did He become one with us? or through what but the death of the body did He loose the chains of death; for the undertaking of death by Christ became the death of death.' [1]

'His death was the life of all.' [2]

The doctrine of redemption from the devil appears in Ambrose, including the idea of a fraud practised upon him. Interesting is the idea that Christ's fasting in the wilderness was a lure to deceive the devil into believing Him weak and an easy prey.

'The snare could not better be broken than by some prey being exhibited to the devil, so that while he hastened to the prey, he might be bound in his own snares. . . . What could be the prey but a body? This fraud had to be practised on the devil, that the Lord Jesus should take a body, and this indeed a corruptible body. . . . And therefore the hunger of the Lord was a pious fraud, that in the case of Him, of whom the devil fearing His greater works was already afraid, he deceived by the appearance of hunger should tempt Him as a man, lest the victory (over him) should be hindered.' [3]

It is noteworthy, however, that Ambrose, besides these ideas inherited from Origen, has others in which the ransom paid to the devil is regarded strictly after the manner of a legal process of debt, to which the devil had a claim, which God was compelled to recognise. Ambrose develops here the imagery of Col. 2:14.

'We were through sin under pledge to an evil creditor, we had contracted a bond of guilt (*chirographum culpæ*), we were owing the penalty of our blood.' [4]

'We were before under a hard usurer, who could not be met and satisfied except by the death of the debtor. . . . We had by our sins contracted a heavy debt, so that we were liable, who before were free.' [5]

This debt Jesus settles by His death.

---

[1] *Ibid.* 3, 11, 84.   [2] 'De Fide Resurrectionis', II, 16.   [3] 'In Luc.' IV, 12, 16.
[4] 'De virginit.' 19, 126.   [5] 'Epist. ad Marcellinam', 41, 7.

'The Lord Jesus came, He offered His death for the death of all, He shed His blood for the blood of every one.'[6]

'The ransom of our liberation was the blood of the Lord Jesus, which of necessity had to be paid to him to whom we were sold by our sins.'[7]

Besides these ideas, however, Ambrose presents also with great emphasis the view of the death of Christ as a sacrifice to God.

'What greater mercy was there than that He offered Himself to be sacrificed for our crimes, that He might wash with His blood the world, whose sin could be blotted out in no other way.'[8]

It is important in this connexion to notice that Ambrose lays stress on the humanity of Christ as the necessary condition of His priesthood and sacrifice.

'The same then is the priest, the same is the victim: now both priesthood and sacrifice is an office of the human condition.'[9]

But Ambrose also supplements the idea of sacrifice with the thought of the satisfaction of the Divine sentence of death pronounced on sinful humanity.

'He underwent death that the sentence might be fulfilled, and that satisfaction might be made to the judgment (satisfieret judicato): the sentence was the curse pronounced upon sinful flesh even unto death. Nothing therefore was done in opposition to the sentence of God, since the condition of the Divine sentence was fulfilled.'[1]

Finally it is interesting and important to observe the way in which Ambrose states the problem, 'Cur Deus homo?'

'What was the cause of the Incarnation, but that the flesh which had sinned might through itself be redeemed?'[2]

There can be no doubt that in the doctrine of Hilary and still more of Ambrose we have to observe a distinct advance in the development of our doctrine along the lines peculiar to the West. It is true that we must not forget that the doctrine of both theologians is lacking in dogmatic precision and fullness. Neither

[6] Ibid. [7] 'Epist. ad Constant.' 72, 8. [8] 'Enarr. in Ps.' 47, § 17.

[9] 'De Fide', 3, 11, 87. [1] 'De fuga seculi', 7, 44. [2] 'De inc. dom. sacr.' 6.

Hilary nor Ambrose, for example, makes it clear upon what Divine attribute the necessity of Christ's sacrifice rests, whether the Divine veracity or the Divine righteousness. Nevertheless it is of the greatest importance that in these theologians, if only in a sporadic way, the somewhat loose and vague religious idea of sacrifice is replaced by the more definite juristic idea of satisfaction. In connexion with the idea of sacrifice it is necessary to emphasise the truth of what Heitmüller speaks of as 'a fact for the most part overlooked, but of the greatest importance for all investigation of ritual, viz. that ritual acts, ceremonies—rites in general are of a manifold significance'.

'Just this', he continues, 'is the attractive and characteristic point in such transactions and processes, that they awake in those who solemnise them manifold sensations and moods, that they admit of manifold interpretations, which need not always thoroughly agree with one another. The rites remain, the views as to their significance change.' [3]

Of no religious rite could these words be truer than of the central rite of sacrifice. [4]

It is therefore of very great importance that here first in the history of theology the concept of satisfaction, and not merely the concept but the term itself, definitely appears as a rational interpretation of the idea of sacrifice. It is to be noted, however, that the idea of satisfaction as found in Hilary, has no association with the term as used by Tertullian in the sense of a merit which avails to pay a debt or with the corresponding concept of Roman private law. Its connexion is rather with the general usage in Roman law, which has been already described, i.e. the meeting of the claim of one who possesses a right. The term in the way that it is used by Hilary and Ambrose means that Christ underwent as a substitute the suffering which sinners should have borne. So Ambrose definitely states the matter.

'That since the Divine decrees cannot be dissolved, the person rather than the sentence might be changed.' [5] To look forward to the future, it is in fact towards the Reformation conception of

---

[3] 'Die Religion in Geschichte und Gegenwart', s.v. Abendmahl, I, 3b.
[4] Cf. 'Man, Sin, and Salvation', pp. 12ff., for the manifoldness of the Biblical ideas of sacrifice. Ethnic ideas have a still wider range.
[5] 'In Luc.' IV, 7.

85

Christ's salvation as a vicarious endurance of punishment rather than to the Anselmic and mediaeval conception of Christ's satisfaction as a merit that pays the debt of sin that the doctrine of Hilary and Ambrose points. We have seen, however, that in Tertullian's writings *pœnitentia* (*satisfactio*) has not merely the significance of a merit availing to pay a debt, but also at times that of one form of penal suffering substituted for another. It is, I think, a mistake to imagine that the notion of satisfaction in Western Catholicism, whether as applied to the practical relation of the Christian to God, or as applied to the work of Christ, was ever quite uniform. The ruling conception of satisfaction no doubt everywhere is that of a merit which pays a debt, but the other idea of a substituted punishment is always in the background, and sometimes as in these earliest applications of the term to the work of Christ comes to the front even before the Reformation.

As regards the practical attitude of the Christian to God in general, Ambrose and Hilary continue the ideas of Tertullian. 'But with Ambrose begins the introduction of them into an increasingly systematised evangelical view of grace, which is finally irreconcilable with the thought of merit.'[6] There is on the one hand a denial of merit in the absolute sense, but on the other hand the firm conviction that through grace merit is made possible, through which we win our salvation according to the rule of a just retribution. In Ambrose, moreover, we find a distinct advance beyond Tertullian in the view that merit is transferable. This idea, which we have seen already to exist in North Africa in Tertullian's time, follows naturally from the legal character of the conception of merit.

'The transition was formed, as appears from Cyprian, by the old conception that the merits, e.g. of the martyrs give them the right to be heard by God in prayer for others.'[7]

Cyprian (Ep. 77, 7) writes to the martyrs imprisoned in the mines: 'Since now your word is more efficacious in prayer . . . beg more earnestly and ask that the Divine regard may accomplish the confession of us all, that God may deliver us with you entire and in glory from the darkness and snares of the world.'

[6] Schultz, op. cit. p. 34.   [7] *Ibid.* p. 36.

In Ambrose the transference of the merits of martyrs (and virgins) is quite axiomatic.[8]

The ideas of Hilary are similar to those of Ambrose, but there is more stress on the grace of God and less on human merit. Faith, the supreme condition of salvation, cannot be merited.[9]

AUGUSTINE

It is universally recognised that in Augustine (A.D. 354–430) we have one of the great turning-points of doctrinal development. Not only does he sum up in himself what has gone before, but he incorporates with it new and original elements of the greatest importance. His writings constitute a storehouse, whence not only the mediaeval theology, but also to a large extent the theology of Protestantism has drawn its materials.

In the first place we may notice Augustine's restatement of the problem of faith and reason.[1] Augustine is not without apologetic thoughts of Christianity as a renewal of the religion of nature.

'What now is called the Christian religion existed formerly among the ancients, nor was it lacking from the beginning of the human race till Christ came in the flesh, from which time the true religion, which was already, began to be called Christian.' [2]

This agrees with the Neoplatonic vein [3] in the theology of Augustine, according to which the essence of Christianity is simply the Logos doctrine. But more characteristic is the view in which Augustine's scepticism of reason leads him to base Christian truth solely upon revelation and in particular upon the Church. In a phrase that later became determinative for the mediaeval theology he says:

'What we understand we owe to reason, what we believe to authority.' [4]

---

[8] *Ibid.* p. 37.   [9] *Ibid.* pp. 41, 42.

[1] Cf. Harnack, D.G., 4th ed., vol. iii, p. 123, n. 4.   [2] 'Retract.' 1, 13, 3.

[3] Augustine, before his final adhesion to the Catholic Church, was first a Manichæan, holding a duality of principles, good and evil : from this position he made his way to Christianity through scepticism and Neoplatonism successively. The 'Neoplatonic vein' in his theology is largest in his earlier works.

[4] 'De utilitate credendi', 11, 25.

87

Then, as regards the sphere of authority, he says:

'I would not believe the Gospel, unless I were moved thereto by the authority of the Catholic Church.' [5]

To the end of his life, however, Augustine continued to hold that belief upon authority is not the highest form of faith. Higher than it is an intuitive understanding of the truth, *intelligere, credere ipsi veritati,*[6] *inhærere veritati.*[7] Faith upon authority is, however, the regular presupposition of understanding. Augustine says in words again determinative of the mediaeval attitude to the subject:·

'If thou canst not understand, believe that thou mayest understand. Faith goes before, understanding follows.' [8]

The next thing which it is important here to observe with respect to Augustine's theology is that by means of his doctrine of original sin he has given a firmer coherence to the understanding of the negative presupposition of the work of Christ. In the Greek theology from Irenæus onwards it was understood that the work of Christ undid Adam's sin, and that mankind was mystically one with Adam. It was also understood that in baptism was given a full forgiveness of all pre-baptismal sin. But Augustine's doctrine of the inheritance of original sin by natural generation from Adam, established it firmly that the chief result of baptism was to wash away original sin, and therefore connected more closely the doctrines of the forgiveness of sins in baptism and of the work of Christ as an undoing of the sin of Adam.

But it is above all by his practical doctrines of grace, justification, merit, and satisfaction that Augustine prepared for fresh conceptions of the work of Christ. He himself, though we owe to him new and important views of Christ's work, was only able to a small extent to connect his doctrine of this subject with his practical doctrines. In particular his doctrine of grace, the most important element in the whole of this sphere, sits very loose to his doctrine of Christ's work. It is not impossible, therefore, in Augustine's case to treat of his practical doctrines before treating of the doctrine of the work of Christ, which ought

---

[5] 'Contra ep. Manich.' 5, 6. [6] 'De utilitate credendi', 2, 25.
[7] *Ibid.* 16, 34. [8] 'Serm.' 118, 1.

properly to form their foundation. We shall, in fact, adopt this order, as it offers the best opportunity of pointing out in Augustine's treatment of the work of Christ, where he has continued along former lines, and where he has attempted to form a basis for his practical doctrines.

As already stated most fundamental of all Augustine's practical doctrines is his doctrine of grace. According to his doctrine of original sin, the fall of Adam had not only involved all humanity (*massa peccati*) in guilt and condemnation, but also infected it with a complete inability to all good. It is the work of grace in justification (Augustine adopts the term from Paul, but gives it his own sense) both to remove by forgiveness the guilt of all sin, especially original sin, and also to renew the will and make it capable of good. The former part, justification as the forgiveness of sins in baptism, is the interpretation of Pauline doctrine common in the Ancient Church before Augustine.

'He who is just, has it as a gift, because he is justified in baptism.'[9] It is a not unnatural, though inexact interpretation of Pauline doctrine. The latter point, the renewal of the will, falls altogether outside the Pauline conception of justification.[1] Augustine evolved it for himself in harmony with the suggestion of the Latin word *justificare*, which he interpreted as *justum facere*: 'Quid aliud est enim, justificati, quam justi facti, ab illo scilicet, qui justificat impium'.[2]

While the remission of sins as an element in justification is of great importance to Augustine, it is on the latter point, the renewal of the will, that the main stress is laid. This was the aspect of grace, whose necessity Augustine discovered for himself by painful experience, and which was hardly present to the minds of the Greek theologians, who were apt to think of the gift of the knowledge of God and of His law as of itself the fundamental grace of the Logos sufficient for all virtue.[3] It is,

[9] Ambrose, 'Ep.' 73, 11.
[1] For which see 'Man, Sin, and Salvation', pp. 114ff.
[2] 'De sp. et Litt.' 25, 45.
[3] Cf. Harnack, D.G., 4th ed., vol. ii, pp. 130, 140ff. It may be observed that Pelagius, who opposed Augustine's doctrines of sin and grace, did so in formal agreement with the previous Greek theology. Yet the doctrine of Pelagius 'was an innovation, because it nevertheless, as a matter of fact, in spite of all accommodations in expression, abandoned the pole of the mystical doctrine of redemption, which the Church had steadfastly maintained side by side with the doctrine of freedom' (Harnack, D.G., 4th ed., vol. iii, p. 201).

however, only with grace as the remission of sins that Augustine can establish any connexion of the work of Christ through the thought of His sacrifice. Grace as renewing the will is thought of primarily as the direct work of God, or of the Logos independently of the Incarnation. The notion later established by the mediaeval theologians that grace as renewing the will, as well as the grace of pardon, was purchased by the merit of Christ found no expression in Augustine's theology.

There is, however, an important series of passages to which Gottschick has called attention,[4] in which stress is laid on the solidarity between Christ as the Head and the Church as His body or members.

'Jesus Christ for no other reason came in the flesh, and . . . was made obedient even to the death of the Cross, than that by this dispensation of most merciful grace He might quicken all those, to whom, established as if members in His body, He is the Head, that they might gain the Kingdom of Heaven.'[5]

'The Word was made flesh, that He might become the Head of the Church.'[6]

'He justifies only His Body, which is the Church.'[7]

'He who believes in Christ . . . Christ enters into him, and is in a way united to him, and he is made a member of His body.'[8]

In the above passages the quickening power of grace is definitely associated with the Incarnation; the theological mediation between the historical work of Christ and the operation of grace is, however, not made evident.

With this failure to establish a clear relation between grace and the work of Christ, we may connect a further ambiguity in Augustine's view of grace, viz. that, while he conceives it, on the one hand, in agreement with the thought that grace proceeds directly from God or the Logos, as predestinarian and independent of Church or sacraments; on the other hand, he conceives it equally as sacramental grace, which properly requires that it should entirely flow from the Incarnation. These two thoughts appear side by side in Augustine, and the relation between them

---

[4] 'Augustins Anschauung von den Erlöserwirkungen Christi', in 'Zeitschrift für Theologie und Kirche', 1901, p. 107.   [5] 'De pecc. mer.' 26, 39.
[6] 'Enarr. in Ps.' 148, § 8.   [7] 'Ep.' 185, 40.   [8] 'Serm.' 144, 2, 2.

is brought to no settlement. They remain in unstable equilibrium, and the attempt to adjust them will be found to be one of the most fruitful causes of developments in the doctrine of the work of Christ.

The actual nature of grace, in so far as it renews the will, Augustine conceives as the infusion of love or charity, the gift of the Holy Ghost. By this infusion not only is the will renewed and made capable of good, but also faith itself is transformed from a mere historical faith into a faith informed with love, and so made saving faith.

In spite of his firm conviction that salvation is all of grace and that in the last resort human merit had no place, Augustine has nevertheless conserved the previous Catholic doctrine of merit, and reconciled it with his doctrine of grace by the idea that grace in renewing the will makes merit possible. Consequently he says:

'When God crowns our merits, He crowns only His own gifts.' [9]

Looked at from one point of view, salvation is of grace; but on the other side equally salvation is merited.

As regards *pœnitentia* (*satisfactio*) Augustine establishes that for light transgressions after baptism, confession of sins in prayer to God is a sufficient satisfaction.[1] Graver sins, however, require due satisfaction (*satisfactio congrua*).[2] In Augustine both conceptions of satisfaction as merit redeeming the debt of sin and as endurance of self-inflicted instead of Divine punishment, stand side by side. Thus on the one hand he writes:

'Many therefore are the forms of almsgiving, which when we accomplish, we are assisted towards the remission of our sins.' [3]

On the other hand Augustine speaks of *pœnitentia* as existing where anyone 'exercises severity towards himself, that being judged by himself, he may not be judged of the Lord'.[4]

So also he says:

'He does nothing, who truly repents, except refuse to allow to remain unpunished the evil done.' [5]

And now at last after these preliminary studies we come to

---

[9] 'Ep.' 194, 5, 19.   [1] 'Ench.' 71.   [2] *Ibid.* 70.
[3] *Ibid.* 72.   [4] 'Serm.' 351, 4, 7.   [5] 'Ep.' 153, 3, 6.

Augustine's actual doctrine of the work of Christ. It is impossible to give a complete account of the enormous variety of views upon this subject, which are to be found scattered throughout his voluminous writings. We shall have to be guided in the matter of selection by the consideration of the place of Augustine in the history of our doctrine, on the one hand as transmitting the ideas of the theology of the past, and on the other hand as frequently presenting new suggestions, new combinations, and new interpretations of former doctrine, often not worked out with any degree of fullness, yet destined to be fruitful in future developments. We shall of course put in the foreground Augustine's own systematic work; but we must also go outside of this to his sermons, epistles, and homiletic works to take account of certain passages which afterwards became the starting-point for further theological developments.

In the first place we shall consider the treatment of our subject in Augustine's complete systematic work, the 'Enchiridion', where the doctrine of the work of Christ is set in relation to his fundamental doctrines of original sin and of grace.

The origin of evils, says Augustine, consists in the turning away of the free will from the unchangeable to the changeable good, which took place first in the angel, then in man (23). Both angels and men are alike justly subjects of damnation for their wickedness. But man has a penalty of his own, viz. the death of the body (25). Moreover, the sin of the first man brought penalty upon the race. Adam 'brought the penalty of death and damnation upon his posterity, which by sinning he had corrupted in himself as it were in its root' (26). Thus the whole *massa damnata* was involved in the eternal condemnation of the rebellious angels. And so it might have justly continued, seeing that man had justly brought the calamity upon himself. So indeed it would have done, were it not that God is not only just but also merciful (27). It pleased God with a view to the order and harmony of the universe to fill up the number of the eternal Jerusalem, depleted by the fall of the angels, by saving some from the mass of sinful humanity (29). This part of humanity, however, could not be saved by the merit of its own works. By the fall the free will had been destroyed, so that man could no longer do what is good. Salvation can therefore only be by grace (30). Faith and regeneration are alike the gifts of the Divine grace (31). The restored free will, therefore, the basis of all merit, is a gift of Divine grace (32).

The human race was thus lying under a just damnation, and all were children of wrath. 'Since men through original sin were under this wrath, and that sin the heavier and more hurtful according as they had added greater or rather more sins, a mediator was necessary, that is a reconciler, who might placate this wrath by the offering of a unique sacrifice, of which all the sacrifices of the law and the prophets were shadows.'

The grace of God through Jesus Christ is in fact reconciliation through a mediator, and the gift of the Holy Ghost whereby we from enemies are made sons of God (33). The Mediator, being born from a virgin, was without original sin (34). He was at once God and man (35). The Incarnation is itself a supreme manifestation of the Divine grace. 'For what did the human nature in the man Christ merit, that it should be so uniquely assumed into the unity of the person of the only Son of God?' The purpose, then, of this extraordinary manifestation of grace is 'that men may understand that they are justified from sin by the same grace, by which it was brought about that the man Christ could have no sin' (36).

Christ, then, exempt from original sin and therefore Himself committing no sin, 'yet on account of the likeness of the sinful flesh, in which He had come, is Himself also called sin, from having to be sacrificed to wash away sin' (41). That He was made sin means that He was a sacrifice for sin, which might avail for our reconciliation.

'He therefore was made sin, that we might become righteousness, not our own but God's, nor yet in ourselves, but in Himself; . . . just as He Himself showed by the likeness of the sinful flesh, in which He was crucified, that the sin was not His own, but ours, and that its ground was not in Himself, but in us; so that, because there was no sin in Him, He might in a way die to sin, while dying to the flesh in which there was a likeness of sin, and since He Himself had never lived according to the old sinful nature, He might signify by His resurrection our new life renewing itself from the ancient death, by which we were dead in sin' (41).

It is in fact this death to sin, and resurrection to new life, that is celebrated in the great sacrament of baptism (42). By it all die to sin, infants to original sin only, adults to original and actual sin (43). So then baptism is a likeness of the death of Christ, and the death of Christ is a likeness of the forgiveness of sins, that, as Christ truly died, we might truly be forgiven, and, as He was truly raised, so we might be truly justified (52).

'Whatever therefore was done in the cross of Christ, in His burial, in His resurrection on the third day, in His ascent into heaven, in His sitting at the right hand of the Father, was so done that the Christian life which is lived here, might be conformed to these things, which were not only mystically said but also done' (53).

This extremely important statement now demands some analysis and comment. As regards the main lines of doctrine as to the work of Christ, it is clear that Augustine resolutely follows Paul. Men were under the wrath of God, and Christ's sacrifice placates this wrath and reconciles us to God. At the same time it is itself a manifestation of the Divine mercy.[6] Augustine moreover distinctly explains the phrase 'He was made sin for us'[7] as meaning, 'He was made a sacrifice for us,' thus defining Paul's doctrine more clearly than does Paul himself, who does not often actually use the terminology of sacrifice. Pauline also, however, is the addition to the doctrine of Christ's sacrifice of the idea of His death as inclusive of ours and of the appropriation of the principle of this death in baptism.[8] Thus Augustine's doctrine in the 'Enchiridion' is fundamentally Pauline.

The following points, however, are developments beyond Paul. Augustine has not only brought the work of Christ into connexion with his doctrines of original sin and of grace, but as a result he has also been able on the one hand to evaluate Christ's birth from a virgin as representing His freedom from original sin and consequent fitness for the work of mediation, and on the other hand he has been led to raise the important

---

[6] Cf. for both aspects Rom. 3:24–26, and 'Man, Sin, and Salvation', p. 119.
[7] 2 C. 5:21.   [8] 'Ench.' 42, 43, 53. See above.

question, hereafter frequently to be discussed, of the ultimate relation of the work of Christ to the Divine grace. This question is, Does the work of Christ by reconciling God procure the Divine grace for men, or is it not finally itself subordinate to it, and a pure manifestation of the Divine grace? Augustine, in spite of his clear doctrine that the sacrifice of Christ obtains for sinners reconciliation with God, regards the whole work of Christ from the Incarnation onward as ultimately purely dependent on the Divine grace. The human nature in Christ in no way merited an assumption into the Divine person: thus the Incarnation is a supreme example of Divine grace, teaching that men are justified by the same grace, which effected the sinlessness of Christ. The natural conclusion from this doctrine is that in the last resort justification depends simply upon the absolute unmerited grace of God, and that therefore the necessity of the work of Christ to bring it about can only be relative. This, moreover, as we shall presently see, is in reality the view of Augustine; though nevertheless he lays great stress on the worth of Christ's sacrifice.

If now we take the 'Enchiridion' as representing Augustine's considered systematic doctrine of the work of Christ, it is evident that it represents an enormous change from the Greek theology. We breathe a different atmosphere. The presuppositions and the conclusions are alike different. The central points are no longer the physical corruption wrought by the Fall, and the Incarnation as in principle the destruction of death and the deification of humanity; but instead we have original sin, justification by grace, and the reconciliation of God by the sacrifice of Christ. The Western type of thought here asserts itself in a fundamental and most striking form.

We have, however, now to supplement what we have learned from the 'Enchiridion' from the other writings of Augustine, in which process we shall discover the great variety of views already alluded to as contained in his works. There is practically no previous form of doctrine which he does not somewhere continue, while there are not a few notable novelties, which lie outside the doctrine of the 'Enchiridion'.

Before, however, we come to these further views, we may first supplement the doctrine of Christ's sacrifice in the 'Echiridion'

by a few passages from Augustine's other writings, in which his
view in this direction is further defined. Specially important is
the following:

'Of thy two evils, one is guilt (*culpa*), the other is punishment (*pœna*): the guilt is that thou art unrighteous: the
punishment that thou art mortal. . . . (Christ) by assuming the
punishment without assuming the guilt, blotted out both the
guilt and the punishment.' [9]

It is to be observed that the sentence here occurring, 'Suscipiendo pœnam et non suscipiendo culpam, et culpam delevit et
pœnam,' is frequently repeated (with slight variations) in Augustine's writings.[1]

Of importance also is the stress which Augustine lays on the
humanity of the Mediator.

'So far as He is man, so far is He the mediator.' [2]

'Nor yet is He the mediator, on this account that He is the
Word . . . but He is mediator in virtue of the fact that He is
man.' [3]

Here most distinctly in opposition to the characteristic Eastern
view of Christ as the God who becomes man in order to deify
humanity, we have indicated the view destined to attain complete
supremacy in the West, that Christ is the man who offers sacrifice
to God, qualified thereto of course by His Divine nature.

So much then for Augustine's reflections along the lines of
the doctrine of sacrifice. Now in the next place we must consider
the alternative statement of the doctrine of justification and reconciliation of God, which Augustine gives in 'De Trinitate', XIII,
where the work of Christ is regarded mainly as redemption from
the devil.[4] This passage in the 'De Trinitate' contains also a
systematic treatment of the work of Christ, though it differs from
that given in the 'Enchiridion' in the important point that it is
not connected with a complete whole of doctrine.

Here Augustine is once more perplexed by the question of
the relation of the grace of God to the need of the placation of
the Divine wrath by a sacrifice.

'What is the meaning of the words, Reconciled by the death

[9] 'Serm.' 171, 3.   [1] Cf. Gottschick, op. cit. p. 181.
[2] 'Conf.' x, 43, 68.   [3] 'De Civ. Dei', IX, 15, 2.
[4] Cf. also a brief incidental statement of this doctrine in 'Ench.' 49.

of His Son? Is it that, when God the Father was angry with us, He looked upon the death of His Son for us and was propitiated (*placatus*) towards us? . . . Unless the Father had been already propitiated towards us, would He, without sparing His Son, have given Him for us?' [5]

In order to meet this difficulty, Augustine tends practically to substitute in part at least for the wrath of God the claim of the devil as the obstacle which is to be met by the death of Christ, prior to our justification and reconciliation with God. His view is that reconciliation with God and justification are alike the just removal of God's retribution upon sin. God's wrath is not a perturbation of the mind, but simply this just retribution.[6] This retribution, however, operates through the claim of the devil upon sinners: so that both reconciliation and justification are equivalent to the legal annulment of this claim by means of the death of Christ.

In Augustine's treatment of this subject the notion of a deceit practised upon the devil disappears in favour of the idea of a legal annulment of his claim. Augustine first explains the justice and the general character of this claim.

'By the justice of God in some sense the human race was delivered into the power of the devil, the sin of the first man passing over by origination into all who are born through the conjugal union of both sexes, and the debt of our first parents binding their whole posterity.' [7]

This delivering up is contained in the course which gives men over to death. God, however, in acting thus 'did not release man from the government of His own power, when He permitted him to be in the power of the devil; since even the devil himself is not outside the power of the Omnipotent'.[8] Augustine's tendency in fact is, while making use of the doctrine of redemption from the devil, to allow the devil as little independence of God as is consistent with a real claim on his part.[9]

The actual process of redemption from the devil Augustine explains in the 'De Trinitate' as follows: He was to be overcome not by might but by righteousness, as was seemly for God, in

[5] 11, 15.　　[6] 16, 21.　　[7] 12, 16.　　[8] *Ibid.*
[9] Elsewhere Augustine calls the devil 'the exactor of punishment'. 'Enarr. in Ps.' 148, 8.

97

order that He might teach men to value righteousness above
might, and not might above righteousness after the manner of
the devil.

'What then is that righteousness by which the devil was
conquered? What but the righteousness of Jesus Christ? And
how was he conquered? Because when he found in Him nothing
worthy of death, he yet slew Him. And certainly it is just that we
whom he held as debtors, should be set at liberty, as believing
in Him, whom he slew without any debt. This is the meaning of
our being said to be justified in the blood of Christ.'[1]

The essence of the matter then is that the devil has to cede
his claim upon men, as amends for the violence used against the
innocent Christ. In connexion with this doctrine we may observe
Augustine's use of a phrase from the Psalms, destined to be
famous in the mediaeval theology.[2] According to the interpretation of the passage adopted by Augustine, it is Christ who speaks,
and says, 'Then I restored that which I took not away' (*Quæ
non rapui, tunc exsolvebam*). The meaning is that Christ pays
the debt of sin, which He did not contract.

To the same effect also Augustine refers to Jn 14:30, 'The
Prince of this world cometh, and hath nothing in me.' The
meaning is that Christ was to pay for us debtors what He Himself did not owe, i.e. was to die at the hands of the devil, and so
earn our release from sin.

Augustine points out here the necessity that Christ should
be both man and God. 'Unless He had been man, He could not
have been slain; unless He had been God, men would have
believed, not that He would not do what He could, but that He
could not do what He would.'[3]

Christ thus conquered the devil by righteousness, not by
might, though the latter way was open to Him; afterwards, however, He conquered him by might also in His resurrection.

If now we review this doctrine of redemption from the devil
as a whole, we see that it serves in reality as an alternative to
the doctrine of sacrifice, one which Augustine is led to adopt
from the past, in order to meet the difficulty of harmonising the
free grace of God as the source of redemption with the necessity

---

[1] 14, 18.   [2] Ps. 69:4.   [3] 14, 18.

of the death of Christ. In the doctrine of Christ's sacrifice this necessity is grounded in the need of the propitiation of the Divine wrath. Here, however, it is based upon the demand of justice, which for Augustine is expressed in the claim of the devil.

In connexion with this it is to be observed that Augustine not only, as we have already seen, finds in this necessity a reason for Christ's being both God and man, but also a reason for His being of Adam's race.

'Assuredly God could have taken upon Himself to be man, in order that in that manhood He might be the mediator of God and man, from some other source and not from the race of that Adam, who bound the human race by his sin; just as He did not create him, whom He first created, of the race of some one else. Therefore He was able either so, or in any other mode that He would, to create yet one other, by whom the conqueror of the first might be conquered. But God judged it better to take upon Him from the very race that had been conquered the man through whom to conquer the enemy of the human race.' [4]

Moreover, as in the parallel doctrine of Christ's work as sacrifice, Augustine here evaluates the virgin birth of Christ as the means by which He had escaped the taint of original sin, which is propagated by ordinary generation, and so was able, as before explained, through His death to conquer the devil.

We may observe that the virgin birth of Christ hereby enters much more essentially into the doctrine of the Incarnation than in the interpretation previously given of it apart from the doctrine of original sin by Gregory of Nyssa, viz. that its miraculous character was calculated along with Christ's subsequent miracles to awaken the devil's cupidity for the soul of Christ.

Finally, however, it is most important to note that while Augustine thus finds a rational necessity for the death of Christ, and also for the accompanying circumstances of His Incarnation, he totally denies that this necessity was absolute. His statement, which is of immense consequence for the further history of doctrine, is as follows:

' We must show, not indeed that no other mode was possible

[4] 18, 23.

to God, to whose power all things are equally subject, but that there neither was nor need have been any other mode more appropriate for curing our misery.'[5]

For this appropriateness Augustine finds many other reasons besides the relative necessity of the death of Christ. These are suggested in 'De Trin.' XIII, 10, 13; 17, 22; but are more fully worked out in other places of Augustine's writings, and we shall therefore first study them in this developed form, finally, however, reverting to the statement of the 'De Trinitate' because of its classical importance. We may sum them up in general as considerations of the subjective or psychological results of the Incarnation.

In the first place we may note that Augustine, while repeating in places the Greek doctrine of the Incarnation, tends to give this a psychological and subjective turn. We find in his writings such statements as:

'He who was God became man to make gods (*deos facturus*) those who were men.'[6]

'For neither should we be made participators of His divinity, unless He became a participator of our mortality.'[7]

But on the other hand Augustine gives a fresh interpretation of the nature of deification, and one very different from the usual Greek idea.

'We are made gods by loving God (*amando deum, efficimur dii*).'[8] In harmony with this he teaches that the deification of mankind in Christ is not natural but adoptive.

'For God wishes to make thee God, not by nature . . . but by His gift and adoption.'[9]

Approximation to God in fact is not physical but ethical.

'We are moved towards Him, who is everywhere present, not spatially, but by good desire and good conduct.'[1]

The nearest thing to this in the Greek theology is the ethical interpretation of deification by Origen. Whoever imitates Jesus, participates in the Divine nature which He bears.[2]

But even this is not quite the idea of Augustine. A new and

---

[5] 10, 13. Cf. the teaching of Gregory of Nyssa, that the patient must not prescribe his cure ('Cat. Magna', 17).　　[6] 'Serm.', 192, 7.
[7] 'Enarr. in Ps. CXVIII', Serm. 16, 6.　　[8] 'Serm.' 121, 1.
[9] *Ibid*. 166, 4.　　[1] 'Doctr. Chr.' I, 10.　　[2] 'De princ.' IV, 31.

warmer note is struck, when he says, 'amando deum, efficimur dii'.

We turn next, however, to consider Augustine's treatment of the Greek doctrine of the Incarnation, not in the shortened or Athanasian form, but in its fuller or Irenæan form. In his theology the Irenæan doctrine of the undoing of Adam's fall by the Incarnation, Passion, Death, and Resurrection of Christ, takes fresh life in combination with the doctrine of Gregory of Nyssa of the Incarnation as a healing process in humanity, the whole being again by Augustine given a subjective or psychological tendency.

The idea of sin as a disease and of Christ as physician and medicine is frequent in Augustine. In this connexion the passage 'De doctrinâ christiana', I, 14, is of special importance. Here Augustine says that 'the medicine of (Divine) wisdom was by His assumption of humanity adapted to our wounds, curing some of them by their opposites, some of them by their similars.'

As examples of the treatment by means of opposites we have the following:

'Seeing therefore that man fell through pride, He applied humility to cure him. We were ensnared by the wisdom of the serpent: we are set free by the foolishness of God. . . . We used immortality so badly as to incur the penalty of death: Christ used mortality so well as to restore us through life. The disease entered a woman's corrupted soul: the remedy came forth from a woman's uncorrupted body.'

As examples of treatment by means of similars Augustine offers on the other hand the following congruities:

'He was born of a woman to deliver us, who were beguiled through a woman; He came as a mortal man to save us, who are mortal men, by death to save us who were dead.'

These passages are especially important as showing how the Irenæan notion of the work of Christ as an undoing of the work of Adam, in the very nature of the case exactly corresponding with and yet also exactly opposed to the sin which it undoes, passed on to the mediaeval theology. The subjective note, however is new. When it is said that Christ's humility heals our pride, this is not Irenæan, but distinctively Augustinian. It may be pointed out that this psychological interpretation of the Incarnation readily merges itself into the simple idea of Christ as example and teacher, which indeed is not infrequent in Augustine.

'He has run, crying out by His words, deeds, death, life, descent, ascent, that we may return to Him.'[3]

'The Lord Jesus Christ commended to us in His passion the labours and tribulations of this age: in His resurrection He commended eternal life and the blessedness of the future age.'[4]

Augustine also says that Christ's sufferings admonish His faithful followers to despise temporal for eternal felicity.[5]

Thirdly, there is one more explanation of the Incarnation and of the work of Christ, which is in a line with the subjective and psychological aspects of the doctrines just described, and is a fresh and important contribution to the history of our subject. It is the doctrine based on Rom. 5:8; 8:32 (afterwards to become the starting-point of the theory of Abelard), which receives its fullest and most characteristic expression in 'De cat. rudibus', 4,7.

'What greater cause was there for the advent of the Lord, than that God should show the love which He has in our case, strongly commending it, because, when we were yet enemies, Christ died for us? This therefore took place, as the end of the precept and the fulfilment of the law is charity, that we should love Him in return, and just as He laid down His life for us, so we also should lay down our lives for the brethren, and if it were difficult for us to love God Himself, at least it should not be difficult for us to love Him in return, when He first loved us and spared not His Only Son, but gave Him up for us all. For there is no greater invitation to love, than to be first in loving.'

Another passage to the same effect is 'De cat. rudibus', 22, 39:

'Who would not strive to love in return, a most just and merciful God, who first so loved men most unjust and proud, that for their sakes He sent His Only Son, through whom He made all things, who was made man, not by the change of Himself but by the assumption of a man, not merely to live with them, but also to be slain for them and by them?'

Finally, the statement of 'De Trin.' xiii, 10, 13; 17, 12, may

<hr/>

[3] 'Conf.' iv, 12, 19. [4] 'Serm.' 217, 3. [5] 'De grat. nov. test.' 5, 13.

now be seen to be no more in general than a mere outline sketch of the foregoing views. It has, however, a peculiar importance of its own, inasmuch as it contains one or two things not previously mentioned, and also because of its direct influence on the mediaeval theology. Its arguments are as follows:

(1) Nothing is more calculated to stimulate our hope of immortality than the manifestation of God's love in the Incarnation.

(2) This manifestation of Divine love (or grace) is peculiarly seen in Christ's assumption of our humanity without prior merits on its part, and indeed in spite of our demerits (cf. 'Ench.' 36).

(3) The Incarnation shows the value set by God on man, and should prevent the idea that the devils, because they are without flesh, are his superior.

(4) The Incarnation is adapted to heal our pride, to teach man how far he has removed from God, and to show the remedial value of suffering.

(5) Christ's death is an example of obedience, His resurrection of its reward.

In the above views of the work of Christ we have then the additional reasons why Augustine finds the Incarnation and death of Christ the appropriate means of redemption. It is characteristic of his theology that while, as we have seen, in his systematic work, the 'Enchiridion', he elevates the doctrine of Christ's sacrifice into the central and fundamental doctrine of Christ's work, yet he abounds in other suggestive and fruitful points of view, which, however, he has not been able to combine together. Enough has been said to show how Augustine's writings constituted a mine, out of which later theologians could extract an abundant material for many doctrinal developments.

We may conclude our account of Augustine by citing a passage from the 'Enchiridion' itself, in which, apart from his systematic treatment of the work of Christ, he has brought together most of his various views on the subject.

'When Adam was made, i.e. as a just man, there was no need of a mediator. When, however, sins had separated the human race far from God, it behoved us through the Mediator, who alone was born and lived and was slain without sin, to be reconciled to God even to the resurrection of the flesh unto eternal life; so that human pride might be reproved and healed by the humility of God, and it might be manifested to man how far he had departed from God, when he was recalled by God incarnate, and an example of obedience might be given to rebellious man by the God-man; and the Only Begotten assuming the form of a servant, which had before deserved nothing, the fount of grace might be opened, and also the resurrection of the flesh promised to the redeemed might be shown beforehand in the Redeemer Himself; and by the same nature which he rejoiced to have deceived the devil might be conquered; and yet man should not glory lest pride should again be born; and whatever else may be perceived and expressed by the advanced in knowledge concerning this great sacrament of the Mediator, or may only be perceived even if it cannot be expressed.'[6]

LEO THE GREAT AND GREGORY THE GREAT

Between Augustine and the mediaeval theology stand the figures of Leo the Great (d. A.D. 461) and Gregory the Great (d. A.D. 604), who both deserve some notice.

Leo is the less important. We may note first the form which the doctrine of merit takes in his hands. His teaching is given with numerous references to his works by Schultz,[7] whose results I here summarise. Leo continues on the one hand the view that almsgiving, fasting, and prayer merit eternal life and avail to atone for post-baptismal sin, but on the other the doctrine that in the last resort all is of grace. 'The Augustinian doctrine of grace hinders Leo as little as Augustine himself from accepting that by merits eternal life can be earned, and satisfaction be made for sins after baptism. This last, however, properly takes place, when the divinely instituted power of the priest and the ecclesiastically instituted penance are guarantee, as otherwise no one would know when his merits really satisfy for his sins.'[8]

The last point is important as illustrating the development in the West of the ideas which led ultimately in the Middle Ages to the establishment of a sacrament of penance.

[6] 'Ench.' 108.   [7] Op. cit. p. 42.   [8] Ibid.; cf. Leo, 'Ep.' 108, 3 ; 168, 2 : 171, 1.

Important also is the way in which Leo not only views the merits of the saints as effective for others, but also brings them into comparison with the work of Christ, only, however, to refuse to put the two things on the same level.

He says on the one hand:

'By so much as we are brought down by our sins, by so much may we be raised by the apostolic merits.' [9]

But on the other hand he says:

'The righteous have received, not given crowns; and from the courage of the faithful have been born examples of patience, not the gifts of righteousness. In each case, moreover, their deaths were each for himself (*singulares*); nor did anyone pay the debt of another by his own end, since among the sons of men the Lord Jesus only has appeared, in whom all have been crucified, all are dead and buried, all again have been raised.' [1]

Leo explained the effect of the merits of the saints in two ways (1) by the influence of their example,[2] (2) by their intercession with God.[3]

As regards the doctrine of the work of Christ Leo affords no new point of view. He is simply a transmitter to posterity of the doctrines already found in Ambrose and Augustine. Moreover, these views are found in Leo principally in his sermons, i.e. rather in a homiletic than in a scientific form.

With Gregory the Great the case is somewhat different. Before, however, we approach his proper doctrine of the work of Christ we must stop to consider his contributions in some outlying regions.

In the first place it is to be observed that he set faith and reason in even stronger opposition to each other than did Augustine. A famous saying of his is often quoted in the Middle Ages.

'Faith has no merit, where human reason affords a test (*experimentum*).' [4]

As regards the doctrines of grace and merit in general Gregory stands in the line of the previous Western theology since Ambrose and Augustine. But in his theology 'is to be found a

---

[9] 'Serm.' 82, 7.   [1] 'Serm.' 64, 3.   [2] *Ibid.* 85, 1.
[3] *Ibid.* 84, 1, 2 ; 85, 4.   [4] 'In Evang.' II, Hom. XXVI.

peculiarly external mode of combining the Augustinian doctrine with the doctrine of merit'.[5] If on the one hand Gregory holds that salvation is all of grace, on the other hand he teaches almost juristically that God 'inquires into the life of men simply by the quantity of merits'.[6]

Like Ambrose and Leo he regards it as axiomatic that the merits of the saints avail for others. Like Leo, however, he views the intercession of the saints with God as the channels through which this availment operates.

'Those who . . . run to the protection of the holy martyrs and press upon their sacred bodies with supplications, pray that they may merit (*promereri*) pardon through their intercession.'[7]

Finally, however, Gregory's actual doctrine of the work of Christ is of some importance. Much of it of course is merely repetition of older ideas. But Loofs[8] has collected from the writings of Gregory a series of passages, in which, as he says, though neither of the terms satisfaction or merit is used, yet the ideas occur which later found their most pregnant expression in these terms:

'Some just men can sometimes meet the manifestations of present censure by the merit of an acceptable innocence, but they are not able by their own virtue to expel from the human race the punishment of imminent death. . . . The Redeemer of the human race, being constituted through the flesh the Mediator of God and man, since He alone appeared as righteous among men and yet even without guilt met the punishment of guilt, has both reproved men of sin and stood in the way of the Divine stroke . . . has reproved the guilt of man by inspiring righteousness, and by dying, has assuaged the wrath of the Judge . . . has given men an example to imitate, and manifested to God in Himself works by which He might be propitiated towards men.'[9]

'Since there was no one, by whose merits the Lord could be propitiated towards us, the Only begotten of the Father, assuming the form of our weakness, alone appeared as righteous, to intercede for sinners.'[1]

'For in interceding for sinners He showed Himself a righteous

[5] Schultz, op. cit. p. 43.
[6] 'Moral', 25, 1, 1, as quoted by Schultz : another reading is 'quality'.
[7] *Ibid.* 16, 51, 64.   [8] D.G., 4th ed., p. 448.   [9] 'Moral', 9, 38, 61.   [1] *Ibid.* 24, 3, 5.

man who might merit forgiveness for others (*qui pro aliis indulgentiam mereretur*).' [2]

'Without intermission the Redeemer slays a holocaust for us, in that He without cessation exhibits His Incarnation to the Father for us. His very Incarnation is the sacrifice of our cleansing, since He shows Himself as man, and intervening blots out man's offences (*delicta*).' [3]

Moreover, it is of great importance to note that 'in connexion with these thoughts the idea, which in Augustine on account of his Neoplatonism did not attain to real recognition, viz. that the grace won by Christ and operative in the saving institution of the Church is the grace of God, is clearly brought to expression'.[4]

Gregory therefore is to be regarded as a distinct stage in the development from Augustine to the Middle Ages. What there emerges into distinct and clear formulation, already finds a more inchoate expression in his writings.

WESTERN ADOPTIANISM

In commenting on the Creed of Chalcedon, I have already referred to the interest of the West in the full humanity of Christ. We have also observed in our study of the Western theologians themselves their corresponding interest in the human aspect of the work of Christ, His cross and passion, which is so emphatically enunciated in the famous doctrine of Augustine, 'In quantum homo, in tantum Mediator'.

It is now necessary, in order to explain certain developments which we shall meet with in the mediaeval theology, to follow up further some manifestations and consequences of the Western interest in the humanity of our Lord. While the Latins Hilary, Ambrose, and Augustine accepted the Greek view, as fixed in the Nicene Creed, according to which the Logos is to be understood as the subject of the historical life of Jesus Christ, they yet at the same time under the influence of Phil. 2:5–11, present a view akin to that later represented in the Greek Church by the Nestorians, in which more independence is given to the humanity

[2] *Ibid.* 24, 2, 4.　　　[3] *Ibid.* 1, 24, 32.　　　[4] Loofs, loc. cit.

of Christ as the *forma servi* over against the *forma Dei*, and in fact the man Christ Jesus is thought of as the subject of actions, whereby He earns for Himself the reward of immortality and Divine glory.

Thus Hilary says:[5]

'Because all this prayer (Save me, O God, by Thy name)[6] proceeds from the character (*persona*) of the servile form, for which servile form, assumed even unto the death of the Cross, He beseeches the salvation of that name which is God's; and, as one to be saved by the name of God, He goes on to add, "and judge me in Thy might". For because of the merit of His humility, since He had emptied Himself, accepting the form of a servant, He was now again seeking in that humility, which He had assumed, the form which He shared with God; when the very man, in whom God had been obediently born, should have been saved by the name of God.'

Ambrose shows less deviation from the orthodox Greek view, yet he too could write:

'It was the man, who cried,[7] being about to die by reason of the separation of the Divinity.'[8]

Augustine, again, expounds Jn 17:1 ('Father, glorify Thy Son') by a reference to Phil. 2:8–11, and says:

'That therefore the Mediator of God and men, the man Jesus Christ, might be glorified by the resurrection, He was first humiliated by the passion. . . . Humility is the merit of glory, glory the reward of humility. But this was done in the form of a servant, but in the form of God there always was and always will be glory.'[9]

Along the same line is the thought of the man Jesus as the supreme example of predestinating grace.

'There is no more illustrious example of predestination than Jesus Himself.'[1]

Similar again is the thought which we have already noticed in the 'Enchiridion':

'Men are to understand, that they are justified from their sins by the same grace, by which it was brought about that the

---

[5] 'Tractatus in Ps.' LIII. 5.   [6] Ps. 54:1.   [7] Matt. 27:46.
[8] 'Expos. in Luc.' 10, 127.   [9] 'In Joh. Tractatus', 104, 3.   [1] 'De dono persev.' 24, 67.

man Christ could have no sin.'[2] Augustine once even wrote of the man Christ as *homo dominicus*,[3] though afterwards he regretted the phrase.[4]

In the subsequent history of thought in the West passages like the above continued to work as a leaven in spite of the general acceptance of the Greek doctrine of the Person of Christ as fixed at Chalcedon. This is shown by the adoptianist controversy in Spain and France in the eighth century A.D., in which the Western interest in the humanity of Christ, expressed in an extreme form, came into collision with the Greek view. The 'adoptianist' view of the Person of Christ was expressed by Elipandus, Archbishop of Toledo, as follows:

'The Son of God Himself according to the form of a servant, which He assumed from the Virgin (in which He is less than the Father, and is not the Adopted of God by nature, but by adoption), is the first-born among many brethren according to the Apostle. Wherefore should He not be called the Adopted, who is equally perfect in all that pertains to us, sin except, as in all that pertains to Himself.'[5]

Elipandus therefore appealed to the Western element in the Chalcedonian Creed in support of his views. Nevertheless his doctrine was rejected at the Counsels of Ratisbon (A.D. 792), Frankfort (A.D. 794), Aix (A.D. 799). The opposition to adoptianism was thus voiced by the leading Carolingian theologian, Alcuin:

'The humanity entered into the unity of the Person of the Son of God and remained the same attribute in two natures under the name of the Son, as it was before in one substance. For in the assumption of the flesh by God, the person of the man perishes, not his nature.'[6]

This is of course the Greek doctrine of the enhypostatic union.

---

[2] 'Ench.' 36, 11. [3] 'De serm. dom.' 2, 6, 20. [4]'Retract.' 1, 19, 8.
[5] Cf. Loofs, 4th ed., p. 456. [6] *Ibid.* loc. cit.

PART II

THE MEDIAEVAL THEOLOGY

CHAPTER 1

PRELIMINARY STUDIES

THE DEVELOPMENT OF THE DOCTRINE OF PENANCE IN THE EARLY MIDDLE AGES

As a preparation to the study of the doctrine of the work of Christ in the Middle Ages, it is necessary first of all to give an account of the development of the doctrine of penance, particularly as regards the modification of the idea of satisfaction.

The penitential system of the Ancient Church was fundamentally one of public penance for mortal sins, i.e. for such sins as were held apart from such penance to exclude from final salvation. As we have already observed, for the ordinary minor sins of daily life nothing more than confession of them to God in prayer was regarded as the necessary condition of the Divine forgiveness.[1]

Even in the Ancient Church, however, a system of private penance came to be established, at first in monastic circles. This aimed not merely at dealing with manifest sins, such as excluded from the Christian Church, but at eradicating the roots of sin in the heart, and involved therefore a penitential discipline for other than mortal sins.

In the early Middle Ages the public to a great extent disappears in favour of the private penance. In connexion with the latter, moreover, there began to appear first in Ireland, then in England, and finally on the Continent a series of penitential books (*libri penitentiales*), directing the priest in his office as spiritual adviser and fixing the amount of satisfaction required in individual cases. Not without some opposition was the supersession of the public by the private penance effected, but in the end it became practically universal. 'From the end of the eleventh century onwards the *pœnitentia* (*publica et*) *solemnis* . . . has become a mere curiosity in the inventory of possible Church

---

[1] Augustine, 'Ench.' 71.

113

procedure against sinners, which in practice was almost entirely put in the background by modern developments.'[2]

Two things in particular concern us in the newer penitential discipline.

The first is the increasing tendency towards the definite transformation of the penitential discipline into a sacrament. Its parts came to be defined as 'contritio cordis, confessio oris, satisfactio operis',[3] and the tendency is for the confession (to a priest) to assume a more and more important position. The theory establishes itself that by confession even mortal sins are transformed into venial sins, which require to be expiated not in hell but in purgatory, unless satisfaction be made for them in the present life. This theory is clearly laid down in the eleventh century Pseudo-Augustinian treatise, 'De vera et falsa pœnitentia'.

'In that (the sinner) of himself speaks to the priest and over-comes his shame by the fear of an offended God, there comes about the forgiveness of the crime. For that which was criminal in the doing becomes venial through confession; and even if it is not purged away at once (i.e. by satisfaction) nevertheless that becomes venial, which as committed was mortal' (10, 25).

The priest appears in the 'De vera et falsa pœnitentia' as the 'nuntius dei' (10, 25), whose is the 'potestas judicis' (15, 30). In this way the discipline of penance becomes essentially a sacrament, since grace operates through the word of the priest in absolution to convert mortal into venial sins, an idea unknown in the Ancient Church.

The other point which concerns us in the newer penitential discipline is the introduction in the penitential books of re-demptions or commutations of the satisfactions proper to various offences. The result of this innovation is to increase the tendency to view the satisfaction from a material point of view, which is immanent from the first in the conception of it as a merit cancelling the debt of sin, and immanent also in the notion of the possibility of a transference of merits. The necessary satis-faction comes more and more to be regarded as something that can be detached from the person and treated upon commercial lines.

The commutations and redemptions of penitential satisfaction

---

[2] Loofs, D.G., 4th ed., vol. i, p. 478.   [3] Op. cit. p. 484.

have thus far their origin in the practice of the Ancient Church that in cases of extraordinary penitence, something of the satisfaction might be remitted.[4] But in the mediaeval practice we come upon a regular tariff of commutations.

In Ireland, as far back as the seventh century, in certain cases fasts were commuted into less exacting penances, such as psalm-singing.[5] It is, however, a stage beyond this, when we find it allowed to substitute for personal fasting the fasting of others.

'He who knows not the Psalms and cannot fast, must choose a righteous man, who may fulfil this for him, and he must redeem this at his own expense and labour.'[6]

A still more extreme instance of the redemption of a satisfaction by means of the fasting of others is found in the 'Canones editi sub Edgardo' (Edgar of England, A.D. 959–975): de magnatibus II; where it is explained how a rich man can accomplish a seven years' fast in three days.

'In the first place let him take to his help twelve men, and let them fast three days on bread and green herbs and water, and let him look out for himself to complete it, as far as he can, seven times one hundred and twenty men, who may fast for him each for three days: then as many fasts are fasted, as there are days in seven years. . . . This is the relaxation of penance for a powerful man and one rich in friends. But a man without power (*infirmus*) cannot act thus; but must look after the matter with more zeal in his own person.'[7]

Yet another mode of redeeming the more exacting satisfaction of fasting is by almsgiving.

'If any one perchance cannot fast and have the means of redemption, if he be rich let him give instead of seven weeks, twenty shillings. If he have not wherewithal to give this, let him give ten shillings. If he be very poor, let him give three shillings. . . . But let each one have regard to what he should give, whether it is to be expended for the redemption of prisoners, or upon the holy altar, or for the Christian poor.'[8]

---

[4] *Ibid.* p. 492. 　　　[5] *Ibid.* p. 493.

[6] 'Pœnitentiale Cummeani', ninth century, in Wasserschleben, 'Die Bussordnungen der abendländischen Kirche ', 1851, p. 463.

[7] Quoted by Loofs, op. cit. p. 494, n. 6.

[8] 'Pœnitentiale Pseudo-Bedæ', c. A.D. 800, cap. 41 ; Wasserschleben, op. cit., pp. 276f.

The above instances give a sufficient idea of the nature of the mediaeval redemptions. The important question has been raised whether in part at least they owe their origin to the system of compositions existing in the secular law of the Irish and more especially of the Teutonic peoples.

The legal system in question turns upon the idea of the honour-price or wergild set upon the life of every free man. Where a man has been killed his family may accept a composition instead of exercising the right of revenge.

In Irish law every man's life was estimated by an *einechlan* or honour-price according to his status. This was reckoned either in cattle or in female bond-slaves, one of the latter being valued at the worth of three oxen. If a man were slain, his honour-price was paid by the family of the slayer to that of the slain, the fine being leviable first on the criminal himself, and then by a regulated system of his relations in order of proximity.[9]

The German ideas were very similar. An injury committed by an individual brings about a state of feud between the kin of the injured and that of the injurer. This feud may be ended by revenge for the injury, or instead the kin of the injured may accept a compensation.

The fundamental case in which the alternative of feud or compensation obtained was that of murder. Here the compensation was the wergild, a compensation fixed according to the rank and position of the murdered man. But compensations for smaller injuries were also fixed: these sometimes were reckoned as fractional parts of the wergild.[1]

Such are the outlines of the secular system of compositions. There is one way at any rate in which undoubtedly it has influenced the ecclesiastical penance. This appears chiefly in the Irish and Anglo-Saxon penitential books, and consists in the fixing of an equivalence between the secular satisfaction and an ecclesiastical penance.

So, for instance, 'Pœnitentiale Theodori', 1, 3, 3: 'He who has often committed theft, is condemned to a penance of seven

---

[9] See Wasserschleben, 'Die Irische Kanonensammlung', 1885, Einleitung, pp. xlixff.
[1] See Brunner, 'Deutsche Rechtsgeschichte', 1887, vol. i, pp. 156ff. ; vol. ii, p. 760, s.v. Wergeld.

years, or as long as the priest shall judge in view of the possibility
of a composition with those he has injured; and he who used
to commit theft, ought under the influence of repentance always
to be reconciled to him whom he used to offend and to make
restitution according to the injury he has done to him, and thus
he will greatly shorten his penance. If, however, he will not or
cannot, he must do penance the fixed time in all completeness.' [2]

So again, *ibid.* 1, 4, 1 : 'If any one shall have slain a man in
revenge of a kinsman, let him repent as a man-slayer seven or
ten years. But if he is willing to pay the kinsmen the wergild
(*pecuniam æstimationis*), his penance will be lighter, i.e. by half
the time.' [3]

In these passages penance and composition are reduced to
a common measure: so far therefore we may say that there is
a tendency to view the ecclesiastical penance as equivalent to a
composition. The disputed question, however, is, whether we
are to recognise beyond this direct but limited influence a more
indirect but much wider one, in which the ideas of the composition
system have affected the general spirit and temper of the penitential discipline in helping to materialise and commercialise the
idea of satisfaction, and thus bring about the practice of
redemptions. This is maintained by Cremer in his essay, 'Der
germanische Satisfaktionsbegriff in der Versöhnungslehre' (St.
Kr. 1893, pp. 316–43), also by Schultz.[4] Loofs, however, is more
cautious. He says:

'It is possible that the system of compositions in secular law
(e.g. the wergild) has given an incentive for the appearance of
these redemptions. But the assumption is not necessary, in view
of the part which alms has always played in the matter of the
(penitential) satisfactions.' [5]

It must be admitted that an influence of the compensation
system upon penance does not seem absolutely demanded, as
there is really nothing in the later ideas of satisfaction, which
has not some starting-point in the thought of the Ancient Church
(value of almsgiving, transference of merits, etc.).

On the other hand, in view of our knowledge of an actual

---

[2] Wasserschleben, 'Die Bussordnungen der abendländischen Kirche', p. 187.
[3] *Ibid.* loc. cit.   [4] Op. cit. pp. 245ff.   [5] D.G., 4th ed., p. 493, n. 3.

direct contact in some cases between the secular and ecclesiastical systems, and of the domination of the idea of wergild over the early mediaeval mind in general, it is hard to think that the development of the ideas of penance is not in some measure due to the influence of the secular system. Nevertheless the point cannot be proved; and so in the end the *non liquet* of Loofs is the safest verdict.

It remains to be added, that the system of redemptions, in spite of its wide extension and development, by no means so dominated the whole field of penance in the Middle Ages as to exclude the quite opposed conception of satisfaction as a voluntary endurance of penal suffering. Especially noteworthy in this connexion is the definition of the 'De vera et falsa pœnitentia,' influential as it is in the determination of much later mediaeval thought:

'Pœnitere enim est pœnam terere' (19, 35).

The aim of penance for the sinner in fact is:

'That he may continually punish, by taking vengeance on himself, the offence he has committed by sinning.'[6]

THE PRINCIPLES OF THE MEDIAEVAL THEOLOGY

In general the Middle Ages constitute a period of great consequence in the history of theology. It is above all other ages the period of systematisation, and herein lies its importance. If it be true that each doctrine only appears in its full significance when viewed as a part of the whole, then the work of the mediaeval theologians, in spite of its limitations, is of the utmost significance. It is true that in Origen's 'De Principiis', Gregory of Nyssa's 'Great Catechism', Augustine's 'Enchiridion' and the 'Exposition of the Orthodox Faith' of John of Damascus we have already systematic works from the Ancient Church. But none of these, not even the last, can compare in thoroughness and completeness with the mediaeval 'Summæ', the influence of whose systematisation is still felt in scientific theology up to the present day.

'All later dogmatic compendia, right up to the nineteenth

[6] *Ibid.*

118

century, are derived in a direct line from the mediaeval "Summæ", and even the most modern dogmatic systems still continue to show in their general shape the original form of the "Summæ", just as the species of animals, which stand to one another in a relation of descent, as soon as the skeleton is disclosed, manifest the structure of the original form.' [7]

The theology of the Middle Ages is usually, in contrast with that of the patristic period, called scholasticism. It is very commonly assumed that the essence of scholasticism lies in the opposition between authority and reason which is fundamental to it, and in the attempt in connexion therewith to give a rational proof of the authoritatively received doctrine. This characteristic of the scholastic theology is, however, not in itself enough to differentiate it from the patristic theology. The opposition of authority and reason and the attempt to give a rational proof of doctrine in some measure characterises all theology, and in particular it markedly characterises the theology of the Western Church from Tertullian onwards.

'Yet there exists a distinction between the mediaeval and the patristic theology. In the period of the Ancient Church its theologians thought within the scheme of the still living philosophic view of the world of the ancients: in the Middle Ages the ecclesiastical tradition and the philosophic culture renewed once again by the help of learned study stand in greater alienation from one another.' [8]

As a consequence the union between authority and reason achieved by the Middle Ages tends to be more formalistic than it was in the patristic period. The extreme opposite in that period to the scholastic method is to be found in the classical Greek theology, where the proof of a doctrine by reason amounts essentially to a discernment of the inner rational essence of the doctrine. The Western theology with its dialectic character approaches nearer to scholasticism, though here also a considerable speculative element was introduced by Augustine.

Again, within the scholastic theology itself there are differences. A speculative tendency is by no means altogether wanting

[7] Heim, 'Das Gewissheitsproblem in der systematischen Theologie', 1911, p. 8.
[8] Loofs, D.G., 4th ed., p. 498.

119

in the Middle Ages. In particular Anselm (d. A.D. 1109) is in many ways more akin to the patristic period than to the later scholasticism. There is the purely scholastic element in Anselm. 'His theologising is often only a "ratione solvere quæstiones", a "satisfacere objectionibus".'[9] But all the same in him the speculative element is dominant. 'His thought included the whole, in a freer and more attractive manner than the systematic work of the formalistically developed later scholasticism. His "libri duo", "Cur Deus Homo", are a brilliant attempt to gather together all the dogmas of the Church in a single central thought; his interlocutor Boso admits in conclusion: "per unius quæstionis, quam proposuimus, solutionem, quidquid in novo verterique testamento continetur, probatum intelligo".'[1]

The thoroughgoing application of the dialectic[2] method to all theological questions begins with Abelard's 'Sic et Non':[3] its success was assured by Peter Lombard's 'Book of Sentences',[4] which became the basis of all later mediaeval theology.

Between Abelard and Lombard, however, Hugo of St Victor (d. A.D. 1141) had endeavoured to find a principle which should gather into one the whole content of Scripture.

'The subject-matter of the entire Scripture is the double work involved in the restoration of man . . . first the work of creation, and second the work of restoration.'[5]

In the theology of the early Franciscan school the same speculative endeavour to reduce the whole of theology to a single principle is apparent. According to Alexander of Hales (d. A.D. 1245) its subject is the doctrine of the *veritas increata*, along with its necessary presuppositions and conclusions.[6]

Thomas Aquinas (d. A.D. 1274) also endeavours to find a conception which shall include the whole of theology. 'Sacred theology does not treat of God and the creatures alike, but of God principally and of the creatures so far as they are referred to God, as to their beginning or their end. In this way the unity of the science is preserved.'[7]

---

[9] *Ibid.* p. 506.   [1] Loc. cit. Cf. Anselm, 'Cur Deus Homo', II, 23.
[2] 'Dialectic' in the Platonic sense of the search for truth on the basis of a recognition of the oppositions of opinion.   [3] Abelard, d. A.D. 1142.
[4] Peter Lombard, d. A.D. 1160.   [5] 'De Sacram.', Prol., cap. II.
[6] 'Summa', Nuremberg, 1482, III, qu. 79, m. 6.   [7] *Ibid.* I, qu. 1, art. 3, ad. 1.

From Alexander onwards, however, the dialectic method introduced by Abelard reigns in the detailed working out of these speculative conceptions. In the great systems of Alexander and Thomas the dialectic element predominates over the speculative as much as the speculative over the dialectic in Anselm. In the critical system of Duns Scotus (d. A.D. 1308) the dialectic element gains still more ground; till finally in the theology of the Nominalists, Occam (d. A.D. 1340), and Biel (d. A.D. 1495), the hope is abandoned of finding any speculative principle in which to gather up the whole of theology, and it takes its place merely as an 'aggregative science', whose task is no more than to arrange in some sort of order the different points of Divine revelation.[8]

It is to be observed, however, that throughout the whole of the scholastic period we meet with a complete confidence in logic and a surprising dexterity in its use. The first form of ancient culture assimilated by the scholastic theologians was the translation by Boethius of Porphyry's introduction to the logical writings of Aristotle. The knowledge of these writings themselves soon followed. The complete Aristotle, however, was unknown in the West till the thirteenth century, when the work of uniting Aristotelianism with the traditional dogma began in the 'Summæ' and the 'Commentaries on the Sentences' of the great schoolmen, Alexander, Bonaventura (d. A.D. 1274), Albert (d. A.D. 1280), and Thomas. It is to be observed, however, that throughout the whole of scholasticism certain material [9] principles accepted as rational were drawn from the Neoplatonic principles embedded in the theology of Augustine. Moreover, in the doctrine with which we are especially concerned the ideas of satisfaction and merit, which we have found in the praxis of the Church, are also taken as rational notions. Thus while logical method reigns supreme throughout the Middle Ages, the material principles accepted as rational come from very various sources.

As regards the nature in detail of the authority on which the mediaeval theology is based, it consists of Holy Scripture, the Creeds, and the Fathers.

The Creeds established as a doctrinal standard in the Middle

---

[8] Cf. Werner, 'Die Scholastik des späteren Mittelalters', vol. ii, pp. 43ff. (Occam) ; vol. iv, pp. 262ff. (Biel).   [9] 'Material' in opposition to formal or logical.

Ages (from the Carolingian period onwards) were three in number. The first was the 'Apostles' ' Creed, the later Gallican form of the earlier Roman Creed, dating from about A.D. 500. The Second was the Nicæno-Constantinopolitanum, with the *filioque* addition (A.D. 589). The third was the 'Athanasian' Creed, which originated in Gaul in the sixth century.[1] The three Creeds are formally recognised as doctrinal standards by Alexander of Hales.[2]

'There are three Creeds, the first the Apostles', the second that of the Fathers, which is sung in the Mass, the third that of Athanasius, which is sung at Prime.'

We have already spoken of the Apostles' Creed in its primitive or Roman form; the only noteworthy changes in the Gallican form are that the clause 'who was born of Holy Ghost and of Mary the Virgin' becomes 'who was conceived of the Holy Ghost, born of the Virgin Mary', and that there is added the clause 'He descended into hell'. The significance of the Nicæno-Constantinopolitanum as a standard of doctrine has also been already estimated. It is now to be added that the Athanasian Creed, as regards its section on the Incarnation, substantially embodies the doctrine of Chalcedon, so that nothing further need here be said of it.

As regards the Fathers, the chief authority is that of Augustine, though many others not only Latin but—in the later scholastics—Greek also, have their place. Anselm at the beginning of the scholastic theology especially relies on the authority of Augustine;[3] and to the end of the Middle Ages Augustine still maintains the same supremacy.

As to the relation between the different authorities of the Scriptures, the Creeds, and the Fathers, there can be no doubt that in general throughout the Middle Ages the fundamental authority was that of Holy Scripture. The Creeds were regarded as summarising Scripture, the Fathers as explaining and unfolding it.

As early as Abelard there appears a sharp distinction

---

[1] See Loofs, D.G., pp. 87, n. 5, 368, 458.
[2] 'Summa', Nuremberg, 1482, pars iii, qu. 82, memb. 5, introd.
[3] 'Monol.', Praef. ; 'Epist.' 68 (Ad Lanfrancum).

between the authority of Scripture and the authority of the Fathers.

'Distinct from the books of later writers is the excellency of the canonic authority of the Old and New Testament. If anything there appears absurd, we may not say the author of the book did not hold the truth, but either the codex is faulty or the interpreter has erred, or thou dost not understand. But in the works of later writers, which are contained in innumerable books, if by chance any things are thought to deviate from the truth because they are not understood as they were meant, yet the reader or hearer has free right of judgment to approve what has pleased or disapprove what has offended him.'[4]

Hugo of St Victor in his 'De Sacramentis' views without question the subject-matter of theology simply as the 'materia divinarum Scripturarum' (Prol.). So also for Alexander of Hales[5] and Bonaventura[6] the matter of theology is the content of Holy Scripture.

Aquinas once more like Abelard distinguishes sharply between the authority of Scripture and that of the Fathers.

'Sacred doctrine uses authorities drawn from Holy Scripture as its natural basis, whence to argue with absolute cogency. The authority of other doctors of the Church, however, it uses as a natural basis for argument, but only an argument with probability.'[7]

Duns Scotus again teaches that 'Holy Scripture sufficiently contains the doctrine necessary for the pilgrim[8]'.[9] He gives eight rational proofs of the authority of Scripture, viz. from prophecy, the harmony of Scripture, the sanctity of the writers, the carefulness of the canonisers, the rationality of the contents, the irrationality of heresies, the stability of the Church, the glory of miracles.

Finally, the Nominalist Occam taught:

'A Christian is not compelled as a necessity of salvation to believe either as a duty or in practice what is neither contained

---

'Sic et Non', Prol.
[6] 'Comm. in Sent.', I, Prol., qu. 2.
[8] *Viator*, one on the way to eternal bliss, in opposition to *comprehensor*, one who has attained it.

[5] 'Summa', I, qu. 1.
[7] 'Summa', I, qu. 1, art. 8, ad. 2.
[9] 'Comm. Oxon. in Sent.', Prol., qu. 2.

in the Bible nor can be inferred as a necessary and clear consequence from the mere content of the Bible.'[1]

An interesting point in connexion with the authority of Scripture is that, whereas towards the beginning of the Middle Ages the system of allegorical exegesis was regarded as an important part of the machinery of the theologian,[2] in the later scholasticism there is a tendency for the allegorical exegesis to disappear behind the literal.

'From it alone can argument be drawn, not from those senses which are according to allegory.'[3] See further on this point Kropatschek, op. cit. pp. 448ff.

So much then as to the authority of Scripture and its relation to that of the Fathers. As to the scholastic view of the relation of the Creeds to the Scriptures, typical is what Aquinas says of the relation to them of the Apostles' Creed, which remained the Creed *par excellence*.

'In Holy Scripture the truth of the faith is contained diffusedly and in various forms, and in some of these obscurely. To draw out the truth of the faith from Holy Scripture therefore long study and exercise are required, to which not all those who need to know the truth of the faith can attain; for many of them, being occupied with other things, have no leisure for study. It is therefore necessary that out of the statements of Holy Scripture something clear should be succinctly gathered for proposal to all to believe. This then is no addition to Holy Scripture, but is rather taken from Holy Scripture.'[4]

As regards the relation of the two other Creeds to the Apostles' Creed we may quote Bonaventura:

'In the Apostles' Creed all those things which it is opportune to believe are sufficiently contained, as far as concerns the main points of belief. . . . The two other symbols, i.e. the Athanasian and that of the Nicene Council have been added for the fuller explanation of the faith, and the confutation of heresy.'[5]

The above statements may be regarded as expressing the

---

[1] Quoted by Kropatschek, 'Das Schriftprinzip der lutherischen Kirche', 1904, p. 440, n. 5.

[2] Hugo of St. Victor, 'De Sacram.', Prol., cap. IV; Alexander of Hales, 'Summa' I, qu. 1, m. 4, art. 4 ; Bonaventura, 'Breviloquium', Proem.

[3] Thomas Aquinas, 'Summa', I, qu. 1, art. 10, ad. 1.

[4] 'Summa', II, 2, qu. 1, art. 9, ad. 1.   [5] 'Comm. in Sent.', III, dist. 25, qu. 1.

general view of the Middle Ages on this subject, when it had become conscious and reflective.

We find, however, in the later scholasticism a tendency to lay stress on the authority of the creeds even independently of that of Scripture.

'For instance, Duns Scotus, who has emphasised the sufficiency of Biblical authority, points at the same time to the symbols of the Ancient Church, which gather up the quintessence of the Scripture for the age following, and also to the compilation of the Canon by the Church, without which no New Testament would be possible. With this then is made lastingly easy the transition to the formula, the Church stands above the Scripture; for there was a Christian Church before there was a Scripture, and in that the Church created the Canon, it thereby "approved and authorised" these books, which it received.' [6]

Along the same lines are the following passages from Biel, the Nominalist:

'A truth is to be called Catholic, either because it is revealed of God, or contained in the Divine Scripture, or because it is received by the Church, or because it is approved by the supreme pontiff, or because it follows from one of the above-mentioned by necessary consequence.' [7]

'Many truths which are not found in the canonical Scriptures, and cannot be deduced by necessary consequence from these only, are Catholic.' [8]

---

[6] Kropatschek, op. cit. p. 442, n. 1.   Reference is made to 'Comm. in Sent.', III, dist. 23, qu. 1, 4 ; 1 dist. 4, qu. 1, 8.   [7] 'Collectorium', III, dist. 25, art. 3, dub. 3.
[8] *Ibid.* IV, dist. 13, qu. 2, art. 1, not. 2.

CHAPTER 2

THE BEGINNINGS OF THE MEDIAEVAL
THEOLOGY

ANSELM

WE begin our account of the scholastic doctrine of the work of Christ with Anselm's 'Cur Deus Homo', which is in many ways determinative of the whole scholastic procedure in this domain, and is moreover epoch-making in the whole history of our doctrine, in that it for the first time in a thoroughgoing and consistent way applies to the elucidation of the subject the conceptions of satisfaction and merit.

From Anselm (d. A.D. 1109), following Augustine, comes the formulation of the fundamental principle of the scholastic method: 'Neque enim quæro intelligere ut credam, sed credo ut intelligam.' [1]

In accordance with this principle is the problem of the 'Cur Deus Homo' stated. It is not indeed rational to establish faith in the Incarnation, but yet to give a rational solution of the question:

' By what reason or necessity God was made man, and by His death, as we believe and confess, restored life to the world' (I, 1).

Anselm begins by rejecting as unsatisfactory various great theories of antiquity.

(1) The recapitulatory theory of Irenæus, in the form in which it has come down to him through Augustine.

(2) The theory of redemption from the devil.

(3) The theory according to which the purpose of the death of Christ was to show how much God loved us.

Incidentally it may be noted that Anselm has very ingeniously cast the 'Cur Deus Homo' into the form of a dialogue, in which he leaves to his interlocutor Boso the task of criticising the above

[1] Prosl., cap. I.   Cf. *supra*, p. 88.

126

traditional theories. As, however, he does not meet Boso's criticisms, they are implicitly admitted to be just.

The first ancient theory to be criticised is thus stated. 'It was fitting that just as through the disobedience of a man death had entered into the human race, so also through the obedience of a man life should be restored; and just as sin, which was the cause of our condemnation, had its origin from a woman, so the author of our righteousness and salvation should be born of a woman; and just as the devil, who had, thanks to his persuasion, conquered man by the taste of a tree, should likewise through the passion on a tree, which he inflicted, be conquered by man' (I, 3).

Anselm adds that there are many other similar reasons of great beauty showing the fitness of the Incarnation. Boso, however, objects that such thoughts, unless some more solid basis of reason can be shown, are like pictures painted on air (I, 4).

Anselm therefore inquires if it be not a sufficiently solid reason for the Incarnation that the human race would have perished, and God's purpose for it been foiled, unless it had been redeemed by the Creator Himself. Boso, however, objects first of all that this deliverance would more reasonably have been made by some other than God, say an angel or a man. God could have made a man without sin, not taken from Adam's sinful race, just as He made Adam at the first, and he might have delivered men. Anselm, however, objects that in such a case man would have become the slave of the angel or man who redeemed him, and so would have failed to be restored to his pristine dignity (I, 5). This leads Boso, however, to find a fresh difficulty. Why is man's deliverance called redemption? The traditional view, of course, was that it was because man was a captive of the devil.

But with regard to this doctrine, Boso urges that as the devil is under the power of God, he can acquire no rights against God by tempting man, his fellow-slave. The bond spoken of in Col.2:14 is not to be interpreted (as it is by Ambrose and Augustine) of an obligation to the devil established by the sin of Adam, but is rather a figure for the Divine sentence which shuts up man to punishment (I, 7).

Finally, as regards the theory that Christ died to show how

much God loved us, what necessity was there for Him to choose this way of showing His love, if it was not the only way of human salvation?

'Your assertion that God has shown in that way how much He loved you, is maintained by no reason, if it is not shown that God could by no means otherwise have saved man. For if He could not have done it otherwise, then perchance it would be necessary that He should show His love in this way; but now, seeing that He can otherwise save man, what reason is there why, to show His love, He should do and endure those things that you allege? Nay, does He not show the good angels how much He loves them, though for them He does not endure such things?' (I, 6).

There must then be some absolute necessity for the salvation of man through Christ's Incarnation and Death. It is not enough to refer merely to the will of God, which must of course be reasonable: the question is whether the Incarnation is reasonable, otherwise it is hard to believe that God willed it (I, 8). And there are so many difficulties in the way. Certainly the difficulty, that the impassible God should have suffered, is none at all; for He suffered according to the passible human nature. But was it right for God to give the innocent to die? Anselm replies that Christ died voluntarily. We must distinguish between what Christ did under obedience to God, and what He bore, not under obedience, but because He maintained obedience. The first was that He immutably kept truth and righteousness in life and speech: this, however, brought on Him Jewish persecution, in enduring which He died. As innocent, however, He deserved not to die, but perceiving that His death was the necessary way of human salvation, He willed to die (I, 9). This, however, brings us back to the point already reached: was it necessary for Christ to die, if men were to be saved?

Anselm demands that there be an absolute necessity for Christ's Incarnation and Death in order to human salvation, thus setting himself in opposition to the authority of Augustine at this point. Nowhere is his theory more revolutionary. Boso represents the traditional view, and again and again presses Anselm by bringing it forward.

Anselm finds the required necessity by means of the consideration that, upon the supposition that man is made for eternal beatitude, he cannot attain to it except by the remission of sins (I, 10).

What, however, is involved in this?

Sin is nothing else than to fail to give to God what is due to Him (*debitum*). This due is the obedience of the will, which constitutes at once man's righteousness and the honour which he owes to God.

'He who does not return to God this honour due to Him, takes away from God what is His own and dishonours God; and this is to sin' (I, 11).

But further, he who has sinned must make satisfaction for sin.

'As long as he does not make good what he has stolen,[2] he remains at fault (*in culpa*): nor is it enough simply to restore what was taken away, but he must for the insult inflicted restore more than he took away. For just as he who injures the health of another, does not do enough, if he restores his health, unless he also makes some recompense for the inflicted injury of pain; so he who violates the honour of anyone does not do enough if he restore the honour, unless, in correspondence with the harm done in dishonouring him, he makes some amends acceptable to him whom he has dishonoured. This also must be noted, that when anyone pays back what he has unjustly taken away, he must give what could not be demanded of him, if he had not stolen another's property. So also every one who sins must pay back the honour which he has stolen from God; and this is the satisfaction which every sinner must make to God' (I, 11).

But cannot God forgive sin without the payment of the honour taken from Him? No, for this would be to admit something out of order (*inordinatum*) in His kingdom. Justice demands that sin should be punished. To the objection that this seems to limit God's omnipotence, Anselm replies that unless God is just, He is not God (I, 12).

The only exception to the rule that sin must be punished is where the sinner voluntarily makes satisfaction for his sin.

---

[2] Quamdiu non solvit quod rapuit—cf. Ps. 69:4, and Augustine's use of the verse n 'De Trin.' XIII, 14, 18 (*supra*, p. 98).

'It is necessary therefore, either that the honour taken away should be repaid, or that punishment should follow' (I, 13).

Either of these courses reclaims for God the honour which He has lost. Man pays back what he has stolen either willingly or unwillingly, and so God has His due (I. 14). There is either 'spontanea satisfactio vel a non satisfaciente pœnæ exactio . . . necesse est, ut omne peccatum satisfactio aut pœna sequatur' (I, 15).

Here Anselm digresses in order to show that sufficient men must be saved in order to fill up the places, in the heavenly city of God, of the angels who fell.[3] From this point of view again Anselm enforces the necessity of satisfaction. How, apart from its being made, can man be fit for the society of the good angels?

Now, however, comes a new principle. Satisfaction must be made according to the measure of the sin: anything else would be out of order. What then can we offer?

'Repentance (pœnitentiam),' replies Boso, 'a contrite and humbled heart, fastings, bodily toils of many kinds, mercy in giving and forgiving, and obedience. Do I not honour God, when for fear and love of Him, in contrition of heart I reject temporal joy, in fastings and toils I trample underfoot the pleasures and ease of this life, when I lavish what is mine in giving and forgiving, and subject myself to Him in obedience?' (I, 20)

Boso obviously has in mind the pœnitentia recognised in the discipline of the Church. Anselm, however, replies, in opposition to the doctrine of Hermas, Tertullian, and others, concerning supererogatory works, that all this is owed to God already apart from the satisfaction of sin (I, 20).

Besides, suppose that all this were not owed, it is not enough. 'Nondum considerasti, quanti ponderis sit peccatum', says Anselm. He measures the weight of sin indirectly. Sin being committed against God is of infinite gravity—for what consideration ought I to bestow even a glance contrary to His will? Clearly then satisfaction according to the measure of sin is impossible to man (I, 21).

Anselm goes on to make a bridge between his new doctrine and the old doctrine that man must conquer the devil. By yielding

[3]Cf. Augustine, 'Ench.' 29 (supra, p. 92).

to the devil man has dishonoured God: he must restore this honour by conquering the devil.

'The victory ought to be such, that, just as while strong and potentially immortal he easily consented to the devil, so as to sin, for which he justly incurred the penalty of mortality, so also, weak and mortal as he has made himself, he should conquer the devil by the difficulty of death, so as in no manner to sin, which he cannot do, as long as, owing to the wound of the first sin, he is conceived and born in sin' (I, 22).

There is then a double reason why man cannot make satisfaction for sin, (1) because as finite he cannot in any case perform the infinite satisfaction required, (2) because he is impotent through sin. This impotence, however, is no excuse, since he has only brought it upon himself. It seems then that there is no way for man to attain to blessedness unless that way be Christ (I, 24, 25).

Christ, however, is that way. God, having created man for perfection, must complete His work. He is not indeed under physical, but is, however, under moral compulsion to do this (II, 4, 5.)

How then can the necessary satisfaction be made, if not by the sinner himself? It must be made by One, who is both man, that He may make satisfaction for man, and God, that His act may have an infinite worth. The answer to the problem is in the God-man of the Creeds, who is perfect God and perfect man, of Adam's race, but as virgin-born, free from sin, and one Person in two natures (II, 6–9).[4]

As a sinless man, though He owes to God the obedience of His life, the God-man is under no obligation to die. If He dies, therefore, it is of His own free will (II, 10 ,11). Here then is the possibility of satisfaction.

'If man sinned through sweetness, is it not fit that he should make satisfaction through bitterness? And if he was with the extremest possible ease conquered by the devil, so that he dishonoured God by sinning; is it not right that man, making satisfaction for sin, should conquer the devil to the honour of God with the extremest possible difficulty? Is it not meet that

Cf. Augustine, 'Ench.' 37–41 ; 'De Trinitate', XIII, 18–23.

he who by sinning so robbed God of himself, that the robbery could not be exceeded, should so give himself to God in satisfaction, that the gift could not be exceeded?

'Man, however, can suffer to God's honour, of his own accord and not by way of debt, nothing more bitter or more difficult than death; and in no way can man give himself to God more entirely than when he gives himself up to death for His honour' (II, 11).

Christ then is in a position to do all this. Anselm adds that there are also many other reasons, why it is befitting that Christ should be found in the fashion of a man and live a human life without sin, which may more easily be understood from His life and works than demonstrated *a priori* by reason. How wisely was it done, that He who was to lead us back to eternal life, should not only teach us, but also offer Himself as an example of patient endurance! (*ibid.*).

But, to return to the subject of Christ's satisfaction, we have seen that His voluntary death is a gift of the necessary painful character. The question is now as to its measure. Is it sufficient to satisfy for all sins, when the least sin is infinite? Anselm measures the value of Christ's death in the same indirect way as he measured the weight of sin. Anselm: 'If that Man were before you, and you knew who He was and it were said to you, unless you kill that Man, your whole world and whatever is not God shall perish; would you do this to save every other creature?' Boso: 'I would not do it, even if an infinite number of worlds were set before me' (II, 14).

In fact, not only the killing, but the least injury of the God-man were the greatest possible sin. The reason is, that whatever happens to His person incomparably outweighs whatever is done apart from it. This then shows the supreme value of the life of the God-man.

'If therefore to give one's life is to accept death, then just as the gift of this life outweighs all human sins, so also the acceptance of this death' (II, 14).

But how can the gift of Christ's life avail for the sin of those who slew Him? They at least according to the previous argument seem to have committed the unpardonable sin. The answer is in 1 C. 2:8: they did it in ignorance (II, 15).

Moreover, the redemption wrought by Christ availed not for His own age only, but for all ages. To show this Anselm uses an important parable. 'For suppose there to be a certain king, against whom the whole people of a certain city of his has sinned, except one alone, who, however, is of their race; so that none of them can do anything to escape the punishment of death; but he, however, who alone is innocent, has such favour with the king that he can, and such love to the guilty that he will, reconcile all who believe in his plan by a certain service, which will greatly please the king, and which he is to perform on a day fixed according to the will of the king. And since not all those who are to be reconciled can assemble on that day: the king grants on account of the greatness of that service, that any who, whether before or after that day shall have confessed that they wish to seek pardon through the work done on that day, and to subscribe to the agreement there established, shall be freed from all past guilt; and if it happens that after this pardon they sin again, then if they wish duly to make satisfaction and suffer correction, they may again receive pardon through the efficacy of that agreement; yet so that no one is to enter the king's palace till that be done, by which his sins are to be forgiven' (II, 16).

This parable is peculiarly valuable as showing the practical application of Anselm's doctrine of the work of Christ. It forms a basis for the first forgiveness, and then again, on the supposition of due satisfaction, for further forgiveness in penance. Moreover, Anselm deduces from his parable the conclusion 'that no soul could enter the celestial paradise before the death of Christ' (ibid.).

In II, 17, 18 Anselm stops in his argument to point out that the Divine predestination of Christ's death does not imply that He died compulsorily, but rather that His will to die was immutable.

Then Boso raises another difficulty. Ought not Christ to die, since He gave an example of patience by dying, and this was well-pleasing to God? Surely He must do what was well-pleasing to God.

Anselm distinguishes, as Tertullian had done long ago, between works demanded and works of supererogation, such

133

as virginity where marriage is lawful. The latter merit a special reward. Christ then performed a work of this kind. He only needed to die because He willed it: He could have done otherwise (II, 18 *b*).

From this point of view, however, it is easy to see how human salvation follows from Christ's death. Christ's voluntary gift of Himself was meritorious: for so great a gift God must make Him a fitting recompense. As the Son of God, however, He Himself wants nothing.

'To whom then could God more fitly grant the fruit and reward of His death, than to those to save whom . . . He became man, and to whom . . . in dying He gave Himself as an example of dying on behalf of righteousness? In vain will they be imitators of Him, if they are not participators of His merit. Or whom will He more rightly make the heirs of His due which He does not need . . . than His kinsmen and brethren, whom He sees, bound by so many and such great debts, wasting away in the depth of their distress; so that there may be remitted to them what they owe for their sins, and granted them what they lack on account of their sins?' (II, 19).

To sum up: in the Divine method of salvation there is a perfect concord of mercy and justice.

'What indeed can be thought of as more merciful than when God the Father says to the sinner condemned to eternal torment, and who has no means of redeeming himself: "receive my Only Begotten Son, and give Him for thyself", while the Son Himself says: "take me, and redeem thyself"? . . . What again is juster, than that He, to whom a price is given greater than every debt, if it is given with right motive, should forgive every debt?' (II, 20).

Such is in outline Anselm's famous theory of the work of Christ. He sets aside altogether the doctrine of redemption from the devil, though he retains in a subordinate place that of Christ's victory over him. The recapitulatory and moral theories he regards as void, unless some more solid theory can serve as a basis for them. This solid basis Anselm finds in the doctrine that Christ made satisfaction for sin and merited salvation. This is the essence of His work, the necessity of which may be seen *a priori*. It is not unimportant, however, that Christ gave us an example: by following this we are qualified to share in His merit.

All histories of doctrine recognise the epoch-making character of Anselm's theory of satisfaction and merit. From this time forward the ideas of satisfaction and merit occupy a central place in the mediaeval doctrine: they were passed on moreover though with notable modifications to Protestantism, where they fill an equally important sphere. It is therefore necessary now to discuss Anselm's theory at some length. We must in the first place clearly distinguish his idea of satisfaction from that of Hilary and Ambrose. These Fathers endeavour to clarify the Pauline doctrine of Christ's redeeming us from the curse of the law, by interpreting it through the *satisfactio* of the Roman public law, which means the endurance of the law's sentence. Anselm, however, is quite without any direct purpose of interpreting Paul, and has before him in the fundamental passage (i, 11), where he explains the notion of satisfaction, the analogy not of public but of private law. He regards satisfaction not as the endurance of punishment, but as a positive gift to God or a performance done to God's honour; though at the same time he admits that it is fit that it should be something hard and difficult in opposition to the pleasure of sin. The main idea, however, is that Christ's work is a positive gift or performance, and hence he can call it not merely satisfaction but merit.

It is generally admitted at the present time that the Anselmic conception of satisfaction is derived not from Scripture but from the ecclesiastical penance. The history of penance, previously given, shows that all the characters of the Anselmic satisfaction above described can be found in the penitential satisfaction. Nor are we left merely to inference in the matter. That Anselm interprets Christ's work in terms of penance is clear for the following reasons:

(1) When Boso proposes in answer to Anselm's question, how man may make satisfaction for sin, the very terms of the ecclesiastical penance (i, 20), Anselm in no way objects to his conception of the nature of satisfaction, but only seeks to show the inadequacy of the ecclesiastical satisfaction in the case in view.

(2) Anselm himself assimilates the satisfaction of Christ to

the penitential satisfaction, in that the satisfaction of Christ brings about the first forgiveness of sins, and any further forgiveness after a lapse must be won by penitential satisfaction (II, 16).

(3) In explaining the meritorious character of Christ's work, he assimilates it to the merit of supererogatory works, such as virginity (II, 18 *b*).

There is no doubt then that the great epoch-making step marked by Anselm in the history of theology consists in the fact, that he first applied to the work of Christ the legal conceptions proper to the ecclesiastical penance. 'Anselm's theory is an evaluation of the work of Christ by means of the conceptual material of the doctrine of penance.'[5] Things had indeed for a long while been tending in this direction; but not till Anselm did the crystallisation of the idea take place.

The above statement would have to be considerably modified if the theory were correct, which has recently been propounded by Gottschick, that in essence the Anselmic theory stands already complete in Augustine, all that is wanting being the express terms satisfaction and merit, and the doctrine of the necessity of satisfaction. Gottschick's theory is contained in his article 'Augustins Anschauung von den Erlöserwirkungen Christi',[6] and summarised in the first of his 'Studien zur Versöhnungslehre des Mittelalters'.[7] According to him, Augustine has already reduced the doctrine of redemption from the devil to a mere doublet of that of Christ's sacrifice, by the thought that that from which Christ redeems us by His death is the Divine punishment, of which the devil is merely the exactor: he has further, in distinction from Hilary and Ambrose with their ideas of Christ's death as the endurance of the sentence of the law, interpreted Christ's sufferings after the analogy of the penitential satisfaction as a self-inflicted punishment, this being the conception of the penitential satisfaction dominant in Augustine's theology. Gottschick refers to Augustine's use of the text so fundamental for Anselm, 'quæ non rapui, tunc exsolvebam',[8] and also to Augustine's sentence, 'suscipiendo pœnam et non

Loofs, D.G., 4th ed., p. 511.
'Zeitschrift für Theologie und Kirche', 1901, pp. 97–213.
[7] 'Zeitschrift für Kirchengeschichte', 1901, pp. 378–84.
[8] Ps. 69:4 ; Augustine, 'De Trinitate', XIII, 14, 18 ; Anselm, 'Cur Deus Homo', I, 11.

suscipiendo culpam, et culpam delevit et pœnam'.[9] It is not clear however (a) that Augustine has reduced the doctrine of redemption from the devil to a mere doublet of the idea of sacrifice; or (b) that the Augustinian doctrine, that Christ has reconciled us to God by His sacrifice, has repaid the debt He did not owe, and borne our punishment without our guilt, in order to remove both punishment and guilt, amounts to so coherent and single a view as Gottschick represents. Moreover, while the suggestion of the text 'quæ non rapui, tunc exsolvebam' has undoubtedly been followed by Anselm, it is begging the question to say that he has been governed by the sentence 'suscipiendo pœnam et non suscipiendo culpam, et culpam delevit et pœnam'. For the remarkable thing about Anselm's theory is his distinction of satisfaction from punishment, and his avoidance of the idea that Christ's satisfaction is the vicarious endurance of our punishment, whether as self-inflicted or inflicted by God. Anselm does certainly approximate to the penal view of satisfaction, when he emphasises that it must be bitter and difficult (II, 11): nevertheless he does not reach it. In fact, in drawing upon the conceptual material of penance, he has not drawn upon the whole of it, but in agreement with the current of thought which we have studied in the Early Middle Ages, dwells upon the view of satisfaction as a positive performance or gift, to the exclusion of the conception of it as the self-inflicted endurance of punishment, which is so fundamental to Tertullian and Augustine. In spite of Gottschick then, the conclusion stands good, that Anselm's originality consists in his application of the conceptual material of penance to the work of Christ: it is going much beyond the evidence to say that Augustine had virtually applied it before him. On the other hand we have to observe that Anselm did not apply the whole conceptual material of penance to the subject; what he omitted was precisely that element in penance which has most affinity with the doctrine of Augustine on the work of Christ.

A further question, however, as to the working out of Anselm's theory: it has been asserted that Anselm is here influenced by the ideas of German law. This view is especially

'Serm.' 171, 3, 3 (*supra*, p. 96).

developed by Cremer in his two essays, 'Die Wurzeln des Ansel-
mischen Satisfaktionsbekriffs',[1] 'Der germanische Satisfaktionsbegriff in der Versöhnungslehre'.[2] We have already seen that
the mediaeval modification of the idea of penance, which
Anselm shares, viz. the increased stress on its positive or
meritorious to the neglect of its penal aspect, has been put down,
though without sufficient reason, to German influence; but other
important elements in the Anselmic doctrine have also been
assigned to the same source.

One point in which German influence is thus held to be
apparent is the substitution of the honour of God for His
righteousness as the Divine attribute demanding satisfaction.
Refusal to tolerate an injury to personal honour was deeply
rooted in the German spirit. As the great pioneer of the study
of German institutions pointed out: 'Hohn und Schmach
duldete kein Freier auf sich.'[3] Yet Tertullian speaks of penance
as honouring God from fear of danger;[4] just as Boso asks:
'Do I not honour God, when because of His fear and love I
reject temporal joy in contrition of heart, trample underfoot in
fastings and toils the pleasures and quiet of this life, lavish what
is mine in giving and forgiving, and subject myself to Him in
obedience?'[5] As Harnack says: 'One must look very closely to
discover in this passage a distinction of shade between Anselm's
God and the injured and angry God of Tertullian'.[6]

Again, there are certainly some striking resemblances between
Anselm's doctrine of satisfaction and the German law of wergild,
especially in the calculation of the amount of the compensation
for injury according to the position of the injured person, and in
the idea of the solidarity of the kin in the matter both of payment and of the receipt of payment. Compare the description
of the German wergild, already given (p. 116). Nevertheless the
idea of the solidarity of the race is also a fundamental principle
in the theology of Augustine, and in particular of his doctrine
of the work of Christ;[7] while we find also in Augustine a

[1] 'Studien und Kritiken', 1880, pp. 7–21.
[2] 'Studien und Kritiken', 1893, pp. 316–45.
[3] Grimm, 'Deutsche Rechtsalterthümer', p. 622.   [4] 'De pœn.' 9 (supra, p. 80).
[5] 'Cur Deus Homo', i, 20.   [6] D.G., 4th ed., vol. iii, p. 392, n.
[7] 'De Trin.' xiii, 18, 23 (supra, p. 99).

remarkable parallel to the Anselmic doctrine that Christ's spiritual kin are the natural heirs of the debt God owes Him. Compare 'Tr. in Ev. Joh.' 2, 13 : 'Whom He wished to make His brothers, them He freed, and made His fellow heirs', together with 'In Ps.' CXXVII, 13 : 'The Church is His brothers and sisters and mother'.

As regards the principle that satisfaction must be according to the position of the injured person, this again is no peculiarity of German law, but belongs just as much to Roman law.[8] In fact it may be regarded as belonging to the *consensus gentium.* In the Code of Hammurabi, for example, offences were graded according to the rank of the injured person relatively to the offender.[9] There is, however, finally, another point where it has recently been contended,[1] that Anselm has been influenced by German law, viz. in his idea of God as the Moral Ruler of the universe. Anselm, though his general idea of satisfaction, in agreement with that of the ecclesiastical doctrine of penance, belongs to the sphere of private law,[2] yet in his anxiety to prove the necessity of satisfaction passes over to the analogy of public law in the thought that God cannot admit anything out of order in His domain (I, 12). Now it is a fact that, while the Roman idea of sovereignty is expressed in the principles of Justinian's Digest, 'Princeps legibus solutus est' (1, 3, 31), 'Quod principi placuit, legis habet vigorem' (1, 4, 1), on the other hand the original Teutonic idea seems to have been that the king was not the fountain of justice, but the guardian of the public peace.[3]

At the same time even here it is not necessary to look for Anselm's idea very far outside of Augustine. God, according to Augustine, is the *ordinator peccatorum,* 'so that those things which would not be sins, except they were against nature, are so judged and ordered, that they are not permitted to disturb or debase the order of nature'.[4]

Gaius, 'Inst. III, 225 ; Justinian, 'Inst.' IV, 4, 9.

Hastings, 'Dictionary of the Bible', extra vol., p. 597.

Seeberg, D.G., 1st ed., vol. ii, p. 53, n. 2 ; D.G., 2nd ed., vol. iii, p. 222 ; 'Die Theologie des Johannes Duns Scotus', 1900, p. 10, n. 1.

[2] 'Cur Deus Homo', I, 11 (*supra*, p. 129).

[3] Stubbs, 'Constitutional History of England', vol. i, p. 199 ; F. de Schulte, 'Histoire du droit et des Institutions de l'Allemagne', French translation from the German, 5th ed. 1882, pp. 39, 95.   [4] 'Contra Faustum' XXII, 78.

To sum up then, the case for a distinct German influence upon Anselm's theory must be dismissed with the verdict 'not proven'.

In conclusion, I may touch on some criticisms of Anselm's theory, and also make some general remarks on the importance of the theological innovation implied by it.

(1) One criticism to which Anselm's theory lies open is that his idea of the absolute necessity of satisfaction conflicts with the principle of private law which he has incorporated, viz. that satisfaction requires the gift to the injured party of 'somewhat, according to his pleasure' (I, 11). In private law, in fact, the measure of the necessity of satisfaction is simply the good pleasure of the offended person, and the necessity, therefore, is not absolute. Anselm, as we have seen, in his endeavour to show the absolute necessity of satisfaction passes over to the standpoint of public law (I, 12). There is, therefore, a fundamental antinomy in Anselm's theory, which the scholastic theology after him largely devotes itself to bringing out.

(2) A second criticism touches Anselm's alternate use of the standpoints of satisfaction and merit. It is true that it can no longer be said with Ritschl, that in passing from the idea of satisfaction to that of merit, Anselm passes from a legal to an ethical point of view, the one being altogether disparate from the other.[5] The researches of Schultz have shown the true and natural relation between satisfaction and merit. Merit is the genus; satisfaction the species, or the form taken by merit where debt exists. Moreover, neither idea in its theological use is strictly legal or strictly ethical. 'The conception of *satisfactio* is no legal idea in the proper sense, and the idea of *meritum* has just as much a legal appearance as that of *satisfactio*.'[6] Nevertheless there is an inconsistency in Anselm's use of the terms satisfaction and merit, which depends on his definition of Christ's satisfaction as corresponding to the exact measure of sin, and upon the view inherited by him from the Ancient Church that the forgiveness of sins and eternal life are two different things.

If Christ's satisfaction only exactly purchases the remission

[5] Cf. Ritschl, 'Rechtfertigung und Versöhnung', 2nd ed., vol. i, pp. 45, 46.
[6] Loofs, D.G., 4th ed., p. 510.

of sins, it is clear that there can be no superfluous merit to win eternal life. The only ways out of the difficulty would be, either with various schoolmen after Anselm to abandon the view that satisfaction is according to the exact measure of sin, or else to equate forgiveness of sins and eternal life, in strict adherence to the maxim of Luther, 'Wo Vergebung der Sünden ist, da ist Leben und Seligkeit.'[7] This last possibility, however, would carry us clean out of the sphere of Anselm's ideas altogether. As it is, it is evident that his theory contains here another antinomy. Ritschl seems to be right when he says:

'The strict consequence of the doctrine of satisfaction through Christ would be the thought that, after this condition of the forgiveness of sins was fulfilled, God, for the sake of His own honour, would lead upon the way of salvation those men who take as an example for themselves Christ's surrender to God. . . . Through the conception of merit, however, the significance of Christ for the men who are to be saved is increased, and a more intimate connexion between them and Christ is suggested, than would follow from the doctrine of satisfaction.'[8]

Anselm, therefore, gains great practical advantages by supplementing the standpoint of satisfaction with that of merit, but he gains them at the expense of a logical fault.[9]

So much then in criticism of Anselm's theory: now for its historical importance. In spite of all continuity with the past, the theory is to be treated as emphatically a new development. We must endeavour to measure the greatness of the change involved in it.

(1) In Anselm's theory the doctrine of the Person of Christ is used in a way fundamentally different from its principal use in antiquity, which use indeed was continually in view during the elaboration of the doctrine by the great Councils. There the emphasis was on the God who employed His humanity as the means, whether of the illumination, or of the deification of humanity. Here the emphasis is on the man, whose work is given an infinite value by his participation in the Divine nature. In antiquity we find something of a parallel to Anselm's view at

[7] *Infra*, p. 291.   [8] ''Rechtfertigung und Versöhnung', 2nd ed., vol. i, p. 45.
[9] Cf. Harnack, D.G., 4th ed., vol. iii, p. 404, n. 2.

this point in the Irenæus doctrine of the victory over the devil of Christ as a man by the help of His Divinity. The Western emphasis on the sacrifice of Christ also prepares the way for the Anselmic view; and still more again Augustine's stress on the humanity of the mediator ('In quantum homo, in tantum mediator', 'Conf.' x, 43, 68), is a preparation for it. Nevertheless, if we take a broad view of the contrast between the new and the old, it is a marked and notable one. There the *God*-man; here the God-*man*.

(2) Dependent upon the above distinction is another. Corresponding to the primacy in the ancient view of the work of Christ of the Divine action in it, is the way in which its result is conceived. This is mystical: in other words Christ's work is thought of as operating in a mode inaccessible to human reason and so proper to Divinity. The death and resurrection of Christ, in fact, act as a ferment in humanity, destroying sin and death and imparting righteousness and immortality. This is the fundamental view of the application of Christ's work, as may be shown by a reference to Gregory of Nyssa,[1] John of Damascus,[2] and Augustine.[3]

Anselm's theory, however, replaces this mystical view with another which is rational and intelligible. Christ gives a gift to God, in return for which God gives eternal salvation. For the purposes of his theory Anselm has to reinterpret the death of Christ as the gift of His life. It is not the death in itself, but the gift made in it, that brings about salvation, and that not directly, but through the reaction of God. This is a totally different view of the work of Christ from the older view, so fundamentally different indeed that it means a theological revolution.

ABELARD

Another great starting-point of the mediaeval doctrine of the work of Christ is found in Abelard (d. A.D. 1142), who possesses a double significance for us, (1) through his general contribution

[1] 'Great Catechism', 35. [2]'Exposition of the Orthodox Faith', vol. iv, 9.
[3] 'Enchiridion', 42.

to system and method in theology, (2) through his direct treatment of the doctrine of the work of Christ.

As regards the first point, Abelard has begun a systematic treatment of theology of a different kind from that of Anselm. In his 'Introductio ad Theologiam' and his 'Theologia Christiana' he has laid the foundations for a scientific treatment of theology in detail, beginning with a doctrine of principles and method, and proceeding to a detailed discussion of the different doctrines upon the basis of carefully selected authorities. His work here remains a torso, in that it only reaches as far as the fundamental doctrine of the Trinity. 'His purpose is with the weapons of dialectic to strike infidels and false dialecticians. . . . Abelard's standpoint is that of apologetic in the widest sense.' [4]

Though Abelard in the above systematic treatises has not carried his work to completion, he has, however, sketched in 'Introd. ad Theol.' I, 1 the outlines of a new arrangement of the whole theological material, which he consciously sets in opposition to the arrangement of Augustine in the 'Enchiridion', and which is of great significance. Augustine had reduced [5] the essence of religion to the three heads 'faith, hope, love'. But Abelard says:

'There are three things, as I think, in which the sum of human salvation consists, viz. faith, love, and the sacrament. Hope, on the other hand, I consider to be included in faith, as the species in the genus.' Abelard therefore is the harbinger of the great development in mediaeval theology of the doctrine of the sacraments. Since, however, in the Catholic view of Christianity the blessings of the Christian salvation are assured to us through the sacraments, this development has a profound retrospective importance for our understanding of the meaning of the mediaeval doctrine of the work of Christ.

Finally, in 'Sic et Non' Abelard has made an even more important contribution to theological system and method, in that he has here arranged the whole material of theology in an ordered system of questions, raised by the apparent discrepancies between the various Biblical and patristic authorities on the various

[4] Bach, 'Dogmengeschichte des Mittelalters', 1873, vol. ii, pp. 45, 46.
[5] 'Ench.' 3.

points. Here above all Abelard has laid firmly the foundation of the typical scholastic method, and has also gathered most of the material afterwards used as a basis of theological operations.

The second point mentioned at the outset was that of Abelard's direct treatment of the work of Christ. This is not found in any of the above systematic works, but in his commentary on the Epistle to the Romans, where, however, it is discussed in the form of a special theological question rising out of the exegesis.[6]

The question is as to the nature of our redemption through Christ, or as to our being justified in His blood. It is exactly the question therefore which Augustine discusses in 'De Trin.' XIII, 10, 13ff., which fundamental passage Abelard clearly has in view in the place before us, as a detailed comparison of the two statements shows.

Abelard, however, begins by rejecting as flatly as Anselm the doctrine of redemption from the devil. His objections to this doctrine are as follows:

(1) Christ redeemed only the elect, but these never were in the devil's power.

(2) If the devil seduced man, his fellow-servant, that gives him no right over man, but makes him rather deserving of punishment. This is the same as Anselm's argument.

(3) The devil could not give man the immortality which he had promised, and so again could have no rights over him.

Abelard sums up:

'By these reasons it seems convincingly proved that the devil had acquired by the act of seduction no right against man whom he seduced, unless perhaps, as we said, in so far as our reasons related to the permission of the Lord, who had given man over to him as jailer or torturer for punishment.'[7]

Man therefore had sinned only against God, whose obedience he had abandoned. If therefore God wished to forgive sin even apart from Christ's passion (as was done many times before the passion and in particular by Christ in His earthly life),[8] then there was nothing to prevent God saying to the torturer, 'I will

---

[6] Lib. II ; col. 833ff. in Migne's edition of the works of Abelard.
[7] *Ibid.* col. 834.   [8] Cf. Lk. 7:47 ; Matt. 9:2.

144

that you punish man no more.' Moreover, the same grace that chose a man without any preceding merits for union with Christ in the Incarnation, could also, without injury being done thereby to the devil, if God had willed it, have freely forgiven men's sins and delivered them from punishment. 'Could not He, who showed man so great grace as to unite him with Himself in one person, expend on him the lesser grace, of forgiving his sins?' [9]

Why then the Incarnation, the sufferings, and the death of Christ? Again, why, when Christ died at the hands of men by a sinful act far greater than Adam's in eating the apple, did not this rather increase God's wrath against men than bring about, as St Paul says, the justification or reconciliation of men? And again, if the solution of these questions be that Christ's blood was given not to the devil, but to God (a ransom is paid for captives not to their torturer, but to their real possessor), does not this create a further difficulty?

'How cruel and unjust it appears, that anyone should demand the blood of the innocent as any kind of ransom, or be in any way delighted with the death of the innocent, let alone that God should find the death of His Son so acceptable, that through it He should be reconciled to the world!' [1]

Abelard's solution of the above difficulties is a fuller development of the ideas of Augustine in 'De Catechizandis Rudibus', 4, 7.

'It seems to us, however, that we are justified by the blood of Christ and reconciled to God, in this, that by this singular grace shown us, that His Son took our nature and persevered in instructing us both in word and deed even unto death, He more largely bound us to Himself by love, so that kindled as we are by so great a benefit of the Divine grace, true charity should henceforth fear nothing at all. . . . And so our redemption is that supreme love manifested in our case by the passion of Christ, who not merely delivers us from the bondage of sin, but also acquires for us the liberty of the sons of God, so that we fulfil all things from love rather than from fear of Him, who, as He Himself bears witness, showed us grace so great that no greater is possible.' [2]

[9] Lib. II ; ed. Migne, col. 835.   [1] *Ibid.* cols. 835ff.   [2] *Ibid.* col. 836.

Such is Abelard's solution of the great question he has set himself. Two benefits proceed from the passion of Christ: (1) the forgiveness of sins, (2) the liberty of the sons of God, which last he interprets to mean the kindling in us of a love towards God, that willingly obeys Him. Abelard does not in the above discussion explain how the two benefits are related the one to the other, nor make it clear how the first benefit, the remission of sins, proceeds from the death of Christ; his argument only shows how that death issues in the second benefit, the awakening of love towards God. The preceding continuous commentary, however, clears up the points in doubt. Abelard there views the remission of sins as the direct result of the kindling of love, and so as the indirect result of the death of Christ. In opposition to Augustine, who made justification include both the remission of sins and the infusion of love, though laying chief stress on the latter, Abelard appears to identify justification simply with the latter, and then says that God has given Christ 'in order that through this righteousness, i.e. charity, we may obtain the remission of sins'. He refers to the words of the Lord,[3] 'Her sins are forgiven, because she loved much.'[4]

As Abelard's formal discussion is naturally to be read in the light of the preceding commentary, it is important to supplement it by means of these additional thoughts just described; and then it becomes evident that he has reduced the whole process of redemption to one single clear principle, viz. the manifestation of God's love to us in Christ, which awakens an answering love in us. Out of this principle Abelard endeavours to explain all other points of view.

It brings him, however, into difficulties with regard to the matter of baptism. The older objective views of the work of Christ formed a natural basis for the remission of sins in baptism, with which rite also the Augustinian doctrine of the infusion of love easily enough connects itself, since this love is regarded as the first fruits of the baptismal gift of the Spirit. But the psychological doctrine of the kindling of the love of God through the death of Christ leads to the problem, how, if the love thus awakened justifies, baptism can yet be necessary to salvation.

[3] Lk. 7:47.   [4] Cf. Lib. II ; ed. Migne, col. 833.

Abelard replies that, unless baptism or martyrdom follows the kindling of love, it must be concluded that perseverance has been lacking. Remission of sins in fact does not take place till baptism, even though love be kindled before baptism. Moreover, in the case of children Abelard has to admit that remission of sins precedes justification, as infants, though clean in God's sight, are not capable either of charity or righteousness, nor can have any merits.[5] Remission of sins therefore in this case at least appears to be independent of the kindling of love. In fact, as Loofs observes, Abelard's new view could not be consistently carried through without more changes than he was prepared to make.[6]

Thus one is not surprised to find side by side with the above fundamental statement on the work of Christ, other passages to which Gottschick has called attention, where Abelard in the traditional way speaks of Christ as a sacrifice for sin, also others again, in which He is said to have borne our sins.[7]

There is, moreover, an important passage, in which Abelard, comparing the results of Adam's sin with those of Christ's obedience, makes use of the principle of merit. If the references to Christ's sacrifice are but short, and the idea they contain undeveloped, the same cannot be said of the treatment of Christ's merit in this passage. The argument is as follows:

'When God made His Son man, He indeed set Him under the law, which He had given in common to all men. And so He as man must according to the Divine precept love His neighbour as Himself, and exercise in our case the grace of His charity, both in teaching us and also in praying for us. . . . But His supreme righteousness required that His prayer should in nothing meet repulse, since the Divinity in union with Him allowed Him to wish or do nothing but what should be. . . . And so, being made man, He is constrained by the law of the love of His neighbour, that He might redeem those who were under the law and could not be saved by the law, and might supply from His own what was wanting in our merits, and just as He was

Cf. *ibid*. col. 837–8.   [6] Cf. D.G., 4th ed., p. 515.
Cf. 'Studien zur Versöhnungslehre des Mittelalters', in 'Zeitschrift für Kirchengeschichte', 1901, p. 425.

singular in holiness, so also He might be singular in His utility in the matter of others' salvation. Otherwise what great thing did His holiness merit, if it availed only for His own, and not for others' salvation?' [8] As Gottschick has pointed out,[9] it is not right here, with Ritschl,[1] to understand the above passage as referring only to the question, how the imperfect merits of the justified may be supplemented. It has a wider reference, and treats of the whole problem of salvation, from the point of view of Christ's merit. The passage is to be regarded therefore as containing a view of Christ's work, not so much supplementary, as alternative to the theory first discussed.

The doctrine of Abelard, in spite of its somewhat fragmentary and sketchy character, in which it contrasts strongly with the fully elaborated theory of Anselm, is nevertheless of the greatest importance and deserves careful study. Its importance indeed has, in view of the striking discussion reproduced at the beginning of this section, been generally conceded. Gottschick, however,[2] by laying stress on the passages in Abelard describing Christ's death as a sacrifice, and again on the passage just quoted touching His merit, endeavours to bring Abelard more into line with the patristic and the scholastic theology in general. But Loofs seems right in asserting in reply [3] the significance of Abelard's discussion, as at least an attempt to reduce the whole doctrine of the work of Christ to a single thought, and that thought one that does not coincide with any main tendency of previous doctrine. The opinion of centuries, whether favourable or unfavourable, has always been impressed by the singular force of this passage. And, if Abelard does in other places present views along different lines, and so himself controvert his own tendency to a simplification of doctrine, this need not prevent our recognising that this tendency exists.

It is, moreover, not only the central thought of Abelard's discussion, viz. that of the moral effect of Christ's death, which is important. Besides the effective criticism which the discussion contains of the doctrine of redemption from the devil, a criticism

---

[8] Col. 865.
[9] 'Studien zur Versöhnungslehre des Mittelalters', in 'Zeitschrift für Kirchengeschichte', 1901. p. 423.　　　[1] 'Rechtfertigung und Versöhnung', 2nd ed., vol. i, p. 50.
[2] Op. cit. p. 428.　　　[3] D.G., 4th ed., p. 515.

in which Abelard stands side by side with Anselm, it introduces what, so far as I know, is a new element into the doctrine of the work of Christ, in that it formally subordinates it to the Augustinian doctrine of predestination. Only the elect are the objects of Christ's redeeming work; its scope is limited beforehand by the Divine decree. We have here a thought destined to play a conspicuous part in the further development of our doctrine.

BERNARD OF CLAIRVAUX

The Middle Age was not content only with an intellectual apprehension of the treasures of the Christian religion as delivered to it by the past: it sought perhaps even more earnestly for an emotional appropriation of them. The movement towards such appropriation, after earlier beginnings, appears in full force in the twelfth century. One manifestation is Abelard's moral theory of the work of Christ, which we have just been studying, where clearly the whole doctrine is arranged so as to secure a definite inner experience of conversion to God. But undoubtedly the most striking and important manifestation of the tendency is in the practical and ascetic writings of Bernard of Clairvaux (d. A.D. 1153), above all in his famous sermons on Canticles.

As Ritschl has pointed out in his essay 'Lesefrüchte aus dem Heiligen Bernhard',[4] Bernard has put forward in these sermons a very remarkable view of the redemptive work of Christ, turning on a new and original evaluation of His Person. Bernard sees in the patience and love of Christ in His human life and passion, not merely the revelation of the love of God, but the actual saving manifestation of His own Divinity. His doctrine is the true Western counterpart of the doctrine of Irenæus and Athanasius, according to which the Incarnation is the saving entrance of God into humanity. Only there the Incarnation and its result are conceived in more physical and objective terms— what God brings into humanity is life and incorruption: here on the other hand they are conceived more subjectively and

"'Gesammelte Aufsätze, Neue Folge', pp. 204ff.

149

psychologically—the entrance of God into humanity is seen in the patience and love, which inspire similiar patience and love in us. Again, as in the case of the Anselmic theory, we may observe the tendency to exchange a mystical and rationally inexplicable doctrine of the saving operation of God in humanity for one that is naturally intelligible. It may be added that the secondary doctrine of Irenæus and Athanasius (which is the primary doctrine of Clement and Origen), where the Incarnation is thought of as the shining of the Divine light in humanity, of course stands much nearer to the new view of Bernard, but is nevertheless more mystical, and less completely intelligible than it.

The principal passages, in which the doctrine we have been summarising is found, are the following:

(1) 'Serm.' 11, 3 (redemption is the filling of man from God through His emptying of Himself).

'Let not what is chief and greatest in the work of our redemption at all recede from the memory of the redeemed. Two things . . . most of all in this work I shall seek to instil into your serious thoughts, . . . its manner and its result. The manner is the self-emptying of God; the result is our being filled from Him.'

(2) 'Serm.' 6, 3 (Jesus shows His Divine nature and power in His miracles and teaching, still more in the patience of His sufferings and in His love to sinners).

'While He does in the flesh and through the flesh the works, not of the flesh but of God, commanding nature and conquering fortune, making foolish the wisdom of men and overcoming the tyranny of the demons, He plainly shows Himself to be Him through whom these same things were made, before, when they were made. In the flesh, I say, and through the flesh, He mightily and manifestly worked miracles, spoke sound words, suffered indignities, and so showed clearly that it is Himself who mightily but invisibly founded the world, wisely rules it and kindly protects it. Then, while He preaches to the unthankful, shows signs to the unbelieving, prays for His crucifiers, does He not clearly show it is Himself, who with the Father makes His sun to rise upon the good and bad, and rains upon the just and the unjust?'

150

(3) 'Serm.' 20, 2 (the love shown in the work of redemption is a greater manifestation of Divine power even than the creation of the world).

'Above all things, I say, kind Jesus, the cup of our redemption, which thou didst drink, makes thee lovable to me. . . . Greatly did the Saviour toil in it, nor in the whole creation of the world did its Author assume so much weariness. The Creator indeed spoke and things were made, He commanded and they were created. But the Saviour in His words endured gainsayers, in His deeds spies, in His torments mockers, and in His death revilers. Behold how He loved.'

Bernard was, however, not only an ascetic writer, originating new ideas, but also a theologian, warmly attached to tradition. As such he wrote a treatise against Abelard ('Tractatus contra quædam capitula errorum Abælardi'), in which he reaffirms in opposition to that writer the doctrine of redemption from the devil, concerning which he says all the doctors since the Apostles agree. Abelard is to know that the devil had not only a power, but a just power over men. Man was justly held captive by him, though the justice was not in man, nor in the devil, but in God (v, 14).

'Man therefore was justly given over to the devil, but in mercy delivered from him; yet in such mercy, that there was not lacking a kind of justice in the very deliverance; though it was also as a result of the mercy of the deliverer that (as befitted the remedies of deliverance) He made use of justice against the usurper rather than power. For what now could man, the servant of sin and the captive of the devil, do of himself to recover the righteousness which he had once lost? There was assigned to him therefore, who had none of his own, the righteousness of another, and this was as follows: The prince of this world came and found nothing in the Saviour, and since none the less he most unjustly laid hands on the innocent, he most justly lost those whom he held; since He, who owed nothing to death, having received the injury of death, rightly freed him, who was liable to it, both from the debt of death and from the dominion of the devil. For with what justice could man a second time be asked for it? If it was man who owed the debt, it was man who

151

paid it. For if one (saith the Apostle) died for all, then all died; so that to wit the satisfaction made by one may be imputed to all, just as the one bore the sin of all: nor is it one who transgressed, and another who satisfied: for the head and the body is one Christ. The head therefore satisfied for the members, Christ for His bowels' (VI, 15).

The above passage repeats the doctrine of Augustine in 'De Trin.' XIII, 10, 13ff., yet with a notable condensation and clarification, and also with some important additions.

(1) Bernard goes beyond Augustine in making use of the idea of satisfaction; though he applies it, not like Anselm with reference to the claim of God, but in harmony with patristic thought with reference to that of the devil.

(2) In order to show the operation for our benefit of Christ's satisfaction, he connects it further with the idea of imputation, and also with the notion, already found with a general reference to redemption in Augustine, of the solidarity of the head and the members in the one body.

(3) Where Augustine speaks of justification and the remission of sins, Bernard, guided by Paul, uses the alternative form of expression, 'Assignata est homini justitia aliena', or as he puts the point in VI, 16, 'justum me dixerim, sed illius justitia'.

These are seminal thoughts destined later to issue in great theological developments.

It is from the point of view of a firm belief in an objective redemption that Bernard is so much opposed to the doctrine of Abelard. The latter he says reduces the whole matter of the Lord's Incarnation, Passion and Death to this: 'That He gave to men by living and teaching an example of life; whilst by suffering and dying He set before us the extreme limit of charity. Did He therefore teach righteousness, and not give it; did He manifest charity, but not infuse it; and did He on these terms return to His own concerns?' (VII, 17).

The opposition between the objective view of redemption and the subjective could not be more clearly stated. Bernard's incisive mind goes straight to the fundamental difference between Abelard's doctrine and what he holds to be the essential doctrine of the past. It is true that the doctors of the past had never taught an objective without at the same time a subjective redemption, and that they had by no means distinguished the way in which these two views conditioned each other. It is true also that Bernard himself as appears from his sermons on Canticles valued greatly the subjective view; while on the other hand Abelard had, as we have seen, by no means exclusively set forth this view, but had in many places left tradition standing. Nevertheless, Bernard feels the force and sweep of Abelard's argument in his fundamental discussion, and how inevitably it tends to reduce all theories of Christ's work to one only, that of the moral influence of His life and death. Such a view of redemption taken alone Bernard regards as in reality denying redemption altogether.

'How is it that he says, that the purpose and reason of the Incarnation was that Christ might illuminate the world with the light of His wisdom, and kindle it to love of Himself? Where then is the redemption?' (IX, 23).

Bernard argues that Abelard's theory implies the denial of the doctrine of original sin. 'If the life which Christ gives is nothing other than His instruction, neither undoubtedly will the death which Adam gave to men likewise be other than his instruction; so that the one educated men by his example to sin, and the other by His example to live well and love Him' (ibid.). He points out, what indeed Abelard had admitted, the inconsistency of the moral theory with the Church's practice of infant baptism: this implies a real and objective redemption, not a subjective process. 'How shall it (the advent of Christ) inflame to the love of God those who do not yet know how to love their own mother?' (IX, 24).

Abelard had not only found difficulties in the idea of our redemption from the devil, but in that other which Augustine in 'De Trin.' XIII, 11, 15, couples with it, the thought of our reconciliation to God. In answer to the problem, how it was that the death of Christ did not increase rather than blot out man's account of sin, Bernard says that it was of such avail as to blot out the sin of the crucifixion with all the rest. And again in answer to the question, how God could possibly take delight in the death of His Son, Bernard gives the noble answer: 'It was not Christ's death that pleased God, but His will in voluntarily dying, and by that death abolishing death, working salvation, restoring innocence, triumphing over the principalities and powers. . . .' (VIII, 20). The Father, says Bernard, did not require the death of His Son, nevertheless He accepted the offering of it; not thirsting for blood, but for salvation, because there was salvation in the blood. It is to be observed that Bernard here does what the patristic theologians had been unable to do: he establishes a clear relation between the ideas of Christ's death as the means of redemption from the devil, and as a sacrifice to God. The death of Christ is accepted by God as an oblation, because it is the way of redemption from death and the devil.

We must note that Bernard for all his stress on an objective redemption nevertheless follows the Augustinian tradition in admitting that the Incarnation was not absolutely necessary for God. Nevertheless from the human point of view it was necessary: this must be enough for us (VIII, 19).

In IX, 25 Bernard sums up his total view of the work of Christ. 'Three principal things I perceive in this work of our salvation: the pattern of humility, in which God emptied Himself: the measure of love, which He stretched even unto death, and that the death of the cross: the mystery of redemption, in which He underwent the death, which He bore. The two former of these without the last are like a picture on the void.'

In the above passage Bernard is moved by the criticism of Abelard to correlate the objective and subjective aspects of redemption in a definite way, which indeed Anselm had already suggested,[5] but which the Fathers had not found necessary. The objective view is the firm basis of the subjective: without the objective the subjective itself must come to nothing.

We must not allow ourselves to be diverted from the essential importance of Bernard's objection to a purely subjective view of the work of Christ by the fact that for him the objective view of redemption was bound up with the notion of a ransom paid to the devil. The fundamental thing to be observed is not the particular form of objectivity favoured by Bernard, but that he has brought into such clear relief the contrast between pure

[5] 'Cur Deus Homo', I, 4.

subjectivity and a subjectivity which rests on an objective basis. Here first in the history of theology, in this controversy between Abelard and Bernard, appears with full consciousness of its importance the opposition of two views of the work of Christ, which still at the present day stand in vital conflict with one another.

RUPERT OF DEUTZ

Rupert of Deutz (d. A.D. 1135), the contemporary of Bernard of Clairvaux, deserves mention not because of a peculiar theory of the work of Christ, but because he was the first to raise an important question, which has a profound bearing upon the doctrine of this subject. This was the question: 'Whether Christ would have become incarnate if Adam had not sinned?'

The thought of an Incarnation independent of the Fall naturally harmonises with those main tendencies of Greek theology, which see in Christ the Life and Light of men, and according to Westcott there are patristic phrases which seem to imply that the idea was to a certain extent realised and discussed by the Eastern Fathers.[6] But the question was not actually raised till the eleventh or twelfth century; from the thirteenth century onwards, however, it became a recognised question of the schools. Its appearance is again like so much that has already been spoken of, a mark of the new intellectual vigour of the age, which in endeavouring to appropriate the inheritance of the past entered often upon bold and fresh lines of speculation, and often also discovered problems where none had been perceived before.

Rupert of Deutz, whose name is connected with the emergence of the question, handles it only in a tentative way, from which it is clear that he had neither received nor was able himself to give a firm and consistent opinion on the subject. His references to it are not cast into systematic form, but take the shape of interpretations of various texts of Scripture.[7]

[6] See his essay, 'The Gospel of the Creation', in 'Commentary on the Epistles of St John', p. 288.

[7] For the passages quoted below I am indebted to Westcott's just-mentioned essay : the pagination given with the quotations refers to this.

In an exposition of Heb. 2:10 [8] Rupert reads *consummari* for *consummare*, and obtains the sense that it was fitting for the Son of God, for whom were all things, and through whom were all things, to be perfected through sufferings. He then goes on to say: 'The first thing to inquire here is whether the Son of God spoken of in this place would have become man or not even if sin, for which we all die, had not intervened' (p. 290). It is certain that in this case He would not have become a mortal man: 'The question is whether God would have become man as the Head and King of all as He now is, and whether this was in some sense necessary for the human race' (*ibid.*).

Rupert further argues from the doctrine of Augustine [9] that the elect saints would certainly have been born if man had not fallen, to the inference that in this case it is absurd to suppose that their Head and King would not have been born also. Sin did not make of none effect the original Divine purpose of Incarnation, but brought the added grace that Christ not only did not shrink from our nature, which He had purposed to assume, but for our sakes even descended to death.

In another place [1] Rupert disputes the doctrine, which we have found stated by Anselm, that man was created to fill the gap caused in the angelic ranks by the fall of some, and says: 'It is more right to say not that man was made for the sake of the angels, but that the angels, as every thing else, were made for a particular man' (p. 291). What does Christ say in Prov. 8:31 but virtually this: 'Before God made anything from the beginning, and when He was making this or that, this was His purpose, that I the Word of God, the Word God (*verbum Deus*) should become flesh, and dwell among men with great love and great humility, which are true delights'? (*ibid.*). The Incarnation therefore is essentially independent of the Fall of man; but again Rupert argues that the Fall did actually redound to the glory of Christ, who may be imagined as saying to the sinner: 'I should not have been such as I am and so great, except for thy sake for the sins of the human race (*causa tui propter peccata generis*

[8] 'Comm. in Matt.' Lib. xiii.   [9] 'De civ. Dei', xiv, 23.
[1] 'De glorif. Trin.' iii, 20ff.

humani). . . . We see, the Apostle says, the Lord Jesus Christ for suffering crowned with glory and honour' [2] (p. 292).

It is clear that the question raised by Rupert has a most important bearing on the doctrine of the work of Christ. If the Incarnation would have taken place even apart from the Fall, then an essential element of His work must be without reference to sin.

[1]'Comm. in Matt.' Lib. xiii (cf. Heb. 2:9).

CHAPTER 3

THE SYSTEMATISATION OF DOCTRINE

Hugo of St Victor

Hugo of St Victor (d. A.D. 1141) is of great significance, not so much for his actual doctrine of the work of Christ, as because from him we obtain the first complete mediaeval system, and have clearly defined for the first time the full context in which the Middle Ages understood Christ's redeeming work.

On the one hand it is of the utmost importance that Hugo has followed out the suggestion of Abelard and has given to the sacraments the place in theology which corresponds to their practical importance in mediaeval Christianity. His whole system in fact, as is suggested by its name 'De Sacramentis Christianæ Fidei', is so arranged that every doctrine converges upon that of the sacraments as the practical means of salvation.

On the other hand Hugo has brought the work of Christ once more into relation with the economy of revelation, proceeding by successive stages from natural law through the written or Mosaic law to the new or Christian law. He has thus set it in the wider context in which it is found in Irenæus and Origen, and has recovered in consequence something of the breadth of treatment so apparent in the earlier Greek theology. It is, however, to be observed that there is a difference. In the Greek theologians the preliminary stages of revelation are directly attributed to the Logos, and so are more closely connected with the historical work of Christ. By Hugo they are rather derived immediately from God Himself, and thus, while supplying a context necessary for the understanding of the mediaeval conception of the work of Christ, do not even indirectly come under that title.

We have already noted elsewhere (p. 120) that Hugo in his system aims to give an account of the doctrine of Holy Scripture, and groups it under the two heads of creation and redemption.

158

The principal matter of Scripture is the work of redemption; yet the doctrine of creation (and of the fall) is the necessary preface.[1]

By putting together various passages from the 'De Sacramentis' we can obtain an idea of Hugo's view as to the nature and the different grounds of theological statement. Faith is perfected, when it proceeds through rational proof to an intuitive understanding (*per veritatem apprehendere*).[2] While the doctrine of creation depends upon the debt of nature, the doctrine of redemption depends upon the debt of grace. 'The former we ought to believe, because we are formed by nature: the latter we ought to believe, because we are redeemed by grace' (1, 10, 5). 'To nature belong reason and the creation (*creatura*); to grace inspiration and doctrine' (1, 3, 31). Hence the doctrine of redemption rests on authority. 'Wherefore after these things we must have regard to those things which authority proves, since human reason, unless illuminated by the Word of God, cannot see the way of truth' (*ibid.*).

Upon the basis of the rational doctrine of creation Hugo then builds the supernatural structure of the doctrine of redemption. The doctrine of the Trinity, its presupposition, is regarded as substantially rational, in view of the image of the Trinity in the mind, and so is included in the doctrine of creation (1, 3, 30). 'The work of redemption is the Incarnation of the Word with all its sacraments.'[3] These sacraments Hugo distinguishes as belonging to the three stages of revelation familiar to us since Irenæus, viz. natural law, the written law, and the new law. It is a peculiar feature of his system that the subject of the work of Christ is introduced twice. It appears the first time before the discussion of the sacraments of natural law and of the written law, chiefly in the form of an abstract discussion of its necessity. The second time it appears before the discussion of the sacraments of the new law, under the head of the doctrine of the Incarnation as actually realised. To obtain a complete view of Hugo's doctrine of the work of Christ it is necessary to put these two isolated sections together.

In the former of them Hugo begins by effecting a curious

---

[1] 1 Prol. 3.   [2] Cf. 1, 10, 4.   [3] 1 Prol.

combination between the new Anselmic doctrine of satisfaction
and the old doctrine of redemption from the devil. He views the
work of Christ as the settlement of a kind of triangular lawsuit,
in which God, man, and the devil are all concerned (1, 8, 4).

'These three therefore, man, God, and the devil, come
together in the cause. The devil is convicted of having done injury
to God, in that he both deceitfully abducted and violently held
His bond servant man. Man similarly is convicted of having done
injury to God, in that he both despised His commandment, and
putting himself under an evil stranger brought on Him the loss
of his service. Moreover, the devil is convicted of having done
injury to man, in that he first deceived him by promising good
things, and afterwards harmed him by bringing upon him evil
things. . . . Man then is justly subject to the devil as regards
his own fault, but unjustly as regards the devil's deceit. If therefore man had a patron, such that by his power the devil could
be brought to judgment, man could justly oppose his dominion.
. . . No such patron, however, can be found but God alone;
but God would not undertake man's cause, because He was still
angry with man for his own fault.'

In this complicated situation what is to be done? Man must
first satisfy God, and thus obtain help against the devil. Here
therefore enters the Anselmic theory of satisfaction, which Hugo
repeats in a condensed form, making, however, some important
modifications in it. He distinguishes between two parts in the
satisfaction made: (a) the placating of God's wrath by the making
good the loss of man's service which took place in Christ's life
of obedience, wherein He rendered to God what was due to Him
from man; (b) the satisfaction made for man's contempt of God
by Christ's voluntarily undergoing the punishment of sin which
He did not deserve. This last does away with man's guilt (reatus),
or liability to punishment.

It will be remembered that Anselm himself suggested such a
distinction. 'He who violates the honour of another does not do
enough if he restore the honour, unless, in correspondence with
harm done in dishonouring him, he make some amends acceptable to him whom he has dishonoured.'[4] In Anselm's hands,

[4] 'Cur Deus Homo', I, 11 (supra, p. 129).

160

however, the distinction came to nothing; whereas Hugo has developed it in a way somewhat anticipatory of the later Protestant doctrine of Christ's satisfaction as consisting both in His active and passive obedience, the resemblance, moreover, extending also to the conception of the satisfactory nature of Christ's death, which is not as with Anselm simply an offering inclining God to remit punishment, but also a substitutionary endurance of our punishment.

Hugo completes his doctrine by returning to the position of the devil after God has been satisfied. The evil one has now no ground of accusation against man, since he never had any right to rule over man, and now moreover man is worthy of deliverance.

Hugo sums up the whole therefore as follows (I, 8, 6 and 7): 'Thus God was made man, that He might deliver man whom He had made, that the Creator and the Redeemer of man might be the same. . . . Wisdom came to conquer wickedness, that the enemy who had conquered by cunning, might be conquered by sagacity. He took from our nature a sacrifice for our nature, that the whole burnt offering to be offered for us might be taken from what was ours, so that redemption might belong to us just in this very thing, that the sacrifice was taken from what was ours. Of which redemption we are indeed made partakers, if we are united by faith to the Redeemer who is become our partner through the flesh.'

Hugo proceeds, however, to point out that God would have done no wrong to men had He left them in their sins to eternal punishment. Salvation in fact depends simply upon the Divine election. There are two kinds of justice. One is the justice of power, according to which God may without injustice treat man as He will, having regard only to the sovereign claims of His own power. The other justice is the justice of equity, which is according to merit; and by it God rewards or punishes him who is the recipient of this justice, even though it be against his will. Justification then takes place by the justice of power, not in accordance with merit. Man is therefore made just by the justice which he receives from God (1, 8, 8).

Salvation, therefore, both in election and justification

161

proceeds from the justice of power. So, however, does the Incarnation itself.

'Wherefore we truly confess, that God could have accomplished the redemption of the human race in another way also, if He had wished. But we confess that the way chosen was the better suited to our weakness, and so God became man, and for man's sake assuming human mortality renewed man by giving him the hope of His own immortality. . . . So that He may be the way in example, the truth in promise, and life in reward' (1, 8, 10).

In the end therefore the necessity of the Incarnation turns out not to be absolute. Election, justification, and the Incarnation, the whole process of salvation in fact in all its parts depends simply upon the sovereign arbitrament of God. It is of great significance that Hugo consciously draws a parallel between the doctrine of election and the doctrine of the atonement: it is another stage on the way to the subordination of the latter to the former which we shall presently find in the theology of Duns Scotus.

We pass on to the second section of the 'De Sacramentis' bearing on our subject. Hugo devotes the whole of Book 2, pt. 1 to the Incarnation, and here are to be found as also in 2, 2, 1 some important passages on the work of Christ.

2, 1, 5 exhibits once more a tendency to explain the whole process of salvation from the one principle of sovereign grace. The Word assumed human nature but without guilt (culpa); that being free from sin, He might become a sacrifice for sin. This was the beginning of the grace, which ends in our salvation.

'That it might be united free from sin to the Word, human nature was cleansed from sin by the same grace by which the Christian is freed from sin, that he may be conjoined to the same nature in Christ His head.'

2, 1, 7 further explains the view of Christ's work as a vicarious endurance of our punishment. In the assumption of human nature at the Incarnation, though guilt was not assumed, the penalty of sin was assumed, not of necessity but by Christ's free will, in order that, because human nature in the Saviour suffered

162

without guilt, the rest of human nature, which was liable to penalty on account of guilt, might be delivered.

More important, however, is a discussion in 2, 1, 6 on the merit of Christ, in which Hugo breaks fresh ground and sets the pattern for the subsequent scholasticism.

The soul of Christ was from the first perfect in wisdom and grace. As regards His merit, however, some assert that the man Christ merited the glory of immortality only through His passion and death, in proof of which doctrine they quote Phil. 2:8, 9. In truth, however, His merit was for us, not for Himself. He merited nothing by His passion, which He did not already merit by His innate goodness from His conception. 'So far as He was man in rank, so far was He good in will. This is merit. If His will was always perfect, so also was His merit always perfect.' Christ then only merited by His passion in a different way what He already merited from His conception. His merit was first in Himself, then in His work. If the passion had not been needed, He would still by His perfect obedience to God have merited without it the glory of immortality. By the passion, however, He has become an example to us who must die, not only calling us to glory, but also showing the way.

Of great significance also is 2, 2, 1, which treats of the grace which is given through Christ, and diffused by the Spirit from the head to the members. Here we find for the first time after the hints and suggestions of Augustine and Bernard a systematic treatment of this important aspect of the work of Christ.

Man was first put under the law of nature, and left to himself. The only result was that through ignorance he erred. The written law came to remedy this ignorance, but could not give strength to man to perform its commandment. 'After these things, therefore, grace was fitly given to illuminate the blind and to heal the weak.' Grace illuminates in order to give the knowledge of the truth, it inflames in order to produce the love of virtue. Hugo says elsewhere (2, 1, 1): 'The time of grace took its beginning from the Incarnation of the Son of God'. Here in 2, 2, 1 he is concerned to show how grace operates.

'Just as the spirit of a man through the mediation of the head descends to quicken the members, so the Holy Spirit comes

163

through Christ to Christians. For Christ is the Head, the Christian the member. The Head is one, the members many, and there is constituted one body from the Head and the members, and one Spirit in one body. . . . By faith we are made members, by love we are quickened. By faith we receive union; by charity we receive quickening. Sacramentally, however, we are united by baptism, we are quickened by the body and blood of Christ. By baptism we are made members of the body, by the body of Christ (in the Eucharist), however, we are made participators in the quickening.'

The doctrine of the work of Christ therefore issues ultimately in that of the Sacraments. As Gregory of Nyssa was the first in the Greek Church, so Hugo of St Victor is the first in the Latin Church to work out this issue in systematic form: Hugo, however, has done it much more fully than Gregory. According to him three things are necessary to salvation both before and after the advent of Christ, viz. faith, the sacraments of faith, and good works (1, 9, 8).

Faith has been manifested before the law (i.e. the law of Moses), under the law, and under grace. Before the law God the Creator was believed in, and redemption was hoped for from Him. Under the law the Person of the Messiah was known, but not definitely as the God-man. Under grace Christ and the mode of redemption are fully known. Under the earlier stages, however, some knew the full truth, and the rest were saved by being joined with them in simple faith and in working righteousness (1, 10, 6).

Each stage, moreover, has its own precepts. The stage of natural law had the two unchangeable precepts of love to God and love to man, which the written law expanded into the three and the seven of the Decalogue (1, 12, 5). To these ten commandments were also added in the written law certain mutable precepts, intended either for discipline and for the increase of devotion or else for the symbolisation of coming truth. The New Testament has further developed the meaning of the Decalogue, has abolished some mutable precepts, and retained others (1, 12, 9).

So far as Christianity is law it is a religion of merit and

164

reward. It is also, however, in all the stages of revelation a religion of sacramental grace. The written law, says Hugo, contains three things, precepts, sacraments, and promises.

'In the precepts there is merit, in the promises reward, in the sacraments assistance' (1, 12,4). *Mutatis mutandis,* this general principle applies also to the other stages of revelation.

We thus come to the doctrine of the sacraments: 'A sacrament is a bodily or material element outwardly presented in sensible form, by likeness representing, by institution signifying, and by sanctification containing a certain invisible and spiritual grace' (1, 9, 2).

Every stage of revelation has its sacraments. Natural law had tithes and sacrifices, the written law circumcision and other rites. Only the sacraments of the New Testament, however, fully correspond to the above definition. They alone are both signs of grace and by benediction channels of grace. The previous sacraments were signs of redemption only, and conveyed grace only indirectly through the mediation of the realities for which they stood. Again, the sacraments of natural law were not instituted but voluntary (*ex voto*): those of the written law, however, like those of the New Testament were instituted (*ex precepto*). The relative inefficacy of the pre-Christian sacraments is shown in that the saints of the Old Testament who had them could not enter heaven till the ascended Christ had opened the gate (1, 11, 5).

The sacraments of the New Testament are therefore alone properly called the sacraments of grace. Hugo connects them with the doctrine of the Incarnation at the point where we finally left it, viz. that Christ is the Head, through whom grace flows to the members. The connecting link is the doctrine of the Church.

'The Holy Church is the body of Christ, quickened by one Spirit and united by one faith, and sanctified. . . . What therefore is the Church, but the multitude of the faithful, the whole society of Christians?' (2, 2, 2).

The Body of Christ, however, has two sides, the Clergy and the Laity (2, 2, 3). It is the former that administer the sacraments, and bear rule in the Church. The administration of the Church, therefore, consists in orders, sacraments, and precepts

165

(2, 2, 5). The Church is in fact a legal and sacramental institution, whose existence depends on the orders of its clergy.

One thing only is missing from the precision of Hugo's doctrine of the sacraments. He does not definitely fix their number. There are three kinds of sacraments:

(1) There are certain in which salvation principally consists and is received: these are Baptism and the Eucharist.

(2) There are others not necessary for salvation, but valuable for the exercise of virtue and the increase of grace, such as the Sprinkling of water and the Receiving of ashes.

(3) There are others instituted for the preparation of persons employed in the sacraments, such as Ordination (1, 9, 7).

Besides Baptism, the Eucharist, and Ordination, however, Confirmation, Extreme Unction, and Matrimony are named as sacraments. Penance is included in the scheme of Hugo's treatise; but does not appear to be included formally by name among the sacraments.

Hugo's doctrine of Penance is as follows. He urges the duty of confession (2, 14, 1). Grace first kindles those dead in sin to inner compunction, and leads them to make confession; which done, they receive from the priest the remission of the debt of damnation. The sinner, however, must still perform the appointed satisfaction or incur the pains of purgatory (2, 14, 3). Here it is to be observed that, while Hugo deduces the remission of eternal punishment from the priestly absolution, the preliminary grace which creates inner contrition is traced directly to the free gift of God. The grace received in Penance is therefore not conceived as entirely sacramental, but a most important part of it lies outside the sacrament.

Apart, however, from difficulties in detail like the above, the general view of Hugo is clear. The Church is on the one hand the body of the faithful, on the other hand it is a legal and sacramental institution. In both aspects it rests upon the foundation of the Incarnation as the culmination of the process of the Divine revelation. Finally, the Church as institution continues the work of Christ for the benefit of the Church as the company of believers, which is, through the Spirit, the recipient of the salvation brought by Him.

Hugo has thus given classical expression to the mediaeval view of Christianity.

'Grace (in the form of the sacraments) and merit (law and performance) are the two centres of the curve of the mediaeval conception of Christianity. This curve, however, is entirely embedded in faith in the Church; for since to it—as no one doubted—were entrusted the sacraments and the power of the keys resulting therefrom, it was not only the authority for the whole construction, but in the strictest sense the continuation of Christ Himself, and the body of Christ, which is enhypostatically united to Him.' [5]

PETER LOMBARD

The other great systematic work of the twelfth century besides the ' De Sacramentis' is Peter Lombard's 'Book of Sentences'.[6] A great importance attaches to this work because of the place which it took during the next three centuries, when it was regarded as the fundamental statement of the doctrine of the Western Church and was made the basis of innumerable commentaries. The book consists in the first place of a compilation of select extracts (*sententiæ*) from Scripture and the Fathers on the various subjects of Christian doctrine, arranged, as in Abelard's 'Sic et Non', which here has given the model, so as to form a system. The cement, however, which is necessary to form these diverse elements into an actual system, and which was wanting in Abelard's work, is furnished in the 'Book of Sentences' in the shape of intercalated comments intended to unite and reconcile the various authorities. Abelard himself and Hugo of St Victor have supplied a good deal of this additional matter. It is clear that the method of the book does not allow great scope for originality, nor indeed was originality the thing aimed at; the intention of the whole is rather to furnish a guide through the labyrinth of existing tradition by means of a careful selection and systematisation. Nevertheless such scope for originality as the scheme allows Lombard makes full use of. It is obvious that

[5] Harnack, D.G., 4th ed., vol. iii, p. 519.   [6] Lombard, d. A.D. 1160.

167

very different accounts might be given of tradition according to the different plans of systematisation adopted, the different passages selected for discussion, and the varying methods of reconciliation made use of in case of divergence between one authority and another.

Lombard's system contains four books. The first has for its subject the doctrine of God, the second that of the Creation and the Fall: in this book is discussed the general relation between grace and free will. The third deals with the Incarnation, and with faith, hope, and love, the fourth with the sacraments and with eschatology.

We shall begin directly with the doctrine of the work of Christ as developed in Lib. III. The redemptive purpose of the Incarnation is defined in general as the bringing in of grace. Of the doctrine of the Incarnation as the medicine of fallen humanity there are some brief reminiscences in III, 2, A: 'Since in man the whole of human nature had been corrupted by vice, He assumed the whole, that is soul and flesh, that He might heal and sanctify the whole'. The authority of John of Damascus is quoted: 'The whole Christ assumed the whole of me, that He might gratify the whole of me with salvation. For what cannot be assumed, cannot be cured.'[7]

There is, however, no development of this line of doctrine. The doctrine of the Incarnation as traditionally accepted from the Ancient Church is, in fact, developed simply as a speculative doctrine of the Person of Christ, apart from the practical motives which had governed the Greek Fathers in enunciating it. So also the discussion of Christ's predestination (Dist. VII) has no direct soteriological connexion. There is, however, soteriological importance in the discussion of the grace of Christ in His humanity, which is contained in Dist. XIII, A.

'It must also be known that Christ according to His humanity received from His very conception the fullness of grace; for to Him the Spirit was given not according to measure, and in Him the fullness of the Godhead dwells bodily. It so dwells in Him, as saith Augustine to Dardanus (Ep. 187, 13, 40), that He is full of grace in every respect. Not so does the Godhead dwell in the

---

[7] Cp. 'Expos. orth. fid.' III, 6.

168

saints. As in our body there is sense in the different members, but not to the same extent as in the head (for in it is sight and hearing and smell and taste and touch; but in the other parts touch only), so in Christ dwells all the fullness of the Godhead, since He is the Head in which are all the senses. In the saints, on the other hand, there is, as it were, touch only; for to them the Spirit is given by measure, since they have received of His fullness. They have received, however, of His fullness, not according to essence, but according to likeness; for they never have received the same grace essentially, but have received a similiar grace. The Child therefore was full of wisdom and grace from His very conception.'

Dist. xv, xvi have also some bearing on our theme. In Dist. xv Lombard teaches that Christ assumed human infirmities, the penalties of sin, without human guilt. In Dist. xvi, again, he teaches that Christ's death was purely voluntary.

The main discussion of the work of Christ, however, is reached in Dist. xviii–xx. Dist. xviii deals with the merit of Christ. Some say that Christ won merit, not for Himself, but for His members only. But it is proved by the authority of Paul,[8] also by that of Augustine[9] and Ambrose (or more properly Ambrosiaster),[1] that Christ merited by the humility and obedience of His passion the glorification of His body and also the impassibility of His soul. Lombard, however, says that all these things which Christ merited for Himself, He merited from the instant of His conception. Christ had more merits in His passion than in His conception; but He had no greater virtue in the many merits than formerly in few.

Further, by His passion Christ merited the name that is above every name. This is the name of God, which He had by nature as God, but merited as man. This name, however, could have been merited without the passion because of His previous virtue. Christ, even if He had become a mortal man, might still have attained the above-mentioned glory. His mortality might have been consumed, and He might have been clothed with the glory of immortality.

[8] Phil. 2:8, 9.   [9] 'In Joh. Ev.' 104, 3.
[1] 'Comment. in ep. ad Philipp.' (on chap. ii, 9–11).

169

Lombard does not say whether these discussions have any reference to the doctrine of Rupert of Deutz as to the possibility of an Incarnation apart from the Fall, but it is obvious that they have a bearing on it. This is particularly clear when we proceed to the next question proposed and the answer returned to it.

'Why then did He will to suffer and die, if His virtues sufficed to merit the above things? For thee, not for Himself. How for me? That His passion and death might be for thee both pattern (*forma*) and cause, the pattern of virtue and humility, the cause of glory and liberty. . . . For He merited for us by the endurance of His death and passion, what He had not merited by the foregoing stages, viz. the entrance to paradise, and redemption from sin, from punishment, and from the devil, and by His death we have obtained these things, viz. redemption and the adoption of the sons of glory. For He Himself in dying became the sacrifice for our deliverance.'

Of these results of the passion and death of Christ Lombard takes first its positive or prospective effect, the opening of paradise. He says that God had decreed because of Adam's sin to close paradise to his posterity, unless his sin of pride should be expiated by a corresponding righteous act of humility. This was accomplished by the perfect sacrifice of Christ, 'who was brought much lower in humility, in tasting the bitterness of death, than the aforesaid Adam had been exalted in pride in enjoying a harmful delight through the eating of the forbidden fruit'. Thus Christ's death fulfilled the Divine decree, and annulled the writing that prevented our entrance into paradise. We are not to understand indeed that He could not have saved us in any other way than by His death; but, if we were to be saved by a sacrifice, no other sacrifice would have availed. 'For all other men were debtors, and scarcely was his own virtue and humility sufficient for each. None of them therefore could offer a sacrifice sufficient for our reconciliation.'

In Dist. xix Lombard comes to the negative or retrospective effects of Christ's passion and death, viz. our redemption from the devil, from sin, and from punishment.

'We are delivered from the devil and from sin by the death of Christ; because, as saith the Apostle, we are justified in His blood; and in that we are justified, i.e. are delivered from sins, we are delivered from the devil, who held us by the chains of our sins.'

Here Lombard first follows the lines of Abelard. We are delivered from our sins, because in the death of Christ there is commended to us the love of God, who gave His Son to die for us sinners, and we are by this pledge of Divine love kindled to love of God, who has done so much for us. Thus we are justified, i.e. freed from sins and made just by the awakening of love in our hearts, love which ensues upon the faith that looks at Christ and His passion, as the Israelites looked at the brazen serpent in the wilderness. By this look we are healed of our sins, and thus are freed from the devil, so that after this life he can find nothing in us to punish.

But now Lombard adds to this line of thought the doctrine of an objective redemption. Christ by His sacrifice has blotted out the guilt (*culpa*), through which the devil held us for punishment. Thus the latter has lost his power over us; and, though he is allowed still to tempt us, he cannot prevail. Christ has bound the strong man, i.e. has restrained him from the seduction of the faithful, 'and thus in the blood of Christ, who answered for the robbery which He did not commit (*qui solvit, quæ non rapuit*), we are redeemed from sin and thereby from the devil'. Here Lombard brings in the doctrine of Augustine that the blood of Christ, who was without guilt, having been shed, all the bond of our guilt by which the devil held us was annulled. The devil in fact was outwitted by Christ. 'What did the Redeemer to our captor? He extended to him His cross as a mouse-trap; He set there as a bait His blood.' Here almost for the last time in the history of theology appears the doctrine of the deceit practised on the devil. Lombard returns, however, to the thought that the devil was conquered, in which he finds the explanation both of the Incarnation and of the death of Christ.

'God therefore was made mortal man, that by dying He might conquer the devil. For unless it had been man who conquered the devil, man, who subjected himself to him of his own accord, would have appeared to be taken from him, not justly, but violently. But if it was man that conquered him, he lost man by

171

manifest right, and in order that man may conquer, it is necessary that God should be in him, to make him immune from sins.'

It will be remembered that Anselm also had retained this last form of the patristic doctrine of redemption.[2]

So much then for redemption from sin and the devil. Lombard next touches on redemption from punishment. Christ has redeemed us from eternal punishment by paying our debt. As regards temporal punishment, we have to wait for our full redemption till the future. But even now we are redeemed from guilt (culpa), though not from punishment, nor yet indeed altogether from guilt. We are not redeemed from it in the sense that it does not exist, but in the sense that it no longer rules over us.

Redemption from temporal punishment takes place as follows: Christ is said to have borne our sins on the cross, i.e. the punishment of our sins, in that through His punishment all temporal punishment owed for sin is entirely remitted in baptism, and is no more exacted from the baptised. Temporal punishment for sins after baptism is reduced in the sacrament of penance by the co-operation of the sacrifice of Christ.

Christ, then, is our Redeemer and Mediator, who reconciles men to God. But we are not to think that God did not love us before this reconciliation. In so far, however, as we were sinners, we were at enmity with God, and His enmity is removed by the Mediator. The whole Trinity is involved in the reconciliation, so far as the exercise of power in the blotting out of sins is concerned: the Son alone is involved in the fulfilment of the obedience, by which according to His human nature those things were accomplished, by believing and imitating which we are justified. Christ then is mediator as man; and all believers are healed of their wickedness, who believing in His humility come to love it, and loving it imitate it.

In Dist. xx Lombard discusses more fully the question already touched on in Dist. xviii, whether God could have redeemed us in any other way than through the death of Christ. Here he repeats what Augustine says in 'De. Trin.' xiii, 10, 13, that the Omnipotent could have saved us in other ways, but this was the

<hr>

[2] 'Cur Deus Homo', i, 22 (supra, p. 131).

172

fittest for healing our misery. What could so encourage us, and deliver us from all despair of immortality, as to know that God loved us so much that His son became incarnate and died for our sake? Moreover, God wished to conquer the devil by justice, not by power, which was done in that the devil lost his right to mankind by slaying Christ, upon whom he had no claim. This idea is developed at length with further quotation from Augustine's 'De Trin.' [3] Hugo of St Victor [4] is also quoted.

Christ's sacrifice, however, was not offered to the devil, but to the Trinity. On the altar of the cross, Himself the priest, He offered the sacrifice of our reconciliation, 'for all, as to the sufficiency of the price; but for the elect alone, as to the efficacy, in that He effected salvation for the elect alone'.

So far as the Jews and Judas gave Christ up to death, their work was evil, since their intention was evil; but so far as the Father surrendered Him, and as Christ surrendered Himself, the work was good, for the intention was good.

Lombard has gathered together in his doctrine of the work of Christ practically the whole tradition of the Latin Fathers, without, however, achieving a complete unification of the same. He has indeed, while passing by Anselm's standpoint of satisfaction, made use of that of merit; but he has not used the conception, so as to unify the whole of his material. What he has given us may, however, be reduced under three main heads: (1) the doctrine in various forms of an objective redemption from the devil, sin, and punishment, with, as its positive (or prospective) result, the opening of the gate of heaven; (2) the revelation of God's love in the death of Christ; (3) the example of His humility. These principal heads, however, by no means exhaust the whole material, which contains many additional incidental points. A particularly important distinction introduced by Lombard is that of the sufficiency and the efficacy of Christ's work: by means of this he deals with the problem introduced by Abelard, as to whether the redemption of the elect alone was the object intended in it. Another point worthy of notice is the connection Lombard establishes between the work of Christ and its particular application in baptism and penance.

[3] XIII, 12–14, 16–18.   [4] 'De Sacramentis', 1, 8, 4.

173

This leads us directly to the next point of our study. In order properly to understand Lombard's formal doctrine of the work of Christ, we must further consider the way in which he has supplemented it (1) with the doctrine of faith, hope, and love, (2) with the doctrine of the sacraments.

(1) The doctrine of Faith, Hope, and Love begins with Dist. XXIII of the third book: 3, 23, A takes up the thread from 3, 13, A.

'Since it was above asserted that Christ was full of grace, it is not irrelevant to inquire whether He had faith and hope, as well as charity. For if He lacked these things, He does not appear to have had the fullness of graces.'

Lombard's view then is, though suggested rather than explicitly developed, that grace manifests itself in the subject in the forms of faith, hope, and love; and that therefore, since grace flows from Christ as the Head to the members of His body, these virtues must appear first in Christ and then in His people.

Consequently we next have a discussion of the nature and mutual relation of faith, hope, and love. Faith is first of all a belief in the Christian verities (3, 23, B). This faith, however, is in itself a *qualitas informis* and not the faith that justifies. Justifying faith is faith which works by love (3, 23, D).

'For charity is the cause and mother of all virtues: if this is wanting, all the rest are possessed in vain; if it is present, all the rest are possessed' (3, 23, I).

Lombard points out that the faith of the Old Testament saints was the same as that of Christians, except that they believed in Christ to come, and we in Christ as come (3, 25, A).

So much then for faith and love in their mutal relations. We come next to hope, which is thus defined:

'Now hope is a virtue, by which spiritual and eternal blessings are hoped for, that is, are expected with confidence (*fiducia*). For hope is the certain expectation of future beatitude, arising from the grace of God and merits preceding both the hope itself, which by nature charity precedes, and the thing hoped for, that is, eternal beatitude. For to hope anything without merit, cannot be called hope, but presumption' (3, 26, A).

In order to bring out the full meaning of all this we must supplement it by a reference to the doctrine of grace and merit

174

in Lib. II, Dist. XXVII. Here Lombard distinguishes between virtue, which is a quality informing the soul, and the act of virtue, which requires the free will. Grace, then, informs the soul with charity, the root of all other virtues, and thereby enables it to put forth meritorious acts. The first of these is the *act* of justifying faith, which accordingly is said to merit justification and eternal life, but only as that act is of grace, and is informed by love.

What then is the love or charity on which all turns? The content of love is defined in the two precepts commanding love to God and to our neighbour, which are the essence of the whole law (3, 27, B). The ceremonial precepts of the Jewish law were only temporary (3, 36, C); but in the Decalogue the two precepts enjoining love of God and of our neighbour are expanded into three and seven commandments respectively (3, 37, A).

Finally, however, the law issues in the Gospel, which is still a law, though a law with a difference. The Apostle calls the Decalogue the letter that killeth:

'Not because it is a bad law, but because by forbidding sin, it increases concupiscence and adds transgression, unless grace delivers, which grace does not so abound in the law as in the Gospel. . . . The letter of the Gospel, however, differs from the letter of the law, because the promises are different. In the one case earthly, in the other heavenly, things are promised. The sacraments are different; for the one only signified, the other conferred grace. The precepts are different, as regards those which are ceremonial. For, as regards the moral precepts, they are the same, but are more fully contained in the Gospel' (3, 40, B).

(2) This leads us then to the doctrine of the Sacraments with which Lib. IV opens. Against the wounds of original and actual sin God has instituted these remedies (4, 1, A). A sacrament is thus defined:

'That is a sacrament properly so called, which is the sign of the grace of God, and the form of an invisible grace, in such a way that it bears its likeness and is itself its cause' (4, 1, B).

Only the sacraments of the Gospel, however, fully correspond to this definition. Those of the law were only signs of grace (*ibid.*).

175

After a brief discussion of the sacraments of the law, especially circumcision, Lombard proceeds to the sacraments of the new law, which he is the first definitely to enumerate as seven. 'These are Baptism, Confirmation, the Blessing of Bread, i.e. the Eucharist, Penance, Extreme Unction, Ordination, and Matrimony. Some of these supply a remedy against sin and confer assisting grace, as Baptism; some are only a remedy, like Matrimony; others support us with grace and virtue, as the Eucharist and Ordination' (4, 2, A).

A most important point is brought out as follows:

'Why were not these sacraments instituted at once after the Fall of man, since in them is righteousness and salvation? We say that the sacraments of grace were not to be given before the coming of Christ who brought grace: for they have obtained virtue from His death and passion' (*ibid.*).

It will be remembered that Lombard in his doctrine of the work of Christ established a connexion between it on the one hand and baptism and penance on the other (3, 19, D). Here, however, it is taught that all the sacraments without exception have virtue from the passion and death of Christ. This co-ordinates the sacraments, and makes them in spite of their great variety parts of one ordered system of grace.

Through Baptism we are cleansed (4, 8, A), and to that end receive the Spirit (4, 7, A). The *res sacramenti*, i.e. the grace conveyed in the sacrament, is justification (4, 3, M). Confirmation bestows the spirit for strengthening (4, 7, A). The Eucharist perfects us in good; since in it Christ Himself, the fountain of all grace, is received (4, 8, A). Penance as interior is a virtue, as exterior is a sacrament: each is the cause of salvation and justification (4, 14, A). The perfection of penance includes three parts, *compunctio cordis, confessio oris, satisfactio operis* (4, 16, A). Extreme Unction is instituted for the remission of sins and the relief of bodily weakness (4, 23, B). Orders convey spiritual power and office (4, 24, K). Matrimony exists for the remedy of concupiscence in the performance of conjugal duty (4, 26, B).

176

CHAPTER 4

THE EARLY FRANCISCAN THEOLOGY

ALEXANDER OF HALES

ALEXANDER OF HALES (d. A.D. 1245), the founder of the early Franciscan school of theology, and called *theologorum monarcha* and *doctor irrefragibilis,* employed the scholastic method introduced by Abelard in his immense 'Summa universæ theologiæ' with 'a virtuosity, which in richness of content, clearness of development, and definiteness of results, is far superior to the treatment of the earlier Summists, and even later has scarcely been surpassed'.[1] It has been usual in histories of theology to pass over Alexander and proceed straight to Thomas Aquinas, as the culminating point of the thirteenth century scholasticism. Harnack, for example, in his great 'History of Dogma' follows this method, saying of Thomas: 'In him his predecessors and contemporaries have disappeared.'[2] But the wisdom of this short cut is questionable. In the most recent literature bearing on mediaeval theology, the originality and importance of Alexander and the difference of the Franciscan theology from that of the Dominican Thomas is coming more and more to be recognised. I may refer especially to the notable work of Karl Heim, 'Das Gewissheitsproblem in der systematischen Theologie', 1911, and to the very important second enlarged edition of Seeberg's 'Dogmengeschichte'. Seeberg says with reference to the doctrine of the work of Christ in particular: 'In the doctrine of the atonement Alexander has set the standard for scholasticism at its zenith.'[3]

Alexander has in fact for the first time combined the new speculative theology of Anselm with the traditional material as collected in Lombard's 'Book of Sentences'. The speculative

---

[1] Windelband, 'Lehrbuch der Geschichte der Philosophie', 3rd ed., p. 259.
[2] D.G., 4th ed., vol. iii, p. 497. [3] D.G., 4th ed., vol. iii, p. 392.

method of Anselm was evidently congenial to Alexander. Nevertheless he adopts it only with considerable reservations. In his doctrine of principles [4] he views the epistemological basis of theology as an immediate experimental intuition of the Supreme Truth *per modum gustus*. In this intuition God is apprehended not only as the true but as the good. With regard to the derivation of other truths from the Supreme Truth, Alexander wavers between the idea that they are already implicitly given in the revelation of the Supreme Truth as consequences that can be speculatively drawn out of it, and the notion that they are given in a supra-rational manner by further revelations from the Supreme Truth.[5] Hence is explained the position which he takes up with regard to the speculative arguments of the 'Cur Deus Homo'. He cannot regard Anselm's reasons as so absolutely convincing that all must admit them; yet they have a necessity for faith.

'There are reasons for the things to be believed, which are strong and apparent, such as those showing in what way God is and is one and omnipotent, which the philosophers prove by many reasons, and there are reasons for the things to be believed, which are not apparent but weak according to human reason, such as those showing in what way Christ was incarnate and suffered, which Anselm introduces in his book 'Cur Deus Homo', as do others: nevertheless, reasons of this kind, when informed through faith infused by God, through the very light of faith acquire strength, so that reasons which appeared to be only based upon congruity and upon God's goodness, by the light of faith appear necessary.' [6] In accordance with this general position Anselm's theory of satisfaction is admitted, and everywhere by Alexander is treated as practically inexpugnable. But at the same time room is made for the fundamental Augustinian position that God could, if He had pleased, have redeemed men otherwise than by the Incarnation. In answering the question, whether human nature could be restored without satisfaction,[7] Alexander distinguishes between God's absolute power and His power with order. 'In considering the Divine power absolutely,

[4] 'Summa', pars I, qu. 1, ed. Nuremberg, 1481.
[5] Cf. Heim, op. cit. pp. 144ff.
[6] Pars III, qu. 78, memb. 5, art. 2, resp. ad 5.
[7] Pars III, qu. 1, memb. 4.

we think of a certain infinite might; and according to that mode there is no limiting the Divine power. And it is granted, that according to this mode it can restore human nature without satisfaction for sin. But in considering the same with order, then we regard it within an order of justice and mercy, and in this mode it is granted that God can do nothing except in accordance with mercy and justice.'

Justice again can be thought of in two ways, either so far as it is equivalent to the Divine essence, or as it is conditioned by respect to the creature, when it connotes the rewarding of each according to his merits. If then we ask, whether God can according to justice remit sin without satisfaction, and refer the term justice to what it principally signifies, i.e. the Divine essence, then what God can do according to His justice is the same as what He can do according to His power, and in this way therefore He can remit without satisfaction.

'But if it be referred to what is connoted, Anselm says that then possibility according to justice is possibility according to congruity of merit; and in this way the same Anselm says: God cannot remit unpunished sin without satisfaction, nor can the sinner attain to a beatitude such as he was to have had before sin' (ibid.).

With these limitations then Alexander accepts Anselm's theory. In pars III, qu. 1, 'de lapsu humanæ naturæ et ejus reparatione', and qu. 2, 'de convenientia incarnationis Christi', he has practically written out the whole of the 'Cur Deus Homo', following Anselm from point to point. He looks, however, beyond Anselm's theory, when in conclusion (qu. 2, memb. 13) he proposes the question raised by Rupert of Deutz as to the fitness of the Incarnation apart from the Fall. Alexander's view, sine præjudicio, is that the Incarnation was even apart from the Fall intended by God, in order that man might be blessed in all his powers, and might apprehend God not only internally by the intellect but externally by the sense. This could not take place unless God should assume a bodily nature, which again could be no other than a human nature. For, as Alexander has already shown (qu. 2, memb. 7), only the microcosm of human nature can contain the various Divine attributes which are manifested

179

in the many things of the world, and at the same time reduce them to unity.

In the following questions Alexander largely follows the guidance of Lombard's 'Sentences'; but he still continues to make use of the 'Cur Deus Homo', working up the Anselmic theory into a new unity with the additional patristic, and especially Augustinian, material drawn from the 'Sentences'. He has in fact drawn firmly the lines of a comprehensive theory of the work of Christ of a much wider scope than the Anselmic theory of satisfaction. Here for the first time in the history of the Latin Church do we obtain a unified view of Christ's work that is anything like as comprehensive as that of the great Greek Fathers. Hugo and Lombard have certainly prepared the way for this wider view; but it was Alexander who achieved it. His merit in this regard has by no means been sufficiently recognised.

The dominating principle of Alexander's whole doctrine of the work of Christ is the Augustinian doctrine of the constitution of Christ as the God-man with a view to the salvation of men by the Divine grace. The theory begins with qu. 3, which deals with the predestination of the Incarnation. Alexander here introduces fresh Augustinian material of the greatest importance for the total view. The meagre reference to the predestination of Christ in Lombard's 'Sentences', III, 10, C, F, does not, as has been pointed out, bring the subject into connexion with the work of Christ, nor touch on the relation of His predestination to ours. Alexander, however, gives the subject of Christ's predestination a commanding position, treating it before even the Incarnation itself, and so makes it, in accordance with his speculative leanings, the key of the whole doctrine. He is here a forerunner of Duns Scotus and the later Franciscan school, and also of the Calvinistic theology.

His doctrine is then as follows: The Son of God is predestinated, so far as He is man (qu. 3, memb. 1). His predestination and that of the elect are one in the Divine foreknowledge. But, as this predestination also connotes the grace and glory to be bestowed on the predestinated, from the temporal point of view there is an order of predestination, 'according to which we say that grace and glory in Christ is the *cause and pattern* of our grace and glory' (memb. 5). In the words 'cause and pattern' we have already the forecast of Alexander's further development of the work of Christ. He follows here lines suggested by Lombard (III, 18, E).

The working out of the scheme is contained in questions 11 and 12, which treat of the grace of Christ. This subject furnishes the preamble to the doctrine of His merit.

There is in Christ first of all (qu. 11, memb. 1), a grace of union. It is not possible for the human creature, by means of God's gift consisting in his natural condition, to be elevated and disposed to the Divine union: therefore grace is necessary to this end. This grace is called the grace of union (*ibid.*). It is twofold: it is a created grace which disposes to union, and an uncreated grace which completes it. The last is the Holy Spirit Himself (qu. 12, memb. 1, art. 1).

But further (qu. 11, memb. 2, 3), there is also grace in Christ, so far as He is Head of the Church and so far as He is a single man. As to the latter Christ lacked no grace possible to man (memb. 3). As to the former Alexander teaches as follows (memb. 2):

So far as Christ is God, He is the giver of grace immediately as the efficient cause; but as man He is the medium of grace in many ways:

(1) By the mode of faith, in so far as the God-man is the object of faith.

(2) By the mode of merit, 'because by His passion he merited from God, that grace should be given to all those who believe upon Him and love Him'.

(3) By the mode of desire or prayer, in so far as He prays for all who believe and desire grace.

(4) By the mode of disposition, as regards His human nature. Before the Incarnation human nature as a whole had become hateful to God because of original sin, but, as assumed by the Son of God into the unity of His Person, it was disposed to grace, as regards the predestinated, by a disposition of congruity or of dignity.

Christ's grace as Head of the Church, so far as it is created,

181

differs in idea, though not in substance, from the created grace of union: so far as it is uncreated and is the Holy Spirit, grace is in both respects one (qu. 12, memb. 1, art. 2).

In qu. 12, memb. 2, art. 3, § 4, Alexander further treats of the flow of grace from Christ the Head into the body of the Church. This takes place in three ways: (1) by the mode of merit, (2) by the mode of example, (3) by the mode of the Head.

(1) 'By the mode of merit there is grace in us from Christ Himself as a man; since it is He who merited for us the grace by which our sins might be remitted, and the grace by which we might know and love Him.'

(2) 'In the second mode He pours grace into us by the mode of example; for, just as we see that the example is related to the copy, and in a certain way the copy is derived from the example; so in Christ Jesus as man there is put before us an example of grace, to which we must fit and conform ourselves.'

(3) 'The third mode of the influence from Him is by the mode of the Head. Now there is a certain love and natural appetite of the head to the members. For the head itself loves the members with a certain natural love. Wherefore the animal spirits, which are in the head, out of this love run down from the head into the members. . . . According to this it is to be said, that the uncreated Spirit by which we have communion with the whole Trinity, i.e. the Holy Spirit, abounds in our Head, i.e. Christ; and the desire of Christ and of His blessed soul is that we should partake of His Spirit. But the Spirit Himself fulfils the desire which Christ has towards us, because of the love which He has towards us.'

Putting together now the above two passages (xi, memb. 2; xii, memb. 2, art. 3, § 4), we obtain a very clear conception of the way in which Alexander understands the work of Christ in general. It is as man that He is Mediator: as God, His work for human salvation in no way differs from that of the whole Trinity. As man, however, His work is twofold. On the one hand He obtains grace for us from God by His merit, intercession, and representation of human nature before God: in this way He is the cause of grace. On the other hand He is the object of faith and the example which we are to copy.

In qu. 16 Alexander goes on further to define the merit of Christ. In memb. 1 he distinguishes five modes of merit:

(1) The term 'merit' is sometimes improperly applied to the case where God rewards the good work of the wicked, as if they had won merit.

(2) The term *meritum de congruo* is used of the case where the saints are said, still being in sin, to merit the first grace (i.e. baptismal grace).

(3) The term 'merit' in the strict sense is used in the case where we make something that was not owed to be owed to us, as where by grace and the free will we merit eternal life.

(4) There is also a merit that makes what is owed to be more owed, as by further works done in grace.

(5) The term 'merit' is also used of the case where what is owed by reason of a habit is made to be owed by reason of an act, 'according to which mode Christ won merit for Himself; for though from the instant of His conception all good was owed to Him by reason of the habitual plenitude of grace, which He possessed, yet, through the succession of time, He made by the act of grace in His excellent works what was owed Him by reason of habit to be owed by reason of act'.

Alexander, however, next inquires, what was the exact difference between meriting by habit and meriting by act. As to the power of the merit, there was no difference; since Christ's charity could know no increase. But there is a difference as to the effect, at least as regards us (memb. 3, art. 2). In particular as regards the passion, Christ merited more by it as regards effect than He had merited before it (memb. 3, art. 3).

This difference is made plain, when Alexander comes to state the effects of Christ's merit, and how His merit is completed by His passion (memb. 4). First of all, Christ merited for Himself His exaltation. The Divine nature could not of course itself be exalted; yet Christ's Divinity could be manifested before the eyes of men, which happened in the resurrection (memb. 4, art. 1, § 1). He also merited the glorification of His body, or more properly indeed that of His soul, upon which the glorification of His body follows as a consequence (§ 2). Finally He merited the name above every name, i.e. the name Jesus or

Saviour (§ 3), and even the name of God, i.e. the manifestation of the name (§ 4).

For us (memb. 4, art. 2) Christ merited the removal of guilt (§ 1), the remission of eternal punishment (§ 2), and of temporal punishment (§ 3). In §§ 1, 2 Alexander introduces as an explanation the Anselmic doctrine of satisfaction [which, it may incidentally be remarked, is another proof that Schultz is right in regarding satisfaction as a species of the genus merit]. Christ's death is a satisfaction for our sin, inasmuch as it is His gift of His life, which is of infinite value in view of His Person and of His infinite charity. In § 3 we meet another aspect of the idea of satisfaction, different from the Anselmic, though equally derived from the practice of penance. Christ's passion is regarded as a voluntary endurance of penal suffering, the greatest possible in the world. This too, however, falls under the general notion of merit, precisely because it is voluntary.

Here then at last in Alexander's doctrine we have outlined the full mediaeval conception of Christ's merit and satisfaction. It is thought of along the lines of the penitential satisfaction in which the repentant sinner punishes himself and offers to God the gift of his self-humiliation and austerity. Not only the notion of the satisfaction as a gift to God, as in Anselm, but also the idea of it as a voluntary endurance of punishment—the whole concrete conception of it as practised in the Church—is utilised by Alexander, who thus importantly modifies the Anselmic doctrine. The fuller development of the idea of satisfaction is reserved for the next question (17), which deals with the Lord's passion. But before proceeding to this Alexander adds a most significant note (§ 4), showing how, from the standpoint he has reached, may be interpreted the old patristic doctrine of the destruction of our death by the death of Christ.

'The question that next rises is, how He destroyed our death by dying; for so say the authorities. . . . Reply: It is to be said that He destroyed death by way of cause. Christ's death is the cause, i.e. the meritorious cause of the destruction of future death in the glorious resurrection. For He destroyed eternal death in those that are His, since He brought it about that they should not fall into it; but He also destroyed the dominion of temporal death in many. For death used so to rule before that men through fear of death turned back; afterwards, however, it was brought about that death was not feared, but they gladly ran to death, as was evident in the case of martyrs.'

Nothing could better show the distance to which the mediaeval theology has moved from the patristic than to compare this short section with the 'De Incarnatione' of Athanasius. The subjective effect of the example of the death of Christ in removing the fear of death remains the same in both. But the mystical idea that the death of Christ is itself our death, so convincing to the Fathers, is to Alexander essentially unintelligible ('so say the authorities') until he has interpreted it by the clear rational notion that Christ by His death merited for men the destruction of death in the resurrection.

From this excursus we return to take up the further development of the doctrine of satisfaction in qu. 17, on the Lord's passion. Here for the second time Alexander works in the material of the 'Cur Deus Homo'. Memb. 3 is on the necessity of the Lord's passion. There was no externally imposed necessity for Christ's passion. He was under no compulsion to suffer and die, as we sinners are. There was only the internal necessity imposed by the end, viz. that of human redemption (art. 1). If men were to be redeemed by the payment of a price, or in other words, if satisfaction was to be made for sin, then Christ needed to die (art. 2). The ultimate necessity for His death was in the immutability of the Divine will, which had fixed on this way of redemption (art. 3).

The reason of this Divine will is given in memb. 4, which treats of the fitness of the passion of Christ. It befitted alike the Divine justice and the Divine mercy. As to the Divine justice, Alexander says:

'It belongs to the Divine justice never to let sin go without punishment. No sin is reduced to order except in punishment. . . . Either therefore sin is reduced to order in accordance with strict justice, so that it is punished eternally, or else by justice with mercy, so that it is punished temporally, and it is in this way that Christ suffered in accordance with justice because human guilt (reatus) could not be paid for by a mere man, as

Anselm proves. For man could not pay, but ought to pay. God could, but ought not. Therefore the God-man had to pay, being man who ought and God who could' (memb. 4, art. 1, § 1).

As regards the Divine mercy, Alexander lays down the principle, that 'the goodness and mercy of God must choose that way, which is best for salvation. But that way is best for salvation, which most has imitators' (§ 2).

The way of the cross is then shown to be the best in this sense. 'It is to be said after Augustine, "De Vera Religione", that all sin arises from the cause that we desire what Christ despised, and because we flee from what Christ endured or desired. Now Christ desired poverty, meanness, and subjection. Men, however, choose riches, pleasures, and honours. If therefore Christ had chosen the way of prosperity, this would not have befitted the Divine mercy, because then there would have been no departure from sin. Christ, however, Himself chose that way, in which there was a departure from sin.

'Or it may be said that the redemption of man was required to be wrought by satisfaction for sin. But satisfaction for sin ought to be penal and afflictive. Wherefore the redemption of man ought to be by a walk in the way not of prosperity, but rather of penal adversity' (ibid.).

Once more then we see that Alexander has modified Anselm's notion of satisfaction. Christ's satisfaction is for him no longer merely a supreme gift to God outweighing the dishonour done to Him by human sin. It must be a gift of endured suffering: 'Satisfaction for sin ought to be penal and afflictive.' It must be a voluntary vicarious penance and self-humiliation before God. Alexander was undoubtedly led thus to modify the Anselmic theory by his recurrence to the patristic doctrinal material, above all to the Augustinian sentence 'Suscipiendo pœnam et non suscipiendo culpam et culpam delevit et pœnam,' This can be shown by a reference to qu. 5, memb. 3, § 2, where Alexander, in discussing how Christ assumed punishment in order to deliver us from both guilt and punishment, teaches that there must be an equivalence of Christ's punishment as satisfaction for sin.

'In the punishment of satisfaction (pœna satisfactoria) two things are necessary, the will and the punishment, and it is not

186

necessary that the punishment, by which one makes satisfaction, should be greater than the punishment for which He makes satisfaction; but that the will joined to the punishment should be greater.' Thus the separation of the body from the soul in the death of Christ in virtue of the will accompanying it is satisfaction for the separation of the soul from God. This is a very different way of viewing satisfaction and the equivalence of satisfaction from that of Anselm. Led by the Augustinian sentence above quoted Alexander makes the *satisfactio* of Christ a penitential *satisfactio* in the full patristic sense, at once a positive gift and a passive endurance, not merely a positive gift only as in Anselm. The equivalence of suffering then comes into view and means have to be found to estimate it. Alexander returns to this point in qu. 17, memb. 2, art. 2, § 1, which deals with the generality of Christ's passion. 'It is to be said, that it is not required in satisfaction to suffer according to every kind of passion, but there is required an equivalence of punishment, that the punishment may be equivalent. Moreover, it is necessary that there be a condignity in the satisfaction.' In what this equivalence of punishment consisted we have already seen; it was in Christ's voluntary endurance. Other factors, however, must come in to make the satisfaction condign; what these are we shall see presently.

To come back to the point whence we digressed, we had followed Alexander in his doctrine of the fitness of the Lord's passion as far as that it befitted both the Divine justice and the Divine mercy (qu. 17, memb. 4, art. 1, § 1, 2). Finally in art. 2 Alexander deals with its fitness as regards us. That Christ suffered at the hands of men, had a fitness in so far as it was especially calculated to manifest His love. 'Wherefore He did not only deliver us from our original sin, but was also alluring us to love, when He endured contradiction of sinners against Himself.[8] Moreover, He prayed for them.' [9]

Memb. 5 of the same question deals with the measure of the passion.

First, as regards its measure in itself (art.1), since Christ's body was perfect and perfectly fitted to His soul, His pain was

---

[8] Heb. 12:3.   [9] Luke 23:34.

very great. Moreover, His passion was against His natural, though not against His rational, will. Its agreement with the latter indeed constitutes the merit of His passion.

As regards the measure of the passion with regard to satisfaction (art. 2), Alexander in part follows Anselm, but in part introduces fresh and important motives. His arguments are worth giving in detail in view of their relation to preceding and following developments. On the one hand it may be argued as follows:

(1) The life of grace is nobler than the life of nature. But by sin the life of grace is destroyed. Christ's death was only a death of nature. How then could it be a satisfaction for sin?

(2) The sin of Adam was universal, because it passed upon all. Christ's death was particular. The latter therefore cannot satisfy for the former.

(3) The sin of those who crucified Christ was as great as the value of His life, i.e. it was infinite: therefore a satisfaction for it at least is impossible.

On the other hand, however, it may be argued:

(1) 'He who suffers is not only man, but also God. If therefore any act whatever of His be weighed, it will compensate for any sin whatever.'

(2) 'Again the measure of merit is according to will and love. If therefore the person making satisfaction is the Person of God, and the love that greatest love, which exceeds all things, then He will be able to satisfy for any guilt whatever.'

The former of these two last cited reasons is of course from Anselm; the second, however, transcends Anselm by making use of Lombard's doctrine of merit (cf. Sent. II, Dist. 27, E), and carries us on to a more inward measure of Christ's satisfaction. Alexander decides in favour of these latter reasons. 'It is to be said that we must consider not how much the Lord suffered, but from how large a basis He suffered. Wherefore, if we consider the circumstances of His Person, because He is the Son of God, and the circumstances of His passion and so on, then the passion of Christ is sufficient for satisfaction of every kind and for all things.'

Alexander therefore replies to the former series of arguments, as follows:

188

(1) The natural death of Christ as man was not a sufficient satisfaction, but since He was also God, it was sufficient.

(2) Christ's satisfaction is as universal as Adam's sin. 'Wherefore Rom. 5 (:19) says, As through the disobedience of the one man, the many were made sinners, so through the obedience of the one, the many were made righteous, i.e. as regards sufficiency, though not as regards efficiency; just as the sun is the sufficient cause of the illumination of all men, yet is not the efficient cause of the illumination in all, for he is not so in the blind.'

(3) The sin of those who crucified Christ was not infinite, inasmuch as it was one of ignorance: they did not intend to take the life of God, but the life of man. Thus the satisfaction of Christ remains universally sufficient.

Qu. 18 proceeds to the effects of the Lord's Passion. These are (1) justification from sins, (2) reconciliation to God, (3) the loosing of the power of the devil, and (4) the opening of the gate of paradise.

Memb. 1 deals with justification.

'The passion of Christ is related to the remission of sins in various ways. For the passion of Christ exists in two ways, in its own essential nature, and in the soul. So far as the passion of Christ exists in its own essential nature, it is related to the destruction of sin in two ways, by the mode of merit and the mode of satisfaction. Now in sin there are two things, the stain and the guilt: the stain, which is deformity or dissimilarity to God: the guilt, which is liability to punishment. The passion of Christ is therefore the meritorious cause of the removal of the stain, because He merited for us grace and all that destroys sin. . . . It is also the cause that makes satisfaction for the liability to punishment. . . . But when the passion of Christ is considered according to the existence which it has in the soul, it also avails for the remission of sin according to four modes, by love, faith, sympathy, and imitation. For by these four modes it is joined to the soul, and has an existence in it. The passion of Christ therefore by love and faith avails for the removal of the stain. But the passion of Christ by sympathy and imitation avails for the destruction of the liability and guilt demanding punishment.'

This happens as follows: it works by love to the end of the

189

removal of the stain, in that it excites to love which covers a multitude of sins. As regards faith it works as efficient cause; for the passion of Christ, operating by faith which is informed by love, avails for the removal of the stain, in adults by their own faith, or in infants by the sacrament of faith, i.e. baptism, through the faith of the Church. As regards sympathy with and imitation of Christ's passion, these work for the removal of the liability to punishment, the former as the meritorious cause of the remission of punishment, the latter in the external act as the cause that makes satisfaction for punishment due.[1]

Alexander points out, however, the limits within which this doctrine is to be understood.

'It is to be said, that God Himself alone is the cause blotting out guilt, as the principal doer and agent. But the passion of Christ belongs to the class of the material cause or of the efficient cause, so far as it is a thing meritorious: because it is not the principal, but a co-operating cause.'

In memb. 2 reconciliation with God is discussed, under the general Augustinian point of view that Christ is Mediator as man. Here Alexander deals with the order of the different aspects of the work of Christ. Scripture has many names for Christ as Mediator, which illustrate the variety of His acts for us as man. There is first the act of union, whereby His humanity is united with the Son of God. Then follows the second act, whereby the human nature of Christ shares in the properties of the Divine nature. This is the act that makes Christ Mediator, and causes to abide in Him fullness of grace. It belongs, however, to fullness to communicate itself: there follows therefore a third act, whereby Christ as Head communicates grace to His members. This is done in particular as follows: Christ illuminates the mind, and awakes the affections; He regenerates us in baptism, and feeds us with doctrine; He redeems us from sin, original and actual; then He removes the flaming sword, or the veil of the mind, which separates us from God; finally He glorifies us.

The treatment of the remaining two effects of Christ's passion may be briefly summarised as follows: The power of the devil

[1] The reference here is to the sacrament of penance. Alexander means that the inner contrition of the penitent, and his external work of satisfaction, are, each in its own way, to be understood as a continuation of Christ's meritorious passion.

is generally lessened, in that true faith has largely banished idolatry. In the faithful he has no power, except what is granted him (memb. 3).

As regards the opening of paradise, the handwriting which excluded us from paradise was Adam's guilt. This had to be blotted out before we could enter paradise, i.e. before we could have the vision of God. This was done by the passion of Christ (memb. 4).

This is the conclusion of the doctrine of Christ's passion. It is very noteworthy how in Alexander's theology the centre of gravity of the whole doctrine of the work of Christ has come to reside in the passion, its merit, and the satisfaction made by it. In the patristic theology it is not the passion, but the death and resurrection of Christ as the destruction of death and beginning of new life for humanity, which most engage attention. In Anselm's theory of satisfaction it is still not the passion, but the death of Christ which is central: the great gift which Christ offers to God as satisfaction for sin is the gift of His life. Peter Lombard indeed begins to lay more stress on the passion; and, so far as he discusses the death of Christ separately from it, he does not do so in connexion with the work of Christ, but rather with reference to the questions, whether there was in it a division of the soul, or of the flesh from the Word (Sent. III, Dist. XXI), and whether Christ in His death was still man (Dist. XXII). Alexander follows Lombard in his similar treatment of the death of Christ (pars III, qu. 19), adding, however, a section (memb. 4 and 5) on the descent into hell, in which he depends on John of Damascus ('Exp. fid. orth.' III, 29, 112). But he has still more than Lombard concentrated attention on the passion itself by interpreting it, as Lombard does not, through the idea of satisfaction, at the same time modifying this idea, as has been shown, so as directly to evaluate the pain and suffering in the work of Christ. Not the death of Christ in itself, but His death as the culmination of His passion, therefore becomes for Alexander the central thing in the work of Christ. This is a great change in the presentation of the doctrine, and worthy of all observation.

How then does Alexander view the other point, so fundamental to the patristic doctrine, viz. the resurrection of Christ?

This is a critical question, in the light of Scripture and the Fathers, not only for him, but for the whole mediaeval theology that contemplates the work of Christ by means of the ideas of satisfaction and merit. Anselm, Hugo, and Lombard had simply left the question alone: it is, however, characteristic of the thoroughness of Alexander that he devotes qu. 20 to the resurrection of Christ, and discusses in memb. 2 the causality and effect of the resurrection. Just as he had previously (qu. 16, memb. 4, art. 2, § 4) reinterpreted the patristic doctrine of the saving effect of the death of Christ, so he does the same here for His resurrection, but at much greater length.

According to art. 1, § 2, 'The resurrection belongs to the class of meritorious cause, but not strictly; to the class of efficient cause, strictly; to the class of material cause, so far as it is believed; to the class of final cause, so far as it is loved, and to the class of formal or exemplary cause, so far as it is contemplated.'

This statement is expanded as follows: The resurrection is a meritorious cause, not strictly, but by way of intercession. Merit is not consistent with complete beatitude, but belongs to servitude: besides, in Christ's passion His merit was already consummated. (In other words, after His resurrection Christ no longer merits, but pleads His merit.) The resurrection is an efficient cause of the general resurrection, or rather Christ Himself in rising is the efficient cause by the mode of agency.[2] The first cause of the general resurrection is God; the mediate cause is the humanity of the Word, or rather the Word Incarnate. The first cause is, however, the very humanity of Christ appearing in glory at the judgment. As to whether the resurrection is a material cause, since it does not justify except as believed, which is not the case with the wicked, it is to be said that it is the cause of resurrection for both, with glorious transformation[3] in the good, so far as it is believed and loved, but without transformation in the wicked. In the former way it is a material cause in the good. In the second way it is an efficient cause in all.

Art. 2 examines the causality of the resurrection in justification. Alexander makes the same distinction as in the case of the

[2] Jn 5:25.　　　[3] 1 C. 15:15.

192

passion, and treats of (1) its causality in itself, (2) its causality in the soul. In itself the resurrection is the cause of justification by the mode of disposition; because the whole of human nature is ordered to the human nature of Christ, wherefore, since Deity is united with humanity in Christ, the whole of humanity is exalted, so that it may be in complete possession of Deity. Human nature is therefore disposed more and more by the Incarnation and the Passion, and still more by the Resurrection, to higher grace. The resurrection is also in itself the cause of justification by the mode of example. Christ's resurrection is an example of our present justification from guilt to grace, and also of our future justification from misery to perfection. In the soul again the resurrection justifies, as it is believed and loved. In these ways then it appears that not only the passion but the resurrection also is the cause of justification. But Christ's resurrection is also a sign of our resurrection, and therefore justification is in Scripture [4] more attributed to the resurrection than to the passion, since the resurrection is not merely, like the passion, the cause, but also the sign and the consummation of justification.

Art. 3 discusses the resurrection of Christ as the cause of the general resurrection of the body. The causality of the resurrection is wider than that of the passion. Christ's sufferings were in order to the justification of the saved, but He was rewarded for them by His resurrection, with judicial power over both good and bad.

Art. 4 deals with the question: Was Christ's resurrection the immediate, or the remote cause of our resurrection? By His passion Christ merited for us justification, resurrection, and glory, both as regards body and soul. There followed at once the deliverance of the souls in Limbo by the descent of Christ's soul into Hades, but the deliverance of bodies waits for His bodily appearance at the last judgment to renew the world. While, therefore, the deliverance of souls followed immediately upon the passion, the resurrection of bodies is separated in time from Christ's resurrection.

Art. 5 inquires whether Christ's resurrection was a necessary or a contingent cause of ours. It was the necessary cause of ours

Rom. 4:25.

in accordance with the Divine fore-ordination, only, however, after the fall the necessary cause because of the Divine justice (i.e. because this required Christ's passion and death).

Finally art. 6 deals with the difference between the causality of the passion and that of the resurrection. The passion of Christ is the meritorious cause of our resurrection and felicity; but His descent into hell and His resurrection are the efficient cause.

This section on the causality of the resurrection is of the utmost importance in the history of theology. What is left here of the old patristic view which is so clear in Gregory of Nyssa's 'Great Catechism' (32) according to which the resurrection works directly like a ferment in humanity? Only a trace, in so far as it is idealised into the view that human nature was increasingly disposed to grace by the Incarnation, Passion, and Resurrection. In the main Alexander has entirely reinterpreted the causality of the resurrection. As regards our resurrection, it is not Christ's resurrection, but rather the Risen Christ at the Judgment that is personally the efficient cause of it, He having obtained the judicial power by His merit. Causality is here not physical but personal. As regards justification, the resurrection no more as with Gregory restores a nature whose dross has been purged by death, but it is strictly the passion that is the cause of justification, and the resurrection is the cause only indirectly by way of its subjective effects. Rom. 4:25 can therefore only mean that Christ's resurrection is symbolically, not actually our justification.

Alexander rounds off his doctrine with a question on the ascension (qu. 23). According to memb. 7, art. 2, § 2, its effects for the Church on earth are as follows: It is the cause of the hope of beatitude, also of spiritual love to Christ according to His Deity; the Spirit could only be given when Christ was ascended, His flesh being an impediment to pure spiritual love of God.

Thus then ends Alexander's express doctrine of the work of Christ, which, however, as in the case of Hugo and in that of Lombard, needs to be completed by some reference to his doctrines of law and grace, and of the sacraments.

(1) Alexander's doctrine of the law. He distinguishes the

eternal law, the law of nature, the law of Moses, and the law of the Gospel.

According to pars III, qu. 26, the eternal law is the order of the universe, and is one with the will of God directed towards the good. It derives its authority, wisdom, and goodness from the three Persons of the Trinity. Its subjects are all rational and irrational creatures alike, the rational in accordance with the freedom of the will, while the irrational obey of necessity. The eternal law is immutable in principle, but variable in execution. The basis of this doctrine is especially Augustine's 'De Vera Religione'.

Qu. 27 treats of natural law, which is the law within the heart of rational creatures. It is in essence one with the uncreated eternal law; but, in so far as it is written in the heart, it is different and is a thing created.

Qu. 28 is on the law of Moses, in which the law of nature was expanded into the Decalogue, while ceremonial and judicial precepts were added. Memb. 1, art. 1, deals with the utility of this law. In the first place, it was given to assist the law of nature. That contained the seeds of righteousness; the law of Moses was added with an authority calculated to bring them to fruition. In the second place, however, it came in to coerce the law of sin in the members. Thirdly, on its ceremonial side it is a figure of the Gospel.

Qu. 60 discusses the law and precepts of the Gospel in general. Here memb. 4 treats of its relation to the law of nature. 'As nature is in order to grace, so the law of nature is in order to the law of the Gospel.' It is not abolished but perfected by the Gospel. 'The law of nature is not a part of the law of the Gospel; yet it is the foundation of it, just as nature is the subject of grace, and therefore it is that whatever the law of nature commands, the law of the Gospel commands, yet by a higher reason.'

Memb. 5 has for its subject the relation of the law of Moses to that of the Gospel. They are one in their general, but different in their individual, conception. As to their agreement, both have behind them the one God, who is a God both of goodness and severity; they have also one end, which is righteousness, and one truth. On the other hand, they differ in that the one was given through a mere man, the other through Christ. The one seeks the common aim by turning man away from evil by fear, the other by working good through love. Finally, truth is in a figure in the law, but plainly revealed in the Gospel.

In memb. 6 Alexander works out still further in detail the difference between the law of Moses and the Gospel. Amongst others, we note that the rewards of the law were temporal, while those of the Gospel are eternal. The law was only given to Israel, whereas the Gospel is for the world. But the great difference, over and above these already stated in memb. 5, is that the Gospel justifies, as the law cannot do, and this because it brings in its sacraments grace, whereas the sacraments of the law were without grace.

Memb. 7 explains how the law is contained in the Gospel. As regards the ceremonial elements, law is compared to Gospel, as sign to thing signified; as regards the moral elements, as plant to fruit. The law of nature was the seed, the law of Moses the plant, the Gospel the fruit.

Memb. 8 treats of the additions made by the Gospel to the law. As regards the meaning of the law, the Gospel adds to the law no new precepts, but adds an elucidation of the precepts. As regards the letter of the law, the Gospel adds to the ceremonial precepts, in so far as fulfilment adds to promise; to the moral precepts it adds the prohibition of the cause and occasion to that of the effect: to the judicial precepts addition is made by the perfection of the imperfect.[5]

(2) Alexander's doctrine of grace. In qu. 69, memb. 2, art. 1, Alexander raises the important question, Whether grace is anything real in the subject of grace, or exists only in the acceptation of the Giver of grace? [6] The reply is, that grace is something in the subject of grace, since he is pleasing to God. But that is pleasing to God, which is deiform, or is made like God. What is hateful to God is want of deiformity, i.e. sin. Thus in the subject of grace there is likeness of God, which merits eternal life, which is complete likeness to God.

The next question (art. 2) is whether grace is uncreated or a thing created. Lombard had identified grace with love or

---

[5] Cf. Matt. 5:33, 39. [6] I.e. does grace exist in us, or in God's attitude to us ?

charity, and both with the Holy Spirit. 'It certainly appears that charity is the Holy Spirit, which informs and sanctifies the qualities of the soul, so that by them the soul is informed and sanctified; without which a quality of the soul is not called a virtue, because it is of no avail to hear the soul' (Lib. II, Dist. 27, F). Alexander is more cautious; he teaches that grace is both uncreated and created. Uncreated grace is the Holy Spirit (*forma transformans*); created grace is the effect of the Spirit in the soul (*forma transformata*).

As regards the natural life of the soul grace is an accident, but as regards its higher life or *bene esse* it is substantial (art. 3). Virtue, again, is related to grace as the ray to the light (art. 4).

Art. 5 touches for the first time on an important distinction, due to Alexander himself, between general grace (*gratia gratis data*) and saving grace (*gratia gratum faciens*). General grace includes any and every gift given without merit, such as the image of God given with creation, or added knowledge. Saving grace is a particular determination of general grace, and means either the first saving gift of grace, as undifferentiated, or the first virtue in which it is manifested, as faith.

In qu. 73, memb. 1, Alexander teaches that 'gratia gratis data', which is not 'gratia gratum faciens', imparts the knowledge of God; it disposes to salvation. Its results are 'fides informis, spes et timor servilis', faith without love, and servile hope and fear (memb. 3).

On the other hand (qu. 70), the effects of 'gratia gratum faciens' are, in so far as it is light, to cleanse, to illuminate, and to perfect (memb. 1); in so far as it is life, to quicken the soul, to make it like God and pleasing to Him (memb. 2); in so far as it is motion, to justify, to awake, to draw out acts of merit (memb. 3). It destroys mortal sin, but leaves the 'fomes peccati' or kindling-matter of sin (i.e. concupiscence), and thus the possibility and even necessity of venial sin (memb. 5). The moment of the expulsion of sin is the same as that of the infusion of grace (memb. 7); as grace comes in, sin departs.

Some further points in connexion with saving grace are discussed in qu. 69, memb. 3, art. 5. The difference between grace before and after the Fall is accidental. The same principle which was the ground of health before the Fall, is the remedy after it.

It is further taught (§ 1), that there is no essential difference between grace before and after the Incarnation; nevertheless there is a different efficacy of grace. Before, grace existed along with the guilt of original sin, which was a hindrance to the vision of God; this hindrance could not be removed except by the passion of the God-man. Further (§ 2), the difference between grace in the child and in the adult is that in the child it informs only, in the adult it both informs and operates. Memb. 5 of the same question deals with the cause of grace. The efficient cause of grace is God. Is there a meritorious cause on our part? Grace according to its definition excludes merit (art. 1). Merit, however, is to be distinguished as 'meritum congrui' and 'meritum condigni'. God is so generous that He allows merit where none strictly exists (art. 2, § 1). What then is the position of him who does what he can (*quod in se est*)? Can he merit grace? No: nevertheless God by reason of the Divine immutability must give him grace (art. 3).

The distinction between 'meritum congrui' (i.e. the disposition for grace which God in His goodness cannot overlook) and 'meritum condigni' (strict merit) is a new creation of Alexander's. It is important to observe that together with his other distinction between general and saving grace, it enables him to modify the Augustinian position that man can in consequence of original sin do no good thing apart from grace. He cannot indeed merit strictly without the 'gratia gratum faciens', but a 'meritum de congruo' is possible in virtue only of 'gratia gratis data', i.e. in one who is not strictly speaking in a state of grace.

(3) Alexander's doctrine of the sacraments. Were sacraments necessary in the state of innocence? (pars IV qu. 1, memb. 2, art. 1).

'Sacraments have been ordained for the apprehension (*intellectus*) of grace, and for the remedy which is given through grace. As far, therefore, as they have been ordained for remedy, they are not necessary in the state of innocence. So far again as concerns the fact that they have been ordained for apprehension, inasmuch as they were (afterwards) added for the apprehension of remedial grace, they were not (then) necessary in this way. But if in them there was an apprehension of a certain grace perfecting unfallen nature, in this way they may be said to be necessary.'

According to art. 2, 'The sacraments were at once necessary after the Fall, and were of vital necessity; wherefore says the gloss on the words, Who is the figure of Him that was to come:[7] "From the side of Christ flowed forth the sacraments, viz. the water of washing and the blood of redemption, through which the Church is saved". Wherefore it is said in Eph. 2(:3): "We were by nature children of wrath", i.e. as the gloss explains, debtors of eternal punishment. The sacraments exist to take away this debt, and especially the sacrament of baptism and the others which have been (instituted) for the remedy of original sin. Besides, since with Abel and Cain there began the division of the spiritual Jerusalem from the city of Babylon, it was necessary that there should be some sacred signs by which the citizens of Jerusalem should be distinguished from the citizens of Babylon.'

According to memb. 3, art. 1 the institution of sacraments is either direct, by Divine precept, or indirect, by Divine counsel (i.e. inspiration): in the latter way were instituted the sacraments of natural law. Only the sacraments of the written law and of grace have the obligation of the precept (art. 2).

Memb. 5, art. 2 discusses whence the sacraments have the virtue of sanctifying. This is above all from faith (§ 1), which perfects the intellect and is the foundation of all good. But from what article of faith in particular? Alexander replies (§ 2): from the passion and resurrection of Christ. The sacraments remove defect and add virtue: 'per appropriationem'[8] it may be said that, while faith in the passion removes defect, i.e. merits remission of sin, faith in the resurrection merits renewal of life through grace moving the will toward good. This mode of speech is, however, only 'per appropriationem'. In general the sacraments have virtue from faith in Christ *simpliciter.*

The above applies to all sacraments: all ultimately have their effect of grace from the passion of Christ. But the pre-Christian sacraments sanctified simply by faith in the passion, of which

[7] Rom. 5:14.   [8] I.e. by *appropriating* a particular cause to a particular effect.

they were symbols. On the other hand the sacraments of the new law, through sanctification or benediction, themselves contain grace (memb. 7).

Qu. 8 expands the above general doctrine of the sacraments, with special reference to the sacraments of the law of the Gospel.

Memb. 3, art. 5, §7 again raises the question, from what is the virtue of the sacrament, and gives a much fuller reply.

'There are many things, from which the sacraments are said to have virtue. One is the institution itself of the Saviour, who instituted them to sanctify. Another is the form of words of Christ and the Church, according to which words are instituted to sanctify, and are uttered by the ministers of the Church. The third is the due action itself of the ministers. The fourth is the passion of Christ with the resurrection. The fifth is the faith itself of the Church concerning the Creator and the Saviour.

'Now, the institution is as it were the first cause; the minister is the second cause, receiving its virtue from the first. The words are by way of instrument; the due action, as it were, is the disposition [9] on the part of the ministers. The passion with the resurrection is as that which gives efficacy to the grace that justifies from punishment as regards its essence, and is a disposition on the part of the Saviour to save fully. Faith again is as it were a disposition on the part of the recipient or of the Church itself.'

Alexander does not hesitate therefore to say that all the Christian sacraments are the cause of grace by reason of the *opus operatum* (memb. 4, art. 1). It is God indeed who alone infuses grace, yet man may dispose to the reception of grace: thus God alone sanctifies, yet the priest, the minister of God, also sanctifies (memb. 3, art. 5, § 2).

The grace given in the sacraments is the 'gratia gratum faciens', it serves both for the healing of the wounds of injured nature and for assistance in good works (memb. 4, art. 2, § 1; cf. memb. 2, art. 2, § 1).

Finally, Alexander has endeavoured, not very successfully indeed, to explain why there are seven sacraments and no more, and to arrange them in an ordered system of grace (memb. 7,

---

[9] I.e. the due action *disposes* the minister to be a channel of grace.

art. 2; cf. memb. 4, art. 1). In memb. 2, art. 1 he distinguishes Baptism and the Eucharist from the rest. All the sacraments of the new law surpass in worth those of the Mosaic law, in so far as they were instituted by Christ and His Apostles; but these two, Baptism which is of the greatest necessity, and the Eucharist, which is of similar necessity—to repair daily infirmities—these are of peculiar dignity, in that they were instituted by Christ Himself.

It may be added that the subject of justification is treated under the head of the sacrament of penance: we have to turn for it to pars IV, qu. 70, 'Of the effect of contrition, which is the justification of the ungodly'. Memb. 1 defines justification as the rectitude of the free will.

According to memb. 2, in order to the justification of the adult contrition is required; inasmuch as all commit, if not actual mortal, yet venial sins. If there were no actual or even venial sins, contrition would not be required, justification having already taken place in baptism by grace and the faith of the Church. Justification is not preceded by, but simultaneous with, contrition (which is repentance induced by the love of God, and thus dependent on the same grace which justifies): hence justification is unmerited as regards 'meritum condigni'. Attrition (i.e. repentance induced by fear of punishment preceding the advent of grace) may, however, merit justification by way of 'meritum congrui'.

Memb. 3 declares that contrition by reason of the grace involved in it purges from guilt. Memb. 4, art. 1 states its further results, as follows:

'The effect of grace taken in itself is to destroy guilt: according as there is joined to it habitual or actual grief of the will together with continued detestation of sin, it blots out eternal punishment: according as there is joined to it pain of sense it destroys the punishment of purgatory under a condition, viz. if that grief suitably corresponds, according as it is accompanied with works of mercy and satisfaction.'

In art. 2, § 3, Alexander says, as regards the remission of temporal punishment, that contrition remits the whole punishment. if it is sufficient; otherwise it remits only a part.

THE FORMATION OF THE MEDIAEVAL SYNTHESIS

Now at last that we have completed our account both of Alexander's doctrine of the work of Christ, and of his complementary doctrines of the law, of grace and of the sacraments, we may stop and review the main features of his scheme, so as to bring out its significance and measure his achievement. It is an immense theological material which he unrolls before us, and there is perhaps a danger that the very wealth of ideas may prevent us from seeing the scheme as a unity. What requires to be done is therefore to consider it in its broad outline.

Alexander's view is based ultimately upon the Divine predestination. There is a relative but not an absolute necessity of the Incarnation and the passion: all necessity in this matter ultimately depends upon the Divine sovereignty. Subject to the Divine decree, however, there was a necessity both of the Incarnation and of the Passion. The Incarnation was necessary even apart from the Fall, in so far as man, a creature of sense as well as intellect, needed a revelation to the senses as well as to the intellect. It agrees with this that the sacraments were necessary even in the state of innocence, in so far as they serve for the apprehension of grace.

The main cause of the Incarnation, however, was sin, which necessitated the passion of Christ. Christ indeed by His charity merited grace even from His conception, but by His acts of love merited it in a different way. The grace merited in both these ways, however, is positive, viz. the infusion of *caritas*, which makes good works possible. So far as grace is the remedy of sin, Christ merited it by His passion alone: by His passion also He merited the opening of paradise to sinners. The passion has also, however, a psychological influence, and the same is true of the resurrection: they serve as example, reveal the love of God, and awaken faith. Finally, the resurrection invests Christ with judicial power.

The complement of the work of Christ as the procuring of grace is the Divine revelation in the law, culminating in the law of the New Testament. The law is accompanied throughout by sacraments, through which grace is given, though only to

202

faith: these sacraments possess virtue from the Lord's passion and resurrection: only the sacraments of the new law, however, contain grace.

Such is the general outline of Alexander's doctrine. In it at last we possess the complete Western parallel to the Greek doctrine of the work of Christ, or, as we may say, the mediaeval synthesis in contrast with the Greek synthesis. Some differences between the Greek theology and Alexander's theology have been noted in our previous study: now, however, we are concerned rather with the similarities occurring along with the differences, similarities which, it may be observed, must necessarily exist between all complete schemes of Christian theology, in so far as they aim at explaining the same ultimate results from the same ultimate causes.

For the Greeks the work of Christ is in the first place the bringing of the knowledge of God and of the law by the Incarnate Logos. Alexander has reminiscences of this view in its wider aspect in his doctrine of the fitness of the Incarnation even apart from sin; but what mainly corresponds to it is his doctrine of the law, which, however, is traced not to the Logos, but to God.

The next point of the Greek view is that by His Incarnation, Death, and Resurrection, Christ has purged away sin, and deified humanity. Finally, He has also in His death paid a ransom to the devil, and has offered a sacrifice of reconciliation to God. All the blessings thus obtained are communicated to mankind in the sacraments: they are, however, properly religious blessings and there remains for the recipients the ethical task of good works, apart from which their possession cannot be assured.

For this complex of ideas Alexander substitutes the Western view that Christ by His merit and satisfaction has obtained grace, including both the remission of sins and the infusion of love which enables the recipient to do good works and merit salvation. Christ has further won for men the opening of paradise. It is not then as in the Greek view salvation itself which in anticipation is conferred on men in the sacraments, as a possession to be assured indeed by good works: what the sacraments confer

203

is rather grace, which makes good works possible and enables salvation to be merited.

There remains in Alexander's scheme the psychological influence of the passion and resurrection in awakening faith and love and stimulating to virtue. This view of the work of Christ is indeed anticipated in the Greek theology so far as Christ is viewed as in His death an example of virtue and as by His resurrection awakening faith (Athanasius); but it is in the West that it receives through Augustine and Abelard its greatest development. It is in general a natural addition to the sacramental view of Christianity, which, however, has no very logical place in its system. There is indeed more place for it in the Greek theology, in so far as there the benefits conferred on man through the sacraments are religious rather than ethical, and man is left to the exercise of his free will to win virtue; a psychological influence of the Incarnation is, however, not altogether incapable of combination with the idea of free will. In the Western scheme where the sacraments confer grace, i.e. the miraculous and supernatural infusion of charity, a natural psychological effect of the Incarnation appears either as itself unnecessary or else to make sacramental grace unnecessary. The same thing, viz. love as the principle of action is viewed as being produced both by a supernatural and a natural cause; and therefore, inevitably, on the principle of the parsimony of reason, the one view must ultimately be reduced to the other. There remains here in fact a problem for subsequent theology, to determine which view is to predominate.

Alexander's theology deserves a prolonged and careful study not only on account of its historical importance, but also because of its real value. The theology of the early Franciscan school may also be studied in his disciple Bonaventura (d. A.D. 1274), of whose doctrine of the work of Christ, Baur has given an account.[1] But it is preferable to study it at first hand in Alexander, if for no other reason than that in Bonaventura we lose the advantage of Alexander's new systematic dispositions. Bonaventura wrote no great theological 'Summa', but only the 'Breviloquium', a compendium of doctrine, and also a commentary on

---

[1] 'Die Christliche Lehre von der Versöhnung', pp. 214ff.

the 'Sentences'. Though the former is a fine work, it necessarily lacks the breadth and fullness of treatment of Alexander's 'Summa', while the latter necessarily conforms to the system of the 'Sentences', and so fails to reproduce the full gain of Alexander's undoubtedly great improvement over Lombard in the matter of combination.

CHAPTER 5

THE DOMINICAN THEOLOGY

THOMAS AQUINAS

WITH Thomas Aquinas (d. A.D. 1274), *doctor angelicus,* we reach the climax of the scholastic movement, and the system which at the present day is recognised as the official theology of the Roman Catholic Church. Thomas is distinguished above all by method and clearness. Moreover, upon the basis of a more thorough study of Aristotle, begun by his master Albert the Great and continued by himself, he has much more completely than either Alexander or Bonaventura succeeded in establishing a working relation between the Peripatetic philosophy on the one hand and the Christian faith on the other. Albert and Thomas were Dominicans, and the Thomist theology was accepted as the theology of the Dominican order in opposition to the Franciscan theology of Alexander and Bonaventura.

In the first place, Thomas defined very differently from Alexander the relation between reason and revelation. While Alexander hesitated between the view that the doctrines of natural theology were the antecedents and the doctrines of revelation the consequences of the intuition of God as the first truth, and the view that the doctrines of revelation were fresh truths not to be deduced by human reason from the first truth, Thomas decided very definitely for the latter alternative, and moreover distinguished very exactly between the spheres of natural and revealed theology. On the one hand reason can prove the existence of God : on the other it cannot demonstrate the ecclesiastical doctrines of the Trinity, creation in time, orginal sin, the Incarnation, the sacraments, purgatory, the resurrection of the flesh, the final judgment, eternal beatitude and damnation.[1]

[1] Cf. Überweg-Heinze, 'Grundriss der Geschichte der Philosophie', 9th ed., vol. ii, p. 302.

Thomas declares the doctrines of revelation to be above reason, but not contrary to reason. Reason can never prove their truth, which rests solely on their Divine authority: if it could, it would overthrow the merit of faith. It can, however, starting from the basis of authority, manifest the implications of revealed doctrine. It can also invariably destroy the reasons assigned by adversaries against the Christian faith; for since the latter rests upon infallible truth, all reasons against it must be fallible.[2]

Thomas has also given a reason why supernatural revelation is absolutely necessary for the salvation of man. It is 'because man is related (*ordinatur*) to God, as to a certain end, which exceeds the comprehension of reason. . . . But the end ought to be foreknown to men, who are required to order their purposes and their actions towards the end. Wherefore it was necessary for man's salvation, that certain things which exceed human reason should be known to him by Divine revelation.'[3]

Two fundamental principles of the theology of Aquinas here appear together. As Ritschl has pointed out,[4] he has combined in his doctrine of God the Neoplatonic conception of His absolute transcendence of the world with the Aristotelian notion of final cause. In the combination, moreover, the former, which expresses God's essential Being, dominates the latter, which denotes His relation to the world. The result is therefore, that 'God's relation to the world and to all that in it is ordered by God, bears the mark of contingency'.[5] By this means, however, a firm philosophical basis is given to the final subordination of all other attributes expressing God's relation to the world to that of His absolute power; so that the Augustinian doctrine to this effect is substantiated against the Anselmic view that God's action is subject to a moral necessity. To this point we shall return, when we come to the doctrine of Thomas on the work of Christ.

Before this doctrine, however, in his system appear the doctrines of law and grace. This arrangement, in which Thomas deviates from his predecessor Alexander, is a result of the determination of his system by the thought that God is the chief end of man. It is in direct pursuance of this thought, that he now

[2] Cf. 'Summa Theologica', I, qu. 1, art. 8.   [3] *Ibid.* qu. 1, art. 1.
[4] Cf. 'Rechtfertigung und Versöhnung', 2nd ed., vol. i, p. 61 (English trans., p. 47).
[5] *Ibid.* p. 62 (English trans., p. 47).

considers law and grace as the general principles, by which man is ordered to his supreme end.

The doctrine of these subjects is developed as follows: The ultimate end of man is beatitude, which consists in the vision of the Divine Being. For man to obtain beatitude, however, good works are necessary. Since the vision of God is beyond all created nature, God alone has it naturally, and without any progress towards it. Angels may acquire it by one motion of meritorious operation. 'Men, however, obtain it by many motions of operations, which are called merits, wherefore according to the Philosopher (i.e. Aristotle), beatitude is the reward of virtuous operations.' [6]

The external principle moving us towards the good is God, who instructs us by the law, and assists us by grace (II, 1, qu. 90, introd.). In qu. 91 Thomas distinguishes first the eternal law, which is the rule of the Divine providence, eternally immanent in the Divine reason (art. 1). Then there is the law of nature, or the light of reason implanted in us by God (art. 2), which is carried out into its particular applications by the human law of the state (art. 3). Finally, there is the Divine law, which is necessary, beyond the law of nature, in order to direct us to eternal beatitude, since this exceeds the nature of man as such (art. 4). This again has the two forms of the old and new law, i.e. the law of the Old Testament and the law of the New Testament (art. 5): 'The new law is the Gospel itself' (qu. 106, art. 1).

The law of nature was a law implanted in the heart; the old law was a written law. The new law contains both characteristics. It is at once written, and implanted in the heart. The latter is its chief characteristic: 'that which is most important in the law of the New Testament, and in which its whole virtue consists, is the grace of the Holy Spirit, which (grace) is given through faith in Christ; and therefore above all the new law is the very grace of the Holy Spirit, which is given to believers in Christ' (loc. cit.). From the law of nature it differs in that this grace is a supernatural gift beyond the light of reason.

With regard to the written part of the new law, this consists of such things as pertain to the grace of the Holy Spirit, either

---

[6] 'Summa Theologica', II, 1, qu. 5, art. 7.

208

as disposing to, or regulative of this grace (loc. cit.). Since grace is mediated to us through the Incarnation, 'therefore it is fitting that the grace flowing to us from the Incarnate Word should be conducted to us by some external sensible channels, and also that from the inner grace, by which the flesh is subdued to the spirit, certain sensible works should proceed' (qu. 108, art. 1).

With regard then to the relation of the old and the new law, beyond the great difference that the new law is accompanied with grace, the following differences emerge. The ceremonial elements of the old law Christ fulfilled, substituting for the shadow the substance. The precepts He fulfilled in general by His work and His doctrine; by His work, in that He kept the law; by His doctrine, (1) in that He explained the true sense of the law, (2) in that He showed how the precepts might be better kept, (3) in that He added to the precepts certain counsels of perfection (qu. 107, art. 2). These last, the ascetic elements in the new law, open a more immediate way to the supernatural beatitude, which is the end of the law; inasmuch as they make complete separation from the world (qu. 108, art. 4).

So much then for the Divine instruction in the law; we now come to the Divine assistance, which is by grace.

According to qu. 110, art. 1, grace means three things: (1) God's love, according to which He holds anyone in favour (*gratum*); (2) any gift of His grace; (3) the thanks, which we return to Him, saying grace. Grace in the second and third senses result from grace in the first sense.

God's grace differs from that of man, in that His will of good to the creature creates some good in the creature: whereas man's grace presupposes wholly or in part some reason for it in the recipient.

God's grace in the first sense is twofold: it is (1) the general love, which He has to all creatures; (2) the special love, by which He draws the rational creature beyond its condition of nature to participation in the Divine good. Hence, that man possesses the grace of God signifies something supernatural in man, coming from God.

Sometimes, however, the grace of God means His eternal love, i.e. the grace of predestination.

According to art. 2, grace in the second of the three senses originally defined, i.e. grace as an effect in man of God's gracious will, is twofold. It is (1) a particular motion in the soul, (2) a habit by which man tends to the supernatural eternal good. In this latter sense it is a quality of the soul.

Grace, as habit, manifests itself in supernatural virtues, as reason in natural virtues (art. 3). Its seat is in the essence of the soul, while the virtues inhabit its diverse powers (art. 4).

In qu. 111, art. 1 grace is distinguished as 'gratia gratum faciens' and 'gratia gratis data'. The first is the grace by which man is brought to God. The second is the grace by which he is enabled to bring others to God. In art. 2 grace is further distinguished as 'operans' and 'co-operans': so far as it renews the will it is the former, so far as it assists it, thus renewed, it is the latter.

According to qu. 112, art. 1 the sole cause of grace is God. The gift of grace exceeds the whole faculty of created nature, and is nothing but a participation of the Divine nature. God alone, however, can deify, which He does by communicating fellowship with the Divine nature through a certain participation of likeness.

The humanity of Christ is the instrument of His Divinity and does not cause grace by its own virtue but by that of the conjoined Divinity, whence it is that the human actions of Christ are saving actions.

As regards the reception of grace, art. 2 teaches that there is a preparation for habitual grace, which consists in the motion of the will to good by general grace or the help of God. Such a preparation is required, as a form can only exist in a matter disposed for it. Art. 3 discusses the question: Is grace necessarily given to him who prepares himself, or does what in him lies? Thomas replies, that, if the preparation be considered in relation to the free will, there is no necessity, as the gift of grace is out of all proportion to human virtue; but, if it is considered in relation to the Divine assistance involved, then there is a necessity, though not of compulsion but of infallibility, inasmuch as God intends that the preparation shall be followed by the gift of grace.

According to qu. 113, introd., the effects of grace are two:

(1) justification, which is the result of operative grace; (2) merit, which is the result of co-operative grace. Qu. 113 deals with justification. It will be remembered that Alexander had defined justification as the rectitude of the free will: Thomas, however, feels himself compelled by ancient theological tradition to raise the question: Whether the justification of the ungodly is the remission of sins? Art. 1 replies that justification is the remission of sins, in so far as it is a change from a state of unrighteousness to a state of righteousness by the remission of sins. Art. 2 then inquires: Whether for the remission of guilt, which is the justification of the ungodly, there is required the infusion of grace? Thomas makes answer that the remission of sins means that God is reconciled to us, which reconciliation consists in the love wherewith God loves us. This love of God is unchangeable and eternal; but its results are variable, in that we sometimes fall away from it, and sometimes regain it. The effect of the Divine love, by which sin is removed, is grace: and therefore there cannot be remission of guilt without infusion of grace.

It is objected that the remission of sin consists in the Divine imputation,[7] while the infusion of grace implies something in us; therefore the infusion of grace is not required for the remission of sins. Thomas answers: That God does not impute sin proceeds from the Divine love, and this implies a certain effect in him to whom sin is not imputed.

In the two following articles Thomas proceeds to show in what sense justification is by faith.[8] The grace infused moves the free will to accept it (art. 3). Its first motion is faith; but concurrent with this is the motion of love, so that faith is informed with charity (art. 4).

Qu. 114 is on merit. According to art. 1, merit implies the rewarding of work in accordance with justice. The possibility of merit lies in the fact that God's justice towards men is not a justice as between equals, but a 'jus paternum' or 'dominativum'. Hence, while there can be no strict merit as between man and God, merit can exist by presupposition of the Divine ordination, which has attached certain rewards to certain works.

The next thing is the relation of merit to grace. According

[7] Ps. 32:1.   [8] Rom. 5:1.

211

to art. 2, man even in the state of innocence could not without grace merit eternal life. This is so (1) because all merit depends upon the Divine ordination; (2) because eternal life is out of all proportion to human nature, and therefore human nature can merit it only by the aid of the supernatural gift of grace. Still less then can man in the state of sin merit eternal life; for here there is the added impediment of sin which alienates man from God, and excludes him from eternal life. The sinner then can never merit eternal life, except he first be reconciled to God by the forgiveness of sins, which takes place by grace.

In grace, however, man can merit eternal life (art. 3). His merit is 'meritum condigni', if the meritorious work be regarded as proceeding from the Holy Spirit; but it is only 'meritum congrui', if it is viewed as proceeding from the free will.

Art. 5 inquires whether it is possible to merit the first grace. The answer is: No; for (1) grace is in itself opposed to merit;[9] (2) grace exceeds the proportion of nature; (3) man in sin is prevented from meriting by sin. According to art. 6, only Christ can merit the first grace for others with 'meritum condigni'; 'since each one of us is moved of God through the gift of grace, to the end that he himself may attain eternal life, and therefore his condign merit does not extend beyond this motion; but the soul of Christ was moved by God through grace, not only that He Himself might attain eternal glory, but also that He might bring others to the same, in so far as He is the Head of the Church, and the author of human salvation'.[1]

It is possible, however, for the saints to merit the first grace for others *ex congruo*.

Finally, art. 7 teaches that no one can merit repentance after a fall. Being out of grace, he has no 'meritum condigni'; while his sin itself impedes the operation of any 'meritum congrui' on the part of others.

The incidental remarks of Thomas upon the humanity of Christ as the instrument of His Divinity in causing grace, and upon the operation of His merit as the Head of the Church point forward for their fuller explanation to the doctrine of Christ and His work in pars III, to which we now proceed. There

[9] Rom. 4:4.   [1] Heb. 2:10.

212

are first some general considerations as to the fitness of the Incarnation (qu. 1). In art. 1 Thomas says: 'It belongs to the nature of the Highest Good to communicate Himself in the highest manner to the creature, which, however, is especially done by this, that "He so joined to Himself a created nature, that one Person is made of the three, the Word, the soul, and the flesh", as Augustine says in his thirteenth book on the Trinity (cf. 17, 22); wherefore it is manifest that it was fitting that God should become incarnate.'

This general reason for the Incarnation would seem to demand its occurrence, even apart from sin. Thomas, however, (art. 3) prefers the opposite view as being more in agreement with Scripture, which constantly speaks of the Incarnation as a remedy for Adam's sin, 'though the power of God is not limited in respect of this; for even if sin were non-existent, God could have become incarnate'.

In art. 2 the reasons for the necessity of the Incarnation are set out at length. While God could have redeemed us in other ways, it is the fittest way of redemption.

Thomas sets out first, after Augustine, its positive effects in restoring human nature. These are:

(1) The establishment of faith by Divine authority.

(2) The elevation of hope, in that God showed His great love by becoming participant of our nature.

(3) The kindling of love by the manifestation of the Divine love.

(4) The giving to man of a Divine example.

(5) The bestowal of the full participation of the Godhead, which is the beatitude of man and the end of human life.

Then there are five other reasons, which refer to the removal of evil:

(1) Man is taught not to think more of the devil than of himself, because the devil is pure spirit.

(2) Again, that human nature has been dignified by the Incarnation, should prevent us from defiling it with sin.

(3) The assumption in Christ of human nature without preceding merits, manifests the Divine grace, and checks presumption.

213

(4) Our pride is healed by Christ's humility.

(5) The Incarnation also delivers men from the bondage of sin by the provision of a satisfaction for sin.

All these reasons come from Augustine and Leo, except that as regards the last there is no mention of satisfaction in the passages from these Fathers quoted in support of it. This last reason anticipates the discussion of the effects of Christ's passion (qu. 48), where in art. 2 His satisfaction is more fully dealt with.

It will be observed that already in these thoughts on the Incarnation Thomas makes the article of the Divine omnipotence the ultimate test of doctrine, both as to the necessity of the Incarnation apart from sin, and as to its necessity altogether. Its necessity can in any case only be relative.

As to the manner of the Incarnation, the union of the two natures in Christ took place by grace.

'Grace is spoken of in two ways: in one way it means the will of God itself giving anything freely; in another way it is the free gift of God itself. Now human nature needs the gracious will of God, that it may be raised into union with God, since this is beyond the power of its own nature. Human nature, however, is raised to union with God in two ways: in the one way by the operation by which, to wit, the saints know and love God: in the other by personal being, which last mode belongs to Christ alone, in whom human nature was assumed for this end, that it may be in the person of the Son of God. Now it is manifest that for the perfection of working, a faculty (*potentia*) must be perfected by a habit: but that a nature has its existence in its substrate does not take place through the mediation of any habit. Thus therefore it is to be said that if grace signifies the will of God itself freely doing anything, or holding anyone to be pleasing or acceptable, then the union in the Incarnation took place through grace, as indeed also does the union of the saints to God through knowledge and love: if, however, grace stands for the free gift of God itself, then the very existence of the union of human nature with the Divine person may be spoken of as a certain grace, in so far as this took place with no preceding merits; not, however, that there is any habitual grace, by the mediation of which such union takes place' (qu. 2, art. 10).

As an individual man, however, Christ possesses habitual grace for three reasons:

(1) Because of the union of His soul with the Word of God, by the closeness of which union it peculiarly participates in the Divine grace.

(2) Because of the nobility of that soul, whose operations could not but attain most closely to God by knowledge and love. Human nature, however, can only so attain by grace.

(3) Because of Christ's relation to the human race. Christ, as man, is Mediator, and must therefore possess grace overflowing to others (qu. 7, art. 1).

Christ consequently possessed all virtues (art. 2) and had all the gifts of the Spirit in the most excellent degree (art. 5). He had also all 'gratiæ gratis datæ' needed to make Him the first and chief Teacher of the faith (art. 7). As man Christ also possessed the gift of prophecy, and foretold the future (art. 8). Christ had in fact the fullness of grace, both as regards its amount and its effects (art. 9).

As communicating grace to others, Christ is the Head of the Church. 'To give grace, or the Holy Spirit, befits Christ, as He is God, by way of authority; but instrumentally it befits Him, as He is man; in so far, to wit, as His humanity was the instrument of His Divinity; and so His actions from the virtue of His Divinity were salvation-bringing for us, in so far as they cause grace in us, both by merit, and by a certain efficacy' (qu. 8, art. 1).

Christ is in the first place the Head of the Church as regards the soul, but secondly as regards the body. He is the latter 'in one way, inasmuch as the members of the body are presented as the weapons of righteousness in the case of the soul of one living through Christ, as the Apostle says;[2] in another way, in so far as the life of glory flows from the soul to the body, according to Rom. 8 (:11)' (art. 2).

'According to its essence the personal grace, by which the soul of Christ was justified, is the same with His grace, according to which He is the Head of the Church, justifying others; they differ, however, in idea' (art. 5).

Finally, Christ alone is in the highest sense the Head of the

[2]Rom. 6:13.

215

Church. 'The inner inflow of grace is from none other than Christ alone, whose humanity has the power of justifying from the fact that it is joined to His Divinity; but the inflow into the members of the Church, as regards its exterior government, may befit others; and in this way certain others may be called heads of the Church' (art. 6).

Thomas reckons the grace of Christ to the perfections assumed together with His assumption of human nature (qu. 7, introd.): He also, however, assumed in the Incarnation certain defects (qu. 14, introd.).

'It was fitting that the body assumed by the Son of God should be subject to human infirmities and defects. And this chiefly for three reasons: in the first place, because to this end the Son of God, having assumed flesh, came into the world, viz. to satisfy for the sins of the human race; now one satisfies for the sins of another, when he takes upon himself the penalty (*pœna*) due for the sin of the other; but bodily defects such as death, hunger, thirst, and so on are the penalty of sin, brought into the world by Adam, according to Rom. 5 (:12); wherefore it was fitting in regard of the end of the Incarnation, that Christ should in our place assume penal characters of this kind, according to Isa. 53 (:4).' The second reason for the assumption of these corporal defects was to show the reality of the Incarnation; the third that Christ might be to us an example of patience (qu. 14, art. 1).

It is to be observed that in the above statement Thomas follows Alexander in defining satisfaction as penal in character. It is in fact the vicarious endurance of another's punishment; 'unus autem pro peccato alterius satisfacit, dum pœnam pro peccato alterius debitam in se suscipit' (loc. cit.).

The active aspect of satisfaction is, however, also recognised as follows: 'Satisfaction for the sin of another has indeed, as its matter, the penalties which one undergoes for the sin of another; but for principle it has the habit of the soul, according to which the soul inclines to the will to satisfy for another, and from which satisfaction has its efficacy; for it would not be an efficacious satisfaction, unless it proceeded from charity' (loc. cit.).

Christ assumed not only bodily defects, but also defects of

216

soul: in particular His soul was passible. 'Therefore He was at once a *comprehensor*, in so far as He had the blessedness proper to the soul, and also a *viator*,[3] in so far as He tended towards beatitude in respect of what was lacking to Him in beatitude' (qu. 15, art. 10).

Christ, as man, was subject to the Father; as appears in that He prayed to the Father, also in that He served Him in His Priesthood (qu. 20, introd.). Thomas discusses the Priesthood of Christ in qu. 22. Christ is a priest, in so far as a priest is mediator between God and the people, offers to God the prayers of the people, and in some way makes satisfaction for sin; all of which in the highest degree apply to Christ (art. 1). Thomas observes: 'Other men have severally certain graces, but Christ as the Head of all, has the perfection of all graces; and therefore, as far as pertains to others, one is legislator, another is priest, and another is king, but all these concur in Christ as the source of all graces' (loc. cit.).

Christ was both priest and victim (art. 2). The result of His work is the expiation of sins. The 'macula culpæ' is destroyed by grace: the 'reatus poenæ' by satisfaction. Both are effected by the priesthood of Christ, by which He procured for us grace and made satisfaction for sin (art. 3).

Christ was not a priest for Himself. He prayed for Himself, and by His passion merited for Himself; but His passion was a sacrifice, i.e. a satisfaction, only for us (art. 4). 'In any priest's offering of a sacrifice two things can be considered, viz. the sacrifice offered, and the devotion of the offerer: the proper effect of priesthood, however, is that which follows from the sacrifice itself. But Christ obtained through His passion the glory of His resurrection, not as it were by the virtue of His sacrifice, which is offered by the mode of satisfaction, but by His very devotion, by which in charity He humbly underwent the passion' (loc. cit.).

Under the same general head of Christ's subjection to the Father is discussed in qu. 24 His predestination, which is thus reduced from the position of supremacy which it occupies in the scheme of Alexander to a subordinate point of interest. Thomas,

[3] See p. 123, n. 8.

however, repeats in arts. 3 and 4 the doctrine of Alexander, that in the eternal act Christ's predestination and ours are one; nevertheless, viewing predestination according to its end, the predestination of Christ is the example and cause of our predestination; the example, in that we are predestinated to be sons of God by adoption as He was predestinated to be Son of God by nature, in each case without prior merits; the cause, in that our salvation was preordained to take place through Jesus Christ.

The next section is on those things which belong to Christ in relation to us (cf. qu. 25, introd.). Here in qu. 26 is discussed His mediatorship. He is the one perfect Mediator, in that by His death He has reconciled man to God (art. 1). Further, He is Mediator as man (art. 2). 'According as He is man, He differs both from God in nature, and from man in dignity both in grace and glory; in so far also as He is man, it befits Him to unite men to God, bringing the commandments and gifts of God to men, and making satisfaction and intercession for men to God; and therefore He is most truly called Mediator, according as He is man' (loc. cit.).

The final section on the Incarnation treats of what the incarnate Son of God underwent or suffered in the nature united to Him. Here Thomas considers (1) what pertains to Christ's advent into the world, (2) what pertains to the progress of His life in it, (3) His departure from the world, (4) what pertains to His exaltation after the present life (qu. 27, introd.). Altogether, he treats of the details of the Gospel history much more fully than Alexander, expanding and enlarging upon the pattern set him by his predecessor.

Under the first of the four heads just mentioned falls the conception of Christ. Christ merited from the very instant of His conception; but what He merited thereby, He merited by the subsequent actions of His life, not, however, that He merited it more, but simply for fresh reasons (qu. 34, art. 3).

Under the head of Christ's life in the world, Thomas discusses His conversation, His temptation, His doctrine, and His miracles (qu. 40, introd.).

'By His humanity Christ wished to manifest His Divinity: and therefore having converse with men (as belongs to man) He manifested to all His Divinity by preaching, by working miracles, and by living innocently and justly among men' (qu. 40, art. 1).

He chose poverty, amongst other reasons, that His Divinity might the more by contrast reveal its power (art. 3). He lived under the law, (1) to approve the old law, (2) to keep it and end it in Himself, (3) to obviate Jewish calumny, and (4) to redeem men from its bondage according to Gal. 4:4, 5 (art. 4).

Christ was tempted that He might overcome the devil and assist us in our temptations, also for our warning and example and to assure us of His sympathy (qu. 41, art. 1).

Among the things pertaining to the end of Christ's life the first to be treated of is His Passion, which receives very full consideration.

Qu. 46, art. 1, discusses its necessity. 'It was not necessary as a matter of compulsion for Christ to suffer, neither as regards God, who ordained that Christ should suffer, nor yet as regards Christ, who suffered voluntarily: it was, however, necessary with a view to its end.' This necessity was threefold: (1) as regards us, who are redeemed by it, (2) as regards Christ, who by the humility of His passion merited the glory of His exaltation, (3) as regards God, whose foreordination of it announced in Scripture must be fulfilled.

Thomas, however, in agreement with his doctrine of the contingency of all that belongs to God's relation to the world, denies that the passion was absolutely necessary for human redemption, and subscribes to the doctrine of Augustine in the 'De Trinitate', XIII, cap. 10, 13 (art. 2).

'Anything can be called possible or impossible in two ways: in one way simply and absolutely, in another way hypothetically. Speaking therefore simply and absolutely, it was possible for God to redeem man in another way than by the passion of Christ; because no word is impossible with God.[4] But from a certain supposition that had been made, it was impossible: for, since it is impossible that God's foreknowledge should be deceived, and His will or ordinance should be broken, granting the foreknowledge and foreordination of God concerning the

---

[4] Lk. 1:37, Vulg.

passion of Christ, it was not at the same time possible for Christ not to suffer, or for man to be delivered in any other way than by His passion' (loc. cit.).

Still more characteristic of his view is the answer which Thomas gives to the objection that God's justice demanded Christ's passion as the necessary satisfaction for human sin, and that God cannot deny His own justice without denying Himself. Thomas says:

'This justice depends upon the will of God, demanding from the human race satisfaction for sin: for, if He had wished to deliver man from sin without any satisfaction, He would have done nothing contrary to justice: for the judge, who has to punish an offence committed against some other, as for instance some other man or the whole state, or the prince above him, cannot without violating justice remit the offence without punishment; but God has no one above Him, but He Himself is the supreme and common good of the universe. And therefore, if He remit sin, which comes under the category of an offence, because it is committed against Himself, He does no one wrong: just as any man whatever, of his mercy, forgives without satisfaction, and does no wrong' (loc. cit.).

This is a very important passage, inasmuch as it contains a criticism of the Anselmic theory of satisfaction, not merely on the religious ground of an instinctive objection to limit the Divine omnipotence (Augustine, Boso, Alexander), but also upon legal grounds. As Anselm had appealed to legal analogies, Thomas meets him with his own weapons. Anselm had at first defined satisfaction in accordance with the rule of private law, but then, in order to demonstrate its necessity, had spoken of God as the Moral Ruler of the universe, who cannot remit sin unpunished. Thomas fixes on the latter point, and supports his view of the contingency of the Divine relation to the world by the analogy of the position of the sovereign, who is not a judge that must execute the law of the state, but is himself the fountain of justice, and is as free to forgive any offence whatever, as a private person is to forgive a wrong against himself. We have seen that the Anselmic idea of the Divine sovereignty has affinity to the German conception of kingship. The Thomist

220

doctrine on the other hand is clearly akin to the Roman notion of the Emperor: 'princeps legibus solutus est' ('Digest', I, 3, 31). The argument of Thomas reduces the two analogies, brought forward by Anselm, to one. The Divine Sovereignty is to be interpreted according to the rule of private law. This is an immensely important position: as long as it remains uncontroverted, the Anselmic doctrine is vitiated at an essential point. It is just round about this point, however, that controversy rages in later attempts to apply legal analogies to the work of Christ.

In qu. 46, art. 3, Thomas, having rejected the absolute necessity of redemption by Christ's passion, goes on to inquire into the fitness of this mode of redemption. 'Any mode is the more fitting for the attainment of an end, in proportion as through it more things combine, which are expedient to the end.' Here, however, many things besides deliverance from sin combine to make the passion the fittest mode of salvation.

(1) It reveals the love of God to man, and incites him to love God, which is the perfection of human salvation.[5]

(2) In the passion Christ gave us an example of obedience, humility, constancy, righteousness, and the rest of the virtues necessary for human salvation.[6]

(3) Christ not only by His passion delivered man from sin, but also merited for him justifying grace and the glory of beatitude.

(4) In that man is bought by the blood of Christ, he has a motive for keeping himself from sin.[7]

(5) Man's dignity is increased, in that as man had been conquered by the devil and merited death, so it was man who conquered the devil, and by dying conquered death.[8]

I pass over the various symbolical congruities which Aquinas, following the Fathers, finds in the fact that Christ died upon the Cross (art. 4), merely observing that among them lingers the old Irenæan idea that, as Adam fell by a tree, so it was meet that Christ should die on a tree.

The next point is more important (art. 5). Christ suffered every possible kind of suffering though not actually every possible suffering. Though the least suffering of His would have sufficed

[5] Rom. 5:8.   [6] 1 Pet. 2:21.   [7] 1 C. 6:20.   [8] 1 C. 15:57.

to redeem humanity, yet as He came to redeem men from every kind of sin, there was a fitness in His suffering every kind of suffering.

Moreover (art. 6), His grief was the greatest possible in this present life. It was both pain of sense and pain of mind and was excessive, the pain of sense because of the extreme painfulness of crucifixion, the pain of mind, because He was satisfying for all the sins of men, because of the sin against Him both of the Jews and His own disciples, and because His suffering was to the point of death. Moreover, His body was perfect and therefore perfectly sensitive, His mental pain had no mitigation, and finally 'the greatness of the grief of Christ may be seen in this, that His passion and grief were assumed voluntarily by Christ to the end of freeing men from sin, and therefore He assumed an amount of grief, as great as was proportionate to the greatness of the fruit which thence followed'.

The importance of the above thoughts shows that Thomas, like Alexander, applies the concrete idea of penance to explain the passion of Christ. Whereas, however, Alexander lays stress on the penal character of Christ's satisfaction, Thomas emphasises His inner pain of mind, which corresponds to the contrition of the ordinary penitent.

'The pain of Christ, however, exceeded all the pain of any and every penitent: both because it proceeded from greater wisdom and love, whence the grief of contrition is increased; and also because His grief was for all sins at once.' [9]

Christ's grief was not diminished by His innocence. The innocent indeed has to grieve not for guilt, but at punishment only; yet His grief at punishment is increased because this is not His due.

Thomas, however, refuses to compare Christ's sufferings with the pains of purgatory or hell. These exceed all evil of the present life, just as the glory of the saints exceeds all present good.

Moreover, Christ's suffering was only in the lower powers of His soul, which were concerned with temporal things: with His higher reason He continued to enjoy the vision of God (art. 7).

In qu. 47 Thomas treats of the efficient cause of the passion.

[9] Is. 53:4.

Art. 2 teaches that Christ died out of obedience for the following reasons:

(1) It befitted human justification that Adam's disobedience should be met by Christ's obedience.[1]

(2) It befitted the reconciliation of God to men,[2] in that Christ was a most acceptable sacrifice to God;[3] but obedience is better than sacrifice,[4] and thus Christ's passion and death fitly proceeded from obedience.

(3) It was fit that Christ should obtain victory by obeying God, as a soldier his leader.[5]

God, then, gave up Christ to suffer (art. 3) according to His eternal counsel,[6] inspiring Him with love so that He willed to die for us,[7] and abandoning Him to His persecutors.[8] The Father gave up His Son, and Christ Himself gave up Himself in love. At the same time Judas gave Him up from envy, Pilate from fear. All these acts were externally the same, but the motives were different. Christ's passion began at the hands of the Jews and was completed at the hands of the Gentiles (art. 4), that its fruits might reach first the Jews, then the Gentiles. The Jewish rulers did not recognise the Divinity of Christ,[9] but this was because of their unwillingness to believe:[1] the Jewish people were seduced by their rulers, and were therefore relatively excusable:[2] still more excusable were the Gentiles who knew not the law. The sin of the Jewish rulers therefore, though not that of their agents, was the greatest possible (arts. 4, 5).

With qu. 48 we reach the very heart of the doctrine of Thomas on the passion. The question deals with its mode as regards its effect.

It operates in the first place by the mode of merit (art. 1). 'To Christ was given grace, not only as to a single person, but in so far as He is Head of the Church, in order that from Him it might overflow to the members; and therefore the works of Christ have the same relation both to Himself and to His members, as the works of another man established in grace have to himself. Now it is manifest, that whoever being established in grace suffers for righteousness' sake, by this very thing merits

[1] Rom. 5:19.   [2] *Ibid*. 10.   [3] Eph. 5.   [4] 1 Sam. 15:22.
[5] Prov. 21:28, Vulg.   [6] Is. 53:6, 10.   [7] *Ibid*. 7, Vulg.   [8] Mt. 27:46.
[9] 1 C. 2:8.   [1] Jn 15:22, 24.   [2] Lk. 23:34 ; Acts 3:17.

223

for himself salvation;[3] wherefore Christ by His passion merited salvation, not only for Himself, but also for all His members.'

The passion in itself, as having its principle from without, was not meritorious; but as voluntarily endured, and thus having its principle from within, it was meritorious.

Christ merited salvation for us from the very beginning of His conception; but there were on our side certain obstacles which hindered the effect of His merits before the passion: to remove these, as will be presently shown (qu. 46, art. 3), the passion was necessary. The passion had an effect which Christ's previous merits did not have, not because His love was increased in the passion, but because it was a work suitable to such an effect.

Arts. 2, 3, 4 then show how it was that the passion had a peculiar merit of its own, and what were the obstacles it removed, which prevented the operation of Christ's former merits.

The passion operated by the mode of satisfaction (art. 2). So Ps. 69:4 teaches; and the proof that Christ in His passion actually made satisfaction for sin is as follows:

'He properly satisfies for an offence, who presents to the offended person, what he loves as much as or more than he hates the offence. But Christ in suffering out of love and obedience, presented to God something more than was required as a recompense for the whole offence of the human race; first indeed, because of the greatness of the love out of which He suffered; secondly, because of the dignity of His life, which He gave as a satisfaction, which was the life of God and man; thirdly, because of the generality of His passion, and the greatness of the grief assumed, as has been said before (qu. 46, art. 6): and therefore the passion of Christ was not only a sufficient, but even a superabundant satisfaction for the sins of the human race.'[4]

Though Thomas lays stress on the grief of Christ in His passion, it is, however, by the agreement of the passion with penitential satisfaction, rather than with penitential contrition, that he explains its operation for others.

'The head and members are, as it were, one mystical person,

---

[3] Mt. 5:10.   [4] 1 Jn 2:2.

and therefore the satisfaction of Christ belongs to all believers as His members. So far as two men even are one in charity, one can satisfy for the other: but the position is not the same as regards confession or contrition: because satisfaction consists in an external act, for which instruments can be adopted, amongst which friends also are counted.'

Thomas easily disposes of the old problem as to the extreme sin of Christ's crucifiers. Christ's love was greater even than their wickedness; and His passion was therefore a sufficient and suberabundant satisfaction even for their sin.

In answer to the objection that satisfaction implies, as an act of justice, an equality with the universal offence expiated, whereas Christ suffered, not as God, but merely in His flesh,[5] Thomas says that because His flesh was assumed by His Divine Person, it had an infinite value.

It will be observed that Thomas in the above section follows Anselm, as regards the definition of satisfaction, and as regards the infinite value given to Christ's satisfaction by His Godhead. Thomas, however, follows Alexander, in attaching the idea of satisfaction to Christ's passion rather than to His death, also in estimating the value of the passion for God from Christ's inner love and grief, as well as from His Divinity. We see, however, that He regards a vicarious contrition as impossible: it is after all only the 'satisfactio operis' that can be vicarious. Finally, when Thomas makes the satisfaction not only sufficient but superabundant, we might be disposed at first to think this an advance beyond Anselm in the same direction: in reality, however, the thought carries us away from Anselm, the essence of whose theory is the necessity of the exact equivalence of satisfaction and sin. Thomas in fact here loosens the close connexion of the Anselmic theory, in agreement with his general principle of the contingency of all that belongs to God's relation to the world.

Art. 3 goes on to teach that Christ's passion operated as a sacrifice.[6] 'Sacrifice in its proper meaning is anything done towards the honour properly owed to God, in order to placate Him.' Christ then in His passion offered Himself for us; and His voluntary endurance of suffering was eminently acceptable

<hr>

[5] 1 Pet. 4:1.   [6] Eph. 5:2.

to God, as proceeding from His charity. In reality therefore Thomas reduces, though he does not say so, the Scriptural idea of sacrifice to an aspect of the ecclesiastical notion of satisfaction, which has been explained in art. 2.

Art. 4, again, teaches that Christ's passion operated by the mode of redemption. This too is reduced to the category of satisfaction. Christ, by satisfying for us, redeemed us both from sin and its penalties, and so from the devil, who held us in the bondage of sin, and had in charge the execution of its penalties: the price, however, was paid not to the devil, but to God.

Our redemption belongs immediately to Christ as man alone; though the first cause of it was the whole Trinity (art. 5).

Finally, according to art. 6 the passion operated by the mode of efficacy.

'The principal efficient cause of human salvation is God; but since, as was said before (qu. 43, art. 2), the humanity of Christ is the instrument of His Divinity; therefore as a consequence all the actions and passions of Christ operate instrumentally in the power of His Divinity to the end of human salvation; and accordingly the passion of Christ is the efficient cause of human salvation.'

From its association with His Divinity, Christ's passion, though corporeal, has yet a spiritual power, and therefore obtains efficacy, not by corporeal, but by spiritual contact, i.e. through faith and the sacrament of faith.[7] In conclusion, Thomas shows how all the different modes of operation are related.

'The passion of Christ, as referred to His Divinity, acts by the mode of efficacy: in reference to the will of Christ's soul, again, it acts by the mode of merit: again, if it is considered as belonging to the flesh of Christ itself, it acts by the mode of satisfaction, in so far as by it we are delivered from the obligation to punishment: again, by the mode of redemption, in so far as we are delivered from the bondage of transgression: once more, by the mode of sacrifice, so far as by it we are reconciled to God.'

Qu. 49 carries us on to the effects of the passion. According to art. 1 we are liberated by it from sin:

[7] Rom. 3:25.

226

(1) By the mode of provocation to love,[8] for love brings the forgiveness of sin.[9]

(2) By the mode of redemption, Christ's merit in His passion being reckoned to the Church, as being one person with its Head.

(3) By the mode of efficacy, inasmuch as Christ's humanity, by which He suffered, was the instrument of His Divinity in expiating sin.

Next (art. 2) we are liberated from the power of the devil:

(1) In so far as man had merited by the Fall to be given over into the power of the devil, he is delivered by Christ's passion, as the cause of the remission of sins.

(2) Again it was God, offended by sin, who had given us over into the power of the devil, but by Christ we were reconciled to God, and so delivered from the devil's power.

(3) The devil wickedly hindered men from obtaining salvation. But the passion of Christ delivered us from his power, in that he exceeded the measure of power granted him by God, in plotting the death of the innocent Christ; so that, as Augustine says,[1] it is just that he should set free in return the debtors whom he held.

It is to be observed that in this place, somewhat inconsistently with what he says in qu. 48, art. 4, Thomas retains, at least in its modified Augustinian form, the doctrine of redemption from the devil.

Again (art. 3) we are delivered from the punishment of sin. We are liberated from the obligation to punishment:

(1) Directly by the mode of satisfaction, since, as a sufficient satisfaction has been exhibited, this obligation is removed.

(2) Indirectly, in so far as the passion of Christ is the cause of the remission of sin, in which is founded the obligation to punishment.

Once more (art. 4), by the passion we are reconciled to God:

(1) In so far as it removes sin, which makes us hateful to God.

(2) In so far as it is a most acceptable sacrifice, placating God, so that He forgives the offence of man.

Again (art. 5) it opened the gate of heaven. Sin, both as original and as actual, prevents our entrance to heaven. Christ's

---

[8] Rom. 5:8.   [9] Lk. 7:47.   [1] 'De Trin.' XIII, 14, 18.

passion delivered us by the payment of a price, not only from original sin, both as regards guilt and as regards obligation to punishment, but also from actual sin, if we have communion with His passion by faith and the sacraments of faith. Before the removal of the obstacle of the guilt of original sin, no entrance into heaven was possible.

Finally (art. 6), Christ by His passion merited His own exaltation. If anyone by a righteous will withdraws from himself what he deserves to have, then he merits that more be added to him as the reward of his righteous will. Christ, in His passion and in the circumstances accompanying His passion, humbled Himself below His proper dignity: He merited by His passion, therefore, His exaltation in His resurrection, ascension, sitting at the right hand of the Father, and judicial authority.

This concludes the extended discussion of the passion, which is almost entirely concerned with its saving value. The death of Christ, however, which comes next (qu. 50), Thomas treats, like Lombard and Alexander, almost entirely as a historical event. In art. 6, however, he discusses its saving value, and comes to terms with the patristic doctrine, just as Alexander had felt bound to do. What a problem the old doctrine presented to the mediaeval mind, centred as it was on the thought of Christ's satisfaction and merit, comes out very clearly in an argument which Thomas finally rejects. 'The passion of Christ wrought our salvation by the mode of merit; but the death of Christ could thus work nothing; for in death the soul, which is the principle of merit, is separated from the body; therefore the death of Christ wrought nothing for our salvation.'

Thomas replies, that the death of Christ, as distinguished from His passion, is the cause of our salvation, not by the mode of merit, but only by the mode of efficiency. By Christ's death His flesh was separated from His soul, but not from His Divinity, by reason of which the flesh of Christ, even as separated from the soul, is of saving virtue for us.

'Now the effect of any cause is properly regarded after the likeness of the cause; wherefore, since death is a certain privation of one's own life, the effect of the death of Christ is looked for in the removal of those things which are opposed to our salvation, which indeed are the death of the soul and the death of the body; and therefore by the death of Christ there is said to be destroyed in us both the death of the soul, which is our sin,[2] and the death of the body, which consists in the separation of the soul.' [3]

This is the same doctrine as that of Gregory of Nyssa.[4] Thomas does not, like Alexander, altogether cut himself loose from the patristic doctrine; nevertheless he relegates it to a somewhat out-of-the-way corner of his system.

Passing on from the death of Christ, Thomas says that, in His descent into hell, Christ liberated by virtue of His passion the Holy Fathers,[5] who were excluded from paradise till the obligation to punishment had been dissolved (qu. 52, art. 6).

Then Thomas comes to the Resurrection of Christ. According to qu. 53, art. 1, it was necessary:

(1) To evince the Divine justice in rewarding His humiliation.

(2) To confirm our faith in the Divinity of Christ.

(3) To elevate our hope, that we too shall be raised like our Head.

(4) To give a pattern for the life of believers.[6]

(5) To fulfil our salvation, that as Christ died to deliver us from evil things, so He might be raised to advance us to good things.[7]

Qu. 56 has for its subject the causality of the resurrection. In art. 1 Thomas discusses 'whether the resurrection of Christ is the cause of the resurrection of bodies'. Here the difficulty of carrying through the Greek view as developed by Gregory of Nyssa comes out very clearly. The resurrection is the cause of our resurrection in the sense that it is first in the *genus* of true resurrection, and that in all resurrection the operative principle is the Word of God, who first quickened His own body, and through it quickens ours, in so far as we are first conformed to Christ's sufferings, and so attain to the likeness of His resurrection. The primary cause of resurrection is therefore God Himself, who could bring about our resurrection apart from that of Christ, just as He could save us apart from His passion;

Rom. 4:25. [3] 1 C. 15:54. [4] 'Cat. Magna', 32.
The saints of the Old Testament. [6] Rom. 6:4. [7] *Ibid.* 4:25.

nevertheless in the actual way appointed by God, the resurrection of Christ operates as a secondary cause of our resurrection, not indeed as the meritorious cause, but as the exemplary and the efficient cause.

In reply to the objection that no cause can act, except on that with which it is in contact, and that our bodies are separated in space and time from that of Christ, Thomas says:

'The humanity of Christ, according to which He rose again, is in a certain sense the instrument of His Divinity, and operates in the power of it; and therefore, just as the other things which Christ did or suffered in His humanity, are salutary to us by the virtue of His Divinity, so also the resurrection of Christ is the efficient cause of our resurrection by the Divine virtue, whose property it is to quicken the dead; which virtue by its presence reaches all places and times; and such virtual contact suffices as the ground of this efficiency.'

There remains, however, the difficulty that unbelievers and sinners also share in the resurrection, and here there is not even spiritual contact. In answer to this objection, Thomas says that God operates here in virtue of His justice, whence Christ as man has judicial authority, and thus the efficiency of Christ's resurrection extends not only to the good, but also to the bad, who are the subjects of His judgment. Here then the resurrection of Christ is an efficient but not also an exemplary cause; since there has been no prior conformation to His death.

Thomas has wrestled much more thoroughly than Alexander with the difficulty as to the causality of the resurrection. His fully developed Aristotelianism, with its sense of the real difference of individuals, makes the traditional doctrine very difficult. He has only by somewhat roundabout ways succeeded in justifying the latter. This remark applies, not only to the above statements of art. 1, dealing with the resurrection of bodies, but also to those of art. 2, which is concerned with the resurrection of souls. Thomas says:

'The resurrection of Christ acts in virtue of His Divinity, which indeed extends itself, not only to the resurrection of bodies, but also to the resurrection of souls; for it is from God that the soul lives by grace, and that the body lives by the soul;

and therefore the resurrection of Christ has instrumentally an effective power, not only in regard of the resurrection of bodies, but also in regard of the resurrection of souls; similarly also it possesses the character of exemplarity in regard of the resurrection of souls, because we ought also according to the soul to be conformed to Christ rising again.'

We complete our long study of the doctrine of Thomas on the work of Christ, by a reference to qu. 57, art. 6, which discusses 'whether the ascension of Christ is the cause of our salvation'. The answer is that it is so:

(1) With regard to us; in so far as it gives us ground for faith, hope, love, and adoration.

(2) With regard to Christ Himself: (i) in so far as He has prepared a way for us to heaven, the Head preceding the members of His body; (ii) in so far as He has entered as our High Priest into heaven to intercede for us; (iii) in so far as He has been exalted to Divine dignity to give gifts to men.

So much then for the doctrine of Christ's work: we come last of all to the doctrine of the sacraments. According to pars III, qu. 60, art. 2, a sacrament 'is a sign of a sacred thing, in so far as it sanctifies men'. Art. 3 teaches that a sacrament is of manifold significance. It signifies our salvation, which implies (1) its cause, the passion of Christ; (2) its form, grace, and the virtues; (3) its end, life eternal.

According to qu. 61, art. 1, sacraments are necessary for salvation:

(1) Because man is naturally led from the sensible to the spiritual.

(2) Because man by sin has subjected himself to bodily things, and the remedy must therefore be applied where the disease exists.

(3) Because man's natural exercise is bodily, therefore in the sacraments wholesome exercise is given him.

Art. 2 maintains that sacraments were not necessary before the Fall, when the soul was subject to God and the body to the soul. For the soul in this state to be perfected through the body, whether in knowledge or in grace, would be contrary to order.

Sacraments were, however, necessary after the Fall, man's

reason having become darkened by sin (art. 3); and were necessary with increase of definition, as sin increased. Saving faith always remaining the same, the sacraments of the written law were more narrowly defined than those of the state before the law. After the coming of Christ, new sacraments became necessary to distinguish between faith in Christ as coming and in Christ as come (art. 3).

According to qu. 62, art. 1, the sacraments of the new law, not only signify, but also cause grace. God is the primary cause of grace, but the sacraments are an instrumental cause. Each adds (art. 2), beyond the general grace which is the basis of the virtues and gifts, some special determination of grace necessary to the Christian life: so, for example, Baptism brings about regeneration, and makes a man a member of Christ.

The sacraments of the new law have their virtue from the passion of Christ (art. 5).

'As was said above (art. 1) a sacrament operates to cause grace by the mode of an instrument; but an instrument is of two kinds; one is separate, as a stick; the other is conjoint, as the hand; now the separate instrument is moved by means of the conjoint instrument, as a stick by the hand. Now the principal efficient cause of grace is God Himself, compared with whom the humanity of Christ is as a conjoint instrument, while the sacrament is as a separate instrument; and therefore it is necessary that saving virtue should flow from the Divinity of Christ, through His humanity, into the sacraments. Sacramental grace, however, appears to be ordained for two things particularly, viz. to take away the defects caused by past sins, in so far as they pass away in act and remain in guilt, and again, to perfect the soul in those things which belong to the worship of God, according to the religion of the Christian life. Now it is manifest, from what has been said before, that Christ freed us from our sins, not only effectively, but by way of merit and satisfaction. Similarly by His passion He originated the rite of the Christian religion, offering Himself as an offering and sacrifice to God.[8] Whence it is manifest that the sacraments of the Church have virtue especially from the passion of Christ,

[8] Eph. 5:2.

232

whose virtue is in a certain way united to us by the reception of the sacraments: in sign of which there flowed from the side of Christ, hanging on the Cross, water and blood, of which the one belongs to Baptism, the other to the Eucharist, which are the chief sacraments.'

Art. 6 proceeds to show why the sacraments of the ancient law, unlike those of the new law, did not confer grace. The virtue of the passion of Christ is united to us by faith and the sacraments. The former mode of union is ideal, the latter external. Now the cause in idea, or final cause, may in time follow the result, not so the external, or efficient, cause. Thus the sacraments could not cause grace before the passion of Christ, but only signified the faith by which we are justified.

In qu. 64, art. 2, Thomas comes to the institution of the Christian sacraments. In general the sacraments may be said to be instituted by God alone, since it is from Him that their virtue proceeds. As regards matters of detail, the things in the sacraments absolutely necessary were instituted by Christ, who is God and man, the rest come through ecclesiastical tradition from the Apostles.

Qu. 65, art. 1, gives reasons why there are just seven sacraments. Five have reference to individual, two to social life; together the sacraments contribute in all ways to perfect man in the Christian religion, and to remedy the defect of sin. Baptism is spiritual regeneration. Confirmation perfects baptismal grace. The Eucharist is spiritual nutriment. Penance restores spiritual health. Extreme unction removes the remains of sin. Ordination gives spiritual power over the multitude. Matrimony secures the multitude.

Art. 4 adds that the sacraments absolutely necessary are Baptism and, supposing mortal sin, penance; also ordination, as the foundation of the Church. The rest are relatively necessary, as by way of spiritual assistance.

The Perfecting of the Mediaeval Synthesis

Initiated by Abelard, Hugo, and Lombard, the mediaeval synthesis of the doctrine of the work of Christ is formed by

Alexander and perfected by Thomas. The main doctrinal outline remains in Thomas the same as in Alexander; but he tends to approximate the doctrine as much as possible to the Greek doctrine. He does not indeed like Alexander recognise the fitness of the Incarnation apart from sin; but he brings out strongly the activity of the Divine Christ in conferring grace through His humanity as a conjoint instrument and the sacraments as a separate instrument, and he describes the effect of sacramental grace as the deification of man. This is in close agreement with the Greek doctrine of the Incarnation; only that the mediaeval view must needs add that the deification which Christ bestows as God, He purchases as man by His merit. The Greeks found no such complementary idea necessary.

The main advances made by Thomas upon Alexander are as follows:

(1) He is more thorough in his use of the Scriptural material. As Alexander is here more thorough than the Greeks, so Thomas than Alexander; he is indeed most exhaustive in this respect. Theology in his hands becomes no mere free construction illustrated from Scripture, but a genuine analysis and synthesis of the Scripture material.

(2) In particular, Thomas has made full use, in his doctrine of the work of Christ, of the details of the Gospel history. Here a line of development, begun by John of Damascus and continuing through Lombard and Alexander, reaches full fruition: the advance made by Thomas on his predecessor is at this point very great.

(3) Thomas is distinguished by the thoroughness of his criticism of the traditional patristic doctrines. Here, however, the advance on Alexander is less marked; still Thomas sums up the progress of criticism from Anselm and Abelard through Lombard and Alexander.

It is desirable to add a word or two on the success of the mediaeval synthesis as completed by Thomas. The amount of detail may easily at first blind us to the greatness of the total scheme. The true analogy of the scholastic system, however, is, as has often been pointed out, the mediaeval cathedral, where immense detail is combined with such strong and noble outlines.

It is important to observe that, besides the worth of the general scheme, the wealth of detail in Scripture material and analytic criticism have great value as preparing the way for further developments. Harnack has indeed described the doctrine of Thomas on the work of Christ, in view of the oscillation between different standpoints which it presents without attaining to complete unity, as being *multa, non multum*;[9] and there is justice in the implied criticism, in so far as the unity of the mediaeval synthesis is still, to a considerable extent, only a unity of aggregation on the basis of authority. Nevertheless the basis of all further simplification and consequent development of doctrine must be admitted to lie in the careful collection and analysis of material made by the mediaeval schoolmen, particularly Alexander and Thomas. Nowhere can the real problems of theology be better studied, by anyone who has sufficient patience, than in the mediaeval scholasticism.

[9] D.G., 4th ed., vol. iii, p. 540.

CHAPTER 6

THE LATER FRANCISCAN THEOLOGY

Duns Scotus

JOHANNES DUNS SCOTUS (d. A.D. 1308) (*doctor subtilis*) is the founder of the later Franciscan school of theology, in distinction from the earlier Franciscan theology of Alexander and Bonaventura and from the Dominican theology of Thomas.

In the theology of Duns the critical element predominates. In the previous scholasticism criticism was mainly directed upon the traditional patristic doctrines, with a view to the substitution of new doctrines in their place. An immanent criticism of these new doctrines, however, begins with Alexander and is greatly increased in Thomas: in Duns Scotus the tide of criticism increases to such a point as practically to make all doctrine appear void of any rational proof other than the reference to the arbitrary sovereign will of God, which has decreed that certain things must be. The principle, already so important in Thomas, of the contingency of the relation of God to the World, becomes the fundamental principle of theology, and all doctrine in consequence is mere matter of authority.

Subject, however, to the Divine decree, the actual place of revealed knowledge in the world-order remains very much the same as in Thomas. On the presupposition that God has ordained that human salvation must take place by way of merit, the Divine revelation is necessary; inasmuch as man could not know by reason that eternal beatitude was to be the reward of merit, there being no proportion between the two; and also inasmuch as he could not know by reason what acts were meritorious and acceptable to God as sufficient for salvation.[1] From the above basis, however, Duns draws a conclusion opposed to that of Thomas,[2] viz. that theology is wholly a practical, not a theoretical

[1] 'Comm. in Sent.' ('Opus Oxoniense'), ed. by Cavellus, Antwerp, 1620. Prol. qu. 1, 8.
[2] 'Summa', qu. 1, art. 4.

science, inasmuch as it is a science simply directive of practice.[3]

It is in accordance with the critical character of the theology of Duns Scotus that he wrote no 'Summa'; but that we have from him only two commentaries on the 'Sentences', the great 'Opus Oxoniense', already referred to, and the shorter 'Opus Parisiense'. The latter is also called 'Reportata', as consisting of notes taken by students from his Paris lectures: the 'Opus Oxoniense' received its form from the hand of Duns himself, and is therefore to be regarded as the primary statement of his doctrine.

That this doctrine appears in the form of a commentary on the 'Sentences' has an important significance for our estimate of the teaching of Duns on the work of Christ, to which we are now about to proceed. While the work of Duns himself is so largely critical, it is to be remembered that the doctrine of the 'Sentences' remains as its basis, and that therefore, where the 'Sentences' are not corrected, they are to be regarded as standing. In this way we come to a somewhat more positive view of the ultimate result of the Scotist criticism than would otherwise be possible. We shall later, when we touch on the doctrine of Duns on the sacraments, have reason to see that this more positive view is the correct one.

With these cautions, therefore, we proceed to the doctrine of Duns on Christ's work. In 'Opus Oxoniense', Lib. III, Dist. 18, qu. unica, he discusses 'whether Christ merited in the first instant of His conception'. First of all he lays down a definition of merit, which is fundamental to the whole subsequent procedure.

'I say that merit is something accepted, or to be accepted in another, for which reward is to be bestowed by the acceptor on him in whom it is, as if it were owed to him in return for that merit, or else on some other for whom he merited' (4).

Next the nature of merit is thus more fully explained. 'Then with regard to what is before us, speaking of merit, so far as it consists in the good willing of the will, I say that Christ merited for us by such a willing; and I say that the root of all merit

[3]'Op. Oxon.' Prol. qu. 4.

consists, speaking strictly of merit, in the love of righteousness of will, not, however, in the love of advantage, nor of the love of righteousness, as it governs the love of advantage. This is clear, because the first object with reference to which anyone in the first place merits is God Himself, according as by the love of righteousness He wishes good to God, as being and well-being, viz. being just and wise, etc.; but the will by the love of advantage has regard to one's own good, and sometimes inordinately, unless it is ruled and governed by the love of justice. Therefore, merit does not consist first of all in the love of righteousness, as it moderates and governs the love of advantage with reference to one's own good: but just as the first demerit of the angels was an inordinate motion and desire of beatitude with regard to God; so merit is a governed motion with reference to God wishing good to Him, and wishing next, with the due circumstances, union with Him in oneself and in others. And therefore everything loved with the love of advantage, if this is not governed and moderated by the love of justice is a demerit, because it is an immoderate desire for one's own good, or else it is a thing indifferent, if there can be a thing indifferent, of which nothing shall be said now (for perchance there can be in so far as it anticipates the love of righteousness): consequently in the love of advantage, unless it is referred to this ultimate end by the love of righteousness, no merit exists' (5).

The way is now prepared for showing how Christ merited.

'Christ in a certain sense was a pilgrim (viator),[4] and was capable of suffering as regards His sensitive nature, and the lower portion of His will:[5] consequently He had many objects present to His senses and the lower portion of His will, with regard to which He could possess a volition contrary to the love of advantage, which is always for the convenience of him, whose it is: consequently by fasting, watching, prayer, and many other such things He could merit, either by performing such things outwardly or wishing such things inwardly for the sake of God' (ibid.).

---

[4] See p. 123, n. 8.

[5] According to IV, Dist. 49, qu. 10, 2, there is a twofold desire in the will, viz. a natural, and a free (or rational).

The objection that Christ was already *in termino* (i.e. in the full enjoyment of beatitude), even as regards the lower portion of His will, Duns sets aside by means of the distinction that this was so as regards impeccability, but not as regards impassibility. But there is a more serious objection.

'Just as in us merit has regard to the intellective part, so is it also in Christ; but in us there is no merit in the inferior portion, unless it has been completely in the superior portion, as is also the case with sin; consequently neither could Christ merit according to the inferior portion only, unless He merited according to the superior portion' (7).

To this Duns replies: 'I say for the sake of argument, that Christ merited according to the superior portion and according to every act of His' (8).

This, however, seems difficult to maintain in view of the accepted doctrine that the blessed do not merit, but enjoy their reward. If Christ could merit even by His beatific vision of God, why should not they? The answer is that merit depends absolutely upon the Divine acceptance. God could, if He chose, treat the beatific act of Michael or of any other of the blessed in heaven as meritorious; actually, however, He does not do so, for the reason that the blessed in heaven are altogether removed from the earthly life, which is the proper sphere of merit. 'With Christ, however, the case was different; in a certain respect He was *in statu viatoris*, and therefore every created act of His was accepted, and meritorious, for those for whom it was offered to God' (9).

This distinction helps Duns further to clear and explain his conception of merit. 'Just as merit neither has regard to nor consists in the very act called forth alone, but in a way in the conditions of the person or the subject calling it forth; so the Divine acceptation not only regards the act, but the accidental conditions of the subject calling it forth' (10).

For instance, two persons may beg pardon of a king for a third, and ask equally well: yet one may not be heard, while the other is for some accidental reason, such as that he is the king's friend. So with Christ the fact that He is so far *extra terminum* is a reason why His beatific act can be accepted as meritorious, in distinction from that of the blessed in heaven.

There is still, however, a further doubt as to whether it is strictly Christ's beatific act, in the enjoyment of the Word in Himself, that is His meritorious act, or rather the same act as it extends to other things seen in the Word, as, for instance, when He loved His mother as seen in the Word, or the other elect thus seen, for God's sake and in God, and even His enemies for God's sake. Altogether then there are three ways in which Christ may be conceived to have merited. Duns says: 'Let the most pleasing way be chosen' (*ibid.*).

It is clear that in place of the firm connexion of the parts of the doctrine of merit found in Thomas, Duns offers us something much looser. The result remains, Christ merited; but the manner of His meriting is by no means so simple as it is in Thomas. In the end Christ appears to merit by an act which it is difficult to view as meritorious; nevertheless accidental circumstances lead God thus to regard it; and the Divine acceptance after all is the only final standard of merit.

Duns next agrees with the former doctors, that Christ merited from the first instance of His conception; since He already had perfect grace, and the object of His action, viz. the whole Trinity, was present to His mind, nor was there any hindrance to His act of volition. There follows the question, as to what He merited. He did not merit for Himself the enjoyment of God; since this was His first act, which could not merit itself. Duns adds, that it would not have been more but less glorious for Christ to have had this union of the soul with God by the way of merit. Did then, as the Master of Sentences declares, Christ merit for Himself the impassibility of soul and body? To this question Duns replies as follows:

'It may be said, in pious agreement with the Master, and by way of a pious gloss upon him, that although He did not merit directly the impassibility of both, yet He merited the removal of the obstacle on account of which these glories were immediately not in Him, viz. the termination of the miracle, which prevented the overflowing of glory to the lower portion of His soul and to His body' (15).

The remainder of what Christ merited is treated of in Dist. 19, qu. unica: 'Whether Christ merited for us all, grace and glory, and the remission of guilt and punishment.'

Here, first of all, Duns gives five (principal) reasons for the negative answer:

(1) The merit of Christ may be held to outweigh the reward of human salvation, and thus there is a disparity which makes a connexion between the two impossible.

(2) On the other hand the merit of Christ was a finite good, since it belonged to Him according to His human nature, whereas the sin of others in so far as it was an offence against God was infinite; so that here there appears to be a disparity the opposite way round, which, however, equally with the former makes the supposed connexion invalid.

(3) The third argument is simply a modification of the second, in so far as the infinity of punishment is substituted for the infinity of sin, and the same conclusion is drawn.

(4) The possibility cannot be denied that the posterity of Adam, inheriting original sin, might extend to infinity, and thus an infinite guilt be produced, which again cannot be compensated by a finite merit.

(5) If Christ's merit were sufficient to confer grace upon all, then all would have obtained grace and glory, which is not the case.[6]

Yet over against all these things the tradition of the Church voiced by Pope Leo declares that Christ, 'just as He found no one free from guilt, so came to redeem all'.[7]

Duns opens the discussion which follows with a reference to the view of Thomas, who recognises in Christ a merit, infinite as regards its sufficiency for the salvation of all, but limited as regards its efficiency for the salvation of those united to Christ by knowledge and love.[8] He also refers to the theory of Anselm, on which the Thomist doctrine as regards sufficiency is founded, viz. that Christ's merit obtains an infinity by reason of the Divine Person Whose it is.[9] The criticism of Duns on the point of sufficiency is as follows:

---

[6] Mt. 22:14.
[8] Cf. 'Summa', III, qu. 48, art. 2, 6.
[7] 'Serm.' XXI, 1.
[9] Cf. 'Cur Deus Homo' II, 14.

'Against this mode of statement I argue, that those statements, in which it is said that the life of Christ was so excellent that it had a certain infinity, appear to be hyperbolical and are to be so explained, seeing that now we speak of the good volition of Christ, by which He merited, and in view of which God accepted His Person for all as regards sufficiency, as they say: because either the good volition of Christ, by which He merited, was just as much accepted as the Person of the Word; or if not, consequently it had not an infinite acceptability, so that it could suffice for an infinite number. If the good volition of Christ was just as much accepted as the Person of the Word, then since the Person of the Word is simply infinite, that good volition was accepted as infinite; but, since God accepts nothing except so far as it has acceptability, consequently that will by reason of its subject had a ground of infinite acceptability; and thus there would be no difference in acceptability between the proper volition of the Word in Himself, and the will of that (i.e. the human) nature in the Word; since as regards what is acceptable there is no greater acceptability: consequently the Word, setting aside the assumed nature, could merit by willing good which is false. And beyond this, it follows that the Trinity could love the volition of the assumed nature as much as the Word Incarnate, which is nonsense, since this is to assume that a creature has as much loveableness as the uncreated, which is false.

'Besides a volition of this kind is no more acceptable to God than it is good: if therefore it was accepted as infinite or for an infinite number, then that will with relation to its subject in the Word was formally infinite:[1] consequently thus the soul of Christ could perfectly enjoy God, or could will with the same regard as the Word with His own will: which is nothing but to assume that the soul was the Word.

'Besides, in itself the principle of that will, taken with every respect to the Word, or to anything else, is finite: consequently both the will was formally finite and limited, and as a consequence was accepted as finite, nor had the Word any causality

[1] I.e. infinite, not merely from some accidental point of view, but in virtue of its form, or intrinsic quality.

242

over that will, which the whole Trinity had not. And if it be granted that the Word has a special influence over that act, yet it does not follow that it is formally infinite and accepted as infinite : because an act thus infinite cannot depend essentially upon any finite causes in completeness, along with an infinite co-operating cause; so that what is created should have an essential causality over that act and not merely an accidental one, such as the assumed nature might have over the volition of the World, and the whiteness of a builder over his building. But the assumed nature had an essential, and not merely an accidental, causality over Christ's will, because according to that nature He merited. Consequently let it be granted that the Word acted specially there, otherwise than the Trinity, yet it does not follow that that act has any ground of infinite acceptance, so that it may avail according to sufficiency for the redemption of an infinite number, but just as the merit was finite in itself, so according to commutative justice it received a finite reward : therefore He did not merit according to sufficiency for an infinite number in the Divine acceptance, just as neither was His merit accepted as infinite, being itself finite' (4).

It has seemed best on account of its extreme importance to give this remarkable criticism in the words of Duns himself, difficult, involved, and thorny as the statement is. It marks the growing gap between the Greek doctrine of the Person of Christ and the new mediaeval doctrine of His human merit.

Seeberg [2] says of the doctrine of Duns on the Person of Christ :

'One may be tempted for a moment so to reproduce the Christology of Duns Scotus, as to conceive of Jesus as a man, who with free will gives Himself to God and is brought by God into a relation of unique communion and absolute dependence, and who possesses in God the truth, which He in detail successively apprehends, and who through His communion with God possesses the power by means of which He immovably, like the blessed in heaven, wills and does the good. This picture would not be absolutely false, yet it would not reproduce the "doctrine" of Duns, in fact not at all accurately—to put it in

[2] 'Die Theologie des Johannes Duns Scotus', p. 274.

modern language—express his feelings. We must not forget that Duns held it possible, that Jesus from the first moment of His conception onwards exercised the moral activity of merit, and that he—in theory at least—in spite of everything, maintained that Christ's human nature was impersonal.'

It is, in fact, in the coexistence side by side of two irreconcilable elements in the doctrine of Duns that its irrationality consists —an irrationality which is met by the appeal to authority. On the one hand, Jesus is a Divine Person, clothed with an impersonal human nature; on the other hand, He is a real human will containing a principle of action independent of the Word. It is out of the discrepancy herein involved that the criticism of Duns, above reproduced, develops itself. If—he says in effect— in order to establish the infinity of the merit of Christ, you take Him strictly as a Divine Person, clothed in an impersonal human nature, then there is in Him no merit at all, nor is there any real difference between His action simply as the Word, and as the Word clothed with humanity. If, on the other hand, you take Him as a human will, as is necessary with a view to the reality of merit, then it is difficult to see how this will of His depends on the Word in any way different from its dependence upon the whole Trinity. Or even, if such special dependence be admitted, since the principle of action is finite, finite it must remain. The two points of view stand sharply apart. Duns ultimately, as we shall see, commits himself to the latter.

We come next to the criticism of the distinction made by Thomas [3] between the sufficiency and the efficiency of Christ's merit, based on the principle that an agent acts in what is disposed to its action and united to the agent. In reply to this position Duns asks, if it means that Christ has not merited for us the first grace, by which we were united to Him. If, however, this be granted, the basis of the distinction is undermined.

Having thus disposed of Anselm and Thomas, Duns proceeds to his own positive statement. Three points are to be considered. First, how Christ merited with regard to efficacy; secondly, how He merited with regard to sufficiency, the words being taken in a fresh sense; thirdly, what He merited.

[3] Cf. 'Summa', III, qu. 48, arts. 2, 6.

Duns deals with the first point by outlining the order of the Divine predestination.

'As regards the first point, I say that the Incarnation of Christ was not by way of occasion,[4] but as the end was seen immediately by God from eternity, so Christ in His human nature, as being nearer to that end, was predestinated before the rest, speaking of the things which are subject to predestination. This, therefore, was the order in the Divine prevision. First God apprehended Himself under the notion of the highest good. In the second act [5] He apprehended all other creatures. In the third He predestinated some to glory and grace, and with regard to the rest exercised a negative act by not predestinating them. In the fourth He foresaw that they would fall in Adam. In the fifth He foreordained or foresaw concerning the remedy, how they might be redeemed by the passion of the Son. Thus then Christ in the flesh, just as also all the elect, was first foreseen and predestinated to grace and glory, before the passion of Christ was foreseen as a remedy against the Fall, just as the doctor first wishes the health of a man, before he ordains the medicine to his healing' (6).

This important argument, in which Duns accepts the position of Rupert of Deutz, that the Incarnation is independent of the Fall, leads obviously to the conclusion that, the passion of Christ being subordinate in the Divine purpose to the salvation of the elect, He must have offered it, and the Trinity must have accepted it, for them alone.

We proceed to the second point, viz. the sufficiency of Christ's merit. Here we have first a summary repetition of the argument already given at length as to the finite nature of the merit of Christ. On the other hand, however, 'just as everything other than God is therefore good, because it is willed by God, and not conversely: so that merit was just as great a good as it was accepted for' (7). Formally, therefore, Christ's merit was not infinite or acceptable for an infinite number; nevertheless, in view of the circumstance that its subject was the Person of the Word, there was a congruity about its being acceptable for an

[4] I.e. the occasion of human sin.
[5] *Signo* (*sc. beneplaciti*), i.e. manifestation of His good pleasure.

245

infinite number. Actually, however, it suffices just for so many and for so much as God willed to accept it for.

As to the third point, Duns teaches as follows: Christ merited for all the first grace, so that our will does not co-operate, except when adults are baptised; and it is the chief point in His merit, that He merits that those, who are not united to Him, should be so. Next, as to penitential grace after a fall into actual sin, although the merit of Christ is here the principal part of the merit required and the total cause of its condignity, yet there is demanded from the recipient of grace, a 'meritum de congruo', such as contrition and compunction for sin. Finally, Christ entirely merited, without the co-operation of any other, the opening of paradise and the removal of the obstacle in the way of our entrance, whether that obstacle was original sin or anything else. Yet, although the obstacle was removed by the passion of Christ, no one (excepting infants, who consequently have the least degree of glory) actually enters heaven without co-operating and using the first grace, which Christ merited for him.

Such then is the positive statement. We return from it to see how Duns disposes of the original (principal) arguments.

(1) As to the argument that the merit of Christ exceeds its reward: If it be granted that He merited according to the inferior portion of the soul, then the reward of the saints is greater than any such merit of Christ. If, however, it be maintained (as it has been), that Christ merited according to the superior portion of the soul, then, where a person merits for others, the reward need not necessarily exceed the merit.

(2) As to the difficulty of a finite merit being set over against the infinity of sin:

(a) Though Christ's merit was formally [6] finite, yet since it joined the elect, by grace and glory, to the infinite God, it could destroy the guilt of sin, or sin itself, which turns man away from the good.

(b) If this is denied, because sin is infinite, the answer is that it is not formally infinite. To maintain this amounts to maintaining a highest evil and a Manichæan God.[7] If, however, the

<hr>

[6] See p. 242, n. 1.   [7] Cf. p. 44, n. 5.

infinity of sin consists in that it is an offence against God, then this is not a formal or intrinsic infinity. But an act of love to God can possess the same kind of infinity from an extrinsic regard. In fact Duns holds it probable that a saint's ardour of love to God may be great enough to counterbalance his inordinate affection in turning away from Him. Especially is this true of the love of the soul of Christ.

(3) As to the infinite punishment due to mortal sin: If the will formally remains in that sin, it is true that it must suffer a punishment extensively infinite. This rule, however, depends simply upon the Divine ordination, and God could punish sin differently, and with a finite punishment, if He willed it.

(4) As to the infinite number of Adam's possible posterity, this difficulty has already been met by anticipation in the main discussion. Duns here therefore merely says that Christ's merit, though finite, could avail for an infinite number, if God so willed; as a matter of fact, however, it avails only for the elect.

(5) As regards the objection, that if Christ's merit had sufficed for all, then all would have been saved, this is easily settled by what has been already said. Christ's passion was offered and accepted, as regards efficacy, for the elect only.

We come now to the last part of the doctrine of Duns on the work of Christ, which is contained in Dist. 20, qu. unica: 'Whether it was necessary that the human race should be restored by the passion of Christ.'

Duns deals with this question by subjecting Anselm's 'Cur Deus Homo' to a most thorough criticism. He reduces Anselm's doctrine to four points:

(1) That it was necessary man should be redeemed.

(2) That he could not be redeemed without satisfaction.

(3) That satisfaction must be made by the God-man.

(4) That the best way was by the passion of Christ.

Under these four heads Duns summarises the argument of the 'Cur Deus Homo'; and then the criticism begins with the words, 'In what Anselm says there appear to be some things doubtful' (7). When, however, Duns has finished, it appears that there is nothing certain.

He takes first the fourth point, and sets against it the familiar

247

authority of Augustine in 'De Trin.' XIII, 10, 13. He also argues
as follows: There was no necessity that Christ should die to
redeem man, except the necessity of consequence. As it is
necessary that I move, if I run; so it was necessary that, if
God had ordained man's redemption by the passion of Christ,
Christ must die. But here the antecedent as well as the consequent
is contingent. Anselm's first point of doctrine in fact is not
sound. The only necessity of man's redemption is to be found in
the Divine predestination.

Then as regards the second point, viz. the necessity of
satisfaction, Duns refers to IV, Dist. 15, qu. 1 (7), where he says
that as regards the absolute power of God, He could allow even
a sinner by mere attrition [8] to merit grace *de congruo,* God
transforming his attrition into contrition, and thus enabling him
to satisfy for sin. Further, even if Christ had not become
incarnate, works of supererogation would have been possible,
if God had in this case also bound us only to the Decalogue:
by such works again satisfaction for sin might have been made.
Nevertheless, according to God's power as subject to order, [9]
satisfaction for sin is necessary, and God has made all further
satisfaction depend upon the satisfaction made by Christ in His
passion.

With regard to the third point, the central point of Anselm's
whole doctrine, Duns says that with all respect to him, his
doctrine here also is untrue. It is untrue that no one satisfies
for sin, unless he offers to God what is of greater value than the
whole creation.

'It was not necessary that the satisfaction for the sin of the
first man should formally [1] exceed the whole creation in magni-
tude and perfection: for it would have sufficed if there had been
offered to God a good greater than was the evil of that man's
sin. Wherefore, if Adam, by grace given him and charity, had
exercised one of many acts of loving God for His own sake, by
a greater effort of the free will than was his effort in sinning,
such love would have sufficed for the remission of his sin, and

---

[8] See p. 201.
[9] See pp. 178ff. for Alexander's explanation of the distinction between God's 'absolute
power' and his 'power with order'.   [1] See again p. 242 , n. 1.

satisfaction would have been made: and thus the proposition is false that he must offer to God something greater than all that for which he ought not to have sinned. But just as he ought not to have sinned for the love of the creature as an object capable of love, so in making satisfaction he ought to offer to God, by touching Him in idea through his act, something greater than is the creature, viz. a love reaching out to God for His own sake; and that love, in its idea, as it is terminated in God, exceeds the love of the creature, just as God exceeds the creature. Wherefore just as he sinned by a love without limit of the less noble object, so he ought to satisfy by a love without limit of the more noble object, and this would have sufficed, at least as regards possibility' (8).

Such an act of love to God, regarded in its idea, i.e. considered with reference to its contemplated end in God, might then have served to make satisfaction for sin. 'Nevertheless that act, by which I am converted to God by love, is not, in its formal aspect, greater than the whole creation, nor even was the created love of Christ, with which He loved God, such' (*ibid.*).

As to Anselm's fourth point, viz. that no one but a man ought to make satisfaction, this again does not appear to be absolutely necessary. One who is not a debtor can make satisfaction for another, just as he can pray for another.

'Wherefore, just as Christ, being an innocent man and not a debtor, made satisfaction, so, if it had pleased God, a good angel could have made satisfaction, offering to God on our behalf, something according to His pleasure, which He might have accepted for all sins: since every created oblation is worth what God accepts it for and no more, as has been said before' (9).

Moreover, a mere man, if he had been miraculously conceived in the same manner as was Christ, and if he had received similar grace, might have made the necessary satisfaction. Nor is Anselm's argument cogent, that in such a case we should have been indebted to him instead of to God. On the contrary, our indebtedness would have been simply to God, he who had made satisfaction being no more than God's instrument, just as our obligation is to God, when the Virgin and the saints have merited on our behalf.

249

Finally, as regards mere possibility, any man might have made satisfaction for himself, since God might have given him, without any merits at all, the first grace which would enable him to win salvation, just as even now He gives him it, without any merits of his own.

The answer to the original question, 'Whether it was necessary that the human race should be restored by the passion of Christ', is therefore as follows: Whatever Christ did in reference to our redemption was only necessary by presupposition of the Divine fore-ordination that would have it so.

'Hence we must believe that that Man suffered for righteousness' sake. For He saw the wickednesses of the Jews, which they committed, and how they were affected with inordinate and distorted affection towards their law, nor would they allow men to be cured on the Sabbath, and yet they would draw out a sheep or an ox out of a well on the Sabbath, and do many other similar things. Christ therefore wishing to recall them all from that error by works and words, preferred to die rather than to remain silent, because the truth had then to be spoken to the Jews, and therefore He died for righteousness' sake. As a matter of fact, however, of His grace He ordained [2] His passion, and offered it to the Father for us, and therefore we are much beholden to Him. For since man could have been otherwise redeemed, and yet of His free will He thus redeemed us, we are much beholden to Him, and more than if we had been thus redeemed of a necessity, and could in no other wise have been redeemed. And therefore, as I believe, He did this especially to attract us to a greater love of Himself, and because He wished man to be more fully bound to God: just as if anyone had first created man, and then instructed him in discipline and in holiness, he would be more under obligation to him, than if he had only created him and another had instructed him, and this is congruity not necessity' (10).

If, however, we wish to 'save' Anselm, we must say that all his reasons proceed upon the presupposition of the Divine fore-ordination, which ordained that man should thus be redeemed: and thus the argument seems to run, that God by His fore-

---

[2] Or 'set in order' (as a sacrifice) : Lat. *ordinavit*.

ordination willed to accept, for the redemption of man, nothing but the death of His Son; yet there was no absolute necessity in the case. Whence says Ps. 130 (:7): 'With Him is plenteous redemption.'

What is supremely interesting in this positive statement is that Duns (anticipated indeed at this point by Anselm, 'Cur Deus Homo', I, 9) first gives a frankly historical view of the cause of the death of Christ. He died to maintain righteousness. Next, however, he accompanies this historical and ethical view of His work with the consideration, that Christ Himself put upon His death the value of a sacrifice to God, Who also accepted it as such. The result is a striking anticipation of the type of theology later developed in the nineteenth century by Ritschl. Moreover, there is another point which is highly noteworthy, viz. that while Duns, as has already been pointed out, most thoroughly carries out the Western anthropological view of the work of Christ, he yet supplies the necessary corrective to the view (here again anticipating Ritschl) by emphasising the immanence of God in His work. Christ is, in His work, human though it be, simply the instrument of God; and therefore our ultimate obligation is not to a man, but to God. In this portion of the doctrine of Duns we have then the outline of a view, whose balance and completeness are in every way remarkable, and which in an extraordinary degree anticipates some of the best modern thought. We see that Duns was far more than a mere critic, and had it in him to develop new dogmatic syntheses. That he did not do so to a greater degree than he has done, is due to his inability after all to break away from tradition.

We have now reached the conclusion of the doctrine of Duns as to the work of Christ. As regards the doctrine of the law, his results in general coincide with those of the previous schoolmen. Men were first under the law of nature: then God added, by way of expansion and elucidation of it, further positive law, first the Mosaic law, and then that of the Gospel. Duns, however, limits the law of nature more than his predecessors do. Not the whole Decalogue, but only, strictly speaking, the first two commandments belong to the law of nature. Moreover, he regards the positive law of the Gospel contained in Scripture as being supplemented by apostolic tradition, and also by the present legislation of the Church: all are alike Divine law. We have before noticed that Duns in his doctrine of Scripture and tradition prepares the way for the later doctrine of the Roman Church.[3]

The principal points of the doctrine of Duns on sacramental grace are contained in 'Opus Oxoniense', IV, Dist. 2, qu. 1: 'Whether the sacraments of the new law have efficacy from the passion of Christ.'

The new law, as the perfection of law, has necessarily the most perfect assistances to grace, i.e. the most perfect sacraments.

Moreover, a second proof, that the new law has the most perfect sacraments, is as follows:

'The most perfect meritorious cause of grace, which the Trinity determined to give to the human race, was Christ, accomplishing His course in this life along with us: now the meritorious cause justly inclines God to grant good to him, for whom such cause merits: moreover, that cause demands more, as manifested, than as promised: therefore in view of the passion of Christ, as manifested and confirmatory of the new law, it was fit that the greatest assistance to grace should be conferred on men, for the time that that law was to be observed' (2).

The perfection of the sacraments of the new law, thus assured, is seen to be both intensive and extensive. The former perfection appears in the completeness with which they signify the truth, the latter in the completeness with which they confer grace. Duns reproduces here the doctrine of Lombard and Thomas, showing how the seven sacraments confer the grace necessary at every stage of the life of the individual Christian, and also the grace necessary for the Church as a community.

Next he agrees with Thomas against Alexander, that all the sacraments were instituted by Christ or God. He, moreover, gives a Scripture proof for this, as follows: Baptism, Mt. 28:19: Eucharist, Jn 6:22f., Mt. 26:17f.; Confirmation, Jn 20:22f.;

[3] See for the doctrine of Duns on the law in general, Seeberg, 'Die Theologie des Johannes Duns Scotus', pp. 484ff.

252

Penance, Jn 20:23, Mt. 16:19; Extreme Unction, Mk 6:13; Matrimony, Mt. 19:4f.; Orders, 1 C. 11:24, Jn 20:23. None but God could institute a sacrament, which is a practical sign of God's proper action.

It is then fixed that the sacraments of the new law are the most perfect possible, and that they were instituted by Christ Himself. Hence, says Duns, follows the solution of the question, if we first understand its meaning; 'for, for a sacrament to have efficacy, is for it to have the effect signified regularly accompanying it: therefore it has efficacy from Him from whom it is, that the effect accompanies it' (6).

This concomitance may take place for two reasons, on account of the principal cause which brings it about, or on account of the meritorious cause which merits it.

'And according to this I say that the sacraments of the new law have efficacy from God alone as principal cause, but have efficacy from Christ suffering, or from the passion of Christ, as meritorious cause' (ibid.).

The first point is clear from the fact that God alone instituted the sacraments, because, if He instituted them, their efficacy can be from no lower cause. For the acts signified by the sacraments are proper to God alone, and can have no second cause. Only God alone therefore can determine Himself to the effects signified by the sacraments.

The second point is clear from III, Dist. 19, and may be shortly proved as follows:

'When man had become an enemy to God through guilt, God determined not to forgive that guilt, nor to give any assistance towards such remission, or towards the obtaining of beatitude, except by means of something offered to Him, which He would accept with more pleasure than that offence was displeasing or disagreeable to Him. Nothing, however, can be found more agreeable to the Trinity than the whole guilt and offence of the human race was displeasing or disagreeable, except there should take place some obedience of a person more beloved, than that whole community which offended through the universal offence had been dear, or ought to be dear, if it had not offended. Such a person so beloved the whole human race could not produce from itself, since it was as a whole God's enemy in one mass of perdition. The Trinity, therefore, determined to give to the human race a person so beloved, and to incline him to the offering of an obedience for that whole race: such a person there is none but Christ, to Whom God gave, not according to measure, the spirit of charity and of grace,[4] and such an obedience is that in which there appears the greatest charity, that is to offer oneself even to death for righteousness' sake: therefore the Trinity granted to man as pilgrim [5] no assistance belonging to salvation, except in virtue of this offering of Christ made on the cross, both by a Person most beloved, and out of the greatest charity. And in this way that passion was the meritorious cause, in regard of meritorious good granted to man as pilgrim' (7).

Duns adds two corollaries. First, it is clear how, in the granting of such remedies necessary to the human race, mercy and truth agree.

'It is a work of the greatest mercy, to grant such remedies to a man who is an enemy: but also it is a mark of the greatest justice, on account of an obedience so pleasing of a Person so beloved, to grant such a remedy to those for whom that Person offered that obedience. It was the greatest mercy in the Person offering, thus to offer Himself for the enemies of the Trinity, Which He supremely loved: but it was also a mark of the greatest justice, both with reference to God and to fallen man: for He would not appear in the greatest degree to love God and His neighbour, unless He were willing to offer that obedience for the sake of so great a common good, viz. the beatitude of man, to which God had fore-ordained him, and had decreed that he should not attain, except through that obedience' (8).

The second corollary is that although the passion of Christ was the meritorious cause of the efficacy of the ancient sacraments, and of the grace granted to the ancient fathers, yet it has a greater efficacy in regard of our sacraments and the grace granted through them, in so far as the obedience of Christ has greater acceptance as manifested, than merely as foreseen.

The above discussion of the efficacy of the sacraments is important in enabling us more adequately to understand Duns'

[4] Jn 3:34.   [5] P. 123, n. 8.

total doctrine of the work of Christ. In the first place, we see that when he is dealing practically with the effect of Christ's passion, he can be much more positive than we might imagine from the extent and incisiveness of his criticism.

It becomes clear that Duns is very much in earnest when in III, Dist. 19 he speaks of 'saving' Anselm—only with the omission of his doctrine of the absolute necessity of the work of Christ. Of course this doctrine was the real nerve of Anselm's theory; but in wishing to destroy it, Duns was one with Alexander and Thomas.

The discussion is also important because of the different attitude towards the grace in the sacraments which we find in Duns, as compared with Thomas. For him, as for Alexander, the grace is not strictly in the sacraments, but they are the sign of it: as he puts it, they are the Divinely appointed sign of its regular concomitance. The sacrament therefore appears less and less to have efficacy in the very nature of things, and to possess it only in virtue of an arbitrary Divine institution.

We may complete our account of the teaching of Duns by a reference to his important criticism of the doctrine of justification. For a succinct account of this I may first most conveniently refer to 'Opus Parisiense', III, Dist. 18, qu. 2: 'Whether God can remit guilt, that is mortal guilt, without the infusion of grace.'

The judgment of Duns is as follows:

'I say that God can do this by His absolute power, but not by His power with order.[6] The first point is proved, in that it includes no contradiction, that sin should be remitted, and grace not given, because when two certain things have a mean between them, it is not necessary that the transition from one extreme to the other should take place without (a passing through) the mean—nay rather a stay may be made at the mean, as in the case of colours; but between the state of guilt and that of grace a mean is included, viz. that a man should be in a state of mere nature, just as Adam was created without any sin, and without justifying grace (gratia gratum faciente); therefore he who is in a state of mortal sin may without any (implied) contradiction be brought back to the same state (as Adam's), because

---

[6] See p. 248, n. 9.

255

this can be done, and is not inconsistent with the matter in itself, and is not therefore impossible to God.

'The second point is proved, because such procedure does not befit the wisdom, goodness, and justice of God in accordance with the order which He has instituted: because He has decreed, that no one should attain beatitude unless he is clothed with grace like a wedding garment, therefore He clothes every man, to whom He remits mortal guilt, with such a garment. Nevertheless, if He had done otherwise, or wished to do otherwise, it would have been just, simply because it pleased Him; yet according to the order mentioned God cannot remit guilt without the infusion of grace. This is also necessary to man in accordance with the state of fallen nature, because, as it is, man cannot progress in good, nor long keep himself from sin, without the assistance of grace, because such nature is weak on account of sin, although perchance in the state of innocence he might be able to stand, and to keep himself without grace' (G).

In 'Opus Oxoniense', IV, Dist. 16, qu. 2, Duns discusses 'whether the remission and expulsion of guilt and the infusion of grace are one change simply'.

This question Duns answers in the negative, for four reasons:

(1) The first can be multiplied while the second remains single. In fact the first is multiple, in so far as God separately forgives each sin committed.

(2) The first can take place without the second, and *vice versa*. God did in fact, without remission of sin, infuse grace into man in the state of innocence and into the good angels. That He can remit sin without infusing grace, is shown as in the argument already given from 'Opus Parisiense'.

(3) There is no formal repugnance between guilt and grace. For the will of the creature has power to bring guilt into existence, or to avoid so doing; but it has no power over the existence of grace. Hence there can be no necessary relation between guilt and grace.

(4) One change only is reckoned, when it takes place from the corresponding privation to the corresponding quality. But from (1) it is clear that guilt, which may be manifold, cannot be the privation corresponding to the quality of grace.

We are carried still farther into the heart of the view of Duns, when he tells us next that neither are the remission of guilt and the infusion of grace two real changes. The infusion of grace is indeed a real change, since it takes place, from the privation of a real quality, to the existence of it. But the remission of guilt is, not a real, but an ideal change (*mutatio rationis*), by which the sinner passes from the state of being under obligation to punishment, for this is what guilt really is, to the state of being without such obligation (18).

It is clear that this doctrine of Duns is of great importance in regard to the doctrine of justification. The two parts of justification, as traditionally distinguished, from Augustine onwards, viz. the remission of sins and the infusion of grace—which Thomas had identified as aspects of one and the same real change—now appeared as logically independent of one another, and merely coexisting by the Divine decree. Moreover, most important of all, the remission of sins, in opposition to the real change of the infusion of grace, is declared to be an ideal change, as indeed guilt itself is ideal and not real. Guilt is in fact a relation in the Divine mind between a certain person and punishment; so that the remission of guilt is the removal in the Divine mind of this relation.

CHAPTER 7

THE END OF THE MEDIAEVAL THEOLOGY

THE NOMINALISTS, OCCAM AND BIEL

THE history of the scholastic theology after Duns Scotus is, in the main, one of dissolution. The greatest schoolman of this period, the Franciscan, William of Occam (d. A.D. 1349), went farther than Duns himself in criticism of the rational proofs of the faith of the Church, resting the support of it more and more upon authority alone. Theology was defined to be, not a proper science, which proceeds from a first principle to necessary conclusions, but simply an aggregative science, i.e. a science improperly so-called, which collects and arranges in order the different independent points of Divine revelation.[1]

There were two factors which contributed to this atomistic point of view:

(1) A Nominalistic philosophy was now adopted by Occam instead of the Realism which had characterised the previous schoolmen, including Duns. Realism assumed that in the concept the mind touched the essence of the thing represented by it: for Nominalism this was not so, but the concept was simply the subjective combination of impressions made by the thing on the human mind. Thus all knowledge was merely an operation with concepts (*termini*), whose accuracy could only be verified by the intuition of the senses. Where, as in the case of revelation, the senses failed to give help, there no such verification was possible. Moreover, knowledge as contained in concepts (*termini*) was inevitably also symbolic, especially where no intuitions were forthcoming. Thus all theological knowledge was only an arrangement of symbols, which never touched the heart of reality. It could therefore hardly be expected that the logic which applied to ordinary natural science should apply to this revealed know-

---

[1] Cf. Werner, 'Die Scholastik des späteren Mittelalters', vol. ii, 1883, pp. 46, 47.

258

ledge. Here was one basis of the increased irrationalism of Nominalism.[2]

(2) Occam adopted from Duns the idea of God as a contingent or arbitrary will, and gave it an even wider scope. He excelled himself in showing, that God could just as well have chosen a thousand other possibilities, instead of the course actually taken by Him. Faith, for example, teaches that God assumed one nature only, viz. the human; but He might just as easily have assumed the nature of an ass, a stone, or of wood. All the actual arrangements of the order of salvation were purely arbitrary.[3]

The relation between Thomas, Duns, and Occam is thus forcibly described in the 'Manual of Catholic Theology', of J. Wilhelm and Thos. B. Scannell (London, 1890), Vol. I, Introd., p. xxviii: 'St Thomas is strictly organic; Scotus is less so. St Thomas, with all his fineness of distinction, does not tear asunder the different tissues, but keeps them in their natural, living connexion; Scotus, by the dissecting process of his distinctions, loosens the organic connexions of the tissues, without, however, destroying the bond of union, and thereby the life of the loosened parts, as the Nominalists did. In other words, to St Thomas the universe is a perfect animal organism, wherein all the parts are held together in a most intimate union and relation by the soul; whereas to Scotus it is only a vegetable organism, as he himself expresses it,[4] whose different members spring from a common root, but branch out in different directions; to the Nominalist, however, it is merely a mass of atoms arbitrarily heaped together. These general differences of modes of conception manifest themselves in almost all the particular differences of doctrine.'

This striking description is true if we look at the actual theology of Thomas, Duns, and Occam: it is, however, to be remembered that the seeds of the subsequent process of dissolution were sown by Thomas himself, in so far as he made the relation of God to the world essentially contingent.

Occam himself in his great commentary on the 'Sentences'

---

[2] Cf. Heim, 'Das Gewissheitsproblem', pp. 202–19 ; Hermelink, 'Die theologische Fakultät in Tübingen', pp. 96–106.　　[3] Werner, op. cit. p. 356 ; Heim, op. cit. p. 212.
[4] The passage referred to is quoted by Seeberg, 'Die Theologie des Johannes Duns Scotus', p. 77.

deals only with a part of the distinctions of the Third Book. We therefore take our account of the Occamist doctrine of the work of Christ from the Commentary of Occam's disciple Gabriel Biel (d. 1475). The commentary is based chiefly upon Occam himself, where that is possible, and is otherwise known as 'Collectorium ex Occamo in iv libros sententiarum'. Biel, like Occam, in his positive theology generally, though not exclusively, follows Duns: the Occamist criticism also is largely a repetition of that of Duns, but is also developed independently, as there is opportunity, from the standpoint of the Nominalist epistemology.

We may notice first of all how Biel deals with the question, whether Christ would have become incarnate, even if man had not sinned (III, Dist. 2, qu. un., dub. 3). Biel first refers with approval to the opinion of Thomas, not in the 'Summa Theologica', but in his commentary on the 'Sentences' (III, Dist. 1, qu, 1), that He alone can know the truth on this question, Who was born and was offered, because He willed it. 'Wherefore', says Biel, 'this question is sufficiently doubtful.' Reference is then made on the one hand to the affirmative answer given by Alexander and Scotus, and on the other hand to the negative reply returned by Thomas ('S. Theol.' III, qu. 1, art. 3); and in conclusion the matter is clinched with a reference to Bonavertura, as follows: 'St Bonaventura says in Lib. III, Dist. 1 that the first opinion (that the Incarnation would have taken place apart from the Fall) rather follows the decision of reason. The second (that it depended on the Fall) rather agrees with Holy Scripture and the authorities of the saints and the reverence of faith. For wherever mention is made of the descent of God (into this world) in either Testament, there is assigned as its reason the deliverance of the human race.'

Biel therefore leaves the point open. It is important, however, to observe that he refutes, on the authority of Occam, the doctrine of Duns which assigns the order of the Divine decrees as a reason for the view that the Incarnation would have taken place apart from the Fall.

'There is no such order in Divine things. But God from all eternity predestinated those whom He chose. He foreknew also those whom He rejected : and at the same time He foresaw merits and demerits, punishments and future rewards : that fiction, therefore, proves nothing.'

Though, however, this reason of Duns and others on the same side are not conclusive, neither are those on the other side. 'That problem, therefore, remains indeterminate, equally probable in either direction, till God shall be pleased to reveal the one doctrine, or the other.'

As regards the grace of Christ (Dist. 13, qu. unica), Biel holds (art. 1), with Occam, against Duns, that there is no absolute limit to any form or quality, but that its degree can always be infinitely increased. Accordingly he teaches (art. 2, concl. 1) that the soul of Christ had not the highest grace possible according to the absolute power of God; nevertheless (concl. 3), it had the highest possible that could be conferred on a creature according to God's power with order.[5]

As regards the grace of union, the habitual grace of Christ, and His grace as Head, Biel holds (dub. 2), that it is a probable opinion that the union itself is really distinct from Christ's habitual grace, while of Christ's grace as Head he says this is the same as His habitual grace, in so far as the latter, in accordance with its fullness, filled the soul of Christ, and is the meritorious cause of our grace, by which He infuses into us the knowledge of God, and the motive principle of love.

We may next notice that Biel lays great stress on the sufferings of Christ (Dist. 15, qu. unica, art. 2, pars 2, concl. 2), viewing them as the means whereby He saved men from the penalties of their sin. He teaches, that Christ experienced grief or pain in every part of His soul, and that this pain was the greatest possible endurable in this life. Biel goes into great detail on this point, and reckons in all the sufferings which Christ endured in His life from infancy onward, till the climax of suffering was reached in Gethsemane and on the Cross. Biel constantly describes the sufferings of Christ as penal (*pœna Christi*), and assimilates His whole passion in the contrition of the penitent. He says, as follows :

'Although the outward suffering of Christ was the greatest

[5] See p. 248, n. 9.

bodily suffering and extreme pain of sense, yet His inward suffering in the rational part of the soul was greater and was of highest excellence. For it was concerning what He supremely hated, viz. the injury and contempt of His Father through the sins of all men as well past, present, and future. None of the repentant ever had so great contrition and grief for his own sins, as in that hour of satisfaction the Lord had for the sins of each and all. For His contrition assumed for us sufficiently blotted out all sins, and paid the whole penalty owed for them.'

Biel further agrees with Thomas ('Summa', pars III, qu. 46, art. 6) that since the Lord voluntarily assumed grief for the sake of delivering mankind from sin, therefore the grief assumed was proportionate to the fruit that followed it, viz. the remission of the sins of all men. Although a smaller degree of suffering would have sufficed by reason of the infinity of the Person of the Sufferer, yet Christ wished to save the human race not by power, but by justice.

'Therefore He not only considered how great virtue His suffering would have because of the Divinity united to His humanity; but He considered how much would suffice according to His human nature for such a satisfaction.'

As regards the merit of Christ, Biel teaches (III, Dist. 18, art. 2, concl. 5) that Christ not only merited in His passion, but, from the very instant of the Incarnation, in His conception.

'Christ in the instant of His conception had all things requisite for merit, viz. a power perfected by the light of glory, as they say, and charity, and the presence of the Object of merit. Nor was there any hindrance: therefore in that instant He had a clear vision and blessed enjoyment of Divinity. But by His enjoyment He merited, as has just been proved;[6] therefore the conclusion is true. For He was in that instant of His conception a man perfected with every grace, and virtue, and meritorious operation.'

But further (concl. 6) it was the same thing which Christ merited in His passion, and before it in His conception. 'The

---

[6] Cf. not. 2, and concl. 2. Charity, the root of merit, has its seat in the superior portion of the soul, while every act of this portion of the soul, as inspired by charity, terminates in God, and is beatific.

proof is: since in the moment of His conception He merited the redemption of the human race and the glory of His own body, by the obedience in which, obeying the Father, He by an act of will offered Himself, to the honour of the Father, to a death to be endured for the redemption of the human race: therefore He merited by this act, and He merited the very same thing by His passion: therefore the conclusion is true.' This doctrine, however, leaves open the doubt as to whether, if Christ merited all at once from His conception, He could merit at all by His passion. Can anyone merit the same thing twice over? Biel resolves this difficulty (dub. 3) by an appeal to the doctrine of Thomas. The same thing may be merited in different ways.

In Dist. 19, qu. unica, Biel accordingly deals with the merit of Christ in His passion. Here he reproduces mainly the doctrine of Duns, but with some noteworthy modifications and developments.

(Concl. 1.) 'Christ sufficiently merited grace and the opening of the kingdom for Adam and his whole posterity. This is proved because the merit of the passion of Christ was sufficient in the Divine acceptation for the remission of all sins, at least of those who believed in Christ and obeyed the law. And while the truth of this stands as a matter of fact and is in itself contingent, and therefore cannot be sufficiently demonstrated (though plausible arguments may be adduced, whereof the blessed Anselm gathers many in his book "Cur Deus Homo"), yet the authority of Scripture is an efficacious proof.' Biel refers to Lk. 19:10, 1 Tim. 1:15, Jn 3:16, Mt. 20:28, Rev. 1:5, and adds: 'And there are innumerable such passages in Scripture, in which it is testified that He merited eternal rewards for those who are united to Him by faith and the sacraments' (Mk 16:16).

(Concl. 2.) 'For those who preceded Him, Christ, by His passion as a sufficient merit, obtained, in so far as it was foreseen, the remission of sins and grace, but in so far as it was exhibited, the opening of the kingdom of heaven and glory.' This doctrine Biel proves by the authority of Mt. 21:9 on the one hand, and of Ps. 68:18 on the other.

(Concl. 3.) 'Although the merit of Christ was in itself simply finite, nevertheless it was accepted as sufficient for an infinite posterity of Adam (if there should be such). The first point is clear from not. 3: since the merit of Christ was an act or a passion of His human nature, and with all the rest of its actions and attributes was a creature, and was in consequence finite. The second point is clear: since Christ's merit was accepted as a sufficient satisfaction and reconciliation for all who obey Him, though they be infinite in number.'

(Concl. 4.) 'By His passion and death, which He offered to the Father for the restoration of men, He efficaciously merited final grace and glory for the predestinated alone.' This is proved by the arguments, that on the one hand only those obtain final grace and glory who obtain them through Christ's passion, and that on the other hand those who obtain these things are the predestinated alone.[7] On this point Biel repudiates, as previously,[8] the doctrine of Duns on the order of the Divine decrees. He says:

'Such priorities are not to be admitted in things Divine, just as neither is there to be admitted a plurality of decreed acts in accordance with the imagination of the Subtle Doctor. For there is but one act in Divine things, indivisible both in fact and in conception (re et ratione), which is the Divine Essence itself, by which act in one single cognition that Essence itself foresaw the Incarnation of Christ, the future beatitude of all the elect, and the Fall and Restoration through Christ's passion. Nor is one thing prior, and another posterior, and therefore there is no such order in things Divine.'

(Concl. 5.) 'Although the passion of Christ principally merited salvation for all the sons of Adam, yet there co-operated from time to time the work of those who were to be saved, by way of meritum de congruo or de condigno.'

'Though the passion of Christ be the principal merit, on account of which is conferred grace, the opening of the kingdom, and glory, yet it is never the only and whole meritorious cause. This is clear: since there always concurs with the merit of Christ some work as meritum de congruo or de condigno on the part of the recipient of grace or glory, if he were an adult having the use of reason, or of some other on his behalf, if he lacks the use of reason.'

Mt. 25:34, Rom. 8:30.   [8] See p. 260.

Biel, however, adds that this is this case *de lege communi*: he makes this reservation to allow for those who have been sanctified in the womb, in which case the passion of Christ was the sole and total cause of the sanctification.

This last conclusion is particularly noteworthy, inasmuch as it brings at last to clear statement what of course is the implicit doctrine of all the schoolmen, viz. that the merit of Christ requires to be supplemented by further merit in order to salvation. No one of the great schoolmen had, however, ventured to say roundly like Biel, that the merit of Christ is never the only and whole meritorious cause of salvation.

In connexion with the above doctrine of Dist. 19, qu. un., it is particularly interesting to notice how simply Biel identifies Christ's merit and His satisfaction. 'Christ's merit was accepted as a sufficient satisfaction and reconciliation for all who obey Him' (concl. 3). Biel's conception of this satisfaction is further elucidated by the answer which he gives (dub. 2) to the traditional question, how we are delivered from guilt, from punishment, from the power of the devil, and from the bond of the writing of the Divine sentence.

'Although the solution of these points is clear from the foregoing, yet for the sake of a short and summary answer, it is to be noted, that through the sin of the first man, by which God was offended with the whole human race, man fell into a state of guilt or obligation to eternal death; and by means of this fell under the power of the devil, as the executioner inflicting the punishment. Now this obligation, in so far as it binds man to pay the penalty of death, is called the writing of the sentence; because just as a writing is an evidence and assurance of a certain debt, so the bond, by which man is under penalty of death by reason of the Divine decree (since it is certain) is metaphorically called the writing of the sentence.[9] But now by the remission of the debt, which is the sentencing of man to punishment because of sin inherited or committed, man is freed from guilt, from punishment, from the power of the devil, and from the bond of the writing of the sentence, because by the remission of the debt he is no longer sentenced to punishment,

[9] Col. 2:14.

265

but is received through grace into friendship with God, and thereby has neither guilt nor liability to punishment, and as a consequence is neither under the power of the devil nor under the bond of the writing. Now this remission is made by the passion of Christ, because the Divine wisdom ordained, not to predestinate fallen man to salvation, and therefore neither to remit his guilt nor his punishment, unless an obedience as acceptable as his guilt was displeasing and unacceptable should be offered by some innocent person: Christ therefore according to His human nature, of His supreme charity voluntarily choosing to die, offered such an obedience to the glory of God; for the human will of Christ proceeding from love so great pleased God more than the sins of all men, not only past, present, and future, but even possible, displeased Him. Therefore on account of a work of Christ so acceptable, which He offered to the Trinity for the reconciliation of man, the Trinity forgave their sins and the guilt of sin to all incorporated in Christ, and ordained anew to glory those formerly ordained to punishment, and thereby delivered them from all the things before mentioned.'

With Dist. 20, qu. unica, we come at last to the central problem, 'whether the restoration of the human race took place of necessity through the passion of Christ as man'.

Here (not. 1) Biel, like Duns, criticises the reasons of Anselm's 'Cur Deus Homo', and says that though they are pious and plausible, 'yet unless they proceed upon the presupposition of the Divine decree, they prove nothing'. They do not, therefore, prove the necessity, taken strictly, either of redemption or of the mode of redemption. As to the first point, there was no more necessity for redemption than there was for creation. 'God could have annihilated, and could still annihilate every rational creature, whether in glory, or in the way of salvation, or under damnation: for just as He contingently created them, so He contingently preserves them.' Thus Anselm's argument, that God must lead man on to beatitude, fails. Again, as to the mode of redemption: 'sin could have been forgiven without satisfaction by mere non-imputation.[1] For by sin, neither is anything existing in God destroyed, nor is the Divine honour in itself diminished,

[1] Ps. 32:1.

266

and so there is nothing that can be restored to God, just as there is nothing that can be taken away from Him. Wherefore the sinner need not remain in guilt, until he make satisfaction, but only till God forgive him the satisfaction which ought to be made; nor, if God were freely to forgive sin without satisfaction, would there be anything out of order in the universe: for the only thing that could be out of order in the universe would be, if anything were to take place or to exist against the will of the Divine good pleasure. For the will of God alone is the rule of all order and justice in the universe.'

In the above arguments as to the necessity of redemption and of the mode of it, even more daring conclusions than those of Duns are drawn from the absolute contingency of all temporal things upon the Divine will. But the second argument contains a further most interesting point. We have already seen (p. 264) how strongly Biel holds the absolute metaphysical unity of the Divine Being; so that he denies any such plurality or order of the Divine decrees as Duns had maintained. Here he turns this same metaphysical doctrine against Anselm's doctrine that sin robs God of His honour and that satisfaction restores it. Anselm, indeed, who shared the same metaphysical doctrine of God, had felt the difficulty Biel points out; but had anticipated it by the distinction:

'It is clear that God, as far as He is in Himself, can be honoured or dishonoured by no one; but any one, as far as he is in himself, appears to do this, when he subjects his will to God's or withdraws it from His.' [2]

Next, Biel comes to the necessity of Christ's satisfaction, it being supposed that satisfaction is the appointed way of redemption. Here he simply repeats the critical reflections of Duns on the natural finitude of Christ's merit, and on the dependence of its enhanced value upon the Divine acceptation.

His final result, then, is that neither the redemption of the human race, nor the mode of it chosen by God was necessary (concl. 1); but that, nevertheless, the mode of redemption through the passion of the Only-Begotten was the fittest of all modes by which the human race could be redeemed (concl. 2). For the

[2] 'Cur Deus Homo', I, 15.

proof of its fitness Biel refers to Lombard, Alexander, Bonaventura, and Thomas.

Gottschick [3] remarks upon the doctrine of Biel on the work of Christ, that there is no need to prove in his case, what rather demanded proof in the case of Duns, that all his critical reflections only play round about the indubitable validity of the tradition derived from Lombard. An interesting proof of this appears in the fact that Biel adds to the 'summary answer', covering the whole ground of the doctrine, previously quoted from Dist. 19, qu. unica, dub. 2, the remark: 'these things can be gathered from Anselm lib. II "Cur Deus Homo")'. As it was with Alexander, Thomas, and Duns, so it is with Biel. It is not the elements of Anselm's view that are criticised, but only the nexus between them.

Biel's doctrine of the law must next engage our attention. He distinguishes between the law of nature and the Divine law as follows (Dist. 37, qu. unica, not. 1):

'The Divine law is obtained by revelation. The law of nature is obtained from the natural light of the intellect.'

'The Divine law concerning one's neighbour of itself governs man to the end of eternal happiness. The natural law governs him to the human felicity of this life. In the remaining points the natural law and the Divine law agree.'

Biel, however, agrees with Duns (concl. 1) that not all the precepts of the Decalogue belong to the law of nature in the strict sense, but only the precepts against the worship of strange gods and against irreverence (concl. 2). It is only the precepts strictly belonging to the law of nature that are absolutely indispensable (concl. 4).

In Dist. 40, qu. unica, Biel states the usual scholastic doctrine as to the superiority of the new law of the Gospel to the law of the Old Testament, alike in precepts, in sacraments, and in promises.

We proceed to the doctrine of the sacraments. In IV, Dist. 1, qu. 1, Biel discusses 'whether the sacraments of the new law are the effective causes of grace'.

Concl. 1 lays it down that 'the sacraments of the new law

---

[3] 'Zeitschrift für Kirchengeschichte', 1903, p. 221.

cause the sacramental effect, which by Divine institution they signify and certify'.

Biel undertakes to prove this by authority and reason, having first defined the 'sacramental effect' as being justifying grace (*gratia gratum faciens*) in every case but that of the Eucharist, where it is the Real Presence of Christ on the altar. The authorities quoted are Augustine, Bernard, Hugo, and Thomas. The rational proof rests on the point, 'that when God instituted the sacraments He determined Himself to produce at the presence of the sacrament, the gracious effect which He would not produce in its absence'. Concl. 2 asserts that 'the sacraments of the new law are not the cause of grace, by reason of their proper nature as assigned them at the first creation of things'. The proof is that the matters of the sacraments had no gracious results before the advent of Christ. Finally (concl. 7) Biel sums up his doctrine as follows:

' The sacraments are *causæ sine qua non* of the sacramental effect. This is clear because they are the causes of the sacramental effect, by the first conclusion, and not the natural causes, or causes by their proper nature, by the second conclusion; therefore they are the *causæ sine qua non*. The consequence holds from the sufficiency of the division. Moreover, by the voluntary Divine institution the sacramental effect is not caused without them—it is, however, caused when they are present— therefore they are *causæ sine qua non*. The consequence holds from the definition of the term, *causa sine qua non*.'

Biel has thus reduced the correspondence between the sacrament and the sacramental effect to the mere *fiat* of the Divine will. It is a good example of the atomising method of the Nominalist scholasticism, and its tendency to treat all things merely as problems in logic. Nominalism gives up all attempt to understand the thing, but is most careful as to the logical definition of the term corresponding to it.

Biel gives the usual scholastic reasons for the number of the seven sacraments, which he thinks it probable were all instituted by Christ (Dist. 2, qu. 1, not. 1, 2). He follows Duns in the doctrine of how they derive their effect from the passion of Christ (dub. 1).

We come finally to Biel's doctrine of justification, which is given in Dist. 4, qu. 1, with reference to Baptism, and Dist. 14, qu. 1, with reference to penance.

Biel teaches (Dist. 4, qu. 1, not. 3) that 'grace and sin are not absolutely and in the nature of the thing contrary one to another, and in consequence do not in the nature of the thing expel one another'.

This is so, because whether a particular act is sin depends simply upon God's will, and a change in this will would make the act no longer sin, and therefore perfectly consonant with the infusion of grace.

Neither are the terms guilt and grace in themselves logically contradictory, but only when taken connotatively, i.e. in the sense that guilt presupposes the Divine rejection, and the gift of grace the Divine acceptance of eternal life. If, however, grace is taken without further connotation simply for the infused quality, and guilt for the sinful act without the thought of the offended God, then there is no repugnance between them.

The corollary is 'that God of His absolute power can remit sin and punishment without the infusion of grace. He can also accept to life eternal and confer the same without grace. . . . But as a matter of fact God, according to His power, as subject to order, can do neither.' [4]

Further light is cast upon the subject in Dist. 14, qu. 1, where Biel inquires (not. 2), what it is that is destroyed when sin is forgiven. Guilt, or the stain of sin, is nothing but the ordination of the sinner to punishment, or more strictly it is the sinner viewed as ordained to punishment, while the offence of the sinner is, strictly speaking, God viewed as angry and ordaining him to punishment. 'The first two are spoken of as being in the sinner by identity, or by predication, not by real inhesion; the third is similarly spoken of as being in God: and they are, therefore, said not to remain, by reason of the forgiveness of sin; for, when sin is forgiven, they no longer stand for the sinner, or for God, and yet nothing is really destroyed or abolished either in the justified sinner, or yet in God.'

Finally (not. 4) 'in accordance with God's power as subject

[4] See p. 248, n. 9.

to order guilt is not remitted; unless at the same time justifying grace (*gratia gratum faciens*) is infused'. 'And hence it is, that between a sinner, under the obligation of punishment, and a righteous man expecting glory, there is no mean, any more than there is between one in grace and out of grace. And notwithstanding the remission of punishment and the gift of grace are distinct changes, because remission is as it were a change in the nature of loss; because it is the cessation of the obligation and the removal of the punishment. On the other hand the gift of grace is a change in the nature of gain, because the creation of grace is also its infusion.'

The result of all this is in the sharpest way to distinguish the two elements united in his conception of justification by Augustine, which Thomas had endeavoured to identify, even more sharply from one another than had been done by Duns. According to Biel the remission of sins and the infusion of grace have no vital connexion, and hang together simply by the Divine *fiat*.

We notice in the above argument the continual stress on the distinction between terms and the things for which they stand, which is fundamental to the epistemologically grounded logic of Occam. This is the instrument by which the Nominalist scholasticism achieves its atomising effect upon the traditional theology.

'Logic', says Occam himself, 'is the most apt instrument of all the arts, without which no science can be had in perfection.' [5]

As to the positive effect which Occam hoped to effect upon theology by his logical criticism it is interesting to read in the same work (III, 1):

'Hence it arises that many, not knowing logic, have publicly taught out of the sayings of the saints and the writings of Aristotle new opinions beyond those vocally expressed in Holy Scripture; and, filling books not a few, have left behind these opinions in their writings.' Here is a programme indicated, which it was given neither to Occam nor Biel to carry out, viz. the simplification of theology by the return from the Fathers and Aristotle to the words of Holy Scripture. Three very different

---

[5] 'Summa totius logicæ', Ven. 1522, vol. i, Preface.

men attempted each in his own way to carry out this programme. They were Erasmus, Luther, and Zwingli.

ERASMUS

The Renaissance was in the first place the literary revival of the culture of the ancient Græco-Roman world, in the second place the appropriation of its ideas and ideals. Under both aspects it appears as a movement of opposition to the culture of the Middle Ages and above all to the mediaeval scholasticism. The great representative of the spirit of the Renaissance upon the field of theology is Erasmus (d. A.D. 1536). As a humanist, he was repelled by the complication and technicality of the mediaeval schoolmen in contrast with the clarity and ease of the classical authors. As a theologian, he wished to simplify theology by a return to the original literary sources of the Christian religion, viz. the writings of the New Testament. What he saw in them in opposition to the elaborate argumentation of the schoolmen was a simple Christian morality, possessing at once its standard and its attractiveness in the example of Jesus Christ. He did not deny the rights of the scholastic theology in its own domain; but he regarded it as the peculiar function of the monastic theologians, and so unnecessary for simple practical Christians. It is a Christianity for laymen which he propounds, in opposition to a Christianity for clerics. Erasmus calls the essential Christian doctrine, which he derives from the New Testament, the 'philosophia Christi'. This he holds to be in agreement with the best of ancient philosophy, such as the doctrines of Plato, Cicero, and Seneca. He has, however, no love for Aristotle, the idol of the schoolmen. Outside the New Testament, the truest Christianity is to be found in the ancient Fathers of the Church, such as Origen, Basil, Chrysostom, and Jerome. The Fathers are better interpreters of the New Testament than the schoolmen: the best of all is Origen; Erasmus specially commends him as a safe guide in allegorical exegesis. He demands, however, of the exegete a wide knowledge of many other things besides theology proper. He must know Hebrew,

272

Greek, and Latin, also dialectic, rhetoric, arithmetic, music, physics, history: the knowledge of dialectic alone is insufficient. The above general ideas of Erasmus are developed in his 'Paraclesis ad lectorem pium', and his 'Ratio seu compendium veræ theologiæ', prefixed to his New Testament (2nd ed. Basel, 1519). See also 'Die religiösen Reformbestrebungen des deutschen Humanismus', by H. Hermelink, 1907, pp. 22–38. The best general statement of the doctrine of Erasmus is in the 'Epistola de philosophia evangelica', prefixed to the later editions of the New Testament (see Hermelink, op. cit. p. 50, where a large part of it is quoted).

Erasmus begins by pointing out with a reference to Rom. 11:33, that the 'philosophia Christi' has nothing to do with the Divine essence. On the other hand no mystery more belongs to us than the Divine plan for the redemption of man. The problem is to explain what was the special value of Christ's Incarnation and teaching. There is so little in the New Testament which is not anticipated either by the Old Testament or the philosophers.

'I will state my opinion, yet so that each may retain his own, if any has anything nearer the truth. Since the Old Testament was a shadow of and as it were a preparatory training for the Gospel philosophy, and since the Gospel doctrine is at the same time the establishment and perfection of nature, as it was first created in purity, it should not seem strange if it was given to certain Gentile philosophers by the power of nature to perceive some things which agree with the doctrine of Christ, when according to the witness of Paul those same men were able from the visible framework of the world to gather those things which are comprehended, not by the eyes, but by the mind, even God's eternal power and divinity. What distinguishing mark, therefore, belongs to that Renewer of all things? There are indeed many such marks. In the first place, that whatever commandments or examples of absolute virtue had been partially given by one and other, He alone both taught and illustrated everything. Nor did He only teach, but He also fixed, inculcated, and by various parables so impressed His doctrine on the minds of all that it could not escape. Moreover, He so illustrated it by behaviour and deeds that His whole life is nothing else than an absolute example of absolute love, modesty, tolerance, clemency, and gentleness. This harmony, this concord of all the virtues, is to be found in none of the saints, save in Christ Jesus alone. Here truly was that Word reduced and brought down to a compend, which at last the Lord manifested upon the earth, in which to recapitulate all things, both in heaven and on earth, that whatever before was sought in so many books and so many saintly lives, might now in compend be derived from Christ alone both far more clearly and more absolutely.'

We see that the simplification of Christian theology proposed by Erasmus amounts essentially to the restoration of the Logos doctrine of the Apologists, only that he has learned from the piety of the Middle Ages to lay more stress on the example of the historical Jesus. In the above passage Erasmus reproduces the doctrine of Justin that in Jesus the whole Logos has become incarnate. The phraseology of the last sentence clearly follows Irenæus, whom Erasmus edited in 1526. But the doctrine of recapitulation has not with him the same realistic meaning as with Irenæus. He does not think of the sanctification of humanity in Christ, but of the complete revelation of the Word in Him.

The Logos doctrine of the Apologists was itself the first attempt to simplify Christianity. The Church had, however, found it insufficient and had united with it, first in the classical Greek theology of Irenæus and Athanasius the idea of the deification of humanity by the Incarnation, then in the Western theology instead of this, the idea of man's redemption by the grace purchased by the satisfaction and merit of Christ. The schoolmen had analysed in minute detail these great conceptions, till the original unities were in danger of being lost in the analysis; and it is no wonder that a desire for simplification should have been expressed even by the analysts themselves. The simplification proposed by Erasmus is, however, inferior to the mediaeval doctrine in that it loses sight of the redemptive aspect of Christianity, which scholasticism amid all its mass of details held firm, and the importance of which Erasmus himself was at times constrained to acknowledge.[6] Was a Christian theology

[6] Hermelink, op. cit. p. 52, n. 13.

possible, which might avoid the complications of scholasticism, and yet retain at its heart the redemptive element as the central thing in Christianity? We must seek the answer to this question in the theology of Luther and Zwingli.[7]

[7] The German mysticism of the fourteenth century, of which the greatest exponent was the Dominican Eckhart (d. A.D. 1327), whose ideas were popularised by Tauler and the 'Theologia Germanica', prepared the way for the theology of the Reformation, in so far as there is manifested in it a tendency to the reduction, in the practical interest, of the complexity of scholasticism to a doctrine of salvation as its essence. This doctrine of salvation was, however, completely different from that of the Reformation, inasmuch as it was essentially independent of history. Salvation is through union with Divine Being : the historical Christ is ultimately only an example of the saving process (cf. Loofs, D.G., 4th ed., p. 621ff.). Eckhart connected his doctrine with the Neoplatonic element in Thomas (supra, p. 207). On Luther's relation to the 'Theologia Germanica' see Ritschl, 'Justification and Reconciliation', vol. i (English trans., p. 105).

PART III
The Older Protestant Theology

CHAPTER 1

THE REFORMERS

LUTHER

LUTHER (A.D. 1483–1546), as he is one of the most important figures in the history of theology, is also one of the most difficult to interpret. His importance lies in the enormous significance of his thought, as the principal though not the sole source of Protestantism. The difficulty of interpreting him is due partly to the comparatively unsystematic character of his thought and to his exuberant variety of statement, partly and still more to the fundamental irrationalism which characterises his doctrine even in its clearest statements, and which becomes almost its hallmark and distinguishing stamp. This peculiar characteristic of Luther's thought has been finely described by O. Ritschl.[1]

'It is the religious intuition, in virtue of which he was in a position to view and feel the sharpest contradictions as in their final basis yet a unity, to identify extremes one with another, and synoptically to comprehend at least their co-existence in one and the same subject. It is the capacity to achieve the boldest reinterpretations of apparently simple facts and connexions, and yet to present them with the most convinced certainty as self-evident equations. It is the high art of the most daring harmonisation, which succeeds in making the *contradictio in adjecto* the dominating starting-point of lines of thought, whose logical consequence then is a match for every objection however keenly critical. It is courage and strength for the religious "nevertheless" in the most perverse form of its expression and application.'

O. Ritschl goes on to inquire what was the origin of this irrationalistic type of view, which is the 'breath of life of Luther's religious thought, and in a certain degree the *principium individuationis* of his entire theology'. He finds it not in any

[1] 'Dogmengeschichte des Protestantismus', vol. ii, 1, p. 85.

previous Christian theology, but in the Bible itself: it comes from the Psalmist with his convinced 'nevertheless',[2] and from the Second Isaiah, Jesus Himself, and Paul with their paradox of the Cross.[3]

'But that Luther was in a position to hear in the Biblical tradition just these notes as the over-tones, and to penetrate with them and with the melody that guides them his own proclamation of Christianity, must be recognised as the result of the staggering religious conflicts, which preceded the winning of his conviction of the grace of God. Just as he had found in the latter the deliverance from that conflict, so evermore for him there went indivisibly together the *mortificatio* of a humiliation, which had led his soul through hellish pains to full submission to God's will even though one of damnation, and the *vivificatio*, which in this very experience of an extremest despair had taught him still just only to hope and trust in God's grace' (*ibid.* p. 86).

Besides, however, this positive origin of Luther's irrationalism in Scripture itself, as interpreted to him by his own remarkable experience, we must also recognise at least a negative preparation for it in the Occamist theology, which was the form of scholasticism in which Luther had been nurtured as student and doctor of Christian theology. As Hermelink well says:[4] 'From the contradictions of the Occamist theology, and especially of the Collectorium of Biel, is to be understood the development of the Reformer.' In fact Luther's central and most characteristic idea —the doctrine of justification by faith alone—which again and again he has emphasised as the fundamental doctrine of the Gospel and as containing in itself all other Christian articles, has undoubtedly not only a positive origin in the Pauline gospel as interpreted by Luther's experience, but also a preparation in the critical reflections which we have already studied in Duns and in Biel, on the abstract possibility of God's justifying the sinner by a non-imputation of sin without at the same time infusing charity.

What, then, is this new fundamental doctrine of Luther's? It is by no means easy to give an account of it, for Luther never

[2] Ps. 72:23.   [3] Isa. 53 ; Lk. 16:15 ; Mk 8:35 ; 1 C. 1:23 ; 2 C. 12:9.
[4] 'Die theologische Fakultät in Tübingen', 1906, p. 127.

reduced it to a single point of view. O. Ritschl, in his work above mentioned, says as follows (p. 147):

'Luther's reformatory doctrine of justification contains the following ideas, which more or less stand in tension with one another. In the first place it is God, who, out of mercy for Christ's sake, justifies—i.e. holds and declares to be righteous—sinners, if they believe. Secondly, God justifies, in that He gives to the sinner justifying faith. Thirdly, faith justifies, so far as it establishes that relation of the sinner to God, which God by means of His imputation holds for righteousness and allows to avail as such. Fourthly, faith justifies, in that it is the righteousness of Christ, entirely alien to sinners, but infused into their hearts, and in so far is the ideal fulfilment of the law. Fifthly, there ever increasingly proceeds from the purity of heart, which thus comes to be in faith, the proper righteousness and fulfilment of the laws of believers, which indeed is never perfect in this life, but in spite of the constant element of sin which it contains, is yet pleasing to God, since the latter is not imputed to them.'

O. Ritschl says that all these thoughts are found in Luther's writings to the end of his life, but that, as time went on, the imputative view, of righteousness before God, gains ground on the rest, inasmuch as it stands in the sharpest contrast to the idea that man can be just before God in virtue of any act or quality of his own.

Such then is the new ferment, working in Luther's theology, and destined to produce a great revolution in the whole traditional system of doctrine. In order properly to understand Luther's principle of justification, and especially its conflict with the preceding Catholic doctrine, the following further points must be noted:

(1) Luther reinterpreted the word grace. Grace meant originally for the Greek Church little more than the gift through the Logos of the knowledge of God and of the promise of immortality.[5] Augustine gave it a deeper meaning in so far as he took it to mean on the one hand the forgiveness of sins, on the other, and this was the chief idea, the infusion of charity which

---

[5] Athanasius, 'De Incarnatione', III, 3–4.

281

makes merit possible. For Luther grace is not a quality of the soul, the *gratia creata* of the schoolmen,[6] which is charity, but God's free unmerited favour to the sinner shown above all in the forgiveness of sins, which, however, is accompanied by the gift of the Holy Spirit.

(2) Luther also gave a new meaning to faith. From the beginning of the systematic theology of the Church faith had been conceived as in itself belief or acceptance of Christian doctrine, especially as embodied in the articles of the Creed. According to Clement and Origen this faith was but a beginning, and in order to become a free principle of virtue needed to be transformed into knowledge. According to Augustine and the schoolmen, on the other hand, belief, in order to become saving faith, needed to be informed by love, the principle of merit. Faith is not in Western Catholicism confidence (*fiducia*). According to Lombard (III, 26, A) such *fiducia* belongs to hope based on merit. Hope apart from merit is presumption. For Luther, on the other hand, faith, though presupposing belief of the articles of the creed,[7] is essentially *fiducia*, confidence or trust in the mercy of God revealed in Jesus Christ.

So much then for Luther's central principle of justification by faith. We have next to try to estimate its reaction upon the complex of doctrine, which we have watched growing up in the Mediaeval Church as the equivalent of the Greek doctrine of the work of Christ. In order that we may do this, I shall make use of three systematic presentations which Luther has given us of practically the whole of Christian doctrine, viz. the Schmalkald Articles (1537), and the Larger and Smaller Catechisms (1529).[8] The Schmalkald Articles have the advantage of presenting Luther's new conception of Christian doctrine in its antithesis to Romanism. The Catechisms, on the other hand, are not polemical or apologetic, but are positive statements of doctrine: these take us into the very heart of Luther's religion. By making use of these three sources, supplemented here and there from other writings of Luther, we may hope to obtain a good general view of his whole Christianity in the form in which he himself

---

[6] *Supra*, pp. 196ff.   [7] Larger Catechism, II, 3, 66–69.

[8] All three works are contained in 'Concordia, Libri Symbolici Ecclesiæ Evangelicæ', Berlin, 1857.

conceived it. It is, however, to be observed that Luther was not by nature a systematic theologian but an original religious genius; and that, even more than is the case with Augustine, his incidental statements constantly exceed the framework of any system even of his own making. This point we shall take further note of with particular reference to the doctrine of the work of Christ.

As regards the proof of his doctrine, Luther, as is well known, appealed to the Scripture alone. The Schmalkald Articles (pars II, art. 2, 15) incidentally contain a peculiarly sharply formulated statement on this point.

'The articles of faith are not to be built up from the words or the deeds of the Fathers. . . . We, on the other hand, have another rule, namely that the Word of God should establish the articles of faith, and none besides, not even an angel.'

Luther, however, found nothing contrary to Scripture in the ancient Creeds. A. Ritschl [9] has laid great stress on Luther's adherence to the Catholic Creeds; and it is of course true and important that Luther did adhere to the traditional Creeds of the Mediaeval Church. In his preface to his treatise, 'The Three Symbols or Confessions of the Christian Faith' (viz. the Apostles' and Athanasian Creeds and the *Te Deum*), Luther says:

'I have *ex abundanti* caused to be published together in German the three symbols or Confessions, which have hitherto been held throughout the whole Church: by this I testify once and for all that I adhere to the true Christian Church, which, up to now, has maintained those symbols, but not to that false pretentious Church, which is the worst enemy of the true Church, and has surreptitiously introduced much idolatry alongside of these beautiful Confessions' (*ibid.* p. 130, n. 1).

Luther has, moreover, taken the Apostles' Creed, along with the Ten Commandments and the Lord's Prayer, in his Larger and Smaller Catechisms, as the basis of instruction on Christian faith and morals. He explains this choice by saying: 'God Himself has given the Ten Commandments, Christ has ordained and taught the Lord's Prayer, the Holy Spirit has composed and conceived the articles of faith in the shortest and most correct

---

[9] 'Justification and Reconciliation', vol. i (English trans., pp. 126ff.).

manner'.[1] Luther, however, regarded the Apostles' Creed and the other Confessions merely as a summary of the truth of Scripture, not as an independent authority.[2]

As regards the interpretation of Scripture, Luther emphasised first of all the necessity of following the literal sense. In controversy with Emser he even said: 'The Holy Ghost is the all-simplest writer and speaker that is in heaven or on earth; therefore His words can have no more than one simplest sense, which we call the Scriptural or literal meaning.'[3] But there was a further important principle which Luther made use of, viz. the distinction between the obscure and the clear passages of Scripture, already found, after Augustine, 'De Civitate Dei', XI, 19; in Duns Scotus, 'Reportata', III, Dist. 24, qu. 1; Biel, III, Dist. 24, qu. un., concl. 6. Luther explains himself on this point in 'De Servo Arbitrio', §§ 3, 4. The *things* contained in Scripture, the Incarnation, the Trinity, Christ's Passion and Eternal Reign are all perfectly plain and clear, though individual *passages* may be obscure. Christ is the essential content of Scripture. How these things are Scripture does not say, nor is it necessary to know.

The above clearness is, however, external only; it requires to be supplemented by internal clearness: 'If you speak of the internal clearness, no man sees an iota in the Scriptures, but he that hath the Spirit of God. All have a darkened heart, so that if they know how to speak of and set forth all things in the Scripture, yet they cannot feel them nor know them; nor do they believe that they are creatures of God, or anything else.'[4] Luther accordingly refused to admit reason as the interpreter of Scripture.[5] It is to be observed that he does not, like Thomas or Duns, argue simply from the natural finitude of reason, but rather from its corruption through sin. As we shall presently see, Luther took the Augustinian doctrine of original sin more rigorously and carried out its consequences more ruthlessly than the schoolmen. Luther did not indeed deny a natural knowledge of God; but this natural knowledge is so poor that it is in fact completest darkness.

[1] O. Ritschl, 'Dogmengeschichte des Protestantismus', vol. i, p. 274.
[2] *Ibid.* pp. 274, 275.   [3] See Beard, 'The Reformation', vol. v, 1907, p. 119.
[4] 'De Servo Arbitrio', Eng. trans. by H. Cole, 1823, p. 17.   [5] *Ibid.* §§ 52, 82.

The following theses from Luther's Heidelberg disputation [6] (theses propounded by himself to be maintained by one of his pupils under his presidency) show his attitude from his central standpoint of justification by faith towards the system of natural theology, including the doctrine of natural law, as developed by the schoolmen:

'19. He is not worthily called a theologian, who beholds the invisible things of God, through these things that are made. 20. But he is worthily so called who understands the visible and back parts of God,[7] as seen through His Passions and Cross. 22. That wisdom, which beholds the invisible things of God, as understood from His works, altogether puffs up, blinds, and hardens. 23. And the law works the wrath of God and slays, curses, charges with guilt, judges, condemns, whatever is not in Christ. 24. That wisdom is not evil, nor is the law to be avoided, but a man without the theology of the Cross makes the worst use of the best things. 25. He is not just, who works much, but he who without works believes much on Christ.'

In a similar 'Disputation against the scholastic theology' (A.D. 1517) [8] Luther deals particularly with the great representative of reason in the Middle Ages, the philosophy of Aristotle. '41. Almost the whole exceedingly bad ethic of Aristotle is hostile to grace. 43. It is an error to say: Without Aristotle a theologian is not made. 44. Rather, a theologian is not made, unless it is done without Aristotle. 50. In brief, the whole of Aristotle is to theology, as darkness to light.'

It was particularly the support given by Aristotle to the doctrine of free will and the consequent mitigation of the Augustinian doctrine of original sin to which Luther objected so vehemently; this will more clearly appear when we come to Luther's doctrine of sin.

After these preliminary statements as to Luther's view of reason and revelation, we proceed to study his general theological outlook, following the lines previously indicated.

In the Schmalkald Articles Luther begins (pars I) by acknowledging as the highest articles concerning the Divine

---

[6] 'Disputatio Heidelbergæ habita' (1518), contained in Stange, 'Die ältesten ethischen Disputationen Luthers', 1904.   [7] Cf. Exod. 33:23.   [8] Also in Stange, op. cit.

majesty the doctrines of the Trinity and the Incarnation, as stated in the Apostles' and the Athanasian Creed. He says: 'Concerning these articles there is no controversy between us and our adversaries, since we on both sides confess them; wherefore it is not necessary that we should now treat at length upon them.'

Pars II deals with the articles which concern the office and work of Jesus Christ and our redemption.

'Here the first and principal article is: that Jesus Christ, our Lord and God, died for our sins, and rose again for our righteousness.[9] And that He alone is the Lamb of God, who taketh away the sins of the world,[1] and that God hath laid upon Him the iniquities of us all.[2] All have sinned, and are justified freely without works or their own merits, by His grace, through the redemption, which is in Christ Jesus, in His blood.[3]

'Since it is necessary to believe this, and it can be acquired and apprehended by no work, law, or merit, it is certain and clear that this faith alone justifies us, as Paul saith.[4] No religious man may recede from this article or grant or allow anything against it, even though heaven and earth and all things be destroyed together. For there is no other name given to man, whereby we may be saved, saith Peter.[5] And by His wounds we are healed.[6] And in this article are set and consist all things, which in our life we teach, testify, and treat of against the Pope, the devil, and the whole world. Wherefore we must be certain of this doctrine, and have no doubt at all of it, even though the Pope, the devil, and all things contrary obtain the right and the victory against us.'

It is important to notice in this section that Luther states the doctrine of the work of Christ as viewed through the principle of justification by faith. To him the two were not two but one. It is just here that the synthetic character of his doctrine, and its difference from the essentially analytic doctrine of the schoolmen appears most momentously. Luther did not regard the scholastic doctrine of the work of Christ as in itself amiss, any more than the doctrine of the Incarnation; what he objected to was the

[9] Rom. 4:24. [1] Jn 1:30. [2] Isa. 53:4. [3] Rom. 3:24.
[4] *Ibid.* 3:18, 26. [5] Acts 4:12. [6] Isa. 53:5.

practical use made of these doctrines. Gottschick well says: 'In relation to Christ's Person and mediatorial work Luther concedes to his opponents that they confess the correct doctrine, and merely contends with them that they should believe it, i.e. take it in practical earnest.' [7] What he found especially amiss in Catholicism was that it did not in his view take the work of Christ in sufficient earnest as the sole ground of salvation, but endeavoured to supplement it with a further ground of salvation in human merit. Accordingly pars II of the Schmalkald Articles contains a polemic against various things in the system of the Roman Church, which to Luther appeared as abuses, in so far as they contradicted the primary article, 'which teaches that Christ alone, and not men's works, saves souls' (art. 2, 12).

How fundamentally Luther agreed with the mediaeval doctrine of the work of Christ, apart from the question of its practical meaning, is shown by his great statement of his own doctrine on the subject in the Larger Catechism (II, 2, 27f.).

'I believe that Jesus Christ, the true Son of God, has become my Lord. What does this mean: To become my Lord? It signifies that He has delivered me by His blood, from sins, the devil, death, and all destruction. . . .

'For when now we had been created by God, and had received from the Father inestimable gifts of every kind, there came the devil, envying our happiness, and drawing us by his devices brought us into open and rebellious disobedience to God, death, and all dangers, so that we lay under His wrath, condemned to perpetual damnation, as we had merited by our guilt. Here there was no longer left any hope of regaining grace, or way of winning salvation, or aid to placate the Father, or way to forgive the sin, till that immortal Son of the immortal Father, pitying in the depth of His kindness our wretched misery and exile, descended from heaven to bring us help, and liberated us from all captivity of sin and death, and the devil, into the freedom of His adoption. Thus then the power of all these tyrants and exactors was dispersed and overthrown, and into their place came Jesus Christ, the author of life and righteousness, salvation, justification, and all goods; who delivered us poor wretched

---

[7] 'Zeitschrift für Theologie und Kirche', 1914. 1st supplementary number, p. 79.

sinners from the jaws of hell, saved us and guaranteed us liberty; won the favour and grace of the angry Father by placating His wrath, and took us as His own possession under His care, to rule and govern us through His justice, wisdom, power, life and beatitude.'

In virtue of all this Christ is 'our Lord'. The rest of the articles in the Creed concerning Him explain the details and conditions of the above-described redemption. Christ was incarnate and born of the Holy Ghost and the Virgin Mary to be the 'Lord of sin'. He suffered, died, and was buried to 'satisfy for me and pay my debt (*culpa*), which I had to pay, not with gold or silver, but with His own precious blood'. None of those things did He do for His own sake, but to become my Lord. Then He rose, ascended, and sits at the right hand of the Father to compel the submission of all the hosts of the devil, till He comes again to redeem us from the evil one.

Luther concludes: 'The whole Gospel which we preach tends to the right understanding of this article, as that in which the sum of our whole salvation and eternal happiness is placed, which because of familiarity and because of its far-and-wide-spreading richness we can never thoroughly enough learn.'

In this extended statement, one of the completest that we have from Luther on the subject,[8] two things are noteworthy. The first is the close formal resemblance to Biel's 'summary answer' to the question: 'How we are delivered from guilt, punishment, from the power of the devil, and the obligation of the writing of the sentence' (III, 19, qu. un., dub. 2). The second is the new atmosphere in which the doctrine is viewed, which is especially felt in the religious appreciation of the title, 'Our Lord', and the convergence of the whole doctrine upon this point: 'all these things, He did for no other reason, than that He might become my Lord'. This religious apprehension of the title is practically the same thing as the doctrine of justification by faith: what we have therefore once more is the interpretation of the old doctrine from the new standpoint.

Pars III of the Schmalkald Articles further unfolds the peculiarity of Luther's doctrine as opposed to Catholicism. In

[8] Cf. Th. Harnack, 'Luthers Theologie', vol. ii, 1886, p. 248.

the first place (art. 1), he insists by way of basis for his new doctrine on a more thoroughgoing adherence to the Augustinian doctrine of original sin. In their anxiety to establish the doctrine of merit, and under the influence of the Aristotelian ethic, the schoolmen had increasingly modified the severity of Augustinianism, so as to admit in man after the fall some liberty to good. Luther says that original sin is not to be measured by reason but solely by the Scripture. He repudiates, amongst other scholastic doctrines, the famous principle of *meritum congrui*: 'That, if a man do what in him lies, God certainly grants him His grace'. This and all such monstrosities have arisen from ignorance of sin and Christ our Saviour, and are mere heathen doctrines not to be borne.

There follows in art. 2, 'De Lege', art. 3, 'De Pœnitentiâ', art. 4, 'De Evangelio', Luther's distinction between the law and the Gospel, so important for the understanding of his conception of the Divine revelation and of the relation of his system to Catholicism.

'We deem that the law was given by God, first that sin might be forbidden by threats and fear of punishment, next by the promise and announcement of grace and benefits. But all this has turned out badly because of the evil disposition which sin has wrought in man' (art. 2, 1).

In fact the law has incensed some against it; and others have been, like the schoolmen, led astray to think that they could keep it in their own strength. Its proper office is, however, to reveal to man original sin and all its fruits.

'In this way he is terrified, hunted, cast down, despairs of himself, and anxiously desires help, nor knows whither to flee; he begins to be angry with God and murmur for impatience' (Rom. 4:15, 5:20) (*ibid.* 4).

This office of the law continues in the New Testament: it causes passive contrition, which is the torment of conscience, the true suffering of the heart and fear of death (art. 3, 2). 'This is the beginning of true repentance' (*ibid.* 3).

'The New Testament immediately adds to this office (of the law) the consolation and promise of the grace of the Gospel, which we must believe' (Mk 1:15) (*ibid.* 4).

289

'When the law alone exercises this its office without the Gospel, nothing but death and hell oppress man, till he altogether despairs' (*ibid.* 7). . . . 'On the other hand, the Gospel brings consolation and forgiveness, not in one way only, but by the Word, the sacraments, and so on' (*ibid.* 8).

The Gospel teaches us that God is infinitely rich and free in His grace and goodness. 'First by the spoken Word, by which it bids the forgiveness of sins be preached in the whole world. And this is the proper office of the Gospel. Secondly by baptism. Thirdly by the reverend sacrament of the altar. Fourthly by the power of the keys, and even by the mutual intercourse and consolation of the brethren' (Mt. 18:20) (art. 4).

The law then contains threats of punishment and promises of grace, which last have no application to man under sin. Its actual principal function is to convict of sin, while the Gospel has as its essence the message of the forgiveness of sins. The sacraments, of which Luther only retains three, viz. baptism, the Eucharist, and penance, gain the meaning of additional ways in which the Gospel is set forth.

We pursue the doctrine of these three sacraments by means of the Schmalkald Articles and the Smaller Catechism. The rest of the seven sacraments of the Mediaeval Church Luther rejects in his treatise, 'De Babylonica captivitate ecclesiæ', as unscriptural.

In the Schmalkald Articles (pars III, 5) Luther defines baptism as the Word of God together with immersion in water according to the Divine institution; and refers to Eph. 5:26, also to Augustine's saying: 'Accedat verbum ad elementum, et fit sacramentum.' He repudiates the Thomist view 'that God has granted and implanted a spiritual virtue in the water to wash away sin'. Yet he does not agree, on the other hand, with Duns 'that in baptism sin is washed away by the assistance of the Divine will, and that this washing is made by the Divine will alone, and by no means by the word'. His endeavour seems to be to steer between these two opposing views, or rather to carry back the doctrine of baptism into the more mystical, less analytic, atmosphere which prevailed in the patristic theology.

Much fuller light on Luther's conception of the meaning of

the sacrament comes from the Smaller Catechism, where Luther teaches as follows (IV, 6):

'Baptism works the forgiveness of sins, delivers from death and the devil, and grants eternal life to all and each, who believe that which the words and the Divine assurances promise.'

The promise is Mk 16:16. Luther adds (IV, 10):

'It is not the water indeed that does such great things, but the word of God, which is in and with the water, and faith, which believes in the word of God added to the water.'

As regards the Eucharist, the Schmalkald Articles (pars III, 6,1) say: 'Concerning the sacrament of the altar we deem that the bread and wine in the Supper are the very body and blood of Christ.'

In attempting further to define the Real Presence of Christ in the sacrament Luther rejects transubstantiation, the doctrine of the schoolmen, and adopts as more Scriptural consubstantiation, which Occam and Biel had maintained to be the more rational doctrine, only that authority taught otherwise. It is notable that at this point Luther does not go back to the mysticism of the patristic theology, but remains a scholastic theologian.

Again, however, the heart of Luther's view comes out in the Smaller Catechism, where he teaches (VI, 6) that the profit of eating and drinking in the Lord's Supper is indicated in the words: 'pro vobis datur et effunditur in remissionem peccatorum'. 'Without doubt, through those words there are given to us in the sacrament the remission of sins, life, righteousness, and salvation. For where there is the remission of sins, there is both life and salvation.' It is not (VI, 8) the eating and drinking but the words that have these results. 'The words are together with the bodily eating the chief and sum of this sacrament. And he who believes these words, has what they say and just as they sound, without doubt, the remission of sins.'

Luther's doctrine on Confession we may sufficiently take from the Schmalkald Articles alone. He says (pars III, 8, 1): 'Since absolution and the power of the keys is a consolation and assistance against sin and an evil conscience, instituted in the Gospel by Christ Himself, confession and absolution are by no means to be abolished in the Church.'

The confession of sins need not, however, be in detail; it is enough to confess oneself in general a miserable sinner (III, 8, 2).

Luther's view is further elucidated, however, by the extended criticism to which he subjects the mediaeval doctrine of penance (III, 3, 10f.). It is at this point that his new doctrine reaches its sharpest practical divergence from the mediaeval system. Luther's doctrine of justification was primarily his answer to the practical question: How may the Christian, who has received the forgiveness of sins at his baptism, be secure of the grace of God and of the forgiveness of post-baptismal sin?

In his criticism of the scholastic doctrine of penance Luther first of all complains of its externality, which he says arises from an insufficient doctrine of original sin and of the consequent sinfulness of the heart. The schoolmen limited the things to be repented of to the outward acts which the free will could do or omit. Luther further says that in the scholastic doctrine of penance the remission of sins is made conditional upon the sufficient performance of the three parts of penance, contrition, confession, and satisfaction.[9] 'Thus in penance man is led to a trust in his own works' (12). Moreover, since none can know whether his contrition is sufficient, it is taught that a man must at least have an imperfect contrition, or *attrition*, as a substitute for contrition, and that this may suffice.[1]

'We see, however, how blind reason feels about and staggers in Divine things, and seeks consolation in its own works according to its own opinion, and altogether forgets Christ and faith. But if the essence of the matter is clearly considered, such contrition (i.e. attrition) is factitious, and is a fictitious thought or imagination proceeding from one's own strength without faith and the knowledge of Christ' (18).

In confession, again, none can know whether he has sufficiently confessed all his own sins.

'Here was no faith, no Christ. And the virtue of absolution was not explained to the penitent, but his consolation was in the enumeration of his sins and in his shame' (20).

Still worse is it with satisfaction. There was no certainty as to the necessary amount of satisfaction.

[9] *Supra*, p. 176. [1] *Supra*, pp. 201, 248.

292

'And yet trust was always put in our work of satisfaction, and if satisfaction could be perfect, the whole trust would have been cast upon that, nor would there have been need of Christ and faith' (23).

It is the same criticism in every case. Faith in Christ is opposed to trust in one's own works, whether these be works of contrition or of confession or of satisfaction. In pars III, 3, 2, Luther distinguishes true repentance from false, as passive from active. The former is a state of mind, into which we are brought against our will by the law. The latter is a work, which we do with our will according to the law. For Luther repentance was but the reverse side of faith: we must despair of ourselves, in order to cast ourselves upon God in Christ. God casts us down in order to lift us up. In this sense Luther said, in the first of his Wittenberg Theses (1517), that the whole life of believers should be repentance.[2] Just as faith (*fiducia*) is the standing condition of the Christian life, so also is repentance. The whole elaborate machinery of the mediaeval penance, therefore, vanishes. If Luther retained confession, there was, as we have seen, to be no compulsory enumeration of all special sins; and the stress was laid on the absolution, or the assurance to the penitent of Divine mercy (pars III, 8, 2).

Luther has fundamentally altered the conception of all the sacraments, in so much as he makes their common content, not grace in the Catholic sense, but essentially *grace as the remission of sins*, as a gospel to be believed, i.e. trusted, by the troubled conscience. All other benefits flow out of this grace: 'Where there is the forgiveness of sins, there is both life and salvation.' In comparison with this great change as to the content of the sacrament, the fact that Luther retains elements of the patristic and even the scholastic theology of the subject is comparatively unimportant: they are counteracted by the telling words, in which the Smaller Catechism interprets the practical working of the sacraments. It is the practical view of the sacraments which sooner or later must determine the metaphysical theory of them: a metaphysic of them, which assumes more than is required by

[2] 'Dominus et magister noster Jesus Christus dicendo : *pœnitentiam agite*, etc., omnem vitam fidelium pœnitentiam esse voluit.' See Gieseler's 'Ecclesiastical History' (English trans., vol. v, p. 227, n. 13).

the doctrine of their operation, is destined to extinction by reason of the rule of parsimony of causes. By his doctrine of the gospel of remission as the fundamental content of the sacraments Luther has in essence broken with the sacramentalism of the Catholic Church.

This is true at least of Luther's drift, if not of his actual achievement. What emerges is in reality a fresh principle of interpretation in regard to the New Testament. The Pauline and Johannine doctrines of baptism and the Lord's Supper are in themselves capable of either a sacramentarian or an evangelical interpretation, according as stress is laid on the syncretistic vehicle of thought used by the New Testament writers, or on their new thought itself.[3] The question is essentially one of values; and the fundamental position of Luther consists in the fact that he is emphatically a creator of new values in the interpretation of the New Testament.

The fresh conception of the sacraments naturally corresponds to a fresh conception also of the ministry and the Church. The work of the ministry is to preach and teach and administer the sacraments (understood as Luther understands them).[4] The Church is the community of believers whose holiness consists in the Word of God and in faith.[5]

After the doctrine of the sacraments, the ministry, and the Church, Luther returns in the Schmalkald Articles (pars III, 13) to the doctrine of justification, which we have already had by implication in the doctrine of the work of Christ (pars II). Luther's system is thus seen to be a closed system, which returns into itself, the doctrine of justification being at once its beginning and end. This time, however, the doctrine of justification is stated, as is natural after the criticism of the scholastic doctrine of merit, with respect to the doctrine of good works. Luther says:

'What I have thus far always and assiduously taught concerning justification, I cannot in the least alter, viz. that we by faith, as Peter says,[6] obtain another heart new and clean, and that God reputes us just and holy for the sake of Christ our

---

[3] Cf. 'Man, Sin, and Salvation', p. 126. [4] Schmalkald Articles, pars III, 10.
[5] Ibid. 12. [6] Ac. 15:9.

294

Mediator. And although sin in the flesh is not yet clean taken away and dead, yet God will not impute that to us or remember it.

'This faith, renewal, and forgiveness of sins, is followed by good works. And what in them is polluted and imperfect, is not regarded as sin and defect, and that again for Christ's sake, and so the whole man, both as regards his person and his works, is, and is called, just and holy of mere grace and mercy, shed, spread, and abounding upon us in Christ. Wherefore we cannot boast of good works, when they are regarded apart from grace and mercy, but, as it is written, "He that glorieth let him glory in the Lord",[7] that is, that he has a merciful God. Thus all things are well. We say, moreover, that where good works do not follow, there faith is false and not true.'

It may be added that Luther presupposed as the standard of good works the Decalogue, which moreover he takes to be naturally written upon the heart of man.[8] Moreover, he holds to the doctrine that good works are rewarded by God, but the consequence of reward does not imply the worthiness of merit, 'seeing that those who do good, do it not from a servile and necessary principle in order to obtain eternal life, but they seek eternal life, that is, they are in that way in which they shall come unto and find eternal life'.[9]

We see from the passage above quoted on justification and good works,[1] that justifying faith involves regeneration, and regeneration has its fruit in good works. Otto Ritschl says:[2] 'Luther uses the expression *justificatio* even in his later writings now and again in so broad a sense that he includes not only the Divine imputation and the faith, in which man obtains a clean heart, but even the renewal of the whole life, beginning and progressing in this faith. In fact Luther speaks of "duæ partes justificationis" in so far as this is, firstly, "gratia per Christum revelata", and, secondly, "donatio spiritus sancti cum donis suis".'

Just here is perhaps the most fundamental antinomy in Luther's theology. It is faith that justifies and not works, and

---

[7] 1 C. 1:31.   [8] Larger Catechism, pars II, art. 3, 67.
[9] 'De Servo Arbitrio', §71, Eng. trans., p. 177.   [1] Schmalkald Articles, pars III, 13.
[2] 'Dogmengeschichte des Protestantismus', vol. ii, 1, p. 148.

not even 'fides caritate formata';[3] yet faith that is without works is false faith. Again justifying faith is itself regeneration, yet again regeneration and indeed faith is the work of the Spirit.[4] All indeed are one, and each depends on the other. Their ultimate unity is synthetic and intuitive. Otto Ritschl rightly points out that it is with these larger implications that justification is to be understood, when Luther declares that all other articles are included in it.[5]

How far, then, has Luther brought about the reduction of theology on a Spiritual basis desiderated by Occam? It is clear that by the principle of justification by faith, the whole elaborate system, built up by the schoolmen on the basis of Augustine in order to reconcile grace and merit, is brought to the ground. The new doctrine, however, which appears in its place is not to be described as simple. It is rather, in agreement with the fundamental irrationalism of which we spoke at the outset, in opposition to the analysis of the schoolmen, synthetic in character, combining within itself diverse elements in the unity of an intuition. This synthetic character comes out very clearly in such sayings as: 'These two belong together, faith and God';[6] 'those three things: faith, Christ, acceptation or imputation, must be joined together'.[7]

We shall now, in conclusion, consider the reaction of Luther's doctrine of justification on his teaching as to the work of Christ. As we have seen, the systematic doctrine of this subject in the Schmalkald Articles and the Larger Catechism differs from that of the schoolmen, especially Biel, only in the angle from which it is viewed. In his sermons and exegetical works, however, Luther by no means kept within this comparatively narrow outline; but was led in the interests of his doctrine of justification to present a variety of views on the subject, in which he partly reverted even to the patristic type of doctrine, and partly developed new lines of doctrine.

In the first place I shall refer to a series of passages from various works [8] in which Luther foreshadows the future doctrine

---

[3] 'Comm. in Gal.', Erlangen ed., vol. i, p. 191.   [4] *Ibid.* vol. iii, p. 156.
[5] 'Dogmengeschichte des Protestantismus', vol. ii, 1, p. 149.
[6] Larger Catechism, I, 1, 3.   [7] 'Comm. in Gal.', vol. i, p. 195.
[8] Quoted by Thomasius, 'Christi Person und Werk', pt. iii, 1862, pp. 284–300.

of Protestant theology, viewing Christ's satisfaction, not like the schoolmen after the analogy of private law as directed to appease God's injured honour, but rather after the analogy of public law as intended to placate His offended righteousness and His violated decree. We have seen that Athanasius, Ambrose, and Hilary all more or less approach this point of view, which moreover appears, though somewhat indefinitely expressed, in various isolated passages in the schoolmen.[9] Still, on the whole, the idea as developed by Luther has a new precision and coherence. Gottschick (loc. cit.) sees in it a natural development from the view of the passion of Christ, as *contritio*, which we found in Biel.[1] 'With the emphasis on Christ's sufferings as such a way is made for the transition to the quite other thought, which becomes operative in Protestantism after the disappearance of the sacrament of penance and therewith of the condition for the understanding of the (mediaeval) idea of satisfaction—the thought that Christ, though voluntarily, has borne the punishment which God laid on Him as substitute, and which is the judgment of God upon our sins.' The change from the mediaeval doctrine of Christ's satisfaction as essentially an active self-oblation to the Protestant view of it as fundamentally a passive endurance certainly runs parallel with the change effected by Luther in the doctrine of contrition, viz. that true contrition is not an active self-humiliation, but a passive sense of the terrors of the Divine judgment. But, again, the forensic view of the Atonement has also a naturally affinity with the forensic doctrine of justification; it has moreover, at least, one clear Biblical starting-point in Rom. 3:25–26, besides being easily construed from other passages such as Gal. 3:3 and 2 C. 5:21. Here after all, is the most natural explanation of its appearance in Luther's theology.

Perhaps the most striking illustration of this form of theory in Luther's works is a passage from a sermon.[2]

'If now indeed out of pure grace our sins are not imputed by God, He has not willed to do this without first His law and His righteousness receiving satisfaction before all things and super-

---

[9] Cf. Ritschl, 'Justification and Reconciliation', vol. i, Eng. trans., pp. 197ff. ; Seeberg, D.G., 1st ed., vol. ii, p. 252, n. 2 ; Gottschick, 'Studien zur Versöhnungslehre des Mittelalters', No. 4 ; in 'Zeitschrift für Kirchengeschichte', 1903, p. 228.
[1] III, Dist. 5, qu. un. ; art. 2, pars 2, concl. 2.　　　　[2] Thomasius, op. cit. p. 287.

abundantly. Such gracious imputation must first be bought and obtained for us from His righteousness. Therefore, since that was impossible to us, He has ordained one for us in our place, who should take upon Himself all punishments, which we had deserved, and fulfil the law for us, and thus turn them from us and reconcile God's wrath.'

Of this passage Seeberg says [3] that it may be taken as a classical presentation of Luther's view of Christ's work as a satisfaction to the Divine righteousness, which he takes to be Luther's fundamental idea as to the work of Christ. He says: 'It is plain, how closely the view adheres to the conceptions, law, fulfilment, and punishment. The firm nexus, which is thus reached, presents an advance closely connected with Luther's general view.' Whether this view is to be taken as Luther's fundamental idea, is, however, dubious, since we do not find it in any of the systematic presentations of his views already studied: again, it is hardly to be found in his great 'Commentary on Galatians'. Nevertheless he repeats it frequently. Many other passages illustrating it are quoted by Thomasius. I select the following examples:

(Another passage from the sermon just referred to): 'Christ . . . Who in thy place and for thee has made satisfaction superabundantly to every Divine command and to God's righteousness' (Thomasius, op. cit., p. 287).

(From another sermon): 'It could not come about, that God's wrath, judgment, and all evil things should be removed and all good be won, without satisfaction having to be made to the Divine righteousness, sin having to be paid for, and death having to be overcome in accordance with justice' (ibid. p. 286).

We may note that the Thomist idea of a superabundant satisfaction recurs in the first and second above-quoted sermon passages: it is also to be found in 'Comm. in Gal.' I, p. 195.

'He could have satisfied for the sins of the world by one least drop of His blood. But now He has satisfied abundantly.'

The remainder of Luther's ideas on the work of Christ we may illustrate from the 'Commentary on Galatians' alone. There is first the use which he makes of the patristic doctrine of the

[3] D.G., 1st ed., vol. ii, p. 257, n. 1.

death of Christ as a redemption from death and the devil. Luther develops along these lines a doctrine of our redemption, from the law, sin, death, and wrath of God, which doctrine he presents in most plastic forms. By including in the series the law and the wrath of God he moreover goes back behind the Fathers and reminds us of the Gnostics.

This patristic-Gnostic form of doctrine may be illustrated from 'Comm. in Gal.' II, pp. 18f.

The doctrine of the Gospel speaks nothing of the works of the law, but of God's mercy, Who, seeing that we were oppressed under the curse of the law and unable to deliver ourselves from it, sent His only Son into the world, and laid upon Him the sins of all men, bidding Him pay and satisfy for them.

'Then comes the law, and says: I find Him a sinner, and such a one indeed as has taken upon Himself the sins of all men, and I see no sin anywhere but in Him, therefore let Him die upon the cross, and so it attacks Him and slays Him. By this means the whole world is purged and cleansed from all sins, and therefore also delivered from death and all evils' (p. 19).

Similarly Christ overcomes sin.

'It, I say, runs upon Christ, and will devour Him, as all others. But it does not see that He is a person of unconquered and eternal righteousness. Therefore in this combat sin must needs be conquered and killed, and righteousness conquer and live' (p. 20).

So again with death and the curse.

'Because life was immortal, even though conquered it came off conqueror, conquering and slaying death' (p. 21).

'So the curse which is the Divine wrath upon the whole world, has the same conflict with the blessing, that is to say with the eternal grace and mercy of God in Christ. The curse therefore fights with the blessing, and would condemn it and altogether bring it to nought, but it cannot do so. For the blessing is Divine and eternal, and therefore the curse must give it place' (*ibid*.).

Finally, here we have salvation (as Irenæus would have said) *in compendio*. As Paul says, Christ spoiled the principalities and powers, and triumphed over them in Himself.[4]

[4] Col. 2:15.

'And this circumstance "in Himself" makes that combat more wonderful and glorious. For it shows that it was necessary that these great things should be accomplished in that one only person of Christ (that is, that the curse, sin and death, should be destroyed, and the blessing, righteousness and life, take their place), and that so the whole creation should be transformed through Him. . . . In so far therefore as Christ reigns by His grace in the hearts of the faithful there is no sin, no death, no curse. But where Christ is not known those things remain' (pp. 21–22).

Luther shows how well he understands the patristic doctrine by pointing out how its very nerve is in the doctrine of the divinity of Christ.

'For to overcome the sin of the world, death, the curse, and the wrath of God in Himself is not the work of any creature but of the Divine power. Therefore He, who has overcome those things in Himself, must be truly and naturally God' (p. 22).

The divinity of Christ in fact, says Luther, is implied in the fundamental article of justification.

'Wherefore, when we teach that men are justified by Christ, that Christ is the conqueror of sin, death, and the eternal curse, we at the same time witness that He is by nature God' (p. 23).

The above passage is one of the most striking reproductions of the patristic doctrine by Luther. We may note, however, before we leave this part of our subject, a remarkable passage, in which he (like Irenæus) passes on from the objective salvation of humanity by the Incarnation to its subjective salvation by the spiritual presence of Christ in the heart.[5]

'As Christ came once corporally at the time appointed, abrogated the whole law, abolished sin, destroyed death and hell, so He comes to us spiritually without ceasing and daily quenches and kills these things in us.

'These things I say that thou mayest know how to answer, when the objection is made: Christ came into the world, and once for all took away all our sins, cleansing us by His blood, what need therefore for us to hear the Gospel, what is the use of absolution and the sacraments? It is true, in so far as thou lookest

---

[5] 'Comm. in Gal.', vol. ii, p. 124.

300

on Christ, the law and sin are in very fact abolished. But Christ is not yet come to thee, or if He is come, yet there are still in thee the remains of sin, thou art not yet all leavened. For where there is concupiscence, heaviness of spirit, fear of death, etc., there still is the law and sin, and Christ is not yet come, who, when He comes, drives out fear and heaviness, and brings peace and quietness of conscience.'

We pass on to various fresh developments of Luther's (besides the doctrine of the work of Christ as the satisfaction of the Divine justice, already treated of), which he has formed with a view to furnish additional grounds for the doctrine of justification in one or other of its aspects. These in some cases so grow out of older views that it is difficult to say whether they should be classed as old or new.

In a noteworthy passage [6] Luther discusses the humiliation of Christ under the law. This passage again strongly reminds us of the Fathers, in that Luther adopts the argument of Augustine [7] only with the substitution of the law for the devil, while once more in agreement with the Gnostics he distinguishes the law as a subordinate power from God as the Highest Power.

Christ redeemed us by being made under the law which held us captive.

'What did He? He is the Lord of the law, and therefore the law has no authority over Him, it cannot accuse Him, because He is the Son of God. When, therefore, He was not under the law, of His own accord He subjected Himself to the law. Then the law exercised over Him all the same tyranny, as over us. . . . Finally, by its sentence it condemned Him to death, and that the death of the cross. This is indeed a wonderful combat, in which the law, a creature, thus joins battle with the Creator, and against all right exercises all its tyranny upon the Son of God, which it exercised upon us children of wrath.'

The law, therefore, stands condemned, and loses its right not only over Christ, but over all them that believe in Him. Christ says to them:

'I could have overcome the law by the highest right, without my hurt, for I am Lord of the law, and it therefore has no right

[6] *Ibid.* pp. 151ff. [7] 'De Trinitate', XIII, 14, 18f.

over me. But I have made myself subject to the law for your sake, who were under the law, taking your flesh upon me; that is, I have beyond all need (*per superabundantiam*) condescended to the same poison, tyranny, and bondage of the law, under which you were bound captive; I have allowed the law to lord it over Me, its Lord, to subject Me, as it ought not, to sin, death, and the wrath of God. Therefore, by a double right I have conquered, overthrown, slain the law; first as Son of God, the Lord of the law; then in your person, which is the same as if you yourselves had conquered the law, for my victory is yours.'

Two important points rise out of this passage:

(1) Through the plastic quasi-Gnostic imagery may be descried the Scotist and Occamist doctrine that God is above all law (*exlex*).

(2) Accordingly, in agreement with the Fathers, Thomas, Duns, and Biel, Luther here maintains that Christ might have overcome the law, and so redeemed us by His mere power.[8] Actually, however, He redeemed us by submitting to the jurisdiction which the law had over us, and was by it condemned as a sinner.

Luther, however, has further representations of the relation of Christ to the law. In another passage he speaks of Christ's obedience to the law as the condition of our redemption.[9]

'He was not made a teacher of the law, but a scholar obedient to the law, that by this His obedience He might redeem those that were under the law. . . . Christ, therefore, was related to the law passively, not actively.' Luther does his best to refute, or at least to limit, the scholastic doctrine which made Christ a legislator, the second Moses, and the giver of the new law.

'Whereas Christ in the Gospel gives commandments and teaches the law, or rather interprets it, this belongs not to the doctrine of justification but to that of good works. Again it is not the proper office of Christ, for which especially He came into the world, to teach the law, but an accidental office.'[1]

It was in fact an office like His working of miracles and one

---

[8] This appears to be Luther's view in general ; cf. Seeberg, D.G., 1st ed., vol. ii, p. 257, n. 2.   [9] 'Comm. in Gal.', vol. ii, p. 155.   [1] *Ibid.* vol. ii, p. 156.

which He shared with others, who were men. His true and proper office was to overcome the law, which is possible only to God (pp. 156–157).

'Christ is accordingly no Moses, no exactor or legislator, but a giver of grace, saviour, and fount of mercy.' [2]

He has in fact abolished for the Christian not only the ceremonial, but also the moral law (I, p. 229), as far as the conscience is concerned (p. 231).

On the one hand: 'Outside of the matter of justification no one can sufficiently magnify the good works commanded by God' (II, p. 100). But on the other hand: 'When we are in this concern, we cannot speak basely and hatefully enough of it (the law)' (II, p. 144).

Even the example of Christ belongs to the law, not to the Gospel (II, p. 331). To put on Christ, says Luther, is taken in two ways, according to the law by imitation, according to the Gospel by new birth (II, p. 126). Yet he admits the use of the example of Christ even for a Christian: 'When we have put on Christ as the robe of righteousness and our salvation, then we must put on Christ also as the garment of imitation' (II, p. 128). But the example of Christ has nothing to do with justification (I, p. 356).

From these fresh ideas of the work of Christ in relation to the law we turn to corresponding fresh views of it as a revelation of God. Here Luther has developed far beyond anything in Augustine or Abelard the thought of the revelation of God's love in Christ. The point where he transcends these predecessors is the thoroughness with which he carries out this thought in opposition to the view of God as revealed in nature and the moral law. We have already seen this opposition in the early passages quoted from the Heidelberg Theses, and are now to find it again strikingly developed in the 'Commentary on Galatians'.

The thought of the revelation of God's love in Christ is the natural immediate presupposition of Luther's view of faith as *fiducia*. If faith and God, and again faith, Christ and imputation, are one, then clearly Christ must be so exhibited in order to justification, as to awaken faith in God. For Luther the Incarna-

[2] *Ibid.* vol. i, p. 260.

tion with the consequent life, death, and resurrection of Christ is above all a revelation of God's love, in which He is manifested as He is not manifested in nature and reason, through which He appears as a lawgiver.

'As many as know not the article of justification, take away from between Christ the Propitiator, and would apprehend God in His majesty by the judgment of reason and pacify Him by their works' (I, p. 47).

We are, therefore, in the matter of justification to seek God only in Christ.

'Wherefore when thou wouldst know and treat of thy salvation, setting aside all speculations on the Divine majesty, all thoughts of works, traditions, philosophy, and even the Divine law, run straight to the manger and the mother's bosom, embrace that babe the little Son of the Virgin, and behold Him being born, sucking, growing up, having conversation among men, teaching, dying, rising again, ascending up above all heavens and having power over all things' (I, p. 50).

But if this is the true revelation of God, the question next arises: How then does the God of the law stand related to the God of the Gospel? One answer is contained in the following passage:

'God's nature is to exalt the humble, to feed the hungry, to enlighten the blind, to console the wretched and afflicted, to justify sinners, to quicken the dead, to save the desperate and damned, etc. For He is an almighty Creator, making all things out of nothing. But that most pernicious plague, man's opinion of his own righteousness, which will not be a sinner, unclean, miserable and damned, but just, holy, etc., prevents God from coming to this His own natural and proper work. Therefore God must use that hammer, to wit the law, to break, beat, pound, and in a word reduce to nothing that beast with its vain confidence, wisdom, righteousness, power, etc., that at length it may learn that it is lost and damned' (II, p. 70).

The law then is a minister of God which prepares the way for grace and justification; but the use of the law is not God's proper work, which is to show mercy. Luther elsewhere speaks of God's terrifying the conscience by the law as His *opus alienum.*[3] These are thoughts whose results, if worked out, must clearly carry us on to a new conception of God, and so prepare the way for a new understanding of the work of Christ, both synthetic rather than analytic like the doctrine of the schoolmen, and so properly corresponding with Luther's synthetic conception of justification.

The following passages from the 'Commentary on Galatians', with their emphasis on the conjunction of contraries in Christianity, and with the suggestion in the last of them that the final reconciliation of the contraries must be through the absorption of one by the other, illustrate the tendency of Luther's thought in such a direction.

'Thus a Christian man is at once righteous and a sinner, a friend and an enemy of God. These contraries no sophists will admit, because they do not hold the true idea of justification' (I, p. 335).

'What can be more contrary, than to fear and dread the wrath of God, and yet to hope in His mercy? The one is hell, the other is heaven, and yet they must be most closely joined together in the heart. In speculation they are easily joined together, but to join them in practice is the hardest thing in the world' (II, p. 108).

'Nothing can be more closely conjoined than fear and faith (*fiducia*), law and gospel, sin and grace. For they are so conjoined that the one is swallowed up of the other. Therefore no mathematical conjunction can be assigned that could approach to this' (II, p. 113).

We see that what Luther has in mind is an inner union of opposites, in which they remain no longer external to each other like bodies in mathematical space, but interpenetrate and permeate each other in the way that is the mark of the spiritual life. The scholastic synthesis of speculation, Luther would say, is after all at best an external union; what is wanted is a new synthesis based on experience, which shall be really synthetic. The criticism of Duns and Occam had dissevered the parts of the scholastic synthesis, till they could no more be rejoined after the manner of Alexander and Thomas. If they were to be rejoined

[3] Isa. 28:21. Cf. Köstlin, 'Luthers Theologie', vol. ii, pp. 55, 64.

305

it must be in a new and more intimate way such as Luther suggests, being 'so conjoined that the one is swallowed up of the other'.

Luther thus suggests a new method of Christian theology, the principle of which is his doctrine of justification by faith with its *coincidentia oppositorum*. Hitherto two methods had prevailed. There was that of the Apologists, Origen and Erasmus, which was to simplify Christianity by reducing it to the Logos doctrine and the doctrine of merit, the Pauline gospel of redemption in all its forms being abandoned. Again there was that of Irenæus and Athanasius, which simply added to the framework of the Apologists an incomplete form of Paulinism, which method of addition was further employed by Alexander and Thomas, who built into the edifice also other Pauline or semi-Pauline elements, viz. Augustine's doctrine of grace, Anselm's theory of satisfaction, and Abelard's doctrine of the revelation of the love of God in the Passion. Luther, however, introducing into the traditional structure his new doctrine of justification by faith, introduces it not as another block to be built in with the rest, but rather as a solvent, before which some elements of the older theology disappear as alien philosophical accretions not belonging to Christianity, while those that remain begin to be transmuted each into the other, and all into the doctrine of justification by faith.

'Luther', says Harnack, 'has so treated the traditional schemata, that he has found expressed in each of them, rightly understood, the whole doctrine.' [4]

It is therefore a new theological method which Luther adumbrates. Christianity is to be neither so simple a thing as it is in the Apologists, nor yet the external union of many parts as with Thomas: on the contrary it is to be a higher form of organism, in which the whole is in every part, and every part is the whole. Whatever also in the traditional doctrine will not conform to the new principle and remains obstinately separate and individual, must be excised as no real part of Christian doctrine.

D.G., 4th ed., vol. iii, p. 835.

Zwingli

Zwingli (A.D. 1484–1531), the father of the Swiss Reformation, who next comes before us, has on the one hand much in common with Erasmus, on the other much also with Luther. To the influence of Erasmus he directly owed the humanistic strain, which characterises all his theological work, and markedly differentiates it from that of Luther, whose early training was in the Occamist scholasticism. What Zwingli has in common with Luther is his return from the mediaeval theology to the Pauline Gospel of justification. Yet even here there was a difference; Luther was led back to the Pauline Gospel above all through his own subjective experience, and thus his final apprehension of it centred in the essentially subjective doctrine of justification by faith. Zwingli, who always emphasised his independence of Luther, came to Paul in the first place rather in the spirit of Erasmus than in that of Luther, in so far as his fundamental desire was to go back to the original sources of Christianity, and understand the Divine revelation in the Scriptures.[5] As the result of his search indeed he found in the sources, not a philosophy like Erasmus, but a Gospel like Luther: nevertheless the difference of starting-point between him and Luther led him to make central not the subjective experience of justification but the objective gospel itself. No doubt justification and the Gospel are only two aspects of the same thing, and the difference between Zwingli and Luther is only one of emphasis. Yet there is a difference, which difference was more accentuated still, when Zwingli in his later theology went back behind the Gospel and made the sovereignty of God his fundamental theological principle.

Another difference between Luther and Zwingli lies in the fact that Zwingli was by nature, what Luther never was, viz. a systematic theologian. Throughout his life Zwingli made frequent efforts to formulate his views in more or less systematic form. In so doing, he appealed from his 'Schlussreden' (1523) onwards to Scripture as the one true basis of Christian doctrine. Nevertheless, like Luther, he accepted the traditional Creeds.

[5] See Gieseler, 'Ecclesiastical History', vol. v, English trans., p. 301, n. 17, 18.

The 'First Sermon preached at Berne' (1528) is based on the Apostles' Creed: the 'Fidei ratio' (1530) refers to the Nicene and Athanasian Creeds.

We shall take our account of the ideas of Zwingli from the 'Commentarius de vera et falsa religione' (1525),[6] which is the completest systematic presentation of the Zwinglian theology. It is noteworthy that Zwingli's humanism leads him to begin (loc. 1. Of the word religion) with a philosophy of religion, derived from reflection upon the Ciceronian definition of *religio* from *relegere*.[7] Cicero says: 'Such as diligently treated of and, so to speak, recounted (*relegerent*), all that belonged to the worship of the gods, were called religious from this recounting (*religiosi dicti sunt ex relegendo*)'. Zwingli then takes religion as that conception which includes the whole of Christian piety: faith, life, laws, rites, and sacraments. Christianity in fact is the true religion. Opposed to it is false religion or superstition. The superstition, which Zwingli has in mind, is Romanism. A definition of religion, not as before verbal, but material, follows (loc. 2. Between whom religion should exist).

'Religion includes two terms (*fines*) ; one, to Whom religion tends; the other, who by religion tends to Him' (p. 640).

These are God and man: to treat of religion we must then acknowledge God and know man.

What God is (loc. 3. Of God) is above human comprehension. The existence of God is, however, manifest to reason. God Himself in fact gave the knowledge of Himself to the heathen.[8] Those who believe in the one true Almighty God do so by His own inspiration. Since the infinite God is as much above man as man is above a beetle, God cannot be known by means of philosophy. If therefore certain philosophers have taught what was true concerning God, that was of God's doing, in that He scattered the seeds of Divine knowledge among the heathen. Since, however, God has spoken to us through His Son and His Holy Spirit much more clearly than He did to the heathen, we must hold to the Divine revelation in the Scripture (*divinis oraculis*).

Man's sin (loc. 4. Of man) lay in his self-love. Because of it

---

[6] 'Corpus Reformatorum', vol. xc, pp. 570ff.
[7] 'De natura deorum', II, 28 (72).   [8] Rom. 1:19.

he is evil by nature. This, however, he only realises, when he believes. Zwingli, like Luther, attacks the schoolmen for allowing fallen man free will. In man's sinful state the existence of religion (loc. 3. Of religion) implies that God recalls errant man to Himself. On man's side religion is piety, adhesion, continual thought how to please God. To trust any other than God is false religion.

Zwingli has already, in his introductory paragraph on the term religion, identified true religion with Christianity. He now, therefore, goes on to this concrete embodiment of religion (loc. 6. Of the Christian religion). He insists on the religious unity of God and Christ. All that has been said of union with God is true of union with Christ, who is the God-man. Everything, however, cannot be treated at once, and the knowledge of God naturally precedes the knowledge of Christ.

'Just as grace is only rightly known, when guilt is established by the law, as Paul says,[9] that is, when guilt is known as measured by the law; so also Christ, Who is the pledge of grace, nay, Who is grace itself, is only rightly taught and known, when we have seen our guilt and learned that through its intervention, the way of ascending to heaven is closed for us. . . . To know Christ rightly we must, therefore, first rightly know ourselves' (p. 675).

'Christ then is the certainty and pledge of the grace of God. This will be clear as follows: We said in our consideration of man, that his condition was so desperate, that he was dead, the slave of sin, and, in a word, of such a nature as to care for none but himself. . . . Whence has arisen a continual despair of coming to God; for how could he, who amidst daily evils felt himself to be liable to bodily death, and thus separated from God by fear of conscience, hope ever to be numbered among those above ? But God was good, and pitying His work formed a plan to undo such a terrible fate. And as His justice being sacrosanct must needs remain no less untouched and unshaken than His mercy, and man was, while in need of mercy, yet entirely liable (*obnoxius*) to the Divine justice, the Divine goodness found a way, whereby, while justice was satisfied, God's heart of mercy might allowably be freely opened without harm to justice. Not

[9] Rom. 7:25.

309

that in this matter He had to take precautions against our enemy, or that the Potter could not of the moistened clay make or refashion a vessel just as He pleased; but that by His example of justice He might take away hesitation and sloth from us, and show Himself to us as He was, righteous, good, and merciful; or lest we should say too much of His counsels, because it so pleased Him' (p. 676).

'Since then God is equally just and merciful, though He inclines to mercy (for His mercies excel the rest of His works), nevertheless His justice must be completely satisfied, that His anger may be appeased. That God's justice must be satisfied, theologians, even recent ones, have rightly taught: "For if thou wouldst enter into life, keep the commandments".[1] But in what way shall man satisfy the justice of God? It is so pure, high, and separate from all blemish; and on the other hand this man of ours is so much nought different from sin and stain, that no one can hope to attain to that measure, which can satisfy the Divine justice' (p. 677).

Zwingli insists that the ecclesiastical satisfactions are insufficient. It is only lack of self-knowledge that prevents the recognition of this.

'At last, therefore, wishing to help our hopeless cause, our Creator sent, to satisfy His justice by sacrificing Himself for us, not an angel, not a man, but His own Son, and Him invested with flesh, that neither His majesty might prevent us from intercourse with Him nor His humility cast us down from hope. For that He is God and the Son of God, who has been sent as our Trustee and Mediator, supports our hope. For what can He not do or has He not, who is God? But that He is man, promises familiarity, friendship, yea relationship and community with us; for what can He deny, who is our brother, who partakes of our infirmity? Unheard of and unexpected as was the event, it was yet intended and ordained from the beginning of human misery. For as God created man by His Son, so by Him also He determined to restore him, when fallen into death, by the Same, that creation and restoration might be of One and the Same' (p. 681).

---

[1] Mt. 19:17.

Christ then is the woman's seed, promised in Gen. 3:15, who should break the serpent's head. In the temptation the devil sought to overcome Him, but Christ won the victory. Having failed here the devil raised the Jews against Him.[2]

Zwingli then draws a comparison between the first and the Second Adam. The Pauline name Second Adam shows how Christ restored man by contrary remedies, satisfying the Divine justice.

(1) Adam was placed in a pleasant garden, but was thrust out on his fall. Christ voluntarily left His equality with the Father to become man, and rule men by His word.

(2) Adam wished to become God, by knowing good and evil. Christ became man to lead us to the knowledge of Him, Who alone is good, and alone knows good and evil.

(3) Adam was seduced by his wife to eat of the forbidden fruit. In Christ Deity overcame human weakness.

(4) Adam stretched out his hand to the forbidden tree, to become blessed and wise, in fact Divine (*deus*). Christ stretched out all His members on the shameful cross, that we by His poverty might become blessed, by His folly wise,[3] by His lack Divine (*dii*).

(5) The author of death stretched out his hand to the fatal tree; the Author of life stretched out His hands on the saving tree.

(6) The sweetness of the apple brought death, the bitterness of the cross life.

(7) The guilty Adam hid himself from God: Christ, to save us, bearing our guilt, manifested Himself to the world.

(8) Adam's tree brought bondage, Christ's freedom.

(9) Adam's transgression brought men down to the level of the beasts. Christ's obedience lifted us from the beasts to be sons of God.

(10) Adam's daring closed paradise. Christ's humility opened heaven.

There are besides, the contrasts drawn by Paul in Rom. 5:15–21, which all again show how our disease was cured by contrary remedies, and how the Divine justice was placated for

Lk. 22:53.   [3] I C. 1:18.

311

us by the righteousness of Christ alone, Who is our righteousness, as He is our life. The Old Testament also contains many prophecies of Christ's advent, life, and death—some clear, some in type, and allegory.

Christ, then, at the fitting time became incarnate in the womb of a pure virgin by the fertilising power of the Holy Spirit alone without the co-operation of the male. There were two reasons why He should be thus born of a virgin: (1) His Divinity could not bear contact with the taint of sin; (2) as a victim He needed to be pure from all stain.

The Virgin, therefore, according to prophecy bore Christ in Bethlehem, and laid Him in a manger. The Divine providence arranged that as Adam by sin had stripped himself, and exposed himself to need, so Christ, Who was to satisfy the Divine justice, should taste want, cold, and all the evils which man has incurred by sin.

'For this was justice, that He, by Whom we had all been created, in Whom there is no sin, from Whom we had departed, should, though innocent, bear those things which we had deserved by sinning, but should bear them for us' (p. 688).

Zwingli illustrates this from the whole life of Christ from manger to cross.

'All of which things we have the more willingly touched upon, that every one who looks may clearly see the righteousness of Christ, which brought a remedy for the wound caused by Adam. For our fixed contention up to now is this argument: that Christ is our righteousness, our innocence, and the price of our redemption. For this He died for us and rose again, that He might declare the mystery of deliverance and confirm our hopes, which, while they see Him dead and not alive again by His own victory, cannot be certified of eternal life beyond this' (p. 691).

Such is Zwingli's account of the Christian religion. He now proceeds to treat of the Gospel (loc. 7). It is, that sins are forgiven in Christ's name, the most joyful news ever heard. 'In Christ's name' means 'by the power or might of Christ'. The Gospel, however, includes besides forgiveness the duty of repentance. The whole work of redemption would be purposeless, if man were not made better thereby. Christ's blood washes away our sin, but with the condition that we should become new creatures. Zwingli says, in verbal agreement with Luther:[4] 'The whole life of the Christian man is repentance. For when is it that we do not sin?' (p. 695). This deeper view of repentance makes the ecclesiastical penance appear as hypocrisy (loc. 8). The true knowledge of oneself is incompatible with the idea of being justified by one's own or others' works. True repentance is inward self-examination, which can only end in drawing man to Christ. This process must go on as long as we bear the weight of the body. To sum up the whole situation:

'All the writings of the Apostles are full of the assertion that the Christian religion is nothing else than a firm hope in God through Christ Jesus, and an innocent life, fashioned after the example of Christ, as far as He Himself grants. . . . That also is plain, that not repentance but hope in Christ washes away sins, and that repentance is watchfulness against falling back into what you have condemned' (p. 705).

Zwingli goes on to discuss the law (loc. 9). It is nothing but the eternal will of God. We are concerned not with the civil law, which changes with time and place, nor with the ceremonial law, which is abrogated by Christ, but with the eternal law written on the heart.

'Those, therefore, who merit under the rule of Christ are bound to those things which charity prescribes: what it does not prescribe, or what does not proceed from it, are no commandments or are useless' (p. 708).

The power of the keys (loc. 12) is nothing but the Gospel itself. The false religion places the power of the keys in priestly absolution. A better view, still obtaining in the Church of Rome, is that the priest is only the instrument of the Divine absolution. The true view, however, is, that the power of the keys is merely a metaphorical name for the comforting of souls, when by the illumination of the Holy Ghost they understand the mystery of Christ.

The Church (loc. 13) is nothing but Christ's people. The sacraments (loc. 15)—Zwingli recognises only Baptism and the

---

[4] *Supra*, p. 293, n. 2.

Lord's Supper as instituted by Christ—are signs or ceremonies, which assure the Church, not ourselves, of our faith. Faith is a reality, and in it the spirit confides in the death of Christ, and requires no external assurance. Baptism is a symbol pledging us to a life in accordance with the rule of Christ. In the Lord's Supper we joyfully prove our trust in Christ's death and thank Him for our redemption.

The above abstract of the 'Commentarius de vera et falsa religione', an abstract made of course from our particular point of view, gives Zwingli's doctrine of the work of Christ along with the practical setting, which enables a comparison of it with the mediaeval doctrine. It will be observed that Zwingli's doctrines of faith and repentance agree essentially with those of Luther. In his doctrine of the law, however, there is none of the quasi-Gnosticism of Luther: on the contrary, the law is the eternal will of God. Accordingly Zwingli lays more stress than Luther on the positive aspect of repentance as life after the example of Christ. But the greatest divergence from Luther is in the doctrine of the sacraments. They are not for Zwingli pledges of the Divine grace, but signs of association among Christians. We have already found this view in Alexander, 'Summa', pars IV, qu. 1, memb. 2, art. 2. Taken as it is by Zwingli to the exclusion of all other ideas, it reduces the sacraments to a much more inessential place than they have even in the doctrine of Luther. In modern phraseology we may say that Zwingli assigns to the sacraments only an ethical, not a religious, value. They belong to the sphere of social influence, not to that of the Divine revelation.

As regards Zwingli's doctrine of the work of Christ we note that, while he makes use of the Irenæan motive that creation and redemption must be by one hand, and while he develops ideas like those of Augustine on the contrary correspondence between the sin of Adam and the obedience of Christ, his main doctrine is a modification of the Anselmic doctrine of satisfaction of the same kind as we have already found in Luther. Zwingli in a very thoroughgoing way elaborates the thought of the need of the reconciliation of mercy and justice, and substitutes the Divine justice for the Divine honour as the attribute in God

314

demanding satisfaction. On the other hand he lays great stress on the subjective aspect of the work of Christ, and its connexion with the Gospel: 'Christ is the assurance and pledge of the grace of God' (p. 676).

It is to be observed that Zwingli, like Luther, abandons Anselm upon the point of the absolute necessity of satisfaction; the necessity was ultimately that of the Divine decree. God did not need to treat with the devil, and might have refashioned man by His sovereign power. Zwingli even suggests that His ultimate purpose, so far as we can understand it, was that of assuaging conscience. It is true that Zwingli has, except in the 'Commentarius', nowhere spoken of the necessity of satisfaction as less than absolute, or suggested that it was subjective rather than objective.[5] Yet it is to be observed that such views fundamentally agree with his doctrine of God, who is so absolutely infinite, as to be above all reach of man's understanding. On this showing, even though satisfaction be a rational necessity from the human, it need not be from the Divine, point of view.

We ask in conclusion: has Zwingli furnished the simplification of theology on the basis of Scripture demanded by Occam? There can be no doubt that on the one hand his doctrine is more Scriptural than that of Erasmus, whose method of simplifying theology is to leave out the idea of redemption. On the other hand, while Zwingli agrees with Luther in his general apprehension of Scripture truth, his theology is simpler than Luther's, in that he is more systematic and less paradoxical, witness his doctrine of the law. So far then Zwingli may be said to have fulfilled the demand of Occam, as neither Erasmus nor Luther had done. Nevertheless, while Zwingli is undoubtedly superior to Erasmus, because more Scriptural, his advantage over Luther in simplicity is at the expense of a real loss. Luther's paradoxes carry the promise of a final synthesis, completer than that of Zwingli. Luther has inherited the gains of the Scotist and Occamist criticism with its keen eye for the antinomies in Christianity, while Zwingli shows a tendency to return to the Thomist type of theology, which the Nominalist criticism has declared in the end to amount to no more than a unity of

[5] Cf. Ritschl, 'Justification and Reconciliation', English trans., vol. 1, p. 204.

315

aggregation. Such a unity of aggregation is indeed plainly exhibited by Zwingli's doctrine of the work of Christ, which brings together patristic, mediaeval, and new evangelical material; nor, although all is viewed in connexion with the doctrine that Christ is our righteousness, is the synthesis of the different elements with this doctrine so intimate as in the parallels in Luther.

CHAPTER 2

THE THEOLOGIANS OF THE REFORMATION

MELANCHTHON

WITH Melanchthon (A.D. 1497–1560) we pass from the Reformers themselves to the theologians of the Reformation. Melanchthon, like Zwingli, was a humanist; it was his work to unite the traditons of Erasmus and of Luther. He has great importance for the history of the Reformation itself, in that under the influence of Luther he drew up the 'Augsburg Confession' (1530), and also published his great 'Apology' for it (1531). In these works, says Loofs,[1] the Gospel of the Reformation has obtained a masterly expression. They are actually earlier in time than the documents we have taken for our exposition of Luther.

The importance of Melanchthon for our doctrine, however, lies not in the 'Augsburg Confession' or in the 'Apology' but in the final edition of his 'Loci Theologici' (1559), in which he has developed his own theology more independently of Luther. The first edition of this great work (1521), like the 'Confession' and the 'Apology', reflected more strictly Luther's ideas. The difference between the earlier and the later theology of Melanchthon is seen especially in the change of attitude with regard to the question of authority and reason. In the first edition he thoroughly shares Luther's irrationalism. Christian doctrine is altogether different from philosophy and human reason. Plato and Aristotle have been the ruin of theology in the times of the Fathers and the Schoolmen respectively.[2] In the last edition philosophy is, however, at least allowed a usefulness in the explication of theology,[3] and the general attitude towards reason is more favourable. It goes along with this difference that while in the first edition Melanchthon intentionally devotes attention

---

[1] D.G., 4th ed., p. 822.   [2] 1st ed., ed. Kolde, 1900, p. 65.
[3] Final ed., ed. Detzer, 1827, vol. i, pp. xvi, 4, 5.

only to the practical doctrines of the Reformation, in the last he enlarges his view to take in their metaphysical presuppositions, both theological [4] and Christological. But this procedure again inevitably brings about a more favourable attitude to ecclesiastical tradition. Thus while in the first edition Melanchthon expresses his purpose as simply to offer a guide to the study of the Scripture, and tells us that the 'Loci Theologici' grew out of lectures delivered on Romans (op. cit., pp. 56–58), in the last edition he says that his intention is to gather the doctrine of the Catholic Church on things necessary, as it is handed down in the apostolic literature and the received writers of the Church (p. vi). In other words there is an express harking back to ecclesiastical tradition. While Melanchthon originally said, 'Besides the canonical Scriptures there are in the Church no genuine writings,' [5] he later refers not only to the Epistle to the Romans, but to Origen, Cyprian, Augustine, John of Damascus, and Lombard. In a word, in Melanchthon's later theology the old landmarks submerged by the flood of Luther's revolutionary thought begin to reappear.

In order therefore to present Melanchthon not merely as the interpreter of Luther, but in his own individuality, we take our account of his theology from the final edition of the 'Loci'. While the first edition is an important monument of the Reformation, the last is the form in which Melanchthon's ideas have worked in history.

The fundamental principle of Melanchthon's theology in all its stages is indeed one.

'There are two parts of Scripture in general, law and Gospel.' [6] 'The whole of Scripture should be distributed under these two chief titles, the law and the promises.' [7] 'These two (the law and the promise of the Gospel) are the chief titles and chief heads of Scripture, to which all other parts can be wisely referred.' [8]

But while the first edition of the 'Loci' contains the famous passage, 'This it is to know Christ, to know His benefits, not, as they (the Schoolmen) teach, His natures, and the modes of the Incarnation' (p. 63), the last edition returns distinctly to the

[4] 'Theological' in the strict sense, i.e. belonging to the doctrine of God.
[5] 1st ed., p. 65. [6] 'Loci', 1st ed., p. 140. [7] 'Apologia Confessionis', IV, 5.
[8] 'Loci', final ed., vol. i, p. 172.

318

scholastic view of the basis of theology. The doctrines of the Trinity and of the Incarnation are introduced as depending on the Scripture and the tradition of the Church (loc. I Of God); while the doctrine of God as Creator has also a rational basis, in that it can be demonstrated from His work in the world (loc. II Of the Creation).

The Son is the Eternal Logos, who has assumed human nature. God has sent Him to be a Redeemer and placate His wrath against sin (I, p. 20). His office also includes the work of teaching according to the command of the Father (p. 34). But Melanchthon does not expand the doctrine of Christ's office, but after a recognition of the Augustinian doctrine of original sin (p. 86) proceeds to his central theme of law and gospel (loc. VI Of the Divine law; loc. VII Of the Gospel).

'The law of God is a doctrine, delivered by God, ordaining, what we are to be and do, and what we should omit, demanding a perfect obedience towards God, and declaring that God is angry and punishes with eternal death those who do not render a perfect obedience' (p. 105).

The law has three species: the Divine law, the law of nature, human law. The Divine laws are those immediately given by God, and are to be found in Moses and the New Testament. The law of nature is a natural knowledge of God and of morals, divinely implanted in the human mind, just as are the principles of numbers. It agrees with that part of the law of God, which is called moral. The law of Moses contained, besides the moral precepts, ceremonial and judicial precepts also. The moral law alone, however, is the eternal and unchanging element in the law. It is summed up in the Decalogue. Altogether the law has three uses: the first is a political use, for the sake of keeping together civil society. Here human law, as based upon the Divine law and the law of nature, has its sphere of operation. The second use of the law is to convince of sin. The third is its use for the regenerate, who are free from the law as regards its curse, but not in so far as its represents the Divine will directing their obedience. The law is so absolute that it admits of no distinction between counsels and precepts. There is one law for all Christians.

319

The law and the Gospel stand in contrast with each other.

'The law, as was said before, is a doctrine demanding a perfect obedience towards God; it does not freely remit sin, it does not pronounce just, that is, accepted with God. except where the law has been satisfied; and though it has promises, yet these require the condition of the fulfilment of the law. On the other hand the Gospel, though it preaches repentance and good works, yet contains the promise of the benefit of Christ, which is the proper and chief doctrine of the Gospel, and is to be distinguished from the law; for it freely remits sins, and pronounces us just, even though we do not satisfy the law' (p. 165).

The law, Melanchthon repeats, has promises, but upon condition. But of the Gospel he further says:

'Quite other is the promise proper to the Gospel. It has not as ground the condition of the law; it does not promise because of the fulfilment of the law, but freely for Christ's sake. . . . Remission and reconciliation or justification are freely given us, that is, not in accordance with our worth; and yet there needed to be a victim on our behalf, therefore Christ was given us and was made a sacrifice, that for His sake we might certainly conclude that we please the Father' (p. 166).

The Gospel was necessary, because after man's fall, though there remained some knowledge of the law, yet sin abides in human nature, and the conscience, if it knows only the law, cannot believe in God's will to forgive. Therefore the Gospel was revealed immediately after Adam's fall,[9] was renewed to Abraham,[1] and was continued by the line of psalm and prophecy.

The sum of the Gospel is contained in the doctrine of grace and justification (loc. VIII), which exhibits the proper benefit of Christ. To neglect it is to transform Christianity into philosophy, to extenuate sin in human nature, and to miss the essential difference between the Christian revelation and philosophy. Melanchthon goes on to define justification, faith, and grace in a completely Protestant sense. The imputative view of justification, which we saw to be the controlling element in Luther's doctrine, is here the only view: Melanchthon justifies it on Scriptural grounds with the help of his humanistic learning.

[9] Gen. 3:15.   [1] *Ibid.* 15:1ff.

320

'Justification signifies the remission of sins and reconciliation, or the acceptation of the person to eternal life; for to the Hebrews to justify is a forensic word. . . . Paul, therefore, took the word justify in accordance with the custom of Hebrew speech in the sense of the forgiveness of sins and reconciliation or acceptation' (p. 177).

Justification is, moreover, of grace (*gratis*): for, although when God forgives sin, He gives the Holy Ghost as the foundation of all virtues, the anxious conscience must not have regard to the virtues which accompany reconciliation. Paul says that we are justified not by works, but by faith in Christ. What does this mean?

'To be justified by works signifies to obtain remission and to be just or accepted before God because of our own virtues and deeds. On the other hand, to be justified by faith in Christ signifies to obtain forgiveness not because of our own virtues, but because of the Mediator, the Son of God' (p. 178).

Faith, then, beholds Christ sitting at God's right hand and interceding for us, views Him as Mediator, and applies His mediatorship to our needs. Faith is, therefore, not merely a historical knowledge, though historical knowledge is implied: it is trust (*fiducia*).

'Faith looks upon Christ, Who must be acknowledged as the Son of the Eternal God, crucified for us, and raised again, etc.; and the history is to be referred to the promise or effect, which is set forth in this article, I believe in the forgiveness of sins. And again, this very article warns us that faith is to be understood as trust: for, for the man who does not trust that his sins are forgiven, these words, I believe in the forgiveness of sins, are said in vain' (p. 179).

Melanchthon again applies his humanistic knowledge to justify the interpretation of πίστις in the sense of *fiducia*. He next proceeds to define grace, once more defending the Protestant sense of the word by the help of the same resource.

'Grace is the remission of sins, or mercy promised for Christ's sake, or free acceptation, which is necessarily accompanied by the gift of the Holy Ghost. It is not difficult for those to determine the meaning of the word, who know the Hebrew expression;

321

for the Hebrew word always signifies favour, sometimes also a gift' (p. 190).

What, however, further requires to be noted is that Paul in his definition of grace always emphasises that it is free (*gratis*), entirely apart from our merit or virtue or deeds. There are four reasons for the exclusion of all these:

(1) That due honour may be given to Christ. To transfer the cause of forgiveness to men's works is both to extenuate men's sins and to imagine that God can be placated, out of Christ. It is to take Christ as a lawgiver or teacher, not as a sacrifice for sin.

(2) Without the exclusion there is no rest for the troubled conscience.

(3) To omit it produces a heathen doubt whether God will hear our prayers, instead of a Christian confidence that He undoubtedly will.

(4) It confuses the law and the Gospel. That forgiveness is free marks the essential distinction between them.

That justification is by faith alone means the same thing as that it is free: the word 'alone' does not exclude contrition or other virtues, but denies that they are the causes of reconciliation with God, and transfers the whole causality to Christ. Justification by faith and free forgiveness are therefore correlative. Melanchthon denies that the figure of *synecdoche* here applies: viz. that we are justified by faith, in so far as it is informed by charity. Forgiveness is gratis, not on account of the fulfilment of the law, as *synecdoche* would imply; in fact the love to God cannot arise, unless first we see that God's wrath is appeased. It is moreover by faith that we receive the Holy Spirit.[2] The remission of sins is not for the inactive (*otiosis*), nor without a conflict and the consolation of the soul by faith.

'Since therefore the Holy Spirit in that consolation produces new activities and new life, this conversion is called regeneration,[3] and a new obedience must of necessity follow' (p. 200).

Thus we reach the subject of good works (loc. IX). Christ clearly taught concerning repentance, and Paul says that we are debtors not to walk after the flesh.[4] 'We are therefore regenerated in reconciliation, that a new obedience may be begun in us'

Gal. 3:14.   [3] Jn 3.   [4] Melanchthon further refers to 1 C. 6:9 ; 1 Jn 3:7, 8.

(p. 203). The works, which we must do, are those according to the Decalogue—they are made possible by the gift of the Holy Spirit. Though sin abides in us, and renders them imperfect, they please God for the sake of Christ, Who offers to God our prayers and worship, and forgives their infirmity. 'Thus for Christ's sake first the person is reconciled, then the works also are accepted' (p. 215). We must do these good works to retain our faith, to avoid punishment, and because they are according to the eternal will of God. God rewards them both here and hereafter, but for Christ's sake. Faith cannot rest on two supports, Christ and our merits. Sin remains in the regenerate against their will; if it remains with their will, the Holy Spirit and faith and grace are lost.

The doctrine of good works then completes the view of law and Gospel. Melanchthon turns now to discuss the subsidiary question of the difference between the Old and New Testaments (loc. x). Both law and Gospel are contained alike in each Testament. The Old Testament, however, was most properly a political constitution under which the law and the promise of the Messiah were safeguarded in Israel. In the New Testament this political constitution is done away, and the ceremonial of the Hebrew law receives its fulfilment in Christ.

We pass on to Melanchthon's doctrine of the Church (loc. XIII) and of the sacraments (loc. XIII).

'The visible Church is the company of those who embrace the Gospel of Christ and rightly use the sacraments, in which God works effectively by the ministry of the Gospel, and renews men to life eternal, in which company, however, many are not regenerate, but (merely) accept the true doctrine' (p. 285).

A sacrament is thus defined:

'According to our present Church usage, sacrament is the name given to a ceremony instituted in the Gospel, that it may be a witness of the promise, which is proper to the Gospel, viz. the promise of reconciliation or of grace' (p. 303).

The doctrine that the sacraments are distinguishing marks of Christian profession Melanchthon holds to be a secular view. Though sacraments have many ends, their principal end is to be tokens of God's will of grace towards us. Such were the sacraments of the Old Testament, and such are now these of the New Testament. Melanchthon accepts as sacraments proper, instituted by Christ, Baptism, the Lord's Supper, and Absolution, all of which signify properly the remission of sins. Next to these he reckons Ordination or the call to the ministry and its public approval. His interpretation of the sacrament of Absolution makes it simply the concrete application of the doctrine of justification by faith. Contrition is terror of conscience in view of the Divine judgment against sin. To awaken it, the moral law must be used; inasmuch as it is the eternal will of God denouncing judgment upon sin. The Gospel also must be applied to accuse the world of its contempt of Christ. Contrition must be followed by faith in Christ. A general, though not a particular, confession of sin is to precede absolution. For the mediaeval satisfaction, Melanchthon substitutes the patient acceptance of affliction and the cross as Divine chastisements, but not as in any way meritorious, which would be to dishonour Christ.

Melanchthon adds a section on the kingdom of Christ (loc. xv).

'The Gospel clearly teaches that the kingdom of Christ is spiritual, that is, that Christ sits at the right hand of the Father and makes intercession for us, and gives remission of sins and the Holy Spirit to the Church, that is, to those that believe in Him and call upon God in trust upon Him; and that He sanctifies them, that He may raise them up at the last day to life and glory eternal. And that we may obtain these benefits, there has been ordained the ministry of the Gospel, by which men are called to the knowledge of Christ; and the Holy Spirit is efficacious, etc.' (II, p. 58).

The above outline shows how well Melanchthon has succeeded in clearly stating in opposition to Catholicism the fundamental position of Protestantism. His theology is undoubtedly founded on Luther's, and retains from him the synthetic view of justification, which is the characteristic and central Protestant doctrine. In detail, however, Melanchthon returns to the analytic methods of the schoolmen. Law and Gospel, contrition and faith, are not as with Luther moments of the same indivisible process, but are clearly separated from one another. Above all justification and regeneration, the forgiveness of sins and the gift of the Spirit, are carefully separated. A great deal of Luther's exuberance of idea has disappeared, and, the fundamental irrationalism of the doctrine of justification by faith once admitted, we are given a clear and rational analysis of what it involves. Not in vain has Melanchthon been called the *præceptor Germaniæ*; he has solved the problem of making Protestantism a teachable doctrine by reducing the paradoxical exuberance of Luther, and reintroducing the logical principle of distinction.

Compared with Zwingli, Melanchthon has on the whole the advantage both as regards matter and form; of matter, in so far as he reproduces Luther, who is superior to Zwingli; of form, in so far as his doctrine is clearer and more finished than that of the Swiss humanist.

By his success in stating the practical doctrines of the Reformation, to such a degree indeed that his outline, while improved in some points by Calvin, has remained the basis of all subsequent Protestant theology, Melanchthon has made the necessary preparation for a new Protestant doctrine of the work of Christ. To the new complex of practical doctrines a new conception of the work of Christ must correspond: to this new conception, however, Melanchthon himself has not yet attained. In his 'Loci' his references to the work of Christ are of the most general character, and are mostly introduced only with immediate practical reference to the doctrine of justification. Such references as there are, however, suggest a reduction of Luther's variety of doctrine to one fixed type. Though Melanchthon recognises the work of Christ as a teacher and also refers to His reign and intercession, the principal point in His work appears to be that as a sacrifice or victim He propitiates the Divine wrath against sinners. In other works Melanchthon develops this last view into a doctrine like that which we have found in Zwingli, modifying the Anselmic theory of satisfaction, and laying great stress on the reconciliation of mercy and justice. Thus in his 'Enarratio Symboli Nicæni',[5] he treats on these lines of the impulsive and final causes of the Incarnation. He says:

'This decree was made by the most free counsel of God, nor

[5] Thomasius, 'Christi Person und Werk', vol. iii, p. 314.

do we so repeat its causes, as if anything were thereby detracted from the freedom of will in God, but it is certain that this decree was made with an admirable wisdom and with the preservation of the order of justice and mercy. Consequently we inquire into its congruous causes whatsoever. Now the first is not obscure. Although God received the human race by His mercy for the sake of His Son's intercession, yet God, since He is just, willed that His justice should be satisfied. So by a wonderful harmonisation of justice and mercy the reconciliation was established. And since the human race had sinned, it befitted the order of justice that one of the human race should pay the penalty, which was the ransom of the rest. It is therefore clear enough why this sacrifice should be a man. The second reason, why He should be God, is the infinite evil of sin; that He might be a ransom of infinite goodness and an equivalent, this Mediator is also God. Thirdly, no created power could alone have borne the wrath of God, and in so great stress of pains have given true praise to Divine justice. This is the secret and great cause, which the devout do not neglect to consider. For in the punishment, which must be a placation, the praise of justice must be rendered to the Punisher: a created power, however, could not have overcome death and restored to us righteousness and life eternal. And since the Mediator must needs be the perpetual guardian of the Church, hearing it at all times and present with the saints everywhere—it is evident that a created power could not be present nor see the groans of our hearts. These things belong only to the Mediator.'

It is observable from the above extract, that Melanchthon, like Zwingli and Luther, rejects the Anselmic doctrine of an absolute necessity of satisfaction.

The 'Formula of Concord'

The period immediately following the Reformation was marked in the Lutheran Church by a number of theological controversies, which were brought to a conclusion by the 'Formula of Concord' (1580).

The 'Concordia' recognises Holy Scripture as the one supreme authority in matters of religion. All other documents, whether ancient or modern, are only to be accepted in subjection to the authority of Scripture, as witnesses of the conservation of the true doctrine in the Church. As such witnesses are recognised the three Creeds, the 'Augsburg Confession' of 1530 with the 'Apology', Luther's 'Schmalkald Articles', and his two Catechisms. The 'Concordia' then proceeds to a determination of the controversies, which have arisen among those theologians, who recognise the 'Augsburg Confession'. There is a shorter statement (*Epitome*), and a fuller (*Solida declaratio*).

The points that concern us, are the doctrine of justification (III) and the doctrine of law and Gospel (V). In the articles on justification the theologians of the 'Concordia' have before them the views of Osiander and Stancarus. Osiander (A.D. 1498–1552) had developed in a one-sided way just those points of Luther's theology which Melanchthon had abandoned. While Melanchthon made justification wholly forensic, Osiander followed the lines of the passage previously quoted,[6] where Luther answers the objection, Christ once and for all took away our sins, what need is there then of the Gospel, absolution, and the sacraments, by saying that in Christ the law and sin are indeed abolished, but that from us the law and sin, fear and heaviness, are not driven out, till Christ comes into us, bringing peace and quietness of conscience. Osiander accordingly maintained[7] that justification by faith takes place by the imputation to us of the righteousness of Christ, inherent in us. This inherence is, however, in principle independent of the historical Christ: it is the indwelling in us of the Eternal Word, that Inner Word of which the external word of the Gospel is only the medium.

Osiander held, like Rupert of Deutz, that the Incarnation of the Word in humanity was decreed independently of the Fall. Men were always intended to have the Incarnate Christ as their Head and King. Adam was made in the image of God, i.e. of Christ, not Christ in the image of Adam. That Adam was thus made in the Divine image means that he was indwelt by the

[6] 'Comm. in Gal.', vol. ii, p. 124.
[7] Cf. Seeberg, D.G., 1st ed., vol. ii, pp. 357-62 ; Baur, 'Christliche Lehre von der Versöhnung', pp. 316-31.

Word, and so partook of the essential righteousness of God. This was the original righteousness of Adam, by which he was justified.

By the Fall, however, this original righteousness of man was lost, until it was restored by the fresh indwelling of the Word, first in Christ, and then in those who believe upon Him. The Incarnation of Christ thus serves to mediate the indwelling of the Word in us; but the righteousness that comes to us through it is 'no work, no deed, no suffering' of man, but the essential righteousness of God Himself. Osiander said that in this Divine righteousness human sin is lost as an unclean drop in the purity of the ocean.

The work of the historical Christ, however, was properly redemption, not justification. Osiander sharply distinguishes the two. Between them he says 'there is a great difference, as can be understood from this, that men can redeem a thief from the gallows, but cannot make him good and just'.[8]

Redemption has two parts:

(1) Christ bore for us in His Passion the wrath of God, and the punishment of sin, and obtained for us the forgiveness of sins.

(2) But, more than this, since, even after that we are born anew, we still sin, and thus would naturally lie open to the condemnation of the law, Christ, in order that the law may not accuse us, has 'fulfilled it absolutely and perfectly for us and for our good, that it (our imperfect fulfilment) may not be reckoned to us, and that we may not be accused, in that we do not in this life perfectly fulfil the law'.[9]

In these two points consists our redemption, which is a thing objective and finished long ago. Osiander says: 'It is manifest that, whatever Christ, as a faithful Mediator, did for our sakes with God, His Heavenly Father, in the fulfilling of the law and in His Passion and Death, was done fifteen hundred years ago and more, when we were not yet born.'[1]

This work, moreover, avails for every one, who belongs to the Church of Christ, entirely apart from his subjective attitude. Redemption, however, is but the prelude to justification, and

---

[8] Baur, op. cit. p. 317, n. 1.
[9] Quoted from Osiander by Seeberg, op. cit. p. 358.
[1] Baur, op. cit. p. 319, n. 1.

328

the negative presupposition of the positive grace of Christ's inherent righteousness, which justifies us. Redemption was accomplished once and for all in the life and death of Christ; justification takes place continually through the indwelling of the Word in fresh believers, as the Gospel is preached.

The agreement of the general outline of Osiander's doctrine with the above-mentioned passage in Luther's 'Galatians' is apparent. Another interesting point is the close correspondence of the ideas of Osiander with these of Athanasius, 'De Incarnatione'. His doctrine of the original righteousness of Adam through the indwelling of the Word is essentially the doctrine of 'De Incarnatione', III, 3, viewed from the standpoint of justification. So also his doctrine, that justification is by the essential righteousness of God, infused into mankind through the Incarnation, and imputed to them as their own, is the Greek doctrine of deification, regarded from the standpoint of justification. The theology of Osiander as a whole is in fact to be regarded as a reinterpretation of the Greek theology, made in order to meet the Reformation problem of justification. It has often been debated whether Osiander's theology is Protestant or Catholic. It is Catholic in virtue of its agreement with the patristic theology; it has, however, little in common with the Mediaeval scholasticism. It is Protestant in so far as there is no calculus of merits, and as justification is made to depend not on our new life nor on *caritas* (*gratia creata*), but on the righteousness of Christ Himself; it is to be observed, however, that this righteousness is not, as in the usual Protestant view, His work. To sum up, Osiander has developed in a one-sided way some valuable thoughts of Luther neglected by Melanchthon, and is the herald of a second type of Protestant theology very different from Melanchthon's, a type of theology, it may be added, which, though it had no success at the time, is yet the precursor of a good deal of modern doctrine. Where, however, Osiander undoubtedly falls short of Luther and of Melanchthon also, is in his clean separation of redemption as a mere logical presupposition from justification as an experience. It is true that Luther alternates the points of view of salvation complete in Christ and salvation energising in us; but it is not in accordance with his fundamental synthesis (preserved by Melanchthon) to speak of redemption as a fact accomplished fifteen hundred years ago, while justification takes place by the imputation of the righteousness of Christ dwelling in us in present experience. In his preference for the Logos doctrine over the doctrine of the Cross, Osiander runs counter to Luther's Heidelberg Theses, and becomes a *theologus gloriæ* rather than a *theologus crucis*.

Stancarus (d. A.D. 1574), the other theologian considered in the 'Formula of Concord', was led, in opposition to Osiander, to go to the other extreme and assert that the righteousness of Christ, by which we were justified, was His righteousness solely according to His human nature. This was simply the doctrine of Augustine and the Schoolmen, that Christ is Mediator as man, viewed from the standpoint of justification. It ran counter to the whole patristic current in Luther's theology.

The 'Concordia' opposes Osiander and Stancarus alike.[2]

'In opposition to both the remaining theologians of the "Augsburg Confession" have taught with unanimous agreement, that Christ is our righteousness not according to His Divine nature only nor yet according to His human nature only, but according to both natures; inasmuch as He (as God and man) by His most perfect obedience delivered us from our sins, justified and saved us.'

The doctrine of justification is further developed as follows (III, 10–15):

'These blessings are offered to us in the promise of the Gospel through the Holy Spirit. But faith alone is the only medium by which we apprehend, accept, and apply them to ourselves. Such faith is the gift of God, by which we rightly acknowledge Christ as our Redeemer in the word of the Gospel, and trust in Him, to wit, that, solely for the sake of His obedience, we have by grace the remission of our sins, and are accounted righteous by God the Father, and are eternally saved. And so these propositions are equivalent and clearly mean the same, when Paul (Rom. 3:28) says: We are justified by faith, or (4:3) faith is imputed to us for righteousness, and when he teaches (5:19) that we are justified

[2] 'Sol. Decl.' Part II, art. 3, sect. 4.

by the obedience of the one Mediator Christ, or that (5:18) by the obedience of one man justification of life comes to all men. For Faith does not therefore justify, because it is so good a work and so excellent a virtue, but because it apprehends and embraces the merit of Christ in the promise of the Gospel; for that must be applied to us if we would be justified by His merit. And so that righteousness, which of mere grace is imputed before God to faith or to believers, is the obedience, Passion, and Resurrection of Christ, by which He satisfied the law on our account and expiated our sins. For since Christ is not only man, but also God and man in one undivided Person, He was as far from subject to the law, as He was (by reason of His Person) free from liability to Passion and Death. For that reason His obedience (not only that, by which He obeyed the Father in His whole Passion and Death, but also that by which for our sake He voluntarily subjected Himself to the law and fulfilled it by His obedience) is imputed to us for righteousness, so that God on account of the whole obedience (which Christ by doing and suffering, in His life and death offered for our sake to His Heavenly Father) forgives our sins, accounts us good and righteous, and bestows on us eternal salvation. This righteousness is offered to us through the Gospel and in the sacraments by the Holy Spirit, and is applied and apprehended by faith: whence believers have reconciliation with God, the forgiveness of sins, the favour of God, the adoption of sons, and the inheritance of life eternal.'

This classical passage is of the greatest importance for the following reasons:

(1) It finally fixes the purely imputative view of justification adopted by Melanchthon as the only doctrine henceforward tenable in the Lutheran Church. (2) In so doing it reduces a number of Scripture views of justification to a common measure of interpretation. (3) In laying stress on the theanthropic character of the Mediator, it proceeds on lines already indicated in controversy with Osiander by Melanchthon's disciple Flacius (cf. Loofs, D.G., fourth ed., p. 872), to an important development of the doctrine of Christ's vicarious obedience. This obedience includes not only the passive obedience of His sufferings and

331

death, but also the active obedience of His life. Anselm had asserted that Christ as man owed God the obedience of His life, and hence could not offer it to the Father for us: the theologians of the 'Formula of Concord' find in Luther's doctrine that Christ, the God-man, is *exlex* the possibility of taking the active obedience of His life also as vicarious. It is to be observed, however, that they insist that the whole obedience, active and passive, is one.[3] 'Wherefore we believe, teach, and confess, that the whole obedience of the whole Person of Christ, which He offered to the Father even to the most shameful death of the cross, is imputed to us for righteousness.' The great difference from Osiander is that this twofold obedience of Christ not merely serves for redemption in Osiander's sense, but is imputed to us in justification. (4) Faith, apprehending the Gospel in word and sacraments, is defined as the medium and instrument of justification. The 'Formula of Concord', however, attributes faith, like Luther, to the work of the Holy Spirit, rather than the reception of the Holy Spirit to faith, as Melanchthon tends to do. It further teaches that renovation or sanctification is also a benefit of Christ the Mediator and the work of the Holy Spirit, but that it does not belong to the article of justification. On this point reference is made to Luther's 'Galatians' (loc. cit. 28). The 'Concordia' concedes to Osiander that there is an essential indwelling of the righteousness of God in us, in so far as the Holy Ghost, who is eternal and essential righteousness, dwells by faith in the justified. But this indwelling is not the righteousness of faith, for the sake of which we are justified: the latter is nothing but the remission of sins and the gracious acceptance of the sinner for the sake only of the obedience and merit of Christ (loc. cit. 54).

The section of the 'Formula of Concord' dealing with the doctrine of law and Gospel may be dealt with much more briefly; it will be sufficient to refer to the 'Epitome' (I, pars v). Here it is said that the distinction between the two is most important. The law is the Divine revelation, teaching us what is pleasing to God, and convincing us of sin. The Gospel is properly the doctrine of Christ's satisfaction and its fruits, especially the remission of sins: in a wider sense, however, it

---

[3] *Ibid.* sect. 56.

includes also the preaching of repentance. But the Gospel proper as well as the law convinces us of sin, inasmuch as Christ's Passion is a supreme exhibition of the Divine wrath against sin: yet it convinces of sin very differently from the mere law, which tends to harden sinners, while the Gospel, in so far as it convinces of sin, reveals to men the spirituality of the law, and impels men to Christ.

'Yet as long as Christ's Passion and death set before the eyes the wrath of God, and terrify man, so long they are not properly the preaching of the Gospel, but the doctrine of Moses and the law, and are the strange work of Christ by which He advances His own proper office, which is to preach concerning the grace of God, to console, and to quicken. These are the properties of the preaching of the Gospel' (loc. cit. 8–10).

In the above doctrine of law and Gospel we have an advance upon Melanchthon, in that his scheme of law and Gospel is filled out with thoughts from Luther. The increasedly synthetic character of the doctrine is apparent.

The importance of the 'Formula of Concord' as the authoritative standard of the developed doctrine of the Lutheran Church is very great. The Reformed Church has no confession, which takes the place of a universal norm in the same sense.[4] What really occupies in the Reformed Church the place of both Melanchthon's 'Loci' and the 'Formula Concordiæ' in one, is Calvin's 'Institutes'. 'Calvin is the most influential bearer of the common Reformed spirit.'[5] It is to be observed that the final edition of Calvin's 'Institutes' (1559) was subsequent to the Osiandrian controversy, but before the 'Formula of Concord'.

CALVIN

Ritschl is said to have called Calvin's 'Institutes' 'the masterpiece of Protestant theology',[6] and they well deserve the name. Here first do we find a complete Protestant system of equal weight with the great mediaeval systems of Catholicism. Moreover,

[4] Cf. Müller, 'Symbolik', 1896, p. 377. [5] Müller, op. cit. p. 379.
[6] Orr, 'The Ritschlian Theology', p. 28, n.

Calvin's system is Protestant through and through, and realises much more adequately than Melanchthon's 'Loci', the synthetic character of Luther's original intuition. For Calvin (A.D. 1509–1564), though he is the great doctor of the Reformed Church, creating the type of theology henceforward peculiar to it in contradistinction from the Lutheran Church, is nevertheless more dependent on Luther than on Zwingli. The very form of the first edition of the 'Institutes' (1535) shows Luther's influence: it followed the lines of Luther's catechisms in treating successively of the Decalogue, the Creed, the Lord's Prayer, and the Sacraments. Calvin has, however, in common with Zwingli, in contradistinction from Luther, the inheritance of the humanistic tradition of Erasmus.

'Calvin, like Zwingli, was a humanist before he became a Reformer, and what he was at first he never ceased to be. On the intellectual side, as a scholar and thinker, his affinities were with Erasmus, though on the religious side they were rather with Luther; indeed, Calvin can hardly be better described than by saying that his mind was the mind of Erasmus, though his faith and conscience were those of Luther.' [7]

Calvin assigns as the purpose of his 'Institutes', to prepare for the study of Scripture.

'I have endeavoured to give such a summary of religion in all its parts, and have digested it into such an order, as may make it not difficult for anyone, who is rightly acquainted with it, to ascertain both what he ought principally to look for in Scripture, and also to what head he ought to refer whatever is contained in it.' [8]

In the preface to the French edition of 1545 Calvin makes use of Erasmus's name of Christian philosophy in order to describe the matter of his summary. It is in fact a Christian philosophy which he offers, though its content is very different from that of Erasmus. True wisdom, he says (I, 1, 1),[9] consists almost entirely of two parts: the knowledge of God and of ourselves. Each part, however, implies the other: here at once the synthetic

[7] Fairbairn, in the 'Cambridge Modern History', vol. ii, p. 349.
[8] 'Epistle to the Reader', 2nd ed., 1539.
[9] This and the subsequent references are to the final edition of the 'Institutes' (1559). The translations are from the version of Beveridge (1845), revised where necessary.

character of Calvin's theology manifests itself. We cannot know ourselves without being led to the recognition of God as Creator and Redeemer. On the other hand, a true knowledge of self is only possible in the light of the knowledge of God. Calvin, moreover, insists that the true knowledge of God is not merely intellectual, but involves religion or piety. It has, however, two degrees. There is first the simple and primitive knowledge of God as Creator, implied in the very course of nature, and which man would have had apart from the Fall. There is, secondly, the peculiar knowledge of God as Redeemer, which after the Fall God has made possible for us in Christ.

As regards the simpler knowledge of God as Creator, it is in the first place written on the heart of man; next, it is taught us by the whole course of nature and providence. Man, however, is so blinded by sin that these natural means of Divine knowledge are insufficient. Hence God has met us with a fresh revelation in Scripture, confirming the prior revelation in nature, and also supplementing it with the further knowledge of Himself as Redeemer. The recognition of the truth of Scripture—it is necessary to receive the Scripture as the very oracles of God— depends not on the authority of the Church, but on the inner testimony of the Holy Spirit in the believer. This testimony alone gives certainty, though there are many other secondary proofs of the authority of Scripture, which result from the reflection of reason upon it. Such are the proofs from its harmony, dignity, simplicity, and efficacy, from the majesty of the prophets, the antiquity of Moses, the fulfilment of prophecy and miracles, the consent of the Church, and the constancy of the martyrs.

From the doctrine of God as Creator, Calvin passes on to the doctrine of man and the Fall. Like Luther, he insists on taking the doctrine of original sin with the utmost thoroughness: there is no free will to good in fallen man. Here then comes in the further knowledge of God as Redeemer (II, 6, 1).

'Since our fall from life unto death, all that knowledge of God the Creator, of which we have discoursed would be useless, were it not followed up by faith, holding forth to us God as a Father in Christ. The natural course undoubtedly was that the fabric of the world should be a school where we might learn piety

335

and from it pass to eternal life and perfect felicity. But after the
Fall, wherever we turn our eyes, above and below, we are met by
the Divine malediction, which, while it seizes upon innocent
creatures and involves them in our fault, of necessity fills our
own souls with despair. For, although God is still pleased in many
ways to manifest His paternal favour towards us, we cannot from
a mere survey of the world infer that He is a Father. Conscience
urges us within and shows that sin is a just ground for our being
disowned, which will not allow God to account or to treat us for
sons. In addition to this are our sloth and ingratitude. Our minds
are so blinded that they cannot perceive the truth, and all our
senses are so corrupt that we wickedly rob God of His glory.'

Thus God is only to be savingly known through Christ the
Mediator. It was so even under the Old Testament: the sacrifices,
the kingdom, prophecy all pointed to the Mediator.

'If, then, the first step in piety is to acknowledge that God
is a Father, to defend, govern, and cherish us, until He gathers
us to the eternal inheritance of His kingdom; hence it is plain,
as we lately observed, that there is no saving knowledge of God
without Christ, and that consequently from the beginning of the
world Christ was held forth to all the elect as the object of their
faith and confidence' (II, 6, 4).

Calvin next shows how the law prepared the way for Christ.
'By the law I understand not only the Ten Commandments, which
contain a complete rule of pious and righteous living, but the
whole system of religion delivered by the hand of God through
Moses' (II, 7, 1). The ceremonies and the kingdom (as was said
before) pointed to Christ: the moral law also prepared for Him,
inasmuch as its first use is to convince of sin. Calvin observes,
however, that the moral law has also a civil use, and a third use
for Christians, in that it instructs them in the Divine will, its
curse being abrogated for them but not its precepts. Calvin
recognises in the Ten Commandments the eternal rule of righteousness naturally imprinted on man's heart. Man's sin, however,
required a fresh promulgation, such as God has given in the
written law (II, 8, 1).

Christ, however, though manifested in type and symbol under
the law, is only clearly revealed in the Gospel (II, 9, 1). Calvin

336

does not set law and Gospel in such extreme opposition as does Luther: his position at this point is nearer to that of Zwingli. He says:

'By the Gospel I understand the clear manifestation of the mystery of Christ' (II, 9, 2). In a wider sense, indeed, it includes all God's promises, even those made in the law. 'Still by way of excellence, it is applied to the promulgation of the grace manifested in Christ' (II, 9, 2). It is a mistake, however, to represent the comparison of law and Gospel as a comparison between the merit of works and the gratuitous imputation of righteousness. The comparison represents truth, but not the whole truth. The Gospel has not succeeded the law in such a sense as to introduce a different method of salvation; when the whole law is spoken of, the Gospel differs only in clearness of manifestation (II, 9, 4).

The Old Testament and the New were, therefore, fundamentally one, though differently administered. The true hope of the Jews was not temporal prosperity. The covenant with them was founded not on their merits, but on the Divine mercy. Moreover, the Jews both had and knew Christ the Mediator, by whom they were united to God and made capable of receiving His promises.

On the other hand there were these differences of administration. In the Old Testament the heavenly inheritance was exhibited under the type of temporal blessings and Christ was typified by ceremonies. In the New Testament types are done away with. Again, under the Old Testament spiritual conversion was the exception, under the New it is the rule. Moreover, the Jews under the Old Testament, being oppressed by ceremonies, had not the liberty belonging to the New Testament. Finally, the Old Testament was particular, the New is universal.

The way is now prepared for the doctrine of the Incarnation and of the work of Christ.[1] Chapter 12 is on the necessity of the Incarnation. It falls into two parts. The first (1–3) gives reasons why the Mediator needed to be both God and Man; the second (4–7) refutes Osiander's thesis that the Incarnation must have taken place even apart from sin. Calvin begins (1):

'It deeply concerned us, that He who was to be our Mediator

[1] II, 12, and 15–17.

should be very God and very man. If the necessity be inquired into, it was not what is commonly called simple or absolute, but flowed from the Divine decree, on which the salvation of man depended. What was best for us, our Merciful Father determined.'

Calvin, therefore, rejects the Anselmic doctrine of an absolute necessity of the Incarnation. He continues, however, to give reasons for the Incarnation. What was necessary was one who could unite God and man. Even apart from sin 'man was of too humble a condition to penetrate to God without a Mediator'. Much more then was a Mediator necessary after the Fall; obviously no sinful man could thus unite man and God, 'All of the sons of Adam, with their parent, shuddered at the sight of God.' The angels themselves needed a head to unite them to God. 'Thus the Son of God needed to become our Emmanuel, i.e. God with us; and in such a way that by mutual union His divinity and our nature might be combined.'

Calvin proceeds (2):

'This will become still clearer, if we reflect that the work to be performed by the Mediator was of no common description, being to restore us to the Divine favour, so as to make us, instead of sons of men, sons of God; instead of heirs of hell, heirs of a heavenly kingdom.'

For this cause especially, also, the Redeemer needed to be both God and man. Only Life could swallow up death. Only Righteousness could conquer sin. Only Almighty Power could conquer the powers of the world and of the air. But Life, Righteousness, and Almighty Power are alone found in God.

Christ's manhood is, however, equally necessary (3):

'Another principal point of our reconciliation with God was, that man, who had lost himself by his disobedience, should by way of remedy oppose to it obedience, satisfy the justice of God, and pay the penalty of sin. Therefore, our Lord came forth very man, adopted the person of Adam, and assumed his name, that He might in his stead obey the Father; that He might present our flesh as the price of satisfaction to the just judgment of God, and in the same flesh pay the penalty which we had incurred. Finally, since as God only He could not suffer, and as man only He could not overcome death, He united the human nature with

338

the Divine, that He might subject the weakness of the one to death as an expiation of sin, and by the power of the other, maintaining a struggle with death, might gain us the victory.'

It is interesting to observe that in all this Calvin presents the fundamental outlines of the patristic doctrine, especially as we find it in Athanasius, Ambrose, and Hilary. He hands on therefore the tradition of the Ancient Church to the Church of the Reformation. In particular, the idea of satisfaction here taught is at once patristic and Protestant. The mediaeval or Anselmic mode of stating the question is quite passed over, and Calvin goes back for his connexions immediately to the Fathers.

In his refutation of Osiander (4–7) Calvin admits that Christ was, as the Eternal Word, the Head alike of angels and men. If man had continued pure, the Word might still have been the Head of the Church without an Incarnation. 'As if indeed He could not, in the same way as angels enjoyed Him for their Head, by His Divine energy preside over men, and by the secret virtue of His Spirit quicken and cherish them as His body, until they were gathered into heaven to enjoy the life of the angels!' (7).

Scripture, moreover, always connects the Incarnation with the necessity of redemption, and we must not be wise above what is written. As to Osiander's argument that Christ was not made in the image of Adam, but Adam in that of Christ, Calvin says that Scripture nevertheless does not refuse to speak of Him as the Second Adam, thus clearly making the Incarnate Christ so far depend on Adam.

Chapter 15 is eminently noteworthy, inasmuch as it introduces us to a new and highly important point of view, viz. that of Christ's threefold office, as Prophet, Priest, and King. Calvin was thoroughly conscious of the importance of this point of view. He says (1):

'In the present day, though the Papists have the words, Son of God, Redeemer of the world, sounding in their mouths, yet, because contented with an empty name, they deprive Him of His virtue and dignity, what Paul says of "not holding the head" is truly applicable to them.[2] Therefore, that faith may find in Christ a solid ground of salvation, and so rest in Him, we must set out

[2] Col. 2:19.

339

with this principle that the office which He received from the Father consists of three parts. For He was appointed both Prophet, King, and Priest; though little were gained by holding the names unaccompanied by a knowledge of the end and use. These too are spoken of in the Papacy, but frigidly and with no great benefit, the full meaning comprehended under each title not being understood.'

Calvin finds all three offices implied by the name Christ (2). Under the law prophets, priests, and kings were all anointed with holy oil. Similarly Christ was anointed as Prophet, Priest, and King. Isa. 61:1, 2, speaks of His prophetic unction. As a prophet, Christ is a herald and witness of the Father's grace, and that beyond all other teachers: His doctrine is perfect and ends the line of prophecy. Moreover, 'the unction which He received, in order to perform the office of teacher, was not only for Himself, but for His whole body, that a corresponding efficacy of the Spirit might always accompany the preaching of the Gospel'.

The kingdom of Christ is spiritual; as such it is eternal (3). It assures the perpetual preservation of the Church against the assaults of the devil and the whole world. It also assures individual believers of immortality. Even in the present life it ensures them comfort and fortitude in their afflictions (4); Christ as King endows His people with all the gifts of the Spirit. He imparts to them in fact His own royal unction (5), with which He was enriched, not privately for Himself, but as the Head of the Church.[3] His sitting at the right hand of God means that He is the vice-regent of the Father to rule and defend the Church, till at last, Christ's office having been completed, God Himself will be the only Head of the Church.[4] 'For the same reason, Scripture throughout calls Him Lord, the Father having appointed Him over us for the express purpose of exercising His government over us through Him.' As He is King and Shepherd of believers, so He will destroy all His enemies.[5] This He does even now, but the full proof of His power will be given at the last judgment.

Calvin comes last to Christ's priestly office (6). He says:

[3] Isa. 11:2 ; Ps. 45:7 ; Jn 3:34, 1:16 ; Eph. 4:7.
[4] 1 C. 15:24, 28.   [5] Ps. 2:9.

340

'With regard to the priesthood, we must briefly hold its end and use to be, that as a Mediator, free from all taint, He may by His own holiness procure the favour of God for us. But because a deserved curse obstructs the entrance, and God in His character of judge is hostile to us, expiation must necessarily intervene, that as a priest employed to appease the wrath of God, He may reinstate us in His favour. Wherefore, in order that Christ might fulfil this office, it behoved Him to appear with a sacrifice. . . . By the sacrifice of His death He wiped away our guilt, and made satisfaction for sin.'

Moreover, the honour of the priesthood was for none other than Christ. He alone, at once Victim and Priest, could both become the fit satisfaction for sin, and be worthy to offer an Only Begotten Son to God. The benefit and efficacy of Christ's priesthood then begins with His death; but He continues to be a perpetual Intercessor. Moreover, through His priesthood, we are not only reconciled to God, but are ourselves constituted priests,[6] and offer to God sacrifices of prayer and praise.

In chapter 16 Calvin add a further view of the work of Christ, arranging the material this time not logically but historically, after the manner of Aquinas, and taking as his guide in so doing the relevant sentences of the Apostles' Creed. After stating (1) in general that Christ is the one ground of our salvation, he proceeds (2) to discuss [7] as a prefatory question, how it can be said that God, who prevents us with His mercy, was our enemy, until He was reconciled to us by Christ. 'For how could He have given us in His only begotten Son a singular pledge of His love, if He had not previously embraced us with free favour?' Here Calvin admits 'there arises some appearance of contradiction'. The solution offered points in the direction of Luther's doctrine of God's *opus alienum*.[8] Scripture usually speaks of God as the enemy of men and of them as accursed, till their sin is expiated by the sacrifice of Christ. But 'such modes of expression are accommodated to our capacity, that we may better understand how miserable and calamitous our condition is without Christ'. These considerations are in fact adapted to convince us of sin, and so to compel us to fly to Christ for

---

[6] Rev. 1:6.   [7] After Augustine, 'De Trin.' XIII, 11, 15.   [8] *Supra*, pp. 304f.

refuge. Calvin, therefore, here gives a psychological explanation of them, which is very noteworthy. He proceeds, however (3–4), to explain that these statements, though accommodated to our weakness, are not said falsely. He repeats after Augustine that God loves the sinner, but hates his sin. He, therefore, in love provides the means of reconciliation to Himself in Christ. Thus there is no real contradiction in the matter.

After this difficulty has thus been cleared up, Calvin comes (5) to the main subject of the chapter.

'When it is asked how Christ, by abolishing sin, removed the enmity between God and us, and purchased a righteousness which made Him favourable and kind to us, it may be answered generally that He accomplished this by the whole course of His obedience.'

Our ground of pardon is the whole life of Christ, but especially His death. That salvation is peculiarly to be ascribed to Christ's death Scripture clearly shows and likewise the Apostles' Creed, 'where a transition is admirably made from the birth of Christ to His death and resurrection'. Nevertheless the obedience of the rest of Christ's life is not thereby excluded. It was this obedience, which included the voluntary humiliation of the Incarnation, that gave value to the sacrifice.

Calvin goes on to explain further the nature of this sacrifice. He lays great stress on the fact that Christ died a judicial death, while Pilate, his judge, at the same time testified to His innocence. Our guilt, then, is seen to have been transferred to Him, and He was a substitute for us. Calvin quotes (once more in the history of theology) Ps. 69:4, 'I restored that which I took not away.'

The proper character of Christ's death appears further (6), in that 'the cross was cursed not only in the opinion of men, but by the enactment of the Divine law'.[9] The whole curse, which on account of our iniquities lay upon us, was taken from us by being transferred to Him. He was a propitiatory victim for sin, on whom the guilt was laid, so that it ceases to be imputed to us.

Calvin goes on to append (7) other explanations of Christ's death. By death Christ delivered us from death and the devil. His death is also the beginning of the mortification of our flesh.

[9] Dt. 21:23.

Next follows (8–12) the discussion of the descent into hell. Calvin rejects the ancient and mediaeval view that Christ descended into hell to set free the souls of the patriarchs; all that 1 Pet. 3:19 implies is, that the death of Christ was made known to the dead. What then is the true explanation of this article of the Creed?

'The Word of God furnishes us with one, not only pure and holy, but replete with excellent consolation. Nothing had been done, if Christ had only endured corporeal death. In order to interpose between us and God's anger and satisfy His righteous judgment, it was necessary that He should feel the severity of the Divine vengeance.' As sponsor and security for the guilty Christ undertook and paid all the penalties, which must have been exacted from them, except only that the pains of death could not hold Him. These penalties were, however, not only bodily but spiritual. Not only was the body of Christ given up as the price of redemption, but there was a greater price—He bore in His soul the tortures of a condemned and ruined man. If Christ's soul had not shared in the punishment, He would have been a Redeemer of bodies only. Calvin produces as Scripture proof for this new interpretation of the descent into hell, Mt. 26:39, 27:46.

In the Creed next follows the Resurrection (13). Without this all else would be ineffective.

'Our salvation may be thus divided between the death and the resurrection of Christ; by the former sin was abolished and death annihilated, by the latter righteousness was restored and life renewed, the power and efficacy of the former being still bestowed by means of the latter.'

Moreover, as the mortification of our flesh depends upon the death of Christ, so also His resurrection is the ground of new spiritual life in us. The resurrection of Christ is also the promise of our resurrection.

The Ascension (14–16) completes what the Resurrection began, and inaugurates the spiritual kingdom of Christ. He now sits at God's right hand as King. By His ascension Christ has opened for us the access to the heavenly kingdom, which Adam had shut. In heaven He intercedes for us, and thence He exercises His kingdom on behalf of His Church. The end of Christ's kingdom is His Second Advent to judgment (17, 18).

Finally (19), Calvin returns to the starting-point of the chapter. There Christ was declared to be the one ground of our salvation: the subsequent analysis has shown that every aspect of salvation is sufficiently grounded in Him.

Calvin closes his discussion of the work of Christ with a chapter (17) dealing with the supplementary question how the merit of Christ is consistent with the absolute grace of God. This chapter first appeared in the final edition of the 'Institutes'.

Calvin says (1):

'I admit that were Christ opposed simply by Himself to the justice of God, there could be no room for merit, because there cannot be found in man a worth which could make God a debtor.' He confirms this position by the authority of Augustine, who teaches that the man Christ Jesus was Himself assumed by the Word without merits of His own. The primary cause of our salvation was therefore the Divine decree; because of His mere good pleasure He appointed a Mediator to purchase salvation for us. Still 'principal and accessory are not incompatible'; and there is nothing to prevent the justification of man being the gratuitous result of the mere mercy of God, and yet being in a subordinate way due to the merit of Christ. There is no contradiction between the two: each stands in equal opposition to all human righteousness.

Calvin supports this conclusion (2–5) by Scripture passages, where our salvation is attributed now to the grace of God, now to the merit of Christ. Finally (6), he briefly touches the question raised by Lombard (III, 18), 'whether Christ merited for Himself or for us'. He says that the inquiry is one of foolish curiosity; but he decides all the same against the idea that Christ merited anything for Himself. Phil. 2:9 cannot be taken in this sense: no man can merit to become Judge of the world, and Head of angels and men. 'The solution is easy and complete. Paul is not speaking of the cause of Christ's exaltation, but only pointing out by way of example to us how it follows as a consequence (upon His death).'[1]

---

[1] It may be observed incidentally that this 'easy and complete' solution is certainly a forcing of the passage, which was correctly understood by Lombard.

344

We pass on to a brief account of Calvin's treatment of the practical effects of the work of Christ. He lays down the following fundamental proposition:

'So long as we are without Christ and separated from Him, nothing which He suffered and did for the salvation of the human race is of the least benefit to us. To communicate to us the blessing which He received from the Father, He must become ours and dwell in us' (III, 1, 1).

Accordingly Christ is called our Head, and we are said to be engrafted into Him. Though this union takes place through faith, yet as all are not believers, we must go higher and attribute it to the secret efficacy of the Spirit, whose chief gift is faith (III, 1, 4).

Calvin defines faith as follows:

'It is a firm and sure knowledge of the Divine favour toward us, founded on the truth of a free promise in Christ, and revealed to our minds and sealed on our hearts by the Holy Spirit' (III, 2, 7).

The true knowledge of Christ consists in viewing Him, as He is offered by the Father, namely, as invested with His Gospel (III, 2, 6). And, therefore, nextly:

'Since faith embraces Christ as He is offered by the Father, and He is offered not only for justification, for forgiveness of sins and peace, but also for sanctification and as the fountain of living waters, it is certain that no man will know Him aright without at the same time receiving the sanctification of the Spirit' (III, 2, 8).

Both justification and sanctification, therefore, require to be treated of as results of faith. Calvin proposes to treat first of sanctification. Repentance and forgiveness of sins are equally parts of the Gospel; but to treat of repentance first, best makes clear how a man is justified by faith alone, and yet holiness is inseparable from the imputation of righteousness by the Divine grace. Repentance always follows faith, and is produced by it. Since forgiveness is with a view to entrance into the kingdom of God, it is impossible to embrace the grace of the Gospel without repentance. Calvin insists that true repentance is not legal but evangelical, not caused by fear of punishment but by sorrow for sin. It is 'a real conversion of our life to God, proceeding from

345

sincere and serious fear of God; and consisting in the mortification of our flesh and the old man, and the quickening of the Spirit' (III, 3, 5). In a word, repentance is regeneration, the renewal in us of the image of God, all but effaced by the Fall (III, 3,9).

The other great benefit proceeding from faith is justification.

'A man is said to be justified in the sight of God, when in the judgment of God he is deemed righteous, and is accepted on account of his righteousness' (III, 11, 2).

Justification by faith is opposed to justification by works. A man is justified by works when his holiness merits an attestation of righteousness before God.

'On the contrary a man will be justified by faith, when, excluded from the righteousness of works, he by faith lays hold of the righteousness of Christ, and clothed in it appears in the sight of God not as a sinner but as righteous. Thus we simply interpret justification as the acceptance with which God receives us into His favour and holds us for righteous, and say that this justification consists in the forgiveness of sins and the imputation of the righteousness of Christ' (III, 11, 2).

Calvin is not to be understood as defining forgiveness and the imputation of Christ's righteousness as two different parts of justification. 'Justification by faith is reconciliation with God, and this consists solely in the remission of sins' (III, 11, 21). But reconciliation and forgiveness of sins take place through the imputation to us of Christ's righteousness, i.e. His expiation and obedience (22, 23).

We come last of all to Calvin's doctrine of the Church and the sacraments. Though God could perfect His people in a moment, He chooses only to bring them to manhood by the education of the Church (IV, 1, 5). The means is in the first place the preaching of the word, which God habitually accompanies with His Spirit; in the second place it is the instrumentality of the sacraments. The preaching of the Word and the administration of the sacraments according to the institution of Christ are marks of the true Church. 'These cannot anywhere exist without producing fruit and prospering by the blessing of God' (IV, 1, 10).

A sacrament 'is an external sign by which God seals on our consciences His promises of goodwill toward us, in order to sustain the weakness of our faith, and we in turn testify our piety towards Him, both before Himself and the angels and also among men' (IV, 14, 1).

Because we are corporeal God leads us to Himself through earthly elements. But there is no sacrament unless the rite is accompanied with the word which explains its meaning, i.e. the promise (IV, 14, 4).

' Sacraments bring with them the clearest promise, and, when compared with the word, have this peculiar advantage, that they represent promises to the life as if painted in a picture' (IV, 14, 5).

Circumcision, purification, sacrifices, and other rites were the sacraments instituted by God under the Jewish dispensation.

'After these were abrogated, the two sacraments of Baptism and the Lord's Supper, which the Christian church now employs, were instituted' (IV, 14, 20). All the sacraments have the same end, viz. to exhibit Christ. There is no essential difference in this respect between the sacraments of the Old and New Testament, only that the sacraments of the New Testament exhibit Christ more clearly.

Baptism attests the forgiveness of sins, not only past but future, teaches that we are united to Christ for mortification and newness of life, and also to be partakers of all His blessings. The Lord's Supper exhibits the great blessings of redemption and even Christ Himself.

'Christ once gave Himself that He might become bread, when He offered Himself to be crucified for the redemption of the world, and He gives Himself daily, when in the Word of the Gospel He offers Himself to be partaken by us, in so far as He was crucified, when He seals that offer by the sacred mystery of the Supper, and when He accomplishes inwardly what He externally designates' (IV, 17, 5).

THE EMERGENCE OF THE PROTESTANT SYNTHESIS

Ritschl's statement that Calvin's 'Institutes' are the masterpiece of Protestant theology is justified, in that Calvin has in them brought the essential Protestant view to a complete and harmonious expression. This is seen especially when we compare him with his predecessors. On the one hand he has eliminated the mediaeval element from Luther's doctrine of the sacraments; while on the other hand he has conserved Luther's religious view of the sacrament as a Gospel in act, and has not followed the merely ethical doctrine of Zwingli on this point. Again, Calvin has realised the synthetic character of Protestantism, as intended by Luther, better than Melanchthon. His view of the application of the benefits of Christ is less analytic than that of Melanchthon: the gift of the Spirit, faith, justification, and sanctification are seen to be all moments in an indivisible process, in which each implies the other. Similarly Calvin's view of Christianity as a whole is more synthetic than that of Melanchthon: law and Gospel are, while distinct, realised by him as a unity as they are not by Melanchthon. At this point, however, it is to be observed that Calvin, influenced by Zwingli, conceives the unity with a leaning towards making law the dominant idea, instead of following out Luther's suggestion that the law is God's *opus alienum,* and another form of the Gospel. What, however, concerns us most of all in Calvin's theology, is the emergence of a new doctrine of the work of Christ, distinct from either the patristic or the mediaeval, viz. the doctrine of the threefold office. This doctrine, the really characteristic Protestant doctrine of the work of Christ, is highly synthetic in character. It has not merely the value of presenting the whole work of Christ in a single view, but also of presenting it in such a manner that it shows how it terminates in the production of faith (*fiducia*) through the Gospel. It is thus of an eminently practical character: the objective aspect of the work of Christ is here duly completed by the subjective aspect.

We have seen that Calvin was himself fully conscious of the advance made by his new doctrine and above all of its practical value for faith. The schema of the threefold office and the deduction of it from the title Christ seem to have originated from Eusebius;[2] but Calvin was the first to employ it in dogmatics. He admits that the titles prophet, priest, and king were spoken

[2] Cf. 'Hist. Eccles.' 1, 3.

348

of in the Papacy, but complains that the full value was not drawn out of them. That he had right on his side in this matter may be seen by reference to Thomas, who, among the great schoolmen, most nearly approximates to the Protestant doctrine. In his 'Summa Theologica', III, qu. 7, art. 8, prophecy is mentioned as one of the graces bestowed on the Incarnate Christ; but the gift of prophecy is here understood not in the broad sense of Protestant dogmatic, but simply with reference to prediction. The teaching of Christ is treated separately in qu. 42. Again the priesthood of Christ is dealt with in qu. 22. In art. 1, ad. 3, Thomas even almost anticipates the Protestant formula. 'Christ, as the Head of all, has the perfection of all graces; and therefore as far as pertains to others, one is lawgiver, another priest, and another king: but all these concur in Christ as in the source of all graces.' But in the complete doctrine of Thomas neither Christ's prophetic nor His priestly office have the relative importance that they have in the Protestant scheme. In particular the doctrine of satisfaction is separately treated. As regards the kingly office, Thomas does not treat it under this name, but in qu. 8, art. 1, treats of Christ as Head of the Church, while His judicial power is treated of in qu. 59. To sum up, Thomas never uses the scheme of a threefold office as a conceptual unity, as does Calvin, who follows Eusebius in perceiving the unity of three offices in the name of Christ. The unity which governs the doctrine of Thomas is not conceptual, but is the intuitional or historical unity of the Apostles' Creed, and what mention of the offices of prophet, priest, and king is found in him is only of secondary importance. The adoption of the formula of the three-fold office instead of the historical order of the Creed marks a great theological progress. Heim says in 'Das Gewissheitsproblem in der systematischen Theologie':

'As a matter of fact the origination of the dogmatic system has been from the beginning onwards a process in which the systematic impulse endeavours to become master of a mass of elements, which were already given by tradition in a certain historical order' (p. 6).

'The systematic thought, which broke into this existing scheme, was like a mountain-spring which seeks its way over a region where primitive stone-blocks lie all round. It has not the power to remove them from the spot, and is content therefore to pour through the gaps which remain free between them. Thus originates a compromise between that general lie of things given by the Biblical narrative, and a tendency to a systematic arrangement of the whole, which proceeds from axioms to consequences' (p. 9).

This last quotation exactly corresponds to the doctrine of the Incarnation and the work of Christ in the 'Summa' of Thomas. The systematic is interspersed with the historical element: the unity of the intuition has not yet been replaced by the unity of the concept. In Calvin's 'Institutes', though the older mode of treatment still remains (III, 16), the new conceptual unity appears, which is presently to displace it altogether. There stands, however, in Calvin as yet a third form of doctrine, the old patristic scheme also (III, 12). How is the doctrine of the threefold office related to this? The Greek scheme of revelation by the Logos and of the destruction of sin and death by the Incarnation, is like the doctrine of the threefold office, conceptual. But the Greek Fathers were not able to control by their formulæ the whole historical material of the life of Christ: although the Logos doctrine is capable of a considerable utility in this direction. It was therefore a real advantage when first Alexander and then Thomas began to work into the theology of the Incarnation more of the historical details. By so doing they indeed made their doctrine less synthetic than the Greek, and ran the risk of making theology appear, as the Nominalists said, to be an aggregative science only. But they prepared thereby for a richer synthesis, conceptual like the Greek synthesis and indeed more of a unity than that, since all its elements run back into the one idea of the 'Anointed' representative of God—a synthesis, moreover, which could more fully than the Greek synthesis include and control the whole historical material of the Gospels. The Protestant synthesis of the threefold office then includes the advantages of both the prior great stages of the doctrine of the work of Christ. It is worthy of note that it is altogether Calvin's own, even within Protestantism. Luther had, indeed, in his 'De Libertate Christianâ', under the influence of 1 Pet. 2:9, treated of Christ as the King and Priest, who communicates His kinghood and priesthood to His people.[3] The Lutheran theologian Strigel had then made dogmatic use of the formula of a twofold office, treating the work of Christ under the two heads of King and Priest.[4] But it was Calvin who first in the 'Geneva Catechism' and then in the 'Institutes' added the head of Prophet, and thus brought the doctrine of the offices into a direct relation to faith through the Gospel.[5]

[3] Luther's 'Primary Works', ed. by Wace and Buchheim, 1883, p. 114.
[4] Schmid, 'Die Dogmatik der evangelisch-lutherischen Kirche', 5th ed., p. 285.
[5] Ritschl, 'Justification and Reconciliation', vol. iii, English trans., p. 417.

CHAPTER 3

THE CONDITIONS
OF THE FURTHER DEVELOPMENT

THE COMPLETION OF THE PROTESTANT SYNTHESIS

THE further development of the doctrine of the work of Christ in the Protestant churches is marked by (a) the general acceptance of the doctrine of the twofold obedience of Christ, as taught in the 'Formula of Concord', (b) the tendency more and more to bring the whole material of the doctrine (including the twofold obedience) under the conceptual scheme of the threefold office. The historical order of treatment indeed remains, but is separated from the doctrine of Christ's work and becomes the doctrine of His two states, that of humiliation or exinanition, and that of exaltation. To the state of exinanition were reckoned Christ's conception, birth, education, conversation upon earth, passion, death, and burial. To the state of exaltation belong His Resurrection, ascension, and return to judgment. The position of the descent into hell was a matter of controversy. The 'Formula of Concord' (IX) followed Luther in taking it literally, and the later Lutheran theology renewed the patristic doctrine of Christ's descent into hell to announce His victory over the Devil; thus it was included in the state of exaltation. The Reformed theologians on the other hand reckoned it to the state of exinanition, interpreting it, partly of the separation of Christ's soul from His body in death, partly of His desolation on the cross.[1]

It is usual to call the orthodox theology of the seventeenth century, in which all these developments took place, with a somewhat depreciatory significance, the Protestant scholasticism. This theology is indeed a scholasticism, in so far as the Lutheran theologians from Gerhard and the Reformed from Keckermann onwards begin to make fresh use of the mediaeval schoolmen

---

[1] Cf. Lipsius, 'Dogmatik', 3rd ed., 1901, p. 480.

and their methods, as also of their great master in philosophy, Aristotle. Nevertheless, this return to scholasticism is made with a full consciousness of the difference that separates the Protestant from the mediaeval theology, nor is there any intention of allowing to Aristotle the same degree of influence as he has in the Middle Ages. Moreover, the current depreciation of the Protestant scholasticism is by no means fully justified. As over against the freer theology of the sixteenth century, that of the seventeenth undoubtedly shows an increased formalism, which sometimes seems to make the form an end in itself: on the other hand there is also a real advance in the thinking out and systematising of the implications of the theological principles of the Reformation.

It will be convenient, before considering the more highly elaborated and complicated forms of the doctrine of the three-fold office, and the conditions under which these have come to be, first of all to obtain a clear notion of the broad outline of the doctrine which is the starting-point of all further developments and is common to the theology of both Confessions. This we may sufficiently do by studying the classical and very succinct presentation of the doctrine in the 'Loci Theologici' (1610–25) of the Lutheran theologian, Gerhard (A.D. 1582–1637).

Gerhard's general theological principles are as follows:[2] He distinguishes natural and supernatural theology. Natural theology arises partly from man's innate knowledge of God, partly from his contemplation of the Creation. Since the Fall, however, the power of natural reason is diminished. Supernatural theology is based upon revelation. Its only adequate and proper principle is Scripture; the articles of faith are not its principle but are derived from Scripture. The property of principles is to be first and unmediated, true, incorrigible, self-evident, irrefutable, and indemonstrable. All these properties belong to Scripture alone. Reason is no second theological principle. Though there are some things which to a certain degree can be known by natural reason, it cannot rise to the mysteries of faith

[2] See Prœmium de natura theologiæ in the Exegesis sive uberior explicatio, prefixed to his 'Loci', ed. 1657.

353

properly so called. The matter of theology is then the truths
revealed in Scripture. Its chief end is the glory of God, its
mediate end the salvation of man. The object and subject about
which it turns is man in so far as he is to be brought to eternal
felicity.

The doctrine of the threefold office is found in vol. I, loc. iv,
cap. viii.

(187) 'The office of Christ is threefold—prophetic, priestly,
and kingly. The prophetic office is that by which Christ revealed
to us the will of God concerning our salvation, which indeed He
executes, first by Himself publishing the Gospel, i.e. the secret
counsel of God concerning the redemption of the human race,
and by purifying the law from the corruptions of the Pharisees;
next by establishing the ministry of teaching in the Church: here
also belongs the institution of the sacraments.'

(189) 'The priestly office of Christ is that by which, inter-
posing Himself between man and God, He reconciled the whole
human race to God, making satisfaction to the Divine law, and
interceding with God; whence the parts of the priestly office are
two, satisfaction and intercession. Satisfaction is that by which
He paid to God a price sufficient for the sins of the whole human
race, and obtained for it righteousness and eternal life; which
satisfaction is to be seen first in the fulfilment of the Divine law,
next in the payment of the due penalties of sin—it is commonly
spoken of as His active and passive obedience, each of which is
a part of the priestly office of Christ.'

(191) 'The kingly office of Christ is that by which He
governs all things in heaven and earth, and above all His
Church.'

(193) 'This kingdom is regarded as belonging either to this
life or the next. In this life it is called the kingdom of power or
of grace: the kingdom of power is Christ's general empire over
all things, to wit, His government of earth and heaven, the
subjection of all creatures to Him, and His dominion in the midst
of His enemies, whom He represses and punishes. The kingdom
of grace is His special work of mercy in the Church, viz. the
mission, illumination, and confirmation of apostles, evangelists,
pastors, and teachers: the gathering of the Church by the preach-

ing of the Gospel, and the dispensation of the sacraments, the regeneration, sanctification and quickening of believers, the application of His merit, the protection and conservation of the pious under the cross and their deliverance, the pouring out of various gifts, etc.'

(194) 'In the next life Christ's kingdom is called the kingdom of righteousness and glory, which is seen in the resurrection of the dead and the universal judgment both of the wicked to damnation and of the elect to eternal life.'

In the above doctrine we have now to recognise not only the characteristic Protestant form of the doctrine of the work of Christ, but a conception which so truly corresponds to the fundamentally synthetic character of Protestant theology that it is a synthesis also of the whole of Christianity. It not merely corresponds to the synthesis of law and Gospel and to the synthetic view of the subjective process of redemption, in which the gift of the Spirit and faith, justification and sanctification are all one; but it also is in reality the same synthesis with each of these others. The whole and the parts, macrocosm and microcosm, are here equal to one another: it is the same synthesis in all cases, only that it is regarded under a different aspect. The schema of the threefold office successfully expresses in the one doctrine of the work of Christ the whole of Christianity, and that as neither the Greek Fathers nor the mediaeval schoolmen were able to do. For in the view of the Greek Church the work of Christ needed to be supplemented by our works; and in the mediaeval view, though it procured sacramental grace which made our works possible, it still ultimately needed the same supplement. But in Protestantism Christ is all and does all; and the doctrine of the threefold office succeeds in so stating the work of Christ as to show this. His work as Prophet, Priest, and King is complete, and leaves no room for anything which is not simply itself in another form.

It is to be observed that what has been said as to the completeness with which the doctrine of the threefold office expresses the Protestant synthesis applies to the doctrine as a whole, and has regard to the balance and mutual co-operation of its parts. It is not meant that the doctrine is a final or perfect statement of

355

Protestantism. Not to speak of the figurative character of the Old Testament types which supply the individual heads of the doctrine, the idea of satisfaction, which it includes, is inherited, though not without modification, from the patristic and the mediaeval theology. It will later appear that for these reasons Protestant theology has not settled down to the doctrine of the threefold office as a final statement of Christianity. Nevertheless it is to be recognised that in this doctrine Protestant theology reaches, if not a final, yet a relative, conclusion, in so far as in the doctrine as a whole we have the perfect reflex of the fundamental Reformation doctrine of justifying faith. Kaftan well says of the doctrine of the threefold office:[3]

'In the setting here given the doctrine of satisfaction obtains a relation to the faith of the individual corresponding to the evangelical knowledge of salvation. The prophetic office continually comes to mediate accomplishment in the Church through the ministers of the Word. And the chief content of the Word is that we now through Christ have a gracious God. The high-priestly intercession and royal dominion of Christ in the kingdom of grace are living present facts, by which faith assures itself of the grace of God in Christ. With all this therefore even in the objective doctrine of salvation the bridge to faith is built.'

As regards the point by point comparison of the new synthesis with the older Greek and mediaeval syntheses, the priestly office corresponds to the mediaeval satisfaction and merit, the kingly office to the mediaeval headship of Christ, both offices together to the Greek recapitulation of the race in Him. The doctrine of the prophetic office, however, differs from the Greek Logos doctrine and the mediaeval doctrine of the law, which are its nearest equivalents, not only in that it includes and indeed centres in the doctrine of the Gospel, but also in that the Protestant theology, following Luther, teaches that Christ brings no new moral law. As Gerhard puts it, He merely 'purified the law from the corruptions of the Pharisees' (loc. cit. 187).

It may finally be pointed out that for us, in the difficult and

---

[3] 'Dogmatik', 3rd ed., 1901, p. 501.

complicated study in which we have been engaged all through the mediaeval and Reformation periods, the attainment of the doctrine of the threefold office marks an alleviation of our task. Inasmuch as this doctrine is a microcosm of the whole evangelical theology, so far as in future we are concerned with this type, it will no longer be necessary to pursue the complementary studies of the doctrines of law and Gospel, of justification, and of the sacraments, which we were compelled to follow in our previous work in the endeavour to bring out the real significance of the formal doctrine of the work of Christ in the Middle Ages, and again to mediate the way from the total mediaeval to the total Protestant point of view. So far as the evangelical doctrine of the threefold office or its practical equivalent henceforward obtains, formal doctrine and real significance coincide. Only therefore where the evangelical view does not fully obtain will it be necessary still to follow the more extended form of treatment; elsewhere we may henceforth limit ourselves to the formal doctrine of our subject only.

INTERNAL CONTROVERSIES

The further development of the doctrine of the work of Christ in Protestant theology depends partly on the interconfessional controversies between the Lutheran and the Reformed Churches, partly on their external controversies with Socinianism and Arminianism.

As regards the interconfessional controversies, we have to note the disputes as to the Person of Christ and as to the extent of the work of Christ. We may take the latter point first. The uniform teaching of the Lutheran Church is that Christ's satisfaction was both a sufficient and efficacious satisfaction for the sins of all men. The Reformed, on the other hand, at least from Beza onwards, show a distinct tendency to restrict the satisfaction of Christ, or at least, if not its sufficiency, yet its efficacy, to the elect. Quenstedt, 'Systema', pars II, cap. iii, memb. 2, sect. 2, qu. 7, quotes Beza, 'Respons. part. 2, ad acta Colloq. Mompelg.', as follows:

357

'I say again, and profess before the whole Church of God, that it is false, blasphemous, and wicked to say that Christ, whether as regards the Divine plan, or as regards the effect, suffered, was crucified, died, and made satisfaction no less for the sins of the damned and those adjudged to eternal judgment than for the sins of Peter, Paul, and all the saints.' [4]

A mediating position was taken up by the Reformed School of Saumur, who taught a hypothetic universality of redemption, i.e. that Christ died for the sins of all men, and efficaciously satisfied for the whole world in the plan of God, so that all should be saved, though only on condition of faith.

Passing on to the controversy on the Person of Christ, we note that while the Lutherans and the Reformed alike accepted the Creed of Chalcedon, they interpreted it differently. Their divergence on this point originated out of the dispute between Luther and Zwingli as to the Lord's Supper. Luther attempted to justify his doctrine of consubstantiation against Zwingli by teaching a real *communicatio idiomatum* between the Divine and human natures in the Person of Christ, in virtue of which Christ's human nature shares in the ubiquity of His Divine nature. Zwingli would only admit a verbal *communicatio idiomatum*, or, as he called it, an ἀλλοίωσις. In his 'Fidei Ratio' (§ 1) he lays great stress on the conservation by each nature of its own properties.

Zwingli has at this point set the pattern for the doctrine of the Reformed Church. Calvin also, though differing from Zwingli in his view of the Supper, followed him as regards the *communicatio idiomatum*. He too holds merely a verbal *communicatio*.[5] The 'Formula of Concord', on the other hand, in fixing the Lutheran doctrine rejects the Zwinglian view as Nestorian,[6] and subscribes to the doctrine of a real *communicatio* as taught by Luther.

The point at which the Christological controversy affected the doctrine of the work of Christ was the question of Christ's

[4] Quenstedt (loc. cit.) even finds traces of the same tendency in Calvin, who says, e.g. in his Commentary on Col. 1:20, that Christ has not made peace for the ungodly, though the benefit of His redemption is offered to them.　　[5] 'Inst.' II, 14, 2.
[6] *Supra*, p. 66.

fulfilment of the law. The Lutherans taught that the God-man in virtue of the *communicatio idiomatum* was altogether above the law, so that His fulfilment of the law was an entirely voluntary and supererogatory self-humiliation. The Reformed on the other hand regard Christ as being, as regards His humanity, under the law like other men.

In connexion with this last difference may be suitably mentioned as partly, though by no means altogether conditioned by it, the doctrine of the Reformed theologian Piscator, who in his 'Theses theologicæ', vol. iii, 1618, opposed the inclusion of Christ's active obedience in the satisfaction of Christ.[7] Piscator had been preceded in his form of teaching by a Lutheran divine Karg, who wrote under the name of Parsimonius, but Piscator's name is always connected with the controversy.

Piscator admitted that the meritorious cause of justification was the obedience of Christ. It was not, however, His active fulfilment of the law, or His active obedience, but only His endurance of suffering and death in obedience to a special mandate of the Father, or His passive obedience. Though Christ according to His Divine nature was the Lord of the law, according to His human nature He was subject to it both by reason of His creatureliness, and, in virtue of His special position as an Israelite, by reason of the covenant between God and His people. Christ then shared the duty of active obedience with the people of God; but if He was as an individual thus bound to the fulfilment of the law, He could not in this respect be the substitute of man.

Piscator further taught that according to the definition of justification given by Paul in Rom. 4:6, 7, the imputation of righteousness and the forgiveness of sins were one and the same. Thus his final conclusion was that the obedience for the sake of which God justifies us, imputes to us righteousness and forgives our sins, was Christ's passive obedience only; though he admitted that Christ's active obedience was a necessary pre-condition of His saving work.

---

[7] Cf. Baur, 'Die Christliche Lehre von der Versöhnung', pp. 352ff. ; Ritschl, 'Justification and Reconciliation', vol. i, English trans., pp. 248ff.

Piscator further argued dialectically against the doctrine of the twofold obedience as follows:

(1) If Christ's active obedience is the meritorious cause of justification and the forgiveness of sins, then His passive obedience was unnecessary, and God was unrighteous in exacting it.

(2) If Christ's active obedience be imputed to us, then we are as free from obedience to the law, as we are free from its curse, because Christ has been made a curse for us. This, however, is impossible, since we are eternally bound to obedience to God as our Creator, Redeemer, and Lord.

(3) Since the imputation of righteousness and the forgiveness of sins are the same, if we are justified by the imputation of Christ's active righteousness, then our sins are forgiven because of it, which is contrary to Heb. 9:22.

(4) If both Christ's active and passive obedience were necessary to complete the satisfaction made for us, then His holiness only obtained part of our redemption, and was therefore imperfect.

(5) The law obliges either to obedience or to punishment, not to both. If then Christ by His death has freed us from punishment, there was no need that He should fulfil the law for us.

Finally, Piscator urged that Scripture everywhere clearly testifies that Christ died for our sins, but nowhere says that He lived a holy life for us.

Piscator's doctrine is interesting, because of its renewed application of dialectic to the doctrine which had been growing up on the basis of Luther's new intuition in the Protestant Church. For a time the power of this intuition had quieted the critical reason, which had attained such striking development in the later Middle Age. But now as the intensity of the vision begins to fade, the critical reason once more awakes and applies itself to the fresh formations of doctrine. Piscator's criticism indeed only goes a part of the way: he finds only one element in the new doctrine irrational and superfluous. The orthodox Mastricht [8] speaks of him as 'in all things else an excellent theologian'. We have next, however, to study the doctrine of

[8] 'Theologia', v, 18, 36.

the man in whom the critical reason was once more fully awake, and who applied the whole energy of his great logical acumen to the destructive analysis of the new orthodoxy.[9]

[9] Quenstedt occasionally includes in the polemic of his 'Systema' the Anabaptists and the mystics Schwenkfeld (A.D. 1490–1561) and Weigel (A.D. 1533–1585), who represent a movement of complete opposition to the developing Protestant orthodoxy, already before Socinus, within the sphere of the Reformation itself. The Anabaptist movement was, as Ritschl says ('Justification and Reconciliation', vol. i, English trans., p. 290), 'as guiltless of theology as it well could be'. Schwenkfeld and Weigel, however, with kindred spirit, present more definition of idea. They pursued the mystical tendency, which had during the Middle Ages accompanied the development of scholasticism (cf. *supra*, p. 275, n. 7), towards a doctrine of salvation independent of history, like the Christian Gnosis of Clement and Origen (*supra*, pp. 36f.). But whereas the mediaeval mystics, like these Fathers, had only aimed at supplementing the ecclesiastical doctrine by an esoteric teaching, Schwenkfeld and Weigel (1) definitely opposed the Protestant doctrine of Scripture by the teaching that the true principle of revelation was the inner Word, of which Scripture was only the external vehicle ; (2) they opposed the Protestant doctrine of justification by a doctrine practically identical with Osiander's (*supra*, pp. 327ff.), in which the historical work of Christ was reduced to a mere presupposition of the real justification which takes place through the essential indwelling of Christ in the heart. Weisse ('Philosophische Dogmatik', pp. 214ff.) has observed that these mystics anticipated in an intuitive and non-scientific way the religious doctrine of modern idealism (cf. Kant and Hegel, *infra*, pp. 519ff.). But what Troeltsch says of Anabaptism ('Die Kultur der Gegenwart', I, iv, 1, p. 516) applies to them also ; the time was not ripe for them, and they were not ripe for the time. Socinus, on the other hand, without their vision, had the science they lacked. The mystical doctrine was handed on to later times by Böhme (A.D. 1575–1625), and above all by the Quakers.

CHAPTER 4

SOCINIANISM

SOCINUS

SOCINIANISM is to be understood as the product of a union between the humanism of Erasmus and the logical criticism of the school of Duns Scotus, effected in a mind liberated by the Reformation from the authority of the Church, but unsubjugated by Luther's new religious principle of justification by faith.

On the positive side Socinus (A.D. 1539–1604), like Erasmus and the Apologists, regarded the content of Christianity as essentially the knowledge of God, the moral law, and the promise of immortality. The doctrine of the Apologists, however, followed by Erasmus, according to which this content is naturally given in human reason, was abandoned by Socinus. For him the moral law only was given in reason, while the knowledge of God and the promise of immortality were mere matter of revelation. Nor is this revelation given, as the Apologists had taught, in the Old Testament. It came first by Jesus Christ, and is contained only in the New Testament. The proof of the authority of the New Testament is historical, and lies simply in the veracity of its writers. The idea of a *testimonium spiritus sancti* is altogether discarded.

It is then from the point of view of this general conception of Christianity that Socinus interprets the New Testament in detail, making use of an exegesis sometimes rather arbitrary to reduce all modes of Apostolic teaching to the same standard. It is, however, to be admitted on the other hand that Socinus not infrequently gives the true interpretation where the previous exegesis was wrong, and that he also correctly brings out the existence in Scripture of passages genuinely supporting his point of view.

The negative side of Socinianism, the keen dialectic derived from the mediaeval scholasticism, is applied as a solvent to the system, which Socinus found competing with his own for recognition as the true doctrine. This is not mediaeval Catholicism, nor yet Lutheranism, but owing to the peculiar sphere of Socinus's labours, the Reformed or Calvinist system.

In the first place, in the anthropology Socinus disallows the Augustinian doctrines of original sin and of predestination, both of which Calvin had adopted. Socinus conceives man as invariably a free moral agent: he is moreover naturally mortal, and immortality is offered to him only as the reward of obedience to the Divine law. Thus the anthropological presuppositions are adapted to the moral scheme of Christianity which Socinus adopts.

Then, next, the doctrines of the Trinity, of the Person and work of Christ, and of justification undergo criticism with a view to the same end. Socinus attacked above all the doctrines of the Godhead of Christ and of His satisfaction for sin. In his Christology Socinus simply drew the conclusions which Duns and the Nominalists had already indicated, and were restrained from adopting only by the external authority of the Church. Harnack says:[1]

'What the Nominalists had stated as an hypothesis, that God could even redeem us by means of a man, is here, now that the authority of the ecclesiastical tradition has gone, accepted as the actual fact. . . . Christ is a mortal man, who has become immortal, though no ordinary man, since He was from the first God's only-begotten Son by the miraculous conception, and was sanctified by the Father, and sent into the world, equipped with Divine wisdom and power, and was finally raised to a power equal to God's own.'

While therefore Socinus renews the moral view of Christianity of the Apologists, he replaces their Logos doctrine by an adoptianist Christology. He explained the peculiar possession of a unique revelation by Jesus by the curious theory that He had at the beginning of His ministry been carried up to heaven, there to receive it. 'Faustus Socinus quotes for this Jn 3:16, 6:38, 62,

[1] D.G., 4th ed., vol. iii, p. 791.

363

compared with Jn 3:21, 8:28, 16:28. He interprets all passages referring to pre-existence of this rapture.'[2]

We proceed to the doctrine of Socinus on the work of Christ. Both his positive doctrine and his criticism of the Calvinist orthodoxy are contained in his great polemic treatise, 'De Jesu Christo Servatore', composed in answer to a Reformed pastor Covetus, of whose presentation of the doctrine of the work of Christ all that needs to be said is that it confines itself practically to the doctrines of Christ's satisfaction and of justification by faith.

Socinus begins (pars I, cap. i) by disputing (with Scripture proofs) the orthodox conception of the Divine justice. That justice of God, which belongs to Him as an essential quality, is not opposed to mercy but 'may be called under another name righteousness and equity . . . to which justice is opposed not mercy but wickedness and iniquity'. There is a justice which is opposed to mercy, and that twofold, as there is a twofold mercy. A twofold justice: there is one mode which God always shows in destroying the wicked, another by which He sometimes according to His law punishes sinners, not completely reprobate, but unrepentant, or again even the repentant, 'the promise of His mercy, by which He has voluntarily in a certain way bound Himself to us, being excluded'. A twofold mercy: there is one mode, by which He pardons the repentant, another that prevents sinners with offers of grace. The former of these modes of each attribute, again, God always shows, the latter He sometimes exhibits at His free will. Now, neither of these modes of justice can be exercised at once with the mode of mercy opposed to it upon the same subject at the same time. For the former justice and mercy require contrary subjects, the one the impenitent, the other the penitent, and they bring about contrary effects, the one destroying, the other saving. The latter pair have the same subject, but their effects are different; so that they cannot coexist at the same time. One offers grace, the other abandons to ruin. 'By the former God gives up much of His right, by the latter He clearly maintains His right.' In Scripture this Divine justice,

---

[2] Schneckenburger, 'Vorlesungen über die Lehrbegriffe der kleineren protestantischen Kirchenparteien', 1863, p. 46.

which is opposed to mercy, bears other names, wrath, fury, indignation, vengeance, etc.; while the name of justice is reserved for God's essential quality of righteousness and equity, which is shown equally in mercy and severity, in both through the keeping of the Divine Word. Vengeance indeed, like mercy, is not an essential quality of God, but simply an effect of His will. Both are subordinate to the true justice of God in carrying out His decrees. Thus the penalties of sin depend simply upon the Divine will, and may be remitted at pleasure. 'For God can, especially since He is Lord of all, abandon as much of His rights as He pleases.' Nor are sinners constituted such by the commission of sin; but it depends simply upon the will of God whether He elects to regard them as such.

It is evident at once that these positions of Socinus with respect to the arbitrary will of God are drawn immediately from Duns: some repeat almost exactly his words in 'Op. Oxon.' IV, Dist. 14, qu. 1.[3] The illustration of the idea by the legal position of God as *omnium dominus* also is not new: it is found in Thomas, 'Summa Theol.' III, 46, 2, ad 3.[4] What on the other hand is new is the correct statement that the Scriptural idea of God's righteousness includes its manifestation not only in punishment but in mercy.[5] This idea, however, finds only an inadequate expression when Socinus identifies it with equity, which as the further development of his doctrine shows really amounts to the reduction of God's position with regard to man 'to the standard of equality between private persons, or of a relation regulated by "reasonableness", such as holds good only in the ethical relations of private life'.[6]

In cap. ii *seq.* follows the positive doctrine of Socinus. Salvation proceeds from the mere will of God in pardoning sinners, but is made known by Christ, the only further condition being our faith and obedience. Hence Christ is in the first place our Saviour, not because He procures salvation, but because He makes it known. He is our Saviour also (cap. iii), because He confirms the truth which He preaches, not only by miracles but

---

[3] Cf., for example, the words in § 7: 'God's being offended or angry is nothing but His will to punish. . . .'

[4] *Supra*, pp. 220f.   [5] Cf. 'Man, Sin, and Salvation', p. 15.

[6] Ritschl, 'Justification and Reconciliation', vol. i, English trans., p. 70.

also by the shedding of His blood, which in a certain way bound God to us as if in a covenant, and finally by His Resurrection, 'the chief point and, as it were, foundation of the whole faith' (cap. v). A comparison of all this with the positive doctrine of Duns (III, Dist. 20) reveals a most striking accord of thought.[7]

Again, Socinus says (cap. iv) that Christ is our Saviour because He is our example. We can imitate Christ, for imitation only means a general resemblance. Just as Duns had said (III, Dist. 19) that to say that the life of Christ was so excellent 'that it had a certain infinity'[8] was a hyperbole, so Socinus asserts that the orthodox view that Christ's virtue differs from ours, as heaven from earth, is hyperbolically stated. The rule, 'that he is said to do justly, whose works are for the most part just', is agreeable both to Scripture and to ethics. God accepts those who correspond to it as just, having regard to our frailty, and not standing on His legal rights.[9]

In cap. VI Socinus still further teaches that Christ is our Saviour, because to Him as man is committed the power of giving eternal life; and in caps. vii, viii he concludes the first part of his work with an explanation of the mediatorship of Christ. It means that He was an ambassador between God and us; but, as the Scripture teaches, He reconciles us to God and not God to us.[1]

Pars II is given up to a discussion of the Scripture proofs of the orthodox doctrine. In the first place 'redemption' in the Scriptures is simply a metaphor for deliverance (cap. i). It is often used both in the Old and New Testaments without any thought of a price being implied. Even where, however, the death of Christ is spoken of as the price of our redemption, this is only by analogy (cap. ii). Our redemption is our deliverance from sin and its penalties. In both cases the death of Christ operates to redeem us in so far as it is an example of obedience, leads us to trust God, and gives us hope of deliverance from punishment. If it is asked (cap. iii) why, since it is the Resurrection rather than the death of Christ which is our deliverance, yet His death rather than His resurrection is spoken of as the price of our redemption,

---

[7] *Supra*, p. 250.　　　　　　[8] *Supra*, p. 242.
[9] Cf. Duns, IV, Dist. 15, qu. 1 (*supra*, p. 248).
[1] Cf. Lombard, III, Dist. 19 (*supra*, p. 172).

the answer is that His death, in view of what it cost, offers the more natural analogy to the price of redemption.

Again (cap. iv), when it is said that Christ bore our sins, Mt. 8:16, 17 shows that 'to bear' can mean to take away. Moreover, that Christ died 'for us' (cap. viii) means, not that He died in our stead, but that He died on our behalf.

Finally, with cap. ix Socinus begins a long discussion of the proof from the Old Testament sacrifices, whose results are thus summarised by Fock.[2]

'The Socinian doctrine admitted indeed that an analogy exists between the Old Testament sacrifices and the sacrifice of Christ: the analogy was not however between it and them all, but only between it and the annual great sacrifice of Atonement, when the High Priest entered into the Holy of Holies. As, however, in that case the slaughter of the sacrificial animal was not regarded as the sacrifice proper, but only as the introduction to the sacrifice, and the latter was rather first accomplished when the High Priest entered into the Holy of Holies with the blood, so also the death of Christ is not properly the sacrifice, but only the introduction to the sacrifice, and this is then first offered when Christ has entered heaven (the Epistle to the Hebrews was appealed to). Besides, those sacrifices also, which were a shadow of the sacrifice of Christ, had by no means the purpose of making satisfaction to God for sins, but were only conditions established by God, under which He would forgive sins. The proper principle of the forgiveness of sins is therefore always the Divine will, and the sacrifice is merely an accidental condition, to which the realisation of that will is joined. The relation is made yet clearer, when it is added that the Old Testament sacrifice was only intended as the means to the forgiveness of lighter sins. It is, however, still maintained that grave sins could be forgiven, and this could naturally then only happen by a volition of the Divine grace, for which God had at least entered into no express covenant, as is the case in Christianity. Thus therefore there lies in the relation of the Old Testament sacrifice to the sacrifice of Christ in no way a sufficient motive for the dogma of satisfaction.'

[2] 'Der Socinianismus', 1847, p. 635.

367

Having thus dealt with the Scripture proofs, in pars III Socinus criticises the satisfaction theory of the Protestant theology. He begins from the position already advanced in pars I, cap. i that God is not to be thought of as Judge but as Lord and Sovereign, or as resembling a private creditor, so that He can freely forgive without requiring satisfaction. Both punitive justice and pardoning mercy are mere effects of His will. If the first resided permanently in Him, He could never forgive at all: if the latter, He could never punish.[3] Both those modes of behaviour are finite quantities: the one destroys the other. The mercy that resides in God is beneficence, as His essential justice is righteousness and equity. Socinus complains justly that the orthodox make much of the Divine justice in the doctrine of the Atonement, nothing in that of predestination. Then he argues that 'punishment is due not to offenders, but to the State' (cap. i). Consequently, on the principle of the 'suum cuique' of Justinian's 'Digest', the mere judge cannot forgive, but the State can, unless some one else is injured thereby; for this principle does not include the rendering of evils, except so far as they are for the benefit of others. It is a different case from the punishment of the innocent. Here both the State and the injured party are affected, in the pardon of the guilty the State alone. To interpret 'suum cuique' otherwise would lead to absolute confusion, for it would prove that debts could not be remitted, the justice of which no one doubts. And what is true of the supreme earthly power is more unreservedly true of God, who is absolutely supreme. From the beginning of His dealings with men (pars III, cap. ii) He has pardoned without satisfaction, innocence of course (i.e. habitual innocence) being required as a condition. *A fortiori* therefore this must hold good under the New Covenant, which is especially the time of grace. How can God be munificent, if He require satisfaction from human nature in Christ? If it be said in giving His Son to make satisfaction, this gift is unnecessary: true liberality would have shown itself in free pardon.

---

[3] Cf. Thomas, 'Summa Theol.' III, 46, 1, 3, where the difficulty is stated that neither mercy nor justice appears to require satisfaction ; since the nature of mercy is to forgive freely, while justice has eternal punishment as its natural result. (Thomas, of course, disallows the objection, saying that Christ's satisfaction was agreeable to both mercy and justice.)

Remission and satisfaction are also contrary in their very idea. The translation of an obligation to a new debtor is not remission but novation. Nor is liberation the same as remission. Liberation ends obligation by payment. Remission is essentially the solution of an obligation without any satisfaction. Pardon (*condonatio*) is even more radically opposed to satisfaction.

Then Socinus teaches, in full agreement with Duns,[4] that God is all the more liberal, in that He not only pardons, but gives His Son to draw us from sin when satisfaction was not necessary. The orthodox theory makes God appear both sordid and cruel. Nor did God give Christ to show His hatred of sin and make it hateful to us. For this the punishment of sinners and the offered reward of eternal life would have sufficed. Finally, Socinus adds that if the satisfaction theory were true, it would have been clear in the Scriptures.

Having thus demonstrated that satisfaction is not necessary, and that its idea conflicts with that of grace, Socinus now proceeds (cap. iii) to criticise the theory that Christ's death constitutes a satisfaction for our sins. If satisfaction were necessary, it must be personal. Eternal death, the penalty of sin, is not transferable like a debt of money. Even in human law punishments are not transferable, or are so only in cases where a special relation exists between the parties, and Christ is in no way related to us more particularly than any one man is related to another. Besides the idea is folly also; it is neither strict justice nor mercy in the sense in which these are effects of the Divine will, and it conflicts with true justice and wisdom.

But further, one death cannot satisfy for many (here again Socinus follows Duns [5]); nor, again, as the orthodox teach, can one man fulfil the law for many. Thus the theory breaks down in another essential point.

Again (cap. iv), Christ's suffering could not have constituted a satisfaction, for the penalty of sin was eternal death, and He rose from the dead. Nor does the theory of the infinite value of Christ's sufferings hold. Firstly, the principle of respect of persons is not equitable. Next, in this case there is no proportion between His sufferings, so short as they were, and those which

---

[4] *Supra*, p. 250. [5] *Supra*, p. 243.

sinners must have endured. Finally, the quality was different: Christ did not suffer, as Calvin says,[6] the pains of the damned. Socinus also repeats the scholastic objection, that if Christ's Deity gives an infinite value to His sufferings, so much need not have been required.[7]

Again, Christ suffered as man, for God is impassible. Hence His sufferings cannot possess infinite value. Even to admit the doctrine of the *communicatio idiomatum* could only yield them a verbal, not a real infinity, whence could only follow a verbal, not a real salvation. Suppose even that the Divine nature suffered, only that which is essential in God is infinite, in which passion is not included. If, again, an infinite time were converted into an infinite extent of punishment, Christ should have suffered infinitely for each and every man.

Again, there can be no satisfaction, unless He who satisfies and those for whom satisfaction is made are of one nature and race. It is said indeed that Christ is true man, but this is not enough. He must satisfy *as man*. If, however, the capacity to satisfy depends on the Divine nature, He cannot do so.

Once more, it is said that satisfaction is paid to the Divine nature. Here is an absurdity: one cannot satisfy oneself. Nor does the doctrine of the Persons in the Trinity help. If the Son satisfies the Father, who satisfies the Son? Besides, what has He to give which is not the Father's? He cannot give His own incommunicable properties; there is left only what He has in common with the Father. Hence, if Christ be Everlasting God, He cannot satisfy.

Now (cap. v) Socinus comes to the other side of the orthodox doctrine, Christ's vicarious performance of the law. Christ was *obnoxius legi*, as others were, and could not therefore satisfy for others by His obedience.[8] Nor does the fact that He voluntarily assumed the obligation make any difference, for this was in view of a reward. Calvin[9] denies what Paul[1] as well as the schoolmen teach, that Christ merited for Himself. But in denying this he really denies that He merited as man at all, for as man He had much to gain. And this is the fact. As being under

[6] 'Inst.' II, 16, 10.   [7] Cf. Thomas, 'Summa Theol.' III, 46, 6, 6.
[8] Cf. Anselm, 'Cur Deus Homo', II, xi.   [9] 'Inst.' II, 17, 6.   [1] Phil. 2:8, 9.

obligation Christ could not merit as man, and all that the Divine nature could do was to help Him to obey, for where there is obligation there is no proper merit. The Divine nature itself could no more obey than suffer, nor can the dignity of Christ's Person make any difference in the matter. Merit, however, can exist in a sense less strict, where there is obligation because of a promise. 'And so in this way Christ may rightly be said to have merited both for Himself and us.' Nothing could more clearly show the fundamental agreement between Socinus and Duns than this passage. *Meritum secundum promissionem* is indeed exactly the Scotist *meritum secundum acceptationem*. Socinus adds (cap. vi) that a theory of acceptation is, however, in spite of Calvin's divergence towards it, contrary to the orthodox belief.

Socinus comes finally (cap. vii), after thus discussing the passion of Christ and His obedience, to His death. This need not be regarded as a satisfaction for sin. Ps. 69:4 is not to be understood as assigning a juridical cause for Christ's death (cap. ix). Socinus here criticises (cap. viii) the orthodox position that death is always the result of sin, and rejects as unjust the doctrine of the imputation of Adam's guilt. He teaches that temporal death is natural to man as such; the wages of sin is eternal death, which Christ did not suffer. And (cap. x) the imputation of our sins to Christ would have been unjust, for imputation of others' guilt is only equitable where there is an imitation of their sin.[2] Imputation, Socinus continues, is not a mere matter of the Divine will, for it involves the rights of individuals, and demands a sufficient cause, in fact desert (*meritum*). So also punishment depends not simply upon the will of God, but on desert. Christ, however (cap. ix), died not because He was in any way bound to die, but simply because God and He willed it. Further (cap. x), that the death of Christ was not exacted as a penalty for sin is shown by the fact that a reward was given to Him. Moreover, if His death had been penal, it could not have been an example for us. It is then to be viewed, not as punishment, but as *affliction*.

In pars iv Socinus criticises the Protestant doctrine of the imputation of Christ's satisfaction through faith. His satisfaction

---

[2] It is noteworthy that this position is reproduced exactly from Thomas, II, 1, qu. 87, 8, where also the same Scripture passages are quoted, viz. Exod. 20:5 ; Ezek. 18:20.

(cap. ii) is not imputed to us as a satisfaction for our sins. For either satisfaction has already been made before this imputation, or, if it do not exist before imputation, then there is no satisfaction to be imputed. Nor can it be imputed for justification, for it constitutes justification.

Nor can this imputation be explained as acceptilation. Acceptilation signifies in Roman law the dissolution of an obligation by mere words. But this excludes a real payment. Even if the word be used less strictly for acceptation, still this latter can find no place where full payment is made. Nor can imputation even be maintained with the sense of application. If it be said that satisfaction was made with the tacit condition, if we should believe, this is not the orthodox doctrine.

Again (cap. iii), the doctrine of the application of the satisfaction of Christ is absurd. If we are to believe in it, it must already have been made, or else we believe what is false. Socinus declares that the whole doctrine of satisfaction is an invention of the schoolmen, and is full of absurdities.

He touches further (cap. v) on the imputation of Christ's righteousness. If satisfaction has been made, nothing further can be necessary. This doctrine is a proof of the unsatisfactoriness of the orthodox view; the difficulty was felt that the Scriptures required holiness, whereas the orthodox view did not, and therefore it was fabricated to cover over the deficiencies of the latter.

But the crowning absurdity (cap. viii) is the idea that by belief in Christ's satisfaction His righteousness is imputed to us; there is no connexion whatever between these matters.

In fact, the Protestant idea of faith is quite wrong; faith is not (cap. xi) the belief that by the death of Christ our sins are blotted out, but rather (cap. xi) obedience to Christ and God and belief in the truth of Christ's message. This justifies, because by it we live justly, and God in His benignity does not impute sin, that is, He forgives the sins of our frailty.

In the remainder of pars iv Socinus seeks to show that his and not the orthodox is the Scriptural view of justification by faith. He ends his great criticism with the consciousness that he has abundantly confuted the received view, and maintained his own. Indeed, human ingenuity could hardly go farther in devising

372

fresh criticism. The above abstract, however, only gives an imperfect conception of the work of Socinus, which must be studied in detail, if its full force is to be felt.

In Socinus's 'Themata de Officio Christi'[3] the doctrine is substantially the same as the positive doctrine of his 'De Servatore', but it is stated in terms of the threefold office. It is most important for the knowledge of the Christian religion (1) to understand truly the nature of Christ, but still more important rightly to determine His office 'since in this most of all consists the knowledge of Christ, without which we cannot obtain eternal life'. The office of Christ (2) is twofold, that which he performed on earth, and that which He performed in heaven. The former (3) is the prophetic office, the latter the kingly, along with the priestly. Christ (4) is frequently called Prophet and King in Scripture, Priest also expressly in the Epistle to the Hebrews.

'The Prophetic Office consists in this, that He both perfectly revealed to us the will of God the Father, and also confirmed it' (5). This will is contained (6) in the New Covenant, which Christ established with men. This differs (7) in many things from the Old Covenant. It differs extrinsically (8); it was not made with Jews only, but has a universal scope. It differs intrinsically (9), firstly as regards precepts, secondly as regards promises. 10–31 describe the difference as to precepts. This consists (a) in the abolition of the ceremonial and judicial precepts of the Mosaic law; (b) in the reinterpretation and perfecting of its moral precepts. Socinus lays great stress on this point, referring at length to Mt. 5–7. The difference further consists (c) in the addition of new moral and ceremonial precepts. 'The moral are to deny onself, to take up one's cross, to imitate Christ' (29). The one ceremonial precept is the Lord's Supper in memory of His death.

Socinus next treats of the difference as to promises. 'We say therefore that the New Covenant has brought to us the clearest promise of life eternal: then next, the promise of the forgiveness of all sins, so far as this can be distinguished *per viam intellectus,* as it is said, from the promise or the obtaining of eternal life: lastly, the promise of the Holy Spirit, to be obtained by all

[3] 'Opera Omnia', 1656, i, 775ff.

373

believers. Since the Old Covenant lacks and lacked all these, and offered an earthly felicity, the superiority of the New Covenant can be easily recognised at this point' (32–3).

In 34–7 Socinus deals with the confirmation of the will of God by Christ. This took place (35) by His holy life, His miracles, and His death at the behest of the Father. His death (36) manifests to us the love of the Father, and so makes us sure of whatever is promised under the New Covenant, which is the reason why the blood of Christ is called the blood of the New Covenant and He Himself the faithful witness. Again the Resurrection, which could not take place without Christ's previous death, assures us of our own resurrection and of the obtaining of eternal life, if we obey Christ. The Resurrection (37) makes us sure of our salvation in a twofold way. We see in it how God delivers those who trust in Him from the most cruel death. It shows us Christ clothed with all authority in heaven and earth, and able to save us from death. Thus we are assured of His power to save us, as we are by His death of His love towards us, and we are secure of eternal life, promised us by Him. The above is the true reason of Christ's death (38): the doctrine of satisfaction is untrue. Redemption, accordingly (39), is not to be understood as redemption by a price from an angry God, but implies simply God's love in delivering us from sin and death. The term redemption is used in Scripture 'not in a strict sense, but metaphorically'. We have (40) already redemption from the bondage of sin, and await that from death.

41–3 treats of justification. 'The manifestation and confirmation of the Divine will by Christ begets in us a lively faith, on account of which we are justified, i.e. are delivered from the guilt of our sins' (41). 'This faith is nothing else than to obey the commandments of Christ in the hope of obtaining life eternal' (42). Justification is only by faith (43), not by works. Justification by works, as spoken of in Scripture, if rightly understood, means the same thing as justification by faith.

44–6 deal with the kingly office. This consists (45) in Christ's sitting after His Resurrection at the Father's right hand and being clothed with all authority, so that He is able in everything to help us. The priestly office (47) is only to be distinguished from

374

the kingly office *per viam intellectus*. When we view the heavenly Christ (48) according to His kingly office, we contemplate His power; when we view Him according to His priestly office, we contemplate His willingness to save us. He does not, however (49), in any strict sense intercede for us.

The priestly office (50) was not assumed till Christ had passed into the heavens. 'Wherefore also we maintain that His expiatory sacrifice was not accomplished on the cross, but is even now being accomplished and achieved in heaven, where Christ is, and where He continually cleanses us from our sins by keeping us back by His word and Spirit from the sins themselves, and defending His own from all evils, so far as they are the real penalties of sins' (51).

Socinus concludes (52) by emphasising once more that an exact understanding of the offices of Christ is most necessary; an error here is far more dangerous than on the question of His nature.

The 'Themata' enable us usefully to compare the doctrine of Socinus with the Protestant synthesis. He admits a real prophet-hood and a real kingship of Christ, but no real priesthood. If he appears to accept the doctrine of justification by faith, it is only an appearance inasmuch as he gives his own interpretation both to faith and justification. Faith is obedience to the commandments of Christ in the hope of the reward of life eternal. It justifies, because God naturally approves such an attitude, and 'if a man does what in him lies' does not exact more. Justification by faith thus becomes only a modification of justification by works. Finally, the Lord's Supper is no means of grace either in the Catholic or the Protestant sense, but the one ceremonial precept of Christianity. Baptism Socinus tended to regard as a merely temporary rite for the reception of Jewish and heathen proselytes in the first days of the Christian Church.[4]

There is no doubt that Socinus marks a turning-point in the history of the doctrine of the work of Christ. What Duns and the Nominalists did for the Catholic, Socinus has done for Protestant doctrine; he had demonstrated its irrationalism. This was naturally not difficult to do, inasmuch as the Protestant doctrine

[4] Schneckenburger, op. cit., p. 59.

contains all the irrational elements of the Catholic doctrine, combined and fused in Luther's intuition with the even more irrationalistic non-Catholic doctrine, justification by faith. The unity of the Protestant doctrine depends upon this intuition: it is psychological, not logical. When therefore the fundamental intuition and psychological basis is wanting, as in the case of Socinus, the synthesis depending upon it can no longer maintain itself.

Socinus, however, has not merely applied the critical method of Duns and Occam; he has also as a jurisprudent made use of legal arguments, and most important of all he has investigated the Scriptural basis of Protestantism by means of the humanist exegesis. The result is that, while he has undoubtedly under-estimated and even falsified the amount of genuine points of contact for the orthodox theory in the New Testament, he has on the other hand for the first time in the history of Christian doctrine clearly established (a) the degree in which terms like 'redemption', etc., are in Scripture limited by their context, so that they cannot be strictly pressed; (b) the fact that much of the orthodox doctrine is not Scripture, but a development from Scripture; and (c) the existence in Scripture of other points of view besides these leading to the orthodox doctrine. Perhaps this last point is the most important of all. The Socinian doctrine is to be understood above all as a return from the Logos Christology to the more primitive Messianic (adoptianist) doctrine, which is clearly visible in passages like Ac. 2:22–36, 3:13–26, 5:30–1, 10:36–43, 13:23–39, and which has also left traces of itself even where it has been superseded by the doctrine of Christ's pre-existence.[5] In this primitive Christology Jesus appears as first in His earthly life the Prophet of the Kingdom of God, and after-wards as being, in reward of His obedience in suffering even unto death, invested with the Messianic dignity by His Resurrection. Socinianism is in part the revival of this primitive view: on the other hand it is no mere revival, but is conditioned by the subsequent history of doctrine. It finally establishes a type of Christianity, which we have already referred to in dealing with Anselm as being opposed to the Pauline mysticism with its sequel

[5] Cf. Rom. 1:4 ; Phil. 2:5–11 ; Heb. 2:9, 5:7–10.

376

in the Irenæan doctrine of recapitulation. Throughout the history of Western Christianity, in Ambrose, Augustine, Lombard, Duns, we can trace the view of Christ as an individual man, who merits glory for Himself, and is an example to others. This view, however, was continually repressed by the weight of ecclesiastical tradition on the side of the view that Christ is no mere individual, but the Second Adam and the summary of the race. With Socinus at last tradition gives way, and the view formerly repressed by it holds the field. Other important elements, however, enter into combination with this Christology to make Socinianism. Amongst these may be mentioned especially the Scotist doctrine that God is arbitrary will, and the doctrine going back through Biel to Alexander,[6] that God accepts him who does what in him lies. The positivism of Socinus, according to which the promise of immortality belongs to the Christian revelation alone, is also the natural consequence of the positivism of Duns and the Nominalists, which, basing itself upon authority, tended to reduce rational theology to a minimum.

To sum up our results: upon the basis of the primitive Christian Messianic doctrine Socinus has developed, by the aid of theologumena derived from Duns and other schoolmen, a theological synthesis, which agrees with the doctrine of the Apologists as to the moral and religious content of Christianity, but not as to the principle of revelation, in that the Apologists present Christianity as a natural, Socinus as a positive, religion. On the other hand the superstructures of Pauline origin, which orthodox Catholicism and Protestantism viewed as the positive Christian revelation beyond the religion of reason, Socinus regards as error and abandons to logical criticism. Christianity therefore is finally presented by him, as by the Apologists, as a religion of law and promise. A qualifying principle of grace is, however, recognised in the form of the doctrine of God's absolute sovereignty, which is inherited from Duns Scotus.

[6] See for Alexander, *supra*, p. 198. Biel taught that a man could, apart from grace, love God above all things, and that such natural love of God might serve as a *meritum de congruo* to obtain the infusion of grace (cf. Loofs, D.G., 4th ed., p. 615).

CHAPTER 5

THE ARMINIAN THEOLOGIANS

ARMINIANISM

ARMINIANISM is most properly to be understood as a *via media* between Socinianism and Calvinism. Its derivation on the one hand from the school of Erasmus is plain enough. It was in attempting to refute the views of the humanist Coornheert (d. A.D. 1590), that Jacob Arminius (d. A.D. 1609), the founder of the new school, was himself converted to a disbelief in Calvinism. Though the controversy between Arminians and Calvinists centred in the question of predestination, yet this was by no means the sole point of difference between Arminianism and orthodoxy. The Lutherans, like the Arminians, held that Christ had died not for the elect alone, but for the whole world, yet their community of doctrine on this point marks no real unity between Lutheranism and Arminianism. On the contrary the first principle of Arminianism is in reality a respect for human reason leading to a disbelief in the view common alike to Lutherans and Reformed, that it is so totally corrupt that it must bow absolutely before Divine revelation. The Arminians believed in the Scriptures as the foundation of theology, but on historical grounds, not on the basis of any *testimonium spiritus sancti*; and moreover the Scriptures were to be rationally interpreted. Their great theologian, Limborch (A.D. 1633–1712), says:[1]

'From these things it appears what is the key by which the obscure meaning of Scripture is to be unlocked; viz. indisputably Scripture itself and right reason. Scripture, indeed, in so far as it is everywhere agreeable to itself, and nowhere contains any contradiction: it is therefore to be so explained, that it may harmonise with itself in all points, and that the sense of the more difficult may be drawn out by means of the plainer passages.

[1] 'Theologia Christiana', I, 12, 4.

378

Right reason; in so far as it is no less from God than Scripture, and is implanted in us as a light, by whose aid we can distinguish the true from the false. For it is not to be believed that Divine revelation can at all conflict with right reason, or that anything can be philosophically true which is theologically false. For, since reason is no less from God than revelation, if these were to conflict with one another, God would be in opposition to Himself. The one light cannot be contrary to the other, but the one is greater than the other. Revelation does not destroy, but perfects reason, to the degree that, what reason alone did not perceive, that it may clearly perceive on the advent of revelation.'

This passage clearly shows the tendency of the Arminian exegesis. Its work was to remove whatever in Scripture might be a stumbling-block to reason. Hence the Arminians are almost as much opposed as Socinus to the Augustinian doctrine of original sin, the negative presupposition of Calvinism.

'Here it is especially two conceptions of the traditional ecclesiastical doctrine which the Arminians oppose, in the first place, that of an implication by means of imputation of Adam's posterity in his guilt through the Fall, nextly that of a total corruption proceeding from the Fall. Against the former conception it is clearly objected that one who was born 1000 years later could not sin along with Adam, and that the transgression of another can be imputed to no one, who has not expressly empowered him to act.[2] As to the other point, the idea of freedom, from which Arminianism set out in its opposition to the doctrine of predestination, did not allow of any thought of a total corruption. . . . Doubt was not cast upon the actuality of corruption, but it was explained through the idea, that after original innocence was lost in Adam, his children were born after his subsequent nature, and were thus created less pure than he, only that they, instead of his natural instinct for good, bring with them into the world a tendency to evil.'[3]

As regards the doctrines of the Trinity and the Person of Christ the older Arminians were essentially orthodox; the later theologians, however, approximated more to Socinianism, preferring, however, rather to remain by the simple assertions of

[2] Limborch, III, 3, 20.   [3] Schneckenburger, op. cit., p. 14.

379

the Creed without speculation. Limbroch says that the dogma of the union of God and man in one person is naturally inexplicable, being without analogy (III, xii, 4).

The Arminian doctrine of the work of Christ seeks a middle way between orthodoxy and Socinianism. There are, however, two different types. The one is the school doctrine represented by Limborch, and amounts essentially to a return to the Scotist doctrine of acceptilation; the other is the new and important theory of the jurist Grotius.

LIMBORCH

In his 'Theologia Christiana', III, xv *seq.,* Limborch discusses the work of Christ under the formula of the threefold office.

'The misery hanging over the human race was, as we said before, the dominion of sin and eternal death. The dominion of sin Christ destroyed by the prophetic office, eternal death by the priestly office, for indisputably by it He has both destroyed the guilt of sin and absolved us from guilt. Both of these things He undertook by the kingly office, for He both prescribes the rules of holiness and provides us with the powers and gifts of the Spirit: by all of which we may resist the snares of sin and the temptations of the Devil; and by His almighty power He actually delivers us from the bonds of death and brings us into a state of happiness; although neither is the priestly office excluded from our deliverance from the power of sin; for by offering Himself as an expiatory sacrifice, He also redeemed us from the dominion of sin' (xv, 1).

The prophetic office was imposed upon Christ by God, and He was equipped by the Father with all things needful for declaring His will. The performance of this office included (1) the announcement of the doctrine of the Gospel, and what belongs to it, (2) the confirmation of that doctrine.

The announcement of the Gospel was partly made by Christ on earth, but is partly made by Him now through His Spirit given to His ministers. The latter point properly belongs to the kingly office, but is treated here to avoid repetition.

'The doctrine of the Gospel is the revelation of the final and most complete Divine will, concerning the eternal salvation of men and the manner of obtaining it' (xvi, 3). Like all other covenants made by God with men the Gospel contains both precepts and promises. It contains precepts in the strict sense. The contra-Remonstrants (i.e. the Calvinists), who practically identify the work of Christ with the priestly office, and teach that Christ made full satisfaction for sins, and also performed the law in our stead, maintain that the Gospel properly contains no precepts, but only repeats those of the law, the performance of which God does indeed from the point of view of the law require of the elect, but which He so accomplishes by the grace of His Spirit, that the precepts are really no more than promises. This view, however, entirely overthrows all necessity of obedience, and puts an end to all zeal for holiness. 'For if Christ does not properly demand obedience from men as the condition of obtaining eternal salvation, but wills to effect it in them, what necessity is there of offering what God does not demand? What anxiety can there be to do that which God Himself promises that He will do in man?' (xvi, 4).

Limborch here enters on the controversy between Socinus and the orthodox as to whether Jesus only purified the law from the corruptions of the Pharisees or whether He added to it.[4] He maintains that mystically, or in its ultimate intention, i.e. sanctity of life and eternal felicity, apart from the question of clearness of expression, the old law is one with the new law; but as to clearness the new law both as regards the ceremonial and the moral precepts is superior to the old. It has fewer ceremonial precepts, and those only with a view to the cleansing of the soul. The moral precepts of the old law also had faults which Christ removed, while He added new precepts never expressed in the old law at all. Moreover, Christ's doctrine was not adapted to the needs of the Jewish state in particular, but was universal in its scope.

The promises of Jesus Christ are especially (1) the forgiveness of sins, (2) the gift of the Holy Spirit, (3) the resurrection from the dead. These with the precepts compose a doctrine, beyond which none more perfect is to be expected.

[4] *Supra*, pp. 356, 373.

As a prophet Jesus also foretold the future, and prayed for the people and the future happy extension of the Divine word. His fulfilment of the prophetic office was marked by His zeal, His freedom and authority in teaching, His wisdom and eloquence, and the clearness of His doctrine.

The continuation of Christ's teaching was (1) by His miracles, (2) by the testimony of Holy Scripture, (3) by the holiness of His doctrine, (4) by the holiness of His life, (5) by His bloody and shameful death.

'It is the mark of a true prophet to lay down His life for the doctrine which He announces by the will of God, and to undergo all kinds of adversities at the hands of men. . . . The death of Christ was therefore, as it were, a seal and confirmation of the covenant, and His blood, as it were, the blood of a covenant sacrifice, by which the New Testament was sealed and guaranteed' (xvii, 19).

At this point the difference between the law and the Gospel becomes clear. They agree (1) in their author, viz. God; (2) in that 'both contain a certain mutual agreement between God and men, in which God demands obedience of man, on the performance of which He promises man a reward' (xvii, 20). But there are also various differences:

(1) The mediator of the one was Moses, of the other Christ.

(2) One was guaranteed by the blood of beasts, the other by that of Christ Himself.

(3) The Gospel surpasses the law, both as regards precepts and promises. The Gospel has fewer ceremonial precepts, while it perfects the law in its moral aspect. The promises are not temporal, but eternal, and not in figure only, but in all plainness.

(4) As regards efficacy, the law could not check sin, the Gospel does this.

(5) As to amplitude, the Gospel is not for Israel only, but for the world.

(6) As to duration, the Old Testament was temporary, the New Testament is eternal.

The prophetic office began with Christ, it was continued by the Apostles, its end is the evangelisation of the world.

In cap. xviii Limborch comes to the priestly office. This was

382

imposed by God on Christ. God, who had of His own accord shown Himself placable, appointed Christ as Priest, by whose mediation He might be fully reconciled to men. Was this by any necessity of His nature, that He might make satisfaction to His vindicative justice? The question might well be dispensed with: why should we ask what God could have done, when we know for certain what He has done? But, as the question has been asked, it is to be maintained 'that God was constrained by no necessity of nature to punish sin, nor therefore can He be said to have been constrained by any necessity of nature to demand satisfaction for the sins which He was to remit. Nay, rather, the Scriptures everywhere preach the gratuitous love of God, and His most free decree, as the source of salvation, whence proceeded, not only the sending of Christ into the world for our redemption, but also the remission of sins itself, now that the sacrifice of Christ has been offered' (xviii, 4).

Nor does this make the passion of Christ superfluous. 'God in accordance with His supreme wisdom chose this way of bringing men to salvation as the fittest, as the most suited to the illustration of His glory, and the conversion of men from their sins to a zeal for holiness. By the grievous passion of His Son, which He has demanded for the redemption of the human race, He indeed showed His wrath against sin; no effect of which would have been seen had no expiatory sacrifice come between: and thus He manifested Himself as a just judge and a rewarder of unrighteousness. At the same time He wished to quicken men to zeal for holiness, seeing that they might easily infer that they can hope for no pardon for their sins, for whose expiation God demanded the bloody death of His only-begotten and beloved Son, unless they seriously say farewell to them and give themselves over wholly to the practice of sanctity. God wished besides that Christ Jesus should be our leader, who by His sufferings might unlock heaven, since He wished us to proceed to heavenly glory through sufferings; so that it might be clear to us that the entrance into heaven is open to us also through sufferings' (XVIII, 5).

The function of the priestly office is (1) oblation, (2) intercession. Benediction, which some add, seems to be comprehended under these two heads, as it is the end of both. Christ's oblation is that in which He offered Himself to the Father as a sacrifice and expiatory victim for our sins. It took place partly on earth, partly in heaven.

'It took place on earth, when He delivered Himself, in order to obey the command of the Father, of His own accord and freely to a bloody and accursed death, and shed His own precious blood as if it were the price of our redemption; which obedience even unto the death of the cross the Father regarded with such favour, that He accepted that blood from the hand of His Son, as if it were a payment in full for our sins, and allowed Himself to be moved by it to bestow on us complete remission of sins' (xix, 2).

'It was perfected and consummated in heaven, because He opened heaven by His blood, which had before been closed, and so entering heaven through His own blood took it, as it were, into the Holy Place, and presented it to God His Father' (xix, 3).

Hence those think too meanly of the death of Christ who regard it merely as the preparation for His oblation, which took place in heaven, and think that the office of priest is not to be attributed to Jesus Christ while on earth.[5] Though Christ is not in so many words called in Scripture a priest on the earth, yet sacerdotal functions are nevertheless attributed to Him in this state, in that His death is viewed as a sacrifice.[6] But the appearance of Christ alive again from the dead in heaven, and His presentation or offering of Himself before His Father, is the consummation of His sacrifice.

Limborch refutes the arguments in favour of the Socinian view, drawn from the Old Testament sacrifices, where the slaying of the victim was only the preparation for its oblation in the sanctuary;[7] he says that the parallel between the Old and New Testaments is not complete. Finally, he answers the question: If the death of Christ is the beginning of His offering, and His appearance in heaven in the consummation of it, why is the remission of sins ordinarily ascribed in the New Testament to the

---

[5] This is of course directed against Socinus (cf *supra*, p. 367), but also against the older Arminian theologian Curcellæus, who here stood nearer to Socinus. Cf. Ritschl, 'Justification and Reconciliation', vol. i, English trans., p. 315.

[6] Eph. 5:2 ; Mt. 20:28, 26:27.   [7] *Supra*, p. 367.

death of Christ alone? The answer is that the oblation in the heavens obtains all its efficacy from the death of Christ. The grounds of this efficacy are: (1) the will of God, which appointed this death and nothing else to be a ransom for the sins of men; (2) the dignity of Christ's Person, as the Son of God; (3) His sinlessness; (4) His perfect obedience; (5) the extremity of His sufferings.

The second part of the work of Christ as Priest is His intercession. This is not the prayer of Christ's earthly life, which belongs to the prophetic office, nor is it a humble supplication to the Father, which would be inconsistent with Christ's royal power; it is therefore nothing but Christ's continual presence before the Father and His application of the forgiveness procured by the offering of His blood. The term intercession is therefore only a figure of speech, and what is implied under it is, strictly speaking, nothing but the continuation of Christ's oblation. Christ's intercession is not, however, to be confounded with the kingly office, for in His intercession Christ deals directly with God, not with men.

Limborch proceeds to define his position by a criticism of the doctrine of the priestly office, as stated by Socinus on the one hand and the contra-Remonstrants on the other. The Socinian doctrine allows Christ no proper priestly office at all, for all that it admits belongs really to His prophetic and kingly work. But Scripture plainly assigns to Christ a priestly office, and not merely that of King or Prophet, the difference being that the Priest deals with God on behalf of men, the King and Prophet with men on behalf of God. Again, Scripture represents Christ's death as a sacrifice, propitiation, and ransom, of all which things Socinus gives no satisfactory explanation. His doctrine makes the death of Christ simply that of a martyr and the confirmation of the truth He preached; and, while this is a true point of view, it is not the whole truth of Scripture. On the other hand, the contra-Remonstrant doctrine of the priestly office has no firm foundation in Scripture. Both merit and satisfaction are unscriptural terms, and as a consequence, 'since they thus nowhere exist in Scripture, but have been devised by men, no one is bound to the meaning of them, any further than it can be furnished from

385

the phrases of Scripture, to elucidate the sense of which they have been applied' (xxi, 1).

The doctrine that the merit of Christ consists in His obedience is both unscriptural and irrational. If Christ satisfied the law for us, then God can demand from us nothing further, not even that we should in faith apprehend His merit. But as a matter of fact both faith and holiness are required for eternal salvation. Again, the idea that satisfaction is an exact payment of the penalties of sin is equally unscriptural and irrational, which appears as follows:

(1) The death of Christ is spoken of in Scripture as a sacrifice, but sacrifices are no plenary satisfactions for sins, but merely the condition of forgiveness.

(2) Christ suffered eternal death, neither extensively in time, nor intensively, since He never despaired under the Divine wrath. But eternal death was the penalty due to our sins.

(3) If Christ had paid the penalty in full, there would have been no room for grace.

(4) Nor under these conditions could God have demanded from us faith and obedience.

Having thus dealt with Socinus and the contra-Remonstrants, Limborch gives his own doctrine, 'which is midway between these two extremes'.

'Our Lord Jesus Christ was a true sacrifice for our sins, and one properly so called, in that He bore the severest anguish and the accursed death of the cross, and afterwards was raised from the dead, and entered by His own blood into the heavenly sanctuary, there presenting Himself before the Father; by which His sacrifice He appeased the Father, who was angry with our sins, and reconciled us to Him. And so He bore for us and in our stead the extremest suffering, and turned away from us the punishment we had deserved' (xxii, 1).

If now it be asked what exactly was the evil which Christ bore in our stead, the answer is as follows: It was not the punishment which we had deserved for our sins, as has already been shown. But He bore extreme misery and a bloody death in our stead, which was in place of the suffering that we ought to have borne. Not that there was a strict equivalence, since we had deserved eternal death. 'But because, though innocent, He took this suffering upon Himself, His sacrifice was so acceptable to God, that He was moved by it to receive us into His grace' (xxii, 2).

Thus the price which Christ paid was paid according to the estimation of God the Father (xxi, 8).

The Divine acceptation of Christ's sufferings for our salvation is further to be understood from the dignity of Christ's Person, as both the eternal Son of God and as the noblest of men (xxii, 5).

In a certain sense therefore Christ may be said to have been punished in our stead, and moreover 'in this sense to have made satisfaction to the Father in our stead, and to have merited right-eousness for us, in so far as He satisfed, not the rigour of the Divine justice, but the will of God, at once just and merciful' (xxii, 2).

This view, says Limborch, does not make light of the sufferings of Christ; but on the other hand it allows for the free grace of God. He further explains his doctrine by saying that what Christ merited for us was the removal of God's wrath, not faith and regeneration. Christ calls us to these, and supplies us with the Divine grace to this end; but He did not merit them, or we should have had them by right, instead of their being laid upon us as a duty. Limborch defends his doctrine against Socinus by saying that the sacrifice of Christ involved no cruelty on God's part, seeing that God had the right of giving Christ to death, as He has absolute rights over every man. Moreover, the Socinians themselves teach that God gave Christ to death as a prophet to confirm the truth of His message. There is therefore no further difficulty in His being given to death as a sacrifice, especially as He Himself also gave Himself willingly.

In cap. xxiv Limbroch proceeds to the kingly office. Christ is King as God, but also as man. His Kingdom as man began at His birth, reached a higher manifestation in His ministry, but culminated in His Resurrection, ascension, and sitting at the right hand of the Father. The functions of Christ's Kingship (cap. xxv) are:

(1) His calling men to participate in His Kingdom, the first act of which was the bestowal of the Holy Ghost on the Apostles, that they might be His ministers for this purpose;

(2) The giving of laws for those called into His Kingdom, in that He demands faith and repentance or holiness of life;

(3) His judicial power, partly exercised now, partly in the world to come.

In all these functions may be observed a difference from those of Christ's priesthood. The priestly functions are exercised towards God, the kingly towards man.

The above account of Limborch's doctrine of the work of Christ may be completed by a note as to the Arminian conception of justification by faith and of the sacraments. In opposition to the orthodox doctrine that in justification Christ's righteousness is imputed to the believer, the Arminians pressed the Scripture phrase that faith was imputed for righteousness (Rom. 4:3, 5).

'The Arminians therefore teach instead of the *per fidem* of the orthodox system a *propter fidem*. That God remits sins to men *propter fidem* is not indeed, as with the Socinians, a mere matter of His good pleasure, but the sacrifice of Christ also in a certain way comes in as a middle term. Careful regard must, however, be had to the object of faith. This is not merely the sacrifice of Christ, or Christ as making satisfaction, but it is the whole Christ as Prophet, Priest, and King, i.e. Christ, in so far as He has given precepts, promises, and threatenings. On account of this relation of justifying faith the same is in its essence already obedience, as with the Socinians, and therefore never appears as justifying, except in so far as works are united with it and are included in it.' [8]

The sacraments are regarded mainly as precepts, and only as means of grace in so far as obedience is exercised in regard to them.

Arminianism, as represented by Limborch in his attempt to mediate between Socinianism and the Protestant orthodoxy, shows an interesting reversion in many points to the mediaeval type of doctrine. Socinus had conceived Christianity as a religion of law and promise, qualified only by God's sovereign grace. Limborch thinks of it as law and promise, qualified by the forgiveness of sins upon the basis of Christ's sacrifice. There is,

[8] Schneckenburger, op. cit., p. 22.

however, no strict satisfaction, nor is satisfaction absolutely necessary, but it is merely, as with the schoolmen, God's chosen way to salvation, which is marked, however, by many points of fitness. By thus abandoning the claim that satisfaction is necessary, Limborch obviates, just as Duns had done before him, the force of the arguments proving its irrationality: Socinus himself had admitted that the Scotist form of the doctrine of Christ's merit was unexceptionable.[9] It is, however, a fresh point that Limborch, while not disputing, as does Socinus, that there is a Scriptural basis for the orthodox doctrines of Christ's satisfaction and merit, nevertheless remarks upon the difference between the implications of Scripture and of these juristic terms: this observation, due to the historical sense of the humanistic exegesis, carries him beyond the mediaeval circle of thought. Finally, while the Arminian and the mediaeval theology agree that the faith which justifies includes love, there is the great difference between them, that the mediaeval sacramentalism is altogether abandoned by the Arminians. Duns and the Nominalists had indeed prepared the way for this, in that they had reduced the giving of grace through the Sacraments to a mere arbitrary Divine decree.[1]

GROTIUS

The theory of Grotius (A.D. 1583–1645), at once a jurist and a theologian, is one of the most important in the whole history of our doctrine. In his 'Defence of the Catholic Faith concerning the Satisfaction of Christ against Faustus Socinus of Siena' (1617), he uses both his exegetical and his juristic science to meet the Socinian criticism of the orthodox doctrine: at the same time he puts forward on the basis of his exegesis and jurisprudence a new theory, which very substantially modifies the orthodox position. He commences (cap. i) with a statement of what he conceives to be the position to be defended.

'The Catholic view is as follows: God, moved by His goodness wonderfully to do us good, in view of the hindrance of our sins, which deserved punishment, determined that Christ

---

[9] *Supra*, pp. 370f.   [1] *Supra* pp. 255, 269.

voluntarily of His own love towards men should endure the severest torments and a bloody and shameful death to pay the penalty for our sins, that, without harm to the manifestation of the Divine justice, through the intermediary of true faith, we might be delivered from the punishment of eternal death.'

This thesis Grotius proceeds to expand in detail in scholastic form and to defend point by point from the Scriptures:

(1) 'The first efficient cause of the matter of which we treat, is God.' [2]

(2) 'The cause which moved God, is firstly mercy.' [3]

(3) 'Secondly, it is our sins as deserving punishment.' [4]

(4) 'The second efficient cause is Christ Himself, in his willingness.' [5]

(5) 'The cause which moved Christ was His $\phi\iota\lambda\alpha\nu\theta\rho\omega\pi\iota\alpha$.' [6]

(6) 'The matter is both Christ's torments before death, and especially His death itself.' [7] The repeated emphasis in Scripture on the death of Christ shows the inadequacy of the view of Socinus, which assigns to it no special and peculiar effect in our salvation.

(7) 'The form is the payment of the penalties for our sins.' [8] For death is the penalty of sin. Grotius admits that man was not naturally immortal: nevertheless he was created for immortality, and only failed of this destiny because of his sin.

(8) 'The end of the whole . . . is twofold, without doubt a dispensation of the Divine justice, and, as far as we are concerned, remission of sins, that is our liberation from punishment.' Grotius appeals to Rom. 3:25-6, and attacks the Socinian view of the Divine justice.[9] The Divine justice of which Paul speaks is righteousness, which has different effects in relation to different objects. Both as regards good and evil deeds its effect is retribution, but this in the case of evil deeds is punishment: the latter is an exercise of the essential justice of God, as He is called just in view of it.[1] It is true that justice often means truth, often also equity, but not in the case of the punishment of sins. 'The end of punishment is the manifestation of retributive justice in regard of sins.'

[2] Jn 3:16, etc.	[3] Rom. 5:8, etc.	[4] *Ibid.* 4:25, etc.
[5] Jn 10:18, etc.	[6] *Ibid.* 15:13, etc.	[7] Isa. 53:5 ; Col. 1:22, etc.
[8] 1 Pet. 2:24.	[9] *Supra*, pp. 364f.	[1] Rev. 16:5, 7.

Grotius also examines the explanations given by Socinus of the connexion between the death of Christ and the remission of sins.[2]

(1) He regards Christ's death as a testimony to the preaching of the remission of sins. This reverses the correct order: it makes the remission the cause of Christ's death instead of *vice versa*. Again, it makes Christ's death only a martyr death. Besides, even the historical cause of His death was not the preaching of remission, but His assertion that God was His Father; and the testimony to His preaching consisted rather in His miracles.

(2) Socinus says that by His death Christ obtained the power to forgive sins, but this is not a Scriptural point of view.[3]

(3) He regards Christ's death as an example, which is correct. But the passages, which so speak of it, are quite distinct from those which connect it with the remission of sins.

(4) Socinus says that the death of Christ is a great persuasion to faith. But in itself it is rather the reverse: it is more the Resurrection, which persuades to faith, as Socinus indeed admits: and if the death be no more than a moment in the process of the Resurrection, how is the Scriptural insistence upon it to be explained, especially in connexion with the remission of sins, with which the Resurrection is not closely associated in the Scriptures?

In this way Grotius clears the ground by disposing of the positive theory of Socinus. Cap. ii commences his own theory, by discussing the general relation between God and man. The question is not merely one of forgiveness; behind this lies the question of punishment. Here God must be considered as *rector,* or supreme governor of the world. To inflict punishment or to liberate from punishment is the act of a *rector* as such. This being admitted, it may be granted to Socinus that God is not to be viewed in this matter simply as a judge ordained under the law. For a judge cannot liberate the guilty from punishment, even by transferring it to another: not because it is in itself unjust, but because it is not in accordance with the law, whose servant

---

[2] *Supra*, pp. 365f.
[3] Grotius refers to 'De Servatore', I, cap. VI, where Socinus teaches that Christ, as a man exalted to heaven, has the power to confer eternal life, and all promised goods. Cf. also 'Themata', § 51 (*supra*, p. 375).

he is. Equity may indeed be exercised by a judge bound to a rule; clemency properly belongs only to the supreme governor.

Socinus, however, though defining God as the supreme sovereign (*summus princeps*), views His relation to man otherwise than as *rector*. He regards Him as the offended party, and again as creditor, and yet again as Lord; though in reality these are all different points of view.[4] Against such doctrine Grotius now advances three points:

(1) To punish is not within the competency of the offended party as such. If God punishes as sovereign, it is not as the offended party. The sovereign punishes, even when the offence is not against himself.

(2) The offended party has naturally no right of punishment. In fact he has not even the right to compel punishment: he is not really in this regard a creditor. Grotius supports this position by the following important argument:

'It is well known that right is twofold, natural or positive: wherefore also every debt must arise from the one source or the other. Natural right consists in the adjustment of things among themselves; of such a character therefore also is natural debt. But positive right is that which originates from the free act of the will: it is twofold, contract and law. Contract is the effect of the power which anyone has over himself and his own affairs; while law is the effect of the power which anyone has over another and his affairs. . . . By nature therefore nothing is owed or can be owed to me by reason of your action, except equality as regards property, that is, that however much I lack because of you, I should receive just as much: this may be called in a word indemnity or restitution.'

But this is a very different case from that of punishment. 'The cause of your natural debt is firstly and in itself not the wickedness of the act, but that I lack something: for even if my lack be from no fault of yours as in the case of a deposit, none the less I am owed restitution. On the other hand the cause of punishment is just the wickedness of the act, not that I lack anything.' From this argument, then, it follows that the right of punishment does not belong to the offended party by the law of nature. Nor

[4] *Supra*, p. 368.

is there any positive law (*jus constitutum*) which gives this right; nor yet any reason why such a law should be made.

(3) 'The right of punishment in the governor is neither the right of absolute sovereignty nor the right of the creditor.' For their ends are different. That of the right of sovereignty or of the creditor is the good of the individual to whom it belongs: that of the right of punishment is the common good. The end of every punishment is simply to maintain and exemplify order. Again, it is never unjust to yield one's private right, nor is anyone called just for exercising it. The reverse is the case with the right of punishment. The difference of the cases is also shown by the fact that the virtue, which yields private right, is different from that which remits punishments: one is liberality, the other clemency.

But when it is said that punishment is owing, does not this imply a creditor? No: it merely implies the idea of fitness in the abstract. If there is anything in the case that answers to the idea of creditor, it is the public good, of which the governor is the servant.

Finally Grotius argues that the Scripture words ἀφιέναι (*dimittere*) and χαρίζεσθαι (*condonare*) imply neither the right of the sovereign nor of the creditor. In cap. iii he proceeds from the examination of the nature of the case to inquire into the rule obtaining in it. Since God is to be regarded as governor, His action must be in general that of jurisdiction. It is not therefore, as Socinus thinks, a question of acceptilation,[5] for that is not an act of jurisdiction; in other words, acceptilation is an affair, not of public, but of private right. More particularly, however, the act in question can be regarded either with a view to, or apart from the Divine sanction. The latter is the ethical aspect of the matter. It is in itself right that sin should be punished; and from this point of view the act becomes the punishment of one for

---

[5] Socinus nowhere says that God's remission of sins for Christ's sake is to be thought of as *acceptilation* : he, moreover, directly denies the fitness of this legal term to explain and justify the Protestant doctrine of the imputation of Christ's righteousness or merit (*supra*, p. 372). The agreement of Socinus with Duns's doctrine of the *acceptation* of Christ's merit (*supra*, p. 371) is a different matter : there has been, however, in the history of doctrine much confusion between acceptation and acceptilation. See further on this point my article 'Acceptilation' in Hastings's 'Encyclopaedia of Religion and Ethics,' vol. i, pp. 61, 62.

the sake of the impunity of another. The former is the legal side. From this point of view the act is one of dispensation, which may be defined as 'the act of the superior, by which the obligation of a law, that still stands, is removed with reference to some particular persons or things'. The sanction is in this case Gen. 2:17, i.e. 'every sinner must bear the penalty of eternal death'.

The Divine act is therefore not the execution of the law; for then no sinner would escape eternal death. Nor yet is it the abrogation of the law; for an abrogated law has lost its obligation, yet unbelievers remain subject to the law. Nor again is it the equitable interpretation of the law; such interpretation shows some fact or person never really to have been within the purview of the law: here, however, all men without exception are by nature children of wrath and subject to the penalty of the law. It remains then that the case can only be one of the relaxation or dispensation of the law.

The question then arises, 'Whether the above penal law is relaxable?' Grotius replies:

'Some laws are either absolutely or by presupposition irrelaxable. Those are absolutely irrelaxable, whose opposite in the very nature of the case involves an immutable wickedness. . . . Such laws, again, are irrelaxable by presupposition, as are established by a fixed decree, which Scripture calls τῆς βουλῆς ἀμετάθετον or ἀμετανόητον, such as the law or the damnation of those who will not believe in Christ.[6] All positive laws, however, are absolutely relaxable: nor must one take refuge in a hypothetical necessity proceeding from a fixed decree, where there is no mention of such a decree.'

Grotius proceeds to meet the objection that his positions conflict with the unchangeableness of God. 'Law is not anything interior in God, or even the will of God, but a certain effect of His will. But it is most certain that the effects of the Divine will are changeable.' Promises indeed may not be broken, because they establish a right on the part of the promiser; and therefore God is the faithful promiser. But is there anything in the above-mentioned penal law which stands in the way of a relaxation? There is first the objection 'that it is naturally just that the

[6] Heb. 3:18.

394

guilty themselves should be punished with a penalty answering to the offence, and that this consequently is not a matter of free will, or relaxable'. Grotius replies that not every negation of what is just is unjust; nor is everything that is called natural strictly such.

'That he who has offended deserves punishment, and is in consequence punishable, follows necessarily from the very relation of sin and the sinner to the superior, and is properly natural. But that every sinner should be punished with such punishment as corresponds to his fault, is not simply or universally necessary, nor properly natural, though agreeable enough to nature. Whence it follows that there is no obstacle preventing the law ordaining this from being relaxable.' There are, nevertheless, grave reasons against relaxation: (1) there is the danger of lessening the authority of the law; (2) the law itself, though not absolute, is fitting. It follows, therefore, not indeed that the law is not to be relaxed, but that it is not to be done lightly. In the case before us, however, there is most serious reason for relaxation: 'For if all sinners had been given over to eternal death, two most beautiful things would have perished altogether from the universe, on the part of men piety towards God, and on the part of God the manifestation of His chief beneficence towards men.'

Cap. iv takes us to the ethical aspect of the question. Grotius groups the objections of Socinus under three heads: (1) those that infer that what we maintain was done was unjust; (2) those that deny that there was any reason for such action; (3) those that deny that what we assert was done at all.

Under (1) there are two points: the injustice may be (a) in the matter, viz. the sufferings of Christ, or (b) in the form, which is punishment.

(a) needs no discussion. Socinus admits that it is not in itself unjust that Christ should suffer, and the mere fact that the Scripture records that He did suffer conclusively proves the same.

(b) is dealt with, as follows:

'I maintain that it is not simply unjust or contrary to the nature of punishment, that anyone should be punished for the sins of others. When I say unjust, it is clear that I speak of such injustice as rises out of the nature of things, not what depends on positive law, that the Divine freedom may in no way be impaired.' Grotius quotes Scripture instances of the transference of punishment in support of his contention.[7] Socinus indeed objects that in Scripture there are no cases of the punishment of the innocent for the guilty. Nevertheless, if some were punished for the sins of others, it makes no difference as to the point at issue whether they had sins of their own; they were punished without regard to their guilt. 'If, however, anyone can be punished in so far as he is innocent, the innocent also can be punished.' The distinction which Socinus draws between punishment and affliction,[8] Grotius dismisses as a mere quibble.

Further, however, Socinus demands at any rate that there be a bond between the guilty and the punished, and denies that there is any such bond between us and Christ.[9] Not only, however, is it true that 'one man is not alien to another', but there is a bond between Christ and us far beyond this general connexion: He is the Head and we are the members.

Grotius now lays down the following proposition: 'It is to be observed that it is essential to punishment that it be inflicted for sin, but not equally essential that it be inflicted on the sinner himself.' This position he illustrates by the analogies of reward, favour, and revenge, which are all transferable without ceasing to be what they are.

Besides, if it were contrary to the nature of punishment to be inflicted on one who has not sinned, this would be a case, not of injustice, but of impossibility. Moreover, 'injustice is properly not an accident of a relation (such as punishment), but of an action (such as is the matter of the punishment)'. This explains 'why it is not equally free to all to punish anyone for another's sin, as it is to reward or favour him for another's merit or good deed. For the act involving reward or favour is a beneficent act, which by its nature is allowed to all. But the penal act is a hurtful act, which is not granted to all, or against all. Wherefore in order that a punishment be just, it is required that the penal act itself fall within the authority of the punisher, which may happen in three ways, either by an antecedent right of the punisher, or by a just and valid consent on the part of him whose punishment

---

[7] Exod. 20:5, etc.   [8] *Supra*, p. 371.   [9] *Supra*, p. 369.

is in question, or through his offence. When in these ways the act is lawful, there is nothing to prevent its then being ordained for the punishment of the sin of another, if only there be some bond between him who sinned and the one to be punished.'

Socinus admits the transference of penalty in money penalties, but says that the reason is that money is transferable, and so money paid by one for another can be regarded, as if it had been first given to him, and then paid by himself: corporal punishment, however, is not thus transferable. The argument of Socinus, however, would prove that no one could be rewarded for the merit of another, nor an unwilling surety be compelled to pay for a defaulting debtor. The distinction he draws is therefore not correct. Grotius further proves against Socinus that corporal punishment was regarded as transferable by ancient law and custom: he particulary notes instances where sureties were admitted in cases of capital punishment. If in general Roman law did not allow sureties for capital punishment, this was because such transactions were regarded not altogether as unjust, but as hazardous. Neither was the rule absolute, nor do modern lawyers so regard it.

Finally Grotius sums up:

'To bring this question to a conclusion, we do not here inquire whether any judge may inflict on anyone any penalties whatever of another's crime. For the law of the superiors takes away this power from the inferior judges. Nor do we inquire whether the highest authority among men may do this with regard to any penalty and any person. For sometimes the Divine law or natural reason stands in the way. But we do exactly inquire whether an act, which is in the authority of the superior, even apart from the consideration of another's offence, may be arranged by the superior for the penalty of another's fault. That this is unjust is denied by Scripture, which shows that God has often done this; by nature, since it is not proved to forbid it; plainly also by the *consensus gentium*. . . . There is therefore nothing wrong in this, that God whose is the highest authority in all matters not in themselves unjust, and is Himself subject to no law, willed to use the sufferings and death of Christ to establish a weighty example against the immense guilt of us all, with whom Christ was most closely allied, by nature, by sovereignty, by surety.'

Indeed this act was not only just, but wise, as the examination of its cause will show.

This cause Grotius discusses in cap. v. It might have been one passing our understanding, nay the will of God had alone been sufficient cause; for things just in themselves God wills because they are so, but other things are just, because He wills them. But as a matter of fact God has plainly revealed the cause. It must, however, be prefaced, that Socinus is unjust in asking that such a cause shall be adduced, as will show that God could not possibly have acted otherwise. 'For such a cause is not required in what God does freely.' Grotius appeals to the classical text, 'Aug. De Trin.' xiii, 10, 13.

Besides, Socinus himself advances no necessary cause of Christ's death: on the contrary the causes that he gives have no vital connexion with it. Scripture, however, shows a sufficient cause, both for God's will to remit eternal punishment, and not to do so otherwise than by the punishment of Christ. God's will to forgive has its cause in the Divine goodness to man; moreover, if men had been left to despair of eternal felicity, religion would have perished. The cause, why God laid punishment upon Christ, is shown by those Scriptures which speak of Him as delivered up, suffering, and dying for our sins. It was 'that God would not remit sins so many and so great without making a conspicuous example'. This was because of His hatred of sin which appears in His wrath: it was also because of His regard for the authority of the law.

God, then, in His love to men, willed to spare those who believe on Christ, at the same time setting up an example against their sins, and choosing in His wisdom the way to display at once various of His attributes. viz. both His clemency and severity, or His hatred of sin and His respect for the law. But besides testifying to the Divine hatred of sin and acting as a deterrent, the sacrifice of Christ reveals the love of God, who thought so much of sin that He gave His only-begotten Son to bear its penalties for us.

Grotius is now in a position further to correct Socinus's view

398

of the Divine justice. What resides in God is retributive justice, on the other hand punishment is an effect of His will: there comes in between the attribute and its effect the free will guided by wisdom.

Again we see how very different a matter is the remission of sins from the mere abandonment of a private right. It is not true, as Socinus says, that the State commits no wrong in forgiving the guilty, unless at the same time it interferes with the right of some individual, or breaks a Divine law[1]: on the contrary relaxation must have a sufficient cause, being not an act of absolute sovereignty, but an act of government, which must be directed to the preservation of order.

Again Socinus says[2] that beside the will of God and Christ no cause can be given for Christ's death, unless it be that He merited to die. The answer is that His death was merited, but impersonally: it was merited by our sins. The transference of the penalty of sin to Christ, however, was an act of the Divine will, not caused by the merit of Christ, who was sinless, but by His extreme fitness to be a penal example, both because of His peculiar union with us, and of the dignity of His Person.

Cap. vi proceeds to the question, whether God willed to punish Christ. Scripture proves this (Rom. 4:25, etc.). When Socinus argues that God has forgiven sin apart from Christ;[3] so far as temporal punishment is in question, it is to be remembered that what is delayed is not abandoned; as regards eternal punishment, there is no proof that there is any remission apart from Christ. Promises of forgiveness under the New Covenant, such as Jer. 31:34, are quite consistent with Paul's doctrine that propitiation is through the blood of Christ.

Socinus, however, has brought objections from the inconsistency of remission and pardon with satisfaction.[4] In the first place, remission is as applicable to punishment as it is to debts; but the former case is one of public, the latter one of private law. Next, Socinus is wrong in saying that remission is inconsistent with any previous payment.

'That this may be understood, we offer a description of the

---

[1] *Supra*, p 368.   [2] 'De Christo Servatore', III, 9. Cf. *supra*, p. 371.
[3] *Supra*, p. 368.   [4] *Supra*, p. 369.

remission of the due (*debitum*), which includes under it two species, viz. debt (*creditum*) and punishment. . . . To remit a due therefore is the act of a creditor or governor, liberating the guilty from the obligation of his punishment or debt. . . . The destruction of an obligation is in law called liberation. This may be preceded, but cannot be followed by payment; for no act can take place concerning what no longer exists. Liberation therefore sometimes happens when some payment precedes, sometimes apart from all payment. But one kind of payment in itself liberates, another kind not in itself. The payment of a thing, clearly the same as was in the obligation, in itself liberates. It is, however, the same thing, whether the guilty person himself pays, or whether another pays for him with the intention that he should be freed: a point which requires to be observed, since if anyone pays the same thing with a different intention, no liberation takes place. Where, therefore, the same thing is paid either by the debtor, or by another in the name of the debtor, no remission takes place; for the creditor or the governor takes no action with reference to the due. Wherefore, if anyone has paid the penalty which he owes, there will here be liberation, but no remission. . . . Another kind of payment, however, does not in itself liberate, for instance, if something other than is in the obligation be paid. But it is necessary for an act of the creditor or the governor to come in also, which act is rightly and usually called remission. Such a payment, however, which can be either admitted or refused, has, when admitted in law, the special name of satisfaction, which is sometimes opposed to payment in the strict sense.[5] And hence is to be sought the real reason, why the substitute for corporal punishment cannot by paying the penalty at once liberate the guilty person; for this delay happens firstly and in itself, not because another pays (that indeed does not hinder liberation, since that is the intention of the payer), but because he pays something other than is in the obligation. For what is in the obligation is the suffering of the offender. . . . Wherefore that from the punishment of one may follow the liberation of another, an act of the governor must intervene. For the law orders that the offender himself be

[5] Grotius here refers to Justinian's 'Digest', 46, 3, 52 : 'Satisfactio pro solutione est.'

400

punished. This act with regard to the law is relaxation or dispensation, with respect to the debtor remission.'

Liberation here, then, takes place not by the substitution of a new obligation (*novatio*), or of a new debtor (*delegatio*), nor yet by the acceptance of a mere verbal payment (*acceptilatio*). This last term belongs to the sphere of private law only, and Socinus is quite wrong in bringing it in here.[6] What takes place is exactly what he denies to be possible, remission preceded by satisfaction. It does not matter whether this precedence is in fact or in the Divine decree; these are the same with God. Socinus is wrong in saying that by satisfaction all debt (*debitum*) is at once removed; this is to confuse satisfaction and strict payment. As it has already been shown, the creditor or the governor has still to admit the satisfaction. Hence a further condition can be imposed along with the admission of a satisfaction as ground of remission; as God indeed has done, in requiring faith in Christ.

Grotius goes on to deal with the difficulty caused by the Scripture command to forgive as God forgives.[7] Does not this imply that He forgives without satisfaction? Grotius replies that God's forgiveness is not completely parallel to ours. God is judge, we are private individuals; hence it does not follow that if we are bidden to forgive freely, God must do the same. Next Grotius comes to the arguments drawn by Socinus from the liberality of God.[8] First the word is out of place; clemency rather is the virtue displayed in remission. But Socinus argues that his view shows God doubly liberal, firstly, in the free pardon of sins, and secondly, in the free gift of Christ; whereas the orthodox theory, making the latter necessary in order to the former, loses one half of this grace. In answer Grotius points out a double beneficence (he will not use the word liberality) implied by the orthodox view, and that a greater than Socinus can adduce; first in the pardon of sins, when, as the death of Christ shows, that meant so much to God; and, again, in giving Christ to die for us.

But further Socinus declares that the orthodox view makes God sordid and grasping: on the contrary it shows His regard for His law. Nor is it right to say that this view makes God cruel. That the sufferings of Christ serve for a satisfaction, makes them

<hr />

[6] *Supra*, p. 393, n. 5.   [7] Cf. Mt. 18:21–35.   [8] *Supra*, p. 369.

no greater: on the contrary it shows their cause, and so rids God of the imputation of cruelty. Grotius adds that while so far he has confined his attention to Christ's satisfaction by His sufferings, he does not mean to exclude the value of His actions also to this end.

The rest of the work, caps. vii–x, contains an examination of the Scriptural basis of the idea of satisfaction. Lest it be thought that the dispute is only as to a word, Socinus objects not merely to the term satisfaction, but to the thing itself, however expressed.

'And thus he repudiates no less than the word satisfaction all these phrases, Christ by His death reconciled God to us, Christ freed us from the hands of Divine justice, giving His blood to God as the price of our redemption, Christ made compensation for our crimes by His obedience, Christ worthily merited that God should grant us the remission of sins, Christ by the loss of His life placated for us the anger of God' (cap. vii).

Even as regards the term satisfaction itself, there is, however, no difficulty in finding its equivalent in Scripture, though expressed in Greek, Hebrew, or Syriac phraseology. 'Thus when Scripture says that Christ was delivered up to death, and bore our sins, i.e. the penalties of our sins, and shed His blood for the remission of sins, all this is in Latin suggestively expressed by the word satisfaction' (ibid.).

Passages to the foregoing effect have been referred to in the course of the previous argument (caps. i–vi). But there are besides four classes of passages with the same significance: (1) those that signify the turning away of wrath; (2) those which speak of redemption by the paying of a price; (3) those which speak of substitution; (4) those which ascribe to the death of Christ expiatory power.

Grotius urges under the first head, 1 Jn 2:2; 4:10; Rom. 3:25, etc., and argues that the idea of propitiation according to classical usage implies the turning away of wrath, and that this is the natural meaning in Scripture, where sinners are said to be under the wrath of God;[9] also that reconciliation is not, as Socinus imagines, of us to God only, but since God was wroth with us,

---

[9] Jn 3:36.

402

also of God to us. Under the second head Grotius presses the force of Mt. 20:28 and 1 Tim. 2:6; 1 Pet. 1:18; 1 C. 6:20; 7:23, and points out that Scripture actually makes mention of the price of our redemption. Under the third head he lays special emphasis on the substitutionary force of ἀντί in Mt. 20:28, but argues that ὑπέρ also often according to its context means 'instead of', 2 C. 5:14, etc. Finally, under the fourth head he argues that the sacrificial language of the New Testament, whether interpreted by Hebrew or classical usage, implies substitution and satisfaction.

Grotius has no difficulty in showing throughout that Socinus is arbitrary in denying the force of these Scriptures in favour of the doctrine of satisfaction. But on the other hand, he himself has hardly realised the full strength of what Socinus says as to the figurative character of Scripture phraseology. It is clear that it is far from logically precise, when two theories of satisfaction so different as the orthodox Protestant doctrine and Grotius's own can each claim to be Scriptural.

The Grotian theory of satisfaction stands out from other theories of the work of Christ by its completely juristic character. It is the work, not merely of a theologian employing juristic ideas, but of a jurist dealing with theology. The legal knowledge of Grotius has enabled him, on the basis of the Roman law to which Socinus appealed, to point out in his arguments some technical errors; just as he has been able in some respects to correct the Socinian exegesis. But it is to be observed that the most damaging criticisms of Socinus upon the orthodox theory, those based on the impossibility of proving an equivalence between the penalties of sin and death of Christ, Grotius does not attempt to meet at all. On the contrary, while professing to defend the Catholic faith against Socinus, he puts forward altogether a new conception of Christ's satisfaction, thus tacitly abandoning the orthodox idea as irrational. He does not adopt the method of Duns, followed by Limborch, and, admitting the irrationality of the idea of strict satisfaction, fall back upon the mere will of God, or at least upon a certain fitness in the method He chose, as a sufficient explanation. In order once more to establish the rationality of satisfaction, he appeals to the

403

philosophy of law, of which he was a distinguished exponent, to give to the idea a completely fresh meaning: on the basis of Rom. 3:24, 25, he develops the thought that the death of Christ is to be understood as a penal example, which God establishes in order to honour the law, while yet pardoning sinners. This penal example, then, is what Grotius means by satisfaction: how different the idea is from that of the Protestant orthodoxy may be seen in that Grotius says that, no strict satisfaction being implied, a further condition of salvation can be demanded of men, viz. faith. Thus indeed Grotius escapes the contradictions which Socinus has shown to lie in the Protestant idea of satisfaction, but he does so at the expense of the evangelical idea of faith, which by the Reformers is conceived as no extra condition, or legal demand, or work, but as pure receptivity: here Grotius shows himself a true Arminian, and nearer to the Catholic than to the Protestant view.

As the theory of Grotius is of the greatest importance, as a really fresh view of the work of Christ, we inquire into the origin of the philosophy of law applied by him to the subject. It may be found almost in entirety in Thomas Aquinas: behind him, however, lie Aristotle and the Roman jurisprudence. We may begin with Aristotle. For him, as for Plato before him, the idea of the State as an organism is fundamental. The State is founded, not simply upon community of place and a compact of mutual forbearance, and for the sake of mutual exchange: these conditions must exist, but do not in themselves constitute a State, which is a community, whose end is the $\epsilon\vartheta$ $\zeta\hat{\eta}\nu$ of all its members, and is complete in itself.[1] Consequently the State must not be governed for the good of the ruler: this is a perversion of its fundamental idea. The State is right $\kappa\alpha\tau\grave{\alpha}$ $\tau\grave{o}$ $\dot{\alpha}\pi\lambda\hat{\omega}s$ $\delta\acute{\iota}\kappa\alpha\iota o\nu$, when its aim is the common profit.[2] Kingly government is the best form of rule. The perfect king is one who is self-sufficient and superabundantly furnished with all that is good: his aim is therefore not his own advantage, but that of his subjects.[3] The special quality of the ruler consequently is prudence, of which statesmanship is only another form.[4] The legislator must specially have a care for the stability of the State; as it is the

---

[1] 'Pol.' iii, 9.   [2] *Ibid.* 6.   [3] 'Eth. Nic.' viii, 10.   [4] *Ibid.* vi, 8.

nature of a bad disposition to love change.[5] Laws must be maintained as long as possible.[6] Aristotle admits, however, that laws cannot be framed to meet all cases.[7] As to the origin of right in general, Aristotle lays down the following important distinction ('Eth. Nic.' v, 10): 'Of that which is just as between citizens, part is natural (φυσικόν), part is conventional (νομικόν). That is natural which has the same validity everywhere, and does not depend on our accepting or rejecting it.'

In the Roman jurisprudence the *jus naturæ*, which is immutable and the expression of eternal reason, is distinguished from the *jus civile*, the mutable law peculiar to any State, enacted for its own government: to the Roman jurists the *jus civile* is, of course, first and foremost the law of Rome.[8] We find also in the Roman jurisprudence the maxim of public utility as the end of legislation in those matters not defined by the law of nature. 'Law (*jus*) is spoken of in various ways: one, in which what is always fair and good is called law, as is the law of nature: the other, what is profitable (*utile*) to all or most in some State, as is the civil law.'[9] This maxim is specially applied to changes in the laws: 'In establishing new arrangements there should be an evident utility, to cause a departure from that law which has long seemed fair.'[1]

We find also in Roman law the notion of a penal example. Cf. 'Digest', 48, 19, 6, §1: 'Which is to be done, that being deterred by the example, they may offend the less.' So again 'Digest', 16, 3, 31: 'For he who has publicly deserved ill, ought also to labour in want, that he may be an example to others to deter them from ill deeds.' I cannot, however, find that this idea was ever applied to qualify the exercise of pardon by the Emperor, as Grotius applies it to the Divine forgiveness. The difference is natural; for Grotius here limits the conception of authority more than would have seemed fit to the Roman jurists. The exercise of pardon by the Emperor was thought of by them as so absolutely unconditioned, that maxims for its direction would have seemed out of

---

[6] *Ibid.* VII, 14.
[6] 'Pol.' III, 16. Ritter and Preller, 'Historia Philosophiæ Græcæ et Romanæ', 4th ed., 1869, p. 325.   [7] 'Pol.' III, 11 ; 'Eth. Nic.' v, 10.
[8] Cf. Gaius, 'Inst.' I, 1 ; Justinian's 'Digest', I, 3, 32, 1.
[9] 'Digest', I, 1, 11 ; cf. I, 1, 1, § 2 ; I, 1, 7, § 1.   [1] 'Digest', I, 4, 2.

place. Socinus rather is exactly in agreement with Roman law when he makes the exercise of pardon a part of the *jus domini*. Yet it is to be observed that Roman law knows the idea of the reverence of the legislator for his own law. 'It is a speech worthy of the majesty of the ruler for the prince to profess himself bound by the laws: to such a degree does our authority depend on the authority of the law, and in truth it is more than empire for royalty to submit to the laws.' [2]

The two streams of the Aristotelian philosophy and the Roman jurisprudence unite in the political philosophy of Thomas Aquinas. According to him (cf. *supra*, p. 208) law is the dictate of reason ('Summa Theologica', II, 1, 90, 1). There is consequently an eternal law in which the Divine law that governs the universe expresses itself (II, 1, 91, 1). In this eternal law the rational creature as such participates (II, 1, 91, 2): this participation constitutes the law of nature. Besides this there exists a human law, which consists of deductions from the first principles of the law of nature, supplying particular determinations in cases which it leaves indeterminate (II, 1, 91, 3). This human law as humanly established (*humanitus posita*) is called positive law (II, 1, 95, 2 and 3). Beyond the law of nature and of man there is also the Divine law, directing man to an end above nature (II, 1, 91, 4).

The law of nature, so far as it participates in the eternal law, is immutable, i.e. it is immutable in its first principles (II, 1, 94, 5); but its particular applications are capable of change, so that human law is always mutable (II, 1, 97, 1). The end of all law is the common good (II, 1, 90, 2). As the dictate of reason, it must tend to the ultimate end of man's being, which is happiness or beatitude: 'Wherefore it is necessary that law should especially have regard to that order, which consists in beatitude. Again, since every part stands in order to the whole, as the imperfect to the perfect, but one man is a part of the perfect community, it is necessary that law should peculiarly have regard to order with a view to the general happiness' (II, 1, 90, 2). Thomas refers to Aristotle, 'Ethic.' v, 1 and 'Pol.' I, 1.

Since human law is mutable, it might seem therefore that it

[2] Cod. IV, Theod. et Valent.

is always to be changed when any improvement in it is possible. But Thomas says: 'Human law is rightly changed, in so far as by its change care is exercised for the common advantage (*utilitati*). Yet the change of the law in itself involves some harm to the common welfare, because custom is of most avail to make laws observed. . . . Wherefore, when the law is changed, the constraining power of the law is lessened, in so far as custom is overthrown: and therefore human law ought never to be changed, unless in some other point as great a recompense is made to the common welfare as the loss which is suffers at that point. This happens when some very great and obvious advantage proceeds from the new statute, or because it is a case of the greatest necessity' (II, 1, 97, 2). Thomas refers in this context both to Aristotle, 'Pol.' II, 6 and to 'Digest', I, 4, 2. In II, 1, 97, 4 he discusses a further point, 'whether the governors of the people (*rectores multitudinis*) have the power of dispensation in the case of human laws'. He says: 'Dispensation properly imports the tempering of some common principle to individual cases. . . . Now it happens sometimes that a precept, which is for the good of the people for the most part, is not suitable to such and such a person or case: because by it either some greater good is prevented, or even some evil brought about . . . therefore, he whose it is to rule the people has the power of dispensation in human law, a power which depends upon his authority, so that, to wit, with regard to the person and cases where the law fails, he should give liberty for the non-observance of the precept of the law.' Thomas says again (ad 3): 'Natural law . . . cannot admit of dispensation: but in the case of the other precepts. . . . sometimes man is the instrument of dispensation. . . . As regards the Divine law, however, every man is in the same position which a private person occupies with regard to the public law, to which he is subject: wherefore just as with human public law, none has the power of dispensation but he from whom the law has its authority, or one to whom he has entrusted it: so with the precepts of the Divine law, which are from God, none has the power of dispensation but God, or one to whom He has especially entrusted it.'

Further, in II, 2, 67, 4 Thomas discusses whether a judge may lawfully remit a punishment (*pœnam relaxare*). He says:

'The judge is prevented for a twofold reason from freeing the guilty from punishment: firstly, from the point of view of the accuser, to whose right it sometimes pertains that the guilty should be punished, for instance, because of some injury committed against him, to undo which right is not within the arbitrament of any judge, for every judge must render to each man his own right: he is prevented in a second way from the point of view of the State, whose authority he exercises. It pertains to the good of the State that ill-doers should be punished: yet in this regard there is a difference between the inferior judges and the supreme judge, to wit, the Emperor, who has entrusted to him the public authority in plenary measure: for the inferior judge has not the power to free the guilty from punishment in opposition to the laws imposed on him by his superior . . . but the Emperor, who has the plenary power in the State, if the injured is willing to overlook the offence, may lawfully forgive the guilty, if it seem to be without hurt to the public advantage.'

It is clear that we have in the three sources just described, viz. the Aristotelian philosophy of the State, Roman jurisprudence, and the political philosophy of Thomas, the very circle of ideas which we have found in Grotius. Direct references, moreover, both in his 'Defensio' and in his famous work 'De Jure Belli et Pacis', where his political philosophy is developed, make clear his indebtedness in each case. See especially 'De Jure Belli et Pacis', Prolegomena, 42, 45, 52, 53; Lib. I, cap. I, 3, 2; cap. I, 9, 2; cap. I, 14, 1. Note also the reference to Thomas and to Duns in the note on cap. I, 10, 1: it may be observed that Duns ('Op. Oxon.' III, Dist. 37, qu. un.) agrees with Thomas that God can dispense with all but the law of nature, though he differs from Thomas as to the content of the latter (cf. *supra*, pp. 251f.). The agreement of Grotius with the doctrines of Thomas as to natural and positive law, dispensation and relaxation, is so close that it may be fairly said that the originality exhibited by Grotius in his 'Defensio' consists in applying these ideas, developed in another connexion by Thomas, to the subject of the work of Christ. The result, however, is to produce a theological view very considerably different from the scholastic doctrine of the work of Christ, which is based on the view, which Socinus follows, that God is to be thought in the matter simply as Sovereign (*princeps*), and which develops the consequences of this view in a thorough-going way. Thomas says that 'God has no superior; He Himself is the supreme and common good' (III, 46, 2), and argues therefore that His relation to man is one of private law. Duns, admitting that a legislator ought to seek in all things the common good, denies that this rule touches God, 'seeing that here the good of the Legislator is simply better than that of the community, whereas in the general case it is not so' (IV, Dist. XIV, qu. 2). On the other hand, Grotius, granting with the schoolmen and Socinus that God is *princeps,* maintains nevertheless that the common good is the end of His action, and so the relation of God to man is one of public law. He does not, like the schoolmen, regard the good of the universe as subsumed in the private good of God, but views it as something independent of Him, an external end towards which He works, though in harmony with His nature.

CHAPTER 6

THE FINAL FORM
OF THE PROTESTANT THEOLOGY

IN order to exhibit the doctrine of the work of Christ in the completed form which it took in the seventeenth century, in view of both the interconfessional controversies and those with the Socinians and Arminians, I select the names of Quenstedt (A.D. 1617–88)[1] as representative of the Lutheran, and of J. H. Heidegger (A.D. 1633–89)[2] for the Reformed orthodoxy. Gass[3] calls Quenstedt 'the high-water mark of (Lutheran) dogmatism', and speaks of his system as a 'pre-eminent work' summing up all its predecessors: 'the personal element disappears in the common spirit which he served'. Of Heidegger Schweizer[4] says that he 'works up the entire treasure of the previous (Reformed) dogmatic in an outstanding manner'. In particular, Heidegger makes use in reasonable measure of the federal method of Cocceius,[5] which distinguished the economy of Divine redemption into two different covenants or modes of religion: '(1) the covenant of nature or of works, i.e. the relation of man to God apart from the ideas of redeeming revelation and grace, as it was realised in its purity before all fell into sin, and though weakened is ever still present; (2) the covenant of grace, from the Fall onwards the only redeeming, truly saving mode of religion, moving through the threefold dispensation before the law, under the law, after the law or under the Gospel'.[6]

QUENSTEDT

According to Quenstedt the general object of theology, i.e. the systematisation of doctrine, is religion.

---

[1] 'Theologia didactico-polemica sive systema theologicum', 1685.
[2] 'Corpus theologiæ Christianæ', 1700.
[3] 'Geschichte der Protestantischen Dogmatik', vol. i, p. 357.
[4] 'Die Glaubenslehre der evangelisch-reformierten Kirche', vol. i, p. 133.
[5] Cocceius (A.D. 1603–69) developed his principles in his book. 'Summa doctrinæ de fœdere et testamentis Dei' (1648).　　　　[6] Schweizer, i, 104.

410

'The Christian religion is the method of worshipping the true God, prescribed in the Word, by which man, ravished from God by sin, is led to God by faith in Christ, as God and man, to be reunited to God, and to enjoy Him for ever.'[7]

The sum of true religion is contained in the Creeds. Besides the six œcumenical Creeds of the Ancient Church (Apostolic, Nicene, Constantinopolitan, Ephesian, Chalcedonian, Athanasian), Quenstedt recognises the various Lutheran symbols summed up in the 'Formula of Concord'.

In theology, however, the sole principle of knowledge is Scripture,[8] not human reason or natural theology.[9] Human reason since the Fall is corrupt, and is out of count as the principle of knowledge in things supernatural. An organic use of reason[1] is admitted for the interpretation of Scripture; but no metaphysical principles are allowed in theology except by way of illustration or of secondary proof.

In cap. v, after the definition of an article of faith as a particular point of revealed doctrine, an important distinction is drawn between fundamental and non-fundamental articles of faith. Those are fundamental which cannot be unknown or denied without the loss of salvation. Those, again, are primarily and absolutely fundamental which must be known: secondarily and less fundamental are those which must not be denied.

Quenstedt adopts the distinction, which goes back to Alexander,[2] of the fundamental articles into antecedent, constituent, and consequent. The constituent articles are the very saving faith itself, viz. the doctrines of God's love to men, the universal merit and satisfaction of Christ, and its appropriation in the individual.[3] The antecedent articles are the necessary presuppositions of this saving faith, such as that the Divine revelation is true: the consequent articles are the various implications of saving faith. Amongst these last Quenstedt places the kingly office of Christ, and the efficacy of the Word and sacraments.

This doctrine of principles is interesting (1) because of the distinction drawn between theology and religion; (2) because of its endeavour to simplify and unify theology by reducing it to

---

[7] 'Systema', pars ı, cap. ıı, sect. 1, Thesis 1.   [8] Cap. ııı, sect. 2.   [9] Porisma 2.
[1] In Grammar, Logic, Rhetoric, etc.   [2] *Supra*, p. 120.   [3] Th. 7.

the saving faith and its implications. Zwingli and Calvin had introduced the idea of religion into theology as a principle of unity: with them religion is implicit theology, and theology explicit religion. In Quenstedt, however, appears the notable idea that theology or the system of doctrine is a means to the end of religion, or the true worship of God. Quenstedt, it is true, again identifies religion with the Creeds, and so after all tends to make religion a less explicated form of theology: nevertheless in making a distinction between the two, he prepares the way for important future theological developments. Further, his notion of fundamental articles, and especially of absolutely fundamental or constituent articles, which are the very saving faith itself, is also a noteworthy advance in the endeavour to understand Christianity synthetically: we cannot but see in this movement towards a central truth the natural outcome of the Protestant principle. It was thoroughly in accordance with the highly synthetic character of Protestantism that Quenstedt should resume the ideas of Alexander as to antecedent, constituent, and consequent articles, with more opportunity of carrying them out to a successful issue. That, however, he includes the doctrine of the kingly office among the consequent articles, instead of in the *fides salvifica* itself, shows that a further theological advance in the synthetic comprehension of Christianity is still necessary.

Quenstedt's doctrine of the work of Christ is contained in 'Systema', pars III, cap. III, membr. 2, and contains two parts, a didactic (sect. 1) and a polemic (sect. 2).

Christ's office, which in general is described as mediatorial, is the function, belonging to the whole Person of the God-man, by which Christ has executed, and still executes in both natures, operating together, all things necessary both for the obtaining and the application of our salvation.

Quenstedt lays great stress throughout on the fact that it is the God-man in both His natures who is the subject of the mediatorial office. Accepting the division of the office of Christ under the three heads of Prophet, Priest, and King, he repeats in each case that the office is to be understood of the God-man in both natures.

412

'The prophetic office is a function of Christ as God-man, by which He has most sufficiently revealed to us by the counsel of the Most Holy Trinity the Divine will concerning the redemption and salvation of men, with the serious intention that in general all may come to a knowledge of heavenly truth.' [4]

From this prophetic office He is called in Scripture Prophet, Evangelist,[5] Master, Rabbi, Teacher, Bishop, etc.

The efficient cause of this office as regards its institution and the approval and destination of Christ for it is the whole Trinity. The Father sent the Son to reveal Him; the Son undertook the revelation; the Spirit anointed Him for the purpose.

The subject-matter of His revelation is, primarily, the truth of the Gospel with a view to the obtaining of faith and salvation by means of it, and, secondarily, the truth of the law, which is necessary to the leading of a holy life. With regard to the law, Christ had to give its true sense, and rescue it from the corruptions of the Pharisees.

Christ's revelation of the Divine will has been made partly immediately, partly mediately. Immediately, so far as Christ taught the Church Himself, and trained His disciples as the future teachers of the Church. Mediately, so far as Christ has made use of the vicarious service of the Apostles and their successors in the Christian ministry.

The end of the prophetic office is the bringing of all men to the knowledge of heavenly truth. An accidental result has been the blinding and hardening of some, the fault of which, however, is entirely with them, not with the Prophet and His work. The Calvinist doctrine, that the blinding and hardening of men other than the elect was directly intended by God, who withheld from them the grace necessary to believe the Gospel, is warmly repudiated by Quenstedt, who calls it 'an impious and execrable gloss and opinion'.[6]

'The priestly office is the function of Christ as God-man, by which He, according to the eternal counsel of God and the undertaking made by Himself, subjected Himself in time for our sakes, in our stead, and for our advantage, to the law of God, and by the perfect fulfilment of it, and endurance of its every penalty,

---

[4] Th. 3.   [5] Isa. 61:1.   [6] Th. 13, Observ. 5.

offered to the Divine justice a perfectly satisfactory obedience, and delivered us from the wrath of God, the curse of the law, sin, and all evils, which obedience He still exhibits to God the Father, and by His intercession obtains for us all necessary goods.'[7]

From the priestly office Christ is called in Scripture Priest, Salvation, Saviour, Jesus. The cause constituting Him a priest is the whole Trinity, but peculiarly the Father.

The priestly office has, then, two parts, viz. Christ's expiatory sacrifice, and His intercession. It was undertaken because of the sin of man, which stank in God's nostrils. Its end is the glory of God and the salvation of men, and its effects are (1) the reconciliation of God and sinful man, (2) our redemption from bondage to the Devil, and (3) our redemption from sin, both as regards its guilt, which is removed in justification, its slavery, which is taken away in sanctification, and its inherence, for the removal of which, however, we still have to hope.

Quenstedt next discusses the two parts of the priestly office in detail. First comes the expiatory sacrifice, or as it is termed in theology the satisfaction, 'by which Christ most perfectly satisfied for all the sins of the whole world and merited salvation'.[8] Then follows the intercession, by which He seeks the application of the salvation won.

It is admitted that the word satisfaction is not to be found in the Scriptures: but its equivalents are abundantly evident. Such are, payment for the robbery of the Divine majesty (Ps. 69:5), bearing our sins (Isa. 53:4), ransom (Mt. 20:28; 1 Tim. 2:6), propitiation (1 Jn 2:2; Rom. 3:24, 25), reconciliation (Rom. 5:10, 11; 2 C. 5:18), redemption (1 Pet. 1:18, 19; 1 C. 6:20; Gal. 3:13), and finally offering, expiation, sacrifice for sins, etc.

Quenstedt proceeds in an important discussion next to distinguish satisfaction and merit.

'The satisfaction and merit of Christ are not equivalents. For (1) the former compensates an injury done to God, expiates iniquity, pays a debt, and most fully delivers from eternal punishments; the latter restores us to a state of Divine good will, and acquires for sinners a gracious reward, or the grace of forgiveness of sins, justification, and life eternal.

[7] Th. 14.   [8] *Ibid.* 23.

414

'(2) The former stands as the cause, the latter as the effect. For merit originates out of satisfaction. Christ made satisfaction for our sins, and for the penalties which they had deserved, and thus merited for us the grace of God, the remission of sins, and life eternal.

'(3) Satisfaction was made to God, the Three in One, and to His justice, not to us, though it was made on our behalf. But Christ merited, and by His merit acquired somewhat, not for the Trinity, but for us.

'(4) The acts of exinanition, such as the fulfilment of the law, the passion and death, etc., are at once satisfactory and meritorious; but the acts of exaltation, such as the Resurrection, ascension into heaven, and sitting at God's right hand, are acts, not satisfactory but meritorious only, i.e. Christ did not make satisfaction for our sins by rising again and ascending into heaven, but by that very thing He merited for us eternal life and unlocked heaven.

'(5) Finally, satisfaction arises out of debt, but merit is a work entirely unowed and free. To it then by opposition corresponds reward or remuneration. Nevertheless all theologians do not observe this distinction, but include in the term merit also the satisfaction of Christ.'[9]

Satisfaction was made to God, the Three in One. For the whole Trinity was wroth with men for their offence, and because of the immutability of the Divine justice, the holiness of the Divine nature, and the truthfulness of the Divine threatenings, could not without satisfaction forgive sins or receive men to grace. The old objection, therefore, that no one can satisfy himself is here of no avail. For the Father being offended, the Son was offended also, nor is there any difficulty in the idea that the offended Son out of mercy should reconcile sinners to the Father.

God is therefore not to be thought of, as the Socinians represent Him,[1] as a mere creditor, but as a most just Judge, who, according to His absolute justice, demands strict satisfaction. The redemption, made to show the Divine justice,[2] proves that the penalty must either be exacted from sinners or from Christ their

[9] Th. 26.   [1] *Supra*, p. 368.   [2] Rom. 3:25.

Surety. If God could forgive sins without satisfaction, there would have been no need of such a redemption price.

Quenstedt follows Anselm [3] very closely in his view of the infinity of sin. 'The infinite God was offended by sin, and because sin is an offence, injury, and violation of the Infinite God, and is, so to speak, a Deicide, it has, in consequence, a certain infinite wickedness, not indeed formally (for considered in itself it can be greater or less) but objectively, and deserves infinite penalties; and so far also demanded an infinite price as satisfaction, which Christ alone could offer.' [4]

It is to be observed that by 'objectively' Quenstedt here means, according to the scholastic usage, 'ideally'. He goes on next to refute the scholastic doctrine that God, since He has no superior, could by His absolute power forgive sin without satisfaction. Such absolute power can neither stand (1) with the nature of God, which must be wroth with sin; (2) with His truth, in that He said to Adam, 'In the day that thou eatest thereof thou shalt surely die'; (3) with His holiness, which must oppose sin; (4) with His justice, which cannot remit sin without punishment.

Christ, then, made satisfaction for all sin, alike original and actual, past and future, venial and mortal, even the sin against the Holy Spirit. He also satisfied for all the penalties of sin, whether temporal or eternal. We are therefore freed by Him not only from punishment, but also from the wrath of God, the curse of the law, the power of the Devil and, finally, from hell and eternal death. The Devil had the power of death as our executioner. Although, then, temporal death still remains for us to undergo, we are delivered from the fear of it, seeing that it is no longer to be regarded as the punishment for our sins, Christ having endured for us both temporal and eternal death.

The satisfaction which Christ made, He made for all sinners without exception; for God truly and seriously wishes all men to be saved, even those who remain unsaved. This, the Lutheran doctrine, Quenstedt fortifies against the Calvinists with many Scriptures (Isa. 53:6; Mt. 20:28; Rom. 8:32; 2 C. 14:15; Heb. 2:9; 1 Tim. 2:6; Jn 1:29; 1 Jn 2:1, 2; Rom. 14:15; 1 C. 8:11; Heb. 6:4; 2 Pet. 2:1), which prove that Christ died

[3] *Supra,* p. 131.   [4] Th. 31.

equally for the elect and the non-elect. The last four texts distinctly refer to His dying for the reprobate.

'The means, by whose intervention the satisfaction was made, is the ransom consisting in the whole obedience of Christ, which includes (1) the most exact fulfilment of the law, (2) the endurance of the penalties deserved by us, the transgressors, or the most bitter passion. For by His doing, Christ expiated the sin, which man had most unjustly committed, and by His suffering bore the penalty, which man was justly to suffer. Hence the obedience of Christ, performed in our place, is usually called twofold: the active, which consists in the most perfect obedience to the law, and the passive, which consists in the most sufficient payment of the penalties which awaited us.' [5]

Both parts of the obedience of Christ were necessary that man might not only be freed from the wrath of God, but also might possess in the imputed righteousness of Christ a righteousness with which to stand before God. The distinction between the active and the passive obedience is, however, not so exact, but that the passive obedience includes the active. Bernard rightly says that Christ's action was passive and His passion active. [6]

The satisfaction of Christ was then a most exact and sufficient payment of all that we owed. Our debt was paid in full. There was no acceptilation.

'This payment of our whole debt, freely undertaken for us by Christ, and imputed to Him in the Divine judgment, was not sufficient from the Divine acceptation. For neither did God in this satisfaction of His free grace accept anything, which was not such in itself, nor did He abate anything of His right in the exaction of the penalty due from us and undertaken by our surety; but what the strictness of His justice demanded, all that Christ in His satisfaction endured; so that He felt the very pains of hell, though not in hell, nor for ever. There is seen indeed a certain temperament of mercy with the Divine justice, and a certain kind of relaxation of the law, in so far as the Son of God Himself offered Himself as surety to make satisfaction, in that

---

[5] Th. 37.

[6] Cf. 'Sermo De Passione Domini' (Feria IV Hebdomadæ sanctæ), 11 : 'Et in vita passivam habuit actionem, et in morte passionem activam sustinuit, dum salutem operaretur in medio terræ'.

the satisfaction offered by Him was accepted as if it were ours, and in that another person was substituted in the place of the debtors, yet all this derogates nothing from the satisfaction itself.

'The satisfaction of Christ is therefore most suffcient and perfect of itself and of its own intrinsic infinite worth; which worth arises (1) because the Person making satisfaction was the Infinite God, (2) because the human nature by the Personal union was made partaker of the Divine and Infinite Majesty, wherefore its passion and death was valued and reckoned of the same worth and price, as if it belonged to the Divine nature.' [7]

The aim of the satisfaction on God's part was on the one hand the manifestation of His justice and on the other the exhibition of His mercy. On our part it was the acquisition of perfect righteousness, eternal redemption, and salvation.

Finally, the period during which Christ made this satisfaction was from the first moment of His exinanition to the end of the three days of His death. All the acts of Christ during this time were satisfactory. His imprisonment for nine months in the Virgin's womb, His hunger, His thirst, etc., were all endured for us and for our sakes.

The second part of the priestly office is Christ's intercession. Here Quenstedt insists against the Calvinists that Christ makes intercession, not only in His human nature, but in both natures. The God-man moreover, pleading His sacrifice, is our sole Intercessor. He makes intercession especially to God the Father, as the Source of the Trinity, the other Persons, however, as one with the Father, not being excluded. The object of His intercession in general is all men. But there is a distinction. He does not intercede for those who have died impenitent, being rather their Judge; but only for those who are alive, whether the elect or the reprobate, with a view to their salvation. More peculiarly, however, Christ intercedes for the elect with a view to their sanctification and increase in spiritual blessings.

The foundation of Christ's intercession is the satisfaction and universal merit of the Intercessor. The form of it consists, however, not merely in the presentation of this merit, but in actual entreaty, though in a manner befitting Christ's Divine dignity.

[7] Th. 39, 40.

418

The end and aim of the intercession is on God's side the manifestation of His glory, and on the side of men the obtaining of salvation and all the blessings won for them by the passion and death of Christ.

The intercession of Christ, moreover, began before the world was, in that He was ordained from eternity as our Priest. Nor will it terminate with the end of the world, but will continue to all eternity—Christ being for the elect an eternal Priest.

Christ in His kingly office rules over all creatures not only as God, according to His Divinity, but also as man, according to His exalted humanity. From this office He is called in Scripture, King, Mighty One, Lord. According to it He rules over all creatures in His Kingdom of power, grace, and glory. Christ is the universal King, with no limit to His sway. It is one and the same power, which He exercises according to His Divine nature and according to His human nature, though the mode is varied. Christ's Divine Kingship is eternal, by His eternal generation; His human Kingship is in time, by the personal union of His humanity with His Divinity, its plenary exercise being in the state of exaltation.

The end and aim of the kingly office is the glory of our King and the salvation of all men. Its duration differs, according as we look at it from the Divine or the human side. Christ's Divine Kingship began when there were subjects to be ruled over; His human Kingship commenced with the first moment of the union of the two natures in Him, its plenary exercise, however, with His exaltation.

In His Kingdom of power Christ rules as God-man: from it He is named in Scripture Lord, the Mighty God, with the government upon His shoulder. In it He rules over all creatures. This Kingdom begins as regards Christ's Divine nature with the Creation: as regards His human nature its plenary exercise begins with His exaltation. 'The Kingdom of power is ordained to the end of the Kingdom of grace. The Messiah rules over the whole earth, but He rules also over His covenanted ones, empurpled with His blood, and delivered from the Kingdom of Satan.' [8]

The Kingdom of grace is administered by a threefold

[8] Th. 77.

hierarchy, (1) in the Church by the ministry, (2) in the State by the magistrates, (3) in the family by parents. Besides, in our common life every Christian is a bearer of this Kingdom.

The Word and the Sacraments are the instrument whereby this Kingdom of grace is exercised. Its object is according to the Divine will all men, but especially believers.

'For by the ministry of the Word and the Sacraments the King Messiah earnestly invites all men to participate in the benefits won by His passion and death, and to repentance, and, if they obey, receives them, justifies and sanctifies them, and by His Spirit rules over the justified, or believers, and defends them against all enemies, and that with all power, all instance, all grace.' [9]

The form of this Kingdom is an absolute monarchy. The kingly acts of Christ consist:

(1) in the appointment of Apostles, Evangelists, and Teachers of the Church, and their illumination, extraordinarily by the Spirit at Pentecost, and ordinarily by the Word;

(2) the gathering of the Church by the preaching of the Gospel and the administration of the Sacraments;

(3) regeneration and justification;

(4) renovation and sanctification;

(5) the bestowal of various gifts;

(6) the protection of believers;

(7) rule in the midst of His enemies, especially by overthrowing their designs, condemning them to hell, and governing even their consciences.

The place of this Kingdom of grace is the world. Its plenary exercise begins with Christ's exaltation. It will be terminated in form, though not in substance, by the end of the world.

In His Kingdom of glory the God-man is called in Scripture the King of Glory. He has this Kingdom from the Father, as He has His others. It is called in Scripture the Kingdom of God. In it Christ uses as His ministers, not only the angels, but the elect, who are His assessors in the last judgment. The subjects of the Kingdom are the good angels, and so far as the purpose of God goes, all men without exception. But only those, who believe

[9] Th. 80.

and persevere to the end, can become citizens of this Kingdom. In it Christ rules gloriously, to the praise of the Divine power, wisdom, mercy, and goodness, to the increase of joy in the angels, the fulfilment of the promises to believers, and the confusion of the devils and the damned. The place we do not know, though it truly exists. The consummation of the Kingdom of glory will be at the general resurrection of the dead, when all the elect shall be gathered and put in possession of their heavenly inheritance. Of this Kingdom there shall be no end.

The above is the content of the didactic section of Quenstedt's doctrine of the threefold office. The polemic section, which follows, is divided into ten questions dealing with particular controversies. In qu. 1 Quenstedt argues against Osiander, Stancarus, Lombard,[1] and Piscator,[2] that Christ is Mediator according to both natures; inasmuch as both natures were necessary to the mediatorial office. In qu. 2 he repudiates the Socinian doctrine,[3] that Christ was caught up into heaven to receive a Divine revelation, as utterly without basis in Scripture and unnecessary. Qu. 3 discusses whether Christ perfectly fulfilled the law in our place. Quenstedt here argues against Piscator and Socinus.[4]

Piscator objects against the orthodox doctrine, that Scripture clearly says that Christ died for us, nowhere that He lived a holy life for us. Quenstedt quotes in reply Mt. 5:17; Rom. 8:3, 4; Jn 17:19, and says further that His holy life is most closely connected with His death.

Again, Piscator and Socinus assert that Christ as man was bound to obey the law, and therefore offered His active obedience for Himself. Quenstedt replies: (1) Christ is Lord of the law.[5] (2) If He were a mere man, the above argument would be true; but His obedience is not merely the obedience of His human nature, but that of His Divine-human Person.

Again, Piscator says that Christ's death was unnecessary, if He satisfied for us by His life. Otherwise we have to admit that He only imperfectly satisfied by His life—which means that His holiness was imperfect. Quenstedt answers that Christ needed to

---

[1] *Supra*, pp. 172, 327, 330.   [2] *Supra*, p. 359.
[3] *Supra*, p. 363.   [4] *Supra*, pp. 359f., 370f.   [5] Mt. 12:8.

make satisfaction both for our guilt by His active, and for our punishment by His passive, obedience. He further says that the fallacy is one of division. Christ's active and passive obedience are two distinct parts of one whole obedience, which is destroyed if either is taken away.

Once more, Piscator urges that the law obliges either to obedience or to punishment, but not to both. Christ, however, has freed us from punishment: there was therefore no need that He should fulfil the law for us. Quenstedt replies that Piscator's dilemma is true, for the case of man before the Fall, but not for that of fallen man: of him the law demands both obedience, in that he is a rational creature, and punishment, because of sin.

Piscator also argues that, if Christ fulfilled the law for us, then we need not obey it. The answer, however, is that Christ did indeed free us from the claim of the law to obedience, yet gives us His Spirit whereby we spontaneously obey it.

Socinus objects, that one can no more fulfil the law for another than he can bear corporal punishment for another.[6] The answer is, that this is true of private, but not of public, persons.

Finally, Socinus argues, that Christ would have needed to fulfil the law as man as many times over as there were sinners to be saved.[7] Quenstedt admits this objection to be valid, if it were not for the Divine decree otherwise, and for the unique position of the God-man.

Qu. 4 discusses, whether Christ as a Prophet increased the moral law with new precepts and thereby made it more perfect. Quenstedt affirms with Gerhard[8] against the Romanists, Socinians, and Arminians,[9] that He only purified the law from Pharisaic corruptions, and explained it, or unfolded its content. Hence Christ is not a second Moses.[1] The Socinian view, both of the precepts and the promises of the Old Testament, limiting their scope to the present life, is false.

The subject of qu. 6 is: whether Christ, in our place, and for our sins, truly and fully satisfied the Divine justice by His death.

---

[6] *Supra*, pp. 369f.   [7] Cf. *supra*, p. 369.   [8] *Supra*, p. 354.
[9] *Supra*, pp. 195, 209, 373, 382.   [1] Jn 1:17.

Here, besides attacking the Scotist doctrine of the acceptation of Christ's merit and the general Romanist doctrine that Christ's satisfaction needs to be completed by ours, Quenstedt deals with Socinus and the Arminians, and even includes the Calvinists in his condemnation, so far as they give place to the Scotist doctrine.[2] Socinus, however, has the chief place among these adversaries: Quenstedt handles him as follows: First come the usual Scripture proofs, much as in Grotius, 'Defensio': Mt. 20:28; 1 Tim. 2:6; Isa. 53:4, 5; Ps. 69:5; 2 C. 5:21; Gal. 3:13; 1 Jn 1:7; Rom. 3:25; Col. 2:14; Rom. 5:10. Next follows a refutation of the enervation of these proof-texts by Socinus: Grotius is here freely utilised. Quenstedt repeats that if the word satisfaction is not in Scripture, the thing is abundantly evidenced. Finally we have a reply to the Socinian dialectic, of which we must carefully set out the chief points:

(1) It is said by Socinus that God can freely forgive, just as we can.[3] Quenstedt first introduces the old scholastic distinction between the absolute power of God and His power with order. Next, he points out that in the latter case, which is what concerns us, God is to be thought of not as a private person, but as the Judge of the whole world. As to the argument that God is not the Judge, but the Supreme Lord of the world, Quenstedt feels the force of it, but says that we must go by Scripture.

(2) As to the difficulty which Socinus makes, about the punishment of one for another,[4] Ezek. 18:4, 20 refers to strict law, not to the equity of the Gospel, which depends upon a special Divine decree.

(3) Socinus objects that the innocent at least cannot be punished for the guilty.[5] This objection is valid, if applied to the case of mere man, or of human judgment. But it is worthless, if applied to the Divine salvation.

(4) Socinus says that no one can be punished for the sins of another, unless those sins are the meritorious cause of the punishment, which is not the case with Christ, Who only died by occasion of our sins, not for them.[6] Scripture, however, teaches otherwise.

[2] Cf. Calvin, 'Inst.' II, 17, 1.
[4] *Supra*, pp. 369, 371, n. 2.   [5] *Supra*, p. 371.
[3] *Supra*, p. 368.
[6] *Ibid.*

(5) According to Socinus Christ did not undergo the debt we owed, this being eternal death.[7] The answer is, that He did undergo it qualitatively, in that God deserted Him.

(6) Socinus says that remission and satisfaction are contrary in their very nature.[8] God, however, is said to remit sins, not in that He receives no satisfaction, but that He does not receive it from us.

(7) The Socinians urge that the guilt of sin still remains unless we believe: therefore Christ cannot have satisfied for it.[9] The answer is, however, that we must distinguish between the obtaining of salvation and the application of the salvation won.

Qu. 7 deals with the interconfessional controversy whether Christ died for all men, expiated the sins of all, and won for all salvation and eternal life.[1] Quenstedt divides his Calvinist adversaries into three classes: (1) the rigid, who say absolutely that Christ satisfied only for the elect; (2) the less rigid, who say that Christ satisfied sufficiently for all, efficiently for the elect only; (3) the School of Saumur,[2] Amyraut,[3] Cameron,[4] etc., who teach hypothetic universalism, that Christ died for all, if only they believe, presupposing, however, an absolute decree of election restricting the gift of faith. Here, in the first place, Quenstedt urges the Scripture proofs for universal redemption, already set out in his didactic section. He points out against the School of Saumur that Scripture nowhere speaks of universal redemption 'on condition of faith'. Besides, what is the object and cause of faith cannot have faith as its condition. As to the strict Calvinist restriction of the 'all', for whom Christ died, to the elect only, there is no warrant for it.

Next Quenstedt refutes the arguments of the Calvinists. They urge that Christ would not pray for the non-elect:[5] it is not therefore possible that He would die for them. The answer is, that we must distinguish between general and special petition: Christ

[7] *Supra*, p. 371.   [8] *Supra*, p. 369.

[9] Quenstedt refers to Schlichthing, 'Comm. in Rom.' III, 24. Cf. also *supra*, pp. 371f., for somewhat similar arguments on the part of Socinus himself.

[1] *Supra*, p. 357.   [2] *Supra*, p. 358.

[3] Moses Amyraut (Amyraldus, A.D. 1596–1664), one of the chief doctors of the School of Saumur.

[4] John Cameron (A.D. 1579–1625). 'The liberalism that distinguished the famous School of Saumur points back to him as its author' (Maury, in 'Realencyclopädie für protestantische Theologie und Kirche', 3rd ed., vol. iii, p. 690).   [5] Jn 17:9.

refused to make the latter only. Again, the Calvinists say that those for whom Christ died, He reconciled to the Father, and those for whom He won reconciliation have not their sins imputed. Scripture, however, does not so teach. The Calvinists object that, if Christ died for all, He died even for those already damned, which was vain. Quenstedt replies that it was not vain, for they could when alive have apprehended Christ's merit. Once more, the Calvinists urge that God was unjust if He demanded payment twice, first of Christ, then of unsaved sinners. The answer is that the latter pay for their further sin of unbelief. Finally, it is said that Christ is only half a Redeemer, if He acquires salvation, but does not apply it. The fault, however, is not in Him but in us.

The eighth question is, whether Christ by His obedience merited anything for Himself. Here Quenstedt attacks Lombard,[6] Thomas,[7] Socinus,[8] and others, That Christ merited only for us follows not only from the dignity of His Person, but from the *communicatio idiomatum,* whereby His human nature (except so far as our redemption required) lacked nothing. Besides, if He merited worship for Himself, how then could He have been worshipped in His earthly life? Moreover, as His merit and satisfaction are really one, if He merited for Himself, then He also satisfied for Himself, which is absurd. Besides, as He transfers the fruit of His merit to us, He can have nothing for Himself. As to the name above every name, He had it already by right. Quenstedt repeats against the Romanists the argument of Calvin,[9] that they confound the relation of antecedent and consequent with that of cause and effect. To the Socinian argument, that if Christ did not merit for Himself He could not merit for us, he replies that He could do this, just because He was not mere man, but God.

Qu. 9 discusses, whether one drop of the blood of Christ would have sufficed for our redemption.[1] Quenstedt says that the phrase has no doubt a pious meaning. One drop of Christ was indeed intrinsically of infinite worth. Nevertheless Scripture alone can teach us as to the actual requirements of God.

[6] *Supra*, p. 169. [7] *Supra*, p. 217.
[8] *Supra*, pp. 370f. [9] *Supra*, p. 344.
[1] Cf. Luther, 'Comm. in Gal.' I, 195 (quoted above, p. 298).

The tenth and final question is, whether Christ even now intercedes in heaven for us. Quenstedt argues against Socinus [2] that Christ truly intercedes: in opposition to the Socinian argument, that Christ as Lord of all needs not to pray, he points out that Scripture does not oppose, but couples, His Lordship and His intercession.

HEIDEGGER

Heidegger's doctrine of principles is contained in his 'Corpus theologiæ Christianæ', loc. I, 'Of theology in general', He admits the existence of natural theology after the Fall, repudiating the Socinian view [3] that there is no natural theology. Revelation, however, is necessary for salvation.

'Revealed theology is the doctrine concerning God, as reconciling sinful man to Himself in Christ, and as He is by the same to be duly known and worshipped: it is sought from God, as He reveals it in His word, and is framed with sincere purpose, as in His sight, for the salvation of sinful man and the glory of the name of God' (14).

The sum and essence of Christian theology (which Heidegger identifies with religion) is defined as follows:

'That without doubt is the true and saving theology and religion, which teaches the true God by proceeding from the true God, i.e. from His indubitable revelation; . . . next, which elicits and sets forth out of the inmost secrets of the Divine will, as disclosed by revelation, that only means, which every right conscience can judge to be suitable to reconcile the sinner to the angry and just Judge and inexorable Punisher of sin by due satisfaction of His justice, and finally unfolds from the same revelation the worship, worthy of the one and only God Who sanctifies the sinner, and alone pleasing to Him' (16).

Theology moreover has a fundamental article. Christ Himself is the foundation of our faith (49), but only as He is believed (50). The fundamental article, therefore, which is one, though differently expressed in various parts of Scripture (51), is this, that Christ is the Saviour of the world (52). Since, however, this

---

[2] *Supra*, p. 375.　　　[3] *Supra*, p. 362.

statement saves not by the mere sound of words, but by its meaning, it implies the doctrines of the Trinity, the Incarnation, sin, the law, the Spirit, and the Resurrection of Christ and ourselves.

We have therefore in Heidegger, as in Quenstedt, the attempt to reduce Christianity to an essential faith and its implications, though in a somewhat different way. Theology and religion are, however, not distinguished.

Heidegger's doctrine of the threefold office is contained in loc. XIX. Like Quenstedt he defines the office of Christ in general as mediatorial.

'That office is a mediation between God and man; or that function of the Mediator, Jesus Christ, which, according to the will of the Father and the unction of the Holy Spirit, He voluntarily undertook to reconcile and save the sinners who had been given to Himself, and, according to both His natures, alone accomplished and accomplishes' (2).

Such is the general definition; where already at the very beginning of the doctrinal statement the special Calvinistic point of view is indicated, in that Heidegger says that Christ undertook His work to save those sinners who had been given Him, i.e. the elect.

The next discussion is that of the Scriptural names describing the mediatorial office. These are innumerable. The chief of them, however, besides the name 'Mediator' are 'Jesus' and 'Christ' or 'Messiah'. Jesus means Saviour. Christ or Messiah signifies anointed. Whereas Quenstedt restricts the name Jesus to the priestly office, and Messiah to the kingly office, Heidegger follows Calvin who applies both names to the office of Christ as a whole before its division into its several parts, and who indeed saw in the name Christ according to its significance, 'the anointed', the common unity of the kingly, priestly, and prophetic offices.[4] There is no doubt that Calvin and Heidegger here express more truly than Quenstedt the Protestant synthesis. Quenstedt's separation of the offices here is parallel with his mistake in reckoning the doctrine of the kingly office among not the fundamental, but the consequent articles.

[4] *Supra*, p. 340.

427

To continue with the statement of Heidegger: the cause of the mediatorial office is the entire Trinity, but each Person operates in a distinct way. The Father, who is the source not only of the Godhead, but also of all its operations, sent the Son into the world to save sinners. To the Holy Spirit is assigned the anointing of Christ with the necessary gifts for His work, though not so as to exclude the operation of the Father, Who also Himself anointed the Son by giving Him His Spirit. Finally, the Son Himself undertook the mediatorial office, and in His own Person carried it out.

This office, moreover, He undertook and executed according to both natures. 'For, just as after the Incarnation there are two natures in the Son of God, and two principles of action in one hypostasis: so the operations of both natures concur in the work of mediation, and the results produced by those operations are attributed to both natures' (15).

Heidegger warmly repudiates the view of Lombard, Thomas, and Stancarus [5] that Christ is Mediator only according to His human nature. Especially noteworthy is his treatment of the time-honoured argument drawn from Augustine in favour of this view.[6]

'It is mere nonsense, not reason, to object that the Mediator, as the mean, ought to be at a distance from God, and so cannot be the Mediator according to His Divinity. For by the same reason He could not be the Mediator according to His humanity, and so could not be Mediator at all. For, as the mean, He must also be at a distance from men. But it is enough that, as God-man, and as performing the mediatorial office, He is at a distance from both God and man. For neither God as such, nor yet man separately, is God-man. And the Mediator is distinguished from God, not according to the nature of His Godhead, but according to the dispensation of His office; just as He is distinguished from man not according to His humanity, but according to the dispensation and relation of the mediatorial office. If Christ cannot

[5] *Supra*, pp. 172, 215, 330.
[6] Cf. Augustine, 'Conf.' x, 42, 67 : 'Now the Mediator between God and man ought to be partly like God, partly like man ; lest being wholly like man, He might be far from God ; or being wholly like God, He might be far from man, and so could not be a Mediator.'

428

be Mediator according to His Godhead, because no one can be a mediator with Himself or for Himself; then neither can He be Mediator according to His humanity, since no one, for whom He acts as Mediator, is the same with Him. It is therefore quite one thing to be the Son of God and another to be Mediator; one thing to be offended as God, another to act as Mediator as God-man' (17).

The work of the Mediator is the reconciliation of man and God, not a mere leading of man to the love of God, as Socinus imagines, but first of all the reconciling of God to man, and only then of man to God.

'For God, not being first reconciled, is so far from what man can love that He rather, as the Judge, Who curses the sinner and threatens him with death, cannot but be dreaded and hated. . . . But when man is reconciled by the blood of Christ, then at length that reconciliation becomes an argument to persuade men of the love of God and a reason for loving Him, thanking Him, and glorifying Him' (23).

Moreover, in this matter of reconciliation the merit of Christ's work must not be separated from its efficacy, as is done by the Remonstrants,[7] 'so that they, as regards the actual reconciliation and salvation of men, leave little or nothing to Christ the Mediator' (24). The Remonstrants assign to the merit of Christ one object, viz. all men and every man; to the efficacy of His work another object, viz. those only who believe and persevere in faith. In this way, however, they altogether overthrow and destroy the idea of merit.

'For they take away (Christ's) merit, since they deny that Christ has merited for anyone the remission of sins, the Holy Spirit, and eternal life, and persist that He has only obtained for the Father the right and the power of compassionating men, and of prescribing to them conditions of salvation such as He will; asserting, moreover, with a rough and harsh voice, that the merit of Christ has not regard to men immediately, and that without injury to it all men can be damned, if no one will observe the prescribed conditions; whilst they deny its efficacy, in that they make calling, faith, and new obedience so depend upon the choice

[7] The Arminians were so called from their manifesto, the 'Remonstrance' of 1610.

of man, that the will of man alone is the cause why some only repent and believe, and others do not; so that this alone and not the grace of Christ is efficacious unto salvation, and this efficiency has reference to salvation, not to faith, since it follows upon, and does not precede, faith inborn without the merit and efficacy of Christ' (24).

Such views, Heidegger declares, work like a gangrene in the Christian religion, make Christ as Mediator a pauper, and crucify Him afresh. On the contrary, the very essence, and the chief glory and fundamental article of Christianity, is that Christ is Mediator and Saviour completely and indivisibly by both merit and efficiency.

'He is Saviour by merit, in that He has obtained salvation for us by His blood;[8] by efficiency, in that He bestows the salvation, which He has obtained, and preserves it, when once bestowed' (25).

The efficiency is the end or fruit of the merit: without it Christ would have died in vain. Neither therefore is the merit wider than the efficiency or the efficiency narrower than the merit. If the efficacy of Christ's merit were left in the hands of men, Christ might lose all fruit of His merit. But, on the contrary, 'righteousness, the forgiveness of sins, and salvation flow to us from the merit of Christ, as the proper effect from the proper cause; and for whom Christ has merited the forgiveness of sins, the Holy Spirit, and life eternal, to those same He grants and applies these gifts' (25).

The office of Mediator is common to every condition of the Church after the Fall. But Christ was in one way Mediator before the Incarnation, and is Mediator in another way after it. Before the Incarnation Christ was Mediator by His future merit. Merit belongs to the order of moral causes, which can operate before they are actually existent. Thus before the Incarnation Christ was Surety and Intercessor for the elect. After the Incarnation, in the state of exinanition Christ was Mediator and Saviour by present merit, and is now in the state of exaltation Saviour by past merit.

The office of the Mediator, as the title Messiah shows, is

[8] Ac. 20:28.

430

threefold, Prophetic, Priestly, and Kingly; for these three orders of men, prophets, priests, and kings, were anointed under the Old Testament. The reason of the threefold office is that Christ, as Prophet, must instruct us by His doctrine concerning salvation, as Priest, must acquire it through His blood by satisfying the law, and as King, must bestow it, when acquired, by His Spirit. The order of the execution of the offices was that named above. First Christ was Prophet in His earthly ministry, then Priest on the cross, now He is King in heaven. But the order of the Divine purpose is different. Here the kingly office comes first, as the end of Christ's mediation, since God before all things gave to Christ as King many brethren to bring to glory. Then follows the priestly office, as the next means to this end, since in this way it was given to Christ to bring in righteousness. Last of all follows the prophetic office, in that it was given to Christ to announce righteousness, salvation, and glory, to the end of the obedience of faith.

'The prophecy of Christ is that, whereby He fully and clearly revealed the will of God concerning our salvation, as it was immediately manifested to Him' (28). Heidegger differs from Quenstedt in making the prophetic office begin under the Old Testament. Christ even then began His work, as the angel of Jehovah appearing to the patriarchs, and revealing the Divine will of salvation. But the chief work of His prophetic office began with His Incarnation, and that indeed from His conception, in inspiring the evangelical canticles that proclaimed His advent among men. Heidegger here repudiates, as unscriptural and as diminishing the glory of Christ in His prophetic office, the notion of Socinus[9] that He needed in the time of His fasting to be caught up into heaven to receive a Divine revelation. The public performance of Christ's work, however, began with His baptism. In the first place, there was an explanation of the true righteousness required by the law. Christ was no new lawgiver, but a teacher and prophet expounding the law.

'Although He brought in a law of faith, and commanded obedience to it, and so far is called Lawgiver, and moreover enjoined legal precepts and the practice of charity, besides

[9] Supra, pp. 363f.

inscribing the law of faith and of the love of God on the hearts of believers; yet He was by no means properly called a lawgiver, bringing in a new law of works, by whose performance sinful man might avail to obtain righteousness and salvation. For otherwise there would have come into being a new God, a new worship, a new God of Israel' (34). Christ came properly, not to destroy the law, but to fulfil it by making satisfaction to it. Heidegger here opposes the Roman teaching that Christ is a lawgiver, also the similar doctrine of Socinus.

Christ indeed commanded not a few things belonging to the love of God and our neighbour, on which the whole law hinges. But His precepts were not exactly new, but were an exposition of the existing law, which moreover He enforced by His example. His precepts were therefore at once old and new. Even the precept of self-denial and bearing the cross was not altogether new, witness amongst other examples the conduct of Moses as illustrated in Heb. 11:25, 26. Christ certainly in His sermon on the mount vindicated the law from the corruptions of the Scribes and Pharisees; but He was far from wishing to add to the old law a new one.

The principal parts of Christ's teaching, however, have to do with the Gospel. Above all things He preached the coming of the Kingdom of God, repentance, and faith. His message especially included the doctrine of the saving grace and mercy of God towards sinners, and that of the sacraments instituted by Himself, as seals of the covenant of grace, and again, that of the Church, etc.

Along with Christ's prophetic doctrine went a Divine efficacy, which was still continued, when after His exaltation He sent the Spirit from heaven, and taught the Church. Christ, moreover, confirmed His message by His miracles, His example, and His martyr-death. Yet Christ is not, as the Socinians think, Saviour in virtue of His prophetic office alone, apart from the priestly and the kingly offices, which give the prophetic office its solid basis. The priestly office especially is the soul of the work of Christ.

'The Priesthood or priestly office of Christ is that, by which He, as being constituted by the Father a Priest, by means of the

432

obedience of His exinanition even unto the death of the cross, in offering Himself up by the Eternal Spirit, made perfect satisfaction to God the Father for the sins of those who were given Him, and continually intercedes with the Same for us' (55).

The external condition of Christ's Priesthood is, that He is an eternal Priest after the order of Melchizedek, appointed by oath: the internal condition is that He was righteous, and had that righteousness, or merit, which the law demands as the basis of a right to life. He is Himself both Priest and Victim; He was in particular an expiatory victim both for sin and for guilt. His sacrifice, like those of the Old Testament, has three parts: (1) the voluntary offering of Himself as a victim, (2) His death, (3) His presentation of His sacrifice in heaven. By His voluntary offering up of Himself Christ won faith for His Gospel, and gave an example of obedience to God and love to men, of hope of the promise of glory, and of humility and patience. By it also He won power over men and grace in the eyes of the Father, enabling Him to exercise a powerful advocacy with God for men. The second part of Christ's sacrifice, His death, is the expiation of our sins and the satisfaction to God for them.

'For God, in that He is of the utmost clemency and mercy, willed to save certain sinners: and in that He is of an equal justice, willed not to save them without the expiation of sin, or the demonstration of His righteousness in punishing sin: and indeed could not do so, since the righteousness, which punishes sin, is natural to Him. . . . Besides, by the Gospel the law or the ordinance of the law is not abrogated, nor without involving the mutability of God could it be. . . . For the law of works, threatening the sinner with death, and promising life to the obedient, could not be otherwise ratified than by an infliction of death on the sinner, or on Him who took the place of the sinner, and by the grant of life to none but the obedient, or to Him who took the place of the obedient, and performed the ordinance of the law' (65).

Heidegger now expends much time in showing that the doctrine of vicarious satisfaction is Scriptural, bringing forward the usual proofs from the death of Christ being called a sacrifice, redemption, ransom, etc. He attacks the Socinian view, that

433

redemption is to be understood as a metaphor.[1] If there is salvation without satisfaction, God has given His law in vain; His holiness, His wisdom, and His veracity all suffer. 'In a word God would in this way simply have denied Himself' (74). Again, Christ would appear to have done no more than any just man, and to have shed His blood in vain, having suffered the penalty of sin without result. Finally, we should have no confidence to appear before the throne of grace in view of the justice of God, who cannot bear to look upon sin. The ends which Socinus attaches to the death of Christ are not according to Scripture:

(1) That the death of Christ is a proof of the forgiveness of sins.[2] On the contrary Scripture makes it the cause of forgiveness. Moreover, Socinus makes Christ's death no more than a martyr's, whereas Scripture makes it unique. Again, Christ's miracles were sufficient proof of the forgiveness of sins: it is the singular eminency of His death, that it is the cause of remission.

(2) That Christ by His death has obtained the right of pardon.[3] This reason Socinus himself overthrows by admitting that Christ possessed it in His lifetime.[4] Besides the Scripture words, expiation, redemption, etc., do not point in this direction.

(3) That in the death of Christ is given us an example of patience and obedience.[5] This is indeed a secondary end of the death of Christ, but does not rank as the primary end.

(4) That Christ's death persuades us to faith, or hope of attaining eternal life, which is necessary to obtain the remission of sins.[6] This reason is absurd. 'For how can the so bloody death of a most innocent man in itself avail to persuade us that the highest joys are prepared by God for those who live holily?' (76). Socinus himself shows the absurdity of his doctrine, by attributing our persuasion to faith directly to the Resurrection, which, however, required that death should precede it. But if this were the meaning of Scripture, it would refer the forgiveness of sins to Christ's Resurrection, ascension, and sitting at the right

---

[1] *Supra*, p. 366.   [2] *Supra*, pp. 365f.   [3] Cf. *supra*, p. 391, n. 3.
[4] In 'De Servatore', II, cap. VI, Socinus says that one reason why Christ is said to have taken away our sins (cf. *supra*, pp. 366f.), is that He, as Mediator, in His lifetime, forgave sins by the authority committed to Him by the Father. Socinus refers to Mt. 9:6 ; Mk 2:10 ; Lk. 5:24.   [5] *Supra*, p. 366.   [6] *Supra*, pp. 365f., 374.

hand of the Father, rather than to His death. The frequent linking of the remission of sins with His death, however, shows that the connexion between them is a close, not a distant, one.

But the Socinians say that satisfaction is nowhere mentioned in Scripture, and is impossible.[7] As to the former point, it is true that Scripture nowhere uses this forensic word to describe Christ's work. 'But the importunity and sophistry of enemies compelled the Church to make use of it to signify the voluntary payment of the penalties which we owed, made for us by Christ as our Surety' (78). If the word be not in Scripture, the thing is there. As to the impossibility of satisfaction, although God could not punish the innocent against his will for the sins of the guilty, there is absolutely nothing to prevent God from punishing him instead of the guilty, where substitution is willingly undertaken. Again, the law forbids the justification of the guilty in himself, but not in view of the expiation of sins by a surety. Moreover, when Christ had undertaken this vicarious satisfaction, He could not, in view of His obedience, suffer eternal death like the damned. The law justifies every one that obeys it, and glorifies everyone who is just. Justice, therefore, presupposing the decree that some should be saved, required that Christ's obedience should be rewarded, and that He should obtain righteousness and life for those for whom He obeyed. He did not therefore undergo eternal death, but, as God, conquered death, and, as just and obedient, obtained His reward. All the Socinian talk about God's absolute power is mere folly. God's absolute power can do what it will, but not what is unworthy of Himself. If God denies His justice, He denies Himself. He is no private creditor, but Ruler of the universe, and to Him as such belongs the law of punishment, which is not that of absolute sovereignty, to punish or leave unpunished, as He pleases. He is a Judge, and must do justice, punishing the guilty and rewarding the meritorious. But it is said that, if God as Ruler and Judge could so far relax His law as to admit a substitute to make satisfaction, then He could relax it so far as to do without satisfaction altogether. Heidegger, however, unlike Quenstedt,[8] will not admit that there is any relaxation of the law at all in

---

[7] *Supra*, p. 369.   [8] *Supra*, pp. 417f.

vicarious satisfaction. He calls this a preposterous opinion, and a clear betrayal of the cause.

'There is therefore to be recognised in the transference of punishment to Christ as Surety no relaxation of the law, but its execution; because, since Christ took our place in bearing punishment, not being separated or divided from us, but most closely joined with us, as Brother appearing on behalf of His brother, . . . whatever He did and suffered for the sake of our salvation, we, as if one with Him, are held to have done and suffered' (81).

Christ's obedience and death are therefore ours. 'In Him we underwent the punishment of sin: in Him we fulfilled the righteousness of the law, are absolved from sin, are pronounced just, and the heirs of life. But by whom? By God, as the just Lawgiver and Judge, not in opposition to, but in agreement with the law, which is eternal, immutable, and irrevocable' (81). There is thus the most absolute satisfaction of God, even in the bestowal of grace.

Finally, the free remission of sins is not opposed to the reality of Christ's satisfaction. 'For it is not simply gratuitous, but with the condition of satisfaction, not indeed on the part of the sinner himself, which alone is incompatible with the grace of forgiveness, but on the part of Another, Christ the Surety' (83).

In order to complete the account of Heidegger's doctrine of the obedience of Christ, we may at this stage conveniently turn to loc. XI, 'Of the covenant of grace', where he explains the necessity and possibility of Christ's obedience, active as well as passive. Christ as our Surety undertook that obedience to the law, which the first Adam owed through undertaking the covenant of works and then violating it. As the Son of God, Christ was subject to no law, but could nevertheless bind Himself to do that which was necessary in order to an efficacious fulfilment of the law by Himself as Mediator. As regards His Divinity, this work was nothing unworthy of God. But since the obedience of the Mediator was a word of the God-man, the concurrence of the Divine nature in it gives infinite worth to the finite obedience of the man. Again, this very obedience, so far as it is subjection under the law, is the work of the Son of God Himself, emptying Himself and taking the form of a servant in obedience to the

Father. To sum up, Christ's exinanition and the efficacy added to His obedience is the work of His Deity: His subjection under the law of the love of God and of His neighbour is the work of His humanity: His complete obedience availing for salvation is the work of His Person, each nature performing its own part in communion with the other. Moreover, the obedience of Christ had to be consummated both by doing and suffering. Since sinful man was bound both to obedience and to undergo punishment, it was demanded of Christ, as the Mediator taking the sinner's place, that He should both do for man what belongs to the law, and suffer for the transgressor of the law that with which the law threatens him.

'This obedience, then, which was to be consummated both in doing and suffering, had to be purely vicarious; so that Christ had neither to fulfil the law for Himself, nor to die for Himself' (18). It is no difficulty, that Christ, as man and as a creature, owed God obedience and subjection. He did not owe it, like Adam, under the covenant of works, as the condition of obtaining eternal life, but, like the angels and the saints in heaven, under no legal condition. Thus His assumption of Adam's place was purely gratuitous.

Such is the doctrine of the twofold obedience as stated in loc. XI: we shall now return to loc. XIX, and take up the argument at the point where we left it. Heidegger proceeds to distinguish between satisfaction and merit, inasmuch as Christ both made satisfaction to the Father, and merited life for us. 'Merit, in general, is a work which is fittingly followed by a reward' (84). Moreover, merit, in the strict sense, is to be understood as a work that obtains some good, not by mere grace and promise, but by justice, according to the measure of its worth and the rule of strict equivalence. A work to which some good is promised out of proportion to its intrinsic worth (as, for instance, the work of Adam, if he had perfectly performed the law) may be called *meritum ex pacto*. But merit, in the strict sense, attaches to Christ's works alone, not indeed to those which were merely natural, but to those which were moral and freely undertaken by Him out of love to God and His neighbour even unto death. Here all the conditions of merit, in the strict sense, are found. Christ's works of obedience were of His own, as the works of the God-man. They were unowed, being freely undertaken by Him as our Surety. They have, on account of the dignity of Christ's Person, an exact equivalence with the reward which they have obtained.

This last point is further worked out as follows: 'Although this merit (of Christ) is not infinite extensively, in so far as all goods are not included within its ambit, since at least He did not merit for Himself, at the instant of His conception, the hypostatic union and the vision of the Word; yet His merit is infinite intensively, since it is so great that it cannot be exhausted or equally compensated by any finite reward' (85). It is to be reckoned in view of the innocence, holiness, and obedience of His human nature, and of the eminency of that nature, not in itself, but as united to the Word, but above all in view of the dignity of the Person of the God-man, Whose holiness, as being truly God, is infinite.

'This dignity of Christ's Person cannot but add much to the value of His obedience and to the acceptability of the same with God, so that it was far more as regards merit and acceptability that this One should suffer, than if the whole human race together had undergone eternal punishment. Yet the value of the merit arises, neither from Christ's obedience alone, nor from the dignity of His Person alone, but from both, and from the right of the Son, Whom the Father loves, in Whom alone He has good pleasure, and Whose glory He seeks, and from the right of the righteous Servant, without exclusion also of His death, in which was the crown and consummation of His obedience' (85).

To take away Christ's vicarious satisfaction, however, is to take away His merit also. The Socinians, Ostorodorus [9] and Veidovius,[1] profess to acknowledge the merit of Christ 'in so far as by His obedience He obtained for Himself glory and heavenly power, and in consequence obtained for us, who believe, eternal salvation, and by His work purchased it as a reward,[2] yet so that this merit is not opposed to the grace of God, but subordinate to it'. Heidegger, however, insists that Christ's merit is merit, in

[9] Ostorodt, d. A.D. 1611. [1] Woidowski, d. after A.D. 1619.
[2] Phil. 2:9 ; Isa. 53:12.

438

the strict sense. The connexion between His obedience and our eternal salvation is no loose one, as the Socinians imagine, but of the closest. Christ merited at once for Himself as Head, and for us as His body, glory and life eternal. Apart from this connexion there was no need for Christ, who was rich, by His work to acquire heavenly power as a kind of reward.

As to the subordination of Christ's merit to the Divine grace, Calvin,[3] taking the word grace loosely, rightly says that 'if anyone wishes to oppose Christ simply and by Himself to the Divine grace, there will be no room for merit'; for without grace there would be no gift of Christ, nor acceptance of His merit by God for human salvation. But as far as concerns the merit of Christ's obedience, there is here no grace nor overlooking of imperfection on God's part, but strict justice.

Finally, neither does it take away the merit of Christ that we assert that He has made satisfaction to God, though we recognise that there is no room for merit in the payment of a debt. For He made satisfaction, not to His own creditor, but to another's, paying a debt for others, in which kind of case satisfaction and merit well agree together.

The effects of Christ's satisfaction and merit were as follows:

(1) Above all, that He manifested the holiness of God as the Justifier of the ungodly without unrighteousness.

(2) He established the gospel of justification by faith, manifesting the love of God, Who gave His Son to die for us.

(3) Besides, He obtained reconciliation with God, and

(4) Deliverance from sin, from the writing over against us, and from bondage to rudiments, together with peace between Jews and Gentiles.

(5) Beyond all this, He merited, for those for whom He made satisfaction, the Holy Spirit, regeneration, and faith.

The Romanists are therefore not much better than the Socinians, in that they limit the effect of the satisfaction of Christ to the removal of original sin and of actual sin before baptism, moreover of mortal sin, but not venial sin, after baptism, and as far as concerns the guilt of sin and the obligation of eternal punishment, but not as concerns that of temporal punishment;

[3] 'Inst.' II, 17, 1.

in that they also assert that for what remains men must make satisfaction for themselves; and in that they deny that Christ in His soul suffered the pains of hell, so as to free us from the tortures of hell.[4]

The Remonstrants [5] also all but abolish the satisfaction and merit of Christ, asserting that Christ died, in order that God the Father might have the right to contract with us anew, on what terms He pleased, concerning forgiveness and justification. But while Christ's obedience and death stand, there can be no other way of obtaining justification; and those, who are justified thereby, are not justified by any legal contract, but purely by grace; and, being united to Christ by faith, are regenerated and purified in heart.

Heidegger goes on to uphold, against the Remonstrants, the limitation of the work of Christ.

'For whom Christ made satisfaction, for the same He offered Himself and died, bore their sins, and bought and redeemed the same for Himself by His own precious blood. For these are parallel phrases in Scripture' (91).

Entirely nugatory is the distinction, that Christ merited, sufficiently for all, but efficiently only for a few. Although in itself the merit of Christ is infinite, yet in the counsel of God it was only paid for those for whom it effected salvation. What kind of efficiency or merit is that which does not produce salvation? What kind of application is it, which is merely in potency and not in act, until the further condition of faith has been realised? The result is, that, if men do not believe, Christ's merit goes for nought.

In dealing with the Scriptural arguments for a universal satisfaction, Heidegger first emphasises the passages in which Christ is said to have died for His friends,[6] or for His sheep, or for many; he then urges that, where Christ is said to have died for all, the sense must be that He died for all the elect. This, he says, is quite clear from the context in such a passage as 2 C. 5:15–19. He points out that in Rom. 11:32; 1 C. 15:22, 'all' can only refer to those who are Christ's.[7] As regards the argu-

---

[4] Cf. *supra*, pp. 171, 172f., 176, 222, 227.
[6] Jn 15:13.
[5] *Supra*, p. 429, n. 7.
[7] Cf. 1 C. 15:23.

ment from passages in which Christ is said to have died for the reprobate, Heidegger takes them one by one and gives them a different sense. 2 Pet. 2:1 refers to not a real redemption, but to an external calling and external inclusion in the Church only. In Heb. 10:29 ἐν ᾧ ἡγιάσθη refers to Christ, not to the unbeliever. Rom 14: 15 does not imply the ruin of those for whom Christ died, but only their attempted ruin.

As regards the argument that Christ died for all, because all are bound to believe in Him, Heidegger says that, while the non-elect are bound to believe the truth concerning Christ, to believe in Him belongs to the elect only. Finally, Heidegger appeals to Christian experience. The foundation of our consolation is to know that Christ died for us; but if Christ died for some who are to be damned, we do not know that we are included in the benefit of His death. It is not in virtue of our common humanity, but of our faith, that we have communion with His death.

The third part of the sacrifice of Christ is the offering in heaven of the sacrifice slain on earth, in that Christ appears before the Father for us, pleading His blood, interceding, and making propitiation.

Christ indeed had already prayed on earth, both for Himself and for others; but His intercession in heaven is altogether of another quality. He no longer falls on His knees, using strong crying and tears, and making deprecatory supplication to an angry Father; but, presenting His sacrifice, He demands in the strength of it, that His heritage be given Him. It is therefore intercession or prayer in a figure, not in the strict sense (though that is not unbefitting Christ as man). It consists in Christ's perpetual advocacy for those who have been given Him.

The Socinians overthrow this heavenly intercession equally with the merit of Christ: (1) in that they deny its basis in Christ's sacrifice on earth, (2) in that they confound it with the Kingship of Christ.

'The Kingly office of Christ is that whereby He governs His Church by His Word and Spirit, and defends and preserves it against all enemies' (98).

The Kingly power deserved to be conferred on Christ, because He had obtained it by His death, and had acquired for Himself

441

as His payment a people for His own possession. It belongs to Christ as Mediator and Saviour of His body. Christ possesses as God, in common with the Father and with the Holy Spirit, an essential Kingdom over all creatures, whom God made by the Word alone, and by the Word preserves and governs. As God-man and Mediator He has a personal Kingdom over the Church or the elect only, in whose hearts He operates by the efficacy of His Word and Spirit. Nevertheless, Christ's mediatorial Kingdom, if regard is had to the fullness of power, which He possesses in it over heaven and earth, differs from His essential Kingdom, not in fact, but in idea only. In it also He is of one substance with the Father; nor can He exercise His personal Kingdom over the Church apart from His essential Kingdom over the world. This personal Kingdom, moreover, Christ even as God maintains not outside of or against, but according to the will of the Father. As God and Mediator, He can do all He will. But He wills nothing, but what is pleasing to the Father. Thus, in that Christ reigns, God does not retire from the throne of His Majesty, or give over His Kingdom to Christ.

Christ performs His office of King differently as God and as Man. As God, He rules in His own right to the edification, protection, and glorification of the Church. He rules as Man, not as Lord of the World, but as the mandatory of the Father, using a finite and dependent power. The Socinians are inconsistent, in that they assign to Christ a dependent power, but make Him use it with an independent will. On the contrary, the will of God and Christ are one.

Christ's Kingdom is not of this world, nor after the manner of this world, but is inward, spiritual, and heavenly. It has a heavenly origin in the Divine Wisdom. Its concern is with heavenly things. Its law is spiritual, written on the heart by the Spirit of God. Its worship is spiritual: its subjects are spiritual men. Its goods are heavenly and spiritual; and its means, the Word of God, His Spirit and faith, are all spiritual. Even its enemies are spiritual, viz. Satan and his Kingdom, over whom Christ triumphs by His cross.

Finally, the Kingdom of Christ is eternal; as Jesus Christ is the same yesterday, today, and for ever. Not even in heaven, after

442

the end of the world, will Christ give up His mediatorial Kingdom. The action of the Mediator will indeed cease to be by merit, as His merit will have done its work; but He will still bestow the gift of life upon His people.

The Socinians corrupt the doctrine of the kingly office, in that they make Christ God's Colleague under the New Testament dispensation only, whereas, according to them, under the Old Testament dispensation God ruled alone.[8] To recite such opinions is to refute them.

The Lutheran and the Reformed Doctrines Compared

We now proceed to institute a comparison between the Lutheran and Reformed doctrines of the work of Christ, as illustrated by Quenstedt and Heidegger respectively.[9]

(1) It is the common doctrine of both Confessions that the mediatorial office is exercised in both natures. Against Lombard, Stancarus, and Piscator they unitedly assert that the office of Christ is *theanthropic*. Nevertheless the greater stress which the Reformed theology lays on the humanity of Christ manifests itself throughout the entire doctrine of His office in various important ways.

(2) As regards the prophetic office, there is a noteworthy agreement between the Confessions as to its fundamentally evangelical character. Both Lutherans and Reformed, in opposition to the patristic, mediaeval, Socinian, and Arminian idea of Christianity as a new law, assert the practical perfection of the Decalogue, and regard Christianity on its moral side as no more than a reaffirmation and true interpretation of the same.

On the other hand, the difference between the Confessions in the conception of Christ's Person [1] comes out in their respective ideas of the efficacy of His teaching. The Lutherans think of it

---

[8] Cf. *supra*, pp. 363, 376, on the Socinian substitution for the Logos doctrine of an adoptianist Christology.

[9] See also Schmid, 'Die Dogmatik der evangelisch-lutherischen Kirche', 5th ed., 1863, pp. 284–312 ; Schweizer, 'Die Glaubenslehre der evangelisch-reformierten Kirche', vol. ii, 1847, pp. 356–412 ; Ritschl, 'Justification and Reconciliation', vol. i, English trans., pp. 234ff.   [1] *Supra*, pp. 357f.

as flowing directly from His Divinity; whereas the Reformed lay stress on the confirmation of His teaching by His holy life and example, and also by the sending of the Spirit into the hearts of believers.

(3) In both Confessions the priestly office, and especially that part of it which is occupied with the work of satisfaction, holds the centre of the field. The *locus de satisfactione* is invariably treated with great care and at great length. The general view of the satisfaction as a *temperamentum misericordiæ et justitiæ* is the same in both Confessions. Both Lutherans and Reformed in general assert an absolute necessity of satisfaction; both trace this necessity to the Divine justice, and in opposition to the Socinian view state that in this question God must be regarded, not as *dominus*, but as Governor and Judge. Quenstedt and Heidegger well illustrate the above statements: there is, however, in some few Reformed theologians a tendency to follow Calvin [2] in making the necessity of satisfaction depend ultimately on the Divine decree.[3] It is to be remembered also that even Quenstedt in one place [4] allows the distinction between *potentia absoluta* and *potentia ordinata*. In general, however, the antithesis to Socinianism causes a return to the extreme Anselmic doctrine of an absolutely necessary satisfaction. So in another place Quenstedt reduces the distinction between *potentia absoluta* and *ordinata* to nothing.[5]

Nextly, however, whatever weakening there may or may not be among the Reformed on the point of the absolute necessity of satisfaction, the Reformed as well as the Lutherans equally assert its infinite value and sufficiency, and also its perfection and sole sufficiency, so that no other satisfaction needs to be added to it or even grounded upon it. The later theology of both Confessions adopts more and more the exact Anselmic doctrine as regards the infinity of Christ's satisfaction. It obtains its infinite value from His Divine nature, and is the exact equivalent of the infinity of sin. Moreover, both Lutherans and Reformed, with a view to exhibiting the equivalence of the sufferings of Christ with the punishment which ought to have been suffered by

[2] 'Inst.' II, 17.
[4] Loc. cit. sect. II, qu. 7. Cf. *supra*, p. 423.
[3] Ritschl, op. cit., pp. 243ff.
[5] Sect. I, Thesis 31. Cf. *supra*, p. 416.

sinners, maintain the doctrine that He bore on the cross the very pains of hell.

The great and controversial difference between the two Confessions is of course as to the extent of Christ's satisfaction. The controversy was mainly fought out on grounds of Scripture, whence texts could be brought on both sides. In reality, however, the settlement of the question turned on the theological difference, that the Reformed allowed the doctrine of predestination at this point a controlling influence over the doctrine of the work of Christ, which the Lutherans did not. The Reformed were from the first more possessed of a systematic interest in theology than the Lutherans. While the Lutherans were content to preserve the experimental and anthropological standpoint of the doctrine of justification by faith, the Reformed preferred to view all things from the ultimate or Divine standpoint, and their method is, not anthropological, but strictly theological. Schweizer has said that the doctrines of justification and of predestination are the mid-points respectively of the Lutheran and the Reformed statements of the fundamental doctrines of Protestantism.[6]

It may here be pointed out in connexion with this difference that the Reformed theology is in general marked by a greater confidence in reason than is the Lutheran, as may be clearly seen in a comparison of the way in which Quenstedt and Heidegger treat the Socinian objections to the doctrine of satisfaction. While Heidegger throughout maintains the rationality of the doctrine, Quenstedt again and again admits that Socinus would be right, were it not for the Divine decree.

As regards the matter of the satisfaction, there is a general agreement that it consists in both the active and passive obedience of Christ. Nevertheless there is a considerable difference between Lutherans and Reformed in their way of stating this common doctrine, a difference which is the result of their different attitude to the doctrine of the Person of Christ. The Lutherans regard Christ as the God-man as altogether above the law. Hence His active, as well as His passive, obedience is purely vicarious. For the Reformed, Christ as man is under the law, consequently

---

[6] 'Die protestantischen Centraldogmen in ihrer Entwicklung innerhalb der reformierten Kirche', vol. i (1854), p. 16.

the vicarious character of His active obedience has to be maintained in a different way. They teach that since Christ only became man for our sakes, His individual fulfilment of the law pertains to His satisfaction and merit just as much as does His suffering and death.

Finally, both Confessions agree in consequence that Christ merited only for us and not for Himself, and disallow the doctrine of Lombard and Socinus on this point.

(4) As regards the kingly office there is a difference between Lutherans and Reformed, which follows from their difference in Christology. The Reformed exclude from the Kingly office of Christ as Mediator the Kingdom of power, as it is defined by the Lutherans, i.e. the dominion of the Logos over the world before and independently of the Incarnation.

Schneckenburger (quoted by Schweizer, 'Die Glaubenslehre der evangelisch-reformierten Kirche', ii, p. 410) thus points out the difference between the two opposing views: For the Reformed 'there can be no talk of the absolute coincidence of the Divine government of the world in general with the Kingdom of Christ, in the sense that the Lutheran system speaks of it as *regnum potentiæ*. Christ as Logos shares in the government of the world, but as God-man He exercises over the world a power which is merely finite. Not what belongs to nature as such, but what has in some degree become the Church, has been delivered over to His Mediatorship.' Christ's gracious sway over the Church includes a victorious dominion over its enemies, such as in the Bible is generally connected with the Messianic office. This is the *regnum potentiæ* in the Reformed sense.

So much then for the comparison of the Lutheran and Reformed scholasticism. If, in conclusion, we ask what it is in both, that carries the whole view of the threefold office, and maintains it against the acutest Socinian dialectic, the reply is that it is Luther's new intuition, the fundamental conviction that Christianity is not partly law and partly grace, but rather a union of opposites, a religion which is all grace, and yet has law in its bosom. It is this conviction which makes the orthodox scholasticism not only impervious to all Socinian attacks, but also resistant even of such a modification of Socinianism as

Arminianism. It is not reason, but the *fides salvifica* as warranted by Scripture, which supports the tremendous fabric. The greater confidence in reason which Heidegger exhibits over against Quenstedt moves after all only within the presuppositions of the *fides salvifica*. Quenstedt is merely more conscious throughout that his doctrine rests upon an antinomy.

Chapter 7

THEOLOGY IN ENGLAND

Hooker and Pearson

In contrast with the theology of the Continent that of the Church of England was in the sixteenth and seventeenth centuries little systematic, but rather Biblical and patristic. Of the Anglican theology of the sixteenth century Gass says as follows:[1]

'It was accustomed to find its office concluded in the exposition, defence, or proof of the Biblical material, without recognising as necessary as a final operation its scientific appropriation. The scientific factor therefore did not maintain the balance with that of Biblical learning. Again, it has already been pointed out that along with this Biblical standpoint was united an extraordinary veneration for ecclesiastical antiquity, and at times also an unlimited idea of the splendour of the Apostolic age. The conviction, that Protestantism aims only at removing inherited errors and abuses, without attempting anything new, finds far sharper expression in the English than in the German Church. Its literature lays the greatest stress on the predicate of Catholicity and on the praise of agreement with the first centuries.'

The Church of England, in fact, retained in her liturgy a special connexion with the past, such as no Continental Protestant possesses, and it was precisely round about this point of contact with antiquity that the theological controversy of the sixteenth century chiefly turned. When Protestantism was re-established under Elizabeth, many of those who had been exiles on the Continent during the Marian persecution, returned with the idea of bringing the Church of England into line with the Protestantism of the Continent. The question was, not primarily of doctrine, but of polity. While the conservative party wished to

---

[1] 'Geschichte der protestantischen Dogmatik', vol. iii, p. 301.

448

retain the liturgy and the Episcopal system connected with it, the Puritans, as they were called, wished to remodel the Church according to the Presbyterian discipline instituted by Calvin at Geneva. The great work of Anglican theology in the sixteenth century is consequently a defence of the existing institutions of the Church of England. It is the famous 'Laws of Ecclesiastical Polity' of Richard Hooker (A.D. 1553–1600), whose primary purpose is to repel the Puritan attack upon the Anglican system. Hooker's appeal is to reason and to ecclesiastical antiquity. His general position, which is based on the mediaeval scholasticism, especially upon Thomas, in that man is under a system of law imposed by God. There is first the natural law which leads him to imitate God's goodness. This, however, in view of sin is insufficient, and God has therefore added in Scripture the super-natural law of faith in Christ; faith that is not without, but includes, hope and love.[2] Scripture, however, does not altogether displace reason. 'The Scriptures which contain the supernatural light, presuppose the existence of a natural light. . . . In the use of this natural light we should not despise the judgment of grave and learned men. Here we learn a reverence for antiquity, and the order established by those who have lived before us.'[3] Upon these principles, then, Hooker defends the Anglican system; his doctrine of the work of Christ is naturally introduced in the exposition of the Sacraments, as their basis. In accordance with his esteem for antiquity both the Incarnation and the Sacraments are interpreted along patristic lines, though the influence of the schoolmen, in particular of Thomas, is also unmistakable.

'The use of Sacraments is but only in this life, yet so, that they here concern a far better life than this, and are for that cause accompanied with grace which worketh salvation. Sacra-ments are the powerful instruments of God to eternal life. For as our natural life consisteth in the union of the body with the soul, so our life supernatural in the union of the soul with God. And forasmuch as there is no union of God with man, without that mean between both, which is both; it seemeth requisite that we must first consider how God is in Christ, then how Christ

---

[2] 'Eccles. Polity', I, 11.   [3] Hunt, 'Religious Thought in England', vol. i (1870), p. 59.

is in us, and how the Sacraments do serve to make us partakers of Christ' ('Eccles. Polity', v, 50).

Hooker, therefore, begins with the Incarnation: if we ask for the cause of this incomprehensible mystery, it 'seemeth a thing unconsonant that the world should honour any other as the Saviour, but Him whom it honoureth as the Creator of the world, and in the wisdom of God it hath not been thought convenient to admit any way of saving man but by man himself' (51). Again, if it be asked, why the Son, rather than the Father or the Holy Ghost, became incarnate: 'Could we, which are born the children of wrath, be adopted the sons of God through grace, any other than the natural Son of God being Mediator between God and us?' (ibid.). Yet the necessity of the Incarnation was not absolute. 'The world's salvation was without the Incarnation of the Son a thing impossible; not simply impossible, but impossible, it being presupposed that the will of God was no otherwise to have it saved than by the death of His own Son' (ibid.).

The Incarnation then took place that Christ might offer a sacrifice in human nature for us, and also that as man He might after His death continue to intercede for us, and rule over us.

'Taking to Himself our flesh, and by His Incarnation making it His own flesh, He had now of His own, although from us, what to offer unto God for us. And as Christ took manhood, that by it He might be capable of death, whereunto He humbled Himself; so, because manhood is the proper subject of compassion and feeling pity, which maketh the sceptre of Christ's regency even in the kingdom of heaven be amiable, He which without our nature could not on earth suffer for the sins of the world, doth now also, by means thereof, both make intercession to God for sinners, and exercise dominion over all men with a true, a natural, and a sensible touch of mercy' (ibid.).

Such is the first summary account of the work of Christ given by Hooker, representing Him as Priest and King. It is not, however, Hooker's whole theory; but requires to be supplemented by passages scattered through the following chapters on the Incarnation and the Sacraments, in which the central thought is the ancient patristic idea of the communication of salvation to humanity, involved in the very Incarnation itself. In the Incarna-

450

tion the Person of the Lord was united, not to a single man, but to humanity in general.

'It pleased not the Word, or Wisdom of God, to take to itself some one person amongst men, for then should that one have been advanced, which was assumed, and no more; but wisdom to the end that she might save many, built her house of that nature which is common unto all, she made not this or that man her habitation, but dwelt *in us*' (52).

Both the natures indeed were with their properties in Christ distinct; yet the human nature derives sundry advantages from its union with the Word. As Hooker puts it, following Thomas ('Summa Theol.' III, 7, 1):[4] 'Christ is by degrees a receiver: first, in that He is the Son of God: secondly, in that His human nature hath had the honour of union with Deity bestowed upon it; thirdly, in that by means thereof sundry eminent graces have flowed as effects from Deity into that nature which is coupled with it. On Christ, therefore, is bestowed the gift of eternal generation, the gift of union, and the gift of unction' (54).

The gift of union and the gift of unction are the fruits of the Incarnation. 'The union therefore of the flesh with Deity, is to that flesh a gift of principal grace and favour. For, by virtue of this grace, man is really made God, a creature is exalted above the dignity of all creatures, and hath all creatures else under it' (*ibid.*). While the person of the Son of God attained nothing by assuming human nature except 'to be capable of loss and detriment for the good of others', human nature was exalted in the Incarnation by union with the Divine nature. 'The very cause of His taking upon Himself our nature, was to change it, to better the quality, and to advance the condition thereof, although in no case to abolish the substance which He took; nor to confuse into it the natural forces and properties of His Deity. . . . For albeit the natural properties of Deity be not communicable to man's nature, the supernatural gifts, graces, and effects thereof are' (*ibid.*).

Finally, the grace of unction replenished both the soul and body of Christ with all things necessary to the economy of salvation which He had undertaken.

[4] *Supra*, p. 215. The correspondence is not exact.

451

We have next to see how the supernatural gifts, graces, and effects of the Incarnation become the property of a special Divine offspring among men. This takes place, firstly, by predestination.

'We are by nature the sons of Adam. When God created Adam, He created us; and as many as are descended from Adam have in themselves the root out of which they spring. The sons of God we neither are all nor any one of us otherwise than only by grace and favour. The sons of God have God's own natural Son as a second Adam from heaven, whose race and progeny they are by spiritual and heavenly birth. God therefore loving eternally His Son, He must needs eternally in Him have loved and preferred before all others, them which are spiritually sithence descended and sprung out of Him' (56).

To this union with Christ by predestination must be added, however, a union by actual sacramental incorporation into the Lord.

'Our being in Christ by eternal foreknowledge saveth us not without our actual and real adoption into the fellowship of His saints in this present world. For in Him we actually are by our actual incorporation into that society which hath Him for their Head, and doth make with Him one Body (He and they in that respect having one name); for which cause, by virtue of this mystical conjunction we are of Him, and in Him, even as though our very flesh and bones should be made continuate with His' (ibid.).

As a consequence, then, of such sacramental incorporation in the body of Christ we are saved by union with Him, and participation in the benefits which human nature in Him receives from union with the Deity.

'Adam is in us an original cause of our nature, and of that corruption of nature which causeth death; Christ as the cause of original restoration to life. The person of Adam is not in us, but his nature, and the corruption of his nature derived unto all men by propagation; Christ, having Adam's nature as we have, but incorrupt, deriveth not nature but incorruption, and that immediately from His own person, into all that belong unto Him. . . . That which quickeneth us is the Spirit of the Second Adam, and His flesh that wherewith He quickeneth. That which

452

in Him made our nature uncorrupt, was the union of His Deity with our nature. And in that respect the sentence of death and condemnation, which only taketh hold upon sinful flesh, could no way possibly extend unto Him. This caused His voluntary death to prevail with God and to have the force of an expiatory sacrifice. The blood of Christ, as the Apostle witnesseth, doth therefore take away sin, because "Through the eternal Spirit He offered Himself unto God without spot". That which sanctified our nature in Christ, that which made it a sacrifice available to take away sin, is the same which quickeneth it, raiseth it out of the grave after death, and exalted it unto glory. Seeing, therefore, that Christ is in us as a quickening Spirit, the first degree of communion with Christ must needs consist in the participation of His Spirit' (ibid.).

But union with Christ affects the body also.

'For, doth any man doubt, but that even from the flesh of Christ our very bodies do receive that life which shall make them glorious at the latter day; and for which they are already accounted parts of His blessed body? Our corruptible bodies would never live the life they shall live, were it not that here they are joined with His body which is incorruptible, and that His is in ours as a cause of immortality, a cause by removing through the death and merit of His own flesh that which hindered the life of ours' (ibid.).

Moreover, Christ both purges away sin and renews men to holiness and immortality; the latter is His primary work, but cannot be done without the other.

'This much no Christian man will deny, that when Christ sanctified His own flesh, giving as God and taking as man the Holy Ghost, He did not this for Himself only, but for our sakes, that the grace of sanctification and life, which was first received in Him, might pass from Him to His whole race, as malediction came from Adam unto all mankind. Howbeit, because the work of His Spirit to these effects is in us prevented by sin and death, possessing us as before; it is of necessity that as well our present sanctification unto newness of life, as the future restoration of our bodies, should presuppose a participation of the grace, efficacy, merit, or virtue of His body and blood; without which foundation first laid, there is no place for those other operations of the Spirit of Christ to ensue.'

Finally, Christ dwells in men by different degrees. All partake of Him, working as the Creator and Governor of the world by providence; not all partake of Him in a saving way. And amongst those who do thus partake of Him, there are degrees of grace. But, wherever He is savingly partaken of, there is both imputation of His righteousness and real habitual infusion of His grace.

'Thus we participate Christ, partly by imputation, as when those things which He did and suffered are imputed unto us for righteousness; partly by habitual and real infusion, as when grace is inwardly bestowed while we are on earth, and afterwards more fully both our souls and bodies made like His in glory.'

The above extended quotations were necessary in order to show the full range of Hooker's doctrine, which contains within it considerably different elements. It is clear that the fundamental stratum is derived from the patristic theology: yet there are elements in it which take us beyond the Fathers. The doctrine of Christ's grace and merit comes from the schoolmen, and Hooker to a certain extent follows them in translating the patristic mysticism into their more rational theory, which, treating Christ as an individual, endeavours to show how the results of His work accrue to others, a point which the patristic doctrine, taking His humanity as not individual but universal, regarded as needing next to no explanation.[5] Finally, in the doctrine of the imputation of Christ's righteousness we have the legacy of the Reformation. In the end, however, the general impression left is that of the massive and unanalytic patristic theory; the elements which take us beyond this appear as mere superficial additions to it, which hardly alter the total effect. There is no doubt that Hooker felt himself substantially in harmony with the Fathers in his view of the work of Christ, and cared little to go beyond them in the attempt either to clarify or to supplement their theory. We may say, then, that the classical theology of the Church of England began its course with what is to all intents

[5] Cf. *supra*, pp. 142, 184f., 191f.

a return to the patristic doctrine of the subject. This result is important, as it gives the key to much that is interesting in the later development of Anglican theology.

In the seventeenth century the inheritance of Hooker begins to be divided between the High Church party on the one hand and the Latitudinarians, the precursors of the Deists, on the other hand. Hooker's appeal was at once to antiquity and to reason, and these two schools appropriated each one of these fundamental elements of his theology. The High Church party emphasised the agreement of the Anglican Church with antiquity, and kept along the lines of the patristic theology, as reintroduced by Hooker. On the contrary, the Latitudinarians kept the appeal to reason, and carried it to results which Hooker had not contemplated. In the seventeenth century, however, systematic theology is still in the background in the Church of England. Gass [6] says of the Anglican theology of this century as follows: 'We may say that Biblical research and the science of ecclesiastical antiquities, Apologetics, Polemics, Patristics along with the writing of monographs on Church history, are those studies in which English theology excelled. A dogmatic literature in the narrower and proper sense even now came into being only in a small degree, and the reasons of this want are clear from the ecclesiastical and scientific conditions. The whole efforts of the Church were from the beginning onwards directed to the establishment and defence of the faith and the polity; in this work and in the scholarly appropriation of material on all sides theological keenness exhausted itself.'

The most famous Anglican dogmatic work of the period is in fact not a systematic theology, but in agreement with the genius of the Church of England an 'Exposition of the (Apostles') Creed', viz. the well-known work of Pearson (d. A.D. 1686).[7] He, though he took the part of the Prayer Book against the Puritans, was not an extreme Churchman, but was thought by the Puritans to have some sympathy with them.[8] While, therefore, in his great work the patristic learning and tradition of the English Church are fully exhibited, it is not surprising to find that his

[6] Op. cit. vol. iii, p. 303.
[7] The first edition of the 'Exposition' appeared in 1659.
[8] Hunt, op. cit. pp. 295, 307, n. 2.

theology is largely dependent on the Protestant theology of the Continent.

It is natural that, in accordance with the plan of Pearson's book as an exposition of the Creed, the material of the doctrine of the work of Christ is introduced in connexion with the different articles of the Creed, particularly in the form of reasons why they should be believed. First of all (art. II), under the head of the words, 'And in Jesus Christ', the doctrine of Christ's Messiahship is unfolded, which leads on to that of His threefold office as Prophet, Priest, and King. This is developed, as it is by Calvin,[9] in connexion with the meaning of the name Messiah. Under the Old Testament prophets, priests, and kings were anointed, and the Divine administration of the people of Israel consisted in these three functions, the prophetical, the regal, and the sacerdotal. In the Messiah, in whom the old dispensation came to an end, the three functions are united, so that Jesus was anointed at once as Prophet, Priest, and King. Such is Pearson's doctrine in full agreement with Calvin: it is characteristic, however, that he supports it by patristic references, the most important of which are to Eusebius.[1]

The significance of the three offices is further explained as follows:

'Again: the redemption or salvation which the Messiah was to bring, consisteth in the freeing of a sinner from the state of sin and eternal death into a state of righteousness and eternal life. Now a freedom from sin in respect of the guilt could not be wrought without a sacrifice propitiatory, and therefore there was a necessity of a priest; a freedom from sin in respect of the dominion could not be obtained without a revelation of the will of God, and of His wrath against all ungodliness, therefore there was also need of a prophet: a translation from the state of death unto eternal life is not to be effected without absolute authority and irresistible power, therefore a king was also necessary.'

There follows a more detailed development of the doctrine under each of the three offices, from which I select three additional quotations:

(1) 'The prophetical function consisteth in the promulgation,

<hr>

[9] *Supra*, p. 339.　　　[1] *Supra*, p. 348, n. 2.

confirmation, and perpetuation of the doctrine containing the will of God for the service of men.'

(2) 'When Jesus had given Himself a propitiatory sacrifice for sins, He ascended up on high, and entered into the Holy of Holies not made with hands, and there appeared before God as an atonement for our sin. Nor is He prevalent only in His own oblation once offered, but in His constant intercession.'

(3) 'This regal office of our saviour consisteth partly in the ruling, protecting, and rewarding of His people; partly in the coercing, condemnation, and destroying of His enemies. First, He ruleth in His own people by delivering them a law in which they walk; by furnishing them with His grace, by which they are enabled to walk in it. Secondly, He protecteth the same, by helping them to subdue their lusts which reign in their mortal bodies; by preserving them from the temptations of the world, the flesh, and the Devil; by supporting them in all their afflictions; by delivering them from all their enemies, whether they were temporal or spiritual enemies.'

Under the words 'His only Son', Pearson brings in the Divinity of Christ as the ground of His making adequate satisfaction for the sins of men. Here he virtually writes out Anselm's argument.

'If we be truly sensible of our sins, we must acknowledge that in every one we have offended God; and the gravity of the offence must needs increase proportionably to the dignity of the party offended in respect of the offender; because the more worthy any person is, the more reverence is due unto him, and every injury tendeth to his dishonour: but between God and man there is an infinite disproportion; and therefore every offence committed against Him must be esteemed as in the highest degree of injury. Again: as the gravity of the offence beareth proportion to the person offended, so the value of reparation ariseth from the dignity of the person satisfying; because the satisfaction consisteth in a reparation of the honour which by the injury was eclipsed; and all honour doth increase proportionably as the person yielding it is honourable. If, then, by every sin we have offended God, who is of infinite eminency, according unto which the injury is aggravated; how shall we ever be sure of our reconciliation unto God, except the Person who hath undertaken to make the reparation be of the same infinite dignity, so as the honour rendered by His obedience may prove proportionable to the offence and that dishonour which arose from our disobedience? This scruple is no otherwise to be satisfied than by a belief in such a Mediator as is the only-begotten Son of God, of the same substance with the Father, and consequently of the same power and dignity with the God Whom by our sins we have offended.'

Belief in the Divinity of Christ is therefore necessary for the confirmation of our faith concerning the redemption of mankind: it is also necessary 'to raise us to a thankful acknowledgment of the infinite love of God, appearing in the sending of His only-begotten Son into the world to die for sinners'.

We can, says Pearson, never make an adequate return for the love of God, unless we have the proper sense of its infinity, which is impossible apart from the recognition of the infinite dignity of Christ.

The conception of Christ, through the Holy Ghost, by the Virgin Mary (art. III), was necessary to His sinlessness, which again was necessary that He might be a sacrifice for sin.

Christ's sufferings (art. IV) were necessary 'for the redemption of lapsed men, and their reconciliation unto God; which was not otherwise to be performed than by a plenary satisfaction to His will'; they were also necessary that Christ 'might purchase thereby eternal happiness in the heavens both for Himself the Head, and for the members of His body. They were, once more, necessary to make Him our compassionate High Priest and our example in suffering'.

Christ's death (*ibid.*) by crucifixion proclaims that he bore the curse for us, and cancelled it. 'The death of Christ is the most intimate and essential part of the mediatorship, and that which most intrinsically concerns every office and function of the Mediator, as He was Prophet, Priest, and King.'

It was necessary, as regards the prophetical office, that Christ should die in order to the confirmation of His doctrine. As regards the priestly office, His death was necessary, both as a satisfaction for sins, and as qualifying Christ for His High Priesthood. As regards the kingly office, it was necessary, that Christ might overcome the principalities and powers, and that He might win the name above every name.

Christ's descent into hell (art. v) is explained as meaning that His soul, being separated from His body, passed into the places below, where the souls of men departed are. This Christ undertook to satisfy the law of death; but because there was no sin in Him, and He had fully satisfied for the sins of others, God did not leave His soul in hell, thus giving security of never coming under the power of Satan to all those who belong to Him.

Christ's Resurrection (*ibid*.) is necessary as the ground of our faith in His Divinity, as manifesting our justification, and as the confirmation of our hope. His ascension (art. vi) also confirms our faith and hope, and exalts our affections heavenward. His sitting at the right hand of God (*ibid*.) manifests His regal power, and also His gracious intercession.

To sum up the results of this exposition of Pearson's teaching: it amounts practically to Calvin's doctrine of the threefold office with the addition of the Anselmic theory of satisfaction. Pearson helps us to realise the existence of another line of tradition in Anglican theology besides that of Hooker.

Owen

Fairbairn has distinguished the Anglican doctrine from the Puritan doctrine, which was opposed to it, by designating the former as *institutional*, the latter as *theological*.

'The earliest controversies in the English Church may be said to have been between two conceptions—whether the actual Church ought to be brought into harmony with the ideal, or whether the actual was not the ideal Church. This of course involved a difference of ideals rather than of actuals: the ideal, in the one case, was theological and abstract, a society constructed according to the mind and will of God; but in the other case it was political and concrete, the society which the wisdom of the past had created and the piety of the present was bound to preserve and administer.' [2]

[2] 'The Place of Christ in Modern Theology', 5th ed., p. 180.

The Puritan theology is, therefore, not bound by the existing institution, its polity and Creeds, but on the contrary, like the Calvinistic theology of the Continent, which it closely follows, aims at a systematic construction of the faith, on the basis of the revelation given in the Scriptures. It was, above all, the idea of absolute predestination, which dominated the greatest of the Puritan theologians, John Owen (A.D. 1616–88), whose treatise on the work of Christ, 'The Death of Death in the Death of Christ' (1647), is entirely consecrated to the complete subjugation of the doctrine to this idea. Owen's treatise is one continuous attack upon the doctrine of universal redemption as taught by the Arminians. Included in the polemic, moreover, are the various schools of Calvinism which had in some degree modified the extreme vigour of its predestinarian doctrine, above all, the School of Saumur with its hypothetic universalism.[3] It is to be observed that while not only the Puritans, but also the Anglicans, had in the Elizabethan era followed Calvin as regards predestination, in the seventeenth century Arminianism had largely become the doctrine of the Anglicans, while the Puritans remained in general true to Calvinism, though with some it was a modified Calvinism.

Owen argues that Christ's work is to be understood from its end or purpose. 'By the end of the death of Christ we mean in general, both—first, that which His Father and Himself intended in it; and, secondly, that which was effectually fulfilled and accomplished by it.'[4] As to the first point, Scripture declares that the end of Christ's work intended by God Himself was the saving of sinners, not indeed of all sinners, but of those who believe, and constitute the Church. As to the second point, the effect and actual product of Christ's work is reconciliation with God, justification, sanctification, adoption, and future glory.

'Thus full, clear, and evident are the expressions in the Scripture concerning the ends and effects of the death of Christ, that a man might think every one might run and read. But we must stay: among all things in the Christian religion, there is scarce anything more questioned than this, which seems to be a most fundamental principle. A spreading persuasion there is

<hr />

[3] *Supra*, p. 358.   [4] 'The Works of John Owen', vol. x, Edinburgh, 1842, p. 157.

of a general ransom to be paid by Christ for all; that He died to redeem all and every one—not only for many, His Church, the elect of God, but for every one also of the posterity of Adam. Now, the masters of this opinion do see full well and easily, that if that be the end of the death of Christ which we have from the Scripture asserted, if those before recounted be the immediate fruits and products thereof, then one of these two things will necessarily follow:—that either first, God and Christ failed of their end proposed and did not accomplish that which they intended, the death of Christ being not a fitly-proportioned means for the attaining of that end (for any cause of failing cannot be assigned); which to assert seems to us blasphemously injurious to the wisdom, power, and perfection of God, as likewise derogatory to the worth and value of the death of Christ;—or else, that all men, all the posterity of Adam, must be saved, purged, sanctified, and glorified; which surely they will not maintain, at least the Scripture and the woeful experience of millions will not allow. Wherefore to cast a tolerable colour upon their persuasion, they must and do deny that God or His Son had any such absolute aim or end in the death or bloodshedding of Jesus Christ, or that any such thing was immediately procured and purchased by it, as we before recounted; but that God intended nothing, neither was there anything effected by Christ —that no benefit ariseth to any immediately by His death but what is common to all and every soul, though never so cursedly unbelieving here and eternally damned hereafter, until an act of some, not procured for them by Christ (for if it were, why have they it not all alike?), to wit, faith, do distinguish them from others' (pp. 159, 160).

The above lengthy quotation practically sums up the whole substance of Owen's book. Against the Arminian position he advances the argument, that its inevitable implication is that Christ's work has in reality done nothing at all, since it has actually and effectively saved no one. This argument is put in many ways and from many points of view, but the different forms which it takes always come back to the same essential point.

After naming the Trinity as the agent in the work of Christ, and assigning to each Person His proper part in it (cf. Quenstedt and Heidegger), Owen distinguishes, as its two parts, Christ's oblation and intercession.

'By His oblation we do not design only the particular offering up of Himself upon the cross an offering to His Father, as the Lamb of God without spot or blemish, when He bare our sins or carried them up with Him in His own body on the tree, which was the sum and complement of His oblation and that wherein it did chiefly consist; but also His whole humiliation, or state of emptying Himself, whether by yielding voluntary obedience unto the law, as being made under it, that He might be the end thereof to them that believe,[5] or by His subjection to the curse of the law, in the antecedent misery and suffering of life, as well as by submitting to death, the death of the cross: for no action of His as Mediator is to be excluded from a concurrence to make up the whole means in this work. Neither by His intercession do I understand only that heavenly appearance of His in the most holy place for the applying unto us all good things purchased and procured by His oblation: but also every act of His exaltation conducing thereto, from His resurrection to "His sitting down at the right hand of the Majesty on High, angels and principalities and powers being made subject unto Him" ' (p. 179).

Having thus defined what he means by these parts of the work of Christ, Owen next lays down the proposition, that although they are to be distinguished in fact and in their immediate issues, yet they are not so to be separated, 'as that the one should not have any respect to any persons or anything, which the other also doth not also in its kind equally respect' (p. 181).

'The sum is, that the oblation and intercession of Jesus Christ are one entire means for the producing of the same effect, the very end of the oblation being that all these things which are bestowed by the intercession of Christ, and without whose application it should certainly fail of the end proposed to it, be effected accordingly; so that it cannot be affirmed that the death or offering of Christ concerned any one person or thing more, in respect of procuring any good, than His intercession doth for the collating of it: for, interceding there for all good purchased, and

[5] Rom. 10:4.

prevailing in all His intercessions (for the Father always hears His Son), it is evident that every one for whom Christ died must actually have applied unto him all the good things purchased by His death' (*ibid.*).

Christ then neither offered Himself nor interceded for any but the elect. All attempts to make a distinction to the effect that He offered Himself, and interceded in a general way for all men, but particularly for the elect, Owen meets by the inquiry as to the intention of Christ, and whether it was or was not carried out. It cannot be but that in Christ's work intention and execution exactly correspond; thus all such distinctions as the above-mentioned come to the ground. As regards the texts of Scripture proposed in favour of his opponents' views, they must be understood with reference to this general and dominating consideration of the correspondence between the intention and the effect of Christ's work.

These arguments bring us to the end of Book I of Owen's treatise. In Book II he returns to treat more fully and directly of the subject of the end of Christ's work, which was at the first announced as the turning-point of the whole consideration, and has been the immanent principle of the argument thus far.

What is this end? The supreme end of the death of Christ is the glory of God and the manifestation of the Divine justice and mercy. The subordinate end is the salvation of the elect. Jesus in His work sought neither His own nor His Father's good. He did not enable God to exercise mercy as He could not otherwise have done. Owen here accepts the Scotist position that the necessity of Christ's satisfaction was contingent upon the Divine decree to manifest His glory by the way of requiring satisfaction, and refers with approval to the classical statement of Augustine, 'De Trinitate' (xiii, 10, 13).[6] It is, however, to be noted that in a subsequent treatise, 'De Divina Justitia' (1653), Owen changed his view on this point, and accepted the absolute necessity of satisfaction, arguing against Twisse and Rutherford, who still maintained the Scotist position.

In the treatise at present before us, however, accepting the Scotist doctrine, Owen goes on to argue that, apart from this

[6] *Supra*, p. 100.

liberty of God to show mercy as He pleases, there are other reasons why the end above assigned it impossible. 'That cannot be assigned as the complete end of the death of Christ, which being accomplished, it had not only been possible that not one soul might be saved, but also impossible that by virtue of it any sinful soul should be saved' (p. 207). It cannot be that the end of the death of Christ was a mere salvability, not salvation. The opponents distinguish between the *impetration* or obtaining of blessings by the oblation of Christ, and the *application* of these blessings: the first was general, just as Christ's merit was universal; the second is particular. Owen states the views of his opponents under three heads:

'First, some of them say that Christ, by His death and passion, did absolutely, according to the intention of God, purchase for all and every man, dying for them, remission of sins and reconciliation with God, or a restitution into a state of grace and favour; all of which shall be actually beneficial to them, provided they do believe. So the Arminians.

'Secondly, some, again [say], that Christ died for all indeed, but conditionally for some, if they do believe, or will do so (which He knows they cannot do of themselves); and absolutely for His own, even them on whom He purposeth to bestow faith and grace, so as actually to be made possessors of the good things by Him purchased. So Camero,[7] and the divines of France, which follow a new method by him devised.

'Thirdly, some distinguish of a twofold reconciliation and redemption—one wrought by Christ with God for man, which, say they, is general for all and every man; secondly, a reconciliation wrought by Christ in man unto God, bringing them actually into peace with Him' (p. 222).

The 'divines of France' are of course the School of Saumur: the third opinion is that of T. More, put forward in this book 'The Universality of God's Free Grace' (1643).

Owen meets all these views with equal opposition; they all, he says, come to the same thing, viz. 'that in respect of impetration Christ obtained redemption and reconciliation for all; in respect of application, it is bestowed only on them who do

---

[7] Cameron. See *supra*, p. 424, n. 4.

believe and continue therein' (p. 223). Owen admits that the distinction between impetration and application is a real one: the paying of the price differs from the freeing of the captives. But the distinction has no place in the intention and purpose of Christ, which includes both equally. There is indeed a condition of the application to us of the benefits of Christ's death, viz. faith, but this very condition is part of His purchase: He has procured for the elect the gift of faith along with all other blessings. Owen admits indeed that the value, worth, and dignity of the ransom which Christ gave Himself to be, and of the price which He paid, was infinite and immeasurable. But His intention and the Father's, with regard to the paying of it, was the salvation of the elect and nothing else; and this is what has to be considered. The whole distinction between impetration and application, as used by the opponents, is irrational. It is contrary to reason 'that a ransom should be paid for captives upon compact for their deliverance, and yet upon the payment those captives not be made free and set at liberty' (p. 233).

Owen asks with regard to the condition of faith, which the Arminians leave to be performed by man, whether it is in his power to perform the condition or not.

'If it be, then have all men power to believe, which is false; if it be not, then the Lord will grant them grace to perform it, or He will not. If He will, why do not all believe, why are not all saved? If He will not, then this impetration, or obtaining salvation and redemption for all by the blood of Jesus Christ, comes at length to this: God intendeth that He shall die for all, to procure for them remission of sins, reconciliation with Him, eternal redemption and glory; but yet so that they shall never have the least good by these glorious things, unless they perform that which He knows they are no way able to do, and which none but Himself can enable them to perform, and which concerning far the greatest part of them He is resolved not to do' (p. 234). Again: 'This condition of faith is procured for us by the death of Jesus Christ, or it is not. If they say it be not, then the chiefest grace, and without which redemption itself (express it how you please) is of no value, doth not depend on the grace of Christ as the meritorious procuring cause thereof: which,

465

first, is exceedingly injurious to our blessed Saviour, and serves only to diminish the honour and love due to Him; secondly, is contrary to Scripture: Tit. 3:5, 6; 2 C. 5:21, "He became sin for us, that we might be made the righteousness of God in Him." And how we can become the righteousness of God, but by believing, I know not. . . . This whole assertion tends to make Christ but a half mediator, that should procure the end, but not the means conducing thereunto. . . . For a close of all; that which in this cause we affirm may be summed up in this: Christ did not die for any upon condition, if they do believe; but He died for all God's elect, that they should believe, and believing have eternal life. . . . Salvation, indeed, is bestowed conditionally, but faith, which is the condition, is absolutely procured' (pp. 234, 235).

Book III contains further arguments against the universality of redemption. The following are the most important:

The main difference between the old covenant of works and the new covenant of grace is that under the former God required the fulfilment of the condition prescribed, but under the latter He promises Himself to effect this condition in those with whom the covenant is made. Only some, however, are brought into this new covenant of grace: the blood of Jesus Christ, therefore, inasmuch as it is the blood of the new covenant, can only apply to them. Again, for whom Christ died, He died as sponsor in their stead. He therefore freed them from anger, wrath, and desert of death: there was no other reason why He underwent death, than thus to free them. It is evident then that He did not die for all, inasmuch as all are not delivered.

Once more, it is clear, in view of the following arguments, that Christ has not satisfied justice for all:

(1) 'For whose sins He made satisfaction to the justice of God, for their sins justice is satisfied, or else His satisfaction is rejected as insufficient. . . . But now the justice of God is not satisfied for the sins of all and every man . . . for they that must undergo eternal punishment themselves for their sins, that the justice of God may be satisfied for their sins, the justice of God was not satisfied without their own punishment, by the punishment of Christ; for they are not healed by His stripes' (p. 247).

(2) 'Christ by undergoing death for us, as our surety, satisfied for no more than He intended so to do. So great a thing as satisfaction for the sins of men could not accidentally happen besides His intention, will, or purpose. . . . But now Christ did not intend to satisfy for the sins of all and every man, for innumerable souls were in hell, under the punishment and weight of their own sins. . . . Now shall we suppose that Christ would make Himself an offering for their sins whom He knew to be past recovery? . . . To intend good to them He could not, without a direct opposition to the eternal decree of His Father, and therein of His own eternal Deity' (pp. 247, 248).

Owen also argues from the ideas of redemption and reconciliation. 'Universal redemption, and yet many to die in captivity, is a contradiction irreconcilable in itself' (p. 258). The reconciliation of God to us and of us to God must answer one another, or there is no perfect reconciliation: 'How can it be, if peace is made only on the one side.' It is therefore apparent that the redemption and reconciliation, achieved by Christ's work, if they are to be real, must be particular.

Next follow arguments from the ideas of satisfaction and merit. Owen discusses carefully the meaning of both words, and in particular examines the Grotian conception of satisfaction; though he only aims to use the two ideas in subordination to his main purpose of combating the notion of universal redemption.

The word 'satisfaction' indeed is not found in the Latin or English Bible with application to the death of Christ. Nevertheless the thing is there, as all admit, except 'the wretched Socinians'.

'Satisfaction is a term borrowed from the law, applied properly to things, thence translated and accommodated into persons; and it is a full compensation of the creditor from the debtor' (p. 265).

'Personal debts are injuries and faults; which when a man hath committed, he is liable to punishment. He that is to inflict that punishment, or upon whom it lieth to see that it be done, is, or may be, the creditor; which he must do, unless satisfaction be made. Now there may be a twofold satisfaction:—First, By a solution, or paying the very thing that is in the obligation, either by the party himself that is bound, or by some other in his stead. . . . Secondly, By a solution, or paying of so much, although in another kind, not the same that is in the obligation, which by the creditor's acceptation stands in lieu thereof' (p. 265).

Now Grotius denies that the payment made by Christ was *solutio ejusdem*. His reasons are: (1) Such a solution, satisfaction, or payment, is attended with actual freedom from the obligation; (2) When such a solution is made, there is no room for remission or pardon.[8]

But the first reason cannot be granted. It is a *petitio principii;* and is indeed the exact opposite of the conviction which for Owen is fundamental, and has dominated his whole argument. He will only admit that there may be time between the procuring of freedom by Christ's work and the actual receiving of it by the sinner. As to the second reason, 'the satisfaction of Christ, by the payment of the same thing that was required in the obligation, is in no way prejudicial to that free, gracious condonation of sin often mentioned' (p. 268).

'God's gracious pardoning of sin compriseth the whole dispensation of grace towards us in Christ, whereof there are two parts:—First, The laying of our sin on Christ, or making Him to be sin for us; which was merely and purely an act of free grace, which He did for His own sake. Secondly, the gracious imputation of the righteousness of Christ to us, or making us the righteousness of God in Him; which is no less of grace and mercy, and that because the very merit of Christ Himself hath its foundation in a free compact and covenant. However, that remission, grace, and pardon, which is in God for sinners, is not opposed to Christ's merits, but to ours. He pardoneth all to us; but He spared not His only Son, He bated Him not one farthing. . . . Remission, then, excludes not a full satisfaction by the solution of the very thing in the obligation, but only the solution and satisfaction by him, to whom pardon and remission are granted. So that notwithstanding anything said to the contrary, the death of Christ made satisfaction in the very thing that was required in the obligation' (pp. 268, 269).

[8] *Supra,* p. 400.

The satisfaction made by Christ 'was a full, valuable compensation, made to the justice of God, for all the sins of all those for whom He made satisfaction by undergoing that same punishment which, by reason of the obligation that was upon them, they themselves were bound to undergo. When I say the same, I mean essentially the same in weight and pressure, though not in all accidents of duration and the like; for it was impossible He should be detained by death' (p. 269).

There is according to Scripture no relaxation of the punishment, but only a commutation of the person. God's relation to the satisfaction of Christ must be considered in a twofold way. With regard to us, He is the party offended and the creditor: with regard to Christ He is the supreme Governor and Lawgiver, 'who alone had power so far to relax His own law, as to have the name of a surety put into the obligation, which before was not there, and then to require the whole debt of that surety' (p. 270). There are, then, two elements in God's action in the matter: first, an act of severe justice as a creditor, requiring His full debt at the hands of the debtor; secondly, an act of sovereignty, translating the punishment from the principal debtor to the surety given by His own free grace. Grotius says [9] that 'the right of punishing in the rector or lawgiver can neither be a right of absolute dominion nor a right of creditor; because these things belong to him, and are exercised for his own sake, who hath them, but the right of punishing is for the good of the community' (p. 271). This reasoning, however, is not applicable to God, whose only end can be His own glory: indeed the good of the community itself is nothing different from this. Again Grotius says,[1] 'Punishment is not in and for itself desirable, but only for community's sake. Now the right of dominion and the right of a creditor are in themselves expetible and desirable without the consideration of any public aim' (ibid.). Owen's answer to this is that, apart from the fact that desirability has nothing to do with the Divine actions, some acts of dominion are in themselves as little desirable as any act of punishment, as for instance the annihilation of an innocent creature, which Grotius will not deny but God may do. Grotius also says:[2]

[9] Cf. supra, p. 393. [1] Ibid. [2] Supra, pp. 393, 394f.

469

'Anyone may without any wrong go off from the right of supreme
dominion or creditorship; but the Lord cannot omit the act of
punishment to some sins, as of the impenitent' (*ibid.*). God,
replies Owen, may, by virtue of His supreme dominion, omit
punishment without any wrong or prejudice. He imputed sin to
Christ, where it was not; and may equally impute no sin, where
it is. Other arguments of Grotius less important are also dealt
with, and then Owen closes his discussion by showing that the
doctrine of satisfaction maintained by himself militates against
the idea of universal redemption. The sacrifice of Christ being
an exact equivalent for the sins of those for whom it was offered
as satisfaction, and the only relaxation of the law being in His
substitution as surety for them, it inevitably follows that God's
justice has no claim against those for whom satisfaction has been
made, or in other words, that those who are to all eternity to be
punished for their sins cannot have been included in the satisfaction.

There is yet one more discussion relative to satisfaction.
Owen meets the objection that election makes satisfaction unnecessary. The elect are already the objects of God's love, and
therefore need no satisfaction, but only the knowledge of God's
favour. The reply is that God's love in election is but a purpose
of favour; satisfaction is the means of its being made actual.

We pass on to what is said of merit. Owen declares that this
subject has really been considered under the head of impetration;
nevertheless he adds some observations on the use of the term.
The word 'merit', like the word 'satisfaction', is not to be found
in the New Testament. Yet the idea is there with reference to
the work of Christ. 'Christ, then, by His death, did merit and
purchase, for all those for whom He died, all those things which
in the Scripture are assigned to be the fruits and effects of His
death' (p. 287).

The following argument against the doctrine of universal
redemption is then added: 'If Christ hath merited grace and
glory for all those for whom He died, if He died for all, how
comes it to pass that these things are not communicated to and
bestowed upon all? Is the defect in the merit of Christ or in the
justice of God?' (p. 288).

Book IV begins with a discussion of the Scripture testimonies urged in favour of universal redemption. Owen's method is to speak of all such passages as 'general and indefinite expressions', and to limit them by the logic of his theory, and by those other passages which agree with it. The book ends with a discussion of some particular arguments urged by the opponents.

(1) That which every one is bound to believe is true; but every one is bound to believe that Jesus Christ died for him; therefore it is true that Jesus Christ died for him. Owen's reply is simply to deny the minor premiss.

(2) The doctrine of particular redemption fills the minds of sinners with doubts as to whether they should believe or not, when God calls them to do so. Owen answers that a man is not bound to believe that Jesus Christ died for him in particular, before he believes in Christ. The command of God to believe is enough to remove all doubts and fears.

(3) It is argued, that the doctrine of universal redemption more exalts God's free grace and the merit of Christ. Owen's reply to this is that the grace that is not effectual is no grace; nor is Christ's merit enhanced by assigning to it a fruit which is a lie.

(4) It is argued, that the doctrine of universal redemption has more of consolation in it. On the contrary, says Owen, to know that all are capable of salvation is no real consolation, but only to believe that we are saved. Consolation in fact is not for unbelievers, but only for believers, whose comfort is in that which distinguishes their position from that of unbelievers.

One cannot close Owen's treatise without feeling admiration for its strong, nervous English, its forcible logic, and its deep religious feeling. McLeod Campbell has expressed the view that, if the idea of strict satisfaction be granted, Owen's logic in favour of the doctrine of particular redemption is unanswerable.[3] If then the result be untenable, the inference is that the premiss itself needs revision.[4]

[3] 'The Nature of the Atonement', 2nd ed., 1867, p. 59.
[4] Cf. McLeod Campbell, loc. cit. : 'That cannot be the true conception of the nature of the atonement which implies that Christ died only for an election among men.'

PART IV
MODERN PROTESTANT THEOLOGY

CHAPTER 1

THE BEGINNINGS OF MODERN THEOLOGY IN ENGLAND AND AMERICA

THE ENGLISH DEISM

No new movement of thought ever begins absolutely unprepared. To a certain extent the most modern theology has its roots in the past. There are no absolute divisions in time or in the history of thought any more than there are between county and county and parish and parish. Nevertheless we may say that modern theology begins with the Deist movement in England.[1] The result of this movement was on the one hand a new philosophy of religion, and on the other the historical criticism of the Scriptures and of the traditional ecclesiastical religion. It is these together that are responsible for modern theology.

The new philosophy of religion was indeed only a modification of the doctrine of the Apologists. It began with the recognition of natural religion, the five points of which are defined at the very outset of the Deist movement by Lord Herbert of Cherbury (d. A.D. 1648), as follows:[2]

(1) That there is a supreme God.

(2) That He is to be worshipped.

(3) That piety and virtue are the principal parts of His worship.

(4) That man should repent of sin, and that, if he does so, God will forgive him.

(5) That there are rewards for the good and punishments for the evil, partly in this and partly in a future state.

Lord Herbert held that these natural religious ideas are innate, or given in the very nature of man: they are 'common notices' (common notions). This is practically the same thing as the doctrine of the Apologists that the work of the Logos in

[1] For the Deist movement see especially Troeltsch, 'Deismus', in 'Realencyclopädie für Theologie und Kirche', vol. iv, p. 533.
[2] Cf. Shedd, 'History of Christian Doctrine,' 1872, vol. i, p. 192.

475

every man is to reveal God and His law, with the promise of immortality: there is, however, added to the Apologetic scheme in the natural religion of Lord Herbert the essentially Christian doctrine of the Divine forgiveness of sins. The general theory of the Deists concerning historical Christianity is the same as that of the Apologists, viz. that it is a republication of the religion of reason. While, however, the Apologists taught that the pure natural religion had been obscured by the demons who had seduced men to idolatry, the Deist doctrine now ascribed the advent of idolatry and superstition to the devices of the priests, who thus take the place of the demons as the corrupters of mankind. And, further, the Deists taught that when once Christianity had brought the religion of reason to light again, the priests had once more corrupted it, and so produced the doctrinal system of the Church with its irrational mysteries. All this was already maintained by Lord Herbert, and was later on enshrined in the famous catchwords 'Christianity not Mysterious', the title of a work by Toland (1696), and 'Christianity as Old as the Creation, or the Gospel a Republication of the Religion of Nature', the title of the famous so-called 'Bible of Deism', the work of Matthew Tindal (1730).[3]

What led the Deists to this reassertion with modifications of the doctrine of the Apologists was the search for a philosophy of religion, which might on the one hand rescue the mind from the perplexity caused by the conflict of confessions since the Reformation, and on the other hand harmonise with the view of the world required by the ever-increasing results of modern science.

There was, however, another problem to be faced. Could it actually be shown historically that Christianity was nothing but a republication of the religion of reason or of nature? Attention to this question led to the attempt to evaluate Christianity as a historical phenomenon, the method adopted being that of the criticism of the original sources of our knowledge of it in the New Testament. I shall attempt to exhibit these critical movements by a reference to John Locke and Thomas Chubb.

[3] Cf. Pfleiderer, 'Geschichte der Religionsphilosophie', 3rd ed., 1893, pp. 108–11, 119–22.

LOCKE

Locke (A.D. 1632–1704) denied the existence of any innate ideas in man. However, he held that the being of God and the duties of natural religion were demonstrable by reason. 'But the articles of the Christian religion belong to another sphere. They come by revelation. They are received by faith, and have nothing to do with the certainty of knowledge. Revelation depends upon the veracity of God.'[4]

There is, however, a chasm to be bridged between the original revelation and the revelation in the individual believer. 'God's veracity is not to be doubted, but we must be certain that it is God who speaks. It is the province of reason to discover the certainty or probability of what is proposed. Christianity is not an immediate revelation. It is only traditional, and proposed to us through the testimony of others. Locke says that those to whom revelation is immediate may have a certainty equal to that of knowledge, but not those who have it through testimony. . . . In another place Locke says that though the Scripture be infallible, yet "the reader may be—nay, cannot but be—very fallible in the understanding of it". The will of God clothed in words is subject to all the uncertainty connected with human language and the human understanding.'[5] Such are Locke's general principles: we have now to see how he applied them in detail.

In his book 'The Reasonableness of Christianity as Delivered in the Scriptures' (1695) the famous philosopher endeavours to mediate between the orthodox Protestant theology and the purely rationalistic religion of the Deists.

'To understand what we are restored to by Jesus Christ, we must consider what the Scripture shows we lost by Adam. This I thought worthy of a diligent and unbiassed search: since I found the two extremes that men run into on this point, either on the one hand shook the foundations of all religion, or on the other hand made Christianity almost nothing. For, whilst some men would have all Adam's posterity doomed to eternal infinite punishment for the transgression of Adam, whom millions had

---

[4] Hunt, 'Religious Thought in England', vol. ii, p. 185. [5] *Ibid.* pp. 186ff.

never heard of, and no one had authorised to transact for him or be his representative; this seemed to others so little consistent with the justice or goodness of the great and infinite God, that they thought there was no redemption necessary, and consequently that there was none, rather than admit of it upon a supposition so derogatory to the honour and attributes of that Infinite Being; and so made Jesus Christ nothing but the restorer and preacher of pure natural religion.' [6]

What Adam lost by his fall, says Locke, was simply bliss and immortality. 'The state of paradise was a state of immortality, of life without end, which he lost that very day that he ate. . . . Death entered then and showed his face, which before was shut out and not known' (p. 3). This and nothing else is the teaching of the New Testament. The sentence of death pronounced on mankind because of Adam's sin is to be understood as referring to the death of the body only. Death here means neither eternal misery, nor the corruption of human nature in the posterity of Adam. The New Testament does not teach that corruption seized on all because of Adam's transgression; but every one's sin is charged upon himself only. Nor can it strictly be said, that in losing immortality the posterity of Adam are punished for his offence. For in taking away from them immortality, God took something to which they had no right: it was a pure gift of His bounty to man. Still merely to lose bliss and immortality is enough to cause man to be spoken of as lost. 'Adam being thus turned out of paradise and all his posterity born out of it, the consequence of it was, that all men should die, and remain under death for ever, and so be utterly lost' (p. 8).

From this estate of death Jesus Christ restores all mankind to life by His Resurrection; that so by Adam's sin they may none of them lose immortality, if only they merit it by their own righteousness. 'For righteousness, or an exact obedience to the law, seems by the Scripture to have a claim of right to eternal life' [7] (p. 8). On the other hand those who transgress the law duly merit death like Adam, and Scripture assures us that all have sinned; so that it follows that no one can by his own righteousness attain to eternal life and bliss.

[6] Ed. London, 1810, pp. 1, 2. [7] Locke refers to Rom. 4:4 ; Rev. 22:14.

478

'This being the case, that whosoever is guilty of any sin should certainly die and cease to be, the benefit of life restored by Christ at the Resurrection would have been of no great advantage (forasmuch as here again death must have seized upon all mankind, because all had sinned: for the wages of sin is everywhere death, as well after, as before the Resurrection) if God had not found out a way to justify some, i.e. so many as obeyed another law, which God gave, which in the New Testament is called "the law of faith" [8] and is opposed to the "law of works" ' (pp. 11, 12).

As to the law of works, Locke follows the traditional doctrine: it is in part the eternal moral law, which, however, was repromulgated by Moses, and is not abrogated by Christ; but above and beyond this it is in part positive ordinance, such as the command to Adam not to eat of the tree of knowledge, or again the ceremonial and political part of the law of Moses: this positive part never possessed more than a limited and temporary obligation.

The law of faith differs from the law of works as follows: 'The law of works makes no allowance for failing on any occasion. . . . But by the law of faith, faith is allowed to supply the defect of full obedience, and so the believers are admitted to life and immortality, as if they were righteous' (p. 15). The moral law, however, remains presupposed by the law of faith; or else this dispensation would have no meaning. Only the Jewish ceremonial law is abrogated by the Gospel.

So far Locke's doctrine is closely allied to that of the Socinians and Arminians. Now comes his own peculiar contribution, in which, however, he is still very much on Socinian lines, except that instead of the complicated Socinian theology, which though it differs *toto cœlo* from that of orthodoxy, still retains its form, he proposes a highly simplified and reduced 'lay' theology. The one and only demand of the law of faith is the belief that Jesus is the Messiah. The tremendous structure of the orthodox dogmatic is replaced by this one solitary proposition. It is a veritable return *ad fontes*.

In order to establish his doctrine Locke adduces as evidence

[8] Rom. 3:27.

simply the Gospels and the Acts of the Apostles. From these it is clear that the only article of faith demanded by Jesus, while He was upon earth, was that of His Messiahship: it is equally plain that this was the one fundamental article of the primitive Church. If now it is said that to believe upon Jesus of Nazareth as the Messiah, is but a historical, and not a justifying or saving faith, the reply is, that men may make what distinctions they please, but they must have a care how they deny that to be a justifying faith, which our Saviour and His Apostles have declared to be so, and have made the condition of eternal life. If, again, it is urged that this faith is no different from that of the devils, who confessed in His lifetime that Jesus was the Messiah, and yet were not saved thereby, the answer is once more that God never offered them this way of salvation, and besides, even if they did thus believe, they did not perform a second condition required by the covenant of grace, viz. repentance. 'Repentance is as absolute a condition of the covenant of grace as faith; and as necessary to be performed as that' (p. 149). It means 'not only a sorrow for sins past, but (what is a natural consequence of such sorrow, if it be real) a turning from them into a new and contrary life' (p. 151).

Such then according to Locke is the scheme of redemption as stated in the New Testament. He now undertakes to show its rationality. Adam was created in the likeness or image of God, part of which was immortality. This, however, he lost for mankind by the Fall. Christ, therefore, who was, as the Son of God, naturally immortal, recovered it for mankind by becoming incarnate, dying, and by His own power rising again. As Christ was sinless, His death can only be interpreted as for others. Hence it demanded a reward, which God gave Him in assigning to Him, as Messiah, an everlasting Kingdom. This Kingdom, however, He could not have without subjects; and to supply these God promised immortality to those who would accept Jesus as the Messiah, and repent of their sins, turning for the future in sincere obedience to the Divine law. They should then have their sins forgiven, and their faith in the Messiah should supply the defects of their obedience, so that they might be made capable of eternal life.

480

In accordance with these views Locke proposes to reduce the doctrine of the work of Christ simply to the one scheme of the kingly office. 'The faith required was to believe Jesus to be the Messiah, the anointed, who had been promised by God to the world. Amongst the Jews (to whom the promises and prophecies of the Messiah were more immediately delivered) anointing was used for three sorts of persons at their inauguration, whereby they were set apart for three great offices, viz. of priests, prophets, and kings. Though these three offices be in holy writ attributed to our Saviour, yet I do not remember that He anywhere assumes to Himself the title of a priest, or mentions anything relating to His priesthood; nor does He speak of His being a prophet but very sparingly, and once or twice, as it were, by the by; but the gospel, or good news of the kingdom of the Messiah, is what He preaches everywhere, and makes it His great business to publish to the world' (pp. 163, 164).

From our Saviour's Messiahship is to be explained what theology had previously reckoned to His prophetic office. 'Thus we see our Saviour not only confirmed the moral law, and, clearing it from the corrupt glosses of the Scribes and Pharisees, showed the strictness as well as obligation of its injunctions; but, moreover, upon occasion, requires the obedience of His disciples to several of the commands He afresh lays upon them, with the enforcement of unspeakable rewards and punishments in another world according to their obedience or disobedience' (p. 177).

Locke now deals with the position of those outside the Christian revelation, a problem which Deism had brought much to the fore. The Jews before Christ were justified by believing on a Messiah to come, just as Christians are by believing on a Messiah that has come. As to the rest of mankind Locke accepts the Deist view. 'God had, by the light of reason, revealed to all that would make use of that light, that He was good and merciful. The same spark of the divine nature and knowledge in man, which making him a man showed him the law he was under as a man, showed him also the way of atoning the merciful, kind, compassionate Author and Father of him and his being, when he had transgressed that law' (p. 193).

This leads naturally to the questions:—What need was there

481

of a Saviour? What advantage have we by Jesus Christ? Locke replies as follows:

(1) We cannot expect completely to understand the Divine wisdom. 'We know little of this visible, and nothing at all of the state of that intellectual world, wherein are infinite numbers and degrees of spirits out of the reach of our ken or guess; and therefore know not what transactions there were between God and our Saviour, in reference to His kingdom. We know not what need there was to set up a head and a chieftain in opposition to the "prince of this world, the prince of the power of the air", etc., of which there are more than obscure intimations in the Scriptures' (p. 195). This is the only place that Locke has for the traditional doctrine of the work of Christ as a transcendent action in the supramundane sphere: he leaves it, however, as a mystery, and so far as his indications point, inclines rather to the views of the Ancient Church than to any more modern doctrine.

(2) Beyond this, however, Locke urges, as the Greeks and in particular Athanasius had done, that there was need of a fresh Divine revelation. 'Though the works of nature in every part of them sufficiently evidence a Deity, yet the world made so little use of their reason, that they saw Him not, where even by the impressions of Himself, He was easy to be found' (p. 196). Christ then brought a fresh revelation of God, and authenticated it by His miracles.

(3) 'Next to the knowledge of one God, maker of all things, a clear knowledge of their duty was wanting to mankind. This part of knowledge, though cultivated with some care, by some of the heathen philosophers, yet got little footing among the people' (p. 201). It seems in fact, that 'it is too hard a task for unassisted reason to establish morality in all its parts, upon its true foundations, with a clear and convincing light' (p. 202). Hence the need for an inculcation of morality more popular in character. 'It is at least a surer and shorter way to the apprehensions of the vulgar, and mass of mankind, that one manifestly sent from God, and coming with visible authority from Him, should, as a king and lawmaker, tell them their duties, and require their obedience, than leave it to the long and sometimes

intricate deductions of reason, to be made out to them' (pp. 202, 203).

(4) Jesus also undertook the reformation of the outward forms of worshipping the Deity; and, doing away with all useless ceremonies, He introduced a spiritual worship of God.

(5) He also brought a great encouragement to a virtuous and pious life by a clear promise of immortality as its reward.

(6) Finally, He brought to men the promise of the assistance of the Holy Ghost. Locke here admits a mystical element into his otherwise (save only for the vague indication of a transcendent mystery in the work of Christ) clear and rationalistic scheme.

With this the positive statement of doctrine closes. There remains, however, a possible objection. 'If the belief of Jesus of Nazareth to be the Messiah, together with those concomitant articles of His Resurrection, rule, and coming again to judge the world, be all the faith required as necessary to justification, to what purpose were the Epistles written? I say, if the belief of these many doctrines contained in them be not also necessary to salvation; and if what is there delivered, a Christian may believe or disbelieve, and yet, nevertheless be a member of Christ's Church, and one of the faithful?' (p. 221).

Here enters the really novel part of Locke's doctrinal method. The close correspondence of the matter of doctrine with that of the Greek Apologists, Clement and Origen, and still more with that of Socinus, is apparent. But he is not writing, like the Apologists, prior to the fixing of the New Testament Canon. Nor does he adopt, like Clement and Origen, to justify his theology, the allegorical method. Nor yet, again, like Socinus, does he compel the New Testament to serve his purpose by a forced exegesis. In contrast with all these theologians, he deliberately makes the basis of his doctrine a critical distinction between one part of the New Testament and another. He harps upon the 'occasional' character of the Epistles. A great deal in them was simply said by way of accommodation of the Christian truth to the special needs of the readers, and has no more than a temporary value.

'It is not in the Epistles we are to learn what are the funda-

mental articles of faith, where they are promiscuously and
without distinction mixed with other truths in discourses that
were (though for edification indeed, yet) only occasional. We
shall find and observe these great and necessary points best in
the preaching of our Saviour and the Apostles, to those who
were strangers, and ignorant of the faith, to bring them in and
convert them to it. And what that was, we have seen already out
of the history of the Evangelists, and the Acts, where they are
plainly laid down, so that nobody can mistake them' (pp. 224,
225).

Such a distinction consciously made between different stages
in the doctrine of the New Testament is of immense importance.
Though present here as yet only in an elementary form it contains
the principle of the modern science of Biblical theology, which,
instead of treating the whole New Testament, and to a considerable extent indeed the whole Bible, as upon the same level,
as did the traditional theology of the Church, notes everywhere
advance and development, differences and shades of doctrinal
apprehension of Christianity, and furnishes dogmatic theology
with an entirely remodelled Scriptural basis from which to
operate.

Locke does not work out in detail the consequences of his
principle of accommodation. But he indicates its possibilities
for the doctrine of the work of Christ, when he says that 'The
setting out and confirming the Christian faith to the Hebrews,
in the Epistle to them, is by allusions and arguments, from the
ceremonies, sacrifices, and œconomy of the Jews, and reference
to the records of the Old Testament' (p. 225). Here we have a
principle stated, which, if admitted, must carry us far indeed in
the restatement of the doctrine of the work of Christ. It has
affinity indeed with the principle under which Clement and
Origen tended to regard some of the theologumena of the New
Testament as more or less allegorical, and has still more affinity
with the doctrine of Socinus as to the metaphorical character
of many New Testament doctrinal passages. But it substitutes
for the arbitrariness of the allegorical method, and the arbitrariness which Socinus often used in working out his metaphorical
principle, the methodic science of historical criticism.

CHUBB

To what the critical principles of Locke were destined to lead, begins to appear in the writings of Thomas Chubb (d. A.D. 1747). Chubb, one of the later Deists, concerns himself, like Locke, more than the early Deists with the Christian revelation and not merely with the religion of reason. He certainly agrees with them that 'whatever is mysterious and unintelligible, so far as it is unintelligible, cannot be revelation in any sense'.[9] Still he seems to admit that Divine revelation may disclose to us things beyond what we might otherwise have known. 'There are a multitude of propositions worthy of the Deity, which are knowable and promulgable, independent of Divine revelation' (p. 8). On the other hand 'there must be something disclosed and made known, that was not known before, to constitute revelation strictly and properly so called' (p. 3). The mere bringing to remembrance, or awakening of the attention to propositions, which otherwise would have been forgotten or neglected, or would not have been sufficiently attended to, can only be called revelation in a loose and improper sense.

Chubb accepts (after consideration) the mission of Jesus Christ and His Gospel as a Divine revelation; while he takes up at the same time a very different attitude to the revelation of the Old Testament, the particularism of which offends him. He says on the one hand: 'It appears, that the Jewish revelation in the gross (whatever may be the case of some particular branches of it) cannot well be admitted as Divine, without offering some kind of violence to the human mind' (p. 29). On the other hand he says : 'It is probable that Christ's mission was Divine; by which I mean, it is probable that Jesus Christ was sent of God to be an adviser and an instructor to mankind, by communicating such useful knowledge to them as otherwise they might not have attained to, and by refreshing their memories, and awakening their attention to such propositions as otherwise might have been greatly neglected by them, even where the highest interest is concerned' (p. 45).

The great question to be determined, then, in regard of the

---

[9] 'Posthumous Works', London, 1748, vol. ii, p. 4.

485

Divine mission of Christ is, what was the message entrusted to Him. Speculation as to His Person Chubb puts aside as irrelevant and misdirected. The transference of attention in the Christian Church from the message brought by Jesus Christ to the Person of the Messenger has brought about nothing but contention, confusion, and manifold mischief, 'Whereas this is a point that we are not interested in, nor concerned with; seeing Christ's message and its importance to us are just the same, whatever His personal character may be . . . the great question with us is, or at least ought to be, what is that important message, which Christ was sent of God to deliver to the world?' (p. 56).

To determine exactly the content of this message is, however, a matter of difficulty. History shows us nothing but conflict of one Christian theology with another, while the New Testament itself, recognised since the establishment of the Canon as the authoritative source of Christian knowledge, is now seen by the critical reason to offer no single answer to the question, What is Christianity?

'Christ's message has been so loosely and indeterminately delivered to the world, that nothing but contention and confusion has attended it, from its first promulgation down to this time, insomuch that what has been deemed to be Christianity in one age, and by one people, has not been so, in and by another. And, as to the books of the New Testament, they have been so far from being a remedy to this evil, that they have been partly the disease, or at least they have contributed to it, as the most opposite and contrary doctrines are capable of being grounded, and have been grounded upon them' (p. 57).

The truth is, that the Christian revelation has come to us entirely through the hands of men, and has been constantly modified in the process of tradition. The oral tradition, which the Church of Rome adds to the written tradition of the New Testament, in order to obtain a sufficient support for the stately edifice of its doctrine, has indeed been rejected by Protestantism; and this was a great advance. But criticism must go farther, and, recognising that the process of modification was at work from the very origins of Christianity, distinguish between different elements in the New Testament itself. 'I say, the Christian revelation is

486

to be collected or gathered from these writings; for as Christ's message is not particularly specified nor ascertained in these books, nor can they in the gross be considered as such; so, consequently, that message can only be gathered or collected from them. The books of the New Testament contain a great deal of matter which is perfectly distinct from, independent of, and quite irrelative to Christ's message; and therefore those books. in the gross, cannot, with any propriety or truth, be called the Christian revelation' (p. 71).

Chubb now distinguishes four parts in the New Testament: (1) the Gospels, containing the history of the ministry of Christ; (2) the Acts of the Apostles, with the history of the ministry of the Apostles; (3) the Epistles, containing apostolic counsel or advice to certain persons or churches; (4) the Revelation, a kind of visionary prophecy of things to come, which he confesses he does not understand, and must therefore leave out of consideration. Of these four parts the Gospels alone form an adequate basis for the determination of Christ's message.

'From these books, I think, the Christian revelation is to be chiefly, if not wholly collected; because they are furnished with materials for that purpose, which are not to be met with elsewhere. In these books we have an account at large of Christ's discourses and parables, and what He from time to time delivered as the will of His father, of which we have no such particular and full account in any other parts of the New Testament. And what we have in these books is at first hand, as from Christ Himself, without anyone's comment upon it, supposing these records to be originally true history, and to have sustained no injury through its conveyance to us: whence, what we have from the Apostles, touching this matter, is at second hand, as from Christ through them, who to say the least were liable to misunderstand their master, as I shall have occasion to show more at large hereafter; nor does the history of their ministry clear up, but rather darken and perplex the subject: so that what is Christ's message, or what is the Christian revelation, strictly and properly so called; this must be chiefly, if not wholly collected from the histories of Christ's ministry, as we have not materials elsewhere to gather it from' (pp. 72, 73).

There is to be observed here the emergence of an immensely important and significant principle. Here is already, in this later Deism, the distinction between the Gospel of Jesus Himself and the Gospel of His Apostles, which constitutes one of the fundamental problems of modern theology. Chubb is indeed following out the return *ad fontes* as recommended by Locke, but he goes farther than the great philosopher. If the latter would have us go back from Paulinism to the pre-Pauline Messianic Christianity of the primitive Jewish Church, Chubb invites us to pass behind even this, and build simply and solely upon the record of the teaching of Jesus in the Gospels. Of course in neither case, in the rough and ready discrimination of the sources, is there as yet an understanding of the complexity of the problems involved; nevertheless there is already the whole programme of criticism, and the outline of the questions which were henceforward to occupy it.

His basis thus critically fixed, Chubb proceeds to sum up in three particulars the substance of Christ's message. (1) Nothing but conformity to the eternal rule of right will render men acceptable to God. (2) If men have greatly departed from it, and have thereby rendered themselves the proper objects of Divine revenge; nothing but repentance and reformation will render them the proper objects of, and will be the ground and reason for, God's mercy to them. (3) God will judge the world in righteousness, and render to every man according to his works.

'These propositions appear, to me, to contain the sum and substance of Christ's ministry: and, as they are altogether worthy of the supreme Deity; so, I think, they may with propriety and truth be called the Gospel of Jesus Christ, or the Christian revelation' (p. 83).

The Acts of the Apostles do not add anything at all to this determination of the Christian message. It is only clear from them that the Apostles limited Christianity to the Jews, and regarded it as nothing but a graft upon Judaism, till St Paul put an end to this state of things by his opposition to such principles. This opposition, however, did not arise out of any special revelation which St Paul had received for abolishing the Jewish law, 'but from the nature of the thing itself, as it obviously appeared to be a law of carnal commandments, which carried with them such a yoke of bondage as was unbearable, and therefore ought to be abolished' (p. 85).

It is to be observed, however, that the doctrine Paul employed to this end, viz. that Christ had abolished the law of ceremonies and nailed them to the cross, is no part of the original Christianity. Otherwise the Apostles could not have viewed Judaism as they did before St Paul's conversion. The same applies to the doctrines that the law was a type of the Gospel and that the Gospel was the completion of the law. Moreover, Jesus Himself never taught so.

With these reflections Chubb obtains a standpoint whence he can deal with the Epistles, especially those of St Paul. 'A great deal of them is altogether irrelative to that message, or else upon some account or other, plainly appears not to have been contained in it. Thus, a great part of St Paul's Epistles consists in showing the weakness and unprofitableness of the Jewish law, and in persuading the people not to submit to it; which surely cannot be conceived to be any part of that Gospel which Christ preached to the Jews in His own person; because, according to the history, He was so far from discharging men from paying obedience to that law, that, on the contrary, He seems rather to have pressed their obedience to it. Nor can what St Paul has said upon this point be any part of the Gospel which Christ gave in charge to His Apostles to publish to the world, because, if that had been the case, then, surely, the Apostles and first Christians would not have maintained the contrary, as we find they did, for some time, viz. till after the conversion of St Paul' (pp. 111, 112).

What, then, of the orthodox Protestant doctrines of the work of Christ, which are supposed to be grounded upon the Epistles, 'such as that men are rendered acceptable to God, and that sinners are recommended to His mercy, either through the perfect obedience, or the meritorious sufferings, or the prevailing intercession of Christ, or through one or other, or all of these?' (p. 112).

Even if men of learning say that these doctrines are plainly contained in the words of the Apostles, they are still to be rejected as contrary to reason and the moral sense; 'and therefore, surely, may fairly be presumed to be no parts of the Christian revelation, whatsoever book they may be contained in, or whomsoever they may have been taught by' (p. 113).

Some learned men indeed (i.e. the Socinians) aver that the above doctrines were not taught by the Apostles. Chubb professes that he is no judge in this matter: only in any case he knows that he cannot receive the Epistles, except so far as they are not contrary to reason, and thus one way or another is under no obligation to believe such doctrines. He is not, however, content to leave the matter here. In order to form a critical estimate of the apostolic teaching he makes use of the idea of accommodation, which we have already observed as thrown out in this connexion by Locke, but which our author applies to the subject in much fuller detail than Locke has done.

'As to the writings of the Apostles, they plainly appear to have been written occasionally, and seem suitable to the exigencies of those upon whose account and for whose sakes they were written; and, as such, it is not unlikely that some of the arguments contained in those writings were arguments only to those to whom they were sent, as they might affect their respective cases only, and as it were reasoning with them upon their own principles' (p. 301).

In fact, the Apostles, in endeavouring to commend the Gospel to the Jews, drew a parallel between the Law and the Gospel. 'For example: As the Jews had their temple, their altar, their high priest, their sacrifices, and the like; so the Apostles, in order to make Christianity bear a resemblance to, and as it were tally with Judaism, found out something or other in Christianity, which they by a figure of speech called by those names' (p. 303). Upon this figurative language, however, some of their followers have built doctrines that are plainly repugnant to truth and reason. 'For example: upon the figurative language of the Apostle this doctrine has been grounded, viz. that God was made placable or merciful to mankind by the sufferings and death of Jesus Christ; which doctrine cannot possibly be true, because God's disposition to show mercy to the proper objects of mercy, arises wholly from His own innate goodness or mercifulness, and

490

not from anything external to Him, whether it be the sufferings and death of Jesus Christ or otherwise' (p. 304).

Let it be observed, as in the case of Locke, only now with more reason, that here is a method of dealing with the traditional doctrine of the work of Christ very different from that of Socinus. Socinus and Chubb indeed agree in repudiating the orthodox doctrine. But their reasons are different. Instead of referring to the legal impossibilities, which Socinus finds in the orthodox theory, Chubb rests his case solely on its moral incompatibility with the idea of God's mercy. But this conception of God's necessary mercifulness is different from the Socinian notion of God, where His mercy flows simply from His arbitrary will.[1] This latter conception of God, which played so great a part in the patristic and mediaeval doctrine as one of its governing principles till Duns Scotus raised it to the rank of the absolute and only true principle of theology as a whole, Chubb critically disallows just in the same way as he rejects the ideas of placation and satisfaction. The introduction of this principle in Rom. 9 is simply an accommodation to Jewish thought. 'The Jews considered God as an absolute sovereign, who makes mere capricious humour and arbitrary will the rule and measure of His actions in His dealings with mankind' (p. 304). This Jewish principle, however, inflicts great dishonour upon the Deity and is false, 'seeing God is so far from making capricious humour, at any time, or in any instance, the rule of His conduct, that on the contrary, He makes the eternal rule of right and wrong the measure of His actions, and in consequence of the rectitude of this Divine conduct, in every nation under heaven, he that feareth God and worketh righteousness is accepted of Him' (p. 305).

Nevertheless, Paul, though no doubt reasoning from other principles in other parts of his writings, has employed this principle in Rom. 9. What then? 'This doctrine, surely, is false; though taught by that great Apostle St Paul' (p. 314). It is 'a difficult thing for men wholly to shake off those principles they have been educated in; and, therefore, they are apt sometimes to reason from those principles, and that seems to have been the case of St Paul here' (p. 314).

[1] Cf. *supra*, pp. 364f.

BUTLER

The great English defence of traditional Christianity against
the Deists is Butler's work, 'The Analogy of Religion, Natural
and Revealed, to the Constitution and Course of Nature'.[2] The
text of the treatise is taken from Origen: 'He who believes the
Scripture to have proceeded from Him who is the Author of
Nature, may well expect to find the same sort of difficulties in
it as are found in the constitution of Nature'.[3] Butler seeks to
show that all evidence of religion is a matter of probability,
which can only lead to moral certainty. It is upon such evidence
that we accept the truths of natural religion, and so upon such
evidence we may well accept revealed religion, i.e. the orthodox
system of doctrine as contained in Scripture. The importance of
Christianity is, that it is not only a republication of the religion
of nature, but also an account of a particular dispensation,
carried on by the Son and Holy Spirit for the redemption of
mankind, not discoverable by reason, and involving new duties
and new precepts. Objections to the scheme of Christianity are
to be answered from the analogy that may be perceived between
it and nature. This argument Butler works out with regard both
to the Christian revelation as a whole, and to its parts in detail.

His argument in the former general reference has been
summarised as follows:

'There is no presumption from analogy against the general
scheme of Christianity. We are acquainted only with a very small
part of the natural and moral system of the universe. It is, then,
no presumption against the truth of what is revealed that it lay
beyond the reach of our natural faculties.'[4]

Butler's defence of the doctrine of the mediation of Christ
against the Deists is contained in 'Analogy', Pt. II, chap. v.[5]

'There is not, I think, anything relating to Christianity, which
has been more objected against, than the mediation of Christ, in
some or other of its parts. Yet, upon consideration there seems
nothing less justly liable to it' (p. 207). In the first place the

[2] Butler, A.D. 1692–1752, 'The Analogy', A.D. 1736.
[3] Butler's *Works*, Oxford, 1897, vol. i, p. 8.
[4] Hunt, 'Religious Thought in England', vol. iii, p. 136.
[5] *Works*, Oxford, 1897, vol. i, p. 207.

principle of mediation belongs to the order of nature. 'There is, then, no sort of objection, from the light of nature, against the general notion of a mediator between God and man, considered as a doctrine of Christianity' (p. 208).

For the further justification of the doctrine of Christ's mediation, however, it is necessary to go back to that system of natural religion, which revelation presupposes. It is a system of Divine moral government, in which vice is punished, either in this world or the next. Analogy leads us to suppose that the future punishments of wickedness may be like those of the present, which take place in the way of natural consequence. However, in the present order the natural consequences of wickedness do not always automatically follow, but may to some extent be avoided by the personal action of the delinquent or by the help of others. There is no reason then to suppose, that with regard to the future punishments of wickedness a relaxation may not be possible. We can hardly, however, imagine that of our own ability we can avert these consequences; even in this world we seldom do this. Analogy leads us to believe that our reformation will be, not indeed useless, but yet insufficient to prevent future punishment. As to the current idea (of the Deists) that repentance is enough, the general tendency among the heathen to supplement it by propitiatory sacrifices seems to show that the Deist view is contrary to common sense.

'Upon the whole, then: Had the laws, the general laws of God's government, been permitted to operate, without any interposition on our behalf, the future punishment, for aught we know to the contrary, or have any reason to think, must inevitably have followed, notwithstanding anything we could have done to prevent it' (p. 214).

Here revelation enters, and confirms our fears as to the unprevented results of wickedness; supposes the world to be in a state of ruin (which supposition, if not provable by reason, is not contrary to it); but finally teaches, what nature might have led us to hope, that the moral government of the universe is not so rigid that there is no room for interposition, and proclaims the interposition of Christ for our salvation through the love of God and His own love. Here there is nothing inconsistent with the Divine goodness. There is, indeed, the strange ruin of mankind. 'But it is not Christianity, which has put us into this state' (p. 216). Moreover, the Scriptural explanation of its origin is not unreasonable. 'That the crime of our first parents was the occasion of our being placed in a more disadvantageous condition, is a thing throughout and particularly analogous to what we see in the daily course of natural Providence' (p. 217).

The Scriptural mode of redemption through the mediation of Christ has already been shown to be in general accordant with the analogy of nature. It now remains to consider the particular type of mediation of which Scripture speaks. Christ is there described as the Revealer of the will of God in the most eminent sense. He is also a propitiatory sacrifice, and as He voluntarily offered Himself, is our High Priest. The view that the latter descriptions are an accommodation to the Jewish point of view is unscriptural. According to the Epistle to the Hebrews, the Old Testament sacrifices were rather intended to suggest and point forward to the great sacrifice of Christ.

Divines accordingly are wont to treat of the office of Christ under three heads:

(1) 'He was, by way of eminence, the Prophet. . . . He published anew the law of nature, which men had corrupted; and the very knowledge of which, to some degree, was lost among them. He taught mankind, taught us authoritatively to live soberly, righteously, and godly in this present world, in expectation of the future judgment of God. He confirmed the truth of this moral system of nature, and gave us additional evidence of it; the evidence of testimony. He distinctly revealed the manner in which God would be worshipped, the efficacy of repentance, and the rewards and punishments of a future life. . . . To which it is to be added that He set us a perfect example, that we should follow His steps' (p. 219).

(2) 'He has a kingdom which is not of this world. He founded a Church, to be to mankind a standing memorial of religion, and invitation to it, which He promised to be with always even to the end. He exercised an invisible government over it Himself, and by His Spirit: over that part of it, which is here militant on earth, a government of discipline. . . . Of this Church all

494

persons scattered over the world, who lived in obedience to His laws, are members. For these He is gone to prepare a place, and will come again to receive them unto Himself, that where He is they may be also, and reign with Him for ever and ever; and likewise to take vengeance on them that know not God and obey not His Gospel' (p. 220).

All objections to the above two heads of doctrine are met by the general considerations in favour of mediation at the beginning of the chapter. There remains, however, the third and most disputed head of doctrine, the priestly office of Christ.

(3) Christ's sacrifice 'was, in the highest degree and with the most extensive influence, of that efficacy for obtaining pardon of sin, which the heathens may be supposed to have thought their sacrifices to have been, and which the Jewish sacrifices really were in some degree, and with regard to some persons. How and in what particular way it had this efficacy, there are not wanting persons who have endeavoured to explain: but I do not find that Scripture has explained it. We seem to be very much in the dark concerning the manner in which the ancients understood atonements to be made, i.e. pardon to be obtained by sacrifices. And if the Scripture has, as it surely has, left this matter of the satisfaction of Christ, mysterious, left somewhat in it unrevealed, all conjectures about it must be, if not evidently absurd, yet at least uncertain. . . . Some have endeavoured to explain the efficacy of what Christ has done and suffered for us, beyond what the Scripture has authorised; others, probably because they could not explain it, have been for taking it away, and confining His office as Redeemer of the world to His instruction, example, and government of the Church. Whereas the doctrine of the Gospel appears to be, not only that He taught the efficacy of repentance, but rendered it of the efficacy which it is, by what He did and suffered for us; that He obtained for us the benefit of having our repentance accepted unto eternal life: not only that He revealed to sinners, that they were in a capacity of salvation, and how they might obtain it; but moreover that He put them into this capacity of salvation by what He did and suffered for them; put us into a capacity of escaping future punishment, and obtaining future happiness. And it is our

wisdom thankfully to accept the benefit, by performing the conditions, upon which it is offered, on our part, without disputing how it was obtained on His' (p. 221).

We are not to judge, antecedently to revelation, whether a Mediator was, or was not, necessary to obtain the remission of eternal punishment; and so neither are we to judge, antecedently to revelation, of the manner in which Christ's mediation may have operated in this matter. It is no objection that we do not see how it was conducive to the end of remission: as long as it cannot be shown to be positively unreasonable, the Scriptural doctrine must stand fast.

As to the objection, that in the revealed scheme of redemption the innocent is punished for the guilty, there is nothing here that is not illustrated continually in the order of nature. Vicarious punishment belongs to this order and is often redemptive. Besides Christ undertook His sufferings voluntarily; whereas in the order of nature those who suffer vicariously often suffer of necessity. Thus the whole objection is worth nothing.

Finally, there is yet another argument to show the folly of human objections to the infinite scheme of redemption, because the utility of the parts is not to us apparent. This is, that our objections are laid against a part of the scheme in which we are not directly concerned. It is in the order of grace, as it is in the order of nature. In both we are instructed in our own duty, not in the secrets of Divine counsels. 'The doctrine of a Mediator between God and man, against which it is objected, that the expediency of some things in it is not understood, relates only to what was done on God's part in the appointment, and on the Mediator's in the execution of it. For what is required of us, in consequence of this gracious dispensation, is another subject, in which none of us can complain for want of information' (p. 226).

Four points are particularly worthy of note in Butler's reply to the Deists with reference to the doctrine of the work of Christ. The first is the stress which he lays on man's incapacity to understand the transcendent side of redemption, while its practical side lies open to him. Here we may trace the influence of the philosophy of Locke. The second point, which is of great interest, is the treatment of the idea of sacrifice. The *rationale* of ancient sacrifice was, in and about the period when Butler wrote, being subjected to fresh investigation.[6] Butler is not so sure as was the older theology, that we fully understand the theory of ancient sacrifice. If indeed he traces its probable origin in general to revelation, still its *rationale* is not evident. Scripture has not explained it. 'We seem to be very much in the dark concerning the manner in which the ancients understood atonement to be made, i.e. pardon to be obtained by sacrifices' (p. 221). This view, of course, fits in with Butler's general scepticism as to our understanding the *rationale* of atonement in the case of Christ; but it is interesting as the precursor of the new investigation of the idea of sacrifice, which has done so much in the nineteenth century to undermine the traditional basis of the orthodox doctrine of atonement. Butler here carries us beyond the Deists. They accepted the traditional interpretation of sacrifice, obviating by their doctrine of accommodation the usual argument drawn from it in support of the orthodox theory. Butler's doubt of that interpretation, however, leaves the way open for further investigation of the idea of sacrifice in general, with the result of the possibility of a consequent modification in the understanding of the New Testament material of the doctrine of the work of Christ.

Thirdly, another noteworthy point in Butler's argument is his justification of the principle of vicarious punishment not from any system of law but from the order of nature: it is forgotten 'that vicarious punishment is a providential appointment of every day's experience' (p. 224). We observe here the introduction of a new argument, destined to take a large place in modern theology.

Finally, another point, closely associated with that just spoken of, is Butler's stress upon the natural consequences of wrongdoing. It was, indeed, no new thought that sin brings suffering according to the very order of nature. But it is a distinct mark of the influence of modern science that this mode of conception should, as it were, be separated from the religious thought of God, and so the natural consequences of sin be distinguished from God's direct punishment of it.

[6] Outram, 'De Sacrificiis,' 1677; Spencer, 'De Legibus Hebræorum ritualibus', lib. III, De ratione et origine sacrificiorum, 1727; Sykes, 'Essay on the Nature, Design, and Origin of Sacrifices', 1748.

JONATHAN EDWARDS

Jonathan Edwards (A.D. 1703–58), the true founder of a distinctive American theology, is interesting, because he too, like Butler, states the doctrine of the work of Christ in view of the Deist controversy. It is, however, a very different line of argument from that of Butler, which he develops in his discourse 'Concerning the Necessity and Reasonableness of the Christian Doctrine of Satisfaction for Sin'.[7] Edwards argues as follows:

(1) 'Justice requires that sin be punished, because sin deserves punishment' (p. 458). Greater sins deserve greater punishment, less sins less punishment; but all sins require punishment according to their demerit.

(2) Sin, viewed as an offence against God, is, however, of an infinite demerit. God must therefore punish it with infinite punishment. 'unless there be something in some measure to balance this desert' (p. 459). Human repentance or sorrow for sin can, however, never reverse the existing balance, since sin is infinite, and there can be no infinite sorrow for sin in finite creatures. To propose that God should pardon sin because of human repentance is no different from asking that He should pardon it with no repentance at all. Repentance is required when sin is pardoned, not as amends for sin, but in view of compensation already made.

(3) Sin strikes at God; it would, if it could, annihilate Him. It must therefore be repaid by God with enmity. As the Ruler of the universe, He must maintain order and decorum in His Kingdom. This is what His justice means.

(4) God's holiness also demands the punishment of sin. As holy, God is opposed to sin, and must be at enmity with the sinner.

(5, 6) God's antipathy to sin must be visibly manifested. 'If there had been only a declaration of God's abhorrence and displeasure against sin, the creature might have believed it, but could not have seen it, unless He should also take vengeance for it' (p. 462).

---

[7] 'Remarks on important theological controversies', chap. VI, *Works*, London, 1817, vol. viii, pp. 458ff.

(7) God's honour requires the punishment of sin. 'If we consider sin as levelled against God, not only compensative justice to the sinner, but justice to Himself, requires that God should punish sin with infinite punishment' (p. 463). The majesty of God must be vindicated by punishment; 'unless there could be such a thing as a repentance, humiliation, and sorrow, proportionable to the greatness of the majesty despised' (ibid.).

(8–10) The Divine law demands the punishment of sin: without a sanction it would be not law, but only counsel. Moreover, the punishment threatened by the law must be executed: otherwise the law is implicity abrogated. Dispensation is so far forth abrogation.

(11–17) God therefore cannot abrogate His law or dispense with it. It would be indecent if the law were to give way to the sinner. To abrogate it would be a slur on its perfection. God's authority would be set aside, and His truth violated by the abrogation of the law.

(18, 19) 'The satisfaction of Christ by His death is certainly a very rational thing' (p. 471). In fact the principle of mediation is a natural principle. It is also a Scriptural principle, since Christ is said to have borne our sins for us.[8]

(20) Some definitions require to be premised.

'By *merit*, I mean anything whatsoever in any person or belonging to him, which appearing in the view of another is a recommendation of him to that other's regard, esteem, or affection' (p. 472). Merit, in short, is whatever recommends, irrespective of intrinsic worth.

' By *patron*, I mean a person of superior dignity or merit, that stands for and espouses the interest of another, interposes between him and a third person or party, in that capacity to maintain, secure, or promote the interest of that other by his influence with the third person, improving his merit with him, or interest in his esteem and regard for that end. And by *client*, I mean that other person whose interest the patron thus expresses, and in this manner endeavours to maintain and promote' (p. 473).

(21) These things premised, Edwards now argues:

[8] Isa. 53:4, 11, 12 ; Heb. 9:28 ; 1 Pet. 2:24.

(i) It is not unreasonable, that respect should be shown to one person in view of his union with another, or, what is the same thing, on account of that second person's merit.

(ii) In such a case the merit of the second person is imputed or transferred to the first; and these persons are so far substituted, the one for the other.

(iii) This will fitly take place, in proportion to the closeness of the union between the two persons.

(iv) It will take place, above all, where the union is the closest possible.

(22) The union is perfect, when the patron's love puts him so fully in sympathy with the client, that he is willing even to be destroyed for his sake.

(23) The patron's intercession will especially avail, if he has manifested his interest in his client at his own expense. His hardships are calculated to purchase good for his client.

(24) Such benefit will accrue to the client, if, above all, the patron pleads his cause, and appeals for him to one by whom the patron is highly regarded: this last person will naturally make the condition that the client should gratefully recognise the great service of the patron. In the special case, where the patron's merit appears in the expense of his own welfare for the good of the client, such expense is in itself the price of the client's welfare; but the merit of the patron is added to the price and gives it moral value. The acceptance of the patron will above all be natural, where the patron goes so far as to take the place of the client, so far as may be consistent with keeping his merit inviolable.

(25) If the client be an offender, the intercession of the patron must be such as to conserve, both his own merit and virtue, and his union with his client. His union with his client must be accompanied by circumstances demonstrating regard for his friend and also for virtue and holiness.

'There is no way that this can be so thoroughly and fully done, as by undertaking himself to pay the debt to the honour and rights of his injured friend, and to honour the rule of virtue and righteousness the client has violated, by putting himself instead of the offender, into subjection to the injured rights and violated authority of his offended friend, and under the violated law and rule of righteousness belonging to one in the client's state; and so for the sake of the honour of his friend's authority, and the honour of the rule of righteousness, suffering the whole penalty due to the offender' (p. 477).

(26–7) The dignity of the patron will naturally be considered. The degree of union with the client required will be in inverse proportion to this dignity of the patron.

(28) The amount of suffering required of the patron will obey a similar rule. The client will be regarded as a member of his body, whom he loves as himself, yet not equally with himself.

'A man loves his little finger as himself, but not equally with the head; but yet with the same love he bears for himself, according to the place, measure, and capacity of the little finger' (p. 479).

The value of the welfare parted with must, therefore, be equal to the value of the welfare obtained, due regard being had to the persons involved.

(29) The last requisite is a perfect cohesion of the client with the patron, or in a word, he must have complete faith in him. Then the intercession of the patron can have no improper consequences.

(30) These things apply to the case of mediation between God and man. The Mediator here must undertake the debt of men, and bear its penalty.

(31) This Christ did.

'Christ suffered the wrath of God for men's sins in such a way as He was capable of, being an infinitely holy Person, who knew that God was not angry with Him personally, but infinitely loved Him' (p. 481).

He could not bear the wrath of God in the same sense as the wicked in hell, who realise God's hatred of them. 'Christ therefore could bear the wrath of God in no other but these two ways, viz. in having a great and clear sight of the infinite wrath of God against the sins of men, and the punishment they deserved; and in enduring the effects of that wrath' (p. 481).

As to the first point, Christ doubtless had a clear view in

His last suffering, both of the hateful nature of the sin of man, and of the dreadful punishment of sin. For, on the one hand, the malignity of sin was never so apparent as when men crucified the Son of God. On the other hand, the sight of the evil of sin, the enduring of temporal death with such extreme pain, God hiding His face, the dying a death that was by God's appointment an accursed death, the having a sight of the malice and triumph of devils, and the being forsaken of His friends, all combined to present to Christ a striking view of the punishment of sin.

'Now the clear view of each of these things must of necessity be inexpressibly terrible to the man Christ Jesus' (p. 482).

This clear view of sin, unbalanced by the sense of God's love (since God forsook Christ), was infinite pain to Him. This was His bearing of our sins, in distinction from His bearing the Divine wrath, which consisted in His sense of the dreadfulness of the punishment of sin.

(32) The latter Christ bore through His pity for, and sympathy with, the elect, fixing the idea of their punishment in His mind as if it were His own; and here, again, He was uncomforted by any sense of the Divine love.

(33) The same ideas, however, which so distressed the soul of Christ, were the motive power of His endurance of such suffering. The more He hated sin, and pitied the elect, the more was He engaged to honour God, and to save the elect by His suffering.

(34) Christ was personally sanctified in His sufferings, His enmity to sin being increased by His experience of its bitterness, and the exercise of His obedience or holiness tending to increase the root of it in His nature.

'Though the furnace purged away no dross, yet it increased the preciousness of the gold; it added to the finite holiness of the human nature of Christ' (p. 485).

Thus He was sanctified,[9] or made perfect in His sufferings,[1] and so was prepared for that high degree of glory and joy to which He was to be exalted.

(35) Christ also endured the effects of God's wrath. 'There

[9] Jn 17:19. [1] Heb. 2:10, v, 9 ; Lk. 13:32.

502

was a very visible hand of God in letting men and devils loose upon Him at such a rate, and in separating Him from His own disciples. . . . Besides, it was an effect of God's wrath, that He forsook Christ' (p. 485).

(36) The only explanation of the sacrificial system of the Old Testament is that it was ordained as a type of the sacrifice of Christ. For there could be no real atonement in the Old Testament sacrifices, yet they were organised to be performed with the greatest pomp, expense, and trouble; what could be the reason for it, but that they were typical of the true atonement?

(37–8) If God's honour ought to be maintained in a degree, why not perfectly? It cannot be argued that God is above receiving satisfaction; He is not above being injured by sin.

(39) 'The satisfaction of Christ, by suffering the punishment of sin, is properly to be distinguished, as being in its own nature different from the merit of Christ' (p. 488).

The idea of satisfaction involves only the equivalence of the punishment suffered, and the union between Christ and others which made it possible for Him to be their representative. By Christ's satisfaction the law is fulfilled independently of His merit or excellency.

(40) 'The blood of Christ washes away sin. So it is represented in the Scripture. But, although the blood of Christ washes away our guilt, it is the Spirit of Christ that washes away the pollution and stain of sin. However, the blood of Christ washes also from the filth of sin, as it purchases sanctification; it makes way for it by satisfying, and purchases it by the merit of obedience implied in it' (p. 489).

(41) 'Late philosophers seem ready enough to own the great importance of God's maintaining steady and inviolate the laws of the natural world. It may be worthy to be considered, whether it is not of as great, or greater importance, that the law of God, that great rule of righteousness between the supreme moral Governor and His subjects, should be maintained inviolate' (p. 489).

No argument against the necessity of strict satisfaction can be drawn from the fact that human rulers sometimes dispense with their own laws, forbear to execute them, and pardon offenders without the suffering of a substitute. Human justice is imperfect: Divine is perfect.

Edwards's discourse is no mere reproduction of the traditional Protestant theology. It contains the following germinal thoughts, all of which have resulted in important developments in modern theology:

(1) A perfect repentance on man's part might have sufficed to satisfy for sin: of such a repentance sinful man was, however, incapable.

(2) Christ's sufferings in bearing the Divine wrath and the burden of human sin are to be understood *psychologically* through His sympathy with, and pity for, men. It was not, however, possible for Him, as an infinitely holy person, to bear the very pains of hell to be endured by the damned.[2]

(3) Christ Himself was perfected by His sufferings, 'the exercise of His obedience or holiness tending to increase the root of it in His nature'.

[2] Cf. Thomas, 'Summa Theol.' iii, qu. 46, art. 6.

CHAPTER 2

THE BEGINNINGS OF
MODERN THEOLOGY IN GERMANY

STEINBART

THE ideas which we have found in inception in Locke and Chubb are carried to a further development in the remarkable work of the German 'Aufklärer', Steinbart (d. A.D. 1809): 'System der reinen Philosophie oder Glückseligkeitslehre des Christenthums' (1778). The 'Aufklärung', or Illumination, in Germany was, as is well known, largely fed and nourished from English sources. During the eighteenth century English philosophical and theological literature, and in particular the literature of Deism, was freely translated into German, and exercised great influence upon the thought of Germany. Steinbart himself acknowledges his indebtedness in particular to the writings of Locke and Foster.[1] The latter was a General Baptist minister of liberal tendencies, who wrote as his chief work a defence of Christianity against Tindal, entitled 'The Usefulness, Truth, and Excellency of the Christian Revelation Defended' (1731). His views, so far as they concern us, were as follows: He maintained the necessity of revelation because of the corruption of human reason.

'Reason may be able to find out many duties of natural religion, but Christianity makes them clearer and gives them authority. We have also in Christianity the revelation of atonement for sin. Christ's death is the ground of forgiveness. This does not mean that Christ appeased His Father, or even that He made reparation to offended justice. It is explained simply that God pardons man for Christ's death, because this was the method He chose to appoint.'[2]

Foster thought 'that an institution so rational and excellent

---

[1] 'Glückseligkeitslehre', 3rd ed., 1786, p. xi.
[2] Hunt, 'Religious Thought in England', vol. iii, p. 253.

as Christianity ought to commend itself to the approbation of all sincere men. The reason why it did not was found in the corrupt doctrine and superstitious worship that prevailed throughout Christendom' (loc. cit.).

Foster, it will be perceived, is nearer to orthodoxy than either Locke or Chubb. Yet he has much in common with the Deists. He made, however, a strong point against Tindal in maintaining that there was nothing irrational in Christianity containing, not merely a republication of the law of nature, but also certain positive precepts. The influence of some of his ideas is clearly traceable in Steinbart's 'Glückseligkeitslehre'.[3]

Steinbart, however, has made a considerable advance upon his English predecessors, both in the way in which he approaches the problems of Christian theology, and in the fullness of material which he brings to their solution. Above all, it is important that on the one hand he introduces a new philosophic starting-point, whence to approach the subject of Christianity, viz. the question of human happiness; and that on the other hand he reduces the content of the Christian revelation itself to one and one only fundamental principle, which he states with the utmost energy, viz. the Fatherhood of God.

In the first place, then, Steinbart investigates what are the conditions of human happiness, and how far it is realised in this world. On the whole his view is optimistic, as might be expected from an eighteenth-century writer.[4] This is a good world, and the occasions of happiness in it exceed those of unhappiness, if only we will duly weigh and consider them. All that Steinbart asks is that there should be an excess of happiness over unhappiness: with the sobriety of the Aufklärung he does not require a perfect happiness. Nevertheless, to the higher happiness, which goes beyond that of the senses and is that of the reason, there are many hindrances. The gratification of the senses cannot bring us true happiness, yet the instincts develop before the reason. Hence the need of an authority, and of moral education. Then,

[3] Cf. further on Foster, Leslie Stephen, 'History of English Thought in the Eighteenth Century', 1876, vol. i, pp. 146f.

[4] The optimism of the English Deism is expressed in the formula of Pope, 'Whatever is, is right' ; while the German Aufklärung was dominated by the optimism of Leibnitz, whose formula was, 'This is the best of all possible worlds.' Cf. Fairbairn, 'The Philosophy of the Christian Religion', 1902, pp. 104ff.

again, men are impressed by the apparent exceptions in the world to the rule that a rational life is the happiest. They are also impressed beyond measure by particular troubles, and cannot rise above them. There is a general lack of reflection. There are bad examples. Finally, there are false religious ideas, which bring much unhappiness. There prevails among men a false conception of God, constructed after the analogy of a human potentate, or of their own selves, viz. that He is an arbitrary and capricious will; so that men torture themselves in order to placate Him. It is easy enough indeed to see how this idea arises.

'The first fundamental conception of the Supreme Being, in which all peoples agree, is the conception of an absolutely all-controlling Power. Every one, then, either abstracts from the mode of action of the potentates of his country the type of thought, which he gives the Deity credit for; or he judges according to his own character, and believes that the Deity acts, as he would act himself, if he had almighty power' (p. 68).

The idea of arbitrariness in God is, however, the prime error in theology. 'All that is arbitrary leads us away from the natural and true way to happiness, confuses the conscience, and necessarily produces a multitude of inner conflicts and therefrom increasing moral anguish' (p. 69). Here, then, to meet these needs and difficulties, and to help men to happiness, enters the Christian revelation.

(1) 'In the first place Christ has sought entirely to remove the practical prejudices concerning arbitrary demands of God upon men, which generally obtained among the Jewish people at the time of His teaching ministry' (p. 71). Paul too has described Moses as a teacher of children, who dealt with men in their minority by sensuous laws and sensuous punishments, till the time of their majority should come, when they might be entrusted to act according to right reason. The heathen also, in spite of the sound doctrine of a few philosophers, were in like manner enslaved to ceremonies, and needed a similar deliverance.

Christianity, moreover, contradicts not only the false notions of God then obtaining, but all such notions.

'This involves: that God according to the teaching of Jesus is entirely to be thought of as a loving Father, therefore Christians

507

are not to be baptised in the name of the Ruler of the World, but of the universal Father;[5] that the spirit of Christianity is called a spirit of sonship and freedom, and that there is expressely demanded as the true character of a Christian a confident love entirely free from all fear' (p. 73). Steinbart is in tremendous earnest with the idea of the Fatherhood of God. He is prepared to use it in a most thorough way as a critical principle, by which to try all religious doctrines.

'Even a human father, when his own needs do not perchance compel him thereto, does not require service from his children; but keeps them only to such practices, whereby they may make themselves more perfect and happier. God, who Himself gives to every one life, breath, and all things, can therefore still less demand any service of His children' (p. 73).

Steinbart means, as the context shows, that God will demand no service, merely for His own gratification, apart from its benefit to His children. The actual Christian law is in fact nothing but love to God and man; nor is asceticism of any value. Christianity does nothing but strengthen and confirm nature and reason: its aim is to stimulate the reason to reflection.

(2) Besides this, however, Christianity 'conveys a supremely excellent and complete morality in a way intelligible to every one' (p. 78). It also introduces this morality with a Divine authority, and enhances the natural motives to virtue with the view of the persistence of the consequences of good and evil in eternity, removing the difficulty raised by the apparent exceptions, where in this life these consequences are not visible. Besides, it offers to unselfish well-doing rewards entirely beyond its merit. Again, it gives us the motive of imitating God our Father. By its prospect into the future it also alleviates our troubles, and assures us that particular troubles, seen in the context of the whole, are nothing but goods.

(3) Finally, Christianity assists the simple by clothing spiritual truth in sensuous and historical forms. Among such forms are to be reckoned the conceptions of Christ as the Incarnate Logos, and as an example of patience duly rewarded by God, and again the conception of His sacrifice on behalf of

---

[5] Mt. 28:19.

men, whereby God has reconciled the world through Him to Himself, so that no satisfactions for sin are necessary for anyone who repents, nor has he to fear any evils except the necessary natural evil consequences of his transgressions, which God never removes, but man can himself gradually lessen by his own industry. Finally, Christ rose on the third day from the dead, which is a greater guarantee of our future resurrection than any philosophical demonstration. In all these instances it appears how beneficial, especially for the multitude, is the clothing of the higher truths of religion in the forms of history. There is, it may be said, no religious or moral need, which the Scriptures do not thus meet; nor must it be forgotten that the whole life of Jesus offers for our imitation the highest pattern of perfection.

'It follows, therefore, that for men practised in thinking the Christian philosophy contains the completest system of directions to happiness, beyond which in the space of eighteen centuries no one has been able to add by thought, or to discover, anything new or better; and that the clothing of these directions in history is for the great multitudes of men the only and safest way to make these higher doctrines of wisdom intelligible and certain' (p. 93).

The simplicity of Christian truth has, however, been obscured by various arbitrary hypotheses, which hinder the influence of Christianity in promoting happiness. Amongst these are the Augustinian doctrines of original sin and of predestination, and the Anselmic doctrine of satisfaction with its later Protestant developments in the doctrine of Christ's twofold obedience, and finally the doctrine of the imputation of Christ's righteousness. We meet with a new phenomenon in the method by which Steinbart criticises these doctrines. 'The history of dogma', says Loofs,[6] 'is a child of the age of the German Aufklärung.' Steinbart, in fact, is no longer content to appeal for the purposes of his criticism merely to texts of Scripture or grounds of reason. In dependence upon Semler,[7] that great father of the historical method, he sets in motion the mode of inquiry which is so familiar to us today, but which was in his time a new and power-

---

[6] 'Dogmengeschichte', 4th ed., p. 1.
[7] Cf. the reference to him in 'Glückseligkeitslehre', p. 105. Semler b. A.D. 1725, d. A.D. 1791.

ful engine of assault. He explains Augustine's doctrine of original sin as the total corruption of humanity through Adam's fall as a survival of his Manichæism.[8] The older and true Christian doctrine was that maintained by Pelagius and the Greeks.[9] Steinbart shows further that Augustinianism had never been accepted by the whole Church either Catholic or Protestant. Luther's acceptance of it was due to the fact that he was an Augustinian monk. Steinbart again endeavours to show that the doctrine of the imputation of Adam's guilt is neither Biblical nor rational. Amongst his arguments the following may be noticed. There is no mention in Scripture of any contract, whereby Adam became our representative: besides, if he were our representative, then not merely his sin would be imputed to us, but also his endurance of its penalty, so that we should be free.

A good deal of the ground of the orthodox doctrine of the work of Christ is certainly cut away by this rejection of Augustinianism. Steinbart, however, proceeds to a direct criticism of the doctrine itself. He begins with an attack on the doctrine of the imputation of Christ's righteousness. If this, as is admitted, was originated by Luther, it is the natural consequence of the Augustinian exegesis and principles.

'For, according to the very same principles, upon which an imputation of the sin of Adam is deduced from Rom. 5, the imputation of Christ's righteousness is also based thereon; and according to the same reasons of law, upon which an alien guilt is imputed to us, an alien righteousness is to be ascribed to us also' (p. 125).

A criticism of these principles is most necessary, if the whole purpose of Christ's religion is not to fail. The source of the confusion of the whole doctrine of the imputation of the righteousness of Christ is to be found in the false, or at least obscure, idea of the reason and purpose of the Divine demands upon men. 'All precepts, which God can give to men, and every father give to his children, either are merely fatherly counsels, by following which the children themselves become more perfect and happy, or are demands of service, whose fulfilment is of no advantage to the children themselves' (p. 126).

[8] Cf. *supra*, p. 87, n. 3.   [9] *Supra*, p. 89, n. 3.

510

The laws of the first class must necessarily be fulfilled by the children themselves; nor can any third party fulfil them on their behalf. The others, which are mere arbitrary demands, may be fulfilled by another. The question now is, whether God has made, and still makes, such demands of service upon men. The Mosaic law indeed contained such precepts: these, however, were simply relevant to the existence of the Jewish state. The Jewish law has, as Paul teaches, no hold upon Christians. What then Paul means by saying, that Christ redeemed us from the Mosaic law, is not that His fulfilment of it was imputed to us, but that He delivered us from the superstition that God demanded such service of us.

Steinbart (p. 130) appeals upon this point to the work of 'my reverend teacher and predecessor in office, Dr Töllner', entitled 'Die thätige Gehorsam Christi untersucht'. This work, published in 1768, had renewed Piscator's objection to the doctrine of Christ's active obedience. Ritschl recognises it as marking the first stage of the German Aufklärung, while Steinbart himself marks a completer development of its principles. Töllner had not denied the doctrine of the passive obedience, though he no longer followed the orthodox interpretation of it as a satisfaction to the Divine justice, but explained it along lines, which are partly Socinian, partly Arminian, and partly new.

'Instead of accepting the forensic idea of righteousness handed down by orthodox tradition, Töllner avows his preference for the idea propounded by Leibnitz that it is goodness tempered by wisdom. From this point of view, he finds satisfaction of God's righteousness to be accomplished in the institution of a representative of men, an institution which partly maintains motives to obedience which arise from the punishment of disobedience, that is to say, in penal example; partly, by instituting an exemplary obedience, makes men worthy and capable of receiving grace, and thus provides for their sanctification. More closely considered, however, the satisfaction given in Christ's passion is not so much an immediate condition of God's bestowal of grace upon men, as it is a means for that sanctification of men upon which the bestowal of grace immediately depends. For that Christ has borne the penalties of sin which we have

511

merited does not free us from the natural punishments which are inseparable from actual sin; this last, therefore, must first be removed in sanctification, before the full bestowal of grace is complete. Sanctification, on the other hand, can again arise only out of the restoration of our confidence in God, which is hindered by the apprehension of the punishments due for sin; Christ's endurance of suffering accordingly is not merely a penal example, but also the guarantee that punishments no longer impend on account of our sins.' [1]

What is particularly noteworthy in the above doctrine of Töllner is the conception of the natural consequences of sin, which are inevitable. Here, as in Butler,[2] we recognise the direct influence of modern science upon the sphere of our doctrine. Steinbart also makes use of this conception, but applies it to go beyond Töllner and repudiate the doctrine of Christ's passive obedience altogether.

What is necessary, he says, is first of all to obtain clear ideas as to the nature of punishment. We must distinguish in every action a physical and a moral side: each has its own consequences. The physical consequences of an action are the same, whether it is an act of moral obedience or of disobedience. The moral consequences require a further distinction: they are either natural or arbitrary. The natural moral consequences are the inward results of the consciousness of having obeyed or disobeyed. The arbitrary are such rewards and punishments as a law-giver chooses to impose: they must be carefully distinguished from the physical consequences which happen independently of any such action on his part. The physical consequences, being independent of the moral quality of the action, can in no way belong to its penalties: apart from the fact of its impossibility, there is consequently no point in the idea that Christ has suffered the physical consequences of sin on our behalf. These consequences can only be ameliorated by our amendment. Christ has redeemed us from them, in so far as He has called us to forsake sin. The natural moral consequences of sin are again of two kinds. Apart from our relation to the Lawgiver, there is

---

[1] Ritschl, 'Justification and Reconciliation', vol. i, English trans., p. 352.
[2] *Supra*, p. 497.

our inner remorse: this natural penalty of sin is, however, highly beneficial to us, as it makes against further sin. Christ cannot, therefore, have freed us from it. Then, with reference to the Lawgiver, along with the consciousness of having offended Him, various disagreeable ideas arise within us, however we conceive Him. If we think of Him as a tyrant, we are afraid: if as a loving Father we are truly contrite. We can therefore explain Christ's great work of redemption, as follows:

He has redeemed the Jews from the idea of God as a tyrant, which was their thought of Him, and from all slavish fear. He has also by His death destroyed the idea of a Satan, or prince of death, such as the Jews had believed in. With respect to the Gentiles, it is not said in Scripture that they were redeemed from punishment; but that God overlooked the time of their ignorance. But to both Jews and Gentiles alike Christ has brought what they needed—to the Greeks Divine wisdom, to the Jews deliverance from legalism, and to both the abolition of the barrier between them.

So much, then, for Christ's relation to the natural moral consequences of our sins. There remain the arbitrary penalties. Has Christ redeemed us from these by a vicarious endurance of them? This idea, says Steinbart, is a very late outgrowth of Augustine's peculiar opinions. It was first brought into the Church at the end of the eleventh century by Anselm, a zealous disciple of Augustine, who based his theory, not upon Scripture, but upon proof *a priori*. Abelard, however, pointed a better way, and, in spite of its general acceptance by the Reformers, Anselm's theory has never wanted opposition. In order to clear up the point, it must be inquired, whether a wise father ever inflicts evils upon his children, except for their amelioration. No theologian will affirm this outside his system. Nevertheless it is contended, that in God there are attributes which are opposed to His goodness, viz. His righteousness and holiness, and that such actions as would in an earthly father be unreason and appalling severity, in God are the expression of a perfect righteousness and holiness. However much God desires to make men happy, His infinite holiness demands satisfaction for the injury done to it.

'Here we have,' says Steinbart, 'the good and evil principle of the Manichees united in our God; two attributes of equal infinity striving against each other, according to which God is impelled equally strongly, in virtue of the one to ameliorate and perfect His rebellious children, in virtue of the other to overwhelm them in misery and ruin. Thus there is in God Himself an eternal contradiction!' (p. 146).

The extreme to which this contradiction can be carried is, however, only apparent when God is conceived in different Persons, in order that He as Father may receive satisfaction from Himself as Son incarnate in Christ. The Bible, however, teaches very differently. Even the Old Testament represents God as merciful and gracious; His holiness and righteousness do not appear as a hindrance to His forgiving sins without satisfaction. The Old Testament sacrifices were not ordained for sinful intentions, but merely for external uncleanness and transgressions. Jesus presents to us God as the Father, without any limitation of His fatherly love. 'Did Christ, who came out of the bosom of the Father, know Him less than Anselm of Canterbury?' (p. 149). Finally, Scripture on all its pages presents the entire mission of Jesus, and all that He has done, not as the cause, but as the effect of the universal grace and love of God.

The theory of Grotius is an improvement on Anselm's; it does not darken God's lovableness so much. But it, too, is against Scripture and reason. Everything depends upon obtaining clear ideas of the holiness and righteousness of God. God's holiness is no special perfection, but simply the absence in Him of any defects in His understanding or goodness. Righteousness is not opposed to goodness, but is a goodness proportionate to the recipiency of its object, or a wise goodness. Steinbart says, like Thomas Aquinas,[3] that in thinking of God we must not compare Him to a subordinate judge under law, but must remember that He is the Supreme Sovereign. There is, then, a proportionateness in God's gifts, in His laws, and in His punishments. His very punishments are calculated in perfect wisdom, and cease, as soon as they are no longer needed. Such, and no other, is the righteousness of God, truly conceived; and there is no opposition

[3] *Supra*, pp. 220f.

514

to it in His love. It is only the wisdom with which His love carries out its purpose of leading men to happiness. The difference between God and human rulers is, that His wisdom, as well as His power, is absolute, and that His dealings with men are therefore always perfect. In the end, therefore, every spirit will attain to the greatest possible happiness; it would detract from the glory of God, if even one were condemned to endless misery. The whole Augustinian and Anselmic philosophy is, therefore, to be rejected. God through the death of Christ, Whom He gave up for us, has declared all propitiation of Himself superfluous, and asks nothing of us, but gladly to receive and enjoy the good which He bestows.

'Thus Christ has by His death for ever freed and delivered, not only the Jews, but all men who believe on Him, from the greatest moral unhappiness, which arises from the torturing ideas of a Deity enraged against us; so that we have nothing more to fear than the natural consequences of our follies, whereby we ourselves, in opposition to God's plan, make ourselves miserable and incapable of higher blessings; just as at the same time by His doctrines He has shown us the way to ever higher stages of happiness, and has illuminated the same by His own life' (p. 161).

Steinbart concludes this discussion, by saying that the doctrine of vicarious satisfaction is the great hindrance to the acceptance of the Christian revelation among thinking men. It is, however, contrary to reason. 'For, no one that has clear ideas of an absolutely perfect righteousness, can possibly be persuaded that the Father of the world will ever inflict on anyone other penal evils, than such as are necessary for his amendment' (p. 162). Nor is the doctrine Scriptural. The simple doctrine of Scripture is, that Christ has redeemed all, and by His death has guaranteed to them the grace of God and the forgiveness of sins, on condition of amendment. We must not raise the questions, which Scripture leaves undetermined, why Christ suffered and died? what was its necessity? etc. 'If a complete knowledge of these things were necessary for salvation, they would have been so clearly explained in the Holy Scriptures that no controversies could arise on the subject' (p. 162).

515

Steinbart later on in his treatise gives the explanation, which we have already found in Locke and Chubb, of the Scriptural references to Christ's priesthood and sacrifice as an accommodation to the Jews. He points out that the early patristic doctrine, however, connected itself rather with the Scripture representations of Christ's death as the means of redemption from the power of the angel of death or the Devil. In any case the modern Christian is not bound by the idea of Christ's death as a sacrifice. 'The doctrine of the sacrificial death of Jesus is the bridge for all those who stand where the Jews were in the time of the Apostles; our thinking Christians already dwell on this side of the water' (p. 288).

At the conclusion of his work Steinbart touches briefly on the relation of Christianity to other religions. A variety of religions appears to lie in the Divine plan of the world; history knows of no time of uniformity in religion. What God values is the development of reason from within, and all revelations are given proportionately to existing knowledge. All religions perform the function of religion, i.e. they yield peace of mind in view of the future, conscientiousness and virtue, though there are many stages of virtue. Not all religions, however, are on the same level, or lead with equal rapidity to the appointed goal. Here, then, is the place of Christianity. 'After the cultured peoples had attained some maturity of reason, Christ appeared, and taught a more spiritual religion' (p. 315).

The above full account of Steinbart's 'Glückseligkeitslehre', so far as it touches our subject, has been given, because it appears to the writer to explain, as does no other book with which he is acquainted, the genesis of the existing problems of modern theology. It was above all in the German Aufklärung that these came into existence. A great deal in Steinbart indeed goes back, as we have seen, to the principles of the English Deism. From that is derived the Biblico-theological method with its distinction of various strata of doctrine in the New Testament. From the later Deism, as exemplified in Chubb, is adopted also the emphasis on the doctrine of God's Fatherhood, as taught by Jesus Himself; though Steinbart makes it even more central and fundamental than does Chubb. From the Deists, too, is taken the

516

principle of the essential oneness of Christianity with the light of reason: Chubb and Steinbart, moreover, both assume that reason teaches the absolute benevolence of God. From Locke and the later Deism also comes the idea of accommodation, with which Steinbart makes so much play. It may be added that, as has already been observed, the important principle of the natural consequences of sin, derived by Steinbart from Töllner, is also utilised in Butler's reply to the Deists in his 'Analogy'.

But, as over against the English writers, the following points appear to be new. In the first place the critical Biblical theology is supplemented by a critical history of doctrine. Then, secondly, Steinbart abandons the Deist idea of an original perfect religion, and adopts instead the notion of an evolutionary religious development and a Divine education of the human race.[4]

The Theology of the Nineteenth Century

The theology of the English Deism and the German Auf-klärung was essentially a return—with, of course, suitable adaptation to new circumstances—from the dogma of the Church, as developed in all its forms from Irenæus onwards, to the moral theology of the Apologists; while the new doctrine of accommodation also is a similar modified revival of the way in which Clement and Origen harmonised Paulinism with their rational theology. The divergences of the eighteenth-century theology from the Apologists, Clement and Origen, are that the speculative Logos doctrine is abandoned, and a Messianic or anthropocentric is substituted for a pneumatic or theocentric Christology; and, again, that the moral theology of the Apologists is enriched by the doctrine of the Fatherhood of God, as taught by Jesus Himself.

Just as, however, the theology of the Apologists, and even that of Clement and Origen was found inadequate by the Church as a complete expression of the Christian religion, and accordingly had to be supplemented by the dogma of the creeds; so

---

[4] Lessing's famous 'Erziehung des Menschengeschlechts', 1780, contains similar thoughts.

again the age of the Aufklärung gives place to an age of renewed interest in and reinterpretation of the ancient dogma and its mediaeval developments. The clear rationality of the Aufklärung makes way for a Romanticism, which finds rationalism shallow and unsatisfying, and which, in the endeavour to look more deeply into the human mind and heart and to interpret the world by what it reads there, returns with a renewed interest to those very doctrines of the past, which the Aufklärung had rejected as irrational. The Romanticist theology substitutes, for the use of the principle of accommodation by the Aufklärung in order to bring Paulinism and the ecclesiastical dogma down to the level of a rational theology, a method of 'penetrative imagination' (to borrow a phrase from Ruskin),[5] which discovers an inner essence in the heart of the dogma altogether transcending mere rationalism. The mysticism of the Greek Church, and the irrationalism of Luther and the Protestant theology, become the principle of a higher reason (*Vernunft*), which regards the logical understanding (*Verstand*) as upon a lower and inferior level of thought. Nevertheless, the new theology has all the same the rationalism of the Aufklärung in its blood. It cannot restore or revive the old doctrines, as though the Aufklärung had never been. On the contrary, its problems are everywhere set by the Aufklärung; and even if it seeks to overcome the latter, it has to do so by first recognising it, and by making use of its methods. Adopting the historical criticism of the Aufklärung, it no longer holds to the forms of the ancient dogma, but dissolves these in favour of a higher truth for which they stand. This truth is, however, not the rational religion of the Aufklärung, but something deeper and more vital.

We have now to give an account of this new theology. It is very commonly called 'modern' theology, since it claims as its own the whole of the nineteenth century; nor has there yet been any further theological development, which falls outside of the lines above described.[6] We are still moving, in theology, between the poles of the Aufklärung and the Romanticism which succeeded it. The primary movement of this modern theology

---

[5] Cf. 'Modern Painters', Part 3, § 2, chap. III.

[6] For the wider sense of the term 'modern theology', see, however, *supra*, p. 475.

belongs to Germany. Baur [7] hardly speaks too strongly when he says: 'The centre of the new movement is the German Protestant Church, and the history of dogma in its last stage coincides altogether with the history of German Protestant theology'. Baur, indeed, is wrong in so far as he refers in the above statement to the whole theological movement from the beginning of the eighteenth century, for he does not sufficiently recognise the importance of the beginnings made in the English Deism; but from the time of the German Aufklärung in the middle of the eighteenth century, what he says is true. There have been, however, important parallel secondary theological movements in England, Scotland, and America, largely dependent, though not entirely so, upon the German development. We shall consider, therefore, first the German, then the English, Scottish, and American theology. There is one fundamental difference between the two movements, in which the primacy of the German movement is manifest, even apart from its historical priority. Speaking generally, we may say that German theology alone in this modern period is fully systematic, in that it aims always at a total view, in which the particular doctrines find their place in a wider connexion. Much of the best English, Scottish, and American theology dealing with the work of Christ is monographic. The German theology alone carries on the great tradition of the mediaeval and the Protestant scholasticism, while the English-speaking theology of the nineteenth century, like the older English theology of the sixteenth and seventeenth centuries, reverts to the patristic method of doctrinal monographs.

KANT

In giving an account of the theology of the nineteenth century, we are met by the difficulty of choosing, out of a whole galaxy of theological luminaries, the best and most sufficient representatives of the movement. But there can be no doubt about our starting-point, which is fixed, just at the end of the eighteenth century, in Kant (A.D. 1724–1804), the great historical connecting link between the Aufklärung and Romanticism. Kant is univer-

---

[7] 'Lehrbuch der christlichen Dogmengeschichte', 3rd ed., 1867, p. 343.

sally recognised as having introduced a new epoch of thought. Nowhere, however, is the influence of the Kantian philosophy more observable than in the fresh theological development resulting from it.

'Kant', says Jodl,[8] 'has become the second Luther. In him is rooted the philosophy of Romanticism, whence the restoration of the historical Church-matters received its final impulses and its scientific formulae.' Bruno Bauch [9] has shown how true it is that Kant was a second Luther, in other words how many of Luther's fundamental moral and religious convictions were renewed by him in philosophic form. Finally, C. H. Weisse [1] says of Kant:

'The epoch-making act of philosophical speculation, by means of which was made possible to the same [2] the creation of such an instrument as the science of the Christian Faith needed for its self-formation, is none other than that great act, which speculation has accomplished through Immanuel Kant, of reflection upon the relation of the pure knowledge of the reason to experience and to the science to be created out of experience, and upon the tasks which are through this relation proposed to the former [3] with reference to the latter.' [4]

Weisse, in fact, recognises in the advent of the Kantian philosophy the beginning of the creation by Christianity of a philosophy 'out of its own midst and out of the depths of its own consciousness', in other words, of a philosophy adequate to its own self-exposition.[5]

The peculiar feature of the Kantian philosophy is, as indicated in the above quotation from Weisse, its careful discrimination of the *a priori,* or purely rational, elements in knowledge from those which are empirical in their origin, and its endeavour exactly to determine the relation between these diverse elements. In his philosophy of religion, accordingly, Kant neither, like the Apologists and the Deists, at once assumes the fundamental religious ideas as rational, nor yet, like the Fathers, the mediaeval Schoolmen, the Protestant theologians, and even Locke, Chubb, and Steinbart, appeals for them, beyond reason, to the external

[8] 'Geschichte der Ethik', 2nd ed., vol. i, p. 552. [9] 'Luther and Kant', 1904.
[1] 'Philosophische Dogmatik', vol. i, § 261, p. 245. [2] I.e. philosophical speculation.
[3] The pure knowledge of the reason. [4] The science to be created out of experience.
[5] Op. cit. vol. i, §§ 9–13, pp. 7–10.

520

authority of the Scriptures; but, on the contrary, he analyses them at every point into their original, rational, and empirical elements, deducing them, on the one hand, from the moral law as given by reason,[6] and, on the other hand, from the empirical facts, not only of man's need for happiness,[7] but also of his natural contrariety to the moral law.[8] We have now to see the way in which Kant, on these bases, built up his philosophy of religion.

In his 'Critique of Pure Reason' (1781), Kant recognised the idea of natural law even more fully than the Aufklärung had done; but he broke with the confidence of the Aufklärung as to the complete rationality of religion. He found that the rational proofs for the existence of God were not demonstrative, having no sufficient basis in experience. In the 'Critique of Practical Reason' (1788), Kant, however, recognised that man is not only as a part of the world subject to natural law, but also as a spiritual being subject to a moral law given in his conscience. He therefore found that the practical reason requires us to believe in our freedom to obey the moral law, in immortality, that we may have time to attain to the infinite perfection which it requires, and in a God, who may reconcile the absolute demand which morality makes upon us with our natural and necessary need of happiness, by causing virtue and happiness to coincide in the supreme good, with which Kant connects the Scriptural name of the Kingdom of God.

'The Kingdom of God is thus that intelligible, moral world, that system through which the co-existence of virtue and happiness is made possible. It cannot therefore, strictly speaking, be said that the Kingdom of God is in the opinion of Kant the highest good; it is rather that supersensuous order of things, through which the highest good is made possible and can come into the possession of men. Men are to "possess" "work", "bring in", the highest good, i.e. virtue and happiness: it is God who makes this possible through the order of His Kingdom.' [9]

[6] At this point Kant touches the Apologists and the Deists.
[7] Here Steinbart had shown the way ; see *supra*, p. 506.
[8] It is the recognition of this fact that, above all, makes Kant 'the second Luther'.
[9] J. Weiss, 'Die Idee des Reiches Gottes in der Theologie', 1901, p. 86. By *intelligible* (in the Kantian sense) is meant, that which is discerned, not by the senses, but by the intellect, or reason, alone.

Kant was able to establish further points of connexion with Christian doctrine, especially in its Protestant formulation. In his book 'Die Religion innerhalb der Grenzen der blossen Vernunft' (1793), the great philosopher recognises the existence in man, in spite of his reverence for the moral law, of a rooted tendency to disobey it. In opposition, therefore, to the Pelagianism of the Aufklärung Kant declares himself essentially on the side of Augustine and Luther, though he cannot accept the Augustinian derivation of the sinful tendency from Adam, but prefers to view it as the result in every case of an 'intelligible act, prior to all experience'.[1] Each man, that is to say, is responsible for his own transgression, but no empirical explanation is sufficient to account for the fact that, from first to last, he is a transgressor.

The question now is, whether and how man, thus discovered to be by nature bad, can be made good. This is not so easy a question as the Aufklärung found it. There is an antinomy here involved. The offender cannot begin to be a good man, as long as he is troubled with the distress of conscience occasioned by his guilt; on the other hand, he cannot be freed from this distress until he has amended his ways. The solution of the antinomy Kant states as follows:[2]

Nothing but a perfect humanity can please God, and so attain felicity. This humanity, well-pleasing to God, is His only-begotten Son, the Word, the Brightness of His glory, etc. It is our duty to raise ourselves to this ideal of human perfection, for which duty the ideal itself can give us strength. But because this ideal is not of our creation, we may say that it has come down to us from heaven, and assumed our humanity. We can only think of it under the form of a man, who not only practises all duties, and by doctrine and example spreads goodness about him, but also is ready for the good of the world to endure all sufferings.

'In practical faith in this Son of God (so far as He is represented as if He had assumed human nature) man can now hope to become acceptable to God, and therewith also blessed' (p. 67). By such faith is meant man's trust in his own allegiance

---

[1] For the meaning of 'intelligible' see preceding note.
[2] 'Die Religion', etc., Zweites Stück, Erster Abschnitt, ed. Vorländer, 1903, pp. 66ff.

to the ideal, and his willingness to endure all sufferings in pursuit of it.

What now is to be said as to the objective reality of this idea? Kant answers: 'The idea has its reality, in the practical reference, entirely in itself. For it lies in our reason in its capacity as a moral lawgiver' (p. 68). Since, however, we must believe in the possibility of the realisation of the idea, an experience must be possible in which an actual example of humanity corresponding to it may be given. If such a man ever really existed, it would not be necessary to think of him as supernaturally born. In fact he would thereby cease to be an example for us, since he would not be in the same circumstances as ours.

Kant now proceeds to certain difficulties as to the realisation of the ideal in us, and to their solution. The first difficulty which appears to hinder the realisation in us of the ideal of humanity, has reference to the holiness of the Lawgiver and our own lack of righteousness. It is solved, in that God first accepts in us the disposition to holiness, until by degrees we realise actual holiness. The second difficulty is to know how we can be sure of the constancy of our good disposition. The solution is, that the disposition itself is the 'Comforter', which confirms us in our faith in its own perseverance, and that this inner witness is guaranteed by our actual progress in good. The third and apparently greatest difficulty is as follows: However in any man the acquisition of a good disposition may have taken place, and whatever perseverance he may show in it, still he began from evil, and his guilt is not extinguished. Even if after his regeneration he commits no more sins, he has not paid for the old ones. Nor is any excess of merit possible, since he can never exceed his duty. The solution here is, that the regenerate man is, in his moral disposition (as an intelligible essence [3]), morally another before his Divine Judge. This new man, who is one with the Son of God, Whom he has received into himself, bears as substitute the guilt of the sins of the old man, in so far as the natural consequences of the latter's sins, of which he is guiltless, come upon him, and he willingly endures them as a sacrifice.

[3] The moral disposition is the 'essence' which reason perceives to underlie the acts apparent to the senses.

Kant goes on to say [4] that Scripture represents the conflict between the good and evil principles under a figure. The world by the Fall became a kingdom of Satan, whose end began with the death of Jesus, Who by His example of virtue and self-sacrifice founds a new ethical community.

The Scriptural doctrine, however, contains an element, which is not found in Kant's previous doctrine, of faith in the ideal Son of God. It is, in its reference, not merely individual but social. Kant also recognised a social element in his philosophical doctrine of religion, which he proceeds now to describe. [5]

A merely individual view of the conflict of good and evil is not sufficient. The evil principle is socially embodied, and thus maintains its mastery over humanity. The good principle therefore must also be socially embodied. The idea of an ethical community is, however, the idea of a people of God under ethical laws, and can be realised only as a Church, 'which, so far as it is no object of possible experience, is called the invisible Church' (p. 115). In the natural order of things the Church always takes its rise from a historical faith, held to be based on revelation. Such a faith may be called an ecclesiastical faith, and is best based upon a holy Scripture. The ecclesiastical faith has, however, as its highest interpreter the faith of pure natural religion. Finally, the gradual transition of ecclesiastical faith into the form of a pure rational faith is the approach of the Kingdom of God. Kant concludes by showing how these general principles correspond to the actual history of religion in Judaism and Christianity. He says:

'If it now be asked: Which age of the entire Church history that we know up to the present is the best, I have no hesitation in replying: It is the present, and that just because the germ of true religious faith, as it is now planted within Christianity, only indeed by some individuals, but still publicly, is permitted more and more to develop unhindered, so that there may be expected to result from it a continuous approximation to that Church uniting all men for ever, which is the visible representation (or schema) of an invisible Kingdom of God upon earth' (p. 152).

[4] Zweites Stück, Zweiter Abschnitt, pp. 88ff.   [5] Drittes Stück, pp. 105ff.

524

J. Weiss [6] has pointed out that, except for one or two passages where the doctrine of the highest good in the 'Critique of Practical Reason' is reproduced, the idea of the Kingdom of God in the 'Religion' is different from that former doctrine. Kant now conceives it simply as an ethical society, whose aim is to establish the supremacy of the good principle over the evil in the world. Reinhard had already in his 'Versuch über den Plan, welchen der Stifter der christlichen Religion zum Besten der Menschheit entwarf' (1781) developed the idea of the Kingdom of God as an ethical community founded by Jesus, a brotherhood for moral ends. Kant, however, only follows Reinhard exactly so far as to recognise his doctrine as a Biblical idea: in his own philosophical doctrine of religion he releases the notion of the Kingdom of God from its connexion with the historical figure of Jesus, and presents it as a universal ethical ideal.

Both conceptions of the Kingdom of God, the view of it as the highest good, an order of things in which under God virtue and happiness are united, and the view of it again as a human community striving for moral ends, now descend as a legacy to the theology of the nineteenth century. It is clear that neither entirely corresponds to the Biblical idea of the Kingdom of God, which is primarily eschatological.[7] Nevertheless Kant's conceptions touch the Biblical idea closely at certain points,[8] and prepare for its further extended use in theology.

As regards the religious doctrine of Kant in general, it is clear that he has carried the separation of Christian doctrine from the historic Christ even farther than Steinbart. He is thus the father of all Modernism, which, distinguishing between the Christ of faith and the Jesus of history, finds the doctrines of the Church profoundly true as ideas, though untrue if understood literally as referring to the historical Jesus.

HEGEL

Before proceeding to the theological development proper in nineteenth-century Germany, we must consider yet one other

[6] Op. cit., p. 87.   [7] 'Man, Sin, and Salvation', pp. 44ff.
[8] Holtzmann, 'Lehrbuch der neutestamentlichen Theologie', 2nd ed., vol. i, pp. 248ff. See in particular p. 265, n. 1.

philosopher, who, along with Kant, has had great influence upon theology. This is Hegel (A.D. 1770–1832), who, following upon lines initiated by Fichte and Schelling, endeavoured to reduce the whole of the Kantian doctrine to a single principle, and out of this principle by a necessary development of thought to explain the universe. This principle is no other than the *coincidentia oppositorum*, which was the unconscious principle of Luther's theology, now raised, however, to the rank of a conscious philosophical principle. For Hegel the ultimate truth of philosophy is the identity of the Infinite and the finite. The Infinite inevitably develops the finite out of itself, and equally inevitably the finite returns into the Infinite. Every finite attempt to express the Infinite proclaims its own insufficiency, and calls for a further endeavour. The forms of abstract logic give place to those of matter and of organic nature, while these in turn give way to the forms of the spiritual life, of which religion is the highest, short of the absolute truth of philosophy. In religion the fundamental truth of the identity of the Infinite and the finite appears in a form adapted to the needs of the common consciousness, in the Christian doctrines of the Person and Work of Christ. Man has in religion an immediate consciousness of his finitude, which being felt by him as separation from the Infinite, manifests itself in the consciousness of sin and guilt, which occasions him the keenest pain. Yet the finite spirit cannot from itself, by its own action, attain reconciliation with the Infinite: it must find the reconciliation as already given and existing, and must accept it as the basis of all its action.

'The unity of subjectivity and objectivity', says Hegel, 'this Divine unity must be as the presupposition for my positing: then first has this a content, which content is Spirit, concrete content —otherwise it is subjective, formal; thus first it obtains true, substantial content.' [9]

This fundamentally unity, as has been stated, exists according to Hegel as the ultimate truth of things. Nevertheless in this form it can only be grasped by means of an elevation to the philosophic

---

[9] 'Vorlesungen über die Philosophie der Religion', ed. Bolland, 1901, p. 638. Hegel means that unless there is first given in reality a unity of the Infinite and the finite, or, what is the same, of the Object with the subject, any mere *thought* of such reconciliation on the part of the subject will be illusory.

standpoint, and is not at once apparent to the common consciousness. It must become thus apparent; but how? Not merely as a thought, for what is only a thought remains subjective and powerless; but as a reality perceivable by the senses, instantly and evidently apparent for the consciousness.

'Thus must this unity show itself for the consciousness in an entirely temporal, perfectly ordinary manifestation of reality, in a man who is "this man", who may at the same time become known as a Divine Idea, not only as a higher being in general, but as the highest, the Absolute Idea, as the Son of God' (p. 641).

This manifestation, however, is not merely necessary, it has become actuality. This has taken place in the Christian Church, in that by its faith Jesus Christ has been recognised as the God-man. This amazing phenomenon has two sides. The essential truth contained in it is the ultimate unity of the Divine and human nature. The form which it takes is the faith of the Church in the Divinity of Christ. "Manifestation is Being for another; this other is the Church' (p. 645).

There are now two views of this historical manifestation. There is first that which is common to all humanity, apart from a religious faith. Here Jesus appears as a human teacher, bringing the doctrine of the Kingdom of God. This doctrine, however, in itself is merely the abstract presupposition of the new religion. It is not the new religion itself. In the new religion it is transformed by being taken up into a concrete whole. 'Christ's doctrine cannot, in its immediacy, be Christian Dogmatic, or Church Doctrine. When the community is founded, and the kingdom of God has attained to its reality, its actuality, then this doctrine can no longer have the same determination as before'[1] (p. 646).

Along with this doctrine of the human Christ belong His moral commandments, which centre in the one commandment of love. To the human aspect of His life also belong the example of Christ and His martyr-death. 'The first point of all is the abstract conformity of the doing, acting, and suffering of this teacher to His doctrine itself,[2] that His life is entirely devoted to

---

[1] The doctrine now enters into new relations, which determine its meaning afresh.

[2] That is, the *conformity*, which reflection perceives, when it *abstracts* first Christ's doctrine, and then His doing and suffering, from His total reality, and finally compares them.

it, that He did not fear death, and by His death sealed this faith' (p. 652).

These are the chief moments of the human manifestation of Christ. But now comes the other and higher point of view, that of Christian faith. 'If we say no more of Christ, than that He is the teacher of humanity and martyr for the truth, we are not yet at the Christian standpoint, not at that of true religion' (p. 645).

What then is this standpoint? Hegel fixes it as follows: 'Through faith this individual is recognised as of Divine nature, whereby the transcendence of God is done away' (p. 645). From this higher point of view in fact all that Jesus does becomes a revelation of God: it is God Himself Who draws near to us and touches us in Him, and so takes us up into the Divine consciousness.

This transformation of the consciousness from human to Divine begins with the death of Christ. 'The death of Christ is the centre about which it turns; in the conception of it lies the difference between the external point of view and that of faith, i.e. the contemplation of it with the spirit, in the spirit of truth, in the Holy Spirit' (p. 653). It is not indeed only with regard to the death of Christ that faith, directed by the Spirit, transforms the common view of His earthly manifestation. The doctrine, the miracles, the whole history, are also conceived and understood from the point of view of faith. But the view of the death is the central point of all. 'The death is, so to speak, the touchstone by which faith proves itself, in that here is essentially expressed its understanding of the manifestation of Christ' (p. 655). On the one hand it is the lot of finite humanity, to which Christ has submitted: His humanity is thus absolutely proved. More than this, the death He died was a death of shame upon the cross: 'humanity is manifested in Him up to the extremest point' (*ibid.*). On the other hand, however, faith recognises that in this death God is revealed, and that the Divine and human natures are one. Thus the significance of death is transformed; the Cross is glorified, and becomes the banner of the new religion.

'There enters now, however, a further determination. God has died, God is dead—this is the most terrifying thought, that all

that is eternal, all that is true, is not, the negation itself exists in
God: the greatest pain, the feeling of absolute hopelessness, the
abandonment of all that is higher is bound up therewith. The
process, however, does not stop here, but there follows the transformation. God in fact maintains Himself in this process, and it
(the process) is only the death of death. God rises again to life,
thus there is a change to the very opposite. The Resurrection
belongs equally essentially to faith: Christ appeared after His
ascension only to His friends: this is not external history for unbelief, this manifestation is rather only for faith. Upon the
Resurrection follows the glorification of Christ, and the triumph
of His exaltation to the right hand of God closes this history,
which in this consciousness is the unfolding of the Divine nature
itself' [3] (p. 656).

But now what does this mean? It means that for those who
attain to this higher point of view, death is dead, finitude is
consumed by being taken up into Infinity. But herewith evil and
sin too are overcome, for they belong only to the finite in separation from God. In this victory over sin and evil the Divine love is
manifested.

'Christ has assumed human finitude, and that in all its forms,
the finitude which in its extremest point is evil. . . . He has, however, assumed it, in order by His death to slay it. . . . Herein
is infinite love, that God has identified Himself with what is
allien to Himself, in order to slay it—such is the significance of
the death of Christ. Christ has borne the sins of the world, has
reconciled God, so it is said' (p. 658).

The process, however, is the necessary process of the Divine
life. Consequently, what is done, is universal in character. Christ
does not make satisfaction to God for our sins, as one independent moral person, acting as a substitute for others. On the
contrary the satisfaction to God consists in this, that finitude,
evil, and sin are in themselves overcome.

'This now is how it stands with regard to the satisfaction
made for us. What is fundamental therein is this, that that satisfaction has happened in and for itself: it is not that an alien

[3] The history of Christ, as taken up into, and interpreted by the above process of
consciousness, appears as the unfolding of the Divine nature.

sacrifice has been brought, not that another has been punished (simply) in order that punishment may have taken place' (p. 660).

Here, however, a difficulty arises. 'Suffering and dying in such a sense is contrary to the idea of moral imputation, according to which each individual has to stand for himself only, each one is the doer of his own deeds' (p. 661).

The solution of the difficulty, however, is at hand. The Christian faith lifts us above the sphere where imputation obtains, viz. the field of finitude.

'In the field of finitude the fixed rule is, that every one remains what he is: if he has done what is evil, then he is evil: the evil is in him as his quality. But already in the sphere of morality, still more in that of religion, the spirit is recognised as free, as affirmative in itself, so that this limitation in it, which proceeds even to that which is evil, is for the infinity of the spirit a non-entity: the spirit can make the done undone, the deed remains indeed in the memory, but the spirit disowns it. Imputation, therefore, does not reach up to this sphere' (*ibid.*).[4]

Such is Hegel's very remarkable interpretation of the Christian doctrine of the work of Christ. It brings together the humanitarianism of the Aufklärung and the idealism of Kant, and relates them to one another as successive stages of truth, in which the lower is only fully understood by the higher. The 'Umkehrung des Bewusstseins', which is characteristic of Hegel, carries us in fact from the standpoint of the Aufklärung to that of Kant. We pass from the history of the human Jesus to that of the Divine Idea, expressed in Him in order that it may be apprehended by us. 'First . . . that which is natural, then that which is spiritual.' [5] It may be freely granted that Hegel has given a most sympathetic interpretation of Christian doctrine, and has done his best by an act of penetrative imagination to arrive at its very essence. He has been able to work into his completed philosophical construction strands from the entire history of Christian doctrine, and to bring them into new relations which cast a great deal of

---

[4] The field of finitude is the domain of the ordinary consciousness, where the spirit is limited in thought and action by existing facts. The spirit is, however, free, in so far as it affirms as true and real its own infinite moral ideals, and refuses to recognise the limitation of facts, including even its own misdeeds. The free spirit thus rises above its past, and rids itself of responsibility for it. [5] 1 C. 15:46.

light on their nature. Especially interesting is the way in which he meets the Socinian criticism of the doctrine of satisfaction by passing on to the Pauline doctrine of mystical identification with Christ, as establishing a higher point of view at which the Socinian objections are no longer valid.

The crucial point in Hegel's reconstruction is, however, that of the connexion of the idealism of faith with the historical figure of Jesus. Hegel has indeed striven very hard to show the necessity for the Incarnation of the Divine Idea in the one individual.

'This individual, who is for the rest the manifestation of the Idea, is "this" unique individual—not certain individuals, for as realised in certain individuals the Divinity becomes an abstraction. "Certain" individuals mean an unsatisfactory excess of reflection, an excess because contrary to the idea of the individual subjectivity. Once is in (the realm of) the concept always, and the Subject must without a choice be realised in one subjectivity. In the eternal Idea there is only one Son; so there is only one, exclusive of the rest, in whom the absolute Idea appears. This perfecting of reality up to the point of immediate unique individuality is the most beautiful point of the Christian religion, and the absolute glorification of finitude is brought to view in it' (p. 643).[6]

The meaning is that, as there is only one eternal Idea, so it must be reflected for us in sensuous form in one point only. Hegel therefore here undoubtedly associates the development of the true religion more closely with the individual figure of Jesus than does Kant. Nevertheless his final view seems to be that this stage of faith is after all only a beginning, and that when the 'Umkehrung des Bewusstseins' takes place, the Idea in its higher form becomes universalised, so that its association with Jesus is now only symbolical.

If then, on the one hand, the Aufklärung may in general be regarded as having renewed in an immanental form (i.e. without the *theologumenon* of the transcendent Logos) the doctrine of

___

[6] This difficult passage may perhaps be paraphrased as follows : As there is only One Infinite Object, it requires in strictness to be *reflected* in only One Subject. A multiplicity of subjects means an unnecessary 'excess of reflection'. The concept of the Object, once formed, is a timeless reality : if *repeated* in time, it appears no more than an abstraction. Thus as there is only One Divine Son in idea, there can be only one, in the strict sense, in history.

the Apologists, that Christianity is the republication of the moral religion of reason, Kant and Hegel may, on the other hand, be viewed as having revived, also in an immanental form, the Gnostic religion of redemption. Like the Gnostics, they have separated the Divine principle of redemption from the historic Jesus, but it is for them no transcendent *Æon Christus*, but an idea immanent in the human mind. We have next, however, to deal with a theologian, who, in opposition to these new Apologists and new Gnostics, renews in immanental form the theology of Irenæus and Athanasius, making the Incarnation of the Divine in the historical Jesus the central point of the Christian religion. This theologian is Schleiermacher, who, a contemporary of Hegel, also starts like him from the Kantian standpoint, but develops his ideas in a different direction.

CHAPTER 3

THE CENTRE OF THE
MODERN THEOLOGICAL MOVEMENT

SCHLEIERMACHER

SCHLEIERMACHER (A.D. 1768–1834) is deservedly called the father of modern theology. His great systematic work, 'Der Christliche Glaube nach den Grundsätzen der evangelischen Kirche in Zusammenhange dargestellt' (1st ed. 1821, 2nd ed. 1831),[1] is the basis of almost all that is best in theology since his time. Kant had indeed in his ethical doctrine given to the modern world a standpoint, whence the ideas of justification and vicarious sacrifice could be understood and appreciated, as they had not been by the Aufklärung. He had also established in his doctrine of the Kingdom of God a point of connexion of great moment between philosophy and the Christian religion. Nevertheless in all this it was only the ideas of Christianity which he regarded as of permanent significance. Its historical elements he viewed as no more than a temporary scaffolding, which had in the history of human thought done good service towards the building of the temple of the Idea in humanity. With Schleiermacher, however, there is a great change. History has for him a deeper meaning than it had for Kant. Christianity is a religion the very essence of which lies in the redemption wrought by Jesus of Nazareth ('Der Christliche Glaube', 2nd ed., § 11).

What did Schleiermacher mean by this, and how did he understand the idea of redemption? He begins at precisely the same point as Kant. He accepts the results produced by the influence of natural science upon philosophy. Man is a part of nature. His knowledge of the world in detail is dependent upon

---

[1] The citations from this work given in the following pages are the present author's translations from the original, available only in German when this book was first published. An English translation by H. R. Mackintosh and J. S. Stewart appeared in 1928 under the title 'The Christian Faith'.

533

his senses. There are also within him natural impulses belonging to this life of the senses. But a spark disturbs his clod. He is also capable of a higher consciousness. That which altogether transcends the senses, the Absolute, the Infinite, makes itself known in him in the feeling of absolute dependence (*schlechthiniges Abhängigkeitsgefuhl*) (*ibid.* §4). This feeling Schleiermacher speaks of as the consciousness of God (*Gottesbewusstsein*), and identifies with the essence of religion, and of all religions. The consciousness of God is intended to permeate the whole of the lower consciousness, and to direct and control it at every point. When it does so completely, there is harmony, joy, and peace in the soul; when it struggles to overcome the lower consciousness there is disharmony, pain, and trouble (§ 5). In humanity in general, however, the ideal state of harmony is not realised. The consciousness of God develops in men more slowly than the lower consciousness (§ 67). Nevertheless so soon as the consciousness of God stirs within us at all, we know that it ought to pervade and control our life; and thus there is no peace for us, as long as it is oppressed and thwarted in its development by the lower consciousness (§ 83). Yet this oppression and hindrance we cannot ourselves overcome, nor can we liberate the consciousness of God in ourselves, so that it attains its rightful position in the soul (§ 86). This is the state of sin and consciousness of guilt.

At this point enters the figure of Jesus as the Redeemer. Redemption is the liberation of the consciousness of God from its oppression by the lower consciousness and the establishment of it in its due supremacy over the soul (§11, 2). Jesus is the archetypal man, in whom the God-consciousness from the first controls the lower consciousness (§93). He is supernatural, in so far as He transcends common humanity; nevertheless His life is not contrary to the true idea of humanity, but is rather the perfect realisation of it (§ 94). Hence, though He is supernatural, He acts naturally in the world by His personal influence, transmitted through the historical channel of the Church. His action is to make others in measure like Himself, to liberate the consciousness of God in them, and to enable it to dominate the lower consciousness, as it did in Him (§ 88). This is the redemption

534

which He brings. Schleiermacher calls the state of redemption, in opposition to the state of sin, the state of grace.

Further light is cast upon the way in which he understands the Christian redemption, by the distinction which he makes between Christianity and other religions. All religions aim at the development of the consciousness of God and the harmony which ensues therefrom. In the lower stages of the evolution of religion, however, the unity of God is seen as refracted into a multiplicity through the variety of nature: at this level, therefore, religion is polytheistic. Christianity, however, is a monotheistic religion (§ 8). Some religions, again, aim simply at establishing harmony in the inner life without affecting our action in the world, which they leave simply to the control of the lower impulses as before. Others aim at controlling conduct as well as feeling. The former are aesthetic, the latter teleological (or ethical) religions. Christianity belongs to the latter class. It aims at the control of the whole life, our actions as well as our feeling. Here Schleiermacher, like Kant, makes connexion with the idea of the Kingdom of God. This is the ultimate aim of the Christian redemption, and individuals are redeemed by Christ to take part in it (§ 9).

The complete definition of Christianity is, then, that it is the monotheistic and teleological religion in which everything is referred to the redemption wrought by Jesus of Nazareth (§ 11). From the Christian standpoint, moreover, it is not to be thought of that in the full sense of the word there can be any other redemption than this which Jesus has brought(§ 14).

Such in broad outline is Schleiermacher's view of the work of Christ. He is the Redeemer in that He establishes the supremacy of the consciousness of God in humanity, and thereby founds the Kingdom of God. We have now to examine in detail the way in which Schleiermacher works out this view. In order to do this satisfactorily we must consider in his 'Der Christliche Glaube' (2nd edition) not only §§ 100–5, in which he formally treats of the work of Christ, but also §§ 86–8, where he deals with the general basis of this and of the other associated doctrines of grace. The first point to be observed in studying those sections is the nature of the proof advanced. The method of Schleiermacher is to appeal, in the first place, not to Scripture but to Christian experience (§ 15), of which in his view Scriptural and ecclesiastical doctrine are alike formulations, only that the doctrine of Scripture is more poetical and rhetorical, while dogmatic theology is more didactic and scientific (§ 16). For the old method of direct proof from Scripture, therefore, Schleiermacher substitutes in reality the attempt to place oneself by sympathy at the point whence Scripture is intelligible as a natural manifestation of the Christian spirit. He can thus allow for the figurative element in Scripture, and avoid the difficulties which the Socinian criticism had shown to follow from the attempt to argue logically, from the express words of Scripture. Schleiermacher establishes as the basis of modern theology a new attitude to Scripture, involving no longer only a grammatico-historical, but also a psychological, exegesis. His method is in essence a return to the 'spiritual' exegesis of Origen, only that the gains of the grammatico-historical exegesis are conserved, in so far as the figures of Scripture are more carefully interpreted. Schleiermacher also, however, employs as proof of doctrine the Creeds and Confessions generally accepted by the Protestant Church (§ 27). His method is to treat them, along with the orthodox Protestant theology which interprets them, as a prior scientific formulation of the Christian experience, which, however, requires criticism and correction. The fundamental principle of Schleiermacher's theology throughout is that objective doctrine and subjective experience must correspond. So far then as doctrine mirrors experience, it is right: so far as it fails to do so, it is, if not absolutely wrong, mere speculation (§ 16, Zusatz).

An important part therefore of Schleiermacher's doctrinal proof consists in the endeavour to show that his positive statement is but the development to its proper consequences of that religious view which is indicated in the Protestant symbols. The complete title of his great dogmatic work in fact is 'Der Christliche Glaube nach den Grundsätzen der evangelischen Kirche im Zusammenhange dargestellt'. (The Christian faith systematically presented according to the fundamental principles of the Evangelical Church.) By the Evangelical Church Schleiermacher meant, not only the Lutheran, but also the Reformed Church. He regarded both branches of Protestantism as being, in spite of their differences, substantially in unity. He stood on the ground of the union of the two Churches, which was initiated in Prussia in 1817. As regards the relation of Protestantism to Catholicism he lays down the following important proposition:

(§ 24, Leitsatz) 'So far as the Reformation was not merely a purification and return from abuses that had stolen in, but there has proceeded from it a peculiar formation of the Christian community, we may by anticipation so conceive the opposition between Protestantism and Catholicism, in such a way that the first makes the relation of the individual to the Church dependent on his relation to Christ, while the latter makes the relation of the individual to Christ dependent on his relation to the Church.'

We are now in a position to proceed with the sections of 'Der Christliche Glaube' above mentioned. Each contains a general proposition or Thesis (Leitsatz), which is followed by a detailed exposition. The Leitsatz of § 87 is as follows:

'We are all of us conscious of approximations to the state of blessedness which manifest themselves in the Christian life, as grounded in a new Divinely-established common life, which counteracts the common life of sin and the misery therein developed.'

Schleiermacher's view of sin, it should be explained, does not end simply with the inability of the individual to free the consciousness of God in him from the hindrance of the lower life. There is a common life of sin, due to the interaction of individuals one upon another, and transmitted as a social tradition from the past (§ 71).[2] This life is the natural state of humanity, to meet which God has established the remedy of the common life of the Church, deriving itself from the life of Jesus.

Upon the above-mentioned experience of an approximation to beatitude Schleiermacher now undertakes to establish his doctrine of the Person and Work of Christ. One difficulty is, that he postulates in Christ a perfect supremacy of the consciousness of God. 'In this common life, which goes back to the work of Jesus, redemption is accomplished by Him by virtue of the communication of His sinless perfection' (§ 88, Leitsatz).

[2] This doctrine of inherited sin (*Erbsünde*) is Schleiermacher's substitute for the traditional doctrine of original sin.

Yet experience can testify only to approximations in our case to beatitude. Can we ever by means of an imperfect result demonstrate a perfect cause? Schleiermacher feels the difficulty, but he says:

'We, nevertheless, hold to this conception (of the absolute perfection of Christ) as the original one and that which has been handed down from the primitive Church to our own, and as at the same time that which both most definitely excludes all surreptitious self-satisfaction, and also is alone consistent with a more serious view of the common life in the state of sin' (§ 88, 1).

In other words, once we undervalue the Redeemer, we begin to undervalue redemption and so to think lightly of sin. Schleiermacher does not, however, deny that a lower view of redemption may still be Christian, provided that we trace to Christ all such experience of blessedness as we have. No strict proof can, however, here be given. For one thing different impressions may be made by the same fact on the various members of the Christian community, so that ultimately we have only our own conviction to point to. Cannot we, however, escape this subjectivity by proof from Scripture? In the first place, most of the Scriptural forms of expression are capable of various interpretation. In the second place, proof from Scripture only shows agreement with the primitive form of Christian faith. This method of proof does not meet our need. All that is possible is psychologically to show how, entirely apart from an external compulsion by means of prophecy or miracle or the like, the belief originally arose and still arises 'that Jesus possesses a sinless perfection, and that in the communion founded by Him there is a communication of the same' (§ 88, 2). If we establish this then it follows of itself that this conviction will involve an ever-increasing beatitude in the community.

What then is here necessary? Firstly, to point out that the doctrine stated does not mean that it is our faith that makes Jesus the Redeemer—faith is no mere subjective view which we take of Him without a sufficient basis in the objective reality of His Person. Secondly, however, we must not say on the one hand that there is in Jesus a perfect consciousness of God, while we yet on the other hand attribute our faith in Him to our own yearning for peace of mind. On the contrary, faith is His work. The founding of the community is not a separate act apart from His consciousness of God. They are indivisibly one and the same. Just as the consciousness of God is in reality an act, so the founding of the community is essentially involved in it. Schleiermacher presupposes the intelligibility of all this in the case of the first disciples, but raises the question, How does Jesus still continue after all these centuries to act in the community of His foundation so as still to create the same faith as that of the primitive Church? The answer is, that His personal activity is replaced by that of the community itself 'in so far as also the picture of Him which we still have in the Scriptures came to be, and still maintains itself, through the community' (§ 88, 2).

No single person in the community indeed is capable of this work. Moreover, the whole community shares in the life of sin. Nevertheless the direct impression of the life of Christ is experienced in it. The individual finds in it the picture of Christ; and in its common life pure impulses from the original source of Christ's sinless perfection continually break forth, even though in action they lose force and become corrupted.

Such then is Schleiermacher's proof of his general view of Christ as Redeemer. It is led entirely from experience: the Scriptures do no more than manifest the agreement of the view with the primitive Christian consciousness. Upon the foundation so laid he now raises the edifice of his doctrine proper of the work or office of Christ ('Von dem Geschäft Christi'), §§100–5. In the first place he makes a further distinction. He now uses 'Redemption' in a narrower sense than heretofore, and opposes it to 'Reconciliation', defining these two aspect of the work of Christ as follows:

'The Redeemer receives believers into the power of His consciousness of God, and this is His redemptive activity' (§ 100, Leitsatz).

'The Redeemer receives believers into the fellowship of His undisturbed beatitude, and this is His reconciling activity' (§ 101, Leitsatz).

(§ 100, 1) The first of these aspects has the logical priority. Since Christianity is an ethical religion, the work of the Redeemer upon us is to be understood as a stimulation of us to free action of our own, which action, however, all the same is His. The more proper activity of the Redeemer is, however, the receiving us into and maintaining us in a state of grace, apart from our activity in the world resulting from this. Schleiermacher repeats that this activity of the Redeemer is through the energy of His sinless perfection or the supremacy of the consciousness of God in Him. But he now adds the important thought that Christ can only direct His consciousness of God against sin, in so far as He enters into the common life of humanity, and in sympathy shares our consciousness of sin, doing this at the same time with a view to its being conquered by Him. We too, as we share in His life, come to share in His victory over sin.

(2) Christ's work in the communication of the consciousness of God is a Divine work, and so is creative. Here Schleiermacher makes play with an idea, which dominates his doctrine of the Person of Christ (§§ 92–9), viz. that the consciousness of God in Christ is the same thing as the immanence of God in Him. (It may be observed that this notion is his equivalent for the traditional doctrine of the Incarnation of the Logos.' Christ, then, like God, creates in us free will, a very inexplicable thing. His will creates a will to be received, or rather to acquiesce in His operation. It must be thought of as a permeative, or better as an attractive power, and like the Divine creative power employed in the origin of the Person of Christ Himself, it is person-forming. Again, like the creative power of God in the world, it is not concerned with individuals except as parts of a whole: it is in fact a continuation of the creative activity by which God created Christ, the ultimate purpose of which was the immanence of God in the entirety of humanity.

(3) Schleiermacher distinguishes his view as mystical, and as the golden mean between the two extremes of a magical and a purely empirical view. The magical view is that which attributes conversion to a personal operation of the Divine Christ, without, however, giving any psychological explanation of it, or assigning any natural channel for it. This has been the view of the sectaries

(the mystical sects),[3] but others (i.e. orthodoxy in its doctrine of the kingly office) have come dangerously near it, though qualifying it with the idea that the Scriptures are a *sine qua non* of the Divine operation. On the other hand the empirical view (that of the Aufklärung) regards Christ as achieving increasing perfection in us by means of doctrine and example. This view, however, thinks too meanly of Christ. Even if His doctrine and example be regarded as perfect, there is wanting the specifically Christian idea of the forgiveness of sins through Him, or comfort is obtained by general means, such as the idea of the mercy of God. At most Christ only serves to bid men cease offering surrogates for the lack of perfection. The whole view is at fault in that it sets philosophy above faith and regards the latter as only a transitional stage.

Throughout § 100 Schleiermacher appeals (in his own sense, of course, of what the appeal means) to Scripture proofs. He views his doctrine as identical above all with the Pauline mystical doctrine of Christ in us, and of our union with Him, whereby we die to sin and live to righteousness (§ 101, 1).

Next comes the discussion of Christ's reconciling work. If His reconciling activity had no connexion with His activity in our redemption, or if reconciliation preceded redemption, the ethical character of Christianity would be affected. As, however, the activity of Christ implies a receptivity or longing in us, His redeeming activity necessarily precedes His activity in reconciliation. For our longing for redemption flows from the consciousness of sin itself, not from the idea of it as a cause of evil (i.e. pain or hindrance to life). [This statement Schleiermacher supports by saying that it must be so 'since evil is not for the individual in any direct connexion with his sin'. In order to clear

<hr/>

[3] Cf. *supra*, p. 361, n. 9. Schleiermacher's statement may be illustrated from Schwenkfeld and from the Quaker thelogian, Barclay. Schwenkfeld (as quoted by Baur, 'Lehre von der Versöhnung', p. 461, n.) says : 'Justifying faith comes not from preaching, but from God in heaven, it does not rest in the fact that Christ has shed His blood for us and paid for our sins, for such faith is an historical, powerless faith, but true faith rests in Christ in God Himself, it stands upon essential Being, and holds to the eternal Truth.' Barclay (A.D. 1648–90) explicitly teaches that 'the evangelical and saving light and grace' of Christ, though it is 'the purchase of His blood', is yet absolutely universal and essentially independent of a knowledge of the Gospel history. He reprimands the Arminians, because they, though teaching a universal redemption, yet made the fruition of it by the individual depend on an historical knowledge ('Apology for the True Christian Divinity', English trans., 1869, Props. V, VI, and VII, Ex. 3).

up this point we must for a moment turn to his doctrine of evil
(§§ 75–8). He regards sin in the world (i.e. the supremacy of
the sense consciousness over the God-consciousness) as disturbing
the ideal order of the world. In the first place, it implies as we
have seen, a sinful society, actuated throughout by bad principles,
which result in the existence of social evils. Secondly, however,
though the laws of nature are not altered by sin, the harmony
of the soul with the world is affected, inasmuch as the universe
is not viewed as a whole as the God-consciousness would prompt,
but is regarded simply in its relation to the life of the empirical
individual. Thus between sin in humanity in general and evil in
the world in general a direct connexion obtains. There is, however, no immediate connexion between the sin of the individual
and the particular evils he experiences.] The reconciling moment
in Christ's activity (that which removes our sense of evil) must
therefore follow upon and out of the redemptive moment in it
(that which lifts us out of the state of sin). Nevertheless the two
are in the closest connexion, and one is not given without the
other.

(2) Reconciliation in fact follows upon redemption in this
way. As in Christ the consciousness of God is the centre of His
Being, and hindrances of His activity come only from without,
and appear merely as temporal determinations of His activity,
so is it with the believer in union with Him. Evils remain for
him only as an indication of the direction of his action, and
occasion no unhappiness. They do not belong to his new life in
Christ.

But there is again the deeper question of the consciousness
of sin, as it is still present in the believer. He relates it, however,
to the common life of universal sinfulness which still has a place
in him, and not to his new life.

'As then the redeeming activity of Christ establishes for all
believers a common activity corresponding to the immanence of
God in Christ; so the reconciling element in Him, viz. the
beatitude of God's immanence in Him, establishes a common
feeling of beatitude for all believers and for each one in particular. In such an one there dies at the same time the former
personality, so far as it meant the isolation of feeling in a bodily

542

unity of life, to which isolation all sympathetic feeling for others and for the community remained subordinated. What, however, remains over as the individuality of the person is the peculiar mode of conception and sensation, which incorporates itself in that new common life as an individualised intelligence, so that the activity of Christ in relation to this element also is person-forming, in that an old man is put off and a new man put on.'

We may, perhaps, distinguish two stages in the process. 'The beginning is the disappearance of the old man with his relation to evil and sin, and thus the disappearance of the consciousness of desert of punishment; so that the first element in reconciliation is the forgiveness of sins. For in the unity of life with Christ all relation to the law ceases, in that there begins the general tendency in opposition to sin, which proceeds from Him.'

The continuation of the process is in the settled possession of beatitude, in that Christ is now the centre of the life, while we recognise that this possession is His gift, who wills that we should enjoy His blessing and His peace. The above distinction, however, does not amount to a real separation of the two elements in the process. Forgiveness implies the blessedness of union with Christ, while the latter also always involves the former, since the general presence of sin continues.

(3) This position is once more mystical, in contrast with the empirical and magical points of view. The empirical point of view makes beatitude to result from amendment; but, as a matter of fact, the evils belonging to the common life of sin do not disappear. Thus beatitude remains only a hope, and is scarcely ever a possession; so that here Christianity has no special advantage over other religions. Neither, if we make beatitude originate only indirectly from Christ, through His bringing about amendment, do we assign to Him any very marked difference from other men.

Magical are all those views of the reconciling activity of Christ, which make the communication of His beatitude independent of reception into fellowship with Him. 'Forgiveness of sins is in fact deduced from the punishment Christ bore, and the beatitude of men itself depicted as a reward, which God grants Christ for that penal suffering.' Schleiermacher does not wish to reject altogether the idea that our blessedness is Christ's reward, nor that there is a connexion between His sufferings and the forgiveness of sins. Both conceptions are, however, magical, if not interpreted through our fellowship with Christ.

'For in this fellowship the communication of beatitude is, as above explained, natural, without it the reward of Christ is an arbitrary Divine act. And this is always something magical, especially when so entirely inward a thing as beatitude is to be brought about from without apart from being established from within. For if it be independent of life in Christ, it can, since the recipient has no source of beatitude in himself, only be in some way infused into each individual from without. Just as magically is the forgiveness of sins wrought, if the consciousness of desert of punishment is to cease, because another has borne the penalty. That indeed in this way the expectation of punishment might be removed, may be thought; but this is only the sensuous element of the forgiveness of sins, and there would still remain the properly ethical element, viz. the consciousness of desert of penalty, which therefore must vanish without any reason, as if removed by enchantment.'

(4) In the above doctrine of redemption and reconciliation the suffering of Christ has not been mentioned. It is in fact only a secondary element in both cases, as is clear from the fact that fellowship with Christ was possible even before His sufferings and death. So far as it does come in, Christ's suffering belongs more immediately to reconciliation, but only mediately to redemption. Schleiermacher, however, takes first its relation to redemption.

'The activity of Christ in founding the new common life could only in reality be manifested in all its perfection—although faith in this perfection could be present even apart from this—if it yielded to no opposition, not even that which might bring about the destruction of the person. The perfection here is not to be found properly and immediately in the suffering itself, but only in the surrender to the same.'

If, however, this climax of suffering is isolated, and the essence of Christ's redeeming activity is viewed as a surrender to suffering for suffering's sake, then we have in this distortion a magical view of Christ's work, since the founding of the new common life is left out of account.

'But now again as regards reconciliation it was for our presentation (of the matter) self-explanatory, that in order to bring about their reception into the fellowship of Christ's beatitude, the longing of those who were conscious of their misery must first be directed to Christ by the impression which they receive of His beatitude. And here the state of things is, that faith in this beatitude could be present without this,[4] but that Christ's beatitude nevertheless was only manifested in its perfection, in that it was not overcome by the plenitude of His suffering, and this all the more as, since this suffering proceeded from the opposition of sin, the sympathy with misery, which everywhere, though without disturbing His beatitude, accompanied the Redeemer since He had entered into the life of sin, must here set in at its highest point. Here it is not the surrender to suffering such as belongs to the redeeming activity, but the suffering itself which becomes the complete confirmation of faith in the beatitude of the Redeemer.'

It is once more, however, a magical distortion of this truth when the absolute necessity of an invincible beatitude in Christ is overlooked, and the reconciling power of His passion is deduced from His voluntary abandonment of beatitude, though but for a moment.

But now there is a further point which follows from the close association of reconciliation and redemption in Schleiermacher's theology.

'The fact that we regard His sympathy with men's misery as the climax of Christ's suffering, already involves that no suffering which does not belong to the redeeming work of Christ can be viewed as belonging to His work of reconciliation, since any such suffering would have no connexion with the reaction of the Redeemer against men's misery, and so could only be reckoned to the work of reconciliation in a magical way.'

The whole suffering of Christ, however, viewed as one, can be regarded as having this connexion with His work of redemption. But to isolate any particular part of Christ's suffering from

---

[4] I.e. without the manifestation of Christ's beatitude in its perfection.

545

the whole, and assign to it a special reconciling value, comes near superstition.

'Least of all is it fitting to set such a special reconciling value upon the bodily sufferings, since these not only in and by themselves stand in the most distant connexion with Christ's reaction against sin, but also according to the testimony of our own feelings it is even now the reward of a temperate moral development and strong piety, that in connexion with a joyous spiritual consciousness, whether it is a person or a common emotion, bodily sufferings are often entirely removed, or at least never penetrate that consciousness and lessen one moment's content of beatitude.'

Finally, Schleiermacher points out that through the twofold work of redemption and reconciliation is realised the perfection of the creation of human nature. The process that began with the forming of the Person of Christ by the immanence of the consciousness of God in Him is continued by every intensive exaltation of the thus formed Divine-human life in its relation to the disappearing common life of sin. In this new life the original destination of humanity is reached, beyond which for a nature like ours there is nothing to be thought of or experienced.

The principal Scripture references in § 101 are to Rom. 8:1; 1 Jn 1:8–9; 2:1–2; Gal. 2:19–21; 5:22–4.

In §§ 102–5 Schleiermacher, according to the theological method already described, further establishes his doctrine by a comparison with that of the Protestant orthodoxy.

'The doctrine of the Church distributes the entire activity of Christ under His three offices, the prophetic, high-priestly, and kingly' (§ 102, Leitsatz).

The division, says Schleiermacher, might at first sight appear arbitrary. We seem to have merely a collection of figures, and not all of these the most obviously suggested by the New Testament. Figurative expressions submit with difficulty to proper limitation, and often create trouble in systematic theology. It turns out, however, on examination that these particular figures are not arbitrarily chosen, but will serve to exhibit the Christian consciousness in terms of the Old Covenant. Because of this historical connexion they are of value, and are not to be neglected; the use of them establishes a connexion with primitive Christianity. On the other hand we no longer stand in the same relation to primitive Christianity as did Judaism, and it is not satisfactory for the modern Christian to be limited to such forms of doctrine only. Hence the need of a restatement of doctrine such as Schleiermacher has already given. What is now requisite is to show the essential unity of that statement 'with that which earlier Christians formed, in that they present the offices of Christ as potentiated transformations of those, through which God's rule was manifested under the Old Covenant'.[5] Schleiermacher says that this unity can only be demonstrated if we take all the three offices together.

'The prophetic office of Christ consists in teaching, prediction, and in the working of miracles' (§ 103, Leitsatz). Christ's teaching, which for the people extended up to His being taken prisoner, but for His disciples up to the ascension, had as its source neither the Jewish law, nor yet, as the empirical school teach, human reason in general; it sprang from His own immediate consciousness of God, which permeated and controlled all His thought. The law and the Messianic expectation were naturally the point of connexion for His proclamation of the Kingdom of God, to be established by Him.

As to the content of His teaching everything was essential, in so far as it belonged to His own presentation of Himself. For only the manifestation of His own proper dignity can effectively invite men into fellowship with Himself. Thus the essence of Christ's doctrine is the doctrine of His Person, which outwardly is the doctrine of His vocation, or of the communication of eternal life in the Kingdom of God, and inwardly the doctrine of His relation to Him Who sent Him, or of God as the Father, Who reveals Himself to and through Him. Christ further speaks of His destination to bring men to God and rule them in the Kingdom of God. What He says, moreover, is not to be dissociated from the 'total impression' of His Person. The immanence of God in Him manifests itself not only in words, but in every form of self-expression. Once more, the predictive

---

[5] Christ's offices are those of the Old Covenant, transformed by being raised to a higher potency.

element in the teaching of Christ is not really different from the rest of His teaching; for in it He could speak only of what was being already fulfilled in His own Person as the Messiah.

Finally, with regard to the miracles of Christ, these no doubt served to confirm His teaching to those who heard Him. But miracles can only perform such a function where they are immediately observed: immediate observation, however, is no longer possible to those who are separated by space and time from the miracles. For us, therefore, the observation of the miracles is replaced by the sight of Christ's spiritual operation in history, which was denied to the first believers. The miracles of Christ in fact did but herald the advent of a new supernatural life: we live in the age when this life is all around us.

'The high-priestly office of Christ includes in itself His complete fulfilment of the law or His active obedience, His reconciling death or His passive obedience, and the representation of believers before the Father' (§ 104, Leitsatz). Here Schleiermacher gives a warning against separating the active and passive obedience, as though the active obedience had filled the life of Christ, while the passive obedience only began with His being taken a prisoner. On the contrary, in all His life the activity of His consciousness of God was present. Moreover, everywhere it was called out by definite occasions which involve passivity, and in action it was limited by hindrances which were felt as suffering. These occasions and these hindrances both came to Christ from the common life of sin, and in the suffering they occasioned Him He felt by sympathy and bore the sin of the world; so that this suffering accompanied Him throughout His whole life. The active and passive obedience were therefore, to speak strictly, united in every moment of His life. The latter signifies the receptivity in Christ, well-pleasing to God and perfectly satisfactory to Him, by which in feeling He entered into the life of sin, the former the activity and sympathy, equally well-pleasing and satisfactory to God, by which He reacted against it in carrying out His Divine vocation.

The essential high-priestly value of Christ's active obedience is as follows: His action alone perfectly corresponds to the Divine will, and purely and entirely expresses the supremacy of

548

the consciousness of God in human nature. This, however, is the basis of our peculiar relation to Him as Redeemer. 'Apart from union with Christ neither any individual man, nor yet any definite part of the common life of humanity, can in and by itself in any period of time whatever be righteous before God or an object of the Divine good pleasure.' No one in living fellowship with Christ is, however, regarded by God, as he is in himself, but as he is inspired by Christ and is a part of His work still in process of development; so that what is not yet united to Christ is nevertheless viewed as related to the same inspiring process of His life, as that which presently is to be inspired thereby. This is the true sense of the often-misunderstood expression, that Christ's obedience is our righteousness, or that His righteousness is imputed to us.

At this point, then, we can distinguish between the prophetic and the high-priestly value of Christ's obedience. To the prophetic office belongs everything of the nature of revelation and self-manifestation both by word and deed, and everything which is directed to men with reference to the opposition between Christ and them, with a view to make them receptive for union with Him. The high-priestly value of Christ's obedience, however, has reference to His union with us, so far as His pure will to do the will of God is effective in us by means of our fellowship with Him, and so far as, therefore, we share His perfection, if not in completion yet in germ; so that our union with Him, though not yet fully apparent, is by God reckoned as absolute and eternal, and is so recognised also by our faith.

There are, however, two points to be guarded against in the usual statement. Firstly, the active obedience of Christ is said to be a perfect fulfilment of the Divine law. The idea of law implies an opposition between a higher commanding and a subordinate imperfect will. In this sense Christ could not be under the law, and even if we say that He voluntarily subjected Himself to the law, yet the idea of opposition between Him and it is left. We must therefore say that the active obedience of Christ was the perfect fulfilment, not of the law, but of the Divine will. So far as the outward precepts of the Mosaic law are concerned, Christ was indeed personally subject to them, but not voluntarily.

(Schleiermacher appears to mean that He was subject to them by His birth as a Jew.) His fulfilment of them was therefore only part of His high-priestly work, in so far as it was a part of His fulfiment of the Divine will.

The second point of divergence is this. We must not say that Christ fulfilled the Divine will 'in our place or for our advantage'. At least we must not say 'in our place' in the sense that we are thereby delivered from the fulfilment of the Divine will; for the chief work of Christ is to inspire us to an ever completer fulfilment of the Divine will. Nor yet must we say it in the sense that a lack of acceptability to God in us can be covered by an excess of acceptability in Christ. For since only the perfect man can stand before God, Christ Himself has nothing in excess to bestow on us.

Nor, again, must we say 'for our advantage' in the sense that Christ's obedience in itself had in any way altered our condition. On the contrary, Christ's entire obedience only avails for us, as it becomes the motive principle of our obedience in fellowship with Him, just as the sin of Adam only results in our condemnation, in so far as it impels us, in our fellowship of nature with him, ourselves to sin.

As regards the passive obedience of Christ we have to remember, first of all, that the connexion in human society between sins and evils is general and not particular. Humanity suffers for the sins of humanity, not each individual for his own. Hence vicarious suffering is possible, in so far as the evils which come upon us are due to others' sins. Christ, then, though sinless, in entering into the common life of sinful humanity vicariously suffered for others. His suffering, moreover, was for the sins of universal humanity, because in accordance with the purpose of His life He felt a general sympathy with the sin of humanity. This sympathy reached its climax, when Jews and Gentiles alike, representing entire humanity, conspired together against His innocence.

'As now this sympathy with human guilt and desert of punishment was the original impulse that set redemption in motion, in so far as every definite human conscious activity is preceded by a determining impression: so now also the maximum increase of this very sympathy was Christ's immediate inspiration to the greatest moment in His office of redemption. And just as from this has proceeded His victory over sin, and as with sin its connexion with evil is also overcome: so we can put like together with like and say that through the suffering of Christ the penalty (of sin) is removed, since in the fellowship of His life of beatitude the evil which is now for the first time in process of disappearance is also at least no longer accepted as punishment.'

This is the true Christian sense of the so much disputed doctrine, that Christ by His free self-surrender to suffering and death has satisfied the Divine righteousness, as that wherein is founded the connexion between sin and evil, and has thereby redeemed us from the penalty of sin. It is now also clear how, apart from the exemplary character of the sufferings of Christ which belongs to His prophetic office, the appropriation of them has always been so fruitful in Christian piety. We can also understand the one-sidedness which concentrates the whole of redemption in this one point.

'For in Christ's suffering even unto death, as occasioned by His faithfulness, is manifested to us His absolutely self-denying love; and in this is present to us in the fullest visibility the mode and manner in which God was in Him, in order to reconcile the world to Himself, as also we feel by sympathy most perfectly through His suffering, how invincible was His beatitude.'

We must not, however, dwell on the mere sufferings of Christ apart from His activity in them, nor again substitute, for the correct formula that Christ by His sufferings has taken away the penalties of sin, the incorrect idea that He has borne the penalty of sin (in the sense of an equivalent for our punishment), in order to satisfy the Divine righteousness. Apart from all other objections, this doctrine breaks down at the point where Christ is supposed to have experienced the Divine wrath.

'For this theory on the one hand takes away all human reality in the human consciousness of Christ, if He is to have possessed as His personal consciousness what in the nature of the case could only exist in Him as sympathy; on the other hand there is undoubtedly here at bottom the presupposition of an absolute necessity of Divine punishments, even apart from a reference to their natural connexion with wickedness, while this notion again is hardly to be distinguished from such a conception of the Divine righteousness as is transferred to God from the rudest human conditions.'

In a footnote Schleiermacher says that he has read with pleasure, that the late J. J. Hess [6] also could not view Mt. 27:46 as a description by Christ of His own misery, but only as the beginning of the Psalm, which He only quoted with a view to what follows in it.

It is to be observed, that in the above passage Schleiermacher accepts the idea of natural law even more thoroughly than the Aufklärer Steinbart, who still leaves room for arbitrary Divine punishments in addition to punishment fixed by the order of nature.[7]

Schleiermacher goes on to express his disapproval of the gathering up of the doctrine of the high-priestly work of Christ in the phrase 'vicarious satisfaction'. He offers his criticism of it, however, in the form of a suggestion as to how it may be modified. 'Instead of relating it, as it stands as a whole, both to the active and passive obedience equally, we must rather divide it, and relate the vicarious element only to the passive obedience, the satisfactory element, on the other hand, only to the active obedience.'

Christ did indeed by His entire work make satisfaction for us: He did it, not, however, instead of us, but rather as the source of our spiritual life. On the other hand His suffering was vicarious, both as regards His sympathy with sinners and in regard to the evils He suffered, which in a general sense, as has been before explained, may be said to have been vicarious.[8] But this vicariousness was not satisfactory; for those who as yet do not suffer for sin must do so, if they are to be united to Christ; and again Christ's suffering of evils does not exclude that of others, but on the contrary those who enter into fellowship with Him must enter into the fellowship of His sufferings, and suffer vicariously with Him for the sins of humanity. If we wish to find one expression for the whole of Christ's high-priestly work we

[6] Of Zürich; A.D. 1741–1828.   [7] *Supra*, p. 512.   [8] Cf. *supra*, p. 550.

may exactly reverse the traditional phrase, and call Him our 'satisfactory vicar', in the sense that He, by His archetypal position in His redeeming activity, so presents before God the completion of human nature, that God by reason of our union with Him only regards us as we are in Him; and again, in the sense that His sympathy with sin, which impelled Him to the work of redemption, and was most perfectly manifested in His death, serves to supplement and perfect our imperfect consciousness of sin. We must, however, be very careful to make clear also that Christ's self-surrender to death is nothing different from His perseverance in the work of redemption. It was no arbitrary act outside of this, such as a voluntary self-infliction of pain to meet the necessity of punishment, a mode of conduct which has been already recognised as contrary to reason.[9] Christ's death was no pattern for the voluntary penances of Romanism, which are transferable from one to another.

As to the intercession of Christ, Schleiermacher says that it is difficult to see how Christ's obtaining goods by intercession from the Father can differ from His bestowal of them as King. A distinction may, however, be observed, if Christ's intercession be supposed to apply to what is properly outside His Kingdom, as for example that men should by the Father's general providence be added to it, or that those already in it may obtain from God's general providence spiritual gifts outside His special Kingdom of grace. Christ's intercession must be thought of as having begun during His lifetime; and, in its continuance beyond this, does not depend upon any particular revelation to us of His present condition, but only on the already established content of His personality and on the worth of it to God. What Schleiermacher appears to mean, is that the Spirit of Christ in us directs and makes effective our prayers, even when they are for spiritual blessings in the domain of general providence, and also that the Person and work of Christ, in their cosmic significance, constitute a continual appeal to God to perfect the work begun in Him.

'The kingly office of Christ consists in this, that all which the

---

[9] The reference is to § 86, 1, where Schleiermacher points out that, since every moment has its duty, time can only be given to self-chastisement at the expense of neglecting duty.

community of believers requires for its welfare continually proceeds from Him' (§ 105, Leitsatz).

The Kingdom of Christ means, first of all, that the intention of Christ was to form a society, of which He is the one Head and Founder. Again, this kingdom is according to His own testimony not of the world. This means that its sphere is in the hearts of men, and that its government is not by external force, or even by sensuous allurements or punishments. Christ's Kingdom is not to be thought of as beginning after He left this earth, or as a kingdom beyond it. Nor is there any difference between His Kingdom as expressed in His earthly life and as it now exists. The rules and directions which He gave then abide now; and His spiritual presence is still mediated by the written Word, with the picture which it contains of His character and work.

The chief difficulty in regard to this office of Christ is rightly to relate it to the general providence of God. The usual division into the kingdom of power, the kingdom of grace, and the kingdom of glory, is here ineffective. In the first place, a kingdom of power apart from the kingdom of grace is not to be admitted as part of our doctrine. It has at least nothing to do with the redeeming activity of Christ, and therefore, even if the idea is found in the New Testament, it is no proper part of the Christian religion. If, again, we interpret Christ's authority as God-man and Redeemer [1] as co-extensive with God's general providence, we come into opposition with the Scriptural passages which represent Him as praying to the Father, and as wishing to establish, in the intercourse of believers with the Father, a direct relation between prayer and its answer. The power of Christ then means only that He inaugurates the kingdom of grace; and it is essentially exhausted in this. It is a power over the world, in so far as believers are taken out of the world to form part of the kingdom of grace; but the power to determine what portion of the world shall be so chosen remains with the Father. As regards the traditional kingdom of glory, Schleiermacher finds no place for this either. Christ is the pattern of our future spiritual glory; but this relation to the Church is not fitly described as a kingdom. Our future glorification proceeds, together with His, from the Father.

---

[1] Cf. Mt. 11:27.

'There remains, therefore, only the one kingdom of grace as a true Kingdom of Christ, which is now also the only one of which we have a real consciousness in our religious states of mind, and of which we also alone, since our active faith must be directed towards it, need a guiding knowledge.' The other two names of the usual division can only be employed, better to define the kingdom of grace. The name, the kingdom of power, may serve to illustrate the universal destiny and scope of the kingdom of grace. The name, kingdom of glory, may indicate the goal of beatitude, to which, as it increases in perfection, the kingdom of grace may advance.

Schleiermacher has applied himself, even more thoroughly and also more successfully than Kant or Hegel, to discover the 'essence' or 'principle' of the Christian religion.

'The expression "principle" ', says Troeltsch,[2] 'belongs only to the modern science of religion, inasmuch as it orginates in general only from our refined modern psychology and the historical thought conditioned by it. It signifies nothing else than the conception of the fundamental impulse that lies behind the individual psychological phenomena and facts, or of the fundamental force which produces them [3] as a unity of spiritual process only recognisable by intuition and divination, yet quite well to be felt: it means the reduction of a connected circle of psychological phenomena to a single fundamental, mostly only instinctive, force, expressing and developing itself in them, which follows in its development an inner tendency of its own, and which only produces its complete content out of its tendency in adaptation and conflict, and yet also is on every side subject to crossing and degeneration.'

These words of Troeltsch exactly describe the way in which, on the *formal* side, Schleiermacher conceives the inner essence of Christianity. His *material* conception of it turns essentially on the notion of personality: it is conceived as a unity, not of logic, but of personal experience, in which the objective and subjective aspects everywhere necessarily correspond to each

---

[2] 'Die Religion in Geschichte und Gegenwart', 1st ed., vol. iv, Art. 'Prinzip religiöses', 1.

[3] The text has 'which they produce'. But the sense seems to require us to read *hervorbringt* instead of *hervorbringen*.

other. Moreover for him personality is not an exclusive but an inclusive idea. The fundamental notion of his whole view is that of immanence, the immanence first of God in Christ, and then of Christ and so of God in us. From this point of view Schleiermacher accordingly finds the doctrine of the Ancient Church 'magical' in so far as its notion of salvation is fundamentally objective and outside of experience, and is only personalised through its application in the sacraments. In so far as the Reformation theology, while adopting the doctrine of salvation through the personal experience of faith, yet maintained at the same time the old objective conception of a salvation independent of experience, Schleiermacher finds this view also 'magical' and unsatisfactory. On the other hand his criticism of the empirical school (viz. the individualistic tendency that runs through the mediaeval criticism on to Socinianism and the Aufklärung) is that it fails to recognise the inclusiveness of personality, and so to find a proper place for the immanence of God and Christ in us.

Schleiermacher has undertaken, on the basis of his central position, a complete reconstruction of theology. His method implies the abandonment of the attempt to put together the Scripture data in an external way, as is done in the great scholastic systems alike of Catholicism and Protestantism. We have instead the endeavour to reconstruct the whole from within by an organic process. The old structures are abandoned to criticism: it is astonishing how largely Socinus is reproduced in this respect by Schleiermacher. Yet the elements of the old theology recur in the new construction, only now in a new context, and united by a fresh set of mediating ideas, many of which are drawn from Kant's reinterpretation of the ecclesiastical dogma. The whole, however, constitutes a revolution in theology. Schleiermacher carries through his immanental view of Christianity in a most thoroughgoing way. Since for him Christianity is entirely a spiritual essence, he has no place in doctrine for the Resurrection and ascension of Christ as external facts (§ 99). Similarly, he dispenses with Christ's Kingdom of power and glory, and retains only His Kingdom of grace. Any idea, that may be found in the New Testament, but which has no direct relation to experience, does not belong to the sphere of Christian doctrine. Schleiermacher would treat such ideas as merely traditional, or at best speculative.

In estimating the value of the theology of Schleiermacher two questions naturally appear to arise. The first is: Is he, and with him modern theology in general, justified in attempting to reduce Christianity to a 'principle'? The second is: If he is to be justified on this point, has he correctly defined the principle of Christianity? Now as regards the first question, there can be no doubt that if there is today to be a theology at all, it must follow the line adopted by Kant and Hegel, and more thoroughly by Schleiermacher, and must endeavour to reduce Christianity to an essence or principle. The previous history of theology shows that the attempt to treat the Scripture upon any other basis is doomed to failure. All systems, which attempt the concatenation of the various logical developments derived from different Scriptural texts, in the end destroy themselves by a process of immanent criticism, which is only the carrying out to its consequences of their own logic.

As regards the second question, there are three points above all to be observed:

(1) Schleiermacher includes in the essence of Christianity, in opposition to Kant and Hegel, the historical Jesus. Christianity is the religion, in which everything is referred to the redemption wrought by Jesus of Nazareth. The inclusion of a historical element in a religious principle has been found unthinkable by the modern liberal theology, of which Biedermann's 'Christliche Dogmatik' is the most outstanding example.[4] Biedermann's watchword is the necessity of separating the principle of Christianity from the Person of Jesus.[5] In defence of Schleiermacher it may, however, be pointed out with Heim in his books 'Das Gewissheitsproblem in der systematischen Theologie bis zu Schleiermacher' (1911) and 'Leitfaden der Dogmatik' (1912) that the principle of the *coincidentia oppositorum*, which governs not

[4] Cf. *infra*, p. 562.
[5] Cf. especially 'Christliche Dogmatik', § 605 : 'The fundamental contradiction in the ecclesiastical Christology . . . is rooted herein, that the Christian principle is immediately identified with the historical personality, whose religious life is the revelation of it in history, and that therefore a spiritual principle is described as a Person. . . .'

only the whole philosophy of Hegel, but also the philosophy of religion of Kant, in so far as it centres in the thought of the identification through faith of the sinner with the ideal son of God, appears to justify also the identification of abstract and concrete, principle and Person.[6] In other words, if the *coincidentia oppositorum* is to be the principle of the higher reason, then Schleiermacher's doctrine appears to be justified by it.

(2) Schleiermacher has been criticised on the other hand by the modern orthodoxy, which finds its most outstanding representatives in the Erlangen school, because of his critical positivism, which allows no transcendental, but only immanental elements in Christian doctrine. It has been argued that his anthropocentric Christology does not guarantee the true Divinity of Christ, and that only a transcendental and theocentric Christology can do so. Was Schleiermacher justified in regarding the perfection of the consciousness of God in Christ as 'ein eigentliches Sein Gottes in ihm', when it appears to be only the supreme case of the Divine immanence in humanity in general?[7] This is a crucial question; but it may at least be pointed out that Schleiermacher was absolutely in earnest with the ascription of Divinity to Christ. The way in which he distinguished the immanence of God in Christ from His immanence in humanity in general, was as follows (§ 94, 2): He regarded the former as related to the latter, in the same way as the latter is related to God's general immanence in nature. Just as the immanence of God in nature is raised in man to the potency of consciousness, so His immanence in man is raised in Christ to the potency of complete energy, i.e. to a complete domination of the lower consciousness. Accordingly Schleiermacher justifies the restriction of the name 'Sein Gottes' to the Divine immanence in Christ on the ground that God's immanence elsewhere is only partial, and is consequently only a suggestion or an idea of God, not God Himself. Till God is realised in the perfection in which He is found in Christ, we have less than God. Nature only contains

---

[6] Cf. Heim, 'Das Gewissheitsproblem', pp. 220–59 ; also the same writer, 'Leitfaden der Dogmatik', pp. 29–32.

[7] Cf. § 94, Leitsatz : 'The Redeemer is accordingly like all men in virtue of the identity of human nature, but is distinguished from all by the constant energy of His consciousness of God, which was a proper Being of God in Him.'

a suggestion of Him, humanity an idea of Him: in Christ He dwells completely, so that the Divine essence is one with His innermost self.

(3) Schleiermacher has also been criticised, above all by Ritschl, for his treatment of the ideas of redemption and reconciliation, on the ground that he has at this point been unfaithful to the central principle of the Reformation, inasmuch as he has, in agreement with Catholicism, made reconcilation dependent upon renewal instead of, as Luther taught, renewal upon reconciliation.[8] It may be worth while, on this important point, to give Schleiermacher's own words (§ 101, 1):

'If this reception into the fellowship of Christ's beatitude were anything independent of our reception into the power of His consciousness of God, or if the latter were supposed to follow from the former,[9] then the teleological [1] character of Christianity would be altered. As, however, in God beatitude and omnipotence are given equal place being mutually interconditioned, and yet also independent of one another: so must also in the Person of Christ the beatitude and the power of His consciousness of God be given equal place in the same way, each conditioning the other, and each independent of the other. Accordingly, we ought to be in a position to say, it must be in the same manner with the activity of Christ, and this would either be simply recognised, or there would be two opposed conceptions of Christianity, the one representing it as an endeavour after beatitude for the sake of the power of the consciousness of God, the other reversing this order, which two conceptions supplemented each other. But since the activity of Christ only arises in so far as a receptivity or a longing precedes it in its object: so also the reconciling activity can only express itself in sequence upon the redeeming activity, since the consciousness of sin in itself, and not of sin as the ground of evil, must be the ground of this longing, since evil, for the individual, does not stand in relation with sin. If therefore we think of the activity of the Redeemer as an influence upon the individual, we can only allow the reconciling moment to follow upon, and out of,

---

[8] Cf. Ritschl, 'Justification and Reconciliation', vol. i, English trans., pp. 485–93.
[9] The context forbids the natural rendering : if the *former* were to follow from the atter.   [1] I.e. ethical, see *supra*, p. 535.

the redeeming moment. Yet we give them equal place, in so far as the communication of beatitude no less that the communication of perfection, is immediately given in our reception into fellowship of life with Christ.'

It is, if we are to be governed by the principles of the Reformation, at this point that Schleiermacher's view is most vulnerable. No doubt the ideal theological statement would be one which showed how Christ at the same moment takes us up into both the blessedness and the power of His consciousness of God. But if there is to be a priority, the evangelical attitude of mind seems to require that power should follow upon beatitude, rather than *vice versa*. We shall presently see how, while the majority of the theologians of the nineteenth century have followed Schleiermacher on this head, some, and especially Ritschl, have endeavoured to modify his doctrine in the evangelical direction. It is noteworthy that Schleiermacher's idea of reconciliation turns, not as we should expect on the removal of the consciousness of guilt (or the experience of the forgiveness of sins), but rather upon the removal of the sense of evils. What he thinks of is, as Ritschl has pointed out, rather reconciliation with evils of the world than reconciliation with God.[2] The root of the defect lies in Schleiermacher's thought of God, whom he thinks of rather simply as the Absolute than as also Personal Spirit.[3]

GERMAN THEOLOGY AFTER SCHLEIERMACHER

The whole of the German theology of the nineteenth century bears the imprint of Schleiermacher. But some of it reproduces his system with less, some with more, modification. It is difficult to find an adequate principle of arrangement, since there

[2] 'Justification and Reconciliation', vol. i, English trans., p. 473.
[3] Cf. 'Der Christliche Glaube', § 8, Zusatz 2, where Schleiermacher says that, since God is only known as mirrored in the religious feeling of absolute dependence, it is impossible from a religious point of view to accord to Theism any advantage over Pantheism. From such a basis no true idea of reconciliation with God can be reached. Ritschl indeed rightly says (loc. cit. *supra*), that in so far as Schleiermacher's idea of redemption implies that the uplifting of the God-consciousness is the free act of the believer, it also implies that he is reconciled to God by this surrender to Him. But, if we keep within the lines of Schleiermacher's system, this implication cannot be made explicit, just for the want of the idea of God as Personal.

is a certain crossing of tendencies as between one school and another. But perhaps we may sufficiently represent the most important movements, as regards the doctrine of the work of Christ, by the following method of treatment:

(1) We shall take first Biedermann as the representative of the Liberal theology, which, while influenced by Schleiermacher, reverts on the most important point of all, the separation of the principle of Christianity from the historical person of Jesus, to the method of Kant and Hegel.

(2) We shall consider next two theologians, Schweizer and Rothe, who have reproduced without essential deviation the system of Schleiermacher. The former, however, has endeavoured to interpret it through the doctrine, introduced by the Aufklärung, of the Fatherhood of God; the latter has endeavoured to approximate it verbally, at least, to orthodoxy, so that he is sometimes reckoned to the 'mediating theology' which is characterised just by the aim of mediating between Schleiermacher and orthodoxy. Rothe accordingly naturally leads on to Dorner who is without doubt a genuine mediating theologian, and as Pfleiderer says, 'the type of the whole school'.[4] We shall therefore consider Dorner next after Rothe.

(3) We shall take in the third place, the very remarkable synthesis between orthodoxy and the theology of Schleiermacher established in various forms by the school of Erlangen. The difference here from the previous types is constituted by a genuine return to the patristic notion of the Incarnation as a ferment in humanity. The school aims at a real revival of the ecclesiastical Christology, in such a form as may be possible in the modern age.

(4) We shall consider next the theology of Ritschl, who out of all the theologians previously mentioned has perhaps his nearest forerunner in Schweizer, but is generally recognised as the initiator of a new and highly distinctive, as well as important, type of theology.

(5) Finally, in order to bring out the peculiarity of the Ritschlian theology, we shall compare with it the work of the contemporary theologians, Lipsius and Kähler.

[4] 'The Development of Theology in Germany since Kant', p. 156.

561

CHAPTER 4

THE LIBERAL AND THE MEDIATING THEOLOGY

BIEDERMANN

BIEDERMANN (A.D. 1819–85),[1] though in agreement with Hegel that the Absolute and the Finite Spirit are ultimately one, and that this union is practically realised in religion, does not regard religion merely as a lower form of the philosophical consciousness. 'Precisely because religious faith is something other than a mere form of secondary knowledge, it can never be rendered obsolete and replaced by any higher kind of knowledge, such as philosophy. Philosophy can exercise a purifying influence upon the theoretical side of religion—on the various modes of conceiving the contents of faith—but can never replace the distinctly religious act of faith itself—the practical elevation of the man to God.'[2]

If, however, in religion the practical union of the finite spirit with the Infinite is achieved, what is Christianity? What is its special *differentia* as a religion? Biedermann answers:[3]

'The Christian religion has its historical basis and fountain-head in the Person of Jesus. This gives both Christianity and its dogma its historically determined, i.e. its positive, character. Indeed the religious principle of Christianity is to be more exactly defined as the religious personality of Jesus, i.e. as that relation between God and the human ego, which in the religious self-consciousness of Jesus has entered as a new religious fact with faith-inspiring power into the history of humanity, and has founded in it the religious community of Christianity.'

The metaphysical basis of this historical foundation-fact of Christianity is the self-manifestation of the Absolute Spirit in the

---

[1] Biedermann's great theological work is his 'Christliche Dogmatik', 1st ed. 1869 2nd ed. 1885.

[2] Pfleiderer, 'The Development of Theology in Germany since Kant', p. 140.

[3] 'Christliche Dogmatik', 2nd ed., § 158.

human finite ego of Jesus. The religious relation which appears in this fact is the principle of divine sonship, which manifests itself in the immediate self-expression of the religious consciousness of Jesus. This is the essential principle of the Christian religion.

'The content of this conception is the content of the Christian principle: Christianity is the religion of the divine sonship which was actually disclosed for mankind in Jesus, and at the same time of the Kingdom of God, which realises itself in this divine sonship, as the final purpose of humanity' (§ 160).

Christ's Messianic consciousness expresses the historical connexion of the new Divine revelation with the Old Testament, as its fulfilment and end.

'The history of the Christian dogma, in the first place that of the dogma of the Person and Work of Christ, secondarily that of the remaining dogmas, which have for content the postulates and consequences of that central dogma, is the historical formulation of the content of that principle into the expression of the faith of the Christian community' (§ 162).

The content of the Christian principle is, however, given in no single historical form which it has taken in the course of its development, but is unfolded in the whole history of dogma. The aim of the science of dogmatic theology is, nevertheless, to express this content in the form of pure thought. Each new dogmatic system is justified, in so far as it is a step towards this goal.

From this point of view Biedermann treats the doctrine of the work of Christ (§ 829ff.). The ecclesiastical doctrine of this subject presents to the imagination the operative power of the Christian principle. The truth of the different moments of the doctrine first becomes apparent by reduction to this essential meaning. As, however, the ecclesiastical doctrine has obtained its form by development from the historical life of Jesus, so as a matter of fact this history forms the original and universally exemplary proof of the doctrine.

'The essence of the doctrine of Christ's *munus propheticum* is the truth, that in the absoluteness of the religious self-consciousness is given for all further historical development the principle of all true religious knowledge, and this in such a way

563

that the historical personality of Jesus, in its definite historical setting, is the exemplary illustration of this truth' (§ 830).

The doctrine of the further mediation of Christ's prophetic office in the Church through the Holy Spirit is the expression of the truth, that the development of religious knowledge from the Christian principle is not complete in any particular historical form, but is a continuous process in which the principle itself is the absolute norm, and each historical form of doctrine only a relative expression of it.

'The essence of the ecclesiastical doctrine of Christ's *munus sacerdotale* is the truth that the absoluteness of the Spirit, at the same time that it becomes the religious consciousness of man, manifests itself in him as the power to remove the contradiction between the natural ego and its destination (i.e. for spiritual freedom). The historical death of Jesus as a sacrifice (in an ethical sense) occasioned the expression of this moment of the Christian principle in the sensuous form of the idea of sacrifice derived from the Old Testament, while it is in essence the abolition of this idea' (§ 832).

'Along with this the moment of Christ's vicarious sacrifice is the expression of the truth, that the *causa efficiens* of reconciliation is not the subjective self-consciousness of the human ego itself, but rather the absoluteness of the Spirit disclosing itself in it for subjective appropriation. Besides this there is the more general ethical truth of the redeeming power of the activity of the innocent in sympathy with the guilty, of which the figure of the Old Testament, and the history of the New Testament, "Servant of God", is the great example' (§ 833).

'The essence of the ecclesiastical doctrine of Christ's *munus regium* is the truth that the absoluteness of the Spirit, disclosing itself within the human self-consciousness, is the effective principle of the continuous domination of nature in the comprehensive meaning of the word, and therewith of the glorification of natural humanity to a Kingdom of God. Of this the Person of Jesus is the individual confirmatory example, and the historical effect of Jesus, viz. Christianity, is the general realisation, fulfilling itself by degrees in the process of the history of the world' (§ 835).

Such are Biedermann's results. His method of proof is given in the whole course of his book, in which he expounds, first the Biblical doctrines of Christianity, and then the ecclesiastical doctrines, as their completion and development: next, he submits the ecclesiastical doctrines to a criticism, the purpose of which is to show that they fail to express the Christian principle and result in insoluble antinomies, because they start upon the wrong philosophical hypothesis of the mutual exclusiveness of God and man: finally, we have the restatement of doctrine, above given, upon the basis of the mutual inclusiveness of the Divine and the human spirit.

ALEXANDER SCHWEIZER

Schweizer (A.D. 1808–88)[4] begins from the position of Schleiermacher, that religion is absolute dependence upon God. He seeks, however, to improve upon his master by representing this dependence as passing through the three successive stages of the religion of nature, the religion of morality, and the religion of redemption. In the religion of nature God is known simply as the Omnipotent Being, on whom the world depends. Where there is no further development to the religion of morality, the religion of nature issues in paganism. When, however, this next development ensues, God is known as the Moral Lawgiver and Ruler of the Universe. This type of religion is most perfectly realised in Judaism: if there is no still further development, it issues in a hard legalism like the Pharisaism under which St Paul groaned, a religion of works and merits, and of fear of the Divine judgment. The final stage of religion, however, for which such legalism prepares the way, is the religion of redemption, in which God is known as the Father, Who establishes in the world the kingdom of His grace. This religion of redemption is Christianity. The work of Christ is its historical realisation. In Him the Christian principle of faith in God as the Father was first incarnate, in order that by the work of the Spirit it might be realised in the Church.

[4] Schweizer's theological system is given in his work 'Die christliche Glaubenslehre nach protestantischen Grundsätzen', 1st ed. 1863–9, 2nd ed. 1877.

Schweizer makes clear his general position as to the relation of Christ to the Christian religion in the following propositions: [5]

(§112, Leitsatz) 'The religion of redemption is in principle completely revealed in Christ, so that it is neither capable of, nor in need of, a further development; the advancing process of its appropriation, however, remains in need of, and is capable of, a continuous development.'

(§ 116, Leitsatz) 'The Christian religious consciousness finds itself in its possession of salvation absolutely dependent upon God as the Father through Christ as the Son of God, who is therefore the only Mediator.' The name 'Son of God' is here to be understood, not in a metaphysical, but in an ethico-religious sense. Jesus is the Son of God, because in Him first of all the principle of the religion of redemption was absolutely realised. The principle of redemption (or Logos) had, however, a development before Christ in the anticipations and prophecies of Christ, in which are to be recognised 'the endeavour of the Logos to become man, a process which accomplishes itself imperfectly and temporarily in the prophets, finally and lastingly in Christ' (§ 116, 1). Once, however, the Logos was thus incarnated in Christ, the principle of redemption and Jesus remain indissolubly one. The notion that the two can be separated rests upon an unsatisfactory view of religion as mere doctrine. The progress of the religion of redemption is in fact inseparable from the continuous influence of the personality of Jesus. It is this, indeed, which gives to the Person of Jesus its peculiar worth.

(§ 118, Leitsatz) 'While an unhistorical, simply conceptual, ideal of human perfection could have value only for the religion of law, Christianity as the religion of redemption rests upon the historical Christ as united with the Christ-Idea.'

There are, however, two modes of the union of the historical Christ with the redemptive Idea.

(§ 123, Leitsatz) 'The process of the unification of Christ with the Christ-Idea manifests itself in His earthly existence, as so faithful a devotion to the increasing burden of His vocation, that the Idea works unhindered through Him; in reward of this

---

[5] 'Die christliche Glaubenslehre nach protestantischen Grundsätzen,' 2nd ed., 1877.

faithfulness it appears as a completely accomplished unification with the Absolute Idea in the state of exaltation.'

In opposition to Schleiermacher, Schweizer regards the exaltation of Christ as having high value for faith. The scientific historical life of Christ may end with His death; but our faith, like that of the early Church, must believe in His victory over the world and death, and in the continuance of His personality, not merely in that of the Idea of Christianity. The permanent identification of His personality with the latter is the fit reward of His faithfulness.

We are now in a position to pass on to the special doctrine of the work of Christ.

(§125, Leitsatz) 'The work of the redeeming activity of Christ is entirely and completely summed up in His regenerating communication of the religion of redemption, which is represented to the imagination as the exercise of the three offices, and is a redemption of man, not of God.'

Schweizer first points out that the communication of religion must be carefully distinguished from the inculcation of doctrine. He next observes that the communication of religion, as a work of Jesus upon men, is not to be supplemented by any work upon God, so as to change His mind towards them. All Christ's work is in fact the outcome of the Father's love. The Reformed Dogmatic rightly saw that Christ in His work was the instrument of the Father's grace, though it was prevented by the force of tradition from carrying this idea completely through. Schweizer endeavours to show that the New Testament passages, upon which the idea of propitiation of, or satisfaction to, God is founded, will not bear the weight of the dogmatic superstructure which has been raised upon them.

(§ 126, Leitsatz) 'Redemption is negatively deliverance from the religion of the law, which rejects sinful men to condemnation, and positively regeneration, through the principle of redemption revealing itself in fulfilment in Christ.'

Schweizer interprets the passages in the New Testament, especially in Paul, which speaks of redemption from the law, etc., in the sense that their real import is deliverance from the *religion* of the law. He opposes vehemently the notion that such redemp-

567

tion is only subjective. 'As existence within the religion of law is no imagination, but corresponds to the real relation of the reasonable creature to God as Lawgiver and Judge, or as Author and Controller of the moral order of the world, so also life in the religion of redemption is the subjective expression of the relationship in which the sonship awakened in us really stands to the fully revealed Fatherhood of God. The influence of Christ as the Revealer and Mediator of this higher principle, therefore, manifests itself as a very real communication of life—which He does not achieve without a heavy day's work, in that He has at the costly ransom-price of His blood redeemed His own out of the religion of the law and saved them by bringing them into the religion of redemption, to make them children of God, to redeem them from the bondage of the law, of sin and its condemnation, and to reconcile them with God—which influence of Christ only regeneratively passes over to the individual, in that the idea of redemption realises itself in him, containing in itself as it does also reconciliation, justification, and sanctification' (§ 127, 2).

Reconciliation to God must not, however, be understood in the sense that any change takes place in Him. 'Christ becomes through His life and death the object of the Divine favour, but only because God remains unchangeably the same, and similarly Christ makes all those regenerated by Him into objects of the Divine favour and grace, since God with eternal unchangeableness graciously receives the men who thus come to Him, in fact His lost sons. Similarly again Christ represents with His complete realisation of the Christian principle His followers who imperfectly realise it, in that He presents them in Himself before God and covers their imperfection; for His perfection guarantees the complete saving power of the life, which is as yet imperfectly realised by them, as that of a life, which also is permeating them and is destined to final victory. Similarly also Christ stands as our Vicar, feeling all human misery due to sin more completely than we do; nay, what is more, He stands making satisfaction instead of His own, as surety for the principle of life, which in them is still imperfect, and is yet operative and destined to victory. In fact, He reconciles God, in so far as the complete sacrifice of His obedience, or of His faithfulness to His vocation, wins the absolute favour of God, in which His people share, though only if they do not leave Him to exercise faithfulness instead of themselves. In one word, this tendency of Dogmatic—to present Christ as Him who wins for us access and acceptance with God, as the Mediator who precedes us before His throne of grace and introduces us there, as the altogether uniquely sublime Patron and Advocate who successfully represents our cause before God —rests on the religious feeling, how much even we, though apprehended and regenerated by Christ, fall short in the full working out of the Christian principle and of its sanctification of all that is within us, and therefore found our confidence in this saving life, not upon our imperfect working out of it, but upon that which has completely appeared in Christ, not upon our own but upon His righteousness, especially upon its most valuable, because most arduous, achievement in the accepted death of the cross' (§ 127, 2).

In accordance with the above general principles, Schweizer now restates the doctrine of the threefold office as follows:

(§ 128, Leitsatz) 'Since Christ has performed in its fulfilment for all men what the prophets performed for the Old Covenant, His redemptive work is described as the prophetic office. It consists essentially in the communication of the saving truth.

(§ 129, Leitsatz) 'To the prophetic office of Christ in accordance with the pattern of Old Testament prophecy also belongs prediction, and that in such fulfilment as corresponds to His Messianic consciousness as Son.'

(§ 130, Leitsatz) 'According to the Old Testament pattern the working of miracles is also reckoned to the prophetic office as a co-operative support of the Messianic mission; it is, however, at the same time ennobled by this. Although Christ did no absolute miracles, He has yet achieved works which appeared as miracles.'

In his repudiation of absolute miracles Schweizer is anxious to conserve the true humanity of Christ and the spiritual character of His mission. Like Schleiermacher he views the Divine indwelling in Him as immanent, not transcendent.

(§ 131, Leitsatz) 'What the priesthood performed Levitically, and therefore imperfectly, for the people of the Old Covenant, Christ in the New Covenant performs ethically and perfectly for humanity. His high-priestly office represents to the imagination as a completed sacrifice Christ's complete self-surrender to the vocation assigned Him by the Father, including an obedience which is everywhere active as well as passive, and is not servile but filial obedience.'

(§ 132, Leitsatz) 'Christ's merit in our behalf can only consist in His accomplished fidelity in His vocation or in His entire obedience up to His death on the cross, but also if we relate this merit to God and conceive it as a satisfaction, it could not dispose the unchangeable God differently from what He was before, since it must itself be ordained as a means of salvation or expiation by the Father's will of love which is eternally one with the Divine righteousness.'

Schweizer refers here with approval to the Reformed tradition which subordinates the merit of Christ to the Divine grace[6] and to the words of Zwingli:

'The Son of God therefore is given to us in proof of God's mercy, as a pledge of pardon . . . that He might certify us of the grace of God.'[7]

(§ 133, Leitsatz) 'Christ's suffering even unto the death of the cross is effective not only as the highest proof of His redeeming love and fidelity in His vocation, which draws us away from evil and awakes us to thankful love in return, not only as the completed moral sacrifice of entire surrender to God and His will; but it also effects the decisive liberation of the Christian religion from the legal religion of Judaism.'

Here Schweizer refers to Abelard as having in contrast with Anselm's doctrine of satisfaction developed the true doctrine of redemption. The passages in the New Testament which speak of redemption are to be understood of redemption from the religion of the law, with all that it involves. As regards the New Testament idea of sacrifice, nothing is farther from Paul's thought than the orthodox idea that sin could only be expiated by a bloody sacrifice. 'On the contrary he speaks of an expiatory sacrifice of Christ in quite another sense, in fact just as also the Apostle himself speaks of himself as a sacrifice in virtue of his

[6] Cf. *supra*, pp. 344, 438f.

[7] Zwingli, 'Fidei Expositio', § 1. Cf. also the similar ideas in the ' Commentarius de Vera et Falsa Religione', *supra*, p. 309.

self-surrender to his vocation and its suffering, and requires of every Christian that he should similarly present himself as a sacrifice to God' [8] (§ 133, 1). Schweizer refers also to Rom. 15:16, where Paul speaks of himself as a priest of the Gospel, presenting to God a sacrifice of the Gentiles: he further quotes Phil. 2:17; 2 Tim. 4:6; 2 C. 12:15; Col. 1:24.

(§ 134, Leitsatz) 'The Kingdom of Christ is His personal spiritual power, which, though in the state of humiliation it is present in concealment, yet is only manifested in Christ's exaltation. The apocryphal descent into hell is, according as the expression is interpreted, to be, or not to be, reckoned to the kingly office.'

Schweizer, however, himself considers 1 Pet. 3:19 too uncertain a basis for a dogma, and is inclined to let the doctrine of the descent into hell go altogether.

(§ 135, Leitsatz) 'Christ has attained to full kingly power in the state of exaltation in the life which He, through the surrender of His life, has won as the Risen One, exalted in heaven to the right hand of God.'

(§ 136, Leitsatz) 'Christ exercises His kingly power, not only through His word and Spirit, but also through His glorified Personality represented in both, ruling the community as the One who is set at God's right hand or has a share in the Divine attributes, also as the One who has become the Measure and Judge of all men.'

The Scriptural doctrines of Christ's exaltation at God's right hand, and of His second coming to Judgment, are pictorial representations of His spiritual sovereignty and immanent power of judgment, as one with the principle of the religion of redemption.

Schweizer adds: (§ 137) 'The redemptive, and as such also reconciling, activity of Christ is united with the principle of the religion of redemption, just as His Person has become one with it.'

Seeberg [9] has spoken of Schweizer's 'brilliant system-building', and has predicted a renewal of interest in his theology.[1] While in

---

[8] Rom. xii, 1.

[9] 'Die Kirche Deutschlands im neunzehnten Jahrhundert', 1904, pp. 250ff.

[1] A revived interest in Biedermann is also prophesied. Seeberg says (loc. cit.):
' The works of Biedermann and Schweizer belong without a doubt to the most remarkable phenomena of nineteenth century theology'.

the main he faithfully follows his master Schleiermacher, the following points of difference deserve notice:

(1) Schleiermacher stood on the ground of the union of the Lutheran and Reformed Churches, and endeavoured to connect his doctrine with the classic theology of both confessions.[2] While Schweizer also occupied the same ground,[3] he attached his doctrine especially to the Reformed theology of the sixteenth and seventeenth centuries, of which he wrote a most thorough and masterly historical account, enriched with abundant original extracts.[4] In this latter work Schweizer presents Schleiermacher himself as the true follower of the Reformed doctrinal tradition.[5]

(2) Schweizer has improved upon Schleiermacher in that he has paid great attention to the reinterpretation, not only of the older Protestant doctrines, but also of the Biblical proof-texts themselves, so as to bring out their religious meaning when viewed through the whole context of the Christian religion. It is a defect in Schleiermacher that, while he has abundantly reinterpreted the ecclesiastical doctrines, he has done much less for the less scientific, more figurative phraseology of the Bible. Here then Schweizer marks a distinct advance on his master.

(3) While Schleiermacher views redemption as the communication by Jesus of the God-consciousness, Schweizer further defines it as the communication of the Christian religion, the central idea of which is the Fatherhood of God. Accordingly he has made a connexion between his own doctrine of the work of Christ and that of Abelard, and has pointed out that both represent Jesus as in the first place the revealer of the Divine love, Who awakes an answering love in return.[6] Ritschl[7] has called attention to Schweizer's notice of Abelard, but is disposed to view not only Schweizer's but also Schleiermacher's doctrine of the work of Christ as a revival of the Abelardian form of doctrine. This view, however, appears to me incorrect. Schleiermacher thinks of Jesus as communicating the Divine life or the consciousness of God, but this is not in itself Abelard's doctrine,

---

[2] *Supra*, p. 536.   [3] 'Die christliche Glaubenslehre', § 92.
[4] 'Die Glaubenslehre der evangelisch-reformierten Kirche dargestellt und aus den Quellen belegt', 1844–7.
[5] Vol. i, pp. 133ff.   [6] 'Die christliche Glaubenslehre', § 133.
[7] Justification and Reconciliation', vol. i, English trans., p. 509.

but is rather a revival of the Johannine and Irenæan theology in one of its main aspects. It is the differentiation of the consciousness of God as the consciousness of God's fatherly love which brings Schweizer so close to Abelard, whom he rightly remembers as the protagonist of his line of thought.

RICHARD ROTHE

The system of Rothe (A.D. 1799–1867) is given in his great work 'Theologische Ethik' (2nd ed. 1867–71). Rothe shows himself a disciple of Schleiermacher, in that he begins from the same point as his master, viz. the consciousness of God as given in the feeling of absolute dependence (§§ 16–17). But Rothe seeks to establish upon this basis a more definite and concrete conception of God by means of the speculative notion of the *causa sui* (§ 23). In this way he reaches a distinction in God between His personality and His nature, corresponding to the distinction in humanity between the ego as the self-determinative principle and the psychical organism of instincts, tendencies, and dispositions, which is its instrument (§§ 27ff.). According to Rothe only the two in harmonious combination, nature as controlled by personality, constitute concrete spirit (§ 29 Anm. 3).

God has created man in order to develop in him the likeness of Himself, in other words in order to communicate to him His own Spirit (§ 114). But man has sinned—as was indeed inevitable, because of his association with matter—humanity has taken the wrong development (§§ 459ff.). Redemption, however, enters through a new head of humanity, whom Rothe calls after Paul the 'Second Adam' (§ 519); it could not be, he says, that God should abandon His creation (§ 515). The Second Adam is (as with Schleiermacher) [8] a miracle rising out of the midst of sinful humanity (§ 533). He is the Archetype of humanity, in Whom first begins the perfecting of the creation; and Who is destined to be the Head of a new humanity, in which this perfecting process is brought to completion. As Rothe, unlike Schleiermacher,[9] accepts the perpetuation of the sinful tendency in humanity

---

[8] *Supra*, p. 534. [9] *Supra*, p. 537.

through heredity and the physical organism (§ 484), he adopts as the explanation of the miracle of Christ's sinlessness the doctrine of the Virgin Birth (§ 534), for which Schleiermacher had no need.[1]

The Second Adam grows up in an atmosphere already prepared for Him by prior revelation, and the process of His religious and moral development is 'at once essentially both a continuous incarnation of God and a continuous deification of man (that is, of the Second Adam), in that the tendency is equally on both sides to become absolutely one with the other' (§ 538, Anmerkung). In this way 'His whole life is an absolutely pure and essential revelation of God' (§ 539). This is the beginning of His redeeming activity, for the precondition of every other redeeming operation upon sinful humanity must necessarily be the purification and awakening of its consciousness of God. But this part of His work involves no special activity beyond that of His life itself: His whole life is itself the revelation (§ 541). The special vocation of the Second Adam is, however, to be the Redeemer of sinful humanity, that is to bring about its redemption from sin, or to destroy first the power of sin over it, and thereby next sin itself within it. This can only be achieved through the establishment of an effective fellowship between God and humanity; for only God is able to destroy sin and its power. The Second Adam has therefore to establish a fellowship between God and humanity in spite of the sin of the latter. In order to do this He has, on the one hand, to maintain His own fellowship with God; this is His *religious* task. On the other hand, He has to establish, by the power of an absolute love for humanity, a bond of union with it; this is His *moral* task. He must without stint or limit give Himself up absolutely to the service of humanity. He must give up all that is His own, even His sensuous life (§ 542). This task is defined for the Second Adam, as it is in the case of every man, by His particular situation in the world. As over against the sinful world He has, on the one

[1] Cf. 'Der christliche Glaube', 2nd ed., § 97, 2. Schleiermacher says : 'The general notion of supernatural generation remains therefore essential and necessary, if the peculiar pre-eminence of the Redeemer is to remain undiminished ; but the closer definition of the same as generation without co-operation of a man has no connexion with the essential elements of the peculiar dignity of the Redeemer, and is therefore in and for itself no part of Christian doctrine.'

hand, to witness for God, on the other, to witness against its sin. This witness inevitably rouses against Him the hate of sinful humanity, and behind that the enmity of the powers of darkness, the demons which rule over sinful humanity. This opposition presents itself to Him as a temptation hindering the development of His life in His vocation, which He has to overcome by persisting in His vocation even to death (§ 543). Thereby He overcame in principle the power of sin and the demons over the world, and this not for Himself, but for and instead of humanity, in other words as its Vicar (§ 544). Along with this completion of His fellowship with sinful humanity, there is included in the task of the Second Adam the establishment of a historical connexion between Him and it through the founding of a special fellowship of redemption (§ § 550, 551). On the other hand, His death sets free from the bonds of matter His perfected spirit, i.e. a personality with a completely developed psychical organism as its instrument. The Resurrection and Exaltation of Christ are virtually one; only that the Exalted Christ continued for a while to make use of His discarded material body. The Exalted Christ and the Holy Spirit are one and the same (§ 548). The double condition for the continuance of Christ in the world is thus given. On the one hand, there is the historical channel of the Church, on the other, the continuance of His perfected Spirit, which though the historical channel finds its way to men's hearts.

We have now, however, to see how redemption is finally accomplished. 'In so far as the Second Adam has through His own religious and moral development essentially qualified Himself, in the sense above explained, to be the Redeemer of sinful humanity, He has herewith immediately at the same time brought about the expiation of human sin' (§ 557). What is meant by this Rothe explains as follows: In the removal of sin two things are involved. There is first the removal of its consequences for the sinner in his relation to God, viz. guilt and punishment, which can only take place through forgiveness. There is also the actual destruction of sin in the sinner, and the establishment in him of a normal religious and moral condition. Each aspect of the matter, however, conditions the other. On the one hand, God cannot forgive one who is still under the power of sin. On the

575

contrary, so long as sin remains in him, God's anger must go forth against it, and manifest itself in the sinner as the consciousness of guilt and alienation from God. On the other hand, a real freedom from sin is impossible apart from the experience of forgiveness. So long as there is a separation from God and a consciousness of guilt, there can be no power to overcome sin. 'Here is an antinomy, the solution of which is absolutely demanded by the very holiness and righteousness of God' (ibid.). These attributes of God in fact must necessarily oppose themselves to sin. But this means, not the destruction of the creature, if any other way to destroy sin can be found, but rather the destruction of sin in the creature, for destruction of the creature would spell the failure of God's plan in creation.

'The removal of sin in the sinner without the annihilation of the latter himself must therefore be in itself a possibility for God; but if this is absolutely conditioned, as was shown before, by a previous forgiveness of sins, then God's holiness and righteousness inevitably require the latter. Only they require at the same time equally inexorably that the anticipatory forgiveness take place in such a way that in it the negating reaction of God against sin shall be included, i.e. (they require) that in themselves the holiness and righteousness of God be absolutely maintained. What is here demanded as the solution of the just exposed antinomy is exactly the expiation, i.e. the making forgivable, of sin (which therefore is just as essentially a necessity for God Himself as a necessity for the sinner), i.e. such a modification of the position towards God of the sinner, unholy as he is on account of his sinfulness, as that, in virtue of it, God in spite of His holiness and righteousness can forgive the sin which still actually clings to him, and disregarding it can enter into fellowship with him' (ibid.).

This expiation can only take a concrete form by God's establishment of a surety, whereby it is guaranteed that in the forgiven sinner the actual removal of sin will follow upon his forgiveness—whereby in fact it is guaranteed that the very forgiveness itself will set in motion the train of events ending in the complete destruction of sin and all its consequences. Just this guarantee, however, is given by the work of the Redeemer as above defined, by His actual victory over sin in His own life and by the establishment of the conditions whereby His Spirit can be transmitted to subsequent humanity. 'To put it in the most general form, that whereby the Second Adam has expiated the sin of humanity, is, therefore, that He has qualified Himself to be the Redeemer of humanity' (*ibid.*). The sacrifice of the Redeemer, as above described, now appears as an expiatory sacrifice, and His perfected personal life as an incomparably great and absolutely universal instrument for humanity in the achieving of its moral task. In other words, it has become both a moral fact and a Divine sacrament. In this way the net result of the life of the Second Adam can be described as *merit*. It has absolute worth as the guarantee of the accomplishment of our religious and moral development; and in so far as God looks at us through this guarantee the forgiveness of sins takes place through the imputation of His merit to us. It is to be observed, however, that the imputation of Christ's merit has to do with a merit established in His relations, not to God, but to us, the members of the old sinful community. The doctrine of Christ's intercession is a symbolic representation of the same idea, that He is our guarantee (§ 558). Finally, in the establishment of an expiation for sin, the Second Adam establishes also a reconciliation between God and sinful humanity, and founds a New Covenant, the first true covenant between God and man.

'This New Covenant rests therefore expressly on the expiation of sin by the Redeemer, and therewith ultimately on the sacrificial death of the latter, as does also the reconciliation' (loc. cit.).

Though Rothe's ideas are fundamentally those of Schleiermacher, his theological method in the 'Theologische Ethik' is notably different. Instead of developing each individual set of doctrines from the common matrix of Christian experience, he adopts, when once his starting-point is taken, the method of *a priori* speculation, and resembles Anselm in the way in which he develops the whole of doctrine in one single sequence.[2] Like Anselm Rothe deduces both the necessity of redemption and the necessary characteristics of the Redeemer from the idea of God and His end in the creation of man. The Redeemer is of course

[2] Cf. *supra*, p. 120.

577

at once identified with Jesus. 'Historically we know this Second Adam as Jesus of Nazareth, the son of Mary' (§ 533, Anm.). But even the historical preparation for Christ in the revelation given to Israel is by Rothe speculatively deduced (§§ 520-32).

It is to be observed that in his reinterpretation of the ecclesiastical doctrines Rothe follows Kant [3] and Schleiermacher. But it is noteworthy that he has abandoned the ecclesiastical term satisfaction for the Biblical word expiation, for which he refers to 1 Jn 2:2, 4:10; Rom. 3:25 (§ 557, Anm. 1). One is reminded of the Arminian preference for the Biblical and vaguer phraseology.

Rothe offers another treatment of Christian doctrine in his posthumous 'Dogmatik' (1870), where, instead of a speculative construction, there is, after the manner of Schleiermacher, a statement and criticism of the doctrines of the Church, with a view to educing from them their essential principle. But Rothe regards the speculative method as the higher: the empirical or critical method has, however, its use in preparing the way for the acceptance of the results of speculation, since the critical treatment of the Church doctrine brings it nearer to the purely speculative science of the 'Theologische Ethik'.[4]

Rothe has also developed in his book 'Zur Dogmatik' (2nd ed., 1869) ideas upon the nature of the Scripture proof of Christian doctrine, intended to meet the situation in theology produced by the criticism of the Aufklärung, by the utilisation of the new basis found for theology by Schleiermacher in Christian experience. Rothe would have us regard the Biblical history itself as the Divine revelation, from which, in its gradual development as a living whole, proof must be led, and not from any isolated individual proof-texts.

DORNER

According to Dorner (A.D. 1809-84), the point from which Dogmatics starts as its immediate source of knowledge is Christian experience or Christian faith. 'The aim, or the problem

---

[3] Cf. the reference to him by name, § 557, note on p. 161.
[4] Cf. Rothe, 'Zur Dogmatik', 2nd ed., pp. 52ff.

is to bring the immediate and matter-of-fact certainty, which faith possesses of its contents, to scientific cognition, or to the consciousness of the internal coherence and the objective verification of these contents.' [5]

The method to be followed is defined as a mean between empirical reflection (Schleiermacher) and productive speculation (Rothe).

'The method of Christian dogmatic theology must not be simply productive, but rather reproductive: still it must not be merely empirical and reflective, but also constructive and progressive. When the enlightened Christian mind is in harmony by its faith and experience with objective Christianity, which faith knows to be its own origin, and which is also attested by the Scriptures and the Scriptural faith of the Church, then such a mind has to justify and develop its religious knowledge in a systematic form' (§ 13).[6]

Dorner distinguishes the doctrines of Christianity into the fundamental and the special. The fundamental doctrines are those of God, man, and religion, together with that of the God-man as a necessary *a priori* truth following from the nature of man as created by God. Dorner regards the idea of God, including that of the Trinity, as rational; but by the Trinity he means the doctrine of the ethically Necessary, the ethically Free, and the Love uniting both, as three aspects of One absolute Personality. Man, as created by God, is on the one hand a part of nature, on the other an immortal spirit destined for union with God.

The special doctrines of Christianity are those of sin and salvation. Dorner teaches that man, though he was good by his original creation, yet became the cause of evil by an act of free will. The evil thus generated became a permanent corruption of human nature, and was handed down according to the laws of heredity from our first parents to the rest of mankind. Dorner holds that this inherited generic sin implies a general need of salvation. It is not, however, personal guilt, and does not settle

[5] 'System of Christian Doctrine', English trans., 1888, § 1.
[6] The translation of this section is taken from Pfleiderer, 'The Development o Theology in Germany since Kant' (1893), p. 157. In all other cases the reference is to the English translation as above, n. 5. The general statement of Dorner's position, up to the point where the direct references to his 'System' begin, is also based upon Pfleiderer (op. cit. pp. 157–62).

a man's final destiny, which depends rather upon his own free decision. The salvation of man as thus involved in the sin of the race is, however, only possible in view of the Incarnation. We have already noticed that Dorner held the Incarnation to be necessary in any case apart from sin. It was required, if man was to attain full communion with God and form a united organism under a central head. As Pfleiderer [7] states the doctrine of Dorner on this point:

'Such a universal head, in whom all the limitations of human individuality are done away, can only be a man in whom God's communication of Himself to mankind is absolutely and universally realised, or in whom God as Logos has become man.'

By God as Logos, however, Dorner does not mean a personal Logos, hypostatically distinct from the Father, but God Himself in His loving will to reveal and communicate Himself to mankind.

To sum up: the Incarnation was necessary even apart from sin, that Christ might be the true and perfect Head of humanity in its relation to God; it was doubly necessary, in order that He might deliver humanity from the state of sin induced by the fall of Adam.

The process of the Incarnation Dorner conceives as follows: There is first a *natural* God-manhood. By an absolute creative act (involving birth from a virgin) God called Christ into being as the Second Adam, a human nature from the first united to God, and thus capable of presenting at every stage of development an archetypal human life (§ 105). Next follows an *ethical* God-manhood. In the course of His life from His birth till His baptism by John, 'Christ's holy nature became a perfect Divine-human character' (§ 107). Finally, we have an *official* God-manhood.

'From the time of His baptism, Christ's matured Divine-human personality passes over into His official God-manhood. Thenceforward, He knows and wills His personal perfection as the absolute revelation of God to the world, making it His obligatory life-work or office by self-revelation and self-communication to be the perfect organ of God's redeeming and perfecting revelation' (§ 108).

[7] 'The Development of Theology in Germany since Kant', p. 162.

580

Dorner (§ 109) accepts the scheme of the threefold office, if rightly understood, as justifiable both historically and intrinsically. In spite of the difference between the usage of the Old and New Testaments as to the titles of King, Prophet, and Priest, a common element is left which justifies their use in Christian theology, on the basis of history. It is, however, important from the point of view of their intrinsic justification to note how the three offices mutually interpenetrate in Christ's action, how each of them requires the aid of the others for its own completion. The offices are not simply co-ordinative or accumulative, but absolutely mutually interpenetrative, both in the state of humiliation and in the state of exaltation; and all Christ's speaking and acting, doing and suffering are to be regarded as belonging to Christ's entire office, and are consequently to be considered under each of the three aspects.

In dealing with the offices in particular, Dorner takes first the kingly office.

'Christ has the full power of the true Messianic King, as even His name affirms (i.e. of King in the divine Kingdom), although in His state of humiliation He exercises it in great measure only in veiled form. He is a king who must first acquire His kingdom; and this cannot be done by mere demonstration of power. Still less are glory and dominion His absolute end; but He places the regal power which He possesses at the service of the spiritual redemption, the result of which will be the kingdom of glory on the consummation' (§110).

Dorner says that the usual method, of beginning with the prophetic, and ending with the kingly office, implies that we do not contemplate Christ's work under the view-point of His official Divine Sonship, and therefore do not connect His Person and work sufficiently closely. According to this ordinary method of treatment then Christ's kingly office on earth is abridged; and the stress falls almost wholly on His heavenly Kingship. The true view of Christ's work, however, requires us to exhibit Christ's kingly consciousness in His earthly life, and also to present His history as the revelation of His Kingship, supplying the fitting attestation that He is the Head of God's Kingdom, in fact the Kings of Kings. 'His very love itself must needs reveal the

581

power of His Person, so far as this was compatible with the ethical character of the process, into which He desires to draw men, and with the suffering which this free process must bring to Him' (§ 110, 1). Christ then begins His official life with the possession of a kingly consciousness. He knows Himself, as united with the creative Logos, to be the true King of men. He displays His power in His gathering of a circle of disciples, and in His appointing for them the office of the Word, Baptism, the Holy Supper, and Church discipline. He also exercises the power of miracles for ethical ends. 'Finally, His high-priestly action and passion also are encompassed by His free power' (§ 110, 2).

At the same time, Christ will only carry out His work with respect for human freedom. 'Hence He will not and cannot at once exhibit the kingdom of heaven as a kingdom of power and glory. The motives for adhering to Him must not be corrupt, which would be inevitable, if He had based it at once on sight, instead of on faith in His person. . . . The soul of His kingly office is *Love*. It demands and initiates a process, the end of which will be the glory and visible triumph of the Kingdom of God' (§ 110, 3).

The kingly office in its working out leads to the prophetic and high-priestly offices. 'Christ is the Prophet as Revealer of Divine truth. He has perfectly revealed as well as fulfilled the Divine Law, and is the consummation as well as the end of prophecy. He is all this because the Divine knowledge is His knowledge, or His Divine-human wisdom; nay, His testimony to the Divine is a testimony to the setting forth of Himself' (§ 111).

Dorner says that in relation to Christ's prophetic office we are not to think of the communication of particular rules and doctrines, but of a totality of self-revelation which presents itself to the spiritual contemplation and lays hold of man in a living way. As to Christ's relation to the Old Testament, He is the perfect prophet, inasmuch as His teaching springs not from isolated workings of the Spirit, but from His Divine-human essence. Christ developed the law by reducing its multiplicity to unity, and making it live in Himself. He is also the end and

582

consummation of Old Testament prediction. So far as He still predicted, He only predicted results already implicitly given in His Person.

Christ's high-priestly office Dorner treats with special fullness. He deals first with the Biblical doctrine. 'The Old Testament does not profess to be the perfected religion of atonement,[8] but to predict it. It predicts that religion in such a way that at the same time it prepares for it by revealing on the one hand the Divine holiness and justice, and on the other the grace which seeks their interpenetration typically in sacrifice, prophetically in the Messianic idea' (§ 112).

'It is the unanimous doctrine of the New Testament, that in Christ alone the atonement is found, and with it the basis for perfect redemption. The means thereto described is the God-pleasing self-sacrifice, offered by Christ for the world in accordance with God's loving will, which desires to see the world reconciled with Himself through the sacrifice. Christ's sacrifice is not considered as a mere attestation of His righteousness and holiness, or as an instructive indication of the fact of God's eternal reconciliation with sinners, or of His eternal readiness to forgive, but rather as the effective cause of our salvation, especially of the forgiveness of sins, so that without prejudice to the pragmatico-historical necessity of His death, a Divine necessity of an official nature also resides in it' (§ 113).

After giving a full history of the ecclesiastical doctrine, Dorner works out his own reasoned apprehension of the above Biblical doctrines as follows (§ 119ff.). Divine justice demands expiation, apart from which mankind is exposed to the Divine retribution, which moreover has no ameliorative effect, but quite the reverse. Sin and guilt, therefore, hinder God's loving purpose of perfecting man in holiness and blessedness.

'But as justice and love exist eternally in God in harmonious interpenetration, so God wills the world to be the scene of the combined revelation of the two so long and so far as the world is still capable of redemption. This is His eternal purpose of atonement, i.e. His purpose to give humanity the possibility of

---

[8] *Versöhnung*. Cf. § 114, note in English translation, vol. iv, p. 1. I have elsewhere rendered 'reconciliation', which I think preferable. The English also occasionally adopts the same translation. The point requires to be noted for the sake of continuity in study.

583

atonement. This possibility is implanted in humanity by the Divine Incarnation in Christ' (§ 119).

Dorner reaches the centre of his theme in § 120, where also he puts forward the idea which is specially characteristic of his doctrine. It is to be observed that it is an extension of Butler's position, that vicarious punishment belongs to the order of nature; [9] Dorner argues more generally that the principle of *vicarious influence* belongs to the order of nature; but he adds that the principle has its supreme application with reference to the relation of Christ to humanity.

'Atonement is only possible through the fact that there are *substitutionary* forces at work for the good of humanity and receptiveness in humanity for those forces. As the Second Adam, or Representative of humanity before God, Christ is the Substitute for humanity outside Him, so far as humanity is defective in religious personality' (§ 120, Leitsatz).

Dorner endeavours to show how widely the principle of substitution is operative within humanity. In the first place it is to be found in the sphere of law, as when one person pays another's debts. Then again it is evident in organic nature, as when one organ suffers in sympathy with another. So also the unborn child has no independent life, but the mother lives vicariously for it, shaping it to independence and maturity. Finally, the principle of substitution is operative in the spiritual domain. All education turns on this principle. The parent's reason lives vicariously in the child, till the latter reaches independence. The receptivity for substitutionary forces is indeed different at different stages of life, and it is possible that forces which are beneficial at one stage may at another injure our individuality. We can, however, never reach a point where there is no receptiveness for Christ. He is the central individual of the race; so that, though His personality cannot absorb our individuality, yet, as we have receptivity for God, so we must have receptivity for Him as the revelation of God and true ideal of humanity.

'This is the meaning of *believing* in Him, the only way in which an evil subjective life-tendency can be plunged, so to speak, into the sacred depth of vital powers possessed of creative

---

[9] Cf. *supra*, p. 497.

force, into the love of One who, belonging to the human race and concentrating its powers in Himself, is mighty to save us and to originate a new life in us' (§ 120, 3).

All this, however, is hardly doubted by any. Substitution and receptivity are generally conceded in the sense that in place of the old man the holy principle that was in Christ must be imparted to us, in order that His life may take the place of the old man.

'But all this has reference merely to the life of sanctification, not of reconciliation. And thus the main question is left: Is not the operation of substitution excluded where the matter in question is the guilt of the subject? It seems as if every one must answer for his free acts, and there were no room therefore for substitution' (loc. cit.).

At this critical point Dorner diverges from Schleiermacher,[1] and reverts, though not completely, to the orthodox view.

'It must be frankly confessed, that a substitutionary work of Christ is not possible for every possible sin and guilt, namely, not for the sin of rejecting Him, for the *finale repudium salutis*, and therefore not for the sin which cannot be regarded at all as the effect of generic sin, because, on the contrary, it is purely personal in kind. Guilt exclusively, and in the full sense personal, God cannot do otherwise than visit on the sinner himself. . . . On the other hand, all other sin and guilt, however great and penal it may otherwise be, is not personal in the full sense: it does not impart this *character indelebilis*; the general state has an ambiguity in it which does not exclude hope. To it, therefore, the Divine justice stands in a different attitude, and not merely is long-suffering compatible therewith, but also the admission of substitutionary powers' (loc. cit.).

Just here is the distinction between human and Divine justice. Human justice can only take cognisance of the act of the individual. God views the individual as a part of the race, and sees how far his responsibility is personal, how far generic.

'The first consequence of this is a far stricter and more deeply penetrating judgment of God on the evil in the world, to wit, the view that on account of the universality of sin and

---

[1] Cf. *supra*, pp. 551f.

585

its power, a common guilt exists, and that even judges, nay, the society that demands the execution of law and justice, are implicated in the common guilt which in God's sight is not appearance but reality. . . . Consequently before the Divine judgment seat, antecedent to the rejection of Christ, all sinners are equal in so far as this, that the difference in the degree of their guilt is not finally decisive, but to the Divine view vanishes again in essential equality as to the universal need of atonement and redemption' (loc. cit.).

But, secondly, the same fact, which unites all in a common condemnation, is also the reason of the hope of salvation.

'We affirm therefore: Substitution still has its place where and in so far as evil is either the result of the inherited evil bias of the race, or may be still included under the common guilt in which we are all implicated, where, therefore, the subject has not yet incurred *the* guilt, which can no longer be reckoned at all part of the generic guilt, because it is purely personal in kind, derivable neither from a corrupt nature nor from temptation by the common spirit of evil, but altogether from free decision. . . . Thus man's capacity for redemption is now defined as receptivity for the substitutionary forces of atonement. . . . The possibility of salvation is restored by this, that humanity in some way carries within itself a saving personal force of universal significance side by side with its common sin and guilt, whose effect is a common punishment. This saving force is able to answer for the whole, because God Himself lives in it, as conversely every individual has receptiveness for it. And this power to make satisfaction in the name of the genus to God's punitive justice, which has reference to the genus, is conferred on the genus by the Son whom God's love vouchsafes to it. He through the act of Divine Incarnation has Divine power to answer for humanity, while He also became a true scion of humanity, as the Son of man, having universal relation to humanity. The fact that humanity in Him transformed this power of satisfaction into reality, thus not merely rendering the Divine forgiveness possible, but actually reconciling God with the world—this is the meaning of His office, which represents at once His ability and right, i.e. His ἐξουσία. The means by which He discharges

586

His office is, that He is able to effect and does effect the satisfaction which is the law of His life as the Centre and Representative of humanity' (loc. cit.).

But what now is the satisfaction which Christ is to make? It is an expiation which 'consists not primarily in righteousness of life, but in voluntary subjection to that law of the Divine justice, which imposes just sufferings on sin and guilt, the centre of which is the Divine displeasure' (§ 121).

This subjection Christ makes, in that He not merely knows the culpability of the world, but by substitutionary love feels with intensest pain the guilt of the world.

'In loving sympathy for us He will feel and bear the penal desert of sin, in a word feel and bear the curse that lies upon us, and the justice of the Divine displeasure with us. To this displeasure He will give the honour due to it in everything which it does and will do, in order by what He does and suffers to vindicate its eternal truth and sacred majesty' (§ 121, 3).

Such honouring of the Divine righteousness is impossible to sinful man, who, firstly, cannot realise the full guilt of sin, and, secondly, is repelled by the Divine justice.

'But what is impossible to man is achieved by the Divine-human Mediator, because He sympathisingly takes our place, and by His Person and work represents to God the expiatory power of humanity' (loc. cit.).

Dorner next considers (a) the subjective purpose of Christ in making the atonement, (b) its objective worth before God. In obedience to God Christ undertook to fulfil the Divine purpose of atonement, which involved the interblending of God's justice and love. The means by which He undertakes this fulfilment is in His sympathy, which transfers itself into the place of humanity so as to bear the Divine displeasure against its sin and guilt (§ 122a). Although, however, His sympathy with humanity and His sufferings through fellowship with sinners ran through His whole life, still His atoning passion was not spread uniformly over His whole life. On the contrary, it came to pass through the historical development of His life, that at the end of it He came into such relation with the sin of the world, as became for Him the point of transition to His high-priestly suffering in the stricter sense, viz. His suffering for the sins of the world. 'The sin of the Jewish and Gentile worlds—and, therefore, the sin of *the world*—here revealed itself in its fundamental forms, confronting Him in typical shape. How does He behave in its presence? . . . He knows what they (men) know not in their conduct, that they stand under God's displeasure and condemnation for hating and reproaching Him. He enters into this condemnation of theirs in feeling, sorrowfully acknowledging it to be just in His deepest soul, and so far, therefore, subjecting Himself to the Divine condemnation, which He recognises' (§ 122*a*, 3).

Christ's purpose of atonement and action in pursuance of it has, moreover, objective worth.

'Contemplating humanity in Christ as making satisfaction to the Divine justice, God sees in Him, who suffered for us, and in love to the Divine justice offered Himself a sacrifice to God, that perfect security for the world, for the sake of which not merely free forgiveness and immunity from punishment, but also life and blessedness, may now be proclaimed and offered to it' (§ 122–6).

With Christ's death His earthly work was finished, but at the same time His Person was spiritually consummated. Thus the lowest stage of His humiliation is also the beginning of His exaltation (§ 123). His descent into Hades marks His attainment of a spiritual form of existence, in which He is independent of space and time (§ 124). Dorner refers to 1 Pet. 3:19, to show how Christ, freed from the limitations of His mortal body, found fresh scope for His ministry of the Word. The Resurrection is the beginning of Christ's transition to a state of heavenly glory, which qualifies Him for the administration of His heavenly office (§ 125). In the ascension of Christ, or His absolute exaltation, the Resurrection finds its conclusion, inasmuch as the exalted God-man is raised above the limits of space and time, the humanity of Jesus having become the free adequate organ of the Logos. This state of exaltation is figuratively expressed as the sitting at the right hand of the Father (§ 126). The glorification of Christ's Person is also the glorification of His threefold office, which is now raised to eternal significance, so as in the process of history to triumph over the limits of space and time. In this office, which He alone carries on and retains as the living Head of God's Kingdom, is realised in the course of history His constantly renewed, spiritual and invisible Second Advent, which, however, will one day visibly burst forth upon us in order to the consummation of His kingdom (§ 127, 1).

Dorner is a true follower of Schleiermacher, in so far as he endeavours to understand the work of Christ, above all through His communication of life. He differs from Schleiermacher on the important point, that he conceives it possible for Christ so to identify Himself with humanity as to share its consciousness of guilt. Schleiermacher admitted the sympathy of Christ with human sin, but would not allow to Him a consciousness of guilt, and refused to regard His vicarious suffering as satisfactory; Christ's satisfaction he placed in His perfect obedience, which is through our fellowship of life with Christ the guarantee of our obedience also. Rothe, virtually agreeing with Schleiermacher, prefers, however, to call this guaranteeing obedience of Christ by the name of expiation; it is what makes our sin forgivable. But Dorner makes the satisfaction or expiation consist above all in Christ's vicarious suffering, or His entrance into humanity's consciousness of guilt and condemnation; in so far, therefore, he approximates to the orthodox Protestant view of satisfaction, only that he abandons the idea of equivalence between Christ's sufferings and ours (§ 121, 3). It is important, however, to observe that, according to Dorner, the expiation is made only for generic, not for fully personal sin: the destruction of personal sin belongs to Christ's prophetic and kingly work, by which He takes men into a fellowship of life with Himself.

CHAPTER 5

THE ERLANGEN SCHOOL

HOFMANN

ANOTHER line of development from Schleiermacher begins with the Erlangen theologian, J. Chr. K. von Hofmann (A.D. 1810–1877), whose chief dogmatic work is his book 'Der Schriftbeweis' (2nd ed., 1857–60).

Hofmann speculatively deduces the whole of Christian theology from the fact of our fellowship with God, as it is grounded upon the fellowship of Jesus Christ with God. In this latter fellowship is expressed the ideal relation between God and man, which as ideal must have a metaphysical basis in the life of God Himself. The eternal will of God is in fact the creation of a Divine humanity, and in the historical Jesus Christ is begun the consummation of this will. But Christ existed in God before the Incarnation: the historical communion of Jesus with God is based upon the inner communion of the Persons in the Trinity.

A first stage towards the final consummation was given in the very creation of man, in that he was made in the Divine image. But the development was broken off, in that man fell through the temptation of the Devil. Nevertheless the ideal relation between God and humanity was not utterly destroyed; but it continued to manifest itself in the pre-Christian revelation, which prepared the way for the coming of Christ.

Hofmann's doctrine of the saving work of Christ is given in the Fünftes Lehrstuck of the Lehrganze, which contains in outline, at the outset of the 'Schriftbeweis', the whole of his system.[1]

We stand in personal communion with God by means of a self-determination on our part, which is the result of an operation proceeding from the man Jesus. 'This operation points back to

---

[1] 'Der Schriftbeweis', vol. i, pp. 45ff.

a self-determination of Jesus, by means of which He became the Mediator of the fellowship of God and humanity, not merely in any one relation within His human existence, but in His very existence as an individual man' (§ 1).

In other words, the saving work of Christ begins in the very act of the Incarnation itself. It begins with, and rests ultimately upon, the act of the pre-existent Christ in taking upon Himself human nature. The purpose of this act is, first of all, to establish within humanity that same fellowship with God which belongs eternally to Christ in His pre-existence. In order, however, to establish this fellowship within humanity, Jesus must enter into a fellowship with humanity, whereby He can communicate to it His own fellowship with God.

'He must, therefore, so have made human nature His own, that He belonged in it to humanity, as it was in consequence of sin, yet without being sinful, and that He possessed it as a means of exercising His eternal fellowship with God, yet an exercising of it, which took place under the conditions of human nature as fixed by creation and by sin' (§ 2). Hofmann, like Rothe and Dorner, considers that the sinlessness of Christ demands His virgin-birth.

The history resulting from the Incarnation follows partly from the form in which the inner relation within God is expressed in it, partly from the purpose for which this relation was thus expressed. In entering into fellowship with sinful humanity Jesus comes under the consequences of sin, and under the wrath of God, as this impends over sinful humanity; nevertheless He maintains to the end His personal communion with the Father under all the consequences of sin, even up to the point of sin's last consequence, which is death. The contradiction between God's love and His wrath against sinners is thus expressed in His life, till it is dissolved in His death. The particular way in which this contradiction worked itself out depended upon Christ's historical place in Israel. Inasmuch as the aim of His life was to express perfect fellowship with God in a sinful world, it was His work first to demand a repentant faith, in fact a faith in the accomplished restoration in Him of the fellowship between God and man. This, however, demanded that He should testify of

591

His own relation to the Father; which accordingly He did. Since, however, Israel rejected this testimony the necessary issue was 'that Jesus suffered death at the hands of His people in their rebellion against the obedience of faith, and indeed, since it was as a people that they opposed Him, the death of a criminal' (§ 5).

Thus came to a climax the contradiction between God's love and God's wrath as expressed in the life of the Incarnate Christ; and at the same time Christ's own fellowship with sinful humanity, in virtue of which He came under all the consequences of sin, also reached its climax. The Father allowed the Son to experience the utmost of what sinful man on his nature-side can experience through the wrath of God, the instrument employed being the hate of the Evil One operative against God in wicked men. Inasmuch as, however, Jesus preserved under all these consequences of sin His personal fellowship with God, there was here dissolved the contradiction between God's eternal will of love and the sin of humanity in its provocation of His wrath; 'since there was now realised a relation between God and humanity, for which the guilt of sin and wrath of God no longer existed, and which was no more exposed to the power of the Evil One, in that it was no longer determined by the hereditary sin of humanity, but by the righteousness of the Son of God, as it had been maintained even to the end within sinful humanity and under all the consequences of sin' (§ 6).

Finally: 'Since death as the deserved consequence of sin belonged to the relation of God and humanity now come to an end, Jesus, in whose Person humanity has become the object of a love of God the Father, which excludes from God Himself wrath because of sin and from humanity the power of the Evil One, cannot have remained subject to death' (§ 7). Yet Christ must remain man, since it is as man that He has brought about the new relation of humanity to God, and therefore He Himself as man must first of all experience its results. Thus Christ's death can be for Him only the transition to a new state of existence in which His human nature becomes the instrument of the communion now both eternally and historically perfected between Himself and the father, so that in Him an unlimited communion between God and humanity is now realised and

592

this very realisation in Him is the means of its realisation in others.

Such is Hofmann's theory. If we express it in terms of the orthodox Protestant doctrine, we may say that for him the work of Christ is essentially an active rather than a passive obedience. It is the active realisation of the true relation between God and humanity in the life of Christ on which the emphasis immediately falls, rather than on the endurance of the penalties of human sin. Nevertheless, in the second place, these come in also, in so far as Christ has to realise this perfect relation to God under the conditions of sinful humanity, so that He actually experiences the consequences of sin as inflicted by the Divine wrath upon humanity. But this is in order that He may be able actually to establish a new relation to God within humanity, rather than because the bearing of these consequences is an end in itself. He bears them in order to come near to man, and in order to overcome them for man's sake, that man may overcome them also, rather than because an abstract justice requires that they should be borne, before mercy can be shown. Hofmann here follows essentially the line of Schleiermacher and stands close also to Rothe: in the stress, however, which he lays on the notion of the Evil One as the instrument of the Divine wrath he goes back to Luther and the patristic theology.

Hofmann drew out the connexion between his doctrine and that of Luther in the second of his 'Schutzschriften für eine neue Weise alte Wahrheit zu lehren', in which he replied to certain theologians of his time, who accused him of unfaithfulness to the principles of the older Protestant doctrine, in that he had abandoned the principle of the *satisfactio vicaria*.[2] In the

---

[2] There were four 'Schutzschriften': I, 1856, II, 1857, III and IV, 1859. Hofmann says of Luther in II, p. 78: 'With him the work of Christ's satisfaction is something quite other than the substitutionary suffering of the punishment, which we ought to have suffered. . . . He so presents the work of Christ's satisfaction, as that God has sent into the world His Son, Who loves Him, in order that, through His love of God and His neighbour, with which He accomplished the work commanded Him, He might fulfil the legal will of God valid for us sinners, and in such righteousness might let come on Him, that He might overcome it, everything which is against us because of our unrighteousness. . . . The question why Christ had to undergo the suffering of death, Luther had no occasion at all to raise, since it was self-evident to him, that Christ, after He had by His Incarnation come under the wrath of God against sinful humanity, must experience all that in virtue of the wrath of God the devil could do against human nature.'

'Schriftbeweis', however, he confines himself, as the name of
the book implies, to the attempt to prove his doctrine from
Scripture. It was his purpose to do this, avoiding the atomistic
method of proof-texts, by an appeal rather to the development of the Divine revelation in the history of the Old
and New Testaments as a whole. His aim is, in other words,
to exhibit his Lehrganze as the essence of the Biblical revelation, gradually unfolded more and more clearly by successive
stages in both Testaments.

THOMASIUS

One of the critics of Hofmann was G. Thomasius (A.D. 1802–
1875), himself also an Erlangen theologian, who, however, sought,
while employing like Hofmann the theological method of
Schleiermacher, to obtain by means of it essentially a 'repristination' of the old Protestant Orthodoxy. The system of Thomasius
is given in his book 'Christi Person und Werk: Darstellung der
evangelisch-lutherischen Dogmatik vom Mittelpunkte der Christ-
ologie aus' (2nd ed., 1856–63). It is noteworthy that Thomasius
writes, not like Schleiermacher from the standpoint of the Union,
but from that of the Lutheran confessions. His statement of our
doctrine begins as follows:

(Einleitung, § 1) The appearance of Jesus Christ in the world
is the centre both of the history of salvation and of the history of
the world. Its essential significance is that it is the reconciliation
of the world with God, and the beginning of a new life within
humanity. The reconciling and restoring significance of this fact
entirely depends upon the Incarnation. Christ's work is based
upon His Person, for it is nothing but His self-manifestation:
Person and work are one. What is given to humanity in the
indivisible unity of the Person and work of Christ is appropriated
to the individual through justifying faith, which is the personal
union of man, as apprehended by the Divine Spirit, with the
Mediator.

(§ 2) As the Person and work of Christ are together the centre
of Christianity, and the essential content of the Christian faith,

both have always been the object and centre of Christian knowledge. This knowledge-of-faith (*Glaubenserkenntniss*) of the Christian Church is summarised in the confession 'that Jesus Christ is God and man in One Person, and that He is the God-man, and as this the Redeemer and Regenerator of humanity'. The Ancient Church has, upon the basis of its faith, formed the individual moments of this confession and fixed it in the Creeds. The Lutheran Church has reshaped it and gathered it together into a true unity. In view, however, of the infinite depth of the matter, it is the work of theology continually to reproduce the Church's Christology in a living way. Such reproduction can only take place in connexion with the delineation of the entire Christian doctrine of salvation, of which the Christology is the centre, with all other doctrines as its presuppositions and consequences.

(§ 3) Three methods of treatment are possible. We may proceed from Scripture, from the ecclesiastical dogma, or from the fact of personal faith. A fourth conceivable way, the purely speculative *a priori* method, Thomasius does not recognise as possible in theology. Of the three admitted methods, the first would involve our obtaining from Scripture a total intuition, which we should then have to prove from it in detail. The total view of the individual, however, depends on his environment. We are thus led next to the second, or historical, method. This method Thomasius rejects, since it does not lead to the development of the Christology together with its presuppositions and consequences, these not being immediately given in the dogma. There remains, therefore, as the only possible method, the procedure from justifying faith or its essential content, the actual communion of the Christian with God (§ § 4, 5). This communion between God and man is more exactly defined as personal, as mediated through Jesus Christ, and as restored. The method of procedure will be to start from this actual communion, then to prove the propositions originating from it from Scripture, finally to prove them from the ecclesiastical consensus. Scripture proof is to be from the spirit, not the letter: ecclesiastical proof, again, is to be from the movement of thought in the formation of dogma. The following account of the doctrine of Thomasius is restricted to the argument from experience: it is to be understood that in his system each section has its corresponding Scriptural and dogmatico-historical proof.

The presuppositions of the Christology (§§ 6–33) are on the one hand eternal, on the other historical. The former are : (1) the Christian idea of God, including the Trinity; (2) the Divine idea of man; (3) the Divine decree of the Incarnation (independently of the Fall). The latter are: (1) the original state and task of man as destined for fellowship with God; (2) his sin, causing the Divine wrath, and his need of redemption; (3) God's relation in Christ to sinful humanity, in virtue of which the eternal decree of Incarnation becomes a decree of reconciliation.

In the Christology (§§ 34–47) Thomasius has made himself famous as the representative of a Kenotic theory, according to which, at the Incarnation, in His entrance into the state of humiliation, the Eternal Logos, retaining His immanent, or moral, Divine attributes of absolute power or freedom, holiness, truth, and love, divested Himself temporarily of His relative, or physical, attributes of omnipotence, omnipresence, and omniscience, in order truly to enter into the form of human life, resuming, however, these relative attributes after the Resurrection in the state of exaltation.

(§ 48) In opening the subject of the work of Christ, Thomasius redefines his experimental starting-point in the light of his previous discussion (§§ 6–47). 'It is . . . a relation of communion of love and life, in virtue of which we, though we are sinners and as sinners are guilty before God, are yet received into His Divine good pleasure, and accepted by Him to grace, and therefore know ourselves reconciled with God, and in faith in this His free love, love Him in return.' This relation is then a reciprocal relation, and is on both sides mediated through Christ, in fact through the exalted Christ, who as the incarnate Son of God is the personal Mediator of our communion with God. For us this communion with God has a *beginning* in time, through a Divine act (baptism), which lies beyond our personal consciousness, and whose significance appears in justifying faith: it has an *end* beyond this present life. Between these two points moves our whole Christian life. Each of these points, however, refers itself to an act of the Mediator, which, while distinct from His continual mediation, is closely joined with it. The first refers back to the past act, by which the relation of God to men has been objectively restored: the second refers forward to the future act, which shall complete this renewed relation. The former act is the sacrifice of the cross: the latter act is Christ's coming again in glory.

(§ 49) In order to a further development of the doctrine of the work of Christ, Thomasius now proceeds from the Christian consciousness of communion with God, in its specification as a consciousness of reconciliation, or of the forgiveness of sins. The question here rises: What is the nature of forgiveness, and how far is sin actually removed for the believer in it? The answer is: Not as a state, nor as a punishment, nor as the power of the Evil One, but only as guilt. Yet in the consciousness of the removal of guilt is the beginning of a new life of victory over sin, death, and the Evil One.

(§ 50) From the nature of guilt it is evident that reconciliation is an urgent necessity of man, but is only possible through an act of God's free love. This appears on the subjective side from the consciousness of guilt. The sinner feels himself alienated from God, under the Divine wrath, and unable in any way to approach God. This consciousness of guilt constitutes the subjective right of dominion of sin, death, and the Devil. But the subjective experience is only the reflex in consciousness of an objective truth. God's holiness cannot allow Him to overlook sin, without negating Himself. But, again, only an act of the Divine free love or grace can make reconciliation possible. God, however, can only intend the removal of guilt along with the further intention of the destruction of the power of sin, death, and the Devil. A forgiveness of sins, which left man under the dominion of these powers without conversion and regeneration, is as contrary to the love of the Holy God as it is to the human conscience.

(§ 51) The nature of guilt, however, also makes it clear that the Divine saving act must be one of satisfaction. The consciousness of guilt is most closely united with that of the desert of punishment. It has led to innumerable attempts on man's part to propitiate the gods, which, however, are felt to be insufficient.

597

Only a Divine act, therefore, can suffice. This act must be no mere declaration of indulgence or amnesty: such an act would not satisfy conscience, but would destroy respect for the law and faith in the righteousness and holiness of God, which would be the destruction of the last bond between the sinner and God. This subjective necessity is again the reflex of an objective truth. Our consciousness of desert of punishment is the manifestation in us of the Divine penal justice, which is the necessary consequence of the Divine holiness. God cannot remove guilt without satisfying His holiness.

(§ 52) A satisfaction through the accomplishment of punishment, viz. the penalty of death, and a removal of guilt in forgiving love seem mutually exclusive. They are, in fact, the extremest contradictions; yet they are found together in the consciousness of the reconciled. Moreover, the difficulty is not merely subjective, but exists also for God. There is in God Himself an inner conflict between love and holiness. The relation between these two Divine attributes is not one of identity, but is a unity which has the principle of difference within it, and is a living harmony. If the two were identical, then holiness would be only another form of love, i.e. educative love (a position which, says Thomasius, here requires no further refutation). If, on the other hand, the two were absolutely opposed, God Himself would be governed by the dualism of His attributes, and there would hence exist for Him the necessity of the realisation of both in a twofold predestination. 'But since both are harmoniously one in God, it follows, that, as soon as they externally come into a real conflict, an inner opposition threatens to rise between them—yet indeed only at once to be removed by God Himself. For a real opposition, God as one with Himself, cannot allow. . . . This removal is the inner essence of reconciliation: it is, therefore, not only a Divine but an intra-Divine act.'

As regards the historical execution of this act, a theory would here be premature, but so much may certainly be affirmed:

'God can in His eternal love only so will (or have willed) the restoration of the communion between Himself and humanity destroyed by sin, as that satisfaction takes place at the same time to His holiness, which demands obedience, and His righteousness,

598

which judges the sinner, i.e. only so as that both His love and His holiness, His grace and His righteousness, come to full realisation and therewith to a mutual balance.' The Divine act can consist neither in the mere remission of sin, nor yet in the mere endurance of the penalty of eternal death, the endurance of which by the sinner would be his ruin: it can only be a third act, in which the Divine sentence is executed, and yet human guilt and the Divine wrath are removed, and the reconciliation of God and the world effected.

'This is expiation. It is distinguished from punishment, in that in it punishment is not merely undergone, but undergone in order to the removal of guilt, and so undergone that this end is thereby attained. While punishment in and for itself delivers over to death him on whom it falls, and therewith excludes him from a blessed communion with God, expiation aims at restoring his relation to the moral order, or if we look deeper still, his relation to God, and therefor to free him from guilt, and therewith from the punishment based upon it.'

Such an expiation for sin, not merely individual, but universal, is beyond the power of sinful humanity. Nothing remains but for God Himself to undertake it, which He does in His love by sending His Son.

(§ 53) The execution of the Divine decree of salvation begins with the Incarnation. The Incarnation itself is already the establishment within humanity of communion with God. In Christ the ideal of humanity is realised. But the Incarnation is not in itself the communion of God with sinful humanity, or reconciliation. The holiness of the God-man is rather only the immediate presupposition or *causa sine qua non* of such communion. Christ's actual holiness is an essential moment of restoration, but only in that it manifests itself in His passive obedience, through which alone restoration can take place, and which is the proper task which brought the Redeemer into the world.

(§ 54) Consequently, neither is Christ's prophetic self-manifestation in itself reconciling; it has rather as its purpose the enabling of mankind to appropriate salvation, and the working within it of faith and repentance. Yet, though it is only

599

Christ's sacrificial death which is reconciling, this death must not be separated from the preceding life.

'It forms with the latter one whole; and just because Christ's death is the offering of this holy life, is it the death of reconciliation. But the expiatory moment is nevertheless in the latter point, in the surrender, in the sacrifice. The preceding life only comes into consideration, in so far as it is one great act of sacrificial passive obedience, which has its climax in the death. In fact, the chief stress so much lies upon the sacrifice that the death (the blood) can almost be spoken of as the whole, through which reconciliation is effected.'

(§ 55) We have then to consider more fully this passive obedience unto death, through which Christ has accomplished reconciliation. It is both a passion and a free action of the Lord. It is a passion, in which Christ suffered from the hate of the world, behind which worked secretly the power of Satan. But there also operated the Divine sentence. God did not merely permit the action of the world and the Devil, but Himself used the powers of the world to execute upon the innocent Christ His wrath against sinful humanity. Moreover, this was not a mere external act.

'What Christ suffers is death, in the fullest and deepest sense of the word, without abatement or reduction, the entire bitterness of this last enemy, bodily and spiritual torment, even to the point of being forsaken of God, i.e. even to that point of separation from God, which could possibly intervene, without destroying the bond of His community of essence with God.'

On the other hand, this suffering of Christ is also His own free act. He sees the necessity of it and freely accepts it. 'Thus He makes the suffering His own act.' It is an act of complete obedience towards God, and holy love towards men, for whose sake He suffers and dies.

'In so far indeed this His act is the absolutely perfect fulfilment of the Divine law, and Christ therein completely and universally satisfies its demands on humanity, though in the form of passive obedience and upon the way of a Saviour's vocation.'

Christ's fulfilment of the law consequently takes the shape of a conflict with sin, death, and the Devil, which was at the same time a conflict with God Himself. Christ had to undergo the Divine wrath, and yet maintain a communion of love with God, in the terrors of judgment keep His hold on the hidden Divine will of salvation, and win mercy from God's penal justice, blessing from His wrath. In this conflict Christ manifested, not only the most perfect righteousness, but an absolute self-sacrifice whereby He was perfected.

'In so far His suffering was of another kind than that in which the unconverted sinner suffers and must suffer, and it was an obedience of another kind than that which the law demands of man as such. It is comparable with repentance in so far as the penitent receives the will of God, which judges sin, into his own will, and voluntarily submits to His judgment. But it is not completely identical with repentance, since the penitent is laden with his own personal sin. It was a great, holy, ethical behaviour, a manifestation of righteousness, such as sinful humanity ought to perform, but could not, and which He alone, the Holy One of God, could.'

(§ 56) We obtain, however, full light upon this great act through reflection upon the Person, whose act it is. Since Christ is God, the reconciliation is a Divine act, as it has been shown that it needed to be; and, since He is man, it also belongs to the race to be redeemed, and is a human act. Then, again, Christ is the God-man, and is as such the representative of humanity before God. Though a single member of humanity, He is also the centre of the entire organism, the realisation of the ideal of humanity.

'In this position, into which He has brought Himself out of holy love, He knows Himself one in solidarity with the race to be represented by Him, whose cause He has made His own. In this position, though personally innocent, He yet assumes the guilt of humanity—not merely that of this or that man: He rather receives the entire guilt of humanity into His own consciousness. He feels the entire opposition to God of human sin as His own pain, infinitely more purely and deeply than any sinful man could feel it, and therewith, in order to expiate it in holy obedience to the eternal will of God, He subjects Himself personally to the wrath of God against sinful humanity, which breaks over Him in His doom of suffering.

601

'In this position, again, the Father, who has destined Him to it, regards Him as one with the race represented by Him, and imputes to Him its sin: He regards it as represented in Him, and imputes to Him the sin of the world. . . .

' . . . Because of this position His action and passion is substitutionary: substitutionary, not in the sense that He externally came into the place of what mankind must do and suffer, nor as if it was an alien equivalent for this, it is rather mankind's doing and suffering, mankind's obedience, which it performs in its Substitute, its sacrifice, which He offers in its name, and which just therefore belongs to it. It has as an individual act at the same time the significance of a common act of humanity: it has this value before God. . . .'

Christ's self-surrender is, moreover, substitutionary, both as Divine and human, in the union of these moments, not, however, as if this significance were an after-thought, in that the metaphysical worth of His Person was afterwards added to the ethical worth of His deed. It has its worth just in that it is the act of this Person.

'If we now unite this knowledge with that previously obtained, viz. that Christ's passion and death was a Divine judgment upon Him, and also His own voluntary act, and again, in the union of these two moments, a sacrifice, we obtain the result: it is the substitutionary sacrifice for the sins of the world. Since it is this, there is accomplished in it the restoration once for all of the sin-disturbed communion between God and man. The moments, however, through which it is accomplished are: satisfaction, expiation, and reconciliation.'

(§ 57) It is, above all, a satisfaction. In that the Redeemer gives Himself up for us, He satisfies the claims of the Divine righteousness upon sinful humanity. He endures the punishment which we ought to have endured, death in the completest sense, or what is the same thing, the essence of eternal death, 'for death is separation, separation of the body and the soul, separation of the whole man from life and from God, and this separation is in itself an eternal one'.

Next, Christ's self-surrender is an expiation. 'Expiation has the aim of removing guilt by undoing sin. Sin, however, is undone, in that its punishment is—not indeed escaped—but so suffered, that the suffering is at the same time the victory over the opposition between the Divine holiness and human sin, which reaches its climax in (the consciousness of) guilt. Expiation therefore has punishment as an essential moment within it, for it is an endurance of the same, yet it differs from punishment, in that (in it) punishment is freely accepted and endured with a recognition of its absolute justification, and with a full accord in the righteousness and holiness manifesting themselves in it—in other words, just in that it is a sacrifice.'

Christ's self-surrender is also our reconciliation.

'Reconciliation is the result, or the consequence, of the foregoing. For since now on the side of humanity in its Substitute, satisfaction is made to both the Divine penal justice and holiness, and such satisfaction as that sin is made good, and guilt is expiated, so also the objective opposition against sinful mankind based upon God's holiness, viz. His wrath (as His absolute reaction against the sinner), is removed, since the negation which provokes it is absorbed, since human guilt is paid for by the blood of Christ, and by Him perfect righteousness is accomplished. The hindrance, which made it impossible for the Divine love to turn to the world with complacency, is done away; it can now without harm to holiness and righteousness turn to it in grace: thus the relation of God to mankind, which was disturbed by sin, is restored in the death of the Lord. Enmity is changed to a relation of peaceful communion. This is reconciliation. This great fact finds its simplest expression in the twofold utterance: "the world is reconciled with God", and "Christ has reconciled God with the world". . . . In Him, its Surety and Representative, through whom it is reconciled with Him, the Father regards and loves it, as freed from sin, delivered from the desert of death, become righteous in accordance with His will of grace.'

Finally, in this great act is accomplished the inner harmonisation of the conflicting essential attributes of God, His holiness and righteousness on the one hand, and His love on the other. The reconciliation of the world is on the one hand the expression of His hatred of sin and wrath against the sinner: it is on the other hand the highest act of His love. Thus the opposition between the

603

Divine attributes, which has its basis in the reaction upon God of human sin, is overcome, not by a one-sided expression of either, but by the full exercise of both.

(§ 58) The same act which has established reconciliation is, in its effect, also redemption from the power of sin, death, and the Devil; yet in such a way that redemption from this threefold result of man's fall from God has as its presupposition the removal of guilt, and is accomplished through it. This takes place, first, objectively, in so far as reconciliation delivers from captivity under these powers; then, subjectively, in so far as victory over them on the part of man is conditioned by the acceptance of reconciliation in faith. Sin is removed as guilt, and its power is broken, in so far as the connexion between it and the Divine wrath is brought to an end; but it is not destroyed altogether at once. Death also remains as bodily death, though its power to separate from God is removed by reconciliation: its energy in this direction lies in the wrath of God: thus expiation also involves victory over death. Finally, as regards Satan, sin makes him ruler, and guilt accuser, of mankind, and God permits both in order to punish mankind. Christ, however, redeems us both from his accusation by the expiation, from his power by the overcoming, of sin.

(§ 59) In order now, next, to pass from the objective to the subjective side of the matter, it is to be observed that the wrath of God is not entirely removed by reconciliation, but remains upon unbelievers. What has been changed is not the actual relation of individuals to God, but that of humanity. But the changed relation of God to humanity is the basis of His changed behaviour to it. 'His will of grace, accomplished through reconciliation, becomes an actual manifestation of grace to it.' This manifestation spreads, since the accomplished reconciliation is eternally present to the Divine regard, both forwards and backwards; backwards in God's patience and suspension of wrath towards the ancient world; forwards, in that with the historical fulfilment of the Divine purpose begins a new economy of salvation and grace; the promise of salvation becoming the gospel of the grace of God in Christ. The new relation of God to humanity, moreover, makes possible a new

604

relation of it to Him, one of trust and repentance, involving an inner communion with the death of Christ and victory over sin.

(§60) With the objective reconciliation, through which humanity has become the object of the Divine grace, arises for the individual members of humanity the possibility of actual reconciliation with God. 'But this possibility ought to become actuality.' This is the aim of the whole process of salvation.

'That this aim ought in accordance with their destiny to be reached by all, follows from the universality of the Divine will of love in Christ.' It is, however, actually realised, though not completely, yet essentially, in the actual communion with God through faith in Christ, which was our starting-point (§ 48). How does this come about? It cannot originate from sinful man.

'It comes into existence through the activity of the same Mediator, who has objectively re-established the (above) communion, and that by a continuous action on His part: He mediates it to us as the Exalted Christ.'

Its objective presuppositions are partly in the fact of the reconciliation once for all accomplished, partly in the relations in which Christ is placed to God and the world by His exaltation. Its immediate precondition, however, is in the Resurrection as the point of transition to His glorification.

'The Resurrection as the act of God upon Him is the Divine justification and sealing of His entire work of redemption in word and deed, the actual confirmation (to the world) of the same, and in particular of the reconciliation accomplished by it—it is the Divine seal upon all this. In so far it is the ground of the possibility and right of faith therein. . . . The question, whether in the work of reconciliation and redemption the eternal will of God has realised itself, and if man may venture to base his salvation upon it—is answered solemnly, openly, irrefutably by the Resurrection of the Lord.'

The Resurrection was also the glorification of Christ's Person, which constitutes Him the eternal High Priest and Head of the Church. As High Priest, He manifests Himself to God as our Representative: as the Head of the Church, He communicates Himself to us.

(§ 61) Christ is the eternal High Priest and Mediator between

God and man on the basis of His sacrifice once for all. As such He is the embodied reconciliation, and in His Person presents humanity as acceptable to God. More than this, He intercedes for the redeemed, which act may be described as an individualising continuation of His high-priestly activity, having the purpose of applying to the individual the grace of God won by His sacrifice. As He has determined once for all the relation of God to humanity, so now He seeks to determine similarly God's relation to the individual members of the redeemed race.

(§ 62) Christ is the Head of the Church on the basis of His exaltation, since this raises Him from the conditions of earthly life to the life of the Spirit and constitutes Him the organising centre of a new humanity. This new humanity is in principle given in His Person, but He now directs His activity to unite individuals with Himself and make them participate in communion with God. In that He unites them with Himself as Head, He unites them with one another: both acts are one.

(§§ 63–5) His work in the application of salvation takes place through an inner spiritual working upon us, of which the first fundamental effect is the establishment of the Church, and of the means of grace, the word and the sacraments. A Divine activity accompanies all the human activities herein implied.

(§ 66) In the word Christ clothes His spiritual manifestation in human form, and makes in it the past history of salvation a living present, His Spirit being immanent in the word. It is the work of the word to create faith and repentance.

(§ 71) As by the word He communicates Himself psychologically to the conscious nature of man, so by the sacraments He communicates Himself to the whole nature of man *geist-leiblich*. Baptism plants men into the organism of the Church, the body of the exalted Christ; the Lord's Supper deepens communion with Him. The word and sacrament apply to the whole man the whole salvation. Without the word the sacrament would be a silent enigma: the word creates the faith which alone saves, and which can save, in case of necessity, even without the sacrament. But the sacrament gives to subjective faith the seal of an objective Divine act, and gives the spiritual life a basis in nature.

I have given the above extended account of the doctrine of Thomasius, because of its importance as a serious effort to justify, from the new standpoint of Schleiermacher, the old Protestant doctrine of the work of Christ. Thomasius has endeavoured to present the essential principle of the old doctrine as the necessary presupposition of our communion with God. In so doing he interprets the sacrifice of Christ, once more in the history of theology, as virtually as vicarious penitence.[3] Like Dorner, he conceives it possible for Christ so to enter into our human consciousness of guilt as to feel Himself one with the Divine condemnation of humanity: in His assent to this condemnation is the essence of the sacrifice by which He expiates sin.[4] But Thomasius goes further than Dorner in that he views this act of Christ as an expiation, not only of generic, but of all sin.[5] The point of difference between Thomasius and the older theology is in his insistence on the absolute identification of Christ with humanity in His sacrifice; here he reverts to the mysticism of the Fathers [6] in order to escape the critical difficulties involved in the scholastic notion of Christ's satisfaction as an equivalent for what mankind ought to have suffered.

FRANK

The third name of the Erlangen school is that of Fr. H. R. Frank (A.D. 1827–94). In his 'System der christlichen Gewissheit' (2nd ed., 1884) he derives the elements of Christian doctrine, including the Trinity, by a process of regressive inference from the experienced fact of regeneration. In his 'System der christlichen Wahrheit' (3rd ed., 1894) he undertakes a systematic arrangement of these elements, which is of a speculative character, and proceeds from the central idea of the purpose of God to create a Divine humanity.

'The Christian truth is the complex of all the realities, which

---

[3] Cf. *supra*, pp. 184, 262. Thomasius, however, understands penitence in the Protestant sense (*supra*, p. 293.). The doctrine of Thomasius is naturally quite independent of the suggestion of Edwards (*supra*, pp. 498f.), which has so greatly influenced British theology (*infra*, p. 666).   [4] Cf. *supra*, p. 587.   [5] *Supra*, p. 589.
[6] *Supra*, pp. 46, 60f., 84.

come to be recognised by the Christian as relative to the establishment of a Divine humanity, this aim itself included' (vol. i, p. 46).

The *principium essendi* of this system is God Himself: the the *principium cognoscendi* is the believing consciousness.

'In this believing consciousness is given and presupposed subjection to the supreme standard of Holy Scripture, and agreement with the testimony of the Church corresponding to it' (p. 83).

It is to be observed that Frank, like Thomasius, writes as a confessional Lutheran.

The Divine humanity is the common purpose both of creation and redemption, which are thus in a sense the execution of a single idea. The necessity of redemption lies in the fact of the Fall. Thus there are actually, including the Fall, three stages in the development of the Divine humanity. Frank calls them respectively: Generation, Degeneration, Regeneration.

The first germs of the development of a Divine humanity are already present in a Divine redemptive revelation before Christ, of which there are obscure traces in heathendom, but which is manifest in the history of Israel, the People chosen to realise the Divine Sonship. In the Incarnation, however, the Second Person of the Trinity actually became man, and through an act of self-emptying transformed His filial consciousness into the forms of a finite developing human consciousness, without, however, losing the consciousness that He was the Son of God, or breaking the identity of His pre-incarnate and incarnate states.

'The Incarnation and self-emptying of the Son of God was necessary in order to the performance of His expiatory obedience, as Mediator of salvation, in His humiliation during His whole earthly life up to the death of the cross. . . . This obedience, involving Christ's temptability and actual temptation, but also His complete sinlessness, was as such, over against the law as at once injunctive and penal, in all points both active and passive, and therewith expiatory' (vol. ii, p. 161).

The necessity of the work of Christ is a necessity only in view of the Divine purpose of redemption. Supporting himself upon various passages of Scripture and on the 'Formula of Concord', Frank takes as the central description of the work of

Christ the idea of obedience, applying this idea to the work of His whole life so as to include both His action and passion. Next, however, he proceeds from this idea, by way of the conception of merit, to the notion of expiation. Nothing is clearer in Scripture or in the Christian consciousness than the notion of Christ's merit. The idea that Christ's obedience is only a revelation of the Divine love is absolutely opposed to Scripture. Nor is the notion of merit in any way opposed to the doctrine of the grace of God. The revelation of God's grace is in the meritorious work of Christ.

The next point, however, is to bring in the suffering of Christ. If the work of Christ has been rightly characterised as obedience and merit, then His suffering enters into it, not as such, but as involved in His obedience. This is made clear by the Scriptural idea of the work of Christ as a victory over the Devil, and also by the Scriptural emphasis on His Person as the ground of our righteousness. Here Frank refers for support to Luther.

Then, again, to bring out the full force of what is implied, we must remember that Christ is the Second Adam. By His Incarnation He entered into the lot of the human race, as it lay after the Fall under the weight of the Divine condemnation. This is seen in His circumcision and in His bearing the yoke of the law, which was given as a counteraction of sin, though at the same time as a preparation for salvation. It is seen further in the work of His earthly vocation, in His temptation by Satan and in the hardships of His ministry, and finally in His supreme passion, which is not to be separated from the rest of the sufferings of His life. Moreover, in the acts of enmity and oppression, to which Christ was subject, we have to see, not merely acts of men, but a Divine counteraction of sin, mediated by Satan and his instruments. Frank takes up the position that there is no evil in the world of whatever kind, which is not ultimately due to the reaction of the Divine holiness against sin.

'In fact, Christ's subjection to the power of Satan and to that of his instruments, especially to death, whose power is in Satan's hands,[7] signifies nothing else than subjection to the Divine will in its reaction against sin, to the Divine sentence of

[7] Heb. 2:14.

609

punishment, to the curse of the Divine law. For death is ordained for the punishment of sin, and can enter nowhere, even though its entrance should anywhere be through the unjust judgment of man, just as it is everywhere through Satan's work and mediation, without such death having to be understood as the reaction of the absolute holy God against the sinful creature' (p. 174).

Christ's death, His supreme passion, undertaken in consequence of His obedience, is moreover the climax of His work: without it all the rest would be incomplete. By it Christ endured the curse of the law in the full sense.[8] Christ's passion was, however, expiatory, not simply in itself as suffering. By suffering in itself, however deep and great, the reaction of God against sin cannot be stayed, but only by suffering undertaken in obedience to the Divine will. In order to understand the expiatory value of Christ's work His active and passive obedience must be taken in the closest unity. This expiatory virtue is now to be more closely defined.

'We understand by the expiation of the Mediator that performance, by which in willing obedience and therefore in sinlessness He took upon Him and satisfied the entire demand of the law, in particular of the offended law, made upon the sinful human race. If we grant the existence of an expiation that takes place in accordance with the demands of the absolute holy God by the coercion of the sinner under the law, to the advantage of the latter but not of the sinner, in contrast with such an expiation that made by Christ is a saving one, to the advantage of the subject of the same, since unity with the Divine will is established in the midst of penal coercion, and therewith the reason of its continuance is taken from the latter' (p. 184).

In other words, Christ in His expiatory obedience not only satisfies the claims of the Divine law, but is also the beginning of a new humanity, obedient to God. Frank lays stress on the human character of Christ's work in virtue of the self-emptying involved in the Incarnation.

Does the above view of the work of Christ include the idea of vicarious satisfaction? This, at any rate, says Frank, is not the point at which to begin. Scripture primarily represents Christ

[8] Gal. 3:13.

610

in His work as identical with us, not as separate from us. It is in fact an abstraction to separate Christ's work from its propagation to the race. To emphasise this point is to make void the old Socinian cavil, that if Christ has satisfied for us, nothing remains for us to do, while on the other hand, if we have to work out our own salvation with fear and trembling, Christ cannot have made satisfaction for us.[9] The above-mentioned abstraction of the one from the many, of Christ from His people, is, however, natural to human reason, and out of it necessarily grows the idea of substitution, which is in so far a reality as it is a legitimate aspect of reality. But substitution must not be understood as if Christ had endured the sufferings of the lost.

'The substitution of the Saviour becomes a precise and fitting idea, if He has paid the ransom which the prisoners must have paid to escape from captivity—not, however, if it was a matter of bearing what the prisoners would have had to endure, if they had not been redeemed. The thought of substitution is correct, and corresponds to the fact, only so long as it can continually be converted again into that of the identity of the subject, in which it has its roots' (p. 194).

Only when this fundamental identity of Christ with the redeemed is borne in mind can we do justice to the element of truth in the idea of vicarious satisfaction. Christ underwent death, and even separation from God,[1] yet not eternal death. Beneath the sense of separation from God was a deeper sense of union with Him.

'He could feel Himself forsaken of God in His Logos-consciousness, containing within itself His human consciousness, only in that He at the same time remained indissolubly united with God, and confessed Him who had forsaken Him as His God' (p. 195).

Hofmann represents the patristic doctrine of Christ's victory over the Devil, so notably revived by Luther, as irreconcilable with the doctrine of vicarious satisfaction.[2] The unification just attained of these aspects of doctrine, however, shows his view to be ungrounded.

---

[9] Cf. Socinus, 'De Servatore', pars IV, cap. V (*supra*, p. 372).
[1] Mt. 27:46.   [2] Cf. *supra*, p. 593, n. 2.

'The overcoming of the Devil, viz. the reducing of him to impotence, as the one who through sin has power over man, and who as executor of the Divine wrath accomplishes upon him the penalty of death, form a unity with that vicarious work of expiation, by which man is delivered from his existing state of guilt and penalty' (p. 196).

The wrath of God and the hostility of Satan are certainly not the same thing, yet they coincide in so far as the one is expressed through the other. Each culminates in Christ's death, so that His free self-subjection to this is at once the final expiation of sin, and the final deliverance from Satan.

'It is a proof of correct understanding of the redemptive work of Christ not to oppose to one another these interrelated moments of its accomplishment; just as we had formerly to object to appeal being made to the love of God from which the work of redemption proceeds, as though it were irreconcilable with an expiation in itself required by God' (p. 198).

Just as expiation includes vicarious satisfaction and redemption, so also it includes reconciliation. Scripture does not relate these different aspects of Christ's work one to another, but calls the whole work by each name. But dogmatic clearness requires their interrelation, which is as follows. The work of expiation satisfies the demands of the Divine law, and so by an absolute necessity there follows, upon the basis of it, reconciliation, viz. the removal of the tension which existed between the enmity of the sinner towards God and the wrath of God against the sinner. Finally, the work of Christ in all these aspects extends according to the Divine idea to the whole human race. It is the abstraction of its subjective effects from the objective work which has led to the question of its particular or universal extent, which question solves itself so soon as it is remembered that it is based upon an abstraction. If anyone remains outside the circle of redemption, it is by his own self-will.

This ends the positive statement of the doctrine. Frank calls attention, however, to the fact that he has not brought in either the category of sacrifice or that of priesthood. The latter idea, he says, so far as it includes Christ's intercession, pre-supposes His exaltation, which belongs to a different place in the theological system. The former notion is not well adapted for use in a theological statement. On the one hand the notion of sacrifice is broader than that of expiation, and on the other everything of importance implied by it has already been included.

The scheme of the threefold office Frank also adjudges entirely unfitted for dogmatic purposes. It divides what ought not to be divided, and is altogether illogical. Moreover, so far as the prophetic and kingly work are to be distinguished from the priestly work, they are best treated in connexion with the exalted Christ.

To this last subject, therefore, Frank now proceeds. Christ's exaltation is the reversal of His exinanition. It transforms the human form of consciousness again into the Divine, so that, however, the ego of the Logos is still conscious of Himself as man. Moreover :

'In the exalted Saviour as the Second Adam the new humanity is in principle given, and all the individual acts in which the life of the Exalted Christ issues have for their purpose the establishment and perfecting of this humanity' (p. 212).

The fundamental function of the exalted state is Christ's Kingship, which, however, is based upon His priestly expiation (p. 161), and includes under itself His priestly intercession and His prophetic work. All these forms of activity had their beginnings in Christ's earthly state, but only with His exaltation do they appear in their perfection (p. 210). In the state of exaltation Christ carries on His prophetic work by means of His ministers. The kingdoms of power and of grace are not to be separated. Christ's power is used in and for the establishment of the new humanity.

Frank rejects the modern view (Schleiermacher) which admits only a work of the historical Christ, and which regards dogmatic assertions as to the work of the exalted Christ as belonging to the realm of the religious imagination.[3] The

---

[3] Schleiermacher regards the doctrine of the states of humiliation and exaltation as entirely untenable. 'It has its origin in a passage of Scripture (Philipp. 2:6–9), which is of an ascetical (i.e. practical), and, if regard is had to the whole context, rhetorical character, and shows no intention that the expressions found in it should be fixed in the form of doctrine' ('Der christliche Glaube', § 105, Zusatz).

operations of the exalted Christ are as historical as those of the Jesus of history. On the other hand, it is the historical life of Christ which gives them their reality: without the basis of the incarnate life there would be no guarantee of their existence as a fact.

Frank, the third theologian of the Erlangen school, may be said to mediate between Hofmann and Thomasius, and to express the final result of the development of the Erlangen theology. This theology is marked by an attempt to reintroduce, though its starting-point is made with Schleiermacher in Christian experience, the transcendent element to be found in the older conceptions of the work of Christ, which with him disappears in favour of the immanence of God in Christ. The result is that once more the Divine operation in Christ appears, as in the patristic theology, as a ferment in humanity, proceeding not merely by psychological, but also by mystical, and even sacramental channels to the regeneration of mankind. We have observed the introduction of a sacramentarian element into the doctrine of the work of Christ in Thomasius; but Hofmann also says that the Church communicates, through baptism, to those who belong to its visible communion, the Spirit of God, which is the operative basis of its common life. He also says that in the Lord's Supper the Church communicates to the participants of the rite the enjoyment of its still future possession of the glorified humanity begun in Christ.[4] Frank also (vol. ii, p. 268) says that the method of Christ's self-communication by the sacraments corresponds to His character as God-man, existing in a spiritual body.

The great object of the Erlangen school is to represent the work of Christ as not merely objective or subjective, but objective-subjective. It is essentially the Realistic mysticism of Irenæus which is revived, as over against a purely spiritual and psychological conception of the work of Christ. To a less extent the same Realistic tendency belongs also to Rothe and Dorner, who as standing between Schleiermacher and the older theology are often called 'mediating theologians'. But it comes to its most decided expression in the modern theology of Germany

[4] 'Der Schriftbeweis', Siebentes Lehrstück, i, 3, 4.

through the Erlangen theologians, and this is what gives their theology its peculiar importance.

It is to be observed that Frank, in bringing the Erlangen theology to completion, stands nearer to Hofmann than to Thomasius.

CHAPTER 6

RITSCHL AND THE MODERN SYNTHESIS

RITSCHL

IT is generally recognised that Albrecht Ritschl (A.D. 1822–89) is the most important German theologian since Schleiermacher. He has, however, left behind him no completed system; but his views are to be gathered from his tractate 'Unterricht in der christlichen Religion' (3rd ed., 1886), which is a kind of modern equivalent of Luther's 'Larger Catechism', and from his great work 'Die christliche Lehre von der Rechtfertigung und Versöhnung'. The first volume of the latter [1] is historical: the second [2] is Biblical: the third [3] contains the constructive theory. This last volume is almost, though not quite, a system of theology. Ritschl said in the preface to the first edition: 'In order to make what is the central doctrine of Christianity intelligible as such, I have been compelled to give an almost complete outline of systematic theology, the remaining parts of which could be easily supplied.'

Ritschl's theology starts from the idea of the Christian religion, as based upon Divine revelation.

'Since the Christian religion originates from special revelation, and actually exists in a special community of believers and worshippers of God, its peculiar idea of God must always be conceived in connexion with the recognition of the Bearer of this revelation and with the appreciation of the Christian community, to the end that the entire content of Christianity may be rightly understood. A doctrinal statement, which sets either the one or the other of these elements on one side, will turn out faulty.' [4]

[1] 1st ed. 1870 ; 2nd ed. 1882 ; English trans. from first edition, 1872.
[2] 1st ed. 1874 ; 3rd ed. 1889, still untranslated.
[3] 1st ed. 1874 ; 3rd ed. 1888 ; English trans. from third edition, 1900 ; 2nd ed. 1902.
[4] 'Unterricht in der christlichen Religion', vol. iv, 1890, § 1, p. 1.

In the above definition of the basis of Christian theology Ritschl differentiates his position from that of Schleiermacher in three points:

(1) He begins, not with the consciousness of God in general, but with the special Christian idea of God as given through Jesus Christ. Thus his doctrine has throughout a more positive character than that of Schleiermacher.

(2) Ritschl complains that Schleiermacher, though making use of the idea of the Church in obtaining the basis of his theology, in so far as he founds it upon the Christian experience, not of the individual, but of the community, yet did not do sufficient justice to this idea in working out his theology, inasmuch as he did not in his notion of redemption sufficiently subordinate the individual to the Church. For Ritschl it is, as we shall see, in the first place the Church, and only in the second place the individual, that is the subject of salvation.

(3) The phrase in the above extract, 'the valuation of the Christian community', suggests the philosophical basis which Ritschl gave to his whole theology, in so far as the recognition alike of the Christian revelation, of Christ as the Revealer, and of the Church as the sphere of revelation, is described as a judgment of value. For Ritschl Christianity has a visible and intramundane aspect: this is its historical side. It has also an invisible and supramundane aspect: this is its religious side, which it reached only through the judgment of value involved in faith. According to Ritschl all religious beliefs, from faith in God downwards, are judgments of value.[5]

In connexion with Ritschl's view of Christianity as a revealed religion is, further, the stress which he lays on the Scriptures as the source of Christian doctrine. Here, however, he defines his position very thoroughly with respect to the problems of historical criticism, both in its application to the Scriptures and to the traditional ecclesiastical theology. Christian theology must indeed, as Schleiermacher says, be stated from the point of view of the Christian community. Inasmuch as, however, in the course of history, the standpoint of the latter has been variously dis-

---

[5] See for Ritschl's theory of value-judgments, 'Justification and Reconciliation', vol. iii, English trans., 2nd ed., pp. 203ff.

placed and alien influences have troubled the purity of the Christian faith, it is necessary to go back to the fundamental statement of the New Testament, which again, for its interpretation, requires an understanding of the Old Testament. Moreover, in the New Testament the Gospels present to us the first cause of the Christian religion in the work of its founder; while the Epistles give us the faith of the primitive community.[6] Ritschl entirely rejects the idea of the Aufklärung that only the 'religion of Jesus' is to be considered true Christianity. On the contrary, especially as regards the doctrines of redemption, the reverse is the case.

'The material of the theological doctrines of forgiveness, justification, and reconciliation is to be sought, not so much directly in the words of Christ, as in the correlative representations of the original consciousness of the community.'[7]

Finally, in connexion with Ritschl's emphasis on the Church as the primary subject of the Christian salvation, there is another point in which he feels himself to occupy a different position from Schleiermacher. This is with regard to the ethical and social character of the Christian religion. Schleiermacher had indeed defined Christianity as a teleological religion, i.e. a religion to be understood through its ethical aim.[8] Ritschl complains that in his actual theology Schleiermacher has not done justice to this point of view. He himself seeks to correct Schleiermacher's defect by including in the definition of Christianity, as a most essential element of the same, the idea of the Kingdom of God.

'Christianity, so to speak, resembles not a circle described from a single centre, but an ellipse determined by two foci.'[9]

These two foci are the ideas of the Kingdom of God and of redemption, as factors of equal moment in the definition of Christianity. Ritschl defines the former of these two ideas as follows:

'The Kingdom of God is the highest good, as assured by God to the community founded by His revelation in Christ; but it is only to be understood as the highest good, in that it is at the

---

[6] See for Ritschl's view of the position of Scripture as the basis of theology, 'Unterricht in der christlichen Religion', § 3.

[7] 'Justification and Reconciliation', vol. iii, English trans., p. 3.

[8] *Supra*, p. 535.   [9] Op. cit. p. 11.

same time to be regarded as the moral ideal, in the realisation of which the members of the community are united together by means of a definite mutual mode of action.'[1]

Ritschl, in fact, understands the Kingdom of God in Kant's sense as a community of men under the rule of God serving each other in love. There is no doubt that in assigning to the conception of the Kingdom of God a fundamental place in theology, Ritschl has made an effective return to the religion of the New Testament. His position has been subsequently criticised in that it has been pointed out that Ritschl ignores the apocalyptic element in the Kingdom of God, which is so prominent in the New Testament.[2] This is true; nevertheless, even when this deduction is made, it remains good that Ritschl has enriched theology with a valuable conception, which if it is not the whole New Testament notion of the Kingdom of God is at any rate a very important, the majority of theologians would say the most important, part of it.

It is further in connexion with the idea of the Kingdom that Ritschl defines the idea of God. He is to be thought of as the Will of love, Who reveals Himself in Christ, in order to realise His Kingdom in the world.[3] His proper name is 'the God and Father of our Lord Jesus Christ'.[4] He is the Father of men, in so far as His aim is the Kingdom of God.[5] All Divine attributes are to be understood through the position of God in respect of the world, herein implied, and no otherwise.[6] God's grace in redemption, or in the forgiveness of sins, is an extension, in accordance with His Fatherly character, of His grace in the establishment of the Kingdom of God.[7] His grace in both respects becomes operative in Jesus Christ. This leads us to Ritschl's view of the work of Christ. It is, in the first place, to found the Kingdom of God, and, in the second, to establish redemption.[8]

He does both by the perfect revelation of God in His life and death, and also by representing before God, as its Archetype, the community of redemption, which realises the Divine Kingdom

---

[1] 'Unterricht', § 5.   [2] Cf. 'Man, Sin, and Salvation', pp. 44ff., 82ff.
[3] Cf. 'Justification and Reconciliation', vol. iii, English trans., pp. 282, 283.
[4] 2 C. 1:3 ; 11:31 ; Rom. 15:6 ; Col. 1:3 ; Eph. 1:3 ; 1 Pet. 1:3. Cf. 'Unterricht', § 11.   [5] 'Unterricht', §§ 12, 13.   [6] Ibid. § 14.
[7] 'Justification and Reconciliation', vol. iii, English trans., pp. 318ff.   [8] Ibid. p. 414.

in the world. Ritschl connects his doctrine with the traditional formula of the threefold office.[9] But he operates a complete readjustment of the offices resulting in a most interesting restatement of the doctrine.[1] In the first place, he subordinates the prophetic and priestly offices to the kingly office, and offers a twofold division, the kingly-prophetic and the kingly-priestly. In the second place, he insists that the whole work should be demonstrated to be essentially contained in Christ's earthly life; so that His activity in His heavenly life can only be conceived as the continuation of His earthly activity. A third point of deviation from tradition is in the distribution of Christ's words, works, sufferings, and death under the offices. Whereas the Protestant orthodoxy divided these in different proportions among the offices, Ritschl insists that, both under the head of Christ's kingly Prophethood, and under that of His kingly Priesthood, the whole material of His life is, though from a special point of view, to be considered. Finally, throughout, Ritschl distinguishes the *ethical* and the *religious* aspects, i.e. the view of Christ's work as a duty undertaken by Him as Founder of the Kingdom of God, and the view of His work as Divinely ordained to this end.

We begin then with the kingly-prophetic office of Christ, and first of all with the ethical view of the same. The first proposition, which Ritschl lays down, is as follows:

'The fundamental condition of the ethical apprehension of Jesus is contained in the statement, that what Jesus actually was and accomplished, that He is in the first place for Himself. Every intelligent life moves within the lines of a personal self-end.'[2]

But is not Christ's work for us? Does it not operate our salvation? If we make use of the traditional standpoint of merit, we may say that Christ's merit in our behalf follows from the merit which He has obtained for Himself. But the standpoint of merit cannot be the final one; Christ's work was taken up by Him as duty, and duty excludes merit. We must therefore state the case as follows:

'In so far as Christ, by His duly ordered speech and conduct, realises His personal self-end, it follows from the special content

---

[9] *Ibid.* pp. 417ff.   [1] *Ibid.* pp. 428ff.   [2] *Ibid.* p. 442.

of the latter that in this form He also realises the ends of others, i.e. has ministered to the salvation of mankind as a whole' (p. 443).

But what is the special content of the personal self-end of Christ? It is determined by His *ethical vocation*,[3] or special duty as an individual in the world, which was to be the Bearer of God's moral Lordship over men, and Founder of the Kingdom of God. This is the vocation of the kingly Prophet; and both Christ's obedience to God and His patience and sufferings are to be understood in connexion with His vocation, and not from such extraneous regards as those adopted by the traditional theology, e.g. that Christ was required to keep the law, or to conform to a Divine ordinance demanding His suffering. Both His doing and suffering are proofs of Christ's loyalty to His vocation; 'and for Christ Himself alone come into account solely from this point of view' (p. 448).

But now the ethical view must be succeeded by the religious view. 'Christ not merely recognises the business of His vocation to be the Lordship or Kingdom of God, He also recognises this vocation as the special ordinance of God for Himself, and His activity in fulfilment of it as service rendered to God in God's own cause' (p. 449).

Thus He is led to regard His sufferings, and finally, when the inevitableness of it becomes apparent, His violent death also, as lying in the Divine purpose, and destined under God's appointment to serve the end of establishing the Kingdom of God.

Such then is the doctrine of Christ's kingly Prophethood, as seen both in the ethical and the religious aspect. It does not depend for proof, however, only on Christ's view of His own vocation and of the sufferings involved in it, but it can be further verified in a double way. It is verified, first, by Christ's actual power over the world, which appears, not so much in His sufferings, as in His patience under suffering, viewed as a victory over the natural limitations of human life.[4] The miracles after all were on quite a limited scale. Christ never attempted any such change in the mechanism of the world as a whole, as had by the prophets

---

[3] Ritschl adopts this term with approval from Schleiermacher (cf. *supra*, p. 547).
[4] Ritschl refers for support to Bernard of Clairvaux (*supra*, p. 150).

been associated with the coming of the Kingdom of God.[5] Not even in the Resurrection does Ritschl seek a proof of Christ's lordship over the world. He accepts it indeed as a consummation, through the power of God, of Christ's life and work, 'the logical completion, thoroughly corresponding to the worth of His Person, of the revelation taking place in Him, which is final with reference to the actual will of God and with reference to the destiny of men'.[6] But Ritschl's view is that the sphere of miracles, not in itself indeed, but because of our lack of the means of explaining it, is withdrawn from scientific explanation. In other words, Christ's miracles and Resurrection belong rather to the Christian faith than to its verification. Christ's lordship over the world through patience in suffering can, however, be verified not only from the account of it in the Gospels, but from the fact that He has left the same type of lordship over the world to His Church. It is a standing factor in the Apostolic experience, and may be our experience too.

We pass on next to the consideration of Christ's kingly Priesthood. Here too there are both ethical and religious aspects. The whole doctrine here, however, demands a most thorough remodelling. The old theology attempts only an ethical interpretation of Christ's work as priest, and brings in the religious point of view only indirectly in so far as Christ's priestly work was initiated by God, and its result is recognised by Him; while 'a religious significance for us is secured to the content or result of this priestly work only through its being taken up into Christ's prophetic activity, and through the corresponding proclamation in the Church of how Christ has determined God to the grace of forgiveness'.[7]

The gravest defect in the traditional representation of the priestly work of Christ lies, however, in the particular ethical standpoint adopted for its interpretation, viz. that of law, which is, as a standard of conduct, directly opposed in Christian experience to the standpoint of religion; while 'the assumption that in God righteousness and grace work in opposite directions is in so far irreligious, that the unity of the Divine will forms an

---

[5] Here Ritschl refers to Mt. 16:1–4.   'Unterricht', § 23, p. 21.
[7] 'Justification and Reconciliation,' vol. iii, English trans., p. 473.

inviolable condition of all confidence in God' (p. 473). The whole notion in fact of a Divine righteousness which is in conflict with the Divine grace is unscriptural.[8]

'God's righteousness is His self-consistent and undeviating action in behalf of the salvation of the members of His community; in essence it is identical with His grace. Between the two, therefore, there is no contradiction to be solved' (pp. 473–474).

Ritschl also opposes the traditional interpretation of the Old Testament sacrifices. His own view was that the sacrifices were to be understood, not as a satisfaction to the Divine justice, but as a covering of the finite creature in His approach to God.[9] There here appears in Ritschl's work a result of the fresh philological and anthropological investigation of the Old Testament ritual, which was so marked a feature of the Biblical scholarship of the latter part of the nineteenth century. Ritschl expresses his opposition to the traditional view of sacrifice, as follows:

'It is unbiblical to assume that any one of the Old Testament sacrifices, after the analogy of which Christ's death is judged, is meant to move God from wrath to grace. On the contrary these sacrifices rely implicitly upon the reality of God's grace to the covenant people, and merely define certain positive conditions which the members of the covenant people must fulfil in order to enjoy the nearness of the God of grace. It is unbiblical to assume that the sacrificial offering includes in itself a penal act, executed not upon the guilty person, but upon the victim who takes his place. Representation by priest and sacrifice [1] is meant not in any exclusive, but in an inclusive sense. Because the priest draws near to God when he brings near the gift, therefore he represents before God those in whose behalf he is acting; it is not meant that because the priest and the sacrifice come near to God, the others may remain at a distance from God. These relations hold even when it is sins of ignorance which give

---

[8] Cf. *supra*, p. 365, n. 5.

[9] The protective covering of the offerers, by the priestly actions, from the face of God, includes in general no reference to their sins, but has respect only to the fact that they are perishable men ('Rechtfertigung and Versöhnung', 2nd ed., vol. ii, p. 204). To translate the Hebrew word *Kipper* (to cover) in the sense of to propitiate is a mistake (*ibid*. pp. 187, 200–3). Cf. Orr, 'The Ritschlian Theology and the Evangelical Faith', 1897, pp. 152, 153.   [1] The English translation has by error 'sacrament'.

occasion for sacrifices: in the latter case forgiveness results from the fact, that with the sacrifice, the priest has indirectly brought the sinners also into the presence of God. Lastly, it is unbiblical to assume that a sacrifice has its significance directly for God, and only under certain other conditions also for men. On the contrary, the sacrificial act is just what combines these two relations' (p. 474).

Ritschl's conclusion is accordingly that the orthodox theory of Christ's priesthood cannot stand. It is ethical, without a religious aspect; and the Biblical basis on which it rests is not sound. Moreover, it fails to supply a satisfactory view of Christ's priesthood even from the ethical side, inasmuch as it overlooks what is so clear in the historical picture of Christ in the Bible, viz. that Christ, before He is a priest for others, is first of all a priest in His own behalf. In other words, He is the subject of personal religion exercising a perfect communion with God, which is the absolute precondition of His being able to bring others into the same communion. This communion Christ maintains first of all by prayer. But His faithful activity in His vocation, and especially His willingness for the sake of His faithfulness to endure death, also fall within the view of His priestly approach to God, inasmuch as they can be considered as the elements of a sacrifice which as priest He offers to God. '

'His conduct therefore is intelligible to Him as a service rendered to God, which in its own way brings Him just as near to God as prayer itself' (p. 476).

But how can His sacrifice have value for others? The doctrine of vicarious punishment in any and every form breaks down upon the rock of Christ's personal innocence. Whatever He endured as the consequences of human sin could be for Him only a testing affliction, not a punishment, since the personal consciousness of guilt was wanting. This criticism is entirely independent of the fact that the notion of a *lex talionis* is no rule of the Christian religion.[2] Nor can the doctrine of vicarious punishment be defended by the assumption that a beginning of satisfaction to God's justice is made in Christ, in order that it may be continued in us, as we are crucified with Christ. For the

[2] *Infra*, p. 632.

sufferings of the Christian are not penal, but disciplinary; so that on the contrary the connexion supposed to exist between Christ's suffering and ours would only seem to show that His suffering also was disciplinary and not penal. Finally, if it is argued that a religious interest attaches to Christ's sufferings viewed as punishment, in that He is our Surety against the wrath and retributive justice of God, He could only be this Surety if we believed that He had in offering satisfaction consciously offered it for each individual. This, however, is impossible. There is nothing to warrant it in the history of Christ's life—nor is there room for such an omniscience within the limits of His human consciousness. Whatever way we view it, the doctrine of vicarious punishment turns out to be indefensible. We must therefore look for another explanation of the significance of Christ's priestly work for others. This explanation Ritschl finds by considering the necessity for the Christian life of justification or the forgiveness of sins. Both for him mean the same thing, viz. the admission of sinners to communion with God. The necessity of justification follows primarily from the direct connexion between justification and eternal life; there is, however, a secondary connexion between justification and the fulfilment of the moral law. Eternal life Ritschl conceives, not as future happiness,[3] nor yet as the mystical vision of God by abstraction from the world,[4] but as the victory over the world which is given by faith in God as our Father, and exercised especially in patience under suffering. In trusting God as our Father, however, we necessarily accept His final end as our own. But this is His Kingdom, of which accordingly we become loyal members, freely obeying the moral law of love. Justification, or the forgiveness of sins, is now the necessary condition of eternal life; inasmuch as only in communion with God can we have the victory over the world, and in view of our consciousness of guilt we cannot have communion with God except by the knowledge that His mind towards us is one of favour in spite of our sin. It is to be observed that Ritschl recognises sin in the forms both of the personal consciousness of guilt and of the common life of sin in which sinners influence

[3] This is the primitive Christian conception. Cf. 'Man, Sin, and Salvation', pp. 44ff., 82ff.   [4] Cf. the doctrine of Thomas, *supra*, pp. 207f.

625

one another for evil: he names this last the 'kingdom of sin' (p. 338). Like Schleiermacher [5] he admits no 'original sin' beyond this social influence of sinners one upon another. Sin, however, is forgivable, because it is ignorance.

'In so far as men, regarded as sinners both in their individual capacity and as a whole, are objects of the redemption and reconciliation made possible by the love of God, sin is estimated by God, not as the final purpose of opposition to the known will of God, but as ignorance' (p. 384).

That God should receive sinners into fellowship with Himself is, therefore, possible by an exercise of His will, which takes shape in a favourable judgment of their case. This is justification; and the only way in which we can enjoy communion with God is by accepting this Divine judgment in faith. Love to God cannot be 'infused'—our attitude to God can only be changed by the knowledge of His attitude to us.

But further: eternal life or the state of victory over the world, which we enjoy through communion with God in justification, is the only state of mind out of which free obedience to the law of love can issue. It may be added that justification, as thus actualised, is the same thing as reconciliation or adoption. The knowledge that God is our Father makes us His sons.

We are now in a position to investigate the connexion which Ritschl sets up between the forgiveness of sins and the work and sufferings of Christ. The forgiveness of sins is mediated to us directly by Christ's priestly position taken as a whole, in that He is conscious 'of standing in the closest conceivable relation to God, and of being called to receive others into the same relation in such a way that their sins shall present no obstacle to their trust in God and God's communion with them' (p. 542).

Inasmuch as Christ's work in His vocation, His sufferings, and death, conditioned, as has already been explained, His nearness to God, they accordingly have value for us as the prerequisite of the exercise of His priesthood. The objection of the Socinians that Christ's sufferings and death cannot condition His exercise of the forgiveness of sins, since He forgave sins in His lifetime,[6] Ritschl deals with along lines already developed

[5] Cf. *supra*, p. 537.   [6] *Supra*, p. 434, n. 4.

626

by Schleiermacher.[7] Christ throughout His life maintained His communion with God—the final perfection of this communion was, however, only established in His death, as constituting its highest proof. The further Socinian objection, that forgiveness was already bestowed by God under the Old Testament dispensation and so can have no necessary connexion with the work of Christ,[8] Ritschl meets by pointing out that the consciousness of communion with God was never steady under the Old Testament, as it is in the New Testament, but was subject to fluctuations, as may be seen in the Psalms. Finally, the view of the Aufklärung that God's forgiveness is a doctrine of natural theology,[9] is met by the assertion that history shows that our knowledge of it proceeds from Scriptural revelation.

The primary object of forgiveness, however, is not the individual, but the community, which was the aim of Christ's life-work. The individual enjoys forgiveness as a member of the community. Ritschl accordingly sums up his whole doctrine of Christ's kingly Prophethood and Priesthood in this connexion as follows:

'In so far as our aim is to understand forgiveness as proceeding from the living will of God the Father, Who permits sinners to draw nigh to Himself, this will is manifested as the grace and the truth in which Christ represents God for men. On the other hand, when what we want is to see forgiveness become operative as the attribute of a community, this aspect of it is guaranteed by the community's Representative, whose inviolably maintained position towards the love of God, which is distinctive of Him, is imputed by God to those who are to be accounted His' (p. 547).

It is, of course, the identical material of Christ's life which is viewed in this double way. Nevertheless, the two aspects are really different. In order, therefore, that a unity may be established between them, one of them must be subordinated to the other. In fact, the priestly office is subordinated to the prophetic office, so as to be even embraced in it, i.e. Christ's representation of

---

[7] *Supra*, pp. 544f.   [8] *Supra*, pp. 368, 399.

[9] The Deist, Lord Herbert of Cherbury, certainly treats God's forgiveness as a doctrine of natural theology (*supra*, pp. 475f.). The Aufklärer Steinbart, however, like the later Deist, Chubb, traces the doctrine to the Christian revelation (*supra*, pp. 488, 507f.), though both certainly regard it as entirely in harmony with reason. Ritschl is hardly fair to the Aufklärung, which in part prepared the way for his own view.

627

us to God follows from His being first of all God's representative to us. The original communion with God, which makes Him God's revelation to us, makes Him also the Head of the Church. In agreement with this subordination of the priestly to the prophetic office, Ritschl points out that the kingly office of Christ is exercised differently under these two aspects, more widely under the prophetic office, more narrowly under the priestly office, since Christ here is properly only Lord of the Church.

It may be pointed out that Ritschl's doctrine here appears to offer a solution of the old and difficult controversy between the Lutherans and Reformed as to the scope of the work of Christ. Both the universalist and the particularist view are seen to be true, though with a different reference. In Ritschl's historical volume the doctrine of Abelard, Duns, and the Calvinists that Christ died for the elect accordingly meets with a favour very unlike the present attitude to it among English-speaking theologians.

In concluding his exposition Ritschl rejects certain modern theories of the work of Christ, as he had previously rejected the traditional Protestant doctrine.

(1) There is, first, the idea that Christ, though He did not bear the punishment of our sins, yet performed for us a vicarious penitence. Ritschl refers to Häring's statement of this theory in his book 'Über das Bleibende im Glauben an Christus' (1880).[1] He refutes this theory by the argument that Christ could not repent of sin without personal consciousness of guilt.

(2) There is, secondly, the view that God in Christ's death condemned human sin, in order to bring men to repentance. Häring, abandoning his earlier position, became a sponsor of this theory in his work 'Zu Ritschl's Versöhnungslehre' (1888). Ritschl says that this amounts to no more than a revival of the Grotian theory of penal example. He had already[2] acquiesced in the criticism passed upon this theory by the Socinian Crell, viz. that it fails on the ground that the suffering of the innocent is affliction, not penalty.[3]

In both these instances, then, Ritschl makes it clear that he

[1] Häring is himself a disciple of Ritschl.
[2] 'Justification and Reconciliation', vol. i, English trans., pp. 311, 312.
[3] Crell simply repeated against Grotius the point of view of Socinus (*supra*, p. 371).

altogether repudiates all attempts to give Christ's suffering a penal character, no matter whether He bears the equivalent of the punishment of sinners or not, or whether an external endurance of sin, or an inner acknowledgment of condemnation is in view. Ritschl's view, in fact, is that there can be no punishment of sin where there is no consciousness of guilt. The primary punishment of sin is exclusion from communion with God: the natural and social evils of life are only felt as punishment by the man who is conscious of guilt.

It may be added that later Häring, still maintaining his second position, has stated a general view in close agreement with Ritschl. In a noteworthy book, 'Zur Versöhnungslehre' (1893), he points out that the New Testament terminology is not adapted to be the means of a scientific doctrine of the work of Christ, and that the Pauline language, in which it is taught that Christ was a sacrifice for us, must be conditioned by the equally Pauline idea that Christ's work is not external to, but inclusive of us. Häring therefore suggests that Christ's work may be best understood under the two heads of Revelation and Representation, the former idea being understood not merely of the communication of doctrine, but of the total effect of His life in bringing men to communion with God. Of these two heads Representation must be subordinated to Revelation. This is essentially Ritschl's doctrine without the formula of the threefold or twofold office.[4]

Three things in particular are observable about the Ritschlian theology. The first is its thoroughly *immanental* character, in which it represents a complete return to Schleiermacher as over against the mediating theologians like Rothe and Dorner and still more in opposition to the Erlangen school. This immanental character appears alike in Ritschl's conceptions of the Kingdom of God, of eternal life, and of the work of Christ. All have their essential sphere *within*, not beyond the terms of humanity.

Secondly, however, Ritschl's theology is distinctly more

---

[4] A later work by Häring is 'Der christliche Glaube' (1906), which is a complete system of theology. Other systematic works in the Ritschlian tradition are Kaftan's 'Dogmatik' and Wendt's 'System der christlichen Lehre' (1907). Of the three, Kaftan's 'Dogmatik' is the most important.

Biblical than that of Schleiermacher. He endeavours more definitely than the latter to understand Christianity as a positive revelation. Ritschl here occupies a middle position between Schleiermacher and the older Protestant theology. While the latter conceives the scheme of Christian doctrine to be given in a circle of ideas to be found in the Bible, and the former views it as the reflex of certain definite experiences, Ritschl regards it as given in those Biblical ideas which can be directly verified in experience. This position was to a certain extent anticipated by such theologians as Quenstedt and Heidegger, with their emphasis on the *fides salvifica* as the essence of Christianity; so that it can be well understood how Herrmann, himself leaning more to the point of view of Schleiermacher, has spoken of Ritschl as 'in reality the last great representative of the orthodox dogmatic, who makes its two precious elements, faith in the sense of the Reformation and the Scripture principle, shine with a brightness they never had before in this connexion in any previous theologian'.[5]

Thirdly, in the theology of Ritschl, as in that of Schweizer, the Abelardian type of doctrine receives the preference over that of Anselm. This is the result of his subordination of the principle of Representation to that of Revelation. Ritschl, like Schweizer, was fully conscious of this connexion with Abelard.

In 'Justification and Reconciliation' (vol. i, English trans. p. 40), he says that 'it appears that the advantage in respect of typical character is to be ascribed to Abelard's view and not to that of Anselm'. Again, in vol. iii, English trans. p. 473, he writes: 'The introduction into the theology of Protestantism since Töllner of the fundamental position of Abelard is a distinct advance upon orthodoxy.'

It is accordingly most of all with Schweizer among previous theologians that Ritschl is in agreement. Like him he conceives the Christian redemption as essentially a transition from the consciousness of sin to the consciousness of grace through the revelation of God's love in Jesus Christ. 2 C. 5:19 supplies the centre of this view: the *immanence* of the love of God in Christ is that on which Ritschl lays such emphasis. His criticism of the

'Zeitschrift für Theologie und Kirche', 1907, p. 25.

Protestant orthodoxy is precisely that 'the immanence of God's love is not set forth just in the love and obedience of Christ; nor is that immanence allowed to have its due place in the connexion of the doctrine'.[6] The difference between Schweizer and Ritschl lies in the further emphasis which the latter lays on the Kingdom of God as the end of the operation of the Divine love. He says of Schweizer:[7]

'If there is any defect that one has reason to complain of, it is that he does not carry far enough the ethical normation of the intuition of Christ; particularly, that His importance as central personality (which is recognised in His vocation) is not measured by reference to the thought of the Kingdom of God, and is apprehended apart from that idea and also apart from the relation between the love of God and the Kingdom of God.'

Herrmann has commented on the *simplicity* of Ritschl's system.[8] Ritschl himself speaks of his work as 'an exposition of Christian doctrine which views and judges every part of the system from the standpoint of the redeemed community of Christ'.[9] In fact, the modern purpose to reduce the system of Christian theology to the unity of a single principle, nowhere receives a more notable exemplification than in the work of Ritschl. He has endeavoured to bring every part of Christian theology under the control of the central idea of the Christian conception of God as revealed in Christ, with its twofold development in the notions of the Kingdom of God and of reconciliation. He rejects the orthodox dogmatic system, including all modern repristination of the same, on the ground that it is not a unity, but is developed from different and inconsistent principles.

'It takes up its standpoint, first of all, in the far-off domain of man's original perfection, which it makes correlative to a certain rational conception of God, correlative, that is, to the necessary twofold recompense which God awards to men, bound as they are to conform to His law. . . . The traditional doctrine

---

[6] 'Justification and Reconciliation', vol. i, English trans., p. 260. (I have, however, substituted 'just' for 'even', as a better rendering of *selbst*.)   [7] Op. cit., p. 510.
  [8] 'Die Kultur der Gegenwart', I, IV, 2, p. 161 : ' The system of Ritschl is distinguished by its simplicity. It is his earnest endeavour to limit himself to the thoughts which really belong to religion.'   [9] 'Justification and Reconciliation', vol. iii, English trans., p. 5.

of man's original state, consequently, implies that theology takes up its standpoint within either a natural or a universally rational knowledge of God which has nothing to do with the Christian knowledge of Him, and is consequently indifferent to the question whether the expositor who expounds the doctrine belongs to the Christian community or not. The nature and the extent of sin, accepted as a fact, is thereafter determined by the standard of the first man's original perfection. Passages of Scripture may be used as well, but that makes no difference, for they are not read in the light of the fact that the Apostle Paul's view of the effect on the human race of the first transgression is determined by its contrast to the effect of Christ upon His community. Traditional theology, in using the passage Rom. 5:12, rather keeps to the lines of Augustine, who, on thoroughly rational grounds, deduced original sin from the sin of the human race, and undertakes to deduce from this the necessity of a redemption, the method of which is brought out by comparing sin with the Divine attribute of retributory righteousness in the purely rational style which Anselm has applied to this topic. Then follows, at the third stage of the traditional theological system, the knowledge of Christ's Person and work, and its application to the individual and the fellowship of believers. Not until it has to deal with this topic does theology take up the standpoint of the community, but it does so in such a way that the above-mentioned rational conception of redemption is held to throughout the exposition of its actual course. No system can result from a method which thus traverses three separate points of view in accomplishing the different parts of its task.' [1]

One is reminded here of Steinbart's attack on Augustine and Anselm from the standpoint of the Christian conception of God.[2] It is evident how the criticism flowing from the Aufklärung is in the veins of the Ritschlian, as indeed of so much modern, theology. Ritschl has particularly attacked the principle of the Divine twofold retribution of rewards and punishments according to merit, as being unfit for use in Christian doctrine. It is in his view an idea of Hellenic religion which was first firmly established within Christianity by the Apologists.[3] St Paul's use

---

[1] *Ibid.* pp. 4, 5.   [2] *Supra*, pp. 513f.   [3] *Op. cit.*, p. 262.

of it in Rom. 2:6f. is merely dialectic: he is arguing with the Roman Christians from their own standpoint.[4] As has already been observed Ritschl defines the Divine righteousness as the consistency of the Divine grace: this position as well as the distinction between punishment and affliction he inherits from Socinianism.[5] He stands, in fact, to the criticism of Socinus and the Aufklärung in the same relation as Luther does to that of Duns and the Nominalists.

Lipsius and Kähler

We can best bring out the full significance of the Ritschlian theology by contrasting it with the work of the two contemporary theologians, Lipsius and Kähler. Kattenbusch [6] has reckoned Lipsius along with Schweizer and Biedermann to the 'liberal' theology: Kähler, on the other hand, he has placed with Rothe and Dorner among the 'mediating' theologians. But the two theologians nevertheless, though in different ways, stand very close to Ritschl. A study of their work is therefore of peculiar value in determining the exact point where Ritschl's theology separates itself from the liberal and the mediating schools. Lipsius may be said to represent the liberal school, and Kähler the mediating school, in their nearest approach to Ritschlianism; and yet, after all, each diverges from that system at a critical point.

Lipsius

Lipsius (A.D. 1830–92) agrees with Ritschl that religious judgments are value judgments. He differs from the latter, however, in holding that the value judgments of religion, as they proceed from experience to what transcends experience, find support in metaphysical reality.[7] Ritschl, on the other hand, refuses any place in theology to metaphysic: he held that any

---

[4] 'Rechtfertigung und Versöhnung', 2nd ed., vol. ii, p. 319.
[5] *Supra*, pp. 364f, 371.
[6] 'Von Schleiermacher zu Ritschl', 3rd ed., 1903.
[7] Cf. Lipsius, 'Philosophie und Religion', 1885.

attempt to support religious faith by metaphysical doctrine must result in the contamination of religious truth with alien points of view.[8]

The general principles on which Lipsius apprehends the work of Christ are laid down in his 'Lehrbuch der evangelisch-pro-testantischen Dogmatik' (3rd ed., 1893) as follows:

(§ 639) 'God's eternal will of salvation and of the establishment of His Kingdom has become historically an object of common and individual experience in the Christian community by means of faith in the Person and work of Christ. The empirical sphere of its operation, therefore, is to be found in the Christian community and in the peculiar religious and moral consciousness which inspires the same.'

(§ 640) Theology must here distinguish between the religious significance of Jesus Christ as the Mediator of the perfect Divine revelation and His ethical significance as the historical Founder of the Kingdom of God and the personal Bearer and Source of the principle inspiring this community. On the other hand, it must justify religious faith in the Divine revelation in Christ by means of the ethical evaluation of His Person as the fundamental embodiment of union with God, or the complete religious relation.

(§ 641) The operation of the religious principle of Christianity or of the Christian spirit in the Church is not immediately identical with the personal work of Christ. On the other hand, however, it is wrong to regard the two as merely accidentally and externally connected, as though the Christian principle had only been first realised in Christ by accident, or as if His work had only provided the external means for symbolising the general operation of this principle in humanity. On the contrary, the Christian principle is the spirit of Christ, and presupposes the complete realisation of the religious relation in His Person, and therewith the complete revelation of the Divine will of salvation in His consciousness.

(§ 642) The eternal truth of the Divine economy of salvation and of the reconciling and redeeming love of God does not therefore depend on the historical Person and work of Christ. On the

---

[8] Cf. Ritschl, 'Theologie und Metaphysik', 3rd ed., 1902.

other hand, the Divine will of salvation is not actually effective apart from the historical revelation of God in Christ as the objective basis of the Christian community.

(§ 643) The inner and abiding connexion of the revelation in Christ and of the operation of the religious principle proceeding from Him makes both inseparable, for the immediate religious view of the Church, which, though originally based upon the relation of the desciples to Jesus in His earthly life, was only completed with His exaltation to be Lord and Head of the Christian community.

In the above statement it is clear how close is the agreement with Ritschl, from whom, however, Lipsius separates himself when he conceives it possible for theology to leave the standpoint of immediate religious faith and take up a metaphysical standpoint, from which it appears that the eternal truth of the Divine will of salvation is independent of the Person and work of the historical Jesus.

The following discussion accordingly deals with (1) the ethical significance of the historical Person of Jesus and His life-work; (2) the religious significance of the Person and work of Jesus Christ for the community; (3) of the religious content of the salvation mediated by Christ.

The first of these themes is dealt with in § § 645–60. The empirical view of history recognises in Jesus of Nazareth the historical founder of the Christian religion and the Christian Church. The special worth of His Person consists in the peculiar religious content of His self-consciousness, which makes Him as the Son of God the exemplary and creative Founder of the community of the Kingdom of God, and also the Personal realisation of the perfect religion and Head of the community. Christ's consciousness of Divine Sonship was at the same time a consciousness of His vocation to found the Kingdom of God, the perfect religious and moral order. His Divine Sonship was, in fact, an immediate unity of religion and morality, of freedom from the world in communion with God, and of the fulfilment of moral duty in love to men.

'Though manifesting itself in the historically and individually conditioned form of a true human consciousness and life, the

religious-moral personality of Jesus, as perfected in death, has
become the realisation of the Christian principle, which is for the
community exemplary and creatively fundamental: while His
work, which is indivisible from His Person, is simply the
execution of His vocational task, viz. by the reception of the
community of disciples into the fellowship of His religious
relation to God to assure it of its reconciliation with God and
its redemption from the world and therewith to found the Kingdom of God' (§ 658).

Christ's historical work of reconciliation and redemption has
reference in the first place to the community as a whole; but the
inner union with the community and with the Kingdom of God
as offered in it, depends on each individual member's personal
assurance of reconciliation and redemption. Lipsius here commends the view of Ritschl,[9] whom he defends in a note to § 659
against the accusation that his doctrine leans too much to
Catholicism.[1] He says:

'To find here a catholicising tendency would only be right
under the presupposition of the identification, as in the older
theology, of the personal work of Jesus Christ with the influence
of the Christian spirit in the community. The fellowship of the
individual with Christ's Person and work is certainly always
historically mediated by the Church; on the other hand, the
operation of the Christian principle in the individual is itself
nothing historical, but depends upon the administration of an
eternal order.'

This, however, is a defence of Ritschl's position which
he himself could not have accepted, since it turns upon the
separation, out of the unity of the view of faith, of a historical
element on the other hand and a metaphysical element on the
other.

Lipsius closes his treatment at this point by observing that
in the relation of the historical work of Christ to the community
is the justification of the Reformed doctrine that the object of His
work is the elect, only that the elect must not be taken to be the

---

[9] *Supra*, p. 627.
[1] Lipsius (loc. cit.) attributes this criticism to Biedermann. But Biedermann himself
says that the Ritschlian only externally, and not really, resembles the Catholic doctrine
('Christliche Dogmatik', 2nd ed., vol. ii, p. 319).

personally predestinated.[2] It may be observed that Lipsius, like Schweizer and Biedermann, stood on the ground of the Union.[3]

There follows next the religious view of the Person and work of Christ (§§ 661–80). This is expressed in the faith of the Church that He is the Christ or the personal Founder of the Kingdom of God and therewith also the religious Reconciler and Redeemer of His people, who in accordance with the Divine will mediates to them communion with God, and so delivers them from the world, sin, and evil. As personal Mediator of reconciliation, Christ is at once for faith the Representative of God to men or the personal Bearer of the Divine revelation, and the Representative of men before God or the personal Bearer of the perfect religion. Lipsius agrees with Ritschl that the former aspect must have religious priority over the latter.

This religious faith in Christ in both its aspects is based upon the ethical view of His Person previously explained. Faith sees in the historical manifestation of the Person of Christ a Divine deed, through which God reconciles the world with Himself, or in which His eternal will of love has become a historical act of love. It recognises, therefore, a peculiar immanence of God in Christ, who is at the same time the Man in perfect union with God and Head of the reconciled community.

As Representative of God to men, Christ reveals God both by word and deed. His revelation of God by word is in the gospel of the Kingdom of God and of reconciliation and redemption, which He preaches. His revelation of God by deed is in the maintenance of the consciousness of God's love, in lowly obedience of love to God, and self-denying loving service of men even unto death; which maintenance at the same time constitutes the actual fulfilment of the Divine will of reconciliation and redemption, through the realisation of the perfect fellowship of God in man in the Head of the new community. The revelation of God's love in Christ's word and deed is also as such the revelation in the community of the Divine principle of salvation, and the founding of the Kingdom of God as freedom from the world.

As Representative of humanity before God, Christ reconciles

---

[2] Cf. the similar view of Ritschl, *supra*, pp. 627f.   [3] Cf. *supra*, pp. 536f.

mankind to God by realising the perfect life of union with God or perfect righteousness, and at the same time by acknowledging in humility the justice of the Divine condemnation of sin, or offering to God a perfect expiation: in both respects the Head vicariously satisfies for the community founded by Him. In fellowship with Christ the community knows itself as reconciled, since fellowship with Him is also communion with God, and the enjoyment of the forgiveness of sins and Divine Sonship.

'This doctrine of the representation of humanity', says Lipsius, is 'the view presented as far back as by Paul, side by side with the juridical idea of substitution, of an ethical representation of the new humanity in Christ, its Head, or the mystical incorporation of believers in Christ.[4] The same thought is expressed by the Reformed doctrine of the *unio cum capite*'[5] (§ 673).

It is to be observed that Lipsius does not hesitate to adopt the doctrine, which Ritschl rejects,[6] of Christ's expiation of sin by an acknowledgment of the Divine condemnation of it as righteous. He here approximates to the mediating theology and Thomasius.[7]

Lipsius gives over the facts of the historical life of Christ to criticism, but considers the religious view of His death and His Resurrection independent of all criticism. In the latter, Christ appears to the faith of the community as its exalted Lord and Ruler of the world. The schema of the threefold office is to be accepted as an imperfect form of the doctrine of Christ's work. Lipsius, however, considers that it cannot be successfully carried through in detail.

Finally, we come to the religious content of the salvation mediated through Christ (§§681–8). This is the perfect religion of Divine Sonship, corresponding to the Divine order of the Kingdom of God, a principle which is a matter of experience in the Christian community and which energises in history as a spiritual power. It is experienced as reconciliation with God, in which all fear of Divine punishment vanishes, and as redemption from the world, the law, and sin.

[4] Cf. 2 C. 5:14, 15.
[6] *Supra*, pp. 628f.
[5] Cf. *supra*, pp. 345, 439.
[7] *Supra*, pp. 587, 601.

Lipsius has the advantage over Ritschl in conciseness and clearness; but is inferior to him in creative power and originality. The points of contact and of difference between the two theologians, which we set out to examine, have already been observed in passing.

KÄHLER

Kähler (A.D. 1835–1912) has besides his system of theology [8] also contributed a special treatise on the work of Christ.[9] I shall take my account of his views, however, from the first-mentioned work, both for the sake of succinctness, and also in accordance with my general plan of utilising, wherever possible, complete systems of theology rather than monographs.

Kähler's general point of view is determined by the title of his book. He seeks to unfold the science of Christian doctrine from the standpoint of the fundamental evangelical article of justification. In assuming this standpoint he is in agreement with Ritschl, as he is also in the emphasis which he lays upon Christianity as a revelation. But whereas Ritschl understands by the Biblical revelation those doctrines of the New Testament which are capable of verification by experience, Kähler holds that the Christian experience of justification involves the 'confession' (a favourite word with him) of the doctrines which the gospel of reconciliation presupposes.

Moreover, instead of defining the truths of Christian faith as value-judgments with a historical basis, Kähler prefers to recognise in them the union of a historical and a suprahistorical element, in which case, in opposition to the positivism of Ritschl, the metaphysical element of doctrine returns again under a new name. Kähler's substitute for the Ritschlian value-judgments of religion, as the form of theological knowledge, is defined by him as follows:

'The scientific knowledge of Christianity is, agreeably to its subject, on the one hand, completely conditioned by historical

[8] 'Die Wissenschaft der christlichen Lehre von dem evangelischen Grundartikel aus im Abrisse dargestellt' (3rd. ed., 1905).
[9] 'Zur Lehre von der Versöhnung' (1898). It is intended as a fuller exposition of the related section of the system. It deals above all with the Scripture proof of the doctrine.

639

insight, on the other hand, never limited to this. Mere philosophical generalisations of its empirical content cannot rise to the suprahistorical in Christianity: there is required a peculiar total view of the historical together with the facts of the inner life depending upon it' (§ 11).

Kähler is, more than any other German theologian whom we have studied in the period after Schleiermacher, a Biblical theologian. He uses wherever possible Biblical forms of expression, instead of those of ecclesiastical origin. But he recognises that the Bible, though it is the standard by which the doctrines of the Church are to be tried, does not itself contain the Christian faith in a scientific form. The scientific proof of the individual propositions of theology depends ultimately on the manifestation of their connexion with the fundamental proposition of Christian conviction, which is the centre of the Scriptural religion, viz. the doctrine of justification.

It is then in this connexion that Kähler develops the doctrine of the work of Christ. In the Person of Christ he recognises a union of the Godhead with humanity 'as a reciprocity of two personal movements, viz. on the one side a generative operation from the standpoint of the eternal Godhead, and on the other a receptive operation from the standpoint of the developing humanity' (§ 388). This is much the same Christology as Dorner's,[1] to whom indeed Kähler appeals (§ 391). It is, according to Kähler, a Christology which is in reality a Soteriology, and shows Christ sufficient for all the needs of salvation. But as the true Christology must be a Soteriology, so also the true Soteriology must be the same. In the historical Christ God has met our double need of a revelation of God and a representation before Him (§ 393). In dependence upon Old Testament types the significance of Christ for salvation has been stated in the form of the threefold office.

'This presentation expresses the indispensable connexion of the guaranteeing (prophetic) revelation and of the guaranteeing (priestly) representation for the sake of the (kingly) creative regeneration for the Kingdom of God' (§ 398a).

All three offices belong, both to the state of exinanition in

---

[1] *Supra*, p. 580.

which the historical, and to the state of exaltation in which the suprahistorical, character of the work of salvation come to view. Theology has had a difficulty in determining to which of the states Christ's death and Resurrection belong: they coincide in fact with the transition from the one to the other.

'Therefore we have first to consider the state of humiliation or the personal development of Jesus under the point of view of His saving work, then His reconciling work of expiation, and finally the state of exaltation or His personal perfecting as the basis of His continuous saving operation' (§ 398c).

To begin with, the Divine self-emptying in the life of Jesus is a special form of the Divine revelation. The Divine self-manifestation is here determined by union with a developing human life, and finds its historical form in Christ's prophetic vocation.

The Divine self-emptying is further manifested in the self-humiliation of the God-man. This consists in Christ's entering without reserve into the relation of humanity to God as determined by finitude and sin.

'His acceptance of the Messianic vocation in baptism demonstrates how He, ripening in faith in spite of temptations, maintained His relation to the Father without disturbance and won complete independence, by means of which He could take up that vocation as prophetic. He comprehended [2] the revelation of God in His manifestation and exercise of a holy love for sinners, but at the same time deepened this love to a representation of sinners in a love unconditionally surrendering itself to God. His revelational activity obtained its confirmation in the Transfiguration, while His representation (of men) issued in to His resolve to suffer death' (§ 404).

This leads us from the consideration of the state of humiliation from the point of view of Christ's saving work on to the historical accomplishment of His 'revelatory substitution' (*offenbarende Stellvertretung*).

'The end of the earthly life of Jesus appears as His act when we set it in the connexion of the entire history of His Divine-human Person. Yet on the other hand this section of His life

[2] I.e. gathered up.

641

definitely stands out from all before it as the historical Divine deed of expiation' (§ 411).

Christ's work of expiation is to be viewed in the unity of two complementary aspects. On the one hand, it is the endurance of the Divine condemnation of sin, on the other voluntary sacrifice. Kähler coins for it the name of 'penal sacrifice' (*Strafopfer*). The penal aspect he defines as follows:

'The deliverance of Christ over to suffering even unto death is a surrender without reservation to the curse pressing upon humanity; His endurance is, however, not only a struggle with powers holding sway in history, but involves an experience of the execution of the Divine wrath. This process has at the same time in the fullest sense the significance of punishment, since it is the means to a restoration of the common life of humanity in correspondence with its destiny; for the judgment is exhausted by the power of the faith of Jesus and His victory is manifested in His Resurrection to exaltation, which demonstrates Him as the Beginner of a new humanity' (§ 414).

The sacrificial aspect of the expiatory work again is thus defined:

'This experience of Jesus bears in itself the essential mark of sacrifice; that is, in it there is accomplished the surrender of His own will to the will of God; it is, however, not complete till the passive obedience or voluntary acceptance of punishment finds its perfecting complement in the active obedience or the surrender of the self to the service of God' (§ 418).

Finally, Kähler sums up both aspects in a section on the substitutionary and revelatory value of the penal sacrifice of Christ. The doctrine of the Church has always connected with the death of Christ the establishment of a new relation of man to God. But it too much separated the work of Christ from the abiding significance of His Person, and allowed it to be forgotten that God is here Himself the Actor.

'This is avoided by an evaluation on all sides of the idea of expiation, for in it revelation can be comprehended together with substitution. Sinners lack the indispensable presuppositions for a life in fellowship with God, since a religious total development of humanity has not taken place and the Divine life-order

642

has not attained to effective validity. God creates in Christ the Substitute in both respects, and this purpose of a substitutionary intervention becomes clear in the Divine dispensation as to the end of Christ's life, if we at the same time take into account the full value of His Person. Just in this surrender of the Son the Triune God accomplishes the full revelation of His holy love' (§ 422).

This brings us to the end of the middle section on the expiatory work of Christ; and we pass on therefore, lastly, to consider the revelatory substitution of the Eternal Mediator, or the manifestation of God's holy love in the perfected Son.

'The founding of the new covenant is not merely the founding of a positive religion, but the abiding opening of access to the Father for all believers, since Christ in the power of His exaltation to the position of equality with God lends an effective presentness to the result of His life-work (*meritum*). The God-man remains the Mediator between humanity and God for all time following, in that He administers His threefold office. The operations of His administration are experienced until His accomplished coming again merely in the appropriation of reconciliation through His Spirit. In their form they constitute the continuation of His prophetic office. Their triumphant success, however, is conditioned by the Exalted Christ's high-priestly representation, and victorious mediation of the communion with God, of every converted sinner, and by His making in His kingly rule the course of history serviceable for the offer of reconciliation' (§ 432).

Kähler's agreement with, and difference from Ritschl will now be plain. Besides his general recognition of a suprahistorical element in the Christian revelation, Kähler, while recognising with Ritschl the necessity for demonstrating the immanence of the love of God in Jesus Christ, yet does not concur in the Ritschlian subordination of Christ's representational to His revelational activity. On the contrary he treats both aspects of His work as of equal dignity, or perhaps even tends to reverse the Ritschlian order, since he speaks of the 'deepening' of Christ's work of revelation to one of representation or substitution. Moreover, Kähler is able to conceive of Christ's entering into the position of humanity to the point of entering into the Divine condemnation, a thing Ritschl was unable to do. In spite therefore of his agreement with Ritschl, at this decisive point he remains apart from him. Kähler speaks of his view in his work 'Zur Lehre von der Versöhnung' as emphasing the *ethical* character of the atonement.[3] He means by this the same idea which we have so often found before in modern theology, of Christ's doing honour to the Divine holiness and justice, yet in such a way that there is no notion on a quantitative equivalence of punishment.

THE MODERN SYNTHESIS

In the German Protestant theology of the nineteenth century, and especially in the work of Schleiermacher and Ritschl, we have to recognise the fourth great doctrinal synthesis, which, as over against the Greek, the mediaeval, and the seventeenth-century Protestant synthesis, we may call 'the modern synthesis'. This new synthesis has taken up into itself the truth of the evangelical experience of the Reformers, of the Socinian criticism, and of the accommodation-doctrine of the Aufklärung, combining them by means of the new philosophy of self-consciousness, which, emerging first in the form of the Kantian criticism, presently reveals itself in the docrines of Hegel and of Schleiermacher as a principle on the immanent union and interpenetration of the opposites of common logic, and thus as the principle of a higher logic adequate to the subject-matter of theology.

This modern synthesis appears as the fulfilment of the tendency, already apparent in the Protestant synthesis of the seventeenth century, towards the statement of Christian doctrine as a whole in which every part is the whole over again, and so all doctrine truly one.[4] Moreover, in the theology of Schleiermacher and that of Ritschl, or rather in the ideal to which both point, but neither entirely reaches, we may recognise the fulfilment of the idea, long ago thrown out by Clement and Origen, of a 'gnosis', which is the essence of the 'pistis' as delivered in

---

[3] Op. cit., pp. 404ff.   [4] *Supra*, pp. 306, 355.

Scripture and ecclesiastical tradition.[5] It is, however, a gnosis which avoids the mistake (repeated, indeed, by Hegel and the liberal theology) of attempting to eliminate the historical from the essence of Christianity. The essence of Christianity, as Kähler puts it, must unite the historical and the suprahistorical in one.

Besides Schleiermacher and Ritschl, who constitute the foci of the new movement, the other theologians whom we have studied contribute their quota towards the development, the goal of which has not yet been completely realised. In spite of all differences the whole movement from Schleiermacher to Ritschl is one. In the whole series of theologies studied, Christian doctrine is treated from the point of view of an experience of communion with God in Christ; and also in general the method of Scripture-proof adopted is no longer merely that from proof-texts, but that from the principles of the Biblical religion. It may, however, be pointed out that the treatment of Scripture-proof is, even in modern theology, not always satisfactory. The danger of relapse into the old method is not always overcome, and one of the most urgent theological needs of the present time is a reinterpretation on psychological lines of the Biblical material of doctrine: this applies to no doctrine more than to the work of Christ.

The differences, as well as the unity, of the modern movement are, however, important. We may illustrate, by means of those between Schleiermacher and Ritschl, considered in the light of the rest of the theological development, the main points in which the ideal of the movement still remains unattained.

(1) Schleiermacher has the advantage over Ritschl, in that his theology, over against Ritschl's positivism, has a metaphysical basis. It is true that Schleiermacher separates theology and metaphysic as sharply as does Ritschl. Nevertheless, since the Infinite which unites all differences is the foundation of his metaphysic, and since he views religion, though not in the form of knowledge, yet in that of the feeling of absolute dependence, as touching this Infinite, Schleiermacher's theology possesses in truth a genuine metaphysical basis, and has behind it at every point the background of reality. On the other hand, Ritschl's

---

[5] *Supra*, p. 35.

statement that religious truth is given in the form of value-judgements is unsatisfactory, unless it be added that in these judgments we touch reality. This is the explanation of the opposition to Ritschl at this decisive point, alike by the liberal, the mediating, and the Erlangen theology. Troeltsch more than any other German theologian has voiced the demand for a metaphysical basis of religion as a guarantee of its reality.[6] What is needed is not a metaphysic apart from religion, or even merely a religious metaphysic: it is a Christian metaphysic and metaphysic of Christianity, such as was desiderated by C. H. Weisse,[7] i.e. a philosophy rising out of the midst of Christianity itself, depending upon the intuition of God in Christ, and proceeding to the apprehension of Christianity and the world through it.

(2) On the other hand, Ritschl undoubtedly has the advantage over Schleiermacher in that, while Schleiermacher leaves the question of the personality of God an open one for religion, he makes close connexion with the New Testament idea of God. Schleiermacher's fault lies in the investigation of the doctrine of God in the first place independently of the intuition of God in Christ: the standpoint thus determined Christian theology must maintain and never abandon even for a moment.

Ritschl has also an advantage over Schleiermacher in the use which he makes of the notion of the Kingdom of God. Again, his advantage consists in that he is in closer connexion with the religion of the New Testament.

What has been said so far concerns the modern synthesis in general: we pass on to consider how it affects the doctrine of the work of Christ.

(1) This is in general rightly considered in modern theology from the standpoint of communion with God. The first result of this shifting of the venue from the court of authority to that of experience is seen in the altered attitude of Schleiermacher and Ritschl to the question of punishment, which is now apprehended not from without but from within. Since it is only in connexion with the consciousness of guilt that evils appear as

---

[6] Cf. his 'Wesen der Religion und der Religionswissenschaft', in 'Die Kultur der Gegenwart,' I, IV, 2, esp. p. 32.   [7] 'Philosophische Dogmatik', vol. i, 1885, §§ 9, 10.

penal, the old juristic method of theology, which considered punishment in abstraction from its relation to consciousness, no longer applies. So far as the mediating and Erlangen theology lose sight of this important truth, they are on retrograde lines. It is noteworthy, however, that even they abandon the strict juristic standpoint and attempt no calculus of merits: modern theology, even where it continues to maintain the doctrine of a satisfaction of the Divine justice in the work of Christ, can only maintain a satisfaction in principle, not in strict equivalence.

(2) The Erlangen attempt partially to reintroduce the idea that the operation of Christ is necessarily mediated through the sacraments, appears also a retrogression. When once it is realised that everything must be interpreted from the standpoint of communion with God in Christ, it becomes clear that the sacraments can only have value *within*, not prior to this communion.

(3) From the same standpoint of communion with God in Christ it also becomes clear that Ritschl's subordination in the doctrine of the work of Christ of the category of Representation to that of Revelation is correct. It is from the standpoint of fellowship with God, implying His revelation to us in Christ, that we think of Christ as our Representative and Substitute. Schleiermacher's doctrine is here essentially the same. The most difficult problem that emerges is that of Christ's identification with us in the consciousness of guilt, which Schleiermacher and Ritschl deny, but the mediating and Erlangen theology affirm. This is a question still awaiting a complete theological solution. On the basis of the concrete conception of personality as the union of opposites, however, the advantage appears to lie with the latter group of theologians. It will be remembered that Lipsius here deviates from Ritschl.

(4) Finally, Ritschl in his endeavour to simplify theology has sometimes forgotten the new concrete conception of personality, and worked too much on the basis of ordinary syllogistic logic. Herrmann has said of him:[8]

'He has not observed that a genuinely religious theology must

[8] 'Christliche Protestantische Dogmatik', in 'Die Kultur der Gegenwart', I, IV, 2, p. 161.

give up the idea of a system of its thoughts. As soon as a religious thought is developed in its logical consequences, it comes into conflict with another, which also belongs to the life of religion.' This opinion of Herrmann is true at any rate in so far as a modern system of theology can no longer be organised upon merely syllogistic lines, but only finally upon the basis of the category of personality. The criticism in consequence to be passed upon Ritschl's theology applies particularly to his entire subsumption of the Divine righteousness in the Divine love, as the *consistency* of the Divine love.[9] The Divine attributes of righteousness and love are rather immediately given at once in the experience of God in Christ, in whose historical life they are manifested in a personal union.[1] Thomasius is here suggestive, when he says that the relation between the Divine holiness and the Divine love is not one of identity, but is a unity which has the difference in it, and is a living harmony.[2]

In conclusion, I may refer to § III of my article 'Justification' [3] as suggesting the lines along which, in view of these various criticisms passed on the German theology of the nineteenth century, I think that the doctrine of the work of Christ is to be further developed.

[9] The fact that the Scriptural idea of righteousness includes its manifestation not only in punishment, but in mercy (*supra*, p. 365), is not a sufficient basis for the complete subsumption of righteousness in love.   [1] Jn 1:17.   [2] *Supra*, p. 598.
[3] 'Dictionary of Christ and the Gospels', vol. i, p. 923.

CHAPTER 7

THEOLOGY IN
ENGLAND AND SCOTLAND UP TO 1860

S. T. COLERIDGE

COLERIDGE (A.D. 1772–1834) occupies in English theology the same position as Kant in Germany: indeed he first introduced into England many of the principles of Kant, upon which his philosophy, as we have it in his 'Aids to Reflection' (1825), is based. Among the objects of the latter work he mentions the following:

'First, to exhibit the true and Scriptural meaning and intent of several articles of faith that are rightly classed among the mysteries and peculiar doctrines of Christianity. Secondly, to show the perfect rationality of all these doctrines, and their freedom from all just objection, when examined by their proper organs, the reason and conscience of man.'[1]

There is little difficulty, says Coleridge, among serious and inquiring persons, with articles of faith such as the Trinity, which may be simply above their comprehension.

'It is only where the belief required of them jars with their moral feelings; where a doctrine in the sense in which they have been taught to receive it, appears to contradict their clear notions of right and wrong, or to be at variance with the Divine attributes of Goodness and Justice, that these men are surprised, perplexed, and alas! not seldom offended and alienated. Such are the doctrines of arbitrary election and reprobation; the sentence to everlasting Torment by an eternal and necessitating decree; vicarious atonement, and the necessity of the abasement, agony, and ignominious death of a most holy and meritorious Person to appease the wrath of God' (p. 137).

Coleridge, however, is well assured of the essential truth of the Christian doctrine of redemption.

[1] Ed. Liverpool, 1883, p. 136.

649

'Where, if not in Christ, is the power that can persuade a sinner to return, that can bring home a heart to God. . . . By the phrase "in Christ", I mean all the supernatural aids vouchsafed and conditionally promised in the Christian Dispensation' (p. 138).

The necessitarianism of Jonathan Edwards, which subjects the moral world no less than the physical to the law of cause and effect, must be absolutely repudiated.[2] So also must the other doctrines of Modern Calvinism, as represented by the same divine, namely, the origination of holiness in power, of justice in the right of property.[3]

Coleridge stands for the reality of the will, as transcending nature and the law of cause and effect. 'If there be aught spiritual in man, the will must be such. If there be a will, there must be a spirituality in man' (p. 117). This is the foundation of all his religious philosophy. He also stands for the originality and ultimate character of the moral law, which cannot be explained in terms of anything else, whether Divine decree or utilitarian philosophy of profit and loss.

From this point of view, then, Coleridge explains the doctrine of original sin. With him as with Kant the corruption of the will is fundamental. But original sin does not mean the inheritance of sin and guilt from Adam, but on the contrary, that, wherever sin exists, it originates from the will, which is not subject to the law of cause and effect, but is free to obey or disobey the moral law.[4]

'The phrase, original sin, is a pleonasm. . . . For, if it be sin, it must be original; and a state or act, that has not its origin in the will, may be calamity, disformity, disease, or mischief; but a sin it cannot be' (p. 234). Original sin is evil having an origin. 'But, inasmuch as it is evil, in God it cannot originate; and yet in some Spirit (i.e. in some supernatural power) it must. For in nature there is no origin. Sin, therefore, is spiritual evil;

---

[2] Edwards sought to defend the Augustinian doctrine of the bondage of the will (cf. *supra*, p. 89) as followed by Luther (*supra*, p. 290) and Calvin (*supra*, p. 335) by resort to a philosophical necessitarianism. 'In the room of an acquired slavery of the will, he teaches a determinism belonging to its very nature' (Fisher, 'History of Christian. Doctrine', 1902, p. 401).

[3] Cf. Edwards, 'Of Satisfaction for Sin', §§ 3–7 (*supra*, pp. 498f.).

[4] Cf. the doctrine of Kant (*supra*, p. 522).

but the spiritual in man is the will. Now, when we do not refer to any particular sins, but to that state and constitution of the will which is the ground, condition, and common cause of all sins; and when we would further express the truth that this corrupt nature of the will must in some sense or other be considered as its own act, that the corruption must have been self-originated;—in this case and for this purpose we may, with no less propriety than force, entitle this dire spiritual evil and source of all evil, that is absolutely such, original sin' (p. 237).

As to the derivation of sin from Adam, Coleridge holds the following view:

'The corruption of my will may very warrantably be spoken of as a consequence of Adam's fall, even as my birth of Adam's existence; as a consequence, a link in the historical chain of instances, whereof Adam is the first. But that it is on account of Adam, or that this evil principle was *a priori*, inserted or infused into my will by the will of another—which is indeed a contradiction in terms, my will in such case being no *will*—this is nowhere asserted in Scripture explicitly or by implication. It belongs to the very essence of the doctrine that in respect of original sin every man is the adequate representative of all men. What wonder then, that where no inward ground of preference existed, the choice should be determined by outward relations, and that the first in time should be taken as the diagram?' (p. 256).

The doctrine of original sin, as the antecedent ground and occasion of Christianity, having been thus stated and explained, the way is open 'to proceed to Christianity itself, as the edifice reared on this ground, i.e. to the great constituent article of the Faith in Christ, as the Remedy of the disease—the doctrine of Redemption' (p. 257). Coleridge says: 'Christianity and Redemption are equivalent terms' (p. 274).

In order to understand the Christian redemption we must not, however, be led away by the mere word redemption, but look at the thing implied.

'Forgiveness of sin, the abolition of guilt, through the redemptive power of Christ's love, and of His perfect obedience during His voluntary assumption of humanity, is expressed, on account of the resemblance in both cases, by the payment of a debt for another, which debt the payer himself had not incurred. Now the impropriation of this metaphor—(i.e. the taking it literally) by transferring the sameness from the consequents to the antecedents, or inferring the identity of the causes from a sameness in the effects—this is the point on which I am at issue; and the view or scheme of Redemption grounded on this confusion I believe to be altogether unscriptural' (p. 282).

In the Christian redemption the Redeemer's act, as the efficient cause and condition of redemption, is transcendent: 'Beyond the information contained in the enunciation of the fact, it can be characterised only by the consequences' (p. 283). It is the consequences of the act of redemption which St Paul endeavours by various metaphors to bring home to the minds and affections of both Jews and Gentiles. A Jew himself, with Jews as his chief opponents, Paul's figures, images, analogies, and references are chiefly of Jewish origin, yet are such also that the most prominent and frequent metaphors are drawn from what was common to the whole Roman world. To this class of images, equally familiar to all, yet having a special interest for Jewish converts, belong the chief metaphors by which Paul illustrates the blessed consequences of Christ's redemption of mankind.

'These are: (1) sin offerings, sacrificial expiation; (2) reconciliation, atonement ($\kappa\alpha\tau\alpha\lambda\lambda\alpha\gamma\acute{\eta}$); (3) ransom from slavery, redemption, the buying back again, or being bought back, from *re* and *emo*; (4) satisfaction of a creditor's claims by a payment of the debt' (p. 284).

Thus, then, Paul states the consequences of the Christian redemption by means of Jewish metaphors. John, on the other hand, the evangelist according to the spirit, i.e. the inner and substantial truth of the Christian Creed, states the fact itself without any metaphor, so far as it is enunciable to the human mind. 'In the redeemed it is a regeneration, a birth, a spiritual seed, impregnated and evolved, the germinal principle of a higher and enduring life, of a spiritual life' (p. 286). This involves also a redemption from spiritual death.

'Respecting the redemptive act itself, and the Divine agent, we know from revelation that He "was made a quickening

652

(ζωοποιοῦν, life-making) Spirit": and that in order to this it was necessary that God should be manifested in the flesh, that the Eternal Word, through whom and by whom the world (κόσμος, the order, beauty, and sustaining law of visible natures) was and is, should be made flesh, assume our humanity personally, fulfil all righteousness, and so suffer and die for us as in dying to conquer death for as many as should receive Him. More than this, the mode, the possibility, we are not competent to know' (p. 287).

Coleridge follows this up with an explanation of St Paul's metaphors. As the Jewish sacrifices removed a civil stain, and restored a man to his place in the commonwealth of Israel, so the Christian regeneration removes the worse stain of sin, and restores us to the family of God. We are delivered from sin and death, hence the terms regeneration and redemption. The Christian salvation is, again, a reconciliation of prodigals to the Father by the intercession of Christ. It may also be expressed in terms of satisfaction. Paul would say in effect: 'You have incurred a debt of death to the evil nature! You have sold yourself over to sin! and relatively to you, and to all your means and resources, the seal on the bond is the seal of necessity! . . . But the Stranger has appeared, the forgiving Friend has come, even the Son of God from heaven: and to as many as have faith in His name, I say—the debt is paid for you! The satisfaction has been made' (p. 289).

There follows, however, a criticism of the doctrines based on taking these metaphors literally, especially that of satisfaction. The orthodox Protestant doctrine of satisfaction is based on the fundamental error of confounding things and persons. It treats sin as literally a debt that can be paid by another, and represents justice as claiming payment of our sin, since we cannot make it, from Christ. 'Is this justice a moral attribute?' asks Coleridge. 'Morality commences with, and begins in, the sacred distinction between thing and person' (p. 291). Debts can be transferred, not so the demerit of sin. The effect of Christ's mediation is no doubt similar to the effect of vicarious satisfaction in the case of debt. In both cases there is deliverance from a grievous burden, and that by the grace of another. But the difference is great. The

reality of redemption is the regeneration of the sinner brought
about by the transcendent operation of the Word 'incarnate,
tempted, agonising (Agonistes ἀγωνιζόμενος), crucified, submitting to death, resurgent, communicant of His Spirit, ascendent,
and obtaining for His Church the descent, and communion of
the Holy Spirit, the Comforter' (p. 297).

Such is Coleridge's doctrine. Its likeness and unlikenesses
with those of Butler and Kant are noteworthy and apparent.[5]
These may be noted, first, with regard to the presupposition of
redemption, viz. human sinfulness. Both Butler and Coleridge
make this a fundamental article, asserting it as a fact of experience, altogether prior to the Christian revelation. But,
whereas Butler thinks merely of human sin, so far as it entails
future punishment and of redemption as remission of penalty,
Coleridge thinks of it as a depravation of the will itself, and of
redemption as regeneration. Here he is in harmony with Kant,
whom indeed in this matter he follows. With regard to the work
of Christ, Butler and Coleridge agree in making it essentially a
transcendent operation, the critical philosophy of Locke affording Butler similar opportunities for so doing, as the philosophy
of Kant, with its distinction between understanding and reason,
gave Coleridge.[6] (Kant himself restricts the transcendent operation on the will to the Divine Idea, limiting the work of the
historical Christ to instruction and example.) There is a difference, however, between Butler and Coleridge in their apprehension of the transcendent nature of the work of Christ. For
Butler this virtually amounts to the doctrine of satisfaction,
accepted by him as a positive revelation, not in itself indeed
unreasonable, but still mysterious. He refuses to allow the
doctrine to be explained away by the Deist theory of accommodation. Coleridge, on the other hand, accepts this Deist theory
as a chief weapon of his warfare to demolish the orthodox theory,
and makes the transcendent operation of Christ consist in His
regeneration and renewal of the will.

[5] Cf. *supra*, pp. 492ff., 519ff.

[6] Locke, founding his philosophy on experience, naturally viewed the spiritual world
as largely transcending the knowledge of reason (*supra*, pp. 477, 480). Kant distinguished
between Understanding (*Verstand*) which interprets the data of the senses, and Reason
(*Vernunft*) which seeks to complete our view of the world by postulating transcendent
principles (*supra*, pp. 518, 520f.).

It is evident therefore, that in the end Coleridge is fundamentally in harmony, not so much with Kant, as with Schleiermacher, and has introduced into English theology the same type of mysticism as Schleiermacher introduced into the theology of Germany. There is little formal similarity between Coleridge and Schleiermacher: the aphoristic style of the former is very different from the close reasoning of the latter. Nevertheless fundamentally there is agreement inasmuch as both make redemption by Christ the centre of Christianity, and identify redemption with regeneration. English theology, therefore, through the influence of Coleridge enters on the same career as that of Germany through the influence of Schleiermacher.

There is indeed one important difference between Coleridge and Schleiermacher as to the thoroughness with which the Kantian criticism is applied to doctrine. While Schleiermacher in consequence of it presents an anthropological Christianity,[7] Coleridge is able to accept the orthodox Christology of the Creeds. English theology in general has here followed Coleridge, and is consequently in closer agreement on the point with the type of theology represented in Germany by the mediating theologians and still more by the Erlangen school, than with that represented by Schweizer and Ritschl which has strictly followed Schleiermacher.

ERSKINE

Along with Coleridge, Erskine of Linlathen (A.D. 1788–1870) was instrumental in the regeneration of British theology in the nineteenth century. This general tendency has thus been characterised by Tulloch:[8]

'Erskine without any indebtedness either to Schleiermacher or Coleridge, and almost as early as either, was in Scotland an apostle of the "Christian consciousness". He led in the great reaction against mere formal orthodoxy, and, for that part of the matter, formal rationalism, which set in with the opening of the third decade of the century. . . . He was rational certainly

[7] *Supra*, pp. 534f, 558.
[8] 'Movements of Religious Thought in Britain during the Nineteenth Century', 1885, p. 138.

655

in comparison with all who saw in Christianity a body of mere doctrines or observances, to be accepted on authority. But he was the very opposite of rationalistic in the sense in which rationalism had prevailed in Germany and England in the eighteenth century. . . . Erskine's religion was *all heart*. He did not understand religion without the living fire of faith and love and obedience animating it all through. It must be a light in his reason, a guide in his conscience—a life within his life—a spiritual power glowing in his whole conduct. This was "internal evidence"—the revelation of Love to love, of Life to life—of God to man, raising him to Divine communion and reflecting upon the Divine likeness.'

Tulloch refers in the words 'internal evidence', which he has placed in inverted commas, to the title of Erskine's first book, 'Remarks on the Internal Evidence for the Truth of Revealed Religion' (1820). Erskine wished to show that Christianity must be self-evidencing in view of the harmony existing between the doctrines it teaches and the moral character it demands.

'The reasonableness of a religion seems to me to consist in there being a direct and rational connexion between a believing of the doctrines which it inculcates, and a being formed by these to the character which it recommends. If the belief of the doctrines has no tendency to train a disciple in a more exact and more willing discharge of its moral obligations, there is evidently a very strong probability against the truth of that religion. In other words, the doctrine ought to tally with the precepts, and to contain in their substance some urgent motives for the performance of them; because, if they are not of this description, they are of no use. What is the history of another world to me, unless it have some intelligible relation to my duties and happiness?' [9]

Here is the same tendency, as we have already found in Schleiermacher and Coleridge, to view the doctrines of Christianity on their experimental and practical side; though this tendency is expressed by Erskine in a simple and popular way without any appeal to a critical philosophy. We are still further reminded of Schleiermacher by Tulloch's characterisation of

[9] Op. cit. 10th ed., 1878, p. 58.

Erskine, as seeking a middle way towards his experimental doctrine between the formal orthodoxy and the formal rationalism of the eighteenth century. It will be remembered that Schleiermacher, describing his conception of Christianity as mystical, regarded it as a *via media* between the magical and the empirical views of the subject.[1]

Erskine applied his principles to the study of the work of Christ in a volume entitled 'The Brazen Serpent' (1831). The doctrine of this book is historically of great importance, in view of the later development of theology in Britain. The treatise is, however, unsystematic in form, and it is somewhat difficult to give an adequate account of its teaching. There is a great deal of repetition; and yet Erskine seldom repeats himself without saying something fresh. Moreover, there is no complete unification of the doctrine. There is instead a succession of deep glances into the heart of the subject, whose unity is not objective, formal, and logical, but subjective—a unity of the temper, spirit, and experience whence they proceed.

The general basis of Erskine's doctrine is that the Incarnation was a Divine light, a word from God, not, however, a spoken word, but a substantial word, the word made flesh (p. 32). The nature of this word is to be understood from the double reflection that in the Incarnation God has taken human flesh, and that, further, this flesh is human nature in general. 'Jesus had no human personality, He had the human nature under the personality of the Son of God' (p. 53). So Erskine teaches, in harmony with the Ancient Church.[2] Moreover, in thus taking human nature, Christ becomes the Second Adam, or new head of the race. As a consequence, 'in the history of the word made flesh, we have a concentrated history of God's actions towards our nature, our flesh; and thus we have a standard by which we may at all times measure the mind of God towards ourselves and every individual of the nature. For that which the Divine nature did to the human nature in Christ, was done to Him in character of head and representative of the human nature; and therefore is to be considered as indicating the mind of God to every man' (p. 32).

What then is the light which the Incarnation sheds upon

[1] Cf. *supra*, pp. 540f., 543f.   [2] *Supra*, p. 68.

human life? In Christ is manifested the Divine pardon of human sin, 'a forgiving love condemning sin—yet bestowing blessing through penal affliction, and life through penal death' (p. 33).

This is the meaning of the sufferings and death of Christ. He dies a penal death; yet God loved Him. He is Himself indeed God incarnate: 'Why does He thus torture and kill the flesh, which He has assumed into so near and indissoluble connexion with Himself' (p. 33).

The suffering was necessary because the nature, which Christ assumed, was a fallen nature, and He thus condemned sin in the flesh.

'He came into it as a new head, that He might take it out of the fall, and redeem it from sin, and lift it up to God; and this could be effected only through sorrow and death, manifesting the character of God, and the character of man's rebellion; manifesting God's abhorrence to sin, and the full sympathy of the new Head of the nature in that abhorrence, and thus eating out of the taint of the fall, and making honourable way for the inpouring of the new life into the rebellious body. Because thus only could there be an open vindication given of the holiness and truth of God, against which the fall was an offence; and thus only could it become a righteous thing in God, in consideration of this new Head of the nature—who had, in that nature, and in spite of its opposite tendencies, vindicated the character of God, and fulfilled all righteousness, to declare the race partaking of that nature forgiven, and to lay up in Him, their glorious Head, eternal life for them all, which should flow into each member, just as He believed in the holy love of God which was manifested in the gift and work of Christ' (p. 35).

Such is the summary statement of Erskine's doctrine given by himself. It is further elucidated in the following pages. In the first place, Erskine criticises the orthodox theory of satisfaction. God has no pleasure in sufferings viewed simply as penal, irrespective of the temper in which they are borne. The sufferings of the rebellious are in fact sin, and as such can give Him no pleasure. But He had pleasure in the sufferings of Christ, first of all in so far as Jesus by them declares the truth of God's character, the holy truth of God to man. He stooped to take our nature. He could be satisfied with nothing less than an exhibition of God's love by actual participation in our humanity.

'God has a personal tender affection for every man, so that He desires union and fellowship with every man. Now the Son declared the love of the Father, by coming into the root of the nature, that part which Adam occupied, and remember that there is a fibre of the root in every branch, in every twig of the tree' (pp. 45, 46).

All Christ's sufferings were the manifestations of Divine love to humanity. 'He loved the Father, and He loved the truth, and He loved man, and wherever He was He saw God dishonoured, the truth despised, and man destroying himself' (p. 48). The fire of holy love burned within Him, and He testified for God and the truth against the evil of the world. 'He spoke not with His tongue only, He was the life of God made manifest in the flesh —He was the life made light, and He walked up and down in that living light, and as it was in a world of spiritual death and darkness that He thus walked, the life in Him continually condemned the death, and the light the darkness' (p. 48). At last He drew upon Himself the hatred of men, till they crucified Him.

'They killed Him, but they could not kill His love; that was stronger than death and stronger than hatred. Blessed be His name: His love conquered. Every action of His being was a part of that warfare of love against hatred, and of righteousness against unrighteousness, which He with perfect success, but with uninterrupted sorrow, waged throughout His life. That warfare could not be carried on without sorrow, it was a continual grieving over sin and ruin, and a continual condemnation of those whom He loved unto the death. For He was every man's brother, and the condemnation was not the condemnation of a stranger, but of a brother' (p. 48).

God, therefore, was pleased with the sufferings of Christ, because they thus manifested the Divine love. But He was also pleased, because they exhibited a triumph over sin and the Devil, within the terms of human nature.

'He waged this hard and successful warfare under all the disadvantages of the fall, not in the power of His own personal

Godhead, but in the power of the Holy Spirit communicated by the Father in continual answer to the continual actings of His faith, as the faith of a dependent creature' (p. 50).

His holiness and His sympathy with men, moreover, make His sufferings expiatory. 'God never was rightly glorified by the penal suffering of the fallen nature, until that suffering was undergone in the Spirit of holy love by one who partook of the fallen nature, and felt for all its sins as if they had been His own, and yet had not personally partaken of them. . . . Now this is the expiation, this is that which put away sin' (p. 54).

Erskine is, however, careful to point out the difference of his doctrine here from that of orthodoxy.

'He did not suffer *for men*, as an individual standing *out* of them, and doing something in their stead, but as one *in* them, as the head of that mass of which they were all partakers, as the root of that tree of which they were all branches' (p. 55).

'Christ came into Adam's place. This is the real substitution' (p. 85).

Once more the Divine Person of Jesus gives glory to His work. Not, however, as giving a weight to suffering, but as manifesting the holy love of God and the sinfulness of sin. The Resurrection proves that Christ's death has indeed put away sin.

'As Christ died as the head of the race, so He rose as the head of the race. He rose as the justified head of the race, with the mark of the cross upon Him, showing that the penalty had been sustained by the *race* in the person of their head' (p. 61).

Moreover, He rose as the righteous head of the race, the King of the Kingdom of God, and the future Judge of all living. This headship He merited by His work.

Erskine's doctrine is completed by his account of the Gospel. The result of Christ's work is that all men are now under a dispensation of forgiving love, in so far as He is in each of us the root of our humanity. Adam before the Fall was under creation love, we are now under redemption love. Erskine calls this love our 'provision'. Christ Himself had a provision, independent of and antecedent to His work, in the strength of which He was to do it—viz. the love and favour of the Father to Himself personally. But our provision is the fruit of His work: it is the federal righteousness which He obtained as a matter not of grace, but of merit.

The Gospel, now, is the declaration of the truth that Christ is one with us in the flesh, and that the race is pardoned in Him. The Gospel believed conveys us into the Spirit of Christ, conforms us to His sufferings and death. Just as we are all in Adam and derive corruption from him, yet not without our own act, so we are in Christ and from His mercy derive righteousness, but also by our own act.

This provision of pardon is the temporary dispensation under which we now are with a view to judgment. The kingdom is a promise to those who live in the light of the pardon, but to none other. Therefore Christianity has from the first associated these two things together, the kingdom and the sacrifice.

Our position at present is therefore thus described: 'It is as if a violent and malicious man were placed in a society of gentle and loving persons, with the intimation "You are placed here for a year, and during that time nothing that you have hitherto been shall ever be remembered, and every act of violence which you may commit shall be met with love, and every offence shall be met with forgiveness. At the end of the period you shall be tried, and if you shall be found to have acquired the life of love, you shall remain always as a member of that gentle society in an increasing happiness, but if you shall be found still to be possessed by the spirit of malice, you shall be cast into outer darkness" ' (p. 64).

Thus Christianity is a religion of reconciliation, yet a moral religion withal: in it mercy and judgment meet together.

The agreement of Erskine's ideas with many older theological conceptions is apparent. There is a noteworthy casting back in general to the patristic type of thought,[3] and in what he says of Christ as the receiver of grace we are reminded of Thomas Aquinas and Hooker.[4] This idea that forgiveness is preliminary and its full fruition in the possession of the kingdom is conditioned by holiness is also ancient and Catholic.[5] On the other hand, the patristic and mediaeval elements are united in Erskine's

---

[3] It is to be remembered that the patristic tradition never died out in Protestantism (cf. *supra*, pp. 298f., 300f., 338f.

[4] Cf. *supra*, pp. 215, 451.   [5] *Supra*, pp. 29, 33.

theology with elements from the later Calvinism.[6] But Erskine seems to have obtained his doctrines by independent Bible study and reflection, and to have been without much knowledge of the previous history of theology. He had no consciousness of the relation of his views to older forms of doctrine.[7] In many points he anticipates the German Erlangen school; but there is an immense contrast between his unsystematic treatise and the scientific precision of the Germans.

MAURICE

F. D. Maurice (A.D. 1805–72), who was born a Unitarian, but joined the Church of England, was influenced both by Coleridge and by Erskine, particularly by the latter. Maurice himself acknowledged this indebtedness to Erskine in dedicating to him the volume 'The Prophets and Kings of the Old Testament' (1852). Erskine's book, 'The Brazen Serpent', particularly attracted Maurice.[8]

Maurice's own doctrine of the work of Christ is summarised in his 'Theological Essays' (1853).

In VII, 'On the Atonement', the subject is laid out under seven heads (pp. 144ff.).

(1) 'It is involved in the very method of theology, as the Bible and the creeds set it forth to us, that the will of God should be asserted as the ground of all that is right, true, just, gracious. . . . It would be accounted heresy in all orthodox schools to deny that the Father sent the Son to be the Saviour of men; that the Father sent forth the Son to be the propitiation for our sins; that Christ, by His life, proved that God is light, and that in Him is no darkness at all.'

These are 'fundamental truths, to which all others must do homage, which no other passages can contradict'. Maurice demands that this should be fully recognised, that complete control of these principles be established over the whole of theology.

(2) 'It is admitted in all schools, Romanist and Protestant,

A notable instance is his use of the doctrine of Christ's federal headship (cf. *supra,* pp. 410, 438f.).   [7] Tulloch, op. cit., p. 144.   [8] *Ibid.,* p. 142.

which do not dissent from the creed, that Christ the Son of God was in heaven and earth, one with the Father, one in will, purpose, substance; and that on earth His whole life was nothing else than an exhibition of this will, an entire submission to it.' This principle again must be fully maintained and allowed the controlling influence proper to it.

(3) 'It is confessed by all orthodox schools, that Christ was actually the Lord of men, the King of their spirits, the source of all the light which ever visited them, the Person for whom all nations longed as their real Head and Deliverer, the root of Righteousness in each man. The Bible speaks of His being revealed in this character; of the mystery which had been hid from ages and generations being made known by His Incarnation.'

From this admitted doctrine, however, Maurice deduces an important inference:

'One who appears as the actual representative of humanity, cannot be a formal substitute for it. We deny Him in the first character by claiming the second for Him.'

(4) 'The Scripture says, "Because the children were partakers of flesh and blood, He also Himself partook of the same". He became subject to death, that He might destroy him who had the power of death, that is the Devil. Here are reasons assigned for the Incarnation and Death of Christ. He shared the sufferings of those whose head He is. He overcame death, their common enemy, by submitting to it. He delivered them from the power of the Devil.'

Christ must not, says Maurice, be put at a distance from us, as bearing sufferings to us inconceivable; it was our actual miseries and griefs into which He entered. He rescued us out of the power of death, an evil accident of our condition, not part of God's original order; out of the power of the Devil, our enemy, not out of the hand of God.

(5) 'The Scripture says "The Lamb of God taketh away the *sin* of the world". All orthodox teachers repeat the lesson. . . . Have we a right to call ourselves Scriptural or orthodox if we change the words, and put "penalty of sin" for "sin", if we suppose that Christ destroyed the connexion between sin and death—the one being the necessary wages of the other—for the

663

sake of benefiting any individual man whatever? If He had, would He have magnified the law and made it honourable? Would He not have destroyed that which He came to fulfil? Those who say the law must execute itself—it must have its penalty, should remember their own words. How does it execute itself, if a person, against whom it is not directed, interposes to bear its punishment?'

(6) 'All orthodox schools have said that a perfectly holy and loving Being can be satisfied only with a holiness and love corresponding to His own; that Christ satisfied the Father by presenting the image of His own holiness and love, that in His sacrifice and death, all that holiness and love came forth completely. . . . How then can we tolerate for an instant that notion of God, which would represent Him as satisfied by the punishment of sin, not by the purity and graciousness of the Son?'

(7) Here in a most characteristic passage Maurice sums up his whole view:

'Supposing all these principles gathered together; supposing the Father's will to be a will to all good; the Son of God, being one with Him, and Lord of man, to obey and fulfil in our flesh that will by entering into the lowest condition into which men had fallen through their sin;—supposing this Man to be, for this reason, an object of continual complacency to the Father, and that complacency to be drawn out by the death of the Cross; is not this, in the highest sense, atonement? Is not the true sinless root of humanity revealed; is not God in him reconciled to man? May not that reconciliation be proclaimed as a gospel to all men? Is not the Cross the meeting-point between man and man, between man and God? Is not this meeting-point what men in all places and times have been seeking for? Did any find it till God declared it? And are we not bringing our understandings to the foot of this Cross, when we solemnly abjure all schemes and statements, however sanctioned by the arguments of divines, however plausible as implements of declamation, which prevent us from believing and proclaiming that in it all the wisdom and truth and glory of God were manifested to the creature; that in it man is presented as a holy and acceptable sacrifice to the Creator?'

Such is Maurice's statement, which has been reproduced

almost *in extenso*, it being already so summary that it can be little further shortened. The agreement with Coleridge, but more especially with Erskine, is plain. The latter agreement is particularly noticeable as regards the general practical conception of the Gospel resulting from the whole system. Like Erskine, Maurice teaches that in Christ men are already pardoned, reconciled, and redeemed, and need further only a consciousness of this—a subjective experience of the objective Divine fact accomplished for them in Christ. Still with the agreement between Erskine and Maurice there is a difference. While both reject the idea of substitution in favour of that of representation, Erskine lays stress on the Incarnation of Christ in the fallen nature of humanity, in which nature He accepted the condemnation of human sin; but Maurice teaches that the surrender of Christ's will to God reveals the true sinless root of humanity. Here is a British parallel to the difference between Schleiermacher and Thomasius as to Christ's 'satisfaction'.[9]

McLeod Campbell

Another disciple of Erskine's was McLeod Campbell (A.D. 1800–72), the dependence of whose doctrine of the work of Christ on 'The Brazen Serpent' is recognised by Tulloch in the following words:

'It ("The Brazen Serpent") contains in germ much of the same thinking which afterwards, in the more powerful reflective mind of Dr McLeod Campbell, expanded into the well-known treatise on the "Nature of the Atonement" ' (op. cit. p. 143).

If, however, Campbell was thus dependent on Erskine, his work, as Tulloch suggests in the above quotation, made a great advance upon his master. 'The Brazen Serpent', as has been said, is unsystematic and full of repetition. The 'Nature of the Atonement', on the other hand, is the most systematic and masterly book on the work of Christ, produced by a British theologian in the nineteenth century. Its style indeed is somewhat heavy; nevertheless, in spite of this it has exercised a great influence

[9] *Supra*, pp. 552, 602f.

upon subsequent theology. Another point of advance upon Erskine also is apparent as soon as we open Campbell's treatise. He begins by orientating himself with reference to previous theology. In Luther's bold imaginative presentation of the work of Christ, as contained in his 'Commentary on Galatians', Campbell finds a suggestive anticipation of his own line of doctrine.[1] Then the Calvinist doctrine, as represented by Owen and Edwards, is examined. Campbell has a great reverence for this type of theology, and considers that the argument of Owen against the Arminians is from his own premises invincible.[2] The great fault, however, of the whole system is that the work of Christ is not so presented as to reveal the love of God.[3] It makes everything subordinate to the arbitrary act of God in election, and an arbitrary act can never reveal character. Again, the whole view of atonement offered by Owen and Edwards is such that a legal is substituted for a filial standing, as the gift of God to men in Christ. Campbell finds, however, in the remarkable admission of Edwards, that a perfect repentance would have availed as an atonement,[4] the hint of a true theory. Unfortunately Edwards only put forward this view as a mere hypothesis, and did not work it out as a substantive theory.

The criticism of the orthodox Calvinism is followed by a consideration of the modification which Calvinism had received in Campbell's own day. Campbell mentions as representatives of this Calvinism the names of Wardlaw, Payne, and Jenkyns.[5] These theologians have abandoned the limitation of the atonement to the elect, and have substituted for the strict satisfaction of justice in the death of Christ by His bearing an exact equivalent of the punishment of sinners, the Grotian notion of an assertion in His death of the principle of the Divine penal righteousness. As a matter of fact, then, by the death of Christ no one is saved, but all may be. These 'modern Calvinists' stand in the matter

---

[1] Cf. *supra*, pp. 298ff.   [2] *Supra*, p. 471.
[3] Cf. Ritschl's precisely similar criticism of the Protestant orthodoxy (*supra*, pp. 630f.).
[4] *Supra*, p. 499.
[5] Campbell refers (see list of works quoted at the end of his book) to Wardlaw, 'Discourses on the Nature and Extent of the Atonement of Christ' (1844) ; Payne, 'Lectures on Divine Sovereignty, Election, the Atonement, Justification and Regeneration, (2nd ed., 1838) ; Jenkyns, 'On the Extent of the Atonement, in its Relation to God, and the Universe' (2nd ed., 1837).

666

practically where the Arminians stood, with whom Owen was contending when he wrote 'The Death of Death'. Campbell praises the universalism of the modern school; though he thinks that Owen has the advantage of them in logic. But he finds that they still retain a view of Christ's work which issues in a legal, not a filial, standing being conceived as God's gift to us in Him. Moreover, in the matter of faith they are more legal than the older Calvinists. The latter represented faith as God's gift to us, while the moderns, like the Arminians, make it in the end a work to be performed by man.

Campbell's own theory is based upon a principle obviously derived from Erskine,[6] which he has stated in the title of Chapter V of his work. It is that *the atonement is to be seen by its own light*. What this means is well illustrated in the following passage:[7]

'We know that, though the Gospel alone sheds clear and perfect light on the evil of man's condition as a sinner, conscience fully recognises the truth of that revelation of ourselves which the Gospel makes to us. Were it otherwise, assuredly its light would be no light to us. So also as to the gift of eternal life. When that gift is revealed to our faith, its suitableness to us, and fitness to fill all our capacities of well-being as God's offspring, is discerned by us in proportion as we are awakened to true self-consciousness, and learn to separate between what God made us, and what we have become through sin. And in like manner I believe that the atonement, related, as it must needs be, retrospectively to the condition of evil from which it is the purpose of God to save us, and prospectively to the condition of good to which it is His purpose to raise us, will commend itself to our faith by the inherent light of its Divine adaptation to accomplish all which it has been intended to accomplish.'

The atonement, accordingly, cannot be understood *a priori* (p. 119), nor yet again from the previous history of religion (pp. 121ff.). The Old Testament sacrifices point forward to it as their antitype, but the antitype explains the type, not the type the antitype. Campbell points out, indeed, elsewhere (p. 180) that

---

[6] Cf. what is said above (p. 657) on the general basis of Erskine's doctrine.
[7] 'The Nature of the Atonement', 2nd ed., 1867, p. 5.

the consideration of the Old Testament sacrifices might have saved men from the idea that atonement was by way of vicarious punishment: the sacrifices were not intended to deliver from punishment, but to purify for worship. In connexion, however, with the relation between type and antitype, reference is made to Heb. 10:1ff., where it is made clear that the essence of the atonement was not that in which it resembled the Jewish sacrifices, but Christ's perfect fulfilment of the will of God (pp. 123ff.).

'We have therefore to trace out the fulfilment of this purpose, Lo, I come to do thy will. In what relation to God and to man did it place the Lord as partaking in humanity?—especially in what relation to men's sins and the evils consequent upon sin to which they were subject?' (p. 125).

Since the second commandment is like the first, 'the spirit of sonship in which consists the perfect fulfilment of the first commandment, is one with the spirit of brotherhood which is the fulfilment of the second' (loc. cit.). Christ's love of the Father involves His love of His brethren as Himself. Through this twofold love we must understand His work.

It presents two parts: (1) Christ's dealing with man on behalf of God, (2) His dealing with God on behalf of man. Each of these two parts, moreover, is to be considered when we deal with the atonement (a) in its retrospective aspect, as a deliverance from sin, (b) in its prospective aspect, as the impartation of eternal life (pp. 127, 128).

First, therefore, we have to consider the retrospective aspect of the atonement, and in particular Christ's dealing here with men on behalf of God (pp. 129ff.). This consists in Christ's revelation of the Father, which was, in view of the sinful opposition of men, itself part of His sacrifice. Christ's sufferings were here necessary in order to the vindication of the name of God and the condemnation of human sin.

But how in this retrospective aspect of His work did Christ deal with God on behalf of men? Here Campbell makes use of the idea he has commended in Edwards, viz. that Christ offered on our behalf a vicarious repentance. The wrath of God against sin requires to be appeased: satisfaction is due to Divine justice.

These things are true, however much the mode of satisfaction has been misconceived.

'If so, then Christ, in dealing with God on behalf of men, must be conceived as dealing with the righteous wrath of God against sin, and as according to it that which was due; and this would necessarily precede His intercession for us' (p. 135).

Just as Christ's long-suffering love was the revelation to men of the forgiving love of God, to which Christ's intercession would be addressed, so Christ's own condemnation of our sins, and holy sorrow over them, indicate that dealing with God's just wrath against sin which prepared the way for His intercession.

'That oneness of mind with the Father, which towards men took the form of condemnation of sin, would in the Son's dealing with the Father in relation to our sins take the form of a perfect confession of our sins. This confession, as to its own nature, must have been a perfect *Amen in humanity to the judgment of God on the sin of man*' (loc. cit.).

Such a condemnation and confession of sin in humanity, which should be a real Amen to the Divine condemnation of sin, only became possible through the Incarnation of the Son of God. Granted this Incarnation, it was, however, not only possible, but inevitable. Though Christ's sufferings must have been very intense, it is not so much their intensity as their nature which is to be considered. They were not penal, but rather a revelation of the nature of God, and hence purifying and cleansing. In them was fulfilled that meeting of sin and righteousness, and that victory of righteousness over sin, of which Luther speaks.[8]

The sufferings of Christ were completed by His intercession. In the light of His knowledge of the Father's heart, He not only said Amen to the Divine condemnation of our sin, but also was encouraged to accompany confession by intercession, not indeed an intercession that aimed at effecting a change in the mind of the Father, but one that expressed a hope for man from that love of God, which is deeper than, and indeed is the real root of, His wrath against sin. To understand, therefore, how the sacrifice of Christ was well pleasing to God, we must consider the response in it not only to the Divine condemnation of sin, but also to the

---

[8] *Supra*, p. 299.

Divine love in its yearning over sinners. Christ's intercession made under the pressure of human sin was part of His sacrifice: its power as an element in the atonement lay in the fact that it was the voice of Divine love coming from humanity.

It will help to make clearer Campbell's exact position, if we observe that he cannot admit that Christ was truly forsaken of God on the cross. There was no exception even here to His experience of abiding in the Father's love, because He kept His commandments. Identification with us therefore does not go so far as absolute desolation. Campbell explains that 'Why hast thou forsaken me?' in the cry on the cross means simply in accordance with the general idea of Ps. 22: 'Why hast thou left me in the hand of the wicked?' (pp. 277ff.).[9]

We are to consider next the prospective aspect of the atonement, viz. its relation to the Divine end contemplated in it (pp. 151ff.). Both parts of Christ's work, His dealing with us on behalf of God, and with God on our behalf, have a prospective as well as a retrospective aspect. Christ's witnessing for God was not only a light condemning human sin, but a light of life for us. His revelation of the Father had for its object our participation in the life of sonship. The revelation of God's Fatherhood and of man's sonship are in fact correlative: the one is reflected in the other. This sonship, moreover, is eternal life, which is not some unknown future blessedness beyond the riches we have in Christ, but the life of sonship itself, which is itself unsearchable infinite riches.[1] Again, Christ's confession of sin, as offered to God for us, must have had in view our participation in that confession as an element in our actual redemption from sin. So also His intercession was not merely for the forgiveness of our sins, but that we might have fellowship with God.

Campbell lays great stress on the due consideration of the prospective aspect of Christ's work. All views of it imply that its ultimate reference was prospective. But not in all is this point equally kept in mind. In the traditional view, for example, Christ's satisfaction and merit are regarded as establishing the remission of sins and the right to eternal life, irrespective of any results

[9] Campbell further points out that the Psalm taken as a whole (see especially v. 24) does not support the notion of separation from God. Cf. the view of Schleiermacher *supra*, p. 552).   [1] Cf. Ritschl's immanental view of eternal life (*supra*, p. 625).

which are to be effective in those who enter into the covenant of grace. Scripture, however, always has these results directly in view, and the acceptableness to God of the work of Christ can only be fully seen when the end of the whole is kept in view, viz. the gift of eternal life or the establishment of fellowship with God. The perfect righteousness of Christ is in fact not the meritorious cause, through its imputation to us, of the gift to us of eternal life. This is altogether too complicated and artificial a combination. On the contrary, the righteousness of Christ is itself the great gift of God to us. Christ in fact becomes the Head of a new humanity, in which He lives as a quickening Spirit, imparting to it that same attitude to God's love and holiness, which was realised in His own sacrifice. The true equivalent of the doctrine of His merit is that, as the root of this new life in humanity, He reveals 'an inestimable preciousness which was hidden in humanity, hidden from the inheritors of humanity themselves, but not hid from God, and now brought into mani-festation by the Son of God. For the revealer of the Father is also the revealer of man, who was made in God's image' (p. 160).

It is not enough, however, that Christ thus reveals a capacity for righteousness hidden in humanity, He must also have power over humanity to impart eternal life. 'Therefore', says Campbell, 'there must be a relation between the Son of God and the sons of men, not according to the flesh only, but also according to the spirit—the Second Adam must be a quickening spirit, and the head of every man be Christ' (loc. cit.). When this is kept in view, the air of legal fiction, which has attached to the identification of Christ with us in the atonement will be removed, and this identification will be seen to be real, and 'fully justify to the enlightened conscience that constitution of things in which Christ's confession of our sins expiates them, and Christ's righteousness in humanity clothes us with His own interest in the sight of God' (p. 161).

In conclusion, Campbell contrasts his theory with the tradi-tional doctrine, in order to show that, so far from being less morally severe and strict, it is really much more so (pp. 188ff.). Dispensation from justice may, with a view to the general good, be possible to a lawgiver and ruler in the exercise of a righteous rule; but our Father can never be satisfied with any accommodation, but must demand from His sons a complete and perfect holiness of life. The work of Christ in fact, as a whole, is calculated to produce in man exactly that holiness which God demands of sinful humanity. Deliverance from punishment is only a secondary result of deliverance from sin.

Such, then, is the atonement, seen by its own light (p. 191). It precludes all accommodation to sin in view of the nature of God and of man alike. It shuts us up to an absolute necessity of coming to God by Christ. But in so shutting us up, it gives us so great a gift in Him that we rejoice to find ourselves shut up to 'so great salvation'.

The fundamental agreement of Campbell's theory with the doctrine of Schleiermacher comes out very clearly in this consideration of the prospective aspect of the atonement. The two theologians are here absolutely at one in conceiving salvation as essentially fellowship with God, brought about by the impartation of the Spirit of Christ: there is, however, the difference that, while Schleiermacher with his philosophical conception of religion speaks in general terms of the communication of the God-consciousness, Campbell, like Ritschl, is more Scriptural, in that he conceives God as the Father, and fellowship with Him as the life of sonship.

In dealing with the retrospective aspect of Christ's work, however, Campbell differs decidedly from both Schleiermacher and Ritschl, who reject the doctrine of a vicarious confession of sin on Christ's part as carrying the idea of His sympathy with men to a point where it becomes unreal and untrue in view of His personal innocence.[2] We have found Campbell's idea in German theology, especially in Thomasius, who, moreover, definitely compares Christ's expiation of sin to an act of penitence.[3] Campbell, however, has expressed the thought of a vicarious repentance with unusual power and wonderful sympathy; it is this element in his theory which gives it a particular distinction amidst cognate forms of doctrine.

[2] *Supra*, pp. 551f., 628f.   [3] *Supra*, p. 601.

CHAPTER 8

RECENT THEOLOGY IN AMERICA AND ENGLAND

BUSHNELL

A SOMEWHAT different type of theory from any of those we have just been studying, though in general agreement with them in attempting to transcend both the traditional orthodoxy and the rationalism of the eighteenth century, is that of the American Congregationalist, Bushnell (A.D. 1802–76). He was influenced both by Coleridge and Schleiermacher. In 'God in Christ' (1849) followed by 'Christ in Theology' (1851) he contended for the economic view of the Trinity as the practical and experimental view. His doctrine is thus summarised by Fisher, 'History of Christian Doctrine', p. 439:

'It is through the medium of three modes of personal action that the ineffable One discloses Himself and comes near to the apprehension of His creatures. The Logos is the self-revealing faculty of the Deity; Father, Son, and Spirit are the *dramatis personæ* through which the hidden Being reveals Himself. In Christ, Bushnell said, God manifests Himself under the limitations of human life—thinking, feeling, suffering with us. The existence of a human spiritual nature, if not expressly denied, was held to be practically of no account.' [1]

Bushnell's chief work on the atonement is 'The Vicarious Sacrifice' (1866), to which 'Forgiveness and Law' (1874) is a supplement. The former book possesses a marked originality. It is the work, not so much of a systematic theologian, but of a great preacher, and has all the force and vigour natural to one who thinks concretely rather than abstractly. The book is full of effective epigrams and phrases. On the other hand, this oratorical power is compensated for by a certain diffuseness and a good deal of repetition.

[1] Cf. the doctrine of Apollinaris in the Ancient Church (*supra*, p. 66).

673

Bushnell has perhaps more than any other modern theologian reproduced the spirit of Abelard's doctrine of the work of Christ. He begins by laying down the principle, that in vicarious sacrifice there is nothing superlative, or above the universal principles of right and duty. On the contrary, it is of the very nature of love vicariously to suffer in helping and healing and in order to help and heal. A mother so suffers: God, the Holy Spirit, the good angels, all redeemed souls, belong to the fellowship of vicarious suffering.

Thus, then, is the work of Christ to be explained. 'Christ', says Bushnell in an epigrammatic sentence, '(is) not here to die, but dies because He is here' (p. 90). He came to heal both the bodies and the souls of men. As He suffered by sympathy in healing human bodies, so also in healing human souls. The healing of bodies, however, was but an outward type of the inner healing: the healing of souls is His great object. He regenerates men, awakens love and patience, and is also the great example. He is not less a regenerator because the Holy Spirit is also a regenerator. The Spirit, in fact, simply continues His influence, and sets men under the impression of His life, character, and death. The question now is: How does Christ achieve this regeneration? Bushnell distinguishes two kinds of power, natural and moral.

'In ordinary cases where a work is undertaken, it signifies nothing more to say that the doer undertakes to be a power to that effect; for whatever is to be done by action, supposes, of course, a power acting. But where there is something to be done, not by action, but by quality of being, or by the worth, and beauty, and Divine greatness of a character, the action is nothing and the power to be effective thus, in simply being what it is, everything' (p. 125).

Regeneration demands not *fiat* force, but moral power, a higher kind of potency, which can work through our consent, and without infringing our liberty. Christ, then, operates in regeneration as the *moral power of God*. He is more than an example, more even than a revealer of God's love, so far as this means simply tender pity and sympathy. In Him the whole moral energy of God is manifested.

There is yet, however, a further distinction. Christ is not merely the moral power of God in the form of a sum of attributes, but in that of the cumulative appeal of a human life. God became incarnate in Him in order to obtain a new kind of power.

'God had a certain kind of power before, viz. that which may be called attribute power. . . . As being infinite and absolute, we ascribe to Him certain attributes or perfections. Such attributes, or perfections, are a kind of abstract excellence, such as we bring out, or generate, by our own intellectual refinements on the idea of God, to answer to our own intellectual demands. Still, as God is infinite, the perfections are distant. We hardly dare think them, if we could, into our finite moulds. We almost reason them away. . . . We make Him great, but we also make Him thin and cold. We feel Him as a platitude, more than as a person. His great attributes become dry words; a kind of milky way over our heads, vast enough in the matter of extension, but evanescently dim to our feeling.

'This result had been mitigated, somewhat, by His works and words and Providence, before the coming of Christ. But the tendency was still to carry back all the more genial impressions thus unfolded, and merge them in the attribute power, by which, as an unseen, infinite Being, we had before contrived to think and measure His character. Till, finally, in the fullness of time, He is constrained to institute a new movement on the world, in the Incarnation of His Son. The undertaking is to obtain through Him, and the facts and processes of His life, a new kind of power, viz. moral power; the same that is obtained by human conduct under human methods. It will be Divine power still, only it will not be attribute power. That is the power of His idea. This new power is to be the power cumulative, gained by Him among men, as truly as they gain it with each other. Only, it will turn out, in the end, to be the grandest, closest to feeling, most impressive, most soul-renovating, and spiritually sublime power that was ever obtained in this or any other world' (pp. 141–3).

This passage contains the very gist of Bushnell's theory. The stress lies above all on the idea that the power of God in Christ is cumulative; it is the total result of His life-history, 'all that He was, felt, suffered, and did' (p. 143). We meet here clearly once

675

more with the 'total impression' of Schleiermacher;[2] the contrast, however, between attribute power and moral power, between the power of the idea and the power of the Incarnation is Bushnell's own. He goes on to show how this moral power is accumulated in the life-history and death of Christ, though the Resurrection first alone sets it in the true light. It is summed up in the 'name' which Christ has won by His achievement.

If now we analyse this power, not into the elements by which it was won, but into the forms which it takes in its effect upon us, we have the following points:

(1) Christ humanises God;

(2) He both awakens the sense of guilt, and draws the confidence of the guilty;

(3) He makes evident by His vicarious sacrifice that God suffers on account of evil, or with and for all created beings under evil. It is especially in the passion and death of Jesus that this is made apparent to us.

What has been said contains in itself already Bushnell's complete view of the work of Christ. He proceeds, however, to bring out its implications by considering its relations both to law and government, between which he carefully distinguishes. On the one hand, there is the eternal and unchangeable moral law of God, the absolute standard of right and wrong, the ideal of righteousness, to which humanity is to be conformed. On the other hand, there is the Divine government of the universe, which is a means that God uses in a sinful world to bring about this conformity to law. The law is impersonal and abstract; the government is personal, nay, is essentially God. While righteousness is conformity to law, justice in the sense of the exaction of penalty belongs not to law, but to government. But to government in the larger sense belongs also redemption.

'Legislation wants redemption for its coadjutor, and only through the Divine sacrifice, thus ministered, can it ever hope to consummate the proposed obedience. Redemption also wants legislation, to back its tender appeals of sacrifice, by the stern rigours of law. Both together will compose the state of complete government' (p. 196).

[2] *Supra*, p. 547.

Justice and mercy are, accordingly, not in opposition; but are collateral means of attaining the same end. Nor does mercy have to satisfy justice before it can do its own work. Justice means in God a deep principle of wrath which girds Him for the infliction of suffering upon wrong-doing. But the principle of wrath is no law to God, that compels Him to inflict so much suffering, till it is satisfied. On the contrary, He has pledged Himself not to give Himself up to wrath, but to exercise mercy. Justice and mercy are, as it were, the two hands of God's constituted government.

'They are to have a properly joint action; one to work by enforcement and the other by attraction, or moral inspiration; both having as their end or office to restore and establish the everlasting, impersonal law' (p. 221).

The antagonism between them is formal, not real; partial, not absolute. As a matter of fact, says Bushnell, both justice and mercy are exercised at once. God dispenses justice, not by direct infliction, but by a law of natural consequences. Now this natural law of retribution is never infringed by mercy; but mercy only interacts supernaturally with justice.

'His new-creating and delivering work of mercy, operating only as by moral power, falls in conjunctively among the retributive causes of nature, and without any discontinuance turns them to a serviceable office in accomplishing its own great designs' (p. 233).

The compensational contrivances of the traditional theology for the saving of God's justice are therefore unnecessary. Mercy does not contradict justice: it honours both the law and justice. The vicarious sacrifice restores men to the precept of the law, bringing them once more into subjection to it. Christ by it reasserts the law, organising a kingdom for it in the world. He again Himself incarnates the precept, and brings it near to men's feeling and convictions by the personal footing He gains for it in humanity. Again, He honours it by His obedience. For what is law but love, and what is love but vicarious sacrifice? Finally, He reveals in His obedience God's obedience to the law. For what is the ultimate ground of the obedience of Christ? The law of love is an eternal necessity for God Himself, prior to His will.

677

'In this manner we are prepared for the conclusion, and even brought down close upon it, that Christ came into the world as the Incarnate Word and Saviour of sinners, just because the eternal, necessary law of love made it obligatory in Him to be such a Saviour' (p. 255).

Christ's work, therefore, makes visible the eternal necessity of love which lies upon God Himself. Accordingly, an immense honour is done to the law by Christ's obedience. It is, in fact, the very law that man had dishonoured which organises redemption.

'The violated law comes back upon us to overwhelm us, by showing us, in Christ, just what goodness was in it' (p. 262).

But, further, the Christian redemption does not diminish the penal enforcements of the law. Not only does it take up the natural consequences of sin and turn them to good, but it also presses the enforcements of the law with new emphasis, and even increases the responsibilities enforced. Christianity, in fact, reinforces the natural penalties of sin by a positive promulgation of future judgment: it also increases the crime of disobedience against law, inasmuch as it appears now not only as against law, but against Christ. The Gospel is therefore infinitely stern, while infinitely gracious.

More than this, however, the Christian redemption effectively maintains the rectoral honour of God. Not, however, as the more recent New England theology [3] has taught, in that Christ has shown by His death 'the same abhorrence to sin that would have been shown by the punishment of the guilty' (p. 306).

This doctrine Bushnell completely rejects.

'Abhorrence to sin expresses almost nothing that would be expressed by punishment. Abhorrence is a word of recoil simply and not a word of majesty. There is no enforcement, no judicial vigour in it' (p. 308).

[3] Bushnell refers to the development of theology in New England after Jonathan Edwards. We may illustrate his point by a reference to Jonathan Edwards, Jr. (A.D. 1745–1801), who taught as follows concerning the Atonement : 'It is a satisfaction to the *general* justice of God, by which is meant that regard to the greatest good, which leads Him, while bestowing forgiveness, to sustain the authority of law. "Christ suffered that in the sinner's stead which as effectually tended to discourage or prevent transgression and excite to obedience as the punishment of the transgressor according to the letter of the law would have done." The end of punishment is the restraining of others from sin The Atonement does this because it shows God's hatred of sin and His determination to punish it' (Fisher, 'History of Christian Doctrine', p. 412).

Abhorrence is, therefore, no fit substitute for punishment. Equally fatal, however, is the objection that in reality no abhorrence at all of sin is expressed in the death of Christ.

'To what in the transaction of the cross can God's abhorrence, by any possibility, fasten itself? Does God abhor the person of Jesus? No. His character? No. His redeeming office? No. The sins of the world that are upon Him? They are not upon Him, save in a figure, as the burden that His love so Divinely assumes' (p. 309).

The fact is that the abhorrence theory, if it is pressed, ultimately reverts to the idea that Christ's sufferings were in some way penal. Only so can they express the Divine abhorrence of sin. The object of the more recent theology has been to escape from the repulsive idea that Christ's suffering was penal: nevertheless this idea is kept in reserve, and forms the true basis of the theory.

With the penal theory of Christ's sufferings, however, Bushnell will hold no terms. Its justice is not just. Moreover, it is not justice or wrath, but righteousness, which is absolute in God. Neither justice nor wrath can claim to be 'satisfied' in the sense of the traditional theory.

Nevertheless, Christ has done enough even in the interests of justice. Christ is incarnated into the curse of the world, so far as He comes into an order of things where suffering follows sin, and so far as He suffers the corporate evil with us. In accepting this lot, He recognises the general course of the Divine justice.

Bushnell rounds off his theory by discussing the idea of justification. He accepts neither the traditional Catholic nor the traditional Protestant theory. Justification is no mere remission of sins or pardon, which latter is in itself 'only a kind of formality, or verbal discharge, that carries no discharge at all' (p. 360). It is real redemption. It is our restoration to the law before government, to the normal state of our being.

'When we are justified by faith or by "yielding our members instruments of righteousness unto God", which is the same thing . . . we are taken by all the foundations of the world, and the governings, compulsions, fears, and judgments that make up the scaffolding of our existence, and have our relations, with

God, only to the law before government: being in it, and the freedom of it, as being in Him and His freedom' (p. 363).

Such justification is the effect of moral power, of Christ operating upon us. Justice still runs its course upon us, but its effects are transmuted by redemption.

Justification, as above described, is 'imputed righteousness', not in the sense that there is any transfer of Christ's merits to us, but in the sense 'that the soul, when it is gained to faith, is brought back, according to the degree of faith, into its original, normal relation to God, to be invested, with God's light, feeling, character—in one word, righteousness—and live derivately from Him' (p. 377).

In others words, the believer is judged, not by his works, but by his general relation of dependence upon God, into which the moral power of Christ lifts him. Luther, Bushnell thinks, felt the truth concerning justification with his heart, but was not capable of bringing it to intellectual expression.

Finally, Bushnell deals with the sacrificial representations of Scripture. It is one of the great merits of his book that throughout there is continual examination of Scripture passages, and Scripture proof. The exegesis, indeed, is sometimes unsound: on the other hand, at times the meaning is most remarkably brought out. Bushnell defines his position in regard to the sacrificial language, used by the New Testament to describe the work of Christ, as follows:

'It is very true that the ancient sacrifices were, and were given to be, types of the higher sacrifice of Christ. Not, however, in the sense that they were such to the worshippers in them, but in that common, widely general, always rational sense, that all physical objects and relations, taken up as roots of language, are types, and are designed to be, of the spiritual meanings to be figured by them, or built up into spiritual words upon them. . . . In this sense the ancient sacrifices were no doubt appointed to be types of the higher sacrifices; visible forms, or analogies, that, when the time is come, will serve as a figure, or basis of words, to express and bring into familiar use, the sublime facts and world-renewing mysteries of the incarnate life and suffering death of Jesus' (pp. 391, 392).

There is no evidence, says Bushnell, that the ancient sacrificial ritual was based upon the idea of substitution. It was, however, in general lustral: it cleansed away ceremonial uncleanness by the sprinkling of blood. Spiritualising this, we come to the true meaning of the sacrificial symbolism in regard to the work of Christ, as also of the other Scriptural figures, judicial, political, commercial, and physical.

'The general conclusion is that all the Scripture symbols coincide, as nearly as may be, in the one ruling conception, that Christ is here in the world to be a power on character—to cleanse, wash, purify, to regenerate, new-create, make free, invest in the righteousness of God, the guilty souls of mankind' (p. 412).

But what of the other ideas connected with sacrifice, such as expiation, atonement, propitiation? Expiation, says Bushnell, is no Scriptural idea at all. Atonement, both in the Old and New Testaments, means the reconciliation of God to the offender, but is used in Christianity only by way of accommodation to the point of view of the sinner.

'Propitiation is an objective conception, by which that change taking place in us is spoken of as occurring representatively in God. Just as guilty minds, thrown off from God, glass their feeling representatively in God; or just as we say that the sun rises, instead of saying, what would be so very awkward to us, and yet is the real truth, that we ourselves rise to the sun' (p. 450).

Such objectification of our inner feelings is common outside of religion.

'We say that a thing is painful, because we suffer pain from it; putting the pain into the thing, which is really in ourselves' (p. 464).

So 'the devil is that objective person, whose reality is the sum of all subjective seductions or temptations to evil' (p. 465).

This objectification of our inner states has an important use.

'If we represented everything subjectively which is subjective, we could do it only by using the most awkward and tedious circumlocutions. In one view these outward projections of what is within are not true, and yet they are all the more vigorously true for that reason' (p. 467).

They take us off from ourselves and our inner states and make us think of God. Thus the altar symbols in particular—

'Compose for us a kind of objective religion; that is, a religion operated for us and before us. In one view they are not true, just as the ten thousand objective expressions of language referred to, are not, and yet there is nothing so sublimely, healthfully true, in the practical and free uses of faith, because we are so simple in them, and so completely carried out of ourselves' (p. 467).

The sacrificial system is, therefore, necessary; but must be kept free from abuse. It is the work of theology to dissipate the wrong associations which have in the course of history gathered around the altar terminology.

Bushnell's later volume 'Forgiveness and Law' (1874) has only secondary importance. He wrote it to correct his former explanation of propitiation. He here attempts to present an objective conception of this point by emphasising the unity of God and Christ in the suffering on the cross. The meaning of propitiation here is, that God by suffering works down and out His own anger against sinners. It is a psychological fact that in striving to help another and suffering for him we cease to be angry with him. We do not of course undertake sacrifice to reduce our anger, but to help others: nevertheless the effect surely follows. True forgiveness, therefore, is by way of propitiation. For it must needs be forgiveness, not in word merely, but in deed. It must be not negative, but positive, expressing itself in redemptive action, which in the circumstances inevitably means suffering and sacrifice. But this, as has been shown, brings about propitiation; thus propitiation is proved to be implied in true forgiveness. There is, however, no expiation. Bushnell is still as much as ever against this idea.

It is a question whether this new doctrine of propitiation, with its extremely anthropomorphic doctrine of God, is any improvement on the former conception. In the following remarks on Bushnell's theology, I shall regard only its original form. The doctrine of the American theologian comes nearer than any other in the English language to that of Schleiermacher and Ritschl. There is the difference, that, as has already been observed, we

682

have in it the work of a strictly systematic theologian, but of an ardent preacher and evangelist. There are minor inconsistencies, which, with more care, might have been smoothed away. For example, Bushnell's account of the relation of God to penalty is not altogether clear. He seems sometimes to think of His action here as altogether personal, the amount of penalty exacted or remitted in each case being determined by His wisdom. At other times he represents Him as acting entirely through natural law; so that penalty is automatic and irremissible. But, in spite of such minor blemishes, Bushnell's doctrine in general forms a noble and consistent whole. Its likeness is perhaps greatest to that of Schleiermacher, with whom Bushnell is in the main in point to point agreement, in spite of the difference in the form of expression. In the interest which he takes in showing how the work of Christ carries out the demand of the moral law, Bushnell approximates to Ritschl: he is more 'teleological' and less 'aesthetic' in his view of the work of Christ than Schleiermacher.[4] In the doctrine of justification, however, he agrees with Schleiermacher, not with Ritschl; yet the way in which he explains the idea of propitiation has affinity with Ritschl's doctrine of justification as the reconciliation of the sinner to God, not of God to the sinner.

DALE

Dale's work, 'The Atonement' (1875), falls next to be considered (I use the 19th ed. 1897); for in it the author had Bushnell's 'Vicarious Sacrifice' continually in view. Dale (A.D. 1829-95) founds his method on a distinction which reminds us at once of Butler, viz. the distinction between the fact and the theory of the atonement.[5] The fact of the atonement means that there is 'a direct relation between the Death of Christ and the remission of sins' (p. 19), or again, that it is 'the objective ground on which God absolves us from sin and delivers us from eternal destruction' (loc. cit.). The theory must unfold the principle and grounds of the above-mentioned relation, or explain why the death of Christ is the basis of the Divine forgiveness.

---

[4] Cf. *supra*, pp. 535, 618.   [5] *Supra*, pp. 495f.

A great part of Dale's book is devoted to the presentation of the Scripture proof of the fact of the atonement. He seeks to establish an improved method of Scripture proof, which takes account of the critical view of things begun by Locke.[6] The 'proof-texts' for the traditional doctrines have been collected and examined so often that no improvement here is possible. Yet proof-texts alone, after all, in view of the 'occasional' character of the New Testament writings, prove very little.

'The frequency and distinctness with which a doctrine is asserted in the apostolic writings is, therefore, no test of its importance. It might even be contended with considerable plausibility that the importance of a doctrine is likely to be in the inverse ratio of the number of passages in which it is directly taught; for the central and most characteristic truths of the Christian Faith are precisely those which the Churches were least likely to abandon' (p. 21).

A new method of proof, therefore, is necessary, which shall consider the New Testament in a broader manner:

'That the Apostles regarded the Death of Christ as a Sacrifice and Propitiation for the sins of the world appears in many passages which yield no direct testimony to this doctrine. It sometimes determines the form and structure of an elaborate argument, which falls to pieces if this truth is denied. At other times it gives pathos and power to a practical appeal. It accounts for some of the misconceptions and misrepresentations of apostolic teaching. It explains the absence from the apostolic writings of much that we should certainly have found in them if the Apostles had not believed that for Christ's sake, and not merely because of the effect on our hearts of what Christ has revealed, God grants us remission of sins. It penetrates the whole substance of their theology and ethical teaching and is the very root of their religious life' (p. 25).

Dale has worked out this thesis at great length and in a very masterly way. After some notice of the history of the doctrine of the atonement, he then proceeds to give his own theory, i.e. his explanation of the relation between the death of Christ and the remission of sins. First, however, he discusses the question

[6] *Supra*, pp. 483f.

whether the remission of sins is possible. The view that the penalties of sin work themselves out automatically seems to forbid this. Dale follows the line of Butler [7] in showing that we ourselves are able to modify the consequences of wrongdoing, both in our own case and in that of others. God also is to be thought of as working personally and directly; He by no means gives over the conduct of the universe to an automatically working system of laws. Remission is therefore possible. But it is also a thing of moment. Dale reprehends Bushnell for his undervaluing of the remission of sins, and his absorption of the idea in the wider idea of regeneration. It is true that remission without regeneration would be in vain. Nevertheless, to say that remission is a mere formality is altogether to undervalue it. The instinct that has made theologians distinguish remission and regeneration is a sound one. The wrath of God is real; and remission of sins, as escape from it, is real also.

We are free, then, to discuss the relation between the death of Christ and the remission of sins. Dale acknowledges that the history of doctrine has shown that the attempt to work out a theory from any one of the Scripture representations of the death of Christ, as ransom, vicarious death, or propitiation, goes astray. These representations are metaphors, which will not bear the weight of a theological theory, but, if pressed, lead us into contradictions. To construct a theory, therefore, 'we must put these descriptions aside, and consider the death of Christ itself, in its real relation to God and man' (p. 359). The Scripture figures will then constitute the authoritative tests of the accuracy of such a theory: 'a theory is false if it does not account for and explain these descriptions, (loc. cit.).

Can we, then, discover in the death of our Lord Jesus Christ anything which promises to throw light on its expiatory power?

'There are three considerations which invest the death of Christ with unique and tragic interest:

'(1) It was the Death of the Son of God manifest in the flesh.

'(2) It was a voluntary Death. He came into the world to die. . . .

'(3) Immediately before His Death, He was forsaken of God:

[7] *Supra*, p. 493.

when we remember the original glory in which He dwelt with the Father, His faultless perfection, and His unbroken communion with the Father during His life on earth, this is a great and awful mystery' (p. 360).

In investigating the connexion between this mysterious death and the remission of the sins of men, Dale proposes to inquire into two questions:

'(1) Whether this connexion can be explained by the existence of any original relation existing between the Lord Jesus Christ and the penalties of sin, or—to state the question more generally —between the Lord Jesus Christ and the eternal law of righteousness, of which sin is the transgression?

'(2) Whether this connexion can be explained by any original relation existing between the Lord Jesus Christ and the race whose sin needed remission?' (p. 361).

The answer to the former question is, firstly, that He is the Judge of the world. But, secondly, He is also the Eternal Word, through whom God made the world. His relation to the eternal law of righteousness is, therefore, wrapped up in that of God Himself to His law. It is an old question, whether the law depends on the will of God, or God, like us, upon the law. Neither is true: the relation between God and the law is unique.

'He is not, as we are, bound by its authority: in Him its authority is actively asserted. . . . In God the law is *alive*: it reigns on His throne, sways His sceptre, is crowned with His glory' (p. 372).

What, again, is the relation between God and the penalties of sin? The end of punishment is not the amelioration of the criminal, nor the deterring of others from similar crime. Punishment, whether Divine or human, is just retribution. God's punishment is not the assertion of His personal honour against injury, but the vindication of the law which lives in Him. The remission of punishment is therefore impossible, unless the law be otherwise vindicated.

'If the punishment of sin is a Divine act—an act in which the identity between the will of God and the eternal law of righteousness is asserted and expressed—it would appear that, if in any case the penalties of sin are remitted, some other Divine act

686

of at least equal intensity, and in which the ill desert of sin is expressed with at least equal energy, must take its place' (p. 391).

The Christian atonement fulfils this necessity. The principle that sin must be punished is not suppressed. It would have been adequately asserted, had God inflicted upon mankind the penalties of transgression. It was asserted in a still grander form by the suffering on the cross of Christ, the Moral Ruler and Judge of men. Nor is this all. The love of the Eternal Father for the Son gives unique value to the work of Christ.

'The mysterious unity of the Father and the Son rendered it possible for God at once to endure and to inflict penal suffering, and to do both under wider conditions which constitute the infliction and the endurance the grandest moment in the moral history of God' (p. 393).

We have not, therefore, here to do with a pardon of sins compensated by the punishment of an innocent man: it is God Himself in Christ who endures suffering instead of inflicting it. It may be noted at this point that Dale in the exegetical part of his book lays great stress on the cry on the cross,[8] which he interprets in the sense that Christ was in reality forsaken of God and takes as establishing the penal character of His sufferings (pp. 60ff.).

There remains the second great question, whether the connexion between the death of Christ and the remission of sins depends on His relation to the human race.

It is not God alone who is concerned in the sacrifice of Christ. It was a sacrifice for us, in which Christ was our Representative. This aspect has not been brought out in the partial conception of the subject already gained. This partial conception, moreover, taken alone seems to suggest that the value of the death of Christ lies in its dramatic character. The theory appears to be somewhat 'in the air'.

'If it can be shown that the original and ideal relation of the Lord Jesus Christ to the human race constitutes a reason why He should become a Sacrifice and Propitiation for our sins, the conception of His Death illustrated in the preceding lecture will rest on more solid and secure foundations' (p. 402).

[8] Mt. 27:46.

Christ is, however, according to Scripture, not merely the Word, through whom God has created the world, but stands in a particular relation to the human race as the ideal and root of humanity.

The following propositions, therefore, hold good:

(1) Christ's submission in the cross to the law is the expression of ours and carries ours with it. He did not submit to the law, that we might be released from its authority, but only from its penalties.

(2) The death of Christ is the objective ground of the remission of sins, because it restored the ideal relation of humanity to God, which had been destroyed by sin.

(3) Also because it involved the actual destruction of sin in all those who believe upon Him.

If to these propositions be added the previously established truth (4) that Christ's death vindicated the eternal law of righteousness and so made possible the remission of sins, then we have a sufficient explanation of all the New Testament metaphors, such as expiation, vicarious death, representative death, ransom, satisfaction, sacrifice for sin. Each is seen to express some one or other aspect of the whole truth.

Dale's powerful book may be said to be perhaps the most forcible restatement in English of the orthodox theory of the atonement. Yet it is by no means the doctrine of the traditional orthodoxy which reappears in it. There is no talk of an equivalence in substituted punishment; what we find is rather in essence the Grotian idea of penal example, though Dale himself does not appear to recognise the affinity of his theory with that of Grotius, for which, though he admits that it has had a great influence on the modern theology of English Nonconformity, he has no good word. He speaks (p. 294) of Grotius, as expressing most perfectly, by expressing in an exaggerated and degraded form, the true character of the Reformation theory. This certainly is not a correct historical judgment; but the passage shows Dales' opinion of Grotius. Yet, as Ritschl has pointed out, the doctrine which explains the death of Christ as a vindication in principle of the Divine justice, without raising the question of the strict equivalence of the sufferings of Christ with those which would have been suffered by sinners, cannot logically be distinguished from the doctrine that the death of Christ was a penal example.[9] The truth is that Dale stood nearer to the 'modern theory of English Nonconformity', as represented by Wardlaw, Payne, etc., than he realised.[1] There is, however, one noteworthy point of difference between Dale's theory and that of Grotius, viz. in the emphasis which Dale lays on the moral unity of the Father and the Son, so that it is God who suffers in the sufferings of Christ.

In the above remarks that aspect of Dale's theory has alone been considered which bulks largest in it, viz. the conception of the death of Christ as a vindication of the Divine righteousness. The other aspects, which are added to this, and are connected with the thought of Christ as the Representative of humanity, are less fully delineated by Dale. We have in them essentially a continuation of the doctrine of Erskine and Maurice. No real connexion is, however, established between this part of Dale's theory and the foregoing, but the two are simply added together. There is no doubt that it is the first-mentioned aspect of doctrine, upon which Dale has spent so much labour, which remains really characteristic of his book. It is this element of his theory also, which is essentially implied in the part of the book, which professes to deal with the Scripture proof of the fact of the atonement. A careful study of this part, probably the strongest and best of the whole work, will show that the supposed distinction between the fact and the theory of the atonement is not sound. The only distinction is between a less or more explicit statement of what is really the same theory throughout. Dale himself admits that the fundamental question, whether the death of Christ has a direct relation to the remission of sins, or whether it was simply a great appeal of God's love to the human race, is a question of theory (pp. 10ff.). Yet in what follows, to establish that for the Apostles the death of Christ had a direct relation to the remission of sins is regarded as the establishment of the existence for them, not of a theory, but of the fact of the atonement (pp. 19ff.). The fundamental value of Dale's book, then, remains the establishment by means of a better form of Scripture

[9] *Supra*, p. 628.   [1] *Supra*, p. 666.

proof of the place in primitive Christianity of the conception, in however indeterminate a form, of substitutionary and expiatory sacrifice. This is a point to be reckoned with by all theories of the school of Schleiermacher and Ritschl, so far as they attempt to establish a connexion with the religion of the New Testament. But, on the other hand, Dale seems to show little appreciation of the work of systematic theology, as the Germans understand it, viz. as the attempt to reproduce the religion of the New Testament in the form of, as Hegel would say, a 'concrete conception', i.e. a conception in which all the parts contribute to the unity of the whole, and are themselves modified in so doing. The establishment of the existence of an idea in the New Testament is, according to this understanding of the matter, not the end as far as theology is concerned. There remains the question, how the idea is modified, when it is associated with and controlled by other ideas, and above all the question, as to which idea is to dominate all the rest. If, for example, the idea of the Fatherhood of God, or, again, that of the Kingdom of God, is to be supreme, then all that Dale says of the New Testament may be true, and yet in the ultimate construction of Christianity as a religion the idea of substitutionary sacrifice may emerge radically modified by the wider context into which it is brought. The 'penetrative imagination',[2] which seeks to apprehend Christianity as a whole, cannot stop at any single idea, however firmly established in the New Testament, as ultimate, unless indeed it be the idea which, after due reflection, is accepted as the dominant principle of the whole; and even that will have to be understood by the way in which it lights up and interprets all the related religious conceptions, which with it compose the religious organism.

WESTCOTT

Westcott's book 'The Victory of the Cross' (1888) is slight in form, being simply six sermons preached during Holy Week. Nevertheless it deserves mention, inasmuch as it contains, though

---

[2] *Supra*, p. 518 (cf. p. 555).

not as clearly stated as would be desirable, a conception of the work of Christ, which is unusual: it has, however, affinities with the doctrine of Rothe. Westcott (A.D. 1825–1901) bases his theory on the representations in the Epistle to the Hebrews, where Christ's sufferings are spoken of as disciplinary for Himself, as purifying for the humanity with which He has become one in the Incarnation, and as perfecting for both.[3] The general point of view implied in Westcott's book is that of the world as a place of discipline for sinful souls, a view which reminds us of Origen,[4] with whose theology Westcott felt great sympathy.[5]

Westcott begins in a way reminiscent of Butler (who, it will be remembered, took the motto of his 'Analogy' from Origen) by considering, first, the scheme of nature as a key to that of grace. He finds that there is in the world a natural fellowship of humanity, and, next, that nature itself shows that the condition of redemption is sacrifice. Then he emphasises the Scriptural doctrine of the unity of humanity in Christ. The Incarnation is the fulfilment of the promise of the creation.

'Humanity however broken into fragments in our eyes is still one. And this one humanity, not the personal manhood of an individual, Christ took to Himself. He fulfilled for man fallen the destiny which was provided for man unfallen. He realised absolutely under the conditions of earth the Divine likeness which neither one man nor all men could reach. He gained for the race that for which they were made' (p. 43).

Christ's life, Westcott says accordingly, was universal in character and experience, and was a Divine life, a life lived in God. In this life, however, the members of Christ's body share: they share it, moreover, that they may reveal it.

But now comes in the place of suffering in the life of Christ. He was perfected through sufferings. He learned obedience by the things which He suffered.

'He learned obedience: He did not learn to obey. There was no disobedience to be conquered, but only the Divine will to be realised. So He carried to the uttermost the virtue of obeying. He fulfilled in action the law which God had laid down for the

[3] Cf. Heb. 2:9–18 ; 4:14–5:10 ; 10:1–18. [4] *Supra*, p. 37.
[5] Cf. his essay 'Origen and the Beginnings of Christian Philosophy', in 'Religious Thought in the West', 1891, pp. 194ff.

being whom He had made in His image: He endured in His Passion every penalty which the righteousness of God had connected with the sins which He made His own. He offered the absolute self-surrender of service and of suffering, through life and through death, fulfilling in spite of the Fall the original destiny of man, and rising in His glorified humanity to the throne of God' (p. 61).

Christ's sufferings, says Westcott, were complete in range and form; were voluntary, were foreseen, and were recognised in their full intensity and in their unnaturalness, as not belonging to the true order of the world, but as being the result of the Fall.

'He gathers into one supreme sacrifice the bitterness of death, the last penalty of sin, knowing all it means, and bearing it as He knows. We indeed can see but little, but we can see this, that He alone, the sinless Son of God who knew perfectly the mind and will of His Father, could bring to Him the offering of perfect obedience and perfect sorrow. He who made every human power, and every human sin, His own by the innermost fellowship of spiritual life could render to God the tribute of absolute service and bear the consequences of every transgression as entering into the Divine law of purifying chastisement' (pp. 68–9).

The Passion, as it was inflicted, is a revelation of human wrongdoing.

'The Passion as it was borne is a revelation of the inexorable sternness of infinite love which, while it gives to pain a potentiality of cleansing grace, requires to the uttermost that retribution which may become a blessing' (p. 69).

Sufferings in themselves, says Westcott (p. 81), are nothing worth. Self-inflicted suffering is simply partial suicide. But sufferings accepted as they come to us by the will of God purify the creature and illuminate life.

'In this sense sufferings are a revelation of the Fatherhood of God Who brings back His children to Himself in righteousness and love. In this sense Christ suffered, knowing the nature of sin, knowing the judgment of God, realising in every pain the healing power of a Father's wisdom' (p. 82).

Westcott's position is made clearer by what he says of the

nature of punishment in general. We materialise spiritual things. We forget that the real punishment of sin is sinfulness.

'So it is we are tempted to regard chastisement as the expression of anger and not as the tender discipline of wisdom. We fail to discern that righteousness and love are, if I may so speak, the two sides of unchangeable holiness as it is seen in relation to the condition of men and in relation to the purpose of God' (p. 77).

Hence we misunderstand the New Testament. Where Christ and the Apostles speak of sin, we think of punishment.

'They represent evil as a barrier which hinders the outflow of Divine love upon the guilty: we think of it as that which entails painful retribution' (p. 78).

When, however, the true view of things, taken in Scripture, is allowed to speak for itself, the traditional theory of satisfaction is seen to be an impossible doctrine of the work of Christ. It falls below the wholeness and simplicity of the Scripture view, which is simply this:

'Christ who took humanity to Himself was able to fulfil the will of God under the conditions of our present earthly life, both actively and passively, raising to its highest perfection every faculty of man, and bearing every suffering through which alone fallen man could attain his destiny' (p. 79).

Christ, however, as the Head of humanity, by the energy of the one life which we all live, could communicate to all who share His nature the fruit of His perfect obedience. His sufferings were not 'outside us'.

'They were the sufferings of One in Whom we live and Who lives in us. Christ gathering the race into Himself suffered for all by the will of God; and in correspondence with this revelation of God's grace, we confess, when we listen to the secret whisperings of our souls, that we need the blessing which it brings, and that it avails for our utmost necessity' (p. 80).

This it does in the following ways: (1) Christ, having exhausted all suffering, bearing it according to the will and mind of God, is able to communicate the virtue of His passion to us. (2) The example of His suffering teaches us self-renunciation, and we have a present sense of His sympathy in our labours.

693

(3) Again, the example of Christ's suffering assures us of a Father's love. Nor is it merely His example, but the power of His life, which brings us into communion with God, vivifying and purifying us at once.

True forgiveness is indeed the energy of love answered by love. The forgiveness which remits a punishment may leave the heart untouched. The forgiveness which remits a sin includes by its very nature the return of responsive gratitude. The believer makes Christ's work his own, and God sees him in the Son of Man. He dies daily, dies into life' (p. 85).

(4) Finally, in sharing Christ's sufferings we also share His joy.

Christ's Kingdom is realised through His cross, His sovereignty is a spiritual, universal, present, Divine, and effective sovereignty, exercised through His people. The complete fulfilment of it, however, is not yet; but for it we wait.

The connexion of Westcott's doctrine with that of Erskine and Maurice is clear. It has also affinity with that of Campbell, only that for the notion of a vicarious repentance is substituted the unity of Christ with us in purifying suffering. As over against Dale, Westcott stands out as fully modern in his conception of punishment. He has firmly grasped the principle, so fundamental for Ritschl, that Divine punishment is not a material but a spiritual thing, no mere external act, but a process in human consciousness.

MOBERLY

The last English theologian that I shall consider is Moberly (A.D. 1845–1903), whose book, 'Atonement and Personality' (1901) continues the line of McLeod Campbell, but restates his theory in terms of modern philosophy, and in view of more recent theological discussions. Moberly also attempts to supplement Campbell's doctrine in points where he considers it defective.

The book begins with a discussion of some fundamental conceptions, viz. Punishment, Penitence, and Forgiveness. Dale's view that punishment is essentially retributive, not reformatory, is rejected. True punishment as the effect of righteousness must deal with persons as individuals and aim at their reformation. The retributive aspect of punishment simply belongs to the imperfection of human justice which cannot deal with individuals, but only with the average. The 'equation' theory of punishment is a corollary from the retributive theory, which reveals the imperfection of the latter.

All punishment, however, is not in experience restorative. Even though it is meant to be so and begins as moral discipline, where it meets with opposition to the discipline, it fails of being reformatory, and becomes simply retribution. Endurance of retribution, says Moberly, in agreement with Erskine, has no atoning tendency whatever.[6] Where, however, punishment is accepted and taken up into the suffering personality as penitence, it really tends to diminish guiltiness.

A corollary from this doctrine is that punishment, as retributive, cannot be predicated of Christ, who was not rebellious against the suffering laid upon Him.

Penitence, in its idea, is a real change of self. A perfect penitence would be such a change of self as would make the past dead, and re-identify the self with righteousness. Righteousness and love would be one in embracing it. Nevertheless such perfect penitence does not exist even in Christians, though Christian penitence points towards it. Yet the existence of even an imperfect penitence is impossible to sinful nature in itself. How then does it exist in Christians? The answer is: it is the indwelling Spirit of the Crucified. It may be observed that the method of argument here reminds us of Schleiermacher, who similary argues back from the imperfect Christian consciousness of God to a perfect God-consciousness as its source.[7]

Moberly continues: Divine forgiveness, again, is not simply remission of penalty. It is not simply not punishing, or treating as innocent. It is an attitude of a Person to a person: there must be a justification for it in the personality of the forgiven. He must be 'forgivable'. God, then, Himself must make the man forgivable. But, again, all experienced forgiveness is provisional.

[6] *Supra*, pp. 658f.   [7] *Supra*, pp. 537ff.

Love is called forgiveness where it is anticipatory, i.e. where it values the desert of any real correspondence with love. Forgiveness is in fact a means to an end, viz. the creation of holiness; and is contingent on the accomplishment of this end. When the end is attained forgiveness is wholly merged in love. Strictly, therefore, forgiveness is a hope equivalent with the hope of personal holiness.

If before we were reminded of Schleiermacher, here we meet with the ideas of Kant. Moberly solves the antinomy of justification in the Kantian way, by the view that justification or forgiveness anticipates sanctification in order that sanctification may be possible, and is ultimately justified by the achievement of sanctification.[8]

The above considerations prepare the way for an understanding of the work of Christ. The fundamental objection to the Christian doctrine is that in the creation of holiness mediation is impossible. It is not clear, first of all, how the unholy can become holy, but in any case—

'How is it conceivable (the mind asks) that any Redeemer's work, or endurance, or goodness, be it what it may, seeing that it is outside of the personalities of men, should touch the point of pressing necessity, which is an essential alteration of what men are? What is wanted is not that there should be a wonderful exhibition somewhere of obedience, or that somebody should be holy: not even that the amount or value of holiness should balance and perhaps outweigh the huge volume of unholiness. What is wanted is that all these particular personalities should be holy, which are in fact the reverse. How can the particular thing which is required be touched by the introduction of another? Here, if anywhere in the world, there can be no question of a fictitious transaction, or an unreal imagining; here, if anywhere, whatever is not vitally and personally real is both mockery and despair' (p. 74).

Moberly appeals to experience. That shows that a friend who will suffer for a sinner is the best hope of his reformation. Logic, in abstracting from experience, here overreaches itself. The objection is, however, not yet fully answered.

[8] Cf. *supra*, p. 523.

'It will be felt that, even if it be not fundamentally impossible, the idea of an atoning mediator is, and must be, incompatible with any profound sense of justice' (p. 76).

This difficulty Moberly meets by demanding, like Hegel, that we rise from the forensic point of view, where personalities are conceived atomically as absolutely separate individuals, to the higher level of thought, where the identification of personalities is seen to be possible.[9] This is illustrated even in our relation to our fellows, which is not so atomic as the forensic point of view assumes. But the identification of the sinner with Christ stands again on a higher level. The Catholic doctrine teaches that Christ is not only identically one with God, but is man, inclusively, not generically.[1] Only Adam can here be compared with Him, but there is a difference.

'What Adam is to the flesh, and, through the flesh, indirectly to the spirit also; that is Christ to the spirit, and, through the spirit, indirectly also to the flesh, of all those, who, as they are partakers, in flesh, of Adam, are made capable of becoming partakers, in Spirit, of Christ' (p. 89).

It is clear that Moberly moves here on a Hegelian basis. The Creeds are interpreted by the ideas, first, that the Infinite Spirit is immanent in the finite spirit, and again that the finite spirit expresses itself in the flesh as its inevitable and necessary other.[2] There is, we are told, no absolute antithesis between spirit and body.

'Neither is body without spirit, nor spirit without body' (loc. cit.).

And again:

'That complete indwelling and possessing of even one other, which the yearnings of man towards man imperfectly approaches, is only possible, in any fullness of the words, to that Spirit of Man which is the Spirit of God: to the Spirit of God, become through the Incarnation the Spirit of Man. No mere man indwells, in Spirit, in, or as, the Spirit of another. Whatever near approach

---

[9] *Supra*, p. 529f.

[1] Cf. *supra*, pp. 65ff. Moberly says : 'His relation to the human race is not that He was another specimen, differing, by being another, from everyone except Himself. His relation to the race was not a differentiating but a consummating relation ' (p. 86).

[2] Cf. *supra*, p. 526.

there may seem to be toward this, is really mediated through the Spirit of Christ' (loc. cit.).

In view of this reinterpretation of the Creeds we are not surprised to discover that Moberly teaches next, in opposition to the Ancient Church,[3] that the humanity of Christ is not impersonal. Rather is He Himself personally expressed in and through humanity. The personal expression of God must of necessity be human. Christ in the Incarnation is not two, God and man; but one, God as man. Consequently, says Moberly, in agreement with McLeod Campbell, He reveals not only the truth of the Divine character, but also the truth of the human character.[4] This He does by His life of obedience to and dependence upon God. Instead of seeking to be independent, which is the essence of sin, He seeks only to reflect the Father. The revelation He makes is not primarily that of the relation of the pre-existent Christ to the Father, but of the Incarnate Christ to God.

The agreement of all this with the immanental theology of Germany is noteworthy. The pre-existence of Christ indeed remains unquestioned, but the practical view of the Incarnation is immanental rather than transcendental. Christ is not conceived as the Divine Person clothed with humanity, but the Man who perfectly reveals God. Here then is the possibility of understanding how He was made sin, how He condemned sin in the flesh. The two impossibilities which would restore man to God are both realised in Him, perfect holiness and perfect penitence. Both are finally accomplished by His death. In the first place, in His dependence by prayer on God in His active obedience, Christ is the perfect reflection of God. His death was necessary for the completion of this aspect of His character, and was the climax of the discipline by which He learned obedience.

But, again, in Christ's death He performed an act of vicarious penitence on behalf of sinners. Vicarious penitence is a fact of experience, when those, who are one with the sinner in nature and love, suffer with and for him in his sin. But perfect penitence is only possible to the perfectly holy; since the perfectly holy alone can see sin as God sees it. Christ then made Himself

[3] *Supra*, pp. 67, 109. [4] *Supra*, p. 670.

one with us in nature, and in love performed the perfect penitence.

'He voluntarily stood in the place of the utterly contrite—accepting insult, shame, anguish, death—death possible only by His own assent—yet outwardly inflicted as penal; nay, more, in His own inner consciousness, accepting the ideal consciousness of the contrite— which is the one form of the penitent's righteousness. . . . He did, in fact and in full, that which would in the sinner constitute perfect atonement, but which has for ever become impossible to the sinner, just in proportion as it is true that he has sinned' (p. 130).

In this vicarious suffering of Christ there is nothing properly penal.

'What would have been punishment *till it became penitence,* is, in the perfectly contrite, only as penitence' (p. 131).

There is, then, in the sacrifice of Calvary really no question of retribution, no external equation of sin and penalty. Christ did not endure the vengeance of God or the damnation of sin. But He accepted death 'as the necessary climax of an experience of spiritual desolation, which, but to the inherently holy, would have been not only material but spiritual death' (p. 133).

But the result was, that, while sin thus slew the mortal element in Christ, it slew itself.

'Where penitence has been consummated quite perfectly, that very consciousness which was heaviness of spirit for sin has become the consciousness of sin crushed and dead' (p. 133).

The question now, however, is how this atonement of Christ can be related to us. As historical, it appears to be outside of us. The objective and the subjective are, however, not opposites, but correlative and inseparable. The atonement was first objective that it might become subjective; it was historical fact that it might become personal experience. How can this be? Belief passes into contemplation and contemplation into love; and by love the objective atonement is made personal experience. What we love ceases to be altogether outside us. Yet the atonement is not a mere appeal to the emotions, nor is an adequate emotional response to it within our power. What is here needed is the doctrine of the Holy Spirit as the indwelling Spirit of Christ; only this can satisfactorily explain the relation of the atonement to man. While the Holy Spirit is personal, He is practically revealed to us as a gift, as the indwelling Spirit of the Incarnate Christ. It is observable how closely Moberly here again, while conserving the Trinitarian metaphysic, in practice follows the Hegelian exposition of the work of Christ.[5]

Finally, the Spirit is ours through the sacraments, which are at once vehicle and symbol; everything here is, in reality, not material, but spiritual.

It is clear that the core and centre of Moberley's theory is inherited from McLeod Campbell. Nevertheless Moberley intends his doctrine to be an advance upon that of Campbell. Admitting that Campbell's theory 'in its real completeness is a very grand one', he finds that it suffers from an 'undue assumption of distinction and antithesis between Christ and ourselves' (p. 406). This shows itself, first, in the tendency to tone down the true idea of a vicarious repentance suggested by Edwards to that of a vicarious confession of sin. It also leads to an explanation of Christ's mental anguish in His passion,[6] such as may seem to match His individual consciousness, as a holy man suffering, rather than what may be called His representative consciousness, as humanity realising penitential holiness (loc. cit.).

Whereas, in fact, Dale misconceives the desolation of Christ on the cross in one direction, understanding it as penal retribution,[7] Campbell equally misconceives it in the opposite direction, denying that Christ was ever truly forsaken of God. Further, Campbell's treatment lacks a reference to the Holy Spirit as the means of our personal identification with Christ, and equally to the sacraments as its vehicle. These defects Moberly has endeavoured to correct by a closer connexion with Catholic tradition on the one hand, and on the other by a more adequate conception of personality. The philosophical medium in which he works is, as has already been pointed out, that of Hegelianism. It is this doctrine, with its general view of the world as the manifestation, at different stages, of one Spirit, which enables Moberly to correct McLeod Campbell's view of the separateness and dis-

[5] *Supra*, p. 528.   [6] *Supra*, pp. 669f.   [7] *Supra*, p. 687.

700

tinctness of Christ as a human individual (the characteristically Western view of His Person) [8] by the idea of Him as an inclusive and pervasive Spirit. It is, again, the Hegelian view of matter as undeveloped spirit which enables Moberly to treat punishment as the first stage in the evolution of penitence, and the sacraments in like manner as the vehicles and symbols of the Spirit. Thus in Moberly's reversion to the Catholic tradition the realistic mysticism of the typical Greek theology is replaced by an idealistic mysticism.[9]

Modern Theology in English

The theology in the English language, which we have just been studying, forms an interesting and valuable parallel to the German theology from Schleiermacher to Ritschl. The fact that the doctrine of the work of Christ is treated mainly in monographs, instead of as in the German theology as a part of a complete theological system, is of less detriment to the value of the English work than might be anticipated, since, especially in the greatest English theories, those of Campbell, Bushnell, and Moberly, the subject is treated essentially from the point of view of the whole of doctrine. As, however, with one exception no new principles emerge in the English work, which have not already been considered in our review of modern German theology, I may refer the reader here for all essential criticism in general to that review. The exception is in the case of Westcott's theory, where in so remarkable a way is developed the idea of Christ's suffering as a purifying discipline for Christ Himself. Westcott's book is too slight for a satisfactory estimate of the value of his idea, which in further working out would certainly need considerable elucidation and clearing from objections. But I regard it as a service of real value that Westcott has called attention to the Biblical material existing for our subject in the Epistle to the Hebrews, which has been in the past either too little utilised, or too much interpreted without regard to its peculiar and distinctive character.

[8] *Supra*, pp. 107f.
[9] As had been the intention of Origen (*supra*, pp. 42f.).

Retrospect

It has been a long and perhaps sometimes a tedious way that I have led the reader. But without a sufficient attention to detail it is impossible to gain a real understanding of the progress of theology. He, however, who will not be discouraged by the mass of material, but will patiently seek to master and understand it, will discover that there has been and is progress in theology.

> Vexilla regis prodeunt
> Fulget crucis mysterium.

These words of the Hymn for the Eve of Passion Sunday happily suggest the goal towards which theology is tending, a view in which the work of Christ and the Christian revelation as a whole shall be seen luminous 'by its own light'.

INDEX

An asterisk indicates major entries.

703

Printed in Great Britain by Thomas Nelson and Sons Ltd, Edinburgh

708

Lightning Source UK Ltd.
Milton Keynes UK
UKOW04f1903181113

221353UK00018B/1600/P